Coping, Personality and the Workplace

A comprehensive review and discussion of all aspects of the coping-personality relationship. For those wishing to enhance or refocus their knowledge, research or practice then this book offers a rich resource for engaging in and improving the quality of working lives.

Philip Dewe, Birkbeck, University of London, UK

Although stress seems to be endemic to modern life, the most interesting question is how, and why, individuals differ in their ability to manage or cope with the stressors they experience. In this volume, Professors Antoniou and Cooper have brought together an impressive array of authors to consider a wide variety of issues related to coping and personality in the workplace. The resulting collection both reviews, and extends, our knowledge of how individuals deal with workplace stressors and will be an important reference for both researchers and practitioners.

E. Kevin Kelloway, Saint Mary's University, Canada;
President-Elect, Canadian Psychological Association

Psychological and Behavioral Aspects of Risk Series

Series Editors: Professor Cary L. Cooper and Professor Ronald J. Burke

Risk management is an ongoing concern for modern organizations in terms of their finance, their people, their assets, their projects and their reputation. The majority of the processes and systems adopted are very financially oriented or fundamentally mechanistic; often better suited to codifying and recording risk, rather than understanding and working with it. Risk is fundamentally a human construct; how we perceive and manage it is dictated by our attitude, behavior and the environment or culture within which we work. Organizations that seek to mitigate, manage, transfer or exploit risk need to understand the psychological factors that dictate the response and behaviors of their employees, their high-flyers, their customers and their stakeholders.

This series, edited by two of the most influential writers and researchers on organizational behavior and human psychology explores the psychological and behavioral aspects of risk; the factors that:

- define our attitudes and response to risk;
- are important in understanding and managing "risk managers"; and
- dictate risky behavior in individuals at all levels.

Titles Currently in the Series Include:

Mental Illness in the Workplace
Psychological Disability Management
Henry G. Harder, Shannon Wagner, and Josh Rash

Creating Healthy Workplaces
Stress Reduction, Improved Well-being, and Organizational Effectiveness
Edited by Caroline Biron, Ronald J. Burke and Cary L. Cooper

Human Frailties
Wrong Choices on the Drive to Success
Edited by Ronald J. Burke, Suzy Fox and Cary L. Cooper

The Fulfilling Workplace
The Organization's Role in Achieving Individual and Organizational Health
Edited by Ronald J. Burke and Cary L. Cooper

Occupational Health and Safety
Edited by Ronald J. Burke, Sharon Clarke and Cary L. Cooper

Coping, Personality and the Workplace

Responding to Psychological Crisis and Critical Events

Edited by

ALEXANDER-STAMATIOS ANTONIOU
University of Athens, Greece

CARY L. COOPER, CBE
Manchester Business School, University of Manchester, UK

Routledge
Taylor & Francis Group

LONDON AND NEW YORK

First published 2016 by Gower Publishing

2 Park Square, Milton Park, Abingdon, Oxfordshire OX14 4RN
52 Vanderbilt Avenue, New York, NY 10017

Routledge is an imprint of the Taylor & Francis Group, an informa business

First issued in paperback 2020

Gower Applied Business Research
Our programme provides leaders, practitioners, scholars and researchers with thought provoking, cutting edge books that combine conceptual insights, interdisciplinary rigour and practical relevance in key areas of business and management.

British Library Cataloguing in Publication Data
A catalogue record for this book is available from the British Library

Library of Congress Cataloging-in-Publication Data
Coping, personality and the workplace : responding to psychological crisis and critical events / [edited] by Alexander-Stamatios Antoniou and Cary L. Cooper.
    pages cm. -- (Psychological and behavioural aspects of risk)
  Includes bibliographical references and index.
  ISBN 978-1-4724-1682-7 (hardback)
1. Job stress. 2. Adjustment (Psychology) 3. Personality and occupation.
4. Employees--Mental health. 5. Psychology, Industrial. 6. Industrial psychiatry. I. Antoniou, Alexander-Stamatios G. II. Cooper, Cary L.
  HF5548.85.C659 2015
  158.7'2--dc23
                                                                                              2015018102

ISBN 978-1-4724-1682-7 (hbk)
ISBN 978-0-367-66852-5 (pbk)

Contents

PART I: CONCEPTUALIZATION AND THEORETICAL FRAMEWORK

PART II: PERSONALITY AND COPING WITH WORK-RELATED STRESS AND PROFESSIONAL BURNOUT

PART III: COPING AND THE ROLE OF RESILIENCE

PART IV: PERSONALITY AND COPING IN EDUCATIONAL SETTINGS

PART V: PERSONALITY AND COPING WITH JOB LOSS

PART VI: SPECIFIC ISSUES ON PERSONALITY TRAITS AND COPING MECHANISMS

List of Figures

List of Tables

List of Contributors

Alexander-Stamatios Antoniou, National and Kapodistrian University of Athens, Greece

Maria Armaou, University of Warwick

Sarah Arpin, Portland State University

Charles C. Benight, University of Colorado Colorado Springs

Paula Brough, Griffith University, Australia

Jesse L. Byrd, Washington State University Vancouver

Roman Cieslak, University of Social Sciences and Humanities, Warsaw, Poland and University of Colorado Colorado Springs

Lenora A. Collins, Department of Psychology, Saint Mary's University, Halifax, Canada

Cary L. Cooper, Manchester Business School, University of Manchester

Marina Dalla, Psychiatric Hospital of Attica, 18 ANO Dependent Treatment Unit

Philip Dewe, Department of Organizational Psychology Birkbeck, University of London

Jennifer K. Dimoff, Department of Psychology, Saint Mary's University, Halifax, Canada

Nico Dragano, Institute of Medical Sociology, Heinrich-Heine University of Dusseldorf

Suzie Drummond, School of Applied Psychology and Griffith Health Institute, Griffith University, Australia

Adrian Furnham, University College London

Nicholas J. Gailey, Washington State University Vancouver

Antigoni Garyfallaki, National and Kapodistrian University of Athens

Esther R. Greenglass, York University, Toronto, Canada

Kaylee J. Hackney, Department of Management, College of Business Florida State University

E. Kevin Kelloway, Department of Psychology, Saint Mary's University, Halifax, Canada

Ellen Kenner, University of RI

Dianna T. Kenny, The University of Sydney, Australia

Bruce David Kirkcaldy, International Centre for the Study of Occupational and Mental Health, Dusseldorf, Germany

Michael P. Leiter, Psychology Department Acadia University, Canada

Magdalena Lesnierowska, University of Social Sciences and Humanities, Warsaw, Poland

Edwin A. Locke, University of Maryland, Los Angeles

Chang-qin Lu, Peking University, PR China

Luo Lu, Taiwan National University, Taiwan

Thorsten Lunau, Institute of Medical Sociology, Heinrich-Heine University of Dusseldorf

Charn P. McAllister, Department of Management, College of Business Florida State University

Cameron T. McCabe, Portland State University

Jeremy D. Mackey, Department of Management, College of Business Florida State University

Diana Malinowska, Jagiellonian University, Poland

Constance A. Mara, James M. Anderson Center for Health Systems Excellence, Cincinnati Children's Hospital Medical Center, Cincinnati, Ohio, USA

Eftychia Mitsopoulou, National and Kapodistrian University of Athens

Cynthia D. Mohr, Portland State University

Kathleen Otto, Philipps University of Marburg, Germany

Joshua C. Palmer, Department of Psychology, College of Liberal Arts Southern Illinois University

Pamela L. Perrewé, Department of Management, College of Business Florida State University

Panagiotis E. Petrakis, Department of Economics at National and Kapodistrian University of Athens, Greece

Tahira M. Probst, Washington State University Vancouver

Tabea Scheel, University of Vienna, Austria

Oi-Ling Siu, Lingnan University, Hong Kong

Ewelina Smoktunowicz, University of Social Sciences and Humanities, Warsaw, Poland

Paul E. Spector, University of South Florida, USA

Sabina Staszczyk, Jagiellonian University, Poland

Aleksandra Tokarz, Jagiellonian University, Poland

Luke Treglown, University College London

Morten Wahrendorf, Institute of Medical Sociology, Heinrich-Heine University of Dusseldorf

Ashley Weinberg, Salford University, UK

About the Contributors

Alexander-Stamatios Antoniou is an assistant professor of psychology at the National and Kapodistrian University of Athens and holds undergraduate degrees (BSc in Psychology and BA in Philosophy) and postgraduate degrees (MEd, MPhil, PhD, PhD) in Psychology, Philosophy, Education and Management from universities in Greece and the UK. The courses he teaches include Social Psychology, Organizational Psychology/Behaviour, Mental Disorders and Psychology of Personality. He has participated as a national coordinator and as a researcher in national and European research programmes. His main research interests include occupational stress and professional burnout, leadership, work values and business ethics, organizational politics, communication networks, etc. His publications include research papers and chapters in refereed academic journals, books and edited volumes and his work has been presented at many national and international conferences.

Maria Armaou is a psychologist and an interest in positive organizational behaviour. She holds a BSc degree in Psychology from the National and Kapodistrian Unversity of Athens, an MSc degree in Occupational Psychology from the University of Nottingham and a PhD in Education from the University of Warwick. Her doctorate research focused on teachers' perceptions of their resources and the use of the definition of job resources to address teachers' sources of support and their professional needs. She has co-authored book chapters related to her research interests and presented her work in international conferences.

Sarah Arpin is a doctoral candidate of applied social psychology at Portland State University. She received her MS from Portland State University in 2012, and her BA in Psychology at Gonzaga University in 2010. Her research examines social and emotional determinants of health. In particular, she investigates the interpersonal and intrapersonal consequences of loneliness over time, including patterns of health behaviour, social behaviour and social cognitions.

Charles C. Benight, PhD, is a professor at the Department of Psychology and the Director of the CU Trauma, Health, & Hazards Center at the University of Colorado, Colorado Springs. Dr Benight utilizes social cognitive theory to investigate the biopsychosocial mechanisms of adaptation to stress and trauma and in the development of innovative technological approaches to assist trauma and disaster survivors.

Paula Brough is a professor of organizational psychology in the School of Applied Psychology at Griffith University, Australia. Professor Brough's research focuses on the evaluation and enhancement of occupational psychological health, with specific interests in occupational stress, well-being and work–life balance. Her research has primarily focused on two issues: (1) reducing experiences of occupational stress within the high-risk industries (e.g. police) and (2) enhancing individual health and organizational performance.

Jesse L. Byrd is an industrial-organizational doctoral student in the Experimental PhD programme at Washington State University. His research interests are focused on organizational intervention research, workplace aggression, production pressure and effective leadership models.

Roman Cieslak, PhD, Associate Professor at the Department of Psychology, University of Social Sciences and Humanities (SWPS), Warsaw, Poland and Senior Research Scholar at the Trauma, Health, and Hazards Center, University of Colorado, Colorado Springs, USA. In his research, he investigates when and how self-efficacy, social support and other resources are used in coping with work stress, job burnout and consequences of traumatic events.

Lenora A. Collins is a personnel selection officer with the Canadian Armed Forces. She received her Masters of Applied Science in Industrial Organizational Psychology from Saint Mary's University. Her research focuses on the role of leaders in promoting resilience and thriving in organizations.

Professor Sir Cary Cooper, CBE
Cary L. Cooper is the author and editor of more than 125 books and is one of Britain's most quoted business gurus. He is The 50th Anniversary Professor of Organizational Psychology and Health at Manchester Business School, University of Manchester, UK. He is a founding President of the British Academy of Management, a Companion of the Chartered Management Institute and one of only a few UK Fellows of the (American) Academy of Management, past President of the British Association of Counselling and Psychotherapy and President of RELATE. He was the Founding Editor of the *Journal of Organizational Behavior*, former Editor of the scholarly journal *Stress and Health* and is the Editor-in-Chief of the *Wiley-Blackwell Encyclopaedia of Management*; now in its 3rd Edition. He has been an advisor to the World Health Organisation, ILO, and EU in the field of occupational health research and wellbeing, was Chair of the Global Agenda Council on Chronic Disease of the World Economic Forum (2009–2010, and currently a member of the Global Agenda Council on mental health of the WEF) and is Immediate Past Chair of the Academy of Social Sciences (comprising 47 learned societies in the social sciences and 90,000 members). He was awarded the CBE by the Queen in 2001 for his contributions to organizational health and safety; and in 2014 he was awarded a Knighthood for his contribution to the social sciences.

Marina Dalla has a doctorate in social psychology from the Department of Psychology, Faculty of Philosophy, Education, and Psychology of the University of Athens, graduated with honours. She has published many papers in the form of journal articles or book chapters in Greek and English and she has different presentations in scientific events, in Greek and in English. Her current research interests focus on acculturation and adaptation of immigrants, resilience and vulnerability of immigrant adolescents, social stigma and mental health of immigrants, immigration and drug abuse. Dr Dalla is a member of International Association for Cross Cultural Psychology, of the Hellenic Psychological Society and the Greek Society for Social Psychology.

Philip Dewe is Professor of Organizational Behaviour in the Centre for Sustainable Working Life, Birkbeck, University of London. He holds a PhD from the London School of Economics. After a period of work in commerce in New Zealand he became a senior research officer in the Work Research Unit, Department of Employment in the United Kingdom. In 1980 he joined Massey University in New Zealand and headed the Department of Human Resource Management until joining the Department of Organizational Psychology at Birkbeck in 2000. He has published widely in the area of work stress and coping.

Jennifer K. Dimoff is a PhD candidate in Industrial/Organizational Psychology at Saint Mary's University in Nova Scotia, Canada, where she completed her MSc in Applied Psychology. Jennifer also holds a BSc (Hon.) in Biology from Queen's University in Ontario, Canada. Jennifer's research focuses on occupational health, leadership and psychological resilience, with an emphasis on the development, implementation and evaluation of workplace mental health interventions.

Nico Dragano is a sociologist with expertise in occupational epidemiology. He is a professor for medical sociology at the University Clinic Düsseldorf. Major fields of interest are occupational health epidemiology, work-related and non-work-related stress, social inequalities in health, cardiovascular disease epidemiology and prevention. He is affiliated with different international research collaborations on work-related stress like the IPD-Work consortium.

Suzie Drummond recently completed her PhD in Organizational Psychology at the School of Applied Psychology at Griffith University, Australia. Her research investigated future-oriented coping and explored its relationships within the framework of the transactional model of stress and coping.

Adrian Furnham was educated at the London School of Economics where he obtained a distinction in an MSc Econ., and at Oxford University where he completed a doctorate (DPhil) in 1981. He has subsequently earned a DSc (1991) and DLitt (1995) degree. Previously a lecturer in psychology at Pembroke College, Oxford, he has been Professor of Psychology at University College London since 1992. He has lectured widely abroad and held scholarships and visiting professorships at, amongst others, the University of New South Wales, the University of the West Indies, the University of Hong Kong and the University of KwaZulu-Natal. He has also been a Visiting Professor of Management at Henley Management College. He has also been made Adjunct Professor of Management at the Norwegian School of Management (2009). He has written over 1000 scientific papers and 80 books. Like Noel Coward, he believes work is more fun than fun and considers himself to be a well-adjusted workaholic. He rides a bicycle to work (as he has always done) very early in the morning and does not have a mobile phone. Adrian enjoys writing popular articles, travelling to exotic countries, consulting on real-life problems, arguing at dinner parties and going to the theatre. He hopes never to retire.

Nicholas J. Gailey is a doctoral student at Washington State University Vancouver where he is studying Experimental Psychology with an emphasis on Industrial and Organizational Psychology. His research interests include positive organizational practices, employee well-being and health, job security, and positive organizational development. Nick is a McNair Scholar Alumni, recipient of the APA Academic Achievement Award in Psychology, and a recipient of the Distinguished Researcher and Diverse Scholars Award.

Antigoni Garyfallaki is a psychologist, with a master's in education (University of Manchester) interested in learning and psychosocial support of children and adolescents with special educational needs. She holds an undergraduate degree from the National and Kapodistrian University of Athens, Department of Psychology, and she has also specialized in Special Education at the same institution. She currently works as a psychologist in special and mainstream secondary education. Furthermore she works voluntarily at the Community Mental Health Centre of Evaggelismos General Hospital, and at the non-profit organization 'One Child One World'.

Esther R. Greenglass is professor of psychology at York University in Toronto, Canada. Her research interests are in the area of stress and coping. More recently, she leads an international consortium of psychologists who study the psychological effects of the recent recession. In particular their research applies theoretical conceptions of stress and coping to an understanding of the ways in which individuals cope with the effects of economic hardship.

Kaylee J. Hackney is a PhD candidate in Organizational Behavior and Human Resource Management at Florida State University. Her current research interests include work–family balance, interpersonal mistreatment and job stress.

E. Kevin Kelloway is the Canada Research Chair in Occupational Health Psychology and Professor of Psychology at Saint Mary's University, Halifax, Nova Scotia. A prolific researcher he is a Fellow of the Association for Psychological Science, the Canadian Psychological Association, the International Association of Applied Psychology and the Society for Industrial/Organizational Psychology. His research interests focus on occupational health psychology, leadership and human resources management.

Ellen Kenner, PhD, is a licensed clinical psychologist and host of the nationally-syndicated radio talk show, 'The Rational Basis of Happiness®'. Her specialty is exploring how to apply the rational, pro-happiness philosophy of Ayn Rand's Objectivism to mental health issues. Dr Kenner has been a speaker at Objectivist conferences for many years and has led workshops on communication, romance and family issues, including 'Romance: Bringing Love and Sex Together', presented in collaboration with co-author Edwin Locke. She makes frequent media appearances. And, as mentioned above, she is co-author, with Dr Locke, of *The Selfish Path to Romance: How to Love with Passion and Reason*. Dr Kenner earned her PhD from the University of Rhode Island and her BA from Brown University.

Dianna T. Kenny, PhD, MA (Sch Couns) BA (Hons) ATCL (Piano) DipEd MAPsS MAPA, is Professor of Psychology and Professor of Music at the University of Sydney, Australia. She has wide research interests and is the author of over 200 publications, including seven books, the most recent of which are *Young Offenders on Community Orders: Health, Welfare and Criminogenic Needs* (Sydney University Press, 2008) (with Paul Nelson), *The Psychology of Music Performance Anxiety* (Oxford University Press, 2011), *Bringing up Baby: The Psychoanalytic Infant Comes of Age* (Karnac, 2013), and *From Id to Intersubjectivity: Talking about the Talking Cure with Master Clinicians* (Karnac, 2014). Her latest book, *God, Freud and Religion* is in press (Routledge, 2015).

Bruce David Kirkcaldy has academic degrees in psychology from the Universities of Dundee and Giessen, as well as postgraduate professional training as a Behavioural Therapist and Clinical Psychologist. He is Director of the International Centre for the Study of Occupational and Mental Health, and runs his own psychotherapy practise specializing in the treatment of anxiety and depressive disorders and psychosomatic ailments. In addition, he has been Visiting Professor for Psychology at the Jagiellonen University, Cracow in Poland. He has published over 200 articles including some 25 book chapters and nine authored/edited books.

Michael P. Leiter (BA Duke; MA Vanderbilt; Phd U of Oregon) is Professor of Psychology at Acadia University in Canada and Director of the Center for Organizational Research & Development that applies high quality research methods to human resource issues confronting organizations. He holds the Canada Research Chair in Occupational Health and Wellbeing at Acadia University. He has published widely on burnout, work engagement and workplace civility.

Magdalena Lesnierowska, PhD student at the Department of Psychology, University of Social Sciences and Humanities (SWPS), Warsaw, Poland. Her research interests include how people cope with stress at work and trauma exposure and why work stress and traumatic events affect whole family systems.

Edwin A. Locke, PhD, is an internationally known and widely published scholar in the field of industrial organizational psychology, with 15 years of clinical experience and more than three decades as a professor of psychology and of management emeritus at the University of Maryland. He has written over 280 books, chapters and articles and is widely cited in psychological literature. Dr Locke, a Fellow of the American Psychological Association and of the American Psychological Society, has been recognized by his peers with many scholarly awards. He frequently speaks at conferences on the topic of setting goals for life and happiness. He is also a scholar and advocate of the works of Ayn Rand, has written and spoken extensively about her philosophy. Dr Locke and Dr Kenner have co-authored the self-help book, *The Selfish Path to Romance: How to Love with Passion and Reason*. Dr Locke earned his PhD from Cornell University and his BA from Harvard University. Dr Locke lives in California.

Chang-qin Lu is an associate professor at the Department of Psychology, Peking University, China. He received his PhD in Industrial/Organizational Psychology from the Institute of Psychology, Chinese Academy of Sciences. His research focuses on work stress, with interests in the jointed roles of self-efficacy and workplace social support among stress process, job insecurity, spillover and crossover effects of work–family conflict/balance, and issues in cross-cultural stress research.

Luo Lu, DPhil, University of Oxford, UK, is currently the Distinguished Professor in National Taiwan University, Taiwan. Her major research interests include: culture and self, subjective well-being, stress and adjustment, occupational health, and other IO psychological topics. She has been awarded the Distinguished Research Award by the Taiwanese government. She has published extensively in journals and edited/authored books and book chapters.

Thorsten Lunau is a junior researcher and PhD candidate at the Institute for Medical Sociology. He holds a master's degree in Sociology, Psychology and Political Science. His major research focuses are health adverse psychosocial working conditions. He investigates the association between psychosocial working conditions and health outcomes (especially mental health). His key research area is the influence of social and labour market policies on psychosocial working conditions.

Charn P. McAllister is a PhD candidate in Organizational Behavior and Human Resource Management at Florida State University. His current research interests include self-regulation, social influence and job stress. His research has been published in the *Journal of Organizational Behavior, Research in Personnel and Human Resources Management* and *Business Horizons*.

Cameron T. McCabe is a doctoral student of applied social psychology at Portland State University. He received his BA and MA in psychology from San Diego State University. His research examines the interplay of stress, social and cognitive processes on daily health and health behaviour.

Jeremy D. Mackey is a PhD candidate in Organizational Behavior and Human Resource Management at Florida State University. His current research interests include interpersonal mistreatment, abusive supervision, job stress and attribution theory. Some of his research has been published in the *Journal of Business and Psychology, Journal of Business Ethics, Journal of Leadership & Organizational Studies, Journal of Managerial Psychology, Journal of Organizational Behavior, Organizational Psychology Review* and *The Leadership Quarterly*.

Diana Malinowska, PhD, is an assistant professor at the Institute of Psychology at the Jagiellonian University, Poland. Her main research interests is in heavy work investment, its motivational and organizational determinants, and she currently examines how the quality of motivation impacts on the relationship between the work context and types of overwork: workaholism and work engagement.

Constance A. Mara is a researcher in the James Anderson Center for Health Systems Excellence at Cincinnati Children's Hospital Medical Center (CCHMC). Her background is in quantitative methodology, social psychology and health. She uses advanced statistical methods to measure and improve health outcomes for children, adolescents and their families.

Eftychia Mitsopoulou works as a Religious Subject teacher at the 2nd Model Experimental Junior High School of Athens. She holds a bachelor's degree in Theology from the Aristotle University of Thessaloniki, a bachelor's degree in Primary Education from the National and Kapodistrian University of Athens, an MPhil in Special Didactics of the Religious Subject from the National and Kapodistrian University of Athens and an MPhil in Psychology and Education from the University of Cambridge. She is currently a PhD student at the Faculty of Primary Education at the National and Kapodistrian University of Athens and specializes in the field of special education and gifted students. She is a member of the British Psychological Society from which she acquired the Graduate Basis for Chartered Membership. Her research interests include: social aspects of special education, resilience of gifted and talented students, the birth and development of stereotypes and prejudice in children, etc.

Cynthia D. Mohr is an associate professor of social psychology at Portland State University. She received her BA from Smith College in Massachusetts in 1991 and her PhD in social psychology from the University of Connecticut in 1999, before working as a postdoctoral research fellow in the Alcohol Research Center at the University of Connecticut Health Center. Her research explores psychosocial influences on subjective well-being and physical health.

Kathleen Otto is full professor of Work and Organizational Psychology at the Philipps University of Marburg (Germany). She holds a PhD in Psychology from the Martin Luther University of Halle-Wittenberg and a master's in Mediation from the University of Hagen. Her research interest lies in the fields of organizational justice, leadership and health, coping with occupational and organizational changes and restructuring, unemployment and job insecurity.

Joshua C. Palmer is a PhD student in Applied Psychology at Southern Illinois University Carbondale. His research interests include the study of leadership characteristics, burnout, ethics and counterproductive work behaviour.

Pamela L. Perrewé is the Haywood and Betty Taylor Eminent Scholar of Business Administration, Professor of Sport Management, and Distinguished Research Professor at Florida State University. Her research interests are in the areas of job stress, coping, organizational politics, emotion and social influence. She has published over 40 books and book chapters and approximately 120 journal articles in journals such as the *Academy of Management Journal* and *Journal of Applied Psychology*.

Panagiotis E. Petrakis is Professor in the Department of Economics at National and Kapodistrian University of Athens, Greece, where he also serves as Director of the International Economics and Development Sector. He is the author of more than 26 monographs in topics related to

European and Greek growth, crisis, and economic policy, entrepreneurship and culture. He also is the author of numerous research articles in prestigious scientific journals.

Tahira M. Probst is an Edward R. Meyer Distinguished Professor of Psychology at Washington State University Vancouver. Her research focuses on economic stress and job insecurity with a particular emphasis on understanding multilevel predictors, moderators and outcomes of these phenomena. She is currently co-editor of *Stress & Health* and sits on the editorial boards of the *Journal of Occupational Health Psychology*, *Military Psychology* and the *Journal of Business and Psychology*.

Tabea Scheel is currently holding a postdoctoral research fellowship (Humboldt Foundation) at the Humboldt-University of Berlin (Germany), Organizational Psychology Department. She obtained her PhD from the University of Leipzig and worked at the University of Vienna. Her work is published in journals such as the *Human Resource Management* and *European Journal of Work and Organizational Psychology*. Her research interests cover psychological contracts, unemployment, error management culture and humour at work.

Oi-Ling Siu is Professor and Head of Department of Applied Psychology at Lingnan University, Hong Kong. Her research interests are in occupational health psychology, specifically occupational stress, safety and work–life balance. She is incoming editor of the *International Journal of Stress Management* and associate editor of the *Journal of Occupational Health Psychology*.

Ewelina Smoktunowicz is a research assistant at the Department of Psychology, University of Social Sciences and Humanities (SWPS), Warsaw, Poland. In her research, she investigates the interactions between work and family domains (crossover and spillover effects) and their consequences for work- and family-related well-being.

Paul E. Spector is Distinguished Professor, and Director of the I/O Psychology and Occupational Health Psychology doctoral programmes at the University of South Florida. He is Point/Counterpoint editor for the *Journal of Organizational Behavior*, associate editor for *Work & Stress*, and is on the editorial board of the *Journal of Applied Psychology*.

Sabina Staszczyk is a PhD student in Psychology at the Jagiellonian University, Poland, working under the supervision of Professor Aleksandra Tokarz. She received her MA in Psychology from the Jagiellonian University, specializing in organizational psychology. Her research is focused on different types of heavy work investment. She is particularly interested in identifying differences between workaholism, passion to work and work engagement.

Aleksandra Tokarz, PhD, is a full professor at the Jagiellonian University, Poland. Key themes in her research include: motivational and emotional mechanisms of creative activity, intrinsic motivation and its properties, methods of arousing motivation for achievements and epistemic motivation, and motivational aspects of work: psychological determinants of motivation to work across age, professional burnout, workaholism. Her research interests include also personality determinants of sport performance.

Luke Treglown is a graduate of Bath University. He is currently a PhD student at University College London.

Morten Wahrendorf is a sociologist with expertise in research methodology. His research areas are work stress, health inequalities, life course epidemiology, comparative welfare research and ageing. He is an attached member of the International Centre For Life-Course Studies in Society and Health (ICLS), and is presently working at the Institute for Medical Sociology, University Düsseldorf, Germany.

Ashley Weinberg is a chartered psychologist, senior lecturer in psychology at the University of Salford and an honorary senior lecturer at the University of Manchester. He has produced three books on well-being at work with Professor Cary Cooper and is editor of *The Psychology of Politicians*. His most recent book, *Stress in Turbulent Times*, highlights the importance of maximizing our psychological resources in times of difficult change and recommends strategies for individuals and organisations.

Foreword

Adrian Furnham

Any applied psychologist will be used to the fact that managers tend to ask them the same questions. The most common are: How can I better motivate my staff? How can I make by staff more resilient? How can I lower absenteeism and raise engagement?

Some jobs are inherently stressful with high demands and low control. They take their toll on people physically, emotionally and behaviourally. Moreover this can effect a person's whole social network. Chronic work stress can lead to chronic problems from hypertension and ulcers to depression. Work stress can have enormous costs and hence there is an interest in trying to reduce it.

Stress is as much subjective as objective. Different people perceive the same job as challenging and exciting, but also demanding and stressful. Much depends on the individual, but there is no doubt that some jobs are potentially very stressful with long hours, demanding bosses and clients.

All of us have coping strategies at, and after, work. Some slump before the television, full wine glass in hand. Others go for a jog or attempt a bit of therapeutic gardening. You can phone a friend, take the dog for a walk, try a bit of meditation. The question is which strategy is best for whom? Can these be taught? Why do some people ruminate while others can leave their stress in the office?

Over the years there has been a great deal of academic and applied interest in how people react to stress. Various overlapping concepts appeared: Coping style, Hardiness, Optimism (Attribution Style), and Resilience. Researchers were interested in identifying those people who had healthy, adaptive coping styles and those who did not. The questions were, first, why was it some people were more resilient than others; second, what was the essence of healthy coping strategies; and, third, how could they be taught to people who did not have them?

The academic questions concerned a parsimonious and veridical description of the process as well as an attempt to measure various concepts. There was also an interest in providing evidence of the efficacy of various intervention techniques.

This research has been made all the more salient by the increased stress and pressure that people experience in the modern workplace.

The chapters in this book look at essentially four issues. The first is personality correlates of coping. It asks the question concerning which personality traits are most closely related to coping strategies. For a long period it was trait Adjustment/Neuroticism/Negative Affectivity that was seen to be the major correlate of coping. People with low adjustment are moody and unstable. They are prone to anxiety, depression and hypochondriasis. They seem easily upset, highly vigilant to social threats and constantly worrying.

The other personality factors were thought of as less important unless people were very high scorers. Thus, the spectrum hypothesis suggests that extremes of normal are (by definition) abnormal, and that people with very high scores on any traits might experience stress. Thus a very high scorer on Conscientiousness may manifest signs of OCD and equally a person who scores very low on Extraversion may appear Schizoid and friendless.

Work on the biological and genetic basis of personality has taken the area forward because it has moved on from an interest primarily on categorization to trying to understand the process. That is researchers are beginning to understand the physiological and psychological mechanisms that account for the behaviours we associate with known personality traits.

The second theme is to explore in some detail the literature in a relevant area like burnout, well-being or resilience. Inevitable, separate literature have grown up around very specific concepts and measures. Some are linked to very different areas of psychology such as clinical, positive and work psychology. They are similar in that they each set out to describe a process, its cause and consequences and how various things can be done to change matters.

Anyone who has the time and inclination to study these little islands in the archipelago of Stress and Coping will note considerable overlap in ideas. They may also be a little disappointed about the "fractionalization" of the field which means that so much work is replicated.

The third theme concerns the consequences for poor coping in different contexts. Different work environments put quite different pressures on individuals. In some there is physical danger and in others considerable time pressures. Different jobs not only provide different sources of stress but also are unique enviroments where stress can have devastating consequences.

A final theme is about intervention, namely how to deal with these issues. Whilst it is not always possible to change jobs to illuminate stress altogether it is possible to devise ways to help individual who have stress. This can be done on an individual, group or organizational level and may have important positive consequences. The question is which techniques work best for whom and why?

There are two dozen chapters in this book written by experts in their field. They differ in length, style and focus, but each takes a up-to-date and critical look at some of the most important issues facing people in the modern workplace.

Introduction

A.-S. Antoniou and C.L. Cooper

Many researchers over the last decades have been interested in the relationship between coping, personality and stress. The outcome is the confirmed connection between these terms and multiple surveys in various fields. Despite the thorough research on this relation, there is still interest in it, innovations and new fields to be explored. In addition, the critiques addressed to the past theoretical frameworks give us the opportunity to take new, innovative pathways.

Coping, Personality and the Workplace shares insights from scholarship around the world, to advance our collective understanding of the conceptualization and theoretical background of these terms, the personality traits, coping strategies and resilience factors affecting the workplace, with a particular emphasis on the role that personality and coping play in responding to stress in educational contexts and in responding to critical events such as coping with job loss, and challenges in the coping process.

Leading scholars and practitioners from 10 countries (Australia, Austria, Canada, China, Germany, Greece, Poland, Taiwan, UK, and USA) provide theoretical and empirical information about coping, personality and the workplace including innovative approaches to theory, measurement and intervention. The information included in the chapters provides fundamental information of interest to scholars, practitioners, students and other professionals.

The following provides a brief description of the information that is included in each section of the handbook:

Conceptualization and theoretical framework. Chapters in this section of the handbook provide important information regarding conceptual issues related to coping and personality in the workplace. The information included in this section is essential in establishing a solid foundation for these concepts. In the first chapter, Dewe overviews the relationship between personality and coping, discusses the challenges surrounding the measurement of the two concepts and focuses on the themes that emerge for the way forward. In the second chapter, Drummond and Brough review the current evidence and discussions concerning future-oriented coping, including the mixed evidence for relationships between coping and personality constructs. Next, Weinberg examines the role of political behaviour in the workplace, the extent to which this reflects aspects of personality and its significance for individual psychological well-being.

Personality and coping with work-related stress and professional burnout. Chapters in this section of the handbook identify and discuss important aspects related to personality, coping and stress and burnout. In the first chapter, Dragano and colleagues explore the role of personality in the frame of contemporary work stress research, and specifically how personality may affect work stress and its consequences for health; they present new data from a longitudinal cohort study of workers in the United States. In the next chapter, Siu and colleagues explore the relationship between two focal social stressors (interpersonal conflict and organizational politics) and psychological strains (job satisfaction and psychological symptoms) and also examine how self-efficacy and active coping might protect employees from negative effects of social stressors.

Next, Locke discusses the conceptualization and the key characteristics of burnout as well as the implications of burnout with an emphasis on the individual and organizational factors that make a person more vulnerable to burnout and the factors that are important for resistance to burnout. Gailey and Probst focus on positive aspects of employee personality that can better enable employees to cope with the workplace stressors. They review a number of positive personality traits, discuss how organizations can promote these strengths within their employees and evaluate the extent to which organizational interventions to promote these positive personality traits have proven successful.

In the final chapter of the section, McCabe and colleagues build on past research and theory by emphasizing perceived responsiveness and other supportive processes in the workplace as central to the development of trust within work relationships. The authors propose perceived responsiveness as one potential mechanism through which social support and supportive behaviours lead to positive outcomes and as a critical determinant of organizational and individual well-being.

Coping and the role of resilience. In the first chapter of this section Treglown and Furnham examine conceptual issues of resilience, and different measures of resilience pointing to the fact that there seems to be no agreed definition and typology of the concept of resilience or the development of an universally applied and psychometrically proven measure. The second chapter by Mara and Greenglass focuses on the study of positive factors that can empower youth to deal with financial strain in times of economic recession. The authors argue that while it is important to understand the negative impact of financial crises, researchers must also devote attention to the positive factors that contribute to individuals successfully dealing with financial and economic adversity in order to promote psychological well-being in times of economic hardship. Next, Armaou and Antoniou investigate teachers' well-being and the role of resilience in the educational context. They argue that individuals' coping strategies and other supportive and non-supportive factors within the contexts of teachers' work need to be adequately addressed for teachers' resilience and their overall well-being at work.

Personality and coping in educational settings. Antoniou and Garyfallaki, in the first chapter of this section argue that personality traits such as low self-efficacy feelings and high stress reactivity make a person perceive a difficult situation as stressful. Coping strategies at the organizational level, class level and personal level, stressors and moderating factors work together to form the background of the coping process for teachers. In the second chapter, Dalla and Antoniou present theoretical and empirical data on the increase of drug use problems, especially for high school students at the upper end of academic performance, the high achievers. Next, Antoniou and Mitsopoulou discuss how personality is pivotal to help us understand why working in the same environment and facing similar stress and demands, does not necessarily mean that all individuals will suffer the same levels of stress. Investigating the individual and organizational factors that play a significant role in coping helps create school contexts that prevent teachers' dropout and foster their commitment to their job.

Personality and coping with job loss. In the first chapter of this section, Probst and Byrd examine different personality constructs that have been found to predict the experience of economic stress and/or assist individuals with coping with these stressors. They look into job insecurity and potential job loss through the lens of positive psychology as a potential opportunity for future growth and development. Scheel and Otto overview the findings on the impact of unemployment on work attitudes and behavior. In particular, the chapter explores the research question, whether unemployment affects coping abilities and strategies (e.g. seeking social support) and related variables.

Specific issues on personality traits and coping mechanisms. In the first chapter of this section, Leiter explores the potential of attachment theory to explaining individual variations among members of workgroups in their perception of and reaction to workplace incivility. The interaction of attachment styles with workgroup conditions and recommendations for measurement and future research are explored. In the next chapter, Petrakis examines the notion of personality traits in the workplace and the role of the connection between organizational culture and the personal traits of the workforce for effective business operation. The relationship between personality traits and productivity is presented as well as whether personality traits change after conditions of economic crisis and business distress.

Next, Hackney and colleagues present the findings of an empirical study that examined the factors that might impact veterans' levels of person-environment fit by investigating the relationships between political skill, job skill transfer, and P-E fit. The results suggested that veterans with high political skill better understand how the skills they learned in the military, and throughout their lifetime, transfer to their civilian organization, allowing them to better fit in with their organization than veterans with low levels of political skill. In the final chapter of this section, Kenny argues that working in the music industry is a stressful occupation and she explores four markers of traumatic stress inherent in the death records of popular musicians.

Challenges in the coping process. In the first chapter of this section, Kirkcaldy et al. critically review interventions for workaholism, and focuses on detailed clinically relevant material to support mental health professionals in their provision of treatment for such ailments. Next, Smoktunowicz and colleagues review the demands that can potentially trigger the negative side of work–family interface and the resources that contribute to its positive side. They focus specifically on personal resources that have the potential to buffer the work–family and family–work conflict and protect individuals from negative consequences. In the final chapter, Dimoff and colleagues discuss the notion of scrambling as the immediate marshalling of resources in response to an acute stressor in order to meet the immediate demands of a crisis. They draw on the crisis response literature, in addition to the literature on coping and stressor-management, in developing a model of scrambling as a process and ability.

In conclusion, we would like to express our many thanks to all those our colleagues who contributed to this new volume. Their expertise and experience has provided original and in-depth insights on critical issues of the working environment. It is a great pleasure for us to welcome once more such an international team of academics, professionals and experts from a number of international universities and institutions. Finally, many credits go to the Gower Publishing staff for their significant advice and support throughout the various stages of this project.

PART I
CONCEPTUALIZATION AND THEORETICAL FRAMEWORK

1

Coping and Personality: Approaches, Measurement and Challenges

Philip Dewe

Introduction

How people cope with stress is, as Aldwin suggests, 'of immediate personal relevance' (Aldwin 2000, p. 73) helping to explain what has been described as a 'boundless enthusiasm for', (Somerfield and McCrae 2000, p. 620) and 'a dramatic proliferation' (Folkman and Moskowitz 2004, p. 745) of, coping research over the last three decades. Re-emerging out of this enthusiasm has been 'a strong interest' in the relationship between personality and coping (Watson, David and Suls 1999, p. 120) and the 'immense importance' of personality in helping to understand how people cope (Vollrath 2001, p. 335). Nevertheless, despite personality being described as revealing its dynamic self under stress (Bolger 1990) and that coping should now be defined as personality in action (Vollrath 2001) research on the coping–personality relationship is not without controversy, debate and challenges. A rich history surrounds coping and personality and this chapter begins by tracing the evolution of this relationship across what Suls and his colleagues describe as three generations of research (Suls, David and Harvey 1996). From what we mean by personality and coping and the debate surrounding how these concepts are defined the chapter then turns to the advances that researchers have made in exploring specific personality traits and coping followed by how coping–personality research has been 'reinvigorated' by the adoption of a more 'unified framework' (Vollrath 2001) for exploring personality described as the five-factor personality model or simply the Big Five (Carver and Connor-Smith 2010; Connor-Smith and Flachsbart 2007; Suls et al. 1996; Watson et al. 1999). None of these developments escape criticism, controversy and challenges and the chapter concludes by exploring some of this unfinished business before looking at the way ahead.

A Short History

In their overview of the history of coping and personality Suls and his colleagues identify three generations of research (Suls and David 1996; Suls et al. 1996). The first they describe as falling under the rubric of *psychoanalytic-ego development-psychology*. Here coping was viewed as a defence mechanism reflecting the way in which the ego dealt with internal conflicts. These mechanisms were assumed to be expressions of personality, reflecting a consistent style of coping (Aldwin 2000, 2007). Hierarchies of defence mechanisms and their type and functions soon followed (see Aldwin 2000; Suls et al. 1996). However, weighed down by their number, range and classification, and beset at times by conceptual, measurement and empirical issues, 'it is scarcely surprising' that this perspective where personality and coping were viewed as the same thing was seen as 'too inflexible' (Suls and David 1996, p. 993) to capture the dynamics of the coping process compelling researchers, if they were to understand the personality–coping relationship, to separate coping from personality.

The psychodynamic perspective of coping did however lead researchers towards exploring 'trait like propensities or styles of coping' (Suls et al. 1996, p. 713). Early work on traits or coping styles was to become beleaguered by the belief that 'they were poor predictors of behaviour'; a belief that soon led to the questioning of the predictive power and role of personality itself (Suls et al. 1996, p. 714). The coming of the second generation of research, initiated somewhat by feelings of discontent with the psychodynamic perspective (Suls et al. 1996), shifted attention to an entirely new focus in understanding the personality–coping relationship. It would, however, be a mistake to believe that the debate surrounding traits was over or that a dispositional view of coping had lost its relevance (Watson et al. 1999), or its potency to be rekindled by advances in our knowledge (Suls et al. 1996; Vollrath 2001). In fact, if anything, as we will see, it remains the one enduring theme throughout any discussion of personality and coping.

The second generation of research describes the *transactional perspective* and takes its name from the work of Lazarus (1966) and his transactional model of stress. The power of Lazarus's work and its significance lies in his process-oriented cognitive-relational view of stress. This view builds on the premise that stress results from the transaction between the individual and the environment. Expressed in this way, argues Lazarus (1990, 1999), stress does not simply reside in the person or in the environment but in the relationship between the two. What distinguishes the transactional model from earlier interactional models of stress is that in the latter person and environment 'retain their separate identities' whereas a transactional relationship offers 'a new level of discourse' where these separate variables are now 'fused into a special kind of relationship' (Lazarus 1998, pp. 188–9) that is imbued with meaning. These meanings Lazarus (1999, 2000) describes link the person and the environment and are expressed through a 'process of appraisal' (Lazarus 2000). It is the appraisal process that shapes the nature of a particular encounter. Two types of appraisal are present separated not by timing but by content as each is engaged together and give the process its dynamic emphasis. The first is *primary appraisal* where the person gives meaning to the encounter and appraises the significant of 'what is at stake' (Lazarus 2001). Secondary appraisal is concerned with 'what can I do about it?' It is where the coping resources are appraised and ways of coping determined.

The role that personality plays in Lazarus's process oriented transactional model has been the focus of considerable debate (Ben-Porath and Tellegen 1990; Costa and McCrae 1990; Krohne 1990; Lazarus 1990; Suls et al. 1996; Watson 1990). If we are concerned with concepts like appraisal, argues Lazarus (1999), then researchers are faced with a dilemma because such concepts reflect a process and therefore imply change rather than stability. While appraisals are 'sensitive to' and 'may vary with personality', Lazarus goes on to argue (1999, pp. 15–16), the idea of process, and therefore the notion of change, should not be obscured by the idea of stability that accompanies the notion of personality traits or dispositional styles. In turning to the role of personality traits in his research Lazarus admits to a 'reluctant yes for neglect' having, as he goes on to argue, given more emphasis to process issues than dispositional issues (1990, p. 42). On the other hand, while not denying the significance of personality in the stress process, it was more a case, as Lazarus points out, that 'other research agenda were more important to us at the time' (1990, p. 42).

While the subtleties of the debate, the detail of the arguments and the commitment and force with which they were expressed are not captured in this summary there does appear to emerge from this debate a call for a 'newer approach to personality traits' (Lazarus 1990, p. 43), an acknowledgement that we may be witnessing a revival and greater acceptance of the role traits play (Ben-Porath and Tellegen 1990), the view that as much attention should now be given to what a person is like as has been given to what a person does (Costa and McCrae 1990) and a shift in focus from an emphasis on 'cognitive and situational determinants of coping' to a growing interest in the role of personality in the stress process (Suls et al. 1996, p. 716). While reviewers generously acknowledge the way Lazarus has inspired researchers (Vollrath 2001), offered much to take forward through his theoretical and empirical work (Brief and George 1991), and that research 'can only benefit from the careful and thoughtful application' of his model (Harris 1991, p. 28) a number of factors were drawing researchers to a third generation of research which saw the *convergence of personality and coping* (Suls et al. 1996). Nevertheless, despite the revival of interest in the role of personality and the growing influence of a new, third generation of research, the second generation is more often thought of as the phase in which personality was more or less 'dropped' from the stress-coping model (Suls and David 1996, p. 996).

A number of factors helped to usher in a third generation of research linking personality to coping. Suls and his colleagues (1996, pp. 719–21) outline these as: (1) empirical work that showed situation variables being generally no better as predictors than traits helping to stimulate more research on traits and behaviour 'in general' and coping 'in particular' (p. 719); (2) the development of the 'Big Five' personality model and its reinvigorating effect on personality research and coping; (3) the recognition that both situational and individual determinants of coping were important in understanding the relationship; and (4) the acknowledgement that no coping strategy should simply be presumed as being inherently good or bad. Other factors that may be added to this list include the growing interest in health psychology and the way in which 'personality traits may act as resources in the stress process' (Vollrath 2001, p. 337), the fact that the third generation approach offered a different way of thinking about the 'interplay' between stressors, personality and coping (Suls et al. 1996, p. 721), the growing acceptance that although 'hardly synonymous' personality and coping overlap as constructs (Suls and David 1996, p. 994), and the discussion around the ways in which personality influences not just the way stress is coped with but how stress itself is experienced (Semmer 2006).

By pointing to the discrete and important role played by personality in the coping process the third generation of research 'represents a significant departure from past efforts' (Suls and David 1996, p. 996). Yet despite this progress unresolved conceptual and methodological issues (Suls et al. 1996) still remain to be resolved. These range from issues surrounding how personality and, more importantly, how coping is defined (Aldwin 2000; Coyne and Gottlieb 1996; Dewe and Cooper 2012; Snyder 1999, 2001; Suls et al. 1996; Suls and David 1996), the structure of coping and issues more generally surrounding the measurement of coping and accompanying operational and interpretive challenges (Coyne 1997; Coyne and Gottlieb 1996; Coyne and Racioppo 2000; Dewe and Cooper 2012; Folkman and Moskowitz 2004; Lazarus 1995; Semmer 2006; Somerfield 1997), and the measurement of traits including the apparent conceptual overlap between them, their structure and unidimensional nature, their relationship to other 'well-established' measures and their presumed uniqueness (Vollrath 2001, p. 337).

Many of these issues reflect the challenges that face all researchers investigating the complexity of the coping process and reflect the continual need to search for innovative and creative ways to advance our knowledge. Much progress has been made but personality does, and has been shown to have a varied role that extends beyond its relationship with coping per se, to include its influence on the nature of stressors themselves, the process of appraisal and the way it, in turn, is moulded by cultures and environments (Semmer 1996, 2006; Suls and David 1996; Suls et al. 1996). As much of this short history has drawn on the work of Suls and his colleagues it is important to acknowledge their analysis and reinforce their conclusion that this 'new look' vision of the third generation seems best placed to meet these challenges (1996, p. 731) Nevertheless, it is still necessary, as Semmer warns, to avoid the tendency of viewing coping as nothing more 'than a problem of idiosyncratic behaviours' and to continue to remind ourselves that not all differences between individuals are differences of personality (1996, 2006, p. 73). We now turn our attention to some of the challenges facing researchers.

Defining Personality

Personality has been described as a very wide ranging concept giving researchers a licence to explore it from a variety of theoretical approaches. It is no wonder then, that personality as Carver and Connor-Smith go on to suggest, 'is easy to observe but hard to pin down' (2010, p. 680). Broadly, personality is defined as 'characteristic patterns of thoughts, feeling and behavior over time and across situations' (Connor-Smith and Flachsbart 2007, p. 1080). At times words like dynamic and systems are used in definitions as in 'dynamic organization within the person' and 'the psychological and physical systems that underlie that person's pattern of action' (Carver and Connor-Smith 2010, p. 680). What emerges is more of a necessity to focus on those key themes that 'are shared by most formal attempts' at defining personality and include the ideas of 'internal, organized, and characteristic of an individual over time' (Watson, Clark, and Harkness 1994, p. 18). Personality concerns individual differences, traits and structure and it was not long before reviewers were drawing attention to broad-based taxonomies, consensual frameworks or working hypothesis of personality (Carver and Connor-Smith 2010; Connor-Smith and Flachsbart 2007; McCrae and John 1992; Vollrath 2001) that offer the building blocks for measuring and organizing personality and which 'may arguably' express those traits necessary to describe personality (DeLongis and Holtzman 2005, p. 1647). So it is time to briefly explore the development and history of these taxonomies.

The utility of a taxonomic or structural approach rests on the way personality traits are systematically, completely and economically classified (Watson and Hubbard 1996) and on the 'essence of structure' as portrayed by patterns of covariation (Watson et al. 1994, p. 19). This type of research has spanned decades, investigated hundreds of traits, reflected on different viewpoints, methodologies and measures, comprehensively investigated what exactly can or could be considered to represent an example of a personality trait, examined structure and hierarchy, and considered issues of consistency, relevance, stability and efficiency. From this research has emerged the 'Big Five' factor model and although this model is now described not just as 'a good starting point' (Connor-Smith and Flachsbart 2007, p. 1080), but as 'an important advancement in the field' (Vollrath 2001, p. 338), as 'essentially correct in its representation' (McCrae and John 1992, p. 176), as having been 'widely adopted as a consensual framework' (Carver and Connor-Smith 2010, p. 681) and 'as arguably the most recognizable contribution personality psychology has to offer today' (McAdams and Pals 2006, p. 204) this does not mean that the 'Big Five' structure has been free from debate and critique or that there is unanimity surrounding the number of factors (Carver and Connor-Smith 2010), or the need to keep searching for new and alternative frameworks even though current research suggests that the 'Big Five' factors 'are important in every aspect of the stress process' (Vollrath 2001, p. 338).

The search for structure has understandably come to dominate personality research. Two approaches known as the 'Big Three' and the 'Big Five' have come to represent this general structural tradition (Carver and Connor-Smith 2010; McCrae and John 1992; Watson and Hubbard 1996; Watson et al. 1994). The 'Big Three' emerged from the seminal work of Hans Eysenck. From a comprehensive series of studies begun in the late 1940s Eysenck identified two factors which he described as Neuroticism and Extraversion (Eysenck and Eysenck 1968). Further work led to a third factor being identified that described Psychoticism or Tough Mindedness; hence the 'Big Three' descriptor (Eysenck and Eysenck 1975; Watson and Hubbard 1996). More work was to follow as researchers continued their work searching for structure and as the 'Big Five' began to emerge it was clear that both models shared what Watson and Hubbard describe as a common 'Big Two' – Neuroticism and Extraversion (1996, p. 743). These authors go on to describe how the 'Big Three' can be transformed into the 'Big Five' by redeveloping Psychoticism into Conscientiousness and Agreeableness and adding a fifth factor describing Openness (Watson and Hubbard 1996, p. 743). This summary cannot capture the rich history and detailed analysis that led to the 'Big Five' but the contributions of those who led this work is well documented by researchers (Costa and McCrea 1985; Digman 1990; John 1990; McCrae and John 1992; Watson and Hubbard 1996; Watson et al. 1994).

While the 'Big Five' has been widely adopted and has received the status of a unifying framework 'that offers a solid and comprehensive basis for the taxonomy of human personality' (Vollrath 2001, p. 338) and a mechanism for developing 'a complete and systematic pursuit of personality correlates' (McCrae and John 1992, p. 177) these tributes have not prevented researchers from exploring and presenting alternative frameworks. Remodelling and transforming factors have led to new five and six factor frameworks being proposed as viable alternatives to the 'Big Five' (see Ashton and Lee 2007; Ashton et al. 2004; Lee and Ashton 2005; Zuckerman, Kuhlman and Camac 1988; Zuckerman, Kuhlman, Joireman, Teta and Kraft 1993). In addition personality researchers are being urged to do more by better integrating the 'Big Five' model into a clearly articulated comprehensive framework for understanding the whole person (McAdams and Pal 2006), recognizing that to capture and understand individuality the 'Big Five' 'may not be comprehensive enough, for it makes the whole of personality to be synonymous with traits' (McAdams 1996, p. 296).

The sentiments in McAdams's work are captured by Mayer when he suggests that those interested in personality need to 'think about the difference between McAdams's question "What do we know when we know a person?" and a more standard "What is personality?"' (1996, p. 351). To McAdams the abstract-conceptual language of traits represents a first level of analysis. If we are to understand someone then, as McAdams (1996) argues, we need to go to another level and, using different methodologies, bring that person to life. Researchers agree that answering the question McAdams sets requires integrating different levels of analysis and reflects a maturing in how personality is explored and our understanding developed (McCrae 1996). It, of course, remains important to continue to develop and organize our knowledge of personality from analysis that spans a number of levels. Nevertheless it is clear that our understanding of traits has been bolstered 'by the widespread acceptance of the five factor model' (McAdams and Pals 2006, p. 204). This is certainly true when it comes to investigating the relationship between personality and coping. Here the 'Big Five' model has been the predominant instrument for such investigations, is regarded as a good starting point (Connor-Smith and Flachsbart 2007), and enables the examination of personality in a reasonably comprehensive manner and so will be the main focus of our review.

Defining Coping

Despite the presence of alternatives the 'Big Five' model is generally accepted as providing a unifying framework for the study of personality. The same cannot be said for coping. There is, perhaps, a sense in the coping literature that some general agreement or synthesis of ideas may surround the classifying of coping strategies in terms of their focus, mode and timing (Dewe and Cooper 2012). However, no consensus exists as to the number and function of strategies that best expresses the nature of coping or whether any agreement can ever be reached without obscuring the richness and complexity of the strategies themselves (Folkman and Moskowitz 2004). Considerable debate also surrounds how best to define coping. The definition most commonly used but not always agreed comes from the work of Folkman and Lazarus and defines coping as 'cognitive and behavioral efforts to manage specific external and/or internal demands that are appraised as taxing or exceeding the resources of the person' (1991, p. 210). A number of themes emerge from this definition including that coping is process-oriented, concerned with what individuals actually think and do, that at the heart of this process is the appraisal or meaning given to the encounter, and that coping involves effort and the availability of coping resources (Folkman 1982). Lazarus goes on to reinforce the idea that coping is all about thoughts and actions and makes it clear that coping 'must be measured separately from its outcomes' (1999, p. 111). There is, Lazarus goes on to add, no one best way to cope, no one coping strategy that is universally effective or ineffective, and that coping is viewed as having two main functions; problem-focused and emotion-focused (Lazarus 1993, 1999, 2001). In short, and with some loss of detail, coping can, as Lazarus suggests, be simplified to 'cognitive and behavioral efforts to manage psychological stress' (1993, p. 237).

Despite clearly expressing the transactional nature of stress and the authority of the appraisal processes that link the individual to the environment many reviewers find the Folkman and Lazarus definition limiting. The essence of this critique lies in the view that restricting coping strategies to only those thoughts and actions that occur within the context of a stressful encounter limits our understanding of what constitutes coping (Coyne and Gottlieb 1996), fails to capture those ordinary, everyday behaviours that help individuals to get along (Aldwin 2000), those that are viewed as management skills (Aldwin 2000), and those whose purpose is not specifically designed to manage a stressful encounter (Snyder 2001). Such criticism questions, how and in what way, coping can be distinguished from everyday adaptation (Costa, Somerfield and McCrae 1996), and whether there is merit in the Lazarus and Folkman suggestion that 'not all adaption is coping' (1991, p. 199). Any conclusion to this debate turns, it seems, on reaching some agreement on the role played by issues like intention, effort and consciousness (Coyne and Gottlieb 1996; Folkman and Lazarus 1991; Snyder 2001). How best any definition expresses the complexity and richness of coping can only be determined by advances in our knowledge (Dewe and Cooper 2012). Such advances cannot be separated from how coping is measured and it is to the question of measurement that we now turn.

Measuring and classifying coping strategies present researchers with a number of challenges. Nowhere in the coping literature is the debate more intense than when reviewers focus their attention on the role and use of coping questionnaires or checklists (Dewe, O'Driscoll and Cooper 2010). No one questions the utility of coping checklists, their convenience, adaptability and efficiency as a means of data collection. While widely used, what lies at the heart of the debate is the criticism that the information they provide is both limited in 'its description and in its explanatory power' (Oakland and Ostell 1996, p. 151). Indeed the intensity of the debate has reviewers questioning whether coping checklists have resulted in the field becoming weighted down by self-evident findings (Coyne 1997), provided researchers with a convenient reason for not bothering to search for other more creative ways of measuring coping (Coyne and Gottlieb 1996), made researchers insensitive to when it is most appropriate to use checklists (Lazarus 1995), and left reviewers to conclude that the only way resolution can be reached is by 'radically refashioning coping research' (Coyne and Racioppo 2000, p. 659).

Sympathetic to the idea that more creativity is needed has led researchers to begin to explore new and innovative ways to measure coping (Lazarus 2000). Nevertheless coping checklists still remain that 'first step' when researching coping (Coyne 1997, p. 327) leaving researchers with the

COPING AND PERSONALITY: APPROACHES, MEASUREMENT AND CHALLENGES   13

challenge of interpreting their data and classifying those coping strategies that emerge (Dewe and Cooper 2012). Classifying coping strategies is seen as a primary goal for most researchers. Using the framework of focus, mode and time (Dewe and Cooper 2012) to classify strategies offers a way forward. However, there is still the issue of whether grouping strategies under a particular descriptor captures the richness and complexity of how strategies are used, how they relate to one another and the different functions they play. It is one thing to classify a strategy according to the data, it is another to understand the way in which that strategy is used within the context of a stressful encounter (Dewe and Cooper 2012). The way that coping strategies are classified influences the way in which we understand how they are being used, the role that they play and how they relate to the context. Any such schema is not without its difficulties and 'is only as good as the measures we use and the interpretations that flow from such measures' (Dewe and Cooper 2012, p. 138).

The primary mechanism for classifying strategies is, more often than not, by focus whilst recognizing that how they are used and when they are used depends on their mode and timing. As discussed previously the origins of classifying coping strategies has its roots in the work of Lazarus and Folkman (1984). It was these researchers who identified through what Folkman later described as a 'useful way of talking about many kinds of coping in broad brushstrokes' two major functions of coping; problem-focused and emotion-focused (Folkman and Moskowitz 2004, pp. 751–2). From this work researchers were to take their cue and although the number and function of strategies were to ebb and flow the work of Folkman and Lazarus set the benchmark and established the standard and basis against which coping strategies were classified. From the volume of work that followed there is now perhaps a sense that attention should shift more towards exploring, across the different studies and all the different classification schema that have emerged, whether a common core of coping strategies can be found.

Reflecting back on their earlier work Folkman identified what she described as 'major gaps in the original formulation' (2011, p. 454) and suggested the addition of three further general categories describing meaning-focused coping, relationship-social focused coping and future-oriented coping. Commenting on the role that meaning plays in coping research (Park and Folkman 1997) the idea of a meaning-focused strategy stems from the way in which individuals attempt to make sense of and search for meaning in a stressful encounter (Folkman and Moskowitz 2007) whereas relationship-social coping reflects the interpersonal aspects of coping and the role of context (Folkman 2011) and future-oriented coping reflects the proactive aspects of coping.

Whether this reflects the beginnings of a 'synthesis of findings' (Folkman and Moskowitz 2004, p. 752) is a matter for debate. However, because of the contextual nature of coping, the ways in which different coping strategies are used, the ways in which they combine and relate to one another and the fact that one strategy may perform a number of different functions means that any attempt to establish a stable set of coping strategies has a certain irony about it because by seeking stability and uniformity across studies we may simply lose the very essence of what it is we are trying to achieve; to identify the richness and complexity of the coping process itself (Dewe and Cooper 2012; Folkman and Moskowitz 2004). Any attempt to arrive at a synthesis of findings 'runs the risk of masking important differences within categories' (Folkman and Moskowitz 2004, p. 752), and proves difficult because the subtleties that distinguish one coping strategy from another 'do not form a neat matrix into which coping can be sorted' (Carver and Connor-Smith 2010, p. 687). This means that the coping literature cannot, in the way that the personality literature can, offer a generally accepted 'consensual' measurement framework, creating another challenge when attempting to understand the personality–coping relationship.

Personality and Coping

Despite the developments in our understanding of stress and coping and the different checklists available to measure coping there is still considerable debate about the structure of coping. It is clear that realizing this ambition of agreeing a common structure remains somewhat unresolved (Suls et al. 1996). No one doubts the utility of checklists but issues still remain as to their explanatory potential, the statistical analysis surrounding how different coping strategies are derived and the innovations necessary to capture the richness and complexity of coping (Aldwin 2000; Coyne and Gottlieb 1996; Dewe and Cooper 2012; Folkman 1982; Oakland and Ostell 1996; Stone and Kennedy-Moore 1992). Coping researchers have, it seems, much to "cope" with when it comes to measurement (Suls and David 1996). It is clear that if we are advance our understanding of the relationship between personality and coping, then the issues of measurement need to be confronted (Suls and David 1996). It is also clear that there is a growing body of advice as to what needs to be done.

At a more general level this advice includes paying more attention to how instructions are worded, the range of items and how they are derived, how they are suitably scored and worded to avoid ambiguity, mixing behaviours with outcomes and resembling more an expression of emotions (Coyne and Gottlieb 1996; Dewe and Cooper 2012; Folkman and Moskowitz 2004; Somerfield 1997). Applying this advice to exploring the personality–coping relationship, then, consideration should be given to whether instructions should be expressed in terms of 'how people usually cope' as styles of coping may have a stronger relationship to personality than encounter-specific coping, how consistency in coping is dealt with as it is, 'at least in part' a function of personality, ensuring that coping items do not overlap with outcomes, and acknowledging that personality may relate not just to the choice of coping strategies but also how effective that choice is used (Suls et al. 1996, pp. 724–6). In a similar vein Suls and David also draw attention to the need to ensure that measures cover a wide range of coping strategies allowing for differentiation between personality traits, acknowledging and understanding how patterns of coping form as this may help to profile different personality traits, recognizing, as others suggest, that using a strategy is different from using it well and accepting that the influence of organizational culture means that 'traits are more easily expressed in some situations than others' (1996, pp. 1000–2).

Two themes emerge from this advice. The first is an operational theme where the emphasis is placed on the design and structure of coping checklists. The second theme is more of a personality–coping relationship one and points to the complexity of the relationship, the contextual issues that surround it and perhaps a subtle questioning of the utility of checklists and the need to be more creative in approach and analysis. What then are the mechanisms that link personality and coping? Perhaps as Watson and Hubbard suggest we should start by turning the question a little by asking 'why should personality and coping be linked' (1996, p. 747)? The answer, these authors suggest, is that since coping responses 'do not differ fundamentally' from other individual responses then it is highly likely that personality traits will have important implications for, and will be significantly linked to, coping (p. 747). Turning back to the original question as to what mechanisms link the two then personality traits are predicted to have both direct (by limiting or 'facilitating the use of specific strategies') and indirect ('by influencing the nature and severity of the stressor experienced or the effectiveness of coping strategies') links to coping (Connor-Smith and Flachsbart 2007, p. 1081).

Although not couched in direct–indirect terms, this theme can be distilled from the work of others who discuss the mechanisms through which personality influences coping. Semmer, for example, describes the influence of personality in terms of the likelihood of experiencing stressors, how they are appraised, the different reactions they produce and the different ways they are dealt with (2006, p. 74). None of these mechanisms are mutually exclusive, he adds, and may have a 'cascading effect' (Suls and Martin 2005) in this way, helping to explain what may make individuals more vulnerable to stressful encounters (Semmer 2006). At the same time Semmer warns against thinking of stress as nothing more than the result of 'idiosyncratic appraisals and coping styles' (1996, p. 52) and regarding all individual differences as only differences between people but recognizing that they can, at times, reflect differences between the cultures that people belong to (Semmer 2006). Vollrath (2001) also points to how personality helps to create, shape and produce stress and the way it is construed and appraised. Again there is a clear sense that more work needs to be done exploring just how all this comes together, what impact different 'constellations' of personality traits have and how these combinations may affect the stress process (Vollrath 2001, p. 342).

The Specifics of Linking Personality to Coping

While personality touches every aspect of the stress process considerable empirical attention has been given to its impact on coping. While we turn our attention to the personality–coping relationship it is as Vollrath suggests a 'complicated task to report on ... because there is no generally accepted model of the dimensions of coping and their organization' (2001, p. 340). It is immediately apparent from the different reviews to grasp the difficulties faced. Almost without exception, reviewers (e.g. Carver and Connor-Smith 2010, p. 685; Connor-Smith and Flachsbart 2007; Vollrath 2001) point to 'the bewildering number of distinctions made' between the broad categories of coping, the blurring that has occurred between coping categories making exact borders difficult to define, the number of coping instruments used, and the differences in coping categories even when each has exactly the same name. On top of this reviewers have also to consider sample characteristics, effect size, reporting bias, methodology and theoretical orientation. Despite all these issues reviewers have provided rich and comprehensive reviews, clearly set out and justified their approach, and systematically identified and discussed their findings. Headline findings follow.

Adapting and building on the reviews by Connor-Smith and Flachsbart (2007) and Solberg Nes and Segerstrom (2006), Carver and Connor-Smith (2010) begin their review integrating personality and coping by suggesting two overall findings. The first, that personality as measured by the 'Big Five' was modestly related to two broad categories describing engagement and disengagement coping. The second, that when using more factor-specific types of engagement and disengagement coping strategies a more nuanced approach emerged. Turning first to the two broad coping categories, extraversion, conscientiousness, and openness were linked to more engagement coping and conscientiousness and agreeableness to less disengagement coping. On the other hand neuroticism was positively linked to disengagement coping.

When the analysis explored the relationship between the 'Big Five' and specific types of engagement coping then extraversion, conscientiousness and openness were strongly related to problem-solving and the same three plus agreeableness were strongly related to cognitive restructuring. Again neuroticism was negatively related to both problem-solving and cognitive restructuring. The pattern for disengagement coping 'is in some ways opposite that of engagement coping' (Carver and Connor-Smith 2010, p. 690) with neuroticism positively linked to all four specific types of disengagement coping with stronger links to withdrawal and wishful thinking than to denial and substance use. On the other hand conscientiousness and agreeableness were negatively linked to denial and substance use while openness showed a more complex relationship with positive links to withdrawal and wishful thinking.

The richness, detail, complexity and thoroughness of these reviews are not captured by these 'reported headlines'. Their comprehensiveness extends to exploring the role of a wide range of moderators and outcomes in addition to pointing to the independent and interactive roles that personality and coping may play in the stress process. Acutely aware of measurement limitations, particularly the need for 'more careful assessing of coping strategies' and alternative methodological approaches (Connor-Smith and Flachsbart 2007, p. 1102), both sets of authors point to the need for more work that 'expands our growing understanding' of the personality–coping relationship and captures those complexities that help to shape the stress process (Carver and Connor-Smith 2010, p. 679). Both offer ways forward that include detailing, scoping and outlining more complex study designs, exploring personality profiles and their combined effects, focusing on facet analysis of Neuroticism, Extraversion and Conscientiousness 'as these are the traits most clearly linked to coping', developing a better understanding of how personality and coping jointly operate and interact and building this knowledge into more effective interventions (Connor-Smith and Flachsbart, 2007, p. 1102).

Carver and Connor-Smith also, in their summary of future directions, reinforce and point to the need for more facet level analysis of personality traits, more emphasis on the interplay between different personality traits in determining coping responses, a more focused exploration of the context within which coping takes place, the manner in which coping responses vary across a stressful encounter and how much of that variability can be accounted for by personality, and the role that cultural differences play in the relationship between personality, coping and outcomes (Carver and Connor-Smith 2010, p. 697). Embedded in the work of these authors are issues surrounding coping effectiveness and how personality influences not just the selection of coping strategies but how they are used, the consistency of their use over time, their competency in using different coping strategies, their flexibility in coping choice and their ability to match coping strategies to the stressors encountered (Carver and Connor-Smith 2010, p. 696). Similarly Connor-Smith and Flachsbart point to the need to develop a better understanding of how 'the joint role of personality and coping determines vulnerability to stressors' as well as the developmental aspects of coping (2007, p. 1102).

Vollrath (2001) also reports on the relation between the 'Big Five' and in this case the use of problem- and emotion-focused coping. Noting the difficulties in establishing precise boundaries between coping strategies and that 'many strategies serve both functions' (p. 340), her review describing 'a broad spectrum of findings' (p. 335) pointed to an association between problem-focused coping and conscientiousness and extraversion. The latter reflecting the 'high energy and activity levels' that accompany extraversion and the former because of its consistent relationship to 'performing at work' (p. 340). Using avoidance strategies and seeking social support as examples of emotion-focused strategies Vollrath pointed to 'a particularly close' relationship between avoidance (e.g. wishful thinking, distraction, denial) and neuroticism and 'a weaker and less consistent' relationship between avoidance and extraversion and conscientiousness (p. 340).

In the case of seeking support the predominant relationship was with extraversion with extraverts appearing 'to seek support successfully' (2001, pp. 340–1). In addition Vollrath (2001) points to the role of personality as a resource in stress, how stressors are selected and shaped by personality, and how personality affects the appraisal process. In the future, Vollrath suggests, there is not just the need to more comprehensively integrate personality into the whole stress process but specifically in relation to coping, exploring its combined and accumulative effect, the different roles both may play, how they relate to one another and their negative and positive impact (2001, p. 342). Vollrath concludes by simply pointing to the importance of personality in understanding stress and coping.

Making the argument that personality 'should become a more central focus of the coping literature' (Watson et al. 1999, p. 119), these authors, as part of their argument, explore the relationship between the 'Big Five' and coping. On the basis of the data reviewed they conclude that neuroticism 'is broadly related' to passive forms of emotion-focused coping, conscientiousness is 'substantially correlated' with problem-focused coping and that extraversion is associated with social support seeking and positive reappraisal. In respect of agreeableness and openness they found only weak links to coping (p. 127). These authors, like others, point to the difficulties surrounding the measurement of coping, that personality influences all aspects of the stress process and that attention needs now to be given to the complexities of the relationship and how it works. In terms of the evidence they reviewed in respect of personality and coping Watson and his colleagues restate their central theme that personality traits, particularly neuroticism, extraversion and conscientiousness, 'should be routinely assessed in research on stress, coping and adaptational outcomes' (1999, p. 135).

There is now a rich history capturing the personality–coping relationship. These 'headline' findings are intended only to provide an overview and are embedded in reviews that are detailed, thorough and explore the role of personality across the stress process. The reviews themselves point to the volume of work being carried out, the creativity of researchers, how personality sits nicely within the transactional stress framework and how personality has re-established its place and affirmed its crucial role in helping to better understand all facets of the stress process. Researchers are already moving forward to explore, for example, the impact of the combined effects of personality types or profiles and coping (Grant and Langan-Fox 2006; Torgersen and Vollrath 2006; Vollrath and Torgersen 2000), what personality tells us about coping by exploring how coping behaviours predict personality (Geisler, Wiedig-Allison and Weber 2009), how the use of daily process methods (DeLongis and Holtzman 2005) and daily experience research (Tennen, Affleck and Armeli 2005) help to better understand the role of personality in the stress and coping process, and the relationship between personality and situational and dispositional coping (Bouchard, Guillemette and Landry-Leger 2004).

In their review Carver and Connor-Smith make the point that there is merit in exploring personality traits other than just the 'Big Five' and give, as an example, the trait of *optimism* (Solberg Nes and Segerstrom 2006), suggesting that optimism 'plugs nicely into the fundamental distinction between engagement and disengagement coping' (2010, p. 695; also Vollrath 2001, p. 337). Carver and Connor-Smith (2010) illustrate this point, by showing from their review, that optimism is positively associated with both broad and factor-specific measures of engagement coping and negatively related to the broad measure of disengagement coping and to different factor-specific aspects of disengagement coping. Another example is *Hardiness* (see Eschleman, Bowling and Alarcon 2010) where its three elements of commitment, control and challenge offer a resource for active coping and a motivation to get things done (Maddi 1999, 2002). Growing out of the positive psychology movement are the traits of *Hope* (Snyder 2000; Snyder, Rand and Sigmon 2005) and the *proactive personality* (Bateman and Crant 1993; Chan 2006).

In the case of the former hope provides pathways for goal-directed thought and agency that motivates to achieve (Snyder and Lopez 2007). A similar theme captures the essence of the proactive personality by distinguishing individuals on the basis of their predisposition to 'take action to influence their environments' (Bateman and Crant 1993, p. 103). *Self–efficacy* is another trait that reflects the aspirations of the positive psychology movement (Bandura 1997; Maddux 2005), explores a person's belief in themselves, their skill to reach and their ability to achieve a goal and is an 'enabling factor that enhances strengths' (Bandura 1997; Snyder and Lopez 2007, p. 178) and coping (Maddux 1995). Hope, optimism and self-efficacy are all elements in, and characteristics of, along with resilience, the concept of psychological capital and the person's 'positive psychological state of development' developed by Luthans and his colleagues (Luthans, Youssef and Avolio 2007, p. 3) – another advance in our understanding of those individual resources that allow people to flourish.

Vollrath in her review of personality and stress comments on what she describes as an 'important line of research focused on the individual difference construct of the Type A Coronary Prone Behaviour pattern' (Vollrath 2001, p. 336). Type A personalities are characterized as 'typically ambitious, persistent, impatient and involved in their work' (Carlson 1999, p. 240), as hostile and irritable (Parkes 1994), and 'aggressively involved in a chronic, incessant struggle to achieve more and more in less and less time' at whatever cost (Pedersen and Denollet 2003, p. 242). In contrast Type B individuals are those 'who are relaxed, patient and rarely overactivated' (Carlson 1999, p. 240). Early reviews (Carlson 1999; Parkes 1994) explored Type A and pointed to its role in helping to understand coping flexibility in relation to stressors. Despite the work that emerged around the potency of the hostility component of the Type A behaviour pattern (Pedersen and Denollet 2003; Williams and Williams 2006), debate and controversy around Type A 'made it unfashionable to include global traits in Coronary Heart Disease (CHD) research' although 'writing off' the role of global traits was viewed as somewhat untimely (Denollet 2005, p. 89). The emerging view was that a more explicit personality driven approach was needed to identify at-risk individuals and account for differences in vulnerability to stress related health problems (Denollet 2000; Pedersen and Denollet 2003).

From the ensuing debate and the belief that it was a little premature to ignore personality traits (Denollet 2005) emerged the Type D personality or distressed personality (Pedersen and Denollet 2003, 2006). Derived from personality theory and empirical findings Type D personality is built around two traits: negative affectivity and social inhibition (Pedersen and Denollet 2006). Those high in negative affectivity tend to experience negative emotions, view themselves in a negative way and continually look at things as inviting trouble (Denollet 2005). Social inhibition refers to the tendency when in social interactions to 'inhibit emotions and behaviours to avoid disapproval by others' (Denollet 2005, p. 89) and has been described as lying as a 'toxic core' of the interpersonal sensitivity disposition (Denollet 2013; Marin and Miller 2013, pp. 974–5). It is this latter trait (social inhibition) in combination with negative affectivity that gives the Type D personality its synergy and its descriminant power (Howard and Hughes 2012; Pedersen and Denollet 2006). There is much to be done and much to learn about interpersonal sensitivity and social inhibition (Denollet 2013) but the Type D distressed personality construct offers a way forward, is personality driven, exhibits 'strong associations with health-related outcomes' justifying it value, supporting its validity and confirming its influence on both cardiovascular and emotional health links (Howard and Hughes 2012, p. 255). It shows clear links to aspects of coping (Polman, Borkoles and Nicholls 2010; Yu, Chen, Zhang and Liu 2011) and provides work stress researchers with another avenue for advancing our understanding of the personality and coping relationship.

Conclusions

This exploration of the relationship between personality and coping was not meant to be exhaustive. Its aim was to present a broad overview aimed at providing an understanding of the issues and the progress being made. As a consequence it does not capture the richness and detail of the work that has been cited nor, at times, the complexity that surrounds the personality–coping relationship. What it does capture is the challenges that researchers have faced and continue to face, the issues that still need resolving, and more importantly possible ways forward. It is clear that one of the stumbling blocks is how coping is measured. It is also clear due to the contextual nature of coping that it may never be possible to arrive at a standardized set of coping strategies that hold across all situations. It may be that, in the future, less emphasis is given to trying to replicate coping strategies and more to exploring how individual strategies come together to form patterns of coping and coping profiles. This is not, of course, a call to abandon the creation of coping components as their utility and their ability to reflect different types of coping is an empirical necessity. However, understanding more about how individual coping strategies work and function together, the role they play in relation to one another and the patterns and profiles they form provides another avenue for understanding the richness and complexity of how coping and personality interact.

A number of themes emerge from the different reviews as to the way forward. While many of these themes have been discussed throughout this chapter they are important enough to be mentioned one more time. The first is, of course, how fundamental personality is to our understanding of coping. While the suggestion that 'coping ought to be redefined as a personality process' (Vollrath 2001, p. 341) will continue to be debated there is no doubt that the influence of personality extends across the whole coping process from its influence on the emergence and shaping of stressful encounters through appraisals, to coping and its effectiveness, to the emotions experienced and the outcomes achieved. In coping research more generally the appraisal of stressful encounters and the effectiveness and competency with which coping strategies are chosen and used have received a less than complete treatment (Dewe and Cooper 2012; Suls et al. 1996). There is now a need to acknowledge the explanatory potential that resides in these processes, their significance in advancing our understanding of the stress process, the crucial role that personality plays in determining both meanings and effectiveness and the fruitfulness of engaging in this type of research.

Turning to the role and use of the 'Big Five' measure, then, the themes that emerge would include, in addition to the idea of shifting attention to and focusing more on extraversion, conscientiousness and neuroticism, developing a better understanding of how the different personality traits relate to one another and the profile they express as it is clear that 'personality does not constitute one trait at a time' (Carver and Connor-Smith 2010, p. 697). In the same way exploring at the level of individual coping strategies how they may pattern or profile in relation to different personality traits, how personality traits are influenced by the context and what it is about the context that allows a trait to be expressed or repressed – the idea of strong or weak contexts (Suls and David 1996). There is also the need to explore the negative and positive aspects of personality traits, how they interact to make individuals more or less vulnerable to stressful encounters, and the type of methods necessary to capture the richness and complexity of the relationship, not forgetting that the more we understand about the interaction between personality and coping then the more effectively we fulfil the obligation we have to those whose working lives we study.

References

Aldwin, C.M. (2000). *Stress, Coping, and Development: An Integrative Perspective.* New York: The Guilford Press.

Aldwin, C.M. (2007). *Stress, Coping, and Development: An Integrative Perspective,* 2nd edn. New York: The Guilford Press.

Ashton, M.G. and Lee, K. (2007). Empirical, theoretical, and practical advantages of the HEXACO model of personality structure. *Personality and Social Psychology Review* 11, 150–66.

Ashton, M.G., Lee, K., Perugini, M., Szarota, P., de Vries, R., Di Blas, L., Boles, K. and De Raad, B. (2004). A six factor structure of personality-descriptive adjectives: Solutions from psycholexical studies in seven languages. *Journal of Personality and Social Psychology* 86, 356–66.

Bandura, A. (1997). *Self Efficacy: The Exercise of Control.* New York: Freeman.

Bateman, T.S. and Crant, J.M. (1993). The proactive component of organizational behavior: A measure and correlates. *Journal of Organizational Behavior* 14, 103–18.

Ben-Porath, Y.S. and Tellegen, A. (1990). A place for traits in stress research. *Psychological Inquiry* 1, 14–17.

Bolger, N. (1990). Coping as a personality process: A prospective study. *Journal of Personality and Social Psychology* 59, 325–37.

Bouchard, G., Guillemette, A. and Landry-Leger, N. (2004). Situational and dispositional coping: An examination of their relation to personality, cognitive appraisals, and psychological distress. *European Journal of Personality* 18, 221–38.

Brief, A.P. and George, J.M. (1991). Psychological stress and the workplace: A brief comment on Lazarus' outlook. *Journal of Social Behaviour and Personality* 6, 15–20.

Carlson, D.S. (1999). Personality and role variables as predictors of three forms of work-family conflict. *Journal of Vocational Behavior* 55, 236–53.

Carver, C.S. and Connor-Smith, J. (2010). Personality and coping. *Annual Review of Psychology* 61, 679–704.

Chan, D. (2006). Interactive effects of situational judgment effectiveness and proactive personality on work perceptions and work outcomes. *Journal of Applied Psychology* 91, 475–81.

Connor-Smith, J.K. and Flachsbart, C. (2007). Relations between personality and coping: A meta-analysis. *Journal of Personality and Social Psychology* 93, 1080–107.

Costa, P.T. and McCrae, R.R. (1985). *The NEO Personality Inventory Manual*. Odessa: Psychological Assessment Resources.

Costa, P.T. and McCrae, R.R. (1990). Personality: Another 'hidden factor' in stress research. *Psychological Inquiry* 1, 22–4.

Costa, P.T., Somerfield, M.R. and McCrae, R.R. (1996). Personality and coping: A reconceptualization. In M. Zeidner and N.M. Endler (eds), *Handbook of Coping: Theory, Research, Applications* (pp. 44–61). New York: John Wiley.

Coyne, J.C. (1997). Improving coping research: Raze the slum before any more building! *Journal of Health Psychology* 2, 153–5.

Coyne, J.C. and Gottlieb, B.H. (1996). The mismeasure of coping by checklist. *Journal of Personality* 64, 959–91.

Coyne, J.C. and Racioppo, M. (2000). Never the twain shall meet? Closing the gap between coping research and clinical intervention research. *American Psychologist* 55, 655–64.

DeLongis, A. and Holtzman, S. (2005). Coping in context: The role of stress, social support, and personality in coping. *Journal of Personality* 73, 1633–56.

Denollet, J. (2000). Type D personality: A potential risk factor refined. *Journal of Psychosomatic Research* 49, 255–66.

Denollet, J. (2005). DS14: Standard assessment of negative affectivity, social inhibition, and Type D personality. *Psychosomatic Medicine* 67, 89–97.

Denollet, J. (2013). Interpersonal sensitivity, social inhibition, and Type D personality: How and when are they associated with health? Comment on Martin and Millar 2013. *Psychological Bulletin* 139, 991–7.

Dewe, P. and Cooper, C. (2012). *Well-being and Work: Toward a Balanced Agenda*. Houndmills: Palgrave Macmillan.

Dewe, P., O'Driscoll, M. and Cooper, C. (2010). *Coping with Work Stress: A Review and Critique*. Chichester: Wiley-Blackwell.

Digman, J.M. (1990). Personality structure: Emergence of the five-factor model. *Annual Review of Psychology* 41, 417–40.

Eschleman, K.J., Bowling, N.A. and Alarcon, G.M. (2010). A meta-analytic examination of hardiness. *International Journal of Stress Management* 17, 277–307.

Eysenck, H.J. and Eysenck, S.B.G. (1968). *Manual of the Eysenck Personality Questionnaire*. San Diego: Educational and Industrial Testing Service.

Eysenck, H.J. and Eysenck, S.B.G. (1975). *Manual of the Eysenck Personality Questionnaire*. San Diego: EdITS.

Folkman, S. (1982). An approach to the measurement of coping. *Journal of Occupational Behaviour* 3, 95–107.

Folkman, S. (2011). Stress, health, and coping: Synthesis, commentary, and future directions. In S. Folkman (ed.), *The Oxford Handbook of Stress, Health, and Coping* (pp. 453–62). Oxford: Oxford University Press.

Folkman, S. and Lazarus, R.S. (1991). Coping and emotion. In A. Monat and R.S. Lazarus (eds), *Stress and Coping: An Anthology* (pp. 207–27). New York: Columbia University Press.

Folkman, S. and Moskowitz, J.T. (2004). Coping: Pitfalls and promise. *Annual Review of Psychology* 55, 745–74.

Folkman, S. and Moskowitz, J.T. (2007). Positive affect and meaning-focused coping, during significant psychological stress. In M. Hewstone, H.A.W. Schut, J.B.F. de Wit, K. van den Bos and M.S. Stroebe (eds), *The Scope of Social Psychology: Theory and Applications* (pp. 193–208). Hove and New York: Psychology Press.

Geisler, F.G.M., Wiedig-Allison, M. and Weber H. (2009). What coping tells about personality. *European Journal of Personality* 23, 289–306.

Grant, S. and Langan-Fox, J. (2006). Occupational stress, coping and strain: The combined/interactive effect of the Big Five traits. *Personality and Individual Differences* 41, 719–32.

Harris, J. (1991). The utility of the transactional approach for occupational stress research. *Journal of Social Behavior and Personality* 6, 21–9.

Howard, S. and Hughes, B.M. (2012). Construct concurrent and descriminant validity of Type D personality in the general population: Associations with anxiety, depression, stress and cardiac output. *Psychology and Health* 27, 242–58.

John, O.P. (1990). The 'Big Five' factor taxonomy: Dimensions of personality in the national language and in questionnaires. In L. Pervin (ed.), *Handbook of Personality: Theory & Research* (pp. 66–100). New York: Guilford Press.

Krohne, H.W. (1990). Personality as a mediator between objective events and their subjective representation. *Psychological Inquiry* 1, 26–9.

Lazarus, R.S. (1966). *Psychological Stress and the Coping Process*. New York: McGraw-Hill.

Lazarus, R.S. (1990). Theory based stress measurement. *Psychological Inquiry* 1, 3–12.

Lazarus, R.S. (1993). Coping theory and research: Past, present and future. *Psychosomatic Medicine* 55, 234–47.

Lazarus, R.S. (1995). Vexing research problems inherent in cognitive mediational theories of emotions-and some solutions. *Psychological Inquiry* 6, 185–96.

Lazarus, R.S. (1998). *Fifty Years of the Research and Theory of R. S. Lazarus: An Analysis of Historical and Perennial Issues*. Mahwah: Lawrence Erlbaum.

Lazarus, R.S. (1999). *Stress and Emotion: A New Synthesis*. London: Free Association.

Lazarus, R.S. (2000). Toward better research on stress and coping. *American Psychologist* 55, 665–73.

Lazarus, R.S. (2001). Relational meaning and discrete emotions. In K. Scherer, A. Schorr and T. Johnstone (eds), *Appraisal Processes in Emotion: Theory, Methods, Research* (pp. 37–67). New York: Oxford University Press.

Lazarus, R.S. and Folkman, S. (1984). *Stress, Appraisal and Coping*. New York: Springer.

Lazarus, R.S. and Folkman, S. (1991). The concept of coping. In A. Monat and R.S. Lazarus (eds), *Stress and Coping: An Anthology* (pp. 189–206). New York: Columbia University Press.

Lee, K. and Ashton, M.C. (2005). Psychopathy, machiavellianism, and narcissism in the Five-Factor model and the HEXACO model of personality structure. *Personality and Individual Differences* 38, 1571–82.

Luthans, F., Youssef, C.M. and Avolio, B.J. (2007). *Psychological Capital: Developing the Human Competitive Edge*. Oxford: Oxford University Press.

McAdams, D.P. (1996). Personality, modernity, and the storied self: A contemporary framework for studying persons. *Psychological Inquiry* 7, 295–321.

McAdams, D.P. and Pals, J.L. (2006) Fundamental principles for an integrative science of personality. *American Psychologist* 61, 204–17.

McCrae, R.R. (1996). Integrating the levels of personality. *Psychological Inquiry* 61, 353–6.

McCrae, R.R. and John, O.P. (1992). An introduction to the five-factor model and its applications. *Journal of Personality* 60, 175–215.

Maddi, S.R. (1999). The personality construct of hardiness: 1. Effects on experiencing, coping, and strain. *Consulting Psychology Journal* 51, 83–94.

Maddi, S.R. (2002). The story of hardiness: Twenty years of theorizing, research and practice. *Consulting Psychology Journal* 54, 173–85.

Maddux, J.E. (ed.) (1995). *Self Efficacy, Adaption, and Adjustment: Theory, Research, and Application.* New York: Plenum.

Maddux, J.E. (2005). Self efficacy: The power of believing you can. In C.R. Snyder and S.J. Lopez (eds), *The Handbook of Positive Psychology* (pp. 277–87). Oxford: Oxford University Press.

Marin, T.J. and Miller, G.E. (2013). The interpersonally sensitive disposition and health: An integrative review. *Psychological Bulletin* 139, 941–84.

Mayer, J.D. (1996). How do we know a person in contemporary frameworks for personality? *Psychological Inquiry* 61, 350–3.

Oakland, S. and Ostell, A. (1996). Measuring coping: A review and critique. *Human Relations* 49, 133–55.

Park, C. and Folkman, S. (1997). Meaning in the context of stress and coping. *Review of General Psychology* 1, 115–44.

Parkes, K.R. (1994). Personality and coping as moderators of work stress processes: Models, methods and measures. *Work and Stress* 8, 110–29.

Pedersen, S.S. and Denollet, J. (2003). Type D personality, cardiac events, and impaired quality of life: A review. *European Journal of Cardiovascular Prevention and Rehabilitation* 10, 241–8.

Pedersen, S.S. and Denollet, J. (2006). Is Type D personality here to stay? Emerging evidence across cardiovascular disease patient groups. *Current Cardiology Review* 2, 205–13.

Polman, R., Borkoles, E. and Nicholls, A.R. (2010). Type D personality, stress, and symptoms of burnout: The influence of avoidance coping and social support. *British Journal of Health Psychology* 15, 681–96.

Semmer, N. (1996). Individual differences, work stress and health. In M.J. Schabracq, J.A.M. Winnubst and C.L. Cooper (eds), *Handbook of work and health psychology* (pp. 51–86). Chichester: John Wiley & Sons.

Semmer, N. (2006). Personality, stress, and coping. In M. Vollrath (ed.), *Handbook of Personality and Health* (pp. 73–113). Chichester: John Wiley & Sons.

Snyder, C. (ed.) (1999). *Coping: The Psychology of What Works.* New York: Oxford University Press.

Snyder, C. (2000). *Handbook of Hope.* San Diego: Academic Press.

Snyder, C. (ed.) (2001). *Coping with Stress: Effective People and Processes.* Oxford: Oxford University Press.

Snyder, C.R. and Lopez, S.J. (2007). *Positive Psychology: The Scientific and Practical Explorations of Human Strengths.* Thousand Oaks: Sage Publications.

Snyder, C., Rand, K.L. and Sigmon, D.R. (2005). Hope theory: A member of the positive psychology family. In C.R. Snyder and S.J. Lopez (eds), *Handbook of Positive Psychology* (pp. 257–76). Oxford: Oxford University Press.

Solberg Nes, I. and Segerstrom, S.C. (2006). Dispositional optimism and coping: A meta analytic review. *Personality and Social Psychology Review* 10, 235–51.

Somerfield, M. (1997). The future of coping research as we know it: A response to commentaries. *Journal of Health Psychology* 2, 173–83.

Somerfield, M. and McCrae, R. (2000). Stress and coping research: Methodological challenges, theoretical advances. *American Psychologist* 55, 620–25.

Stone, A. and Kennedy-Moore, E. (1992). Assessing situational coping: Conceptual and methodological considerations. In H. Friedman (ed.), *Hostility Coping and Health* (pp. 203–14). Washington, DC: American Psychological Association.

Suls, J. and David, J.P. (1996). Coping and personality: Third time the charm? *Journal of Personality* 64, 993–1005.

Suls, J. and Martin, R. (2005). The daily life of the garden-variety neurotic: Reactivity, stressor exposure, mood spillover and maladaptive coping. *Journal of Personality* 73, 1485–509.

Suls, J., David, J.P. and Harvey, J.H. (1996). Personality and coping: Three generations of research. *Journal of Personality* 64, 711–35.

Tennen, H., Affleck, G. and Armeli, S. (2005). Personality and daily experience revisited. *Journal of Personality* 73, 1465–82.

Torgersen, S. and Vollrath, M. (2006). Personality types, personality traits, and risky health behaviors. In M. Vollrath (ed.), *Handbook of Personality and Health* (pp. 215–34). Chichester: John Wiley & Sons.

Vollrath, M. (2001). Personality and stress. *Scandinavian Journal of Psychology* 42, 335–47.

Vollrath, M. and Torgersen, S. (2000). Personality types and coping. *Personality and Individual Differences* 29, 367–78.

Watson, D. (1990). On the dispositional nature of stress measures: Stable and nonspecific influences on self-reported hassles. *Psychological Inquiry* 1, 34–7.

Watson, D. and Hubbard, B. (1996). Adaptational style and dispositional structure: Coping in the context of the five-factor model. *Journal of Personality* 64, 738–74.

Watson, D., Clark, L.A. and Harkness, A.R. (1994). Structures of personality and their relevance to psychopathology. *Journal of Abnormal Psychology* 103, 18–31.

Watson, D., David, J.P. and Suls, J. (1999). Personality, affectivity and coping. In C.R. Snyder (ed.), *Coping: The Psychology of What Works* (pp. 110–40). New York: Oxford University Press.

Williams, R.B. and Williams V.P. (2006). The prevention and treatment of hostility. In M. Vollrath (ed.), *Handbook of Personality and Health* (pp. 259–76). Chichester: John Wiley & Sons.

Yu, X., Chen, Z., Zhang, J. and Liu, X. (2011). Coping mediates the association between Type D personality and perceived health in Chinese patients with coronary heart disease. *British Journal of Behavioral Medicine* 18, 277–84.

Zuckerman, M., Kuhlman, D.M. and Camac, C. (1988). What lies beyond E and N? Factor analysis of scales believed to measure basic dimensions of personality. *Journal of Personality and Social Psychology* 54, 98–107.

Zuckerman, M., Kuhlman, D.M., Joireman, J., Teta, P. and Kraft, M. (1993). A comparison of three structural models of personality: The big three, the big five and the alternative five. *Journal of Personality and Social Psychology* 65, 757–68.

Future-Oriented Coping and Personality

2

Suzie Drummond and Paula Brough

Introduction

Significant progress in both the theoretical and applied aspects of occupational stress has occurred over the past decade, illustrated by the emergence of new research models and their accompanying generation of research activities (e.g. Brough, O'Driscoll, Kalliath, Cooper and Poelmans 2009; Demerouti, Bakker, Nachreiner and Schaufeli 2001; Dollard, Shimazu, Bin Nordin, Brough and Tuckey 2014). However, coping research has achieved far more modest outcomes. Discussions continue concerning the most appropriate definitions, measurements and taxonomies of coping (e.g. Brough, O'Driscoll and Kalliath 2005a; O'Driscoll, Brough and Kalliath 2009). Indeed coping has become such a 'difficult' construct to research that it is often excluded from stress investigations altogether. This exclusion is in stark contrast to the recognition of the centrality of coping to the stress process as was originally defined by Folkman, Lazarus and colleagues. The transactional stress and coping theory (Lazarus 1966) and more recent theories such as Edwards' (1988) cybernetic coping theory both defined coping as an individual response maintaining a state of equilibrium and thus preserving well-being. Exactly *how* these coping responses fit within the psychological stress process and how coping should be best measured remains under discussion (e.g. Brough, Dollard and Tuckey 2014).

Several decades of coping research has succeeded in drawing our attention to the identification of coping as a *state-based* or a *trait-based* (dispositional) individual response and the corresponding qualitative and/or quantitative measurement techniques which accompany these responses (Brough, O'Driscoll and Kalliath 2005b). However it is noticeable that many researchers fail to identify the basic type of coping they propose to assess and this oversight partly explains the lack of adequate progress in coping research. Some recent discussions suggest, for example, that *future-oriented proactive coping* may be a significant advancement to coping research (Aspinwall 2004; Folkman and Moskowitz 2004). Future-oriented coping identifies ways in which individuals can best cope with an anticipated future stressor such as an examination, medical procedure or work restructure. Hence the focus in future-oriented coping is training individuals to cope with *future* stressors, as opposed to evaluating the coping strategies individuals used to manage past stressors.

In this chapter we review the current evidence and discussions concerning future-oriented coping, including the mixed evidence for relationships between coping and personality constructs. We also present some small original empirical research which explores the stability over time of the most widely used future-oriented coping measure (the Proactive Coping Inventory [PCI];

Greenglass, Schwarzer, Jakubiec, Fiksenbaum and Taubert 1999a; Greenglass, Schwarzer and Taubert 1999b), and we assess the associations over time between future-oriented coping and some key personality constructs. The aim of this chapter is to collate and extend current discussions of future-oriented coping.

Future-Oriented Coping

Recent attention has focused on how individuals cope with *future* stressors and this is commonly described as *future-oriented coping*. Future-oriented coping is comprised of different types of coping behaviours, but the most prominent are *proactive coping* and *preventive coping*. Schwarzer (2000) defined proactive coping as efforts aimed at building up resources to enhance one's potential and opportunities for personal growth that might arise due to a future event. An example of proactive coping is undertaking skills training to improve the likelihood of gaining a job promotion. Proactive coping is therefore driven by challenge appraisals (Schwarzer and Knoll 2003) and is related to active goal management (Schwarzer 2000). Preventive coping includes the accumulation of resources to assist in reducing the severity of the impact of a future event. Stockpiling food, water and other necessary items in the event of a cyclone or flood is a good example of preventive coping. Preventive coping is akin to risk management, where the risks are seen as broad, with individuals accumulating resources 'just in case'. Therefore, preventive coping is driven primarily by threat appraisals.

Currently, the most widely used measures of proactive and preventive coping are the subscales within the PCI (Greenglass et al. 1999a, 1999b). The PCI consists of seven subscales, six of which measure different elements of future-oriented coping, namely proactive coping, preventive coping, reflective coping, strategic planning, emotional support seeking, instrumental support seeking, and one subscale assesses avoidance coping. The PCI was developed on the premise that coping is a multidimensional construct operating simultaneously at cognitive and behavioural levels. Coping is, therefore, conceptualized as an 'approach to life, an existential belief that things will work out … because the individual takes responsibility for outcomes' (Greenglass et al. 1999a, p. 5). In this regard, the various future-oriented coping constructs measured by the PCI are considered to be dispositional measures of coping, reflecting the types of coping *styles* that people would generally utilize, rather than situation-specific coping actions. Therefore, the PCI reveals the tendency to which people are likely to utilize one or more future-oriented coping styles. Only limited (cross-sectional) research has discussed the full PCI, warranting Folkman's (2009) call for establishing the stability of the PCI subscales over time to support its assertion as a dispositional measure. One of the aims of the empirical research we report in this chapter, therefore, was to test the stability of the PCI subscales over time.

Coping and Personality

Personality has long been recognized as having an influence on coping styles and behaviours (Carver and Connor-Smith 2010; Connor-Smith and Flachsbart 2007; Costa and McCrae 1990; Hewitt and Flett 1996; O'Driscoll and Brough 2010; Penley and Tomaka 2002). Traditional forms of coping (i.e. reactive coping such as problem-focused, emotion-focused and avoidance coping) have often been reported as mediating the relationship between personality and health and work-related outcomes. For example, Carver et al. (1993) found that optimism predicted an increase in emotion-approach coping, which in turn reduced distress over time in a sample of breast cancer patients. Similarly, Knoll, Rieckmann and Schwarzer (2005) reported that neuroticism increased negative affect over time by increasing evasive coping, and decreased positive affect over time by decreasing positive coping. Furthermore, Chang (2012) demonstrated support for maladaptive perfectionism increasing burnout of hospital nurses by increasing emotion-focused coping. Studies such as these provide support for the role that coping plays in mediating the effect of personality on outcomes.

However, not all studies have found support for these relationships. Inconsistent results have been reported depending on whether coping is measured as a dispositional or situational variable, that is, whether coping styles or coping strategies are the focus. Additionally, the use of cross-sectional and longitudinal study designs also appears to influence whether significant mediation effects are observed (see Brough et al. 2005b). For example, Knoll et al. (2005) tested the long-term mediating relationships between neuroticism, coping and positive and negative affect using both situational and dispositional forms of coping. Knoll et al. reported that dispositional coping did not mediate the relationships, but that situational coping did. Conversely, Panayiotou, Kokkinos and Kapsou (2014) reported that dispositional forms of active coping and avoidance coping significantly mediated the cross-sectional relationship between agreeableness and distress, and dispositional avoidance coping also mediated the cross-sectional relationship between neuroticism and distress. These examples illustrate the inconsistent results regarding the mediating role of dispositional coping between personality and outcomes. The empirical research described in this chapter, therefore, seeks to clarify the long-term impact of dispositional coping.

As proactive and preventive coping are both dispositional constructs, it is also important to understand if these future-oriented coping styles operate as mediators between personality and outcomes. In comparison to reactive coping, limited research has examined the mediating effects of proactive and preventive coping with personality, and none of these studies have employed longitudinal designs. For example, Griva and Anagnostopoulous (2010) found that proactive coping mediated the relationship between optimism and anxiety, and between self-esteem and anxiety, thereby modelling optimism and self-esteem as preceding proactive coping. Similarly, Chang and Chan (2015) reported that proactive coping mediated the relationship between optimism and burnout, while Albion, Fernie and Burton (2005) found support for the mediating role of proactive coping between proactive attitude and self-efficacy. Furthermore, Stanojevic, Krstic, Jaredic and Dimitrijevic (2013) reported that proactive coping mediated the relationship between optimism and satisfaction with life, and self-efficacy and satisfaction with life. Based on these examples, optimism was clearly found to work with proactive coping in the prediction of health and work-related outcomes.

No published studies could be located that tested preventive coping and personality variables in the same manner, which highlights a significant gap in this literature. Simple correlation analyses have demonstrated preventive coping is related to personality and health outcomes, suggesting that mediating effects may occur. For example, Ouwehand, de Ridder and Bensing (2006) reported positive correlations between preventive coping and future orientation and goal orientation, while Sohl and Moyer (2009) found preventive coping was positively related to optimism. Negative relationships have also been reported for preventive coping with perceived stress (Hu and Gan 2011) and depression (Gan, Yang, Zhou and Zhang 2007). Further research on these relationships is clearly warranted to provide insight into the relationships between personality and future-oriented coping. The study described in this chapter contributes to current knowledge and understanding about the role of future-oriented coping with personality variables, as well as providing an insight into the mediating relationships when coping is measured dispositionally and longitudinally.

Research Aims and Hypotheses

There were two primary aims of this empirical research: (1) to establish the stability of the PCI to provide evidence for its use as a dispositional measure of future-oriented coping; and (2) to examine the mediating effects of proactive and preventive coping between personality and psychological health, over time. To achieve these aims, we tested two hypotheses:

> Hypothesis 1: The Proactive Coping Inventory will demonstrate adequate test-retest reliability coefficients to demonstrate its stability over time.

> Hypothesis 2: Proactive and preventive coping will mediate the relationship between personality variables and psychological strain over time, after controlling for baseline levels of psychological strain.

Method Participants and Procedure

The research was advertised to undergraduate students at an Australian university via emails, lectures and on course websites. In exchange for participation, participants received course credit (first year participants only) or were entered into a draw to win $150 cash (all other participants). Two hard copy surveys were distributed to volunteer participants with a six-month time lag. A total of $N = 179$ useable surveys were returned at Time 1 (53% response rate) and $N = 125$ useable surveys were returned at Time 2 (58% response rate). Of these, $N = 67$ were matched across the two administrations. The response rates are representative of the average response rates in academic settings (Baruch 1999). Surveys were matched across the two time points using a unique code provided by each participant.

Participants ranged in age from 17 to 44 years ($M = 23.45$; $SD = 7.04$) and were primarily female ($n = 58$; 87%), Caucasian ($n = 51$; 76%), and lived at home ($n = 43$; 64%). Most respondents were in the first year of university ($n = 48$; 72%) and were enrolled full-time ($n = 64$; 96%) in a Psychology degree ($n = 64$; 96%). A series of multivariate analysis of variance (MANOVA) procedures were conducted to determine whether differences existed on (1) the demographic variables, (2) the personality variables, and (3) the PCI subscales and psychological strain between completers versus non-completers (i.e. respondents who completed only Time 1 surveys versus those who completed both the Time 1 and Time 2 surveys). The results revealed there were no significant differences for psychological strain, the demographic or personality variables, but significant differences did exist on the PCI subscales ($F[8, 170] = 2.22$, $p = 0.03$, Pillai's trace $= 0.10$; partial $\eta^2 = 0.10$). Respondents who only completed the Time 1 surveys reported higher levels of preventive and reflective coping compared to the respondents who completed both surveys.

Measures

Future-oriented coping. The PCI (Greenglass et al. 1999b) contains 55 items and seven scales. Table 2.1 indicates the subscales, example items, number of items, and reliability coefficients as reported by Greenglass et al. (1999a). Responses were scored on a 4-point scale ranging from 1 (*not at all true*) to 4 (*completely true*). Greenglass et al. (1999a) reported reliability coefficients ranging between 0.61 and 0.85 across Canadian and Polish-Canadian samples.

Table 2.1   PCI subscale items, examples and reliability coefficients

Subscale	No. of items	Example item	Reliability
Proactive Coping	14	*I am a 'take charge' person*	0.80–0.85
Preventive Coping	10	*I prepare for adverse events*	0.79–0.83
Reflective Coping	11	*I imagine myself solving difficult problems*	0.79–0.80
Strategic Planning	4	*I make a plan and follow it*	0.71
Emotional Support Seeking	5	*Others help me feel cared for*	0.64–0.73
Instrumental Support Seeking	8	*I ask others what they would do in my situation*	0.84–0.85
Avoidance Coping	3	*When I have a problem I like to sleep on it*	0.61–0.74

Note: Reliability coefficients reported by Greenglass et al. (1999a).

Optimism. Optimism was measured using the 10-item Revised Life Orientation Test (LOT-R; Scheier, Carver and Bridges 1994). Participant responses were made on a 5-point scale ranging from 0 (*strongly disagree*) to 4 (*strongly agree*), with higher scores representing greater optimism. Example items include '*I am always optimistic about my future*' and '*If something can go wrong for me, it will*' (negatively worded). Reliability coefficients ranging from 0.70 to 0.81 have been reported in the literature (Geers, Helfer, Kosbab, Weiland and Landry 2005; Mäkikangas, Kinnunen and Feldt 2004; Scheier et al. 1994).

Neuroticism. Neuroticism was measured with the NEO-Five Factor Inventory (NEO-FFI; Costa and McCrae 1992). Participants indicated their agreement or disagreement to 12 items on a 5-point scale ranging from 1 (*strongly disagree*) to 5 (*strongly agree*). High scores reflect higher levels of neuroticism. Reliability coefficients ranging from 0.81 to 0.88 have been reported (Costa and McCrae 1992; Eaton and Bradley 2008; Jones, Banicky, Pomare and Lasane 2004).

Past and future orientation. The Temporal Orientation Scale (TOS; Jones et al. 2004) was used to measure past and future orientation. A total of 10 items pertaining to past orientation ('*I think about the past a lot*') and future orientation ('*I keep working at a difficult, boring task if it will help me to get ahead*') were included. Responses were scored on a 7-point scale ranging from 1 (*not true of me*) to 7 (*very true of me*). Jones et al. (2004) reported average reliability coefficients of 0.80 (past orientation) and 0.72 (future orientation).

Goal orientation. The tendency to set goals and make plans was assessed using the Goal Orientation scale (Malouff et al. 1990). Responses were scored on a 5-point scale ranging from 1 (*strongly disagree*) to 5 (*strongly agree*) to 15 items such as '*I often plan for the future*'. Reliability coefficients ranging from 0.73 to 0.86 have been reported in the literature (Jones et al. 2004; Ouwehand et al. 2006).

Psychological strain. The 12-item General Health Questionnaire (GHQ-12; Goldberg 1972) was used to assess generic psychological strain. Participants responded to a list of 12 affective statements concerning their psychological health over the past few weeks relative to their usual level of health. Responses were scored on a 4-point scale ranging from 0 (*not at all*) to 3 (*much more than usual*) to questions such as '*Lost much sleep over worry?*' Higher scores indicated higher levels of psychological strain. Acceptable reliability coefficients ranging from 0.85 to 0.91 have been reported in the literature (Kalliath, O'Driscoll and Brough 2004; Mansell, Brough and Cole 2006).

Data analysis. The data were analysed via bootstrapping with the PROCESS macro (Hayes 2013) in SPSS version 21. For each analysis, 5,000 bootstrap resamples and 95% bias corrected confidence intervals were utilized. Heteroscedasticity-consistent standard errors (HSEs) were also calculated to account for the slight deviations from normality (Edwards and Lambert 2007). To provide a more stringent measure of mediation, Time 1 psychological strain was included as a covariate in each analysis, and both types of coping were included simultaneously as mediators to account for their shared effects on the outcome variable. Based on recent recommendations in the literature (Hayes 2013; Zhao, Lynch and Chen 2010), an indirect effect was judged to be significant if the confidence intervals did not contain zero.

Results

The means, standard deviations and alpha reliability coefficients are reported in Table 2.2. All variables exhibited acceptable means and standard deviations, and demonstrated good internal consistency (i.e. $\alpha = 0.70$ or above), however the measurement of avoidance coping was not reliable (T1 $\alpha = 0.43$; T2 $\alpha = 0.50$). Each of the PCI subscales demonstrated test–retest reliability coefficients ranging between $r = 0.60$ to $r = 0.78$. These values were within Schorr's (2001) guidelines that recommend trait measures should exhibit stability coefficients between 0.60 and 0.80. Therefore, Hypothesis 1 regarding the stability of the PCI subscales was supported.

Table 2.2   **Means, standard deviations and reliability coefficients at Time 1 and Time 2 for personality and coping variables**

	Time 1		Time 2		Test–retest
	Mean (SD)	Alpha	Mean (SD)	Alpha	reliability
Past Orientation	3.85 (1.19)	0.79	3.55 (1.14)	0.77	0.67
Future Orientation	4.49 (1.07)	0.74	4.64 (0.99)	0.75	0.77
Goal Orientation	3.63 (0.63)	0.87	3.66 (0.56)	0.90	0.85
Neuroticism	2.91 (0.77)	0.87	2.76 (0.78)	0.89	0.88
Optimism	2.53 (0.82)	0.89	2.60 (0.82)	0.89	0.83
Proactive Coping	2.95 (0.44)	0.85	3.06 (0.41)	0.85	0.78
Preventive Coping	2.82 (0.49)	0.83	2.93 (0.44)	0.80	0.72
Reflective Coping	2.84 (0.43)	0.83	2.97 (0.43)	0.84	0.74
Strategic Planning	2.83 (0.62)	0.78	3.03 (0.51)	0.72	0.60
Instrumental Support	3.01 (0.57)	0.89	3.17 (0.52)	0.88	0.76
Emotional Support	3.16 (0.62)	0.80	3.30 (0.52)	0.77	0.70
Avoidance Coping	2.72 (0.53)	0.43	2.72 (0.56)	0.50	0.64
Strain	1.05 (0.58)	0.91	0.84 (0.42)	0.85	0.59

Note: Test–retest reliability coefficients are significant at $p < 0.001$.

The correlation results are presented in Table 2.3. As expected, significant correlations were observed for all personality variables and proactive coping at Time 1 and Time 2 in the expected directions. Only future orientation and goal orientation at both Time 1 and Time 2, and neuroticism at Time 1 were significantly related to preventive coping. Proactive coping was associated with reduced psychological strain at both Time 1 and Time 2, but preventive coping was only associated with reduced strain at Time 1. These results demonstrate that proactive coping exhibits stronger associations with personality and psychological strain compared to the same relationships with preventive coping.

Table 2.3   Correlations between T1 personality, coping and strain, and T2 coping and strain

	1	2	3	4	5	6	7	8	9	10
1. T1 Past Orientation										
2. T1 Future Orientation	0.04									
3. T1 Goal Orientation	0.01	0.51***								
4. T1 Neuroticism	0.63***	-0.17	-0.11							
5. T1 Optimism	-0.52***	0.15	0.03	-0.65***						
6. T1 Proactive Coping	-0.43***	0.50***	0.48***	-0.66***	0.55***					
7. T2 Proactive Coping	-0.32**	0.40***	0.43***	-0.53***	0.52***	0.78***				
8. T1 Preventive Coping	-0.14	0.53***	0.52***	-0.31**	0.24	0.50***	0.45***			
9. T2 Preventive Coping	-0.13	0.38***	0.46***	-0.21	0.05	0.36***	0.47***	0.72***		
10. T1 Strain	0.60***	-0.12	0.01	0.75***	-0.70***	-0.57***	-0.48***	-0.27*	-0.17	
11. T2 Strain	0.47***	-0.08	0.04	0.63***	-0.55***	-0.53***	-0.42***	-0.15	0.02	0.59***

Notes: $^*p < 0.05$; $^{**}p < 0.01$; $^{***}p < 0.001$.

Indirect effects. Hypothesis 2 tested the mediating effects of proactive and preventive coping between personality and psychological strain over time. The results of the bootstrapped analyses are presented in Table 2.4. Preventive coping was not a significant mediator of any of the relationships between personality and strain. Proactive coping, however, acted as a significant mediator for the effects of personality on strain for each of the personality variables except neuroticism. The effects were such that future orientation, goal orientation and optimism decreased psychological strain over time by increasing proactive coping, and past orientation increased strain over time by decreasing proactive coping. Taken together, these results provided partial support for Hypothesis 2.

Table 2.4   Bootstrapped indirect effects for Time 1 personality predicting Time 2 strain via Time 1 proactive and preventive coping

	Via proactive coping		Via preventive coping	
	b (SE b)	CI	b (SE b)	CI
Past – Coping	**-0.155 (0.048)**	**-0.251, -0.060**	-0.057 (0.053)	-0.162, 0.049
Coping – Time 2 Strain	**-0.319 (0.135)**	**-0.589, -0.050**	0.112 (0.109)	-0.105, 0.329
Indirect effect	**0.050 (0.027)**	**0.009, 0.118**	-0.006 (0.010)	-0.039, 0.004
Direct effect	0.049 (0.044) -0.040, 0.138			
Future – Coping	**0.204 (0.053)**	**0.098, 0.309**	**0.242 (0.059)**	**0.125, 0.360**
Coping – Time 2 Strain	**-0.391 (0.139)**	**-0.668, -0.114**	0.087 (0.116)	-0.144, 0.318
Indirect effect	**-0.080 (0.036)**	**-0.165, -0.021**	0.021 (0.028)	-0.028, 0.083
Direct effect	0.045 (0.046) -0.046, 0.136			
Goal – Coping	**0.334 (0.082)**	**0.169, 0.498**	**0.402 (0.072)**	**0.258, 0.547**
Coping – Time 2 Strain	**-0.465 (0.154)**	**-0.773, -0.157**	0.050 (0.114)	-0.178, 0.278
Indirect effect	**-0.155 (0.061)**	**-0.297, -0.054**	0.020 (0.044)	-0.066, 0.109
Direct effect	0.160 (0.086) -0.012, 0.332			
Neuroticism – Coping	**-0.377 (0.059)**	**-0.494, -0.259**	**-0.201 (0.076)**	**-0.352, -0.050**
Coping – Time 2 Strain	-0.222 (0.145)	-0.511, 0.068	0.119 (0.103)	-0.086, 324
Indirect effect	0.084 (0.054)	-0.017, 0.200	-0.024 (0.024)	-0.08, 0.010
Direct effect	**0.193 (0.084) 0.025, 0.361**			
Optimism – Coping	**0.294 (0.058)**	**0.178, 0.411**	0.142 (0.093)	-0.043, 0.328
Coping – Time 2 Strain	**-0.295 (0.145)**	**-0.585, -0.005**	0.116 (0.103)	-0.090. 0.322
Indirect effect	**-0.087 (0.043)**	**-0.179, -0.010**	0.017 (0.021)	-0.006, 0.081
Direct effect	-0.104 (0.077) -0.259, 0.050			

Note: 95% bias corrected confidence intervals. Significant effects are bolded.

Discussion

Hypothesis 1 tested whether the PCI subscales would be stable over time by examining the test–retest coefficients over a six-month time lag. As per Schorr's (2001) recommendations, the PCI subscales were within the acceptable ranges for trait measures (i.e. between $r = 0.60$ and 0.80). These results provide support for the consideration of the PCI as a dispositional measure of coping. One area of concern, however, was the low reliability for avoidance coping at both time points. These results suggest that respondents had difficulty reliably answering the avoidance coping items, possibly because they do not fit with the overall emphasis of the PCI, which is concerned with active, positive forms of coping with the future. Other research has also reported difficulties with the avoidance coping subscale. For example, Roesch et al. (2009) reported the avoidance coping subscale had less than acceptable reliability (i.e. $\alpha = 0.57$), and Cantwell, Scevak, Bourke and Holbrook (2012) also reported that the avoidance coping subscale failed to load on a single factor during CFA procedures and was therefore removed from their study. While the results of this study provide support for the stability of the PCI over time, they also indicate further work is required to achieve a reliable avoidance coping subscale.

Hypothesis 2 tested the mediating relationships between personality, future-oriented coping and psychological strain over time. The results partially supported this hypothesis, demonstrating that proactive coping mediated the relationship between past orientation, future orientation, goal orientation and optimism with psychological strain over time. Preventive coping was not a significant mediator of any of these relationships. The results demonstrated that when the personality variable had a beneficial impact on the outcome (i.e. reduced psychological strain) the inclusion of proactive coping enhanced this effect, such that personality increased proactive coping, which in turn reduced levels of strain. Conversely, when personality had a detrimental impact on the outcome (i.e. increased psychological strain), the inclusion of proactive coping worsened this effect, such that personality (specifically past orientation) decreased proactive coping, which then increased levels of strain.

These results are consistent with existing research, demonstrating that positive, approach types of coping can have beneficial impacts on outcome variables by transmitting the positive effects of personality. For example, proactive coping was found to carry the effects of optimism to psychological strain, similar to Griva and Anagnostopoulous (2010) and Stanojevic et al. (2013). Goal orientation was also found to have a beneficial outcome by increasing proactive coping, supporting research by Porath and Bateman (2006) who reported that learning and performance goal orientations increased performance by increasing proactive behaviour, and Parker, Martin, Colmar and Liem (2012) who found that mastery goal orientation decreased burnout by increasing problem-focused coping. Similarly, our results extend the findings of Fortunato and Furey (2011) who reported that future-focused thinking was associated with less depression, while past-focused thinking was associated with more anxiety and depression. The results reported here demonstrated that the effects of future orientation and past orientation were transmitted through proactive coping to psychological strain in a similar direction. The added benefits of the results of this study are that these effects were found for a measure of dispositional future-oriented coping in a longitudinal sample. The results therefore directly contribute to the scarce literature on longitudinal future-oriented coping research by demonstrating these effects are present over time.

In regards to the lack of significant mediating effects for preventive coping, prior research has often reported that preventive coping is less influential compared to proactive coping, particularly when included simultaneously in analyses. For example, when preventive coping was included with proactive coping in a model predicting social well-being, preventive coping was not a significant predictor (Zambianchi and Bitti 2013). Similarly, Sohl and Moyer (2009) suggested that the relationships between preventive coping and outcomes may be due to its shared variance with proactive coping. The results of the current study were consistent with this suggestion by the finding that preventive coping was not a significant mediator when tested simultaneously with proactive coping. These results suggest that preventive coping was not uniquely important in transmitting the effect of the personality variables included in this study on psychological strain. Further research with other variables will be important to increase insight into the impact of preventive coping.

Neuroticism revealed it was a stronger direct predictor of psychological strain than the effect through proactive or preventive coping. This is consistent with Mirnics et al. (2013) who reported that the direct effect of neuroticism on psychopathology was more strongly evident than an indirect effect through dispositional coping. Interestingly, Bouchard, Guillemette and Landry-Léger (2004) found that the mediating effect of coping between neuroticism and psychological distress was significant when coping was measured as a situational construct. These examples may point to a mediating effect when coping is measured situationally, but a stronger direct effect for neuroticism when coping is measured dispositionally. Clearly these relationships need further testing to clarify how neuroticism interacts with future-oriented coping in the prediction of psychological ill-health.

Limitations and future research. As the majority of research into future-oriented coping has been cross-sectional, this study contributes to the literature by incorporating measurements over time, and illustrating the stronger effect of proactive coping as compared to preventive coping in reducing psychological strain. There are, however, two notable limitations. Firstly, the small sample size restricted the complexity of the analyses that could have been conducted. While bootstrapping via the PROCESS macro is an acceptable method for testing indirect effects, larger samples would enable testing via complex procedures such as structural equation modelling. We acknowledge that a small sample size is also equated with a greater impact of non-normality and less power to detect significant effects (Field 2013), which may have contributed to some of the non-significant relationships.

Secondly, each personality variable was investigated as a separate predictor. Personality traits do not occur in isolation, and may act in a causal sequence to influence each other. For example, being optimistic may increase levels of future orientation which may in turn influence coping; or being higher in neuroticism may lead to a higher past orientation which might then decrease future-oriented coping. Testing these relationships in more detail in future research would be informative to clarify how exactly personality is related to future-oriented coping.

Conclusion

This chapter has provided insight into a new area of coping research: future-oriented coping. We considered current research findings in this area, including the mixed results for the associations between future-oriented coping and personality. We presented original longitudinal empirical research to provide evidence for the dispositional nature of the PCI, as well as to investigate the mediating relationships between future-oriented coping, personality, and psychological strain. The results revealed that the test–retest coefficients for the PCI were consistent with those expected of trait measures, and that proactive coping was superior to preventive coping in acting as a mediator between various personality traits and psychological strain over time. Overall, the study demonstrated that future-oriented coping operates in a similar manner to reactive coping in mediating the effects of personality on psychological strain. Finally, we also provided evidence for the mediating effects of dispositional coping in a longitudinal sample.

References

Albion, M.J., Fernie, K.M. and Burton, L.J. (2005). Individual differences in age and self-efficacy in the unemployed. *Australian Journal of Psychology*, 57, 11–19.

Aspinwall, L.G. (2004). Proactive coping, wellbeing, and health. In N.J. Smelser and P.B. Baltes (eds), *International Encyclopedia of the Social & Behavioral Sciences* (pp. 16447–51). Oxford: Elsevier.

Baruch, Y. (1999). Response rate in academic studies – a comparative analysis. *Human Relations*, 52, 421–38.

Bouchard, G., Guillemette, A. and Landry-Leger, N. (2004). Situational and dispositional coping: An examination of their relation to personality, cognitive appraisals, and psychological distress. *European Journal of Personality*, 18, 221–38.

Brough, P., Dollard, M. and Tuckey, M. (2014). Theory and methods to prevent and manage occupational stress: Innovations from around the globe. *International Journal of Stress Management*, 21, 1–6.

Brough, P., O'Driscoll, M. and Kalliath, T. (2005a). Evaluating the criterion validity of the Cybernetic Coping Scale: Cross-lagged predictions of psychological strain, job and family satisfaction. *Work & Stress*, 19, 276–92.

Brough, P., O'Driscoll, M. and Kalliath, T. (2005b). Confirmatory factor analysis of the Cybernetic Coping Scale. *Journal of Occupational and Organisational Psychology*, 78, 53–61.

Brough, P., O'Driscoll, M., Kalliath, T., Cooper, C.L. and Poelmans, S. (2009). *Workplace Psychological Health: Current Research and Practice*. Cheltenham: Edward Elgar.

Cantwell, R.H., Scevak, J.J., Bourke, S. and Holbrook, A. (2012). Identifying individual differences among doctoral candidates: A framework for understanding problematic candidature. *International Journal of Educational Research*, 53, 68–79.

Carver, C.S. and Connor-Smith. J. (2010). Personality and coping. *Annual Review of Psychology*, 61, 679–704.

Carver, C.S., Pozo, C., Harris, S.D., Noriega, V., Scheier, M.F., Robinson, D.S., Ketcham, A.S., Moffatt, F.L. and Clark, K.C. (1993). How coping mediates the effect of optimism on distress: A study of women with early stage breast cancer. *Journal of Personality and Social Psychology*, 65, 375–90.

Chang, Y. (2012). The relationship between maladaptive perfectionism with burnout: Testing mediating effect of emotion-focused coping. *Personality and Individual Differences*, 53, 635–9.

Chang, Y. and Chan, H.-J. (2015). Optimism and proactive coping in relation to burnout among nurses. *Journal of Nursing Management*, 23(3), 401–8.

Connor-Smith, J.K. and Flachsbart, C. (2007). Relations between personality and coping: A meta-analysis. *Journal of Personality and Social Psychology*, 93, 1080–107.

Costa, P.T. Jr. and McCrae, R.R. (1990). Personality: Another 'hidden factor' in stress research. *Psychological Inquiry*, 1, 22–4.

Costa, P.T. Jr. and McCrae, R.R. (1992). *NEO PI-R Professional Manual*. Odessa: Psychological Assessment Resources, Inc.

Demerouti, E., Bakker, A.B., Nachreiner, F. and Schaufeli, W.B. (2001). The job demands-resources model of burnout. *Journal of Applied Psychology*, 86(3), 499–512.

Dollard, M., Shimazu, A., Bin Nordin, R., Brough, P. and Tuckey, M. (eds) (2014). *Psychosocial Factors at Work in the Asia Pacific*. London: Springer.

Eaton, R.J. and Bradley, G. (2008). The role of gender and negative affectivity in stressor appraisal and coping selection. *International Journal of Stress Management*, 15, 94–115.

Edwards, J.R. (1988). The determinants and consequences of coping with stress. In C.L. Cooper and R. Payne (eds.), *Causes, Coping and Consequences of Stress and Work* (pp. 233–63). Chichester: John Wiley.

Edwards, J.R. and Lambert, L.S. (2007). Methods for integrating moderation and mediation: A general analytical framework using moderated path analysis. *Psychological Methods*, 12(1), 1–22.

Field, A. (2013). *Discovering Statistics using IBM SPSS Statistics and Sex and Drugs and Rock 'n' Roll*. (3rd edn). London: Sage Publications.

Folkman, S. (2009). Questions, answers, issues, and next steps in stress and coping research. *European Psychologist*, 14, 72–7.

Folkman, S. and Moskowitz, J.T. (2004). Coping: Pitfalls and promise. *Annual Review of Psychology*, 55, 745–74.

Fortunato, V.J. and Furey, J.T. (2011). The theory of MindTime: The relationships between future, past, and present thinking and psychological well-being and distress. *Personality and Individual Differences*, 50, 20–4.

Gan, Y., Yang, M., Zhou, Y. and Zhang, Y. (2007). The two-factor structure of future-oriented coping and its mediating role in student engagement. *Personality and Individual Differences*, 43, 851–63.

Geers, A.L., Helfer, S.G., Kosbab, K., Weiland, P.E. and Landry, S.J. (2005). Reconsidering the role of personality in placebo effects: Dispositional optimism, situational expectations, and the placebo response. *Journal of Psychosomatic Research*, 58, 121–7.

Goldberg, D.P. (1972). *The Detection of Psychiatric Illness by Questionnaire*. Oxford: Oxford University Press.

Greenglass, E., Schwarzer, R., Jakubiec, D., Fiksenbaum, L. and Taubert, S. (1999a). *The Proactive Coping Inventory (PCI): A Multidimensional Research Instrument*. Paper presented at the 20th International Conference of the Stress and Anxiety Research Society, Krakow, Poland.

Greenglass, E., Schwarzer, R. and Taubert, S. (1999b). *The Proactive Coping Inventory (PCI): A Multidimensional Research Instrument*. Retrieved 22 October 2008 from http://userpage.fu-berlin.de/~health/greenpci.htm.

Griva, F. and Anagnostopoulous, F. (2010). Positive psychological states and anxiety: The mediating effect of proactive coping. *Psychological Reports*, 107, 795–804.

Hayes, A.F. (2013). *Introduction to Mediation, Moderation, and Conditional Process Analysis: A Regression-based Approach*. New York: The Guilford Press.

Hewitt, P.L. and Flett, G.L. (1996). Personality traits and the coping process. In M. Zeidner and N.S. Endler (eds), *Handbook of Coping: Theory, Research, Applications* (pp. 410–33). New York: John Wiley & Sons.

Hu, Y. and Gan, Y. (2011). Future-oriented coping and job hunting among college students. *The Psychological Record*, 61, 253–68.

Jones, J.M., Banicky, L., Pomare, M. and Lasane, T.P. (2004). *A Temporal Orientation Scale: Focusing Attention on the Past, Present and Future*. Unpublished manuscript. University of Delaware.

Kalliath, T.J., O'Driscoll, M.P. and Brough, P. (2004). A confirmatory factor analysis of the General Health Questionnaire – 12. *Stress and Health*, 20, 11–20.

Knoll, N., Rieckmann, N. and Schwarzer, R. (2005).Coping as a mediator between personality and stress outcomes: A longitudinal study with cataract surgery patients. *European Journal of Personality*, 19, 229–47.

Lazarus, R.S. (1966). *Psychological Stress and the Coping Process*. New York: McGraw-Hill.

Mäkikangas, A., Kinnunen, U. and Feldt, T. (2004). Self-esteem, dispositional optimism, and health: Evidence from cross-lagged data on employees. *Journal of Research in Personality*, 38, 556–75.

Malouff, J., Schutte, N., Bauer, M., Mantelli, D., Pierce, B., Cordova, G. and Reed, E. (1990). Development and evaluation of a measure of the tendency to be goal oriented. *Personality and Individual Differences*, 11, 1191–200.

Mansell, A., Brough, P. and Cole, K. (2006). Stable predictors of job satisfaction, psychological strain, and employee retention: An evaluation of organizational change within the New Zealand customs service. *International Journal of Stress Management*, 13, 84–107.

Mirnics, Z., Heincz, O., Bagdy, G., Surányi, Z., Gonda, Z., Benko, A., Molnar, E., Jakšić, N., Lazary, J. and Juhasz, G. (2013). The relationship between the Big Five personality dimensions and acute psychopathology: Mediating and moderating effects of coping strategies. *Psychiatria Danubina*, 25, 379–88.

O'Driscoll, M. and Brough, P. (2010). Work organisation and health. In S. Leka and J. Houdmont (eds). *Occupational Health Psychology* (pp. 57–87). Chichester: Wiley-Blackwell.

O'Driscoll, M., Brough, P. and Kalliath, T. (2009). Stress and coping. In S. Cartwright and C. Cooper (eds), *The Oxford Handbook of Organizational Well Being* (pp. 237–66). Oxford: Oxford University Press.

Ouwehand, C., de Ridder, T.D. and Bensing, J.M. (2006). Situational aspects are more important in shaping proactive coping behaviour than individual characteristics: A vignette study among adults preparing for ageing. *Psychology and Health*, 21, 809–25.

Panayiotou, G., Kokkinos, C.M. and Kapsou, M. (2014). Indirect and direct associations between personality and psychological distress mediated by dispositional coping. *The Journal of Psychology: Interdisciplinary and Applied*, 148, 549–67.

Parker, P.D., Martin, A.J., Colmar, S. and Liem, G.A. (2012). Teachers' workplace well-being: Exploring a process model of goal orientation, coping behavior, engagement, and burnout. *Teaching and Teacher Education*, 28, 503–13.

Penley, J.A. and Tomaka, J. (2002). Associations among the Big Five, emotional responses, and coping with acute stress. *Personality and Individual Differences*, 32, 1215–28.

Porath, C.L. and Bateman, T.S. (2006). Self-regulation: From goal orientation to job performance. *Journal of Applied Psychology*, 91, 185–92.

Roesch, S.C., Aldridge, A.A., Huff, T.L.P., Langner, K., Villodas, F. and Bradshaw, K. (2009). On the dimensionality of the proactive coping inventory: 7, 5, 3 factors? *Anxiety, Stress & Coping*, 22, 327–39.

Scheier, M.F., Carver, C.S. and Bridges, M.W. (1994). Distinguishing optimism from neuroticism (and trait anxiety, self-mastery, and self-esteem): A reevaluation of the Life Orientation Test. *Journal of Personality and Social Psychology*, 67, 1063–78.

Schorr, A. (2001). Subjective measurement in appraisal research: Present state and future perspectives. In K.R. Scherer, A. Schorr and T. Johnstone (eds), *Appraisal Processes in Emotion: Theory, Methods, Research* (pp. 331–49). Oxford: Oxford University Press.

Schwarzer, R. (2000). Manage stress at work through preventive and proactive coping. In E.A. Locke (ed.), *The Blackwell Handbook of Principles of Organizational Behavior* (pp. 342–55). Oxford: Blackwell Publishers Ltd.

Schwarzer, R. and Knoll, N. (2003). Positive coping: Mastering demands and searching for meaning. In S.J. Lopez and C.R. Snyder (eds.), *Positive Psychological Assessment: A Handbook of Models and Measures* (pp. 393–409). Washington, DC: American Psychological Association.

Sohl, S.J. and Moyer, A. (2009). Refining the conceptualization of a future-oriented self-regulatory behavior: Proactive coping. *Personality and Individual Differences*, 47, 139–44.

Stanojevic, D., Krstic, M., Jaredic, B. and Dimitrijevic, B. (2013). Proactive coping as a mediator between resources and outcomes: A structural equations modeling analysis. *Applied Research in Quality of Life*, November, 1–15.

Zambianchi, M. and Bitti, P.E.R. (2013). The role of proactive coping strategies in time perspective, perceived efficacy on affect regulation, divergent thinking and family communication in promoting social well-being in emerging adulthood. *Social Indicators Research*, March, 1–15.

Zhao, X., Lynch, J.G. Jr. and Chen, Q. (2010). Reconsidering Baron and Kenny: Myths and truths about mediation analysis. *Journal of Consumer Research*, 37, 197–206.

3

Politics, Personality and Surviving the Workplace

Ashley Weinberg

Introduction

'Politics is a dirty word', we are told: 'Anyone who is a politician should not be trusted'. And so the cycle of disbelief in the people and processes that govern so many countries and organizations continues. Yet herein lies a common self-deception. Whether we like it or not, we are all politicians! Let anyone who has never attempted to persuade another person nor support a course of action nor resolve a dispute show their hand. For those who are less public in their dealings, who has never prioritized one piece of information over another, nor secretly given to charity nor conformed to what others think because it suited their aims? Politics is essentially about exercising – privately or publicly – some kind of control, influence or power. Whether it is at the level of the individual, group or organization, political acts are part of our everyday dealings. There is a clear purpose to this, as 'political animals' we naturally keep aware of opportunities as well as threats to our survival. In this sense politics may indeed be a 'dirty' word, because it is something we may not wish to advertise, but is actually fundamental to ensuring we can survive and prosper. This chapter examines the role of political behaviour in the workplace, the extent to which this reflects aspects of our personality and its significance for individual psychological well-being.

What is political behaviour? Far from exclusively being a set of arts attributable to less desirable human habits, it comprises activities such as building social networks, gaining the support of influential others, self-promotion (Buchanan and Badham 2008), relating to others, employing analytical skills (Silvester, Wyatt and Randall 2013), controlling information and using rules and structures to one's advantage (Morgan 2006). The use of each presumes we are capable of understanding politics as it is enacted in our workplaces. Naturally there may be resistance to recognizing these as political skills as these resemble the features of 'how I get my job done', but this is curiously close to how political skills are defined, i.e. 'the ability to effectively understand others at work and to use such knowledge to influence others to act in ways that enhance one's personal and/or organizational objectives' (Ferris et al. 2005, p. 127). Depending on the specific job, such things that underpin the social expectations of the workplace can be distinguishable from those aspects of the job which give it its title. In other words, political skills may be considered separate from the purely technical aspects of work which overtly define our roles as engineers, customer service agents, machine operators, social workers, etc. However organizational politics surround us and to varying degrees engage us, as the dynamics of our workplaces flex to daily and strategic demands. 'I love my job, but I hate the politics of this place' is a common mantra and a heartfelt expression of emotion about this extrinsic feature of work. It is noteworthy that even those who actually have the job of politician and would be considered as 'better than others at "doing" organisational politics' (Kwiatkowski 2012, p. 55) are not exempt from the frustrations it brings.

Arguably it is impossible to escape involvement in the politics which characterize human relations in at least some part of our daily work. Indeed politics is the lifeblood of the psychological contract which directly describes unmet or violated expectations connected with work and mediates how we may respond (Conway and Coyle-Shapiro 2012). For example a teacher may feel happy that they have enjoyed a rewarding day encouraging their students, yet at the end of it discover that factors beyond their control have blocked funding for an educational trip they had planned; an electrician may have successfully fixed all the electrical faults they were asked to mend, but goes home worrying about a complaint from a customer who refuses to pay for the work done. In other words, the nature of the job task may not be the challenge to the employee, but instead the conditions surrounding this aspect of work clearly have the potential to fulfil or frustrate. If political behaviour is the medium we use to facilitate our goals and/or those of our organization, this is often seen as an added dimension to our job, but is actually fundamental in helping us achieve satisfactory work outcomes. As such, the influence of political behaviour on job satisfaction, as well as on well-being, cannot be underestimated (Malik, Danish and Ghafoor 2009). This begs the question of how well equipped are we to deal with this type of political challenge?

In fact there are apparent similarities between political awareness and functioning and those factors highlighted by known models of personality. Emotional Intelligence (EI), which emphasizes the capacity for intra- and interpersonal insights and their use to achieve goals, has received considerable attention since the turn of the century, while Machiavellianism, which is centred around deceptive capacities, has been widely researched for almost 50 years (Christie and Geis 1970). It is tempting to consider these traits as opposite sides of the same coin – with EI viewed as positive and Machiavellianism as negative – however they have been found to be distinct (Austin, Farrelly, Black and Moore 2007; Dahling, Whitaker and Levy 2009). As such it can be expected that both politically oriented traits can play important, albeit different, roles in influencing individual well-being at work. Perhaps this is no coincidence, as the ability to calculate at some level what is good for achieving our own goals is likely to have implications for our own psychological and physical health. Indeed this is fundamental to our survival. Our social antennae are attuned to potential opportunities and threats, so political behaviours are required to make the most of the former and to minimize the latter. However given our inclination towards social groupings – inside and out of the workplace – it is particularly relevant to examine the respective roles of EI and Machiavellianism.

Various models of EI have been proposed of which Goleman, Boyatzis and McKee's (2002) mixed model is probably the best known, featuring self-awareness and self-regulation (oriented towards the person), social awareness and social skills/management (highlighting social competencies). Goleman et al.'s model differs from Mayer and Salovey's (1997) ability-focused approach, combining aspects of ability and personality, but similarly incorporates the capacity to recognize and regulate emotions. Bar-On's (2005) emotional-social intelligence model is another mixed model which includes stress management and general mood. For the purposes of this chapter, reference will be made to components of Goleman's model, thus avoiding the potential for duplication between Bar-On's conceptualization of stress and the psychological health outcomes featured later. Machiavellianism provides a stark contrast to EI and has as its main features the capacity to ascribe cynicism to the motives of others, a lack of adherence to ethical behaviour and the desire to manipulate others for gain (Dahling, Kuyumcu and Librizzi 2012) which therefore promotes a short-term focus to problems. It is not considered a personality disorder (Kessler et al. 2010). This trait is rooted in self-interest (Furnham 2008) and it is not surprising that controversy has long surrounded the inspiration for it, which is the work 'On Principalities' by Niccolo Machiavelli, written in 1513 and given the title 'The Prince' by the publisher after the author's death (Parks 2009).

For illustrative purposes, it is useful to consider the operation of EI and Machiavellianism in the workplace example of the teacher. The teacher who receives bad news about their cancelled trip may feel under-valued for the extra work which had been invested in the idea, frustration that an educational opportunity had been missed, as well as disappointment on behalf of the enthusiastic students. Any or all of these emotions may motivate the teacher to seek an appointment with the head of the school to query the decision and begin a search for alternative ways of funding the trip. These actions may not be considered 'teaching', but are necessary for the personal and public reasons given. These are political actions and have the potential to yield a solution to the problem, or indeed further discontent. The stance of the individual teacher is likely to be influenced not only by insight into their own motives. These would include the degree of importance attached to the educational goal, the ability to cope with unmet expectations, as well as their own levels of emotional intelligence and Machiavellianism. In other words, 'I am here to teach but am denied the resources which will help me deliver the best teaching to the students, so how do I feel inclined to address the situation?' In theory at least, emotionally intelligent actions by the teacher should result in exploration of the alternatives and careful communication of the outcome to students without resulting in conflict with the school or its pupils and their families. However a more Machiavellian approach might lead to leaking news about insufficient support for education to local media to try to force the situation. Given the potential for the situation to end positively or negatively for all concerned – including the teacher and school's working relationship and respective reputations – attention to the relevant political processes and implications is clearly important. Preparation for treading the fine line between a more or less successful political outcome would not have featured in the teacher training qualification and yet it has the greater potential than most technical errors in class for a negative impact on the teacher's psychological health and career prospects. This example is designed to illustrate how important political awareness can be, yet how this is often overlooked in preparing workers for organizational life. Without relevant training, individuals are more reliant on the inclinations of their personality to guide their reactions to events. The respective implications for well-being of higher levels of EI or Machiavellianism are considered next in relation to categories of political activity identified by relevant researchers into organizational life. First it is important to consider the shared territory between political behaviour and psychological health.

Control is so often found to be the key to our psychological well-being, featuring in established models of mental health (e.g. Rotter 1966; Warr 1989), as well as psychosocial theories of the workplace (e.g. Hackman and Oldham 1976; Karasek 1979). Within these perspectives, control may be referred to as autonomy and the process by which it is gained as empowerment. As such it can be hard to divine how much relative importance should be afforded to individual perceptions of control or instead to more objectively assessed criteria. Either way it is known that employees' well-being stands to benefit from perceiving they have (e.g. Leach, Wall and Jackson 2003) or are objectively assessed as having (e.g. Randall, Griffiths and Cox 2005) greater control over their job. The key implication for individual psychological health is that this positively encourages an enhanced sense of self-efficacy and self-worth, i.e. 'I did that; I made that happen'. Positive outcomes for well-being are based on competence ('I can do this well'), aspiration ('I want to do this'), positive affect ('I feel good'), personal growth ('I can learn how to do this') and a sense of purpose ('I am making a difference') (Ryff 1989; Warr 1987), along with an absence of limiting factors such as cognitive weariness and psychosomatic complaints (van Horn, Taris, Schaufeli and Schreurs 2004). Whilst it is unlikely that all of these facets of psychological health will be serviced by any given occupational context, awareness of the range of influential factors for well-being is necessary to understand the function of political behaviours. For the individual experiencing unsatisfactory conditions, political actions may provide a route to addressing such deficits. Large scale research studies have shown the negative impact on mental health of having little or no control over work-related events, from downsizing in the Finnish civil service (Vahtera et al. 2004) to job insecurity across 16 European countries (Laszlo et al. 2010). Even in circumstances where we may have little control over events, some level of involvement makes a positive difference leading to reduced incidence of depression, heart disease and smoking (Karasek and Theorell 1990). Such examples illustrate the significance of political considerations for our well-being and how effectively we cope with challenges within the job. When considering political activities in the remainder of this chapter it will be seen that these are not ostensibly or exclusively about enacting direct control. However it is suggested that their role in creating or maintaining a sense of control does underpin the link with positive experiences of mental health. Figure 3.1 presents a simplified model of how this might operate in practice. Personality traits recognized as politically important are highlighted, i.e. EI and Machiavellianism, and their relevance to shaping political behaviours at work is also shown. In turn their anticipated links with psychological health outcomes are indicated. The contents of Table 3.1 and the commentary which follows it expand on this theoretical framework.

Political skills have been variously studied among ostensibly political and non-political occupations (e.g. Buchanan and Badham 2008; Morgan 2006; Silvester et al. 2013), however their links with the psychological health of the actors have been less well studied. Table 3.1 highlights how political behaviours commonly used in the workplace link with psychosocial constructs of known relevance to psychological health outcomes in the workplace.

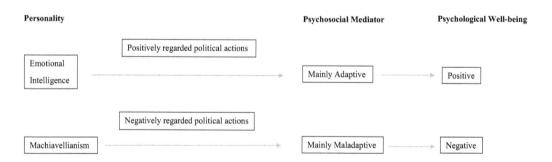

Figure 3.1   Politically oriented personality traits leading to psychological health outcomes

Table 3.1   **Hypothesized links between 12 political activities and predicted psychological health outcomes mediated by psychosocial factors in the workplace**

Political activity	Psychosocial mediator(s)	Psychological health outcome (predicted)
Building social networks	Social support	+ve
Gaining support of powerful others	Management support	+ve
Self-promotion	Job advancement/personal growth	+ve
Using rules to one's advantage	Perceived control	+ve
Understanding organizational culture	Perceived control	+ve
Taking a lead role	Autonomy	+ve/-ve
Controlling information	Autonomy	+ve/-ve
Relating to others	Social support	+ve
Handling conflict	Emotional labour	+ve/-ve
Analytical skills	Perceived control/competence	+ve
Manipulating others	Lack of social support	-ve
Coping	Perceived control/self-esteem	+ve

Note: Based on political skills highlighted by Buchanan and Badham (2008), Morgan (2006) and Silvester et al. (2013).

The analysis of social behaviour at work which follows explores the contents of Table 3.1 in turn and highlights political activities and their implications for our experience of the workplace and of psychological well-being.

Building social networks around us is likely to be a natural consequence of being around others and is not necessarily a conscious act in itself. In this way the gregarious individual likely to score high on extraversion will be socially oriented for the purposes of assessing this aspect of their emotional intelligence. Those who score higher in Machiavellianism are less likely to invest energy in this activity unless they see the benefit of a particular social network. Whichever predisposition leads to engaging in social contact, the result is the opportunity for increased social support and as the Whitehall studies of UK civil servants have shown this carries positive potential for psychological health (Stansfeld, Fuhrer and Shipley 1998). In addition the beneficial impact of social support on individuals' determination to persist in the face of challenges at work (Warr 2007) and its facilitation of employees' identity with the wider workforce (Wood 2008) have shown how political considerations such as drive towards a common goal and unity with others can positively impact on well-being. On an organizational scale, building social networks can mirror the positive impact of social support as a coping strategy utilized by individuals in talking about, validating and hopefully addressing the problems they face.

Gaining the support of powerful others in the workplace is likely to mean developing positive working relationships with one's line manager and/or with other colleagues at a more senior level in the organization. In this way the employee should feel comfortable within their job role as well as perceiving a greater degree of organizational support (Rhoades and Eisenberger 2002). In fact the impact of relationships with managers on the individual worker's psychological health has been highlighted in the research literature to the extent that the UK's Health and Safety Executive (HSE 2004) included this type of support in its management standards for tackling stress at work. Furthermore the UK's National Institute for Clinical Excellence (NICE) has been developing guidelines for managers recognizing the direct effect of their behaviour on the mental health of employees reporting to them (NICE 2013). Managing one's own relationships is a core component of the construct of emotional intelligence as much as recognizing opportunities for advancement for gain are central to Machiavellianism. One may suppose that those scoring high on each predisposition will fare well in drawing support to their cause. However, in practice, the resulting behaviours can range from being confident about expressing opinions or even sharing a joke with a manager to having a realistic expectation of support from the manager for a new idea. What is likely to differ between those high in either trait is the capacity for deep or surface acting of the relevant emotions and with this the risk of appearing insincere or obviously fawning. The natural cynicism and short-term focus which informs the Machiavellian approach may actually undermine their desired impact on the manager.

Similarly effective *self-promotion* requires careful management of one's own emotional display, whether this is in the course of putting oneself forward to lead or to seek an actual job promotion. The emotionally intelligent individual is likely to have sufficient concern for the impact of their behaviour and with raised levels of self-awareness more embarrassing tactics for putting oneself forward are more readily avoided. Ambition is not the sole domain of the Machiavellian approach, for its purpose to facilitate positive outcomes for the individual is clear to all; however the manner in which it is expressed and pursued sends clear messages to fellow workers and managers alike. There are competitive organizational cultures in which the respectful treatment of others is overlooked in favour of raw methods of advancement, so it would be less surprising to see Machiavellianism reaping more rewards where there is a lack of regulation of employee behaviour. The banking sector, both before and since the economic crisis of 2007–8, has achieved a dubious reputation in this regard. However more recent recognition by some financial institutions of the negative impact of an unforgiving working culture on mental well-being has increased desire for psychologically healthier working (City of London 2014). Generally job promotion opportunities are seen as desirable and are likely to be linked to positive past achievements. Where this is assessed in terms of dealings with others, the individual with a reputation for integrity based on their inclination towards social awareness should do comparatively well, although the deceptively charming individual has the chance to succeed where this depends on a strong interview performance (Furnham 2008). Whichever way self-promotion is achieved, improved health prospects can be expected to follow from the resulting enhanced levels of autonomy further up the organizational hierarchy (Marmot, Bosma, Hemingway, Brunner and Stansfeld 1997) or simply enhancing one's life options through increased income (Gardner and Oswald 2007).

This political activity is linked to *taking a lead role*, which is likely to attract those with a range of motivations for exercising power. However the additional responsibility of such a task is that of bringing others along with you and as mentioned earlier this can be achieved in more than one manner, with those scoring high in emotional intelligence likely to try less formal routes to achieve organizational goals with their employees (Kessler et al. 2010). The most effective style of leadership depends in no small part on the circumstances in which it is required. The organizational equivalents of war and of peace carry their own risks for individual and collective well-being. However the effect of leadership on those who are expected to follow is also bound up in the success of the enterprise at hand. Thus leadership which fails to convey its aims, to win trust, to inspire or continue to energize employees is likely to flounder, not least because its impact is unhealthy for organizational survival and therefore collective well-being. One may imagine that the increased chances of such results following the implementation of an unethical Machiavellian approach. On the other hand emotionally intelligent leadership is likelier to recognize the need for careful handling of employees, particularly in change scenarios (Travaglione and Cross 2006). The impact on the psychological health of the individual taking the lead role has been the focus of many case studies, but given the considerable number of variables in operation, the definitive answer remains elusive. We might expect that being a leader bolsters one's sense of control and self-esteem, but psychological risks historically accompany such an overtly political role – as one

American President John Quincy Adams famously stated, 'The four most miserable years of my life were my four years in the presidency'.

The adage that 'information is power' points to the political nature of actions which acquire, use and manage the flow of knowledge – in other words boosting control over a situation in the short- or long-term. *Using rules to one's advantage, understanding organizational culture, deploying analytical skills and controlling information* each exemplify the capacity of the individual to shape his/her future by gathering and utilizing the necessary resources. Gaining an understanding of 'how things work around here' (Bower 1966) is underpinned by a predisposition towards more than being inquisitive as it requires the motivation and skills to connect with those who already possess or govern access to this information. To this end and from different motivational viewpoints, both emotionally intelligent and Machiavellian individuals will recognize the importance of building working relationships and alliances. However difficulties with trust as well as the inclination to break with protocol and to stray into unethical practice provide significant risks to the success of the more Machiavellian-minded. The ability to analyse quantities of complex information is recognized by those who have it, and their colleagues, as significantly correlated with conscientiousness (Silvester et al. 2013). The drawback for those inclined to manipulate data for unethical purposes is that there is a negative correlation between conscientiousness and Machiavellianism (Lee and Ashton 2005) which increases their chances of making mistakes and getting caught. The step represented by controlling information is reliant on subjective judgement and as such is potentially open to abuse. Again the overlap between managing (EI-related) and manipulating (Machiavellian-related) relationships with others is apparent, but the outcome for the individual in possession of the information is an increased perception of control and therefore a likely boon to well-being.

The activities of *relating to others* and *handling conflict* are considerations of daily living and by virtue of this they also represent the most commonplace of political behaviours. For those who remain sceptical that we are all indeed politicians, this is the 'acid test'. Social behaviour naturally leads us into dealings with family, friends and colleagues, which inevitably provides opportunities for positive contact as well as challenges. The key difference between those inclined towards emotionally intelligent or Machiavellian practices lies in what these relations mean to that individual. In simple terms the person with raised EI is more likely to genuinely enjoy relations with others and as well as possessing a liking for others may be more able to show this too. Machiavellian priorities make this harder for the individual to experience and to display. This can lead to quite different approaches to conflict where resolution also means different things. On the one hand, higher EI may indeed result in the peaceful resolution (or even prevention) of a potential conflict situation, however this presupposes that the process is required to be peaceful. It can be equally likely there are those for whom specific or ongoing conflict is seen as an alternative political approach to a problem, perhaps preferring to prioritize the use of threat or force over any attempt to win 'hearts and minds'. Machiavelli's 'The Prince' famously ponders this advice to would-be rulers in a range of scenarios, suggesting that both might and persuasion should reside in our political armoury. Indeed one could argue that leadership is loosely categorized according to this model, with transactional and transformational styles representing quite different motivations for the use of power (Burns 1978) and transformational styles showing more positive effects on employees compared to other approaches (Kelloway, Turner, Barling and Loughlin 2012). Whilst considerable debate exists around the most effective approach to leadership, it is used here to highlight the likely (but not exclusively) differing priorities for the personality traits under discussion. What the political activities of relating to others and handling conflict say about those for whom EI or Machiavellianism is dominant, is not only linked to how they deal with others but how much this is informed and influenced by how they view themselves.

Reviews of relevant research suggest that higher emotional intelligence is linked to increased levels of well-being (Schutte, Malouff, Thorsteinsson, Bhullar and Rooke, 2007) and to a reduced risk of depression among men (Salguero, Extremera and Fernandez-Berrocal 2012) and lower levels of anxiety among men and women (Lizeretti and Extremera 2011). This is consistent with holding a positive view of oneself and experiencing accompanying feelings of self-worth and self-esteem (Mikolajczak and Luminet 2008). With enhanced understanding of one's own emotions as well as awareness of those of others, it is logical to predict more frequently positive social interactions for the high-EI individual. A different picture emerges for Machiavellianism which is negatively correlated with subjective well-being (Jones and Paulhus 2009). A relationship between this trait and depression is less obvious, however proneness to high anxiety and disconnection from emotions (Jones and Paulhus 2009) convey a more negative self-image and a lowered sense of well-being than experienced by those possessing higher levels of EI. Within a work context, Machiavellianism is linked with increased job strain and reduced job and career satisfaction (Jones and Paulhus 2009), as well as impaired employee performance (O'Boyle, Forsyth, Banks and McDaniel 2012). Taken as a whole, the commentary thus far on the relative likelihood of success or failure in work of those individuals so predisposed, suggests more positive outcomes for psychological well-being where EI is higher and more negative ones where Machiavellianism dominates. However this conclusion is not clear-cut in relation to each category of political activity (see Table 3.1), nor is the certainty of the predicted outcome given the range of individual and organizational variables involved. Nevertheless the list of political behaviours examined here omits an important component (although readers may have additions of their own in mind). The category proposed by this author is that variously known as coping or resilience – in other words actions which directly protect or promote the well-being of the individual.

Can *coping* be a political activity? The answer lies again with definition and motivation. If supporting a cause is political in nature, then it is not unreasonable to suggest that the cause can be 'you'. By taking steps to safeguard one's psychological health or enhance one's capacity to deal with challenges from the psychosocial environment, the potential to survive is increased. The need to perform this political function for ourselves is no less great than in the modern workplace (Weinberg and Cooper 2012) and it is no coincidence that different forms of coping have received considerable focus. This is not to say that the impact of work has previously been easier on workers' mental health, but that the options for coping have altered. In the UK in days before employment legislation and associated employee rights, the voice afforded to disgruntled workers was noticeably limited. This is exemplified by the action of an apprentice chimney builder who worked for a particularly cruel employer. Such was the young employee's fear that he dared not share his thoughts out loud, but so intense was his sense of dissatisfaction and injustice that he wrote his honest thoughts about the employer on a piece of paper and inserted it into the brickwork behind the fireplace as he was fixing it in place. This silently defiant act went unnoticed by others for over 100 years until the fireplace was being replaced and the letter discovered. Acts such as this were regarded as examples of stoicism and now find their equivalent in what is widely referred to as 'resilience'. This describes the capacity to use emotions to help us bounce back from negative events (Tugade, Frederickson and Feldman-Barrett 2005). The overlap between resilience and coping goes further than this as appraisal of the incoming threat to the individual is implicit in both the ability to embrace a challenge and to mobilize resources to meet it (Lazarus and Folkman 1984). This begs the question about individuals' knowledge of their capacity to cope. The self-awareness integral to higher EI may furnish the individual with positive emotional resources (Tugade et al. 2005) which are less accessible to the person with higher Machiavellianism. The Conservation of Resources theory (Hobfoll 1989) highlights the preventative potential of preparing to cope.

As such the political activities examined in this chapter, whether deployed in advance of, or in response to, an emerging problem could be regarded as forms of resilience or coping in their own right. However this does not guarantee that professional politicians who routinely use political actions, are inoculated against psychological strain in their own job. Indeed the impact of changes at work over which national politicians have reduced levels of control have been observed to have just as negative an effect on their mental health as in parallel scenarios for other occupational groups facing job uncertainty (Weinberg 2013). It would appear that recognition of the explicit need to look after one's psychological health should have no exemptions and therefore deserves its own category in the list of political activities in Table 3.1. Without positive mental health, our longer term capacity to maintain all other behaviours – political or not – is ultimately limited.

Conclusion

The forms of coping and features which make up individual resilience are linked to the facets of psychological well-being considered previously in this chapter (Ryff 1989; Warr 1987) and if deployed successfully will service our needs accordingly. For the teacher mentioned earlier, the challenge to the psychological contract is clear and some readjustment of expectation is required by the individual and/or the organization to avoid dissatisfaction spiralling into derailment. This example also underlines the potential importance of training employees in how to deal with politically charged events at work. Herriot and Pemberton's (1995) advice to the employee in such a situation, to 'get out, get safe or get even' encapsulates a stark range of options, but it is arguable that each has its merits for psychological well-being. However the influential role of personality cannot be overlooked, for as it shapes our behavioural style, it also has the capacity to promote outcomes for the betterment or detriment of mental health. Within the specific context of work, attempts at modelling emotionally intelligent behaviours have yielded promising research outcomes (Nelis, Quoidbach, Mikolajczak and Hansenne 2013). The debate about freedom to express 'natural' dispositions cannot be far behind. It should be noted that for ease of contemplation, only the roles of EI and Machiavellianism have received extended attention here and this may risk conveying the impression that 'if x, then y'. Clearly if taken in isolation this would be too simplistic, as the potential impact of other aspects of personality, individual differences and job context cannot be ignored. Notwithstanding this limitation, it is hoped that by focusing on the role of selected personality traits in the context of work, this chapter has made explicit 'political' activities, emphasizing their commonplace nature, their clear implications for psychosocial factors at work and in turn their potentially key role in determining our well-being. However successful or otherwise this enterprise, it is hoped that enough evidence has been presented to convince the undecided that political behaviour is not just for those who work in the job of 'politician' – for we are all politicians in our own social sphere.

Acknowledgements

I would like to thank Lottie Weinberg for her assistance with proofreading and design features of this chapter.

References

Austin, E.J., Farrelly, D., Black, C. and Moore, H. (2007). Emotional intelligence, Machiavellianism and emotional manipulation: Does EI have a dark side? *Personality and Individual Differences*, 43, 179–89.

Bar-On, R. (2005) The Bar-On model of emotional-social intelligence. *Psicothema* 18, supplement 13–25.

Bower, M. (1966) 'Company philosophy: The way we do things around here'. Available at: http://www.inc.com/articles/2003/04/25365.html. Accessed 7th July 2015.

Buchanan, D.A. and Badham, R.J. (2008). *Power, Politics and Organizational Change: Winning the Turf War.* London: Sage.

Burns, J.M. (1978). *Leadership.* New York: Harper & Row.

Christie, R. and Geis, F.L. (1970). *Studies in Machiavellianism.* New York: Academic Press.

City of London (2014). Best practice in promoting employee health and well-being in the City of London. Available at: http://www.cityoflondon.gov.uk/business/economic-research-and-information/research-publications/Documents/Research-2014/employee-health-and-wellbeing-in-the-city-of-London-technical-report.pdf. Accessed 7th July 2015.

Conway, N. and Coyle-Shapiro, J.A.-M. (2012). The reciprocal relationship between psychological contract fulfillment and employee performance and the moderating role of perceived organizational support and tenure. *Journal of Occupational and Organizational Psychology*, 85(2), 1–23.

Dahling, J., Kuyumcu, D. and Librizzi, E.H. (2012). Machiavellianism, unethical behavior and well-being in organizational life. In R.A. Giacolone and M.D. Promislo (eds), *Handbook of Unethical Work Behaviour: Implications for Individual Well-being* (pp. 183–94). New York: M.E. Sharpe Inc.

Dahling, J., Whitaker, B. and Levy, P. (2009). The development and validation of a new Machiavellianism scale. *Journal of Management*, 35, 219–57.

Ferris, G.R., Treadway, D.C., Kolodinsky, R.W., Hochwarter, W.A., Kacmar, C.J., Douglas, C. and Frink, D.D. (2005). Development and validation of the political skill inventory. *Journal of Management*, 31, 126–52.

Furnham, A. (2008). *Personality and Intelligence at Work: Exploring and Explaining Individual Differences at Work.* Hove: Routledge.

Gardner, J. and Oswald, A.J. (2007). Money and mental wellbeing: A longitudinal study of medium-sized lottery wins. *Journal of Health Economics*, 26(1), 49–60.

Goleman, D., Boyatzis, R.E. and McKee, A. (2002). *Primal Leadership: Realising the Power of Emotional Intelligence.* Boston: Harvard Business School Press.

Hackman, J.R. and Oldham, G.R. (1976). Motivation through the design of work: Test of a theory. *Organizational Behaviour and Human Performance*, 16, 250–79.

Health and Safety Executive (HSE) (2007). *Managing the Causes of Work-related Stress: A Step-by-step Approach using the Management Standards*, 2nd edn. London: HSE.

Herriot, P. and Pemberton, C. (1995). *New Deals.* Chichester: Wiley.

Hobfoll, S.E. (1989). Conservation of resources: A new attempt at conceptualising stress. *American Psychologist*, 44(3), 513–24.

HSE (2004). What are the management standards? Available at: http://www.hse.gov.uk/stress/standards/. Accessed 7th July 2015.

Jones, D.N. and Paulhus, D.L. (2009). Machiavellianism. In M.R. Leary and R.H. Hoyle (eds), *Individual Differences in Social Behavior* (pp. 93–108). New York: Guilford.

Karasek, R.A. (1979). Job demands, job decision latitude, and mental strain: Implications for job redesign. *Administrative Science Quarterly*, 24, 285–308.

Karasek, R.A. and Theorell, T. (1990). *Healthy Work; Stress, Productivity and the Reconstruction of Working Life.* New York: Basic.

Kelloway, E.K., Turner, N., Barling, J. and Loughlin, C. (2012). Transformational leadership and employee psychological well-being: The mediating role of employee trust in leadership. *Work & Stress*, 26(1), 3955.

Kessler, S.R., Bandelli, A.C., Spector, P.E., Borman, W.C., Nelson, C.E. and Penney, L.M. (2010). Re-examining Machiavelli: A three-dimensional model of Machiavellianism in the workplace. *Journal of Applied Social Psychology*, 40(8), 1868–96.

Kwiatkowski, R. (2012). Politicians and power: MPs in the UK parliament, In A. Weinberg (ed.), *The Psychology of Politicians* (pp. 39–58). Cambridge: Cambridge University Press.

Laszlo, K.D., Pikhart, H., Kopp, M.S., Bobak, M., Pajak, K., Malyutina, S., Salavecz, G. and Marmot, M. (2010). Job insecurity and health: A study of 16 European countries. *Social Science Medicine*, 70, 867–74.

Lazarus, R. and Folkman, S. (1984). *Stress, Appraisal and Coping*. New York: Springer Publications.

Leach, D.J., Wall, T.D. and Jackson, P.R. (2003). The effect of empowerment on job knowledge: An empirical test involving operators of complex technology. *Journal of Occupational and Organizational Psychology*, 76, 27–52.

Lee, K. and Ashton, M.C. (2005). Psychopathy, Machiavellianism, and narcissism in the Five-Factor Model and the HEXACO model of personality structure. *Personality and Individual Differences*, 38, 1571–82.

Lizeretti, N.P. and Extremera, N. (2011). Emotional intellitgence and clinical symptoms in outpatients with generalised anxiety disorder. *Psychiatry Quarterly*, 82(3), 253–60.

Malik, M.E., Danish, R.Q. and Ghafoor, M. (2009). Relationship between age, perceptions of organisational politics and job satisfaction. *Journal of Behavioural Sciences*, 19(1–2), 23–40.

Marmot, M.G., Bosma, H., Hemingway, H., Brunner, E. and Stansfeld, S. (1997). Contribution of job control and other risk factors to social variations in coronary heart disease incidence. *Lancet*, 350, 235–9.

Mayer, J.D. and Salovey, P. (1997). What is emotional intelligence? In P. Salovey and D. Sluyter (eds), *Emotional Development and Emotional Intelligence: Implications for Educators* (pp. 3–13). New York: Basic Books.

Mikolajczak, M. and Luminet, O. (2008). Trait emotional intelligence and the cognitive appraisal of stressful events: An exploratory study. *Personality and Individual Differences*, 44, 1445–53.

Morgan, G. (2006). *Images of Organization*. London: Sage.

Nelis, D., Quoidbach, J., Mikolajczak, M. and Hansenne, M. (2009). Increasing emotional intelligence: (How) is it possible? *Personality and Individual Differences*, 47(1), 36–41.

NICE (2013) Workplace policy and management practices to improve the health of Employees. Available at: http://www.nice.org.uk/guidance/ng13. Accessed 7th July 2015.

O'Boyle, E.H., Forsyth, D.R., Banks, G.C. and McDaniel, M.A. (2012). A meta-analysis of the dark triad and work behaviour: A social exchange perspective. *Journal of Applied Psychology*, 97, 557–79.

Parks, T. (2009). *Introduction to The Prince by N. Machiavelli*. London: Penguin.

Randall, R., Griffiths, A. and Cox, T. (2005). Evaluating organizational stress-management interventions using adapted study designs. *European Journal of Work and Organizational Psychology*, 14, 23–41.

Rhoades, L. and Eisenberger, R. (2002). Perceived organizational support: A review of the literature. *Journal of Applied Psychology*, 87, 698–714.

Rotter, J.B. (1966). Generalized expectancies for internal versus external control of reinforcement. *Psychological Monographs*, 91, 482–97.

Ryff, C.D. (1989). Happiness is everything, or is it? Exploration of the meaning of psychological well-being. *Journal of Personality and Social Psychology*, 57, 1069–81.

Salguero, J.M., Extremera, N. and Fernandez-Berrocal, P. (2012). Emotional intelligence and depression: The moderator role of gender. *Personality and Individual Differences*, 53(1), 29–32.

Schutte, N.S., Malouff, J.M., Thorsteinsson, E.B., Bhullar, N. and Rooke, S.E. (2007). A meta-analytic investigation of the relationship between emotional intelligence and health. *Personality and Individual Differences*, 42, 921–33.

Silvester, J., Wyatt, M. and Randall, R. (2013). Politician personality, Machiavellianism, and political skill as predictors of performance ratings in political roles. *Journal of Occupational and Organizational Psychology*, 87(2), 258–79.

Stansfeld, S., Fuhrer, R. and Shipley, M.J. (1998). Types of social support as predictors of psychiatric morbidity in a cohort of British Civil Servants (Whitehall II Study). *Psychological Medicine*, 28, 881–92.

Travaglione, A. and Cross, B. (2006). Diminishing the social network in organizations: Does there need to be such a phenomenon as 'survivor syndrome' after downsizing? *Strategic Change,* 15(1), 1–13.

Tugade, M.M., Frederickson, B.L. and Feldman-Barrett, L. (2005). Psychological resilience and positive emotional granularity: Examining the benefits of positive emotions on coping and health. *Journal of Personality,* 72(6), 1161–90.

Vahtera, J., Kivimaki, M., Pentti, J., Linna, A., Virtanen, M., Virtanen, P. and Ferrie, J.E. (2004). Organisational downsizing, sickness absence and mortality: 10-town prospective cohort study. *BMJ,* 328, 555.

van Horn, J.E., Taris, T.W., Schaufeli, W.B. and Schreurs, P.J.G. (2004). The structure of occupational well-being: A study among Dutch teachers. *Journal of Occupational and Organizational Psychology,* 77, 365–75.

Warr, P.B. (1987). *Psychology at Work,* 3rd edn. London: Penguin.

Warr, P.B. (1989). *Work, Unemployment and Mental Health.* Oxford: Clarendon.

Warr, P.B. (2007). *Work, Happiness and Unhappiness.* Mahwah: Erlbaum.

Weinberg, A. (2013). A longitudinal study of the impact of changes in the job and the expenses scandal on UK national politicians' experiences of work, stress and the home-work interface. *Parliamentary Affairs.* doi: 10.1093/pa/gst013, 1–24.

Weinberg, A. and Cooper, C.L. (2012). *Stress in Turbulent Times.* Basingstoke: Palgrave-Macmillan.

Wood, S. (2008). Job characteristics, employee voice and well-being in Britain. *Industrial Relations Journal,* 39(2), 153–68.

PART II
PERSONALITY AND COPING WITH WORK-RELATED STRESS AND PROFESSIONAL BURNOUT

4

Links between Personality, Work-Related Stress and Health

Nico Dragano, Morten Wahrendorf and Thorsten Lunau

Introduction

Work-related stress and its consequences for health and well-being have been studied intensively in the past. A large number of experimental and observational studies have demonstrated that exposure to stress at work increases the risk to develop various somatic diseases like cardiovascular disease and mental disorders like depression (Bonde 2008; Gilbert-Ouimet et al. 2014; Kivimaki et al. 2012; Kraatz et al. 2013; Magnusson Hanson et al. 2008; Nakata 2012; Netterstrøm et al. 2008). Yet, the majority of existing studies use theoretical concepts of work stress that put the focus on stress-inducing characteristics of the work environment to describe stress at work. Even if theoretical models recognize that stress has an important individual dimension, personal factors – such as personality traits – are seldom explicitly included in research. This has recently been criticized by researchers who argued that personal characteristics may have an important impact, both on the perception of a working situation and on individual coping strategies (Törnroos et al. 2012). Along these lines, it is of scientific interest to improve the understanding of links between personality, the work environment, stress and health, and thus, to have a fuller picture of stressful working conditions. In addition, knowledge about how personality affects work-related stress and its effects on health may also help to improve existing occupational stress interventions. Accounting for individual variations of stress perception, coping and vulnerability could help to design tailored interventions which address the specific needs of the different personalities at work more appropriately.

In this chapter we therefore set out to explore in more detail the role of personality in the frame of contemporary work stress research. More specifically, the next section will first describe basic ideas about stress and stress-related disease in general. Then existing theoretical ideas and methodological approaches within 'conventional' occupational epidemiology to investigate stress at work will be outlined. On this basis, we will explore how personality may affect work stress and its consequences for health. Finally, as empirical research is still limited in this area, we will present some new empirical findings on links between personality, work stress and health. They are based on data from a longitudinal cohort study of workers in the United States.

WORK-RELATED STRESS IN
CONVENTIONAL OCCUPATIONAL HEALTH RESEARCH

Stress is a psychobiological response of the organism to a real or expected internal or external threat (i.e. stressor). The main purpose of the biological stress reaction is an on-the-spot activation of energy and awareness needed for a sudden fight-or-flight response in face of an acute danger. Important physiological systems, like the cardiorespiratory and the metabolic system are involved in order to maximize fitness, muscle power and energy supply. As soon as the cause of the stress reaction disappears – hopefully due to a successful accomplishment of the situation – recovery starts as an inherent part of the stress response. Normally, a stress response which is followed by an appropriate recovery has no long-term consequences for the normal functioning of the biological and psychological systems involved. But there are cases in which stress can become dysfunctional, for example when a stress response is so intense that trauma occurs or when a stress response has a prolonged duration without appropriate recovery or when the stress system is frequently activated by repetitive stressors (McEwen 1998, 2000). As a consequence, the temporal biological, psychological and behavioural changes which occur during stress may become chronic. For example, blood pressure and heart rate rise under stress. If this occurs frequently, the regulation of blood pressure or heart rate variability may become chronically impaired (Jarczok et al. 2013). Further risks are associated with specific stress-related hormones such as cortisol or adrenalin which are important for an acute stress response, though, can also have negative consequences for health if they last longer (Liao et al. 2013). Moreover, chronic stress has found to be related with health damaging behaviours like a sedentary lifestyle or smoking (Fransson et al. 2012; Heikkilä et al. 2012).

In view of the potential harms of a dysfunctional stress response it is important to identify their origins in more details. One important domain in this respect is certainly work and employment. It is the core assumption of most concepts of work stress that specific aspects of the work environment may trigger stress reactions which are chronic, repeated or prolonged, and therefore health damaging. The work environment, broadly speaking, includes the organization of work, specific task profiles, social interactions at work or employment relations. Stressors can be located in all domains. Examples of single work-related stressors are an overwhelming high pace of work, tight deadlines, frequent interruptions, conflicting tasks, emotionally demanding work, conflicts with supervisors or colleagues or an insecure employment contract (Cartwright and Cooper 2009; Niedhammer et al. 2012). All those situations, or environments, may cause threat as they challenge capacities of emotional and functional self-regulation as well as the control over important personal resources (like positive social relations, autonomy, promotion prospects or income security).

Next to these single stressors, theoretical models of work stress have been developed to delineate specific patterns or aspects of the psychosocial work environment with particular consequences for health. These have been shown to be associated with chronic stress reactions in particular. Among these models, the demand-control model and the effort-reward imbalance model are the most frequently used in occupational epidemiology (Karasek 1979; Karasek and Theorell 1990; Siegrist 1996). We therefore describe their theoretical notions in more detail, as they will be used to measure work-related stress in the following empirical analyses on associations with personality factors.

The demand-control model focusses on the task profile and assumes that stress is caused by an unfavourable combination of high demands at work and low levels of control (Karasek 1979; Karasek and Theorell 1990). More specifically, the model assumes that the combination of high demands and low control (a combination also labelled as 'job strain') is particularly stressful, because it limits the experience of autonomy at work and – at the same time – exerts continued pressure. Demands include both psychological (e.g. high pace of work) and physical demands, while control at work is measured in terms of skill discretion (e.g. ability to develop new skills) and decision latitude.

As a complementary model, the effort-reward imbalance model focusses on the work contract and the underlying principle of 'social reciprocity' (Siegrist 1996). It claims that an imbalance between high efforts spent and low reward received in turn could induce stress in the affected individual. Rewards include money, esteem at work and career opportunities (job promotion and job security). Apart from the balance between efforts and rewards, the model also includes an intrinsic component termed 'overcommitment'. This component describes a disposition of the individual which is particularly characterized by a high personal need for being rewarded (material and immaterial), a tendency to exhaust oneself at work, and of being constantly concerned by work-related problems even during leisure time. Taken together, both work stress models cover different aspects of the work environment, where lack of autonomy (high demand and low control, 'job strain') and frustration of rewards (imbalance between high efforts and low rewards, 'effort-reward imbalance') matter most. There is convincing evidence that work stress measured in terms of the two work stress models induces psychobiological stress reactions and dysfunctional behaviours like sedentary lifestyle or smoking (Chandola et al. 2010; Fransson et al. 2012; Heikkilä et al. 2012; Jarczok et al. 2013; Liao et al. 2013; Nakata 2012). In this perspective, the individual stress reaction is the intermediate factor linking the work environment and health. This link has been confirmed by a large number of experimental and observational studies which found pronounced associations between job strain or effort-reward imbalance and subsequent diseases (Bonde 2008; Kivimaki et al. 2012) and work-related health outcomes such as disability or sick leave (Juvani et al. 2014; Laine et al. 2009; Ndjaboué et al. 2014).

THE ROLE OF PERSONALITY IN CONVENTIONAL WORK STRESS CONCEPTS

As described above, there are a number of pathways which underlie the association between psychosocial work stress and stress-related diseases. But where and how does personality come into play?

To give an answer to this question we briefly describe the concept of personality as it is conceptionalized in modern psychology. Personality is a concept used to characterize generalizable patterns of behaviours, emotions, attitudes and perceptions of an individual. According to the psychological literature, these aspects are considered to be relatively stable over time, in other words, they are traits rather than states. One well known example for a systemic classification of generalizable personality traits is the five factor model of personality (McCrae and Costa 1999). This model is an attempt to structure the complexity of personality traits. It distinguishes five global dimensions of personality by which each individual can be described: Extraversion, Neuroticism, Conscientiousness, Agreeableness and Openness. Individuals score high or low on the respective dimensions (extraversion vs. introversion; neuroticism vs. emotional stability; conscientiousness vs. lack of conscientiousness; agreeableness vs. hostility; openness to experience vs. closedness to experience).

Associations of the 'Big Five' personality dimensions with health are obvious, in particular with mental health. As an example, neuroticism is characterized by traits such as fearfulness, irritability, low self-esteem, social anxiety, poor inhibition of impulses and helplessness. Further, persons who score high on the neuroticism scale have a tendency to experience feelings of insecurity and negative, distressing emotions. All these factors may then predispose for manifest diseases like depression or anxiety disorders. Importantly, it is also plausible that the Big Five personality traits will influence the way an individual acts in working life as well (Ozer and Benet-Martínez 2006).

In that respect, studies have investigated the association between certain aspects of personality and work related outcomes. A well-known example is the 'Type D' personality, which characterizes individuals with high levels of competitiveness, chronic anger and hostility. Some previous studies found that employees with a Type D personality were at higher risk for negative work-related outcomes such as sick leave or disability retirement (Mols and Denollet 2010; Mommersteeg et al. 2012). However, these studies did not directly address whether work stress is an intermediate factor linking personality traits with health or work-related outcomes. Similarly, traditional work stress research mainly focuses on the work environment while in general personality is not addressed explicitly. This applies for the two work stress models described above and for other models of work stress alike, such as the model of organizational injustice. In case of the effort-reward imbalance model 'overcommitment' may be seen as one attempt to include a personal component. Yet, in contrast to personality concepts within psychology, overcommitment does not describe different personalities in general. Rather, it supplements the above-mentioned extrinsic sources of effort and reward by an intrinsic component, which is primarily manifested at work (Vearing and Mak 2007). It should also be noted that most studies do not consider this component when measuring work stress according to the effort-reward imbalance model and that more specific assumptions about the nature of the association between extrinsic effort/rewards and the intrinsic component still needs to be studied.

Taken together, it seems necessary to adopt a perspective that integrates both work stress research and psychological research. Although some attempts have been made in the recent past in that respect, a clear conceptual basis is still missing (Törnroos et al. 2012). To address this shortcoming, it seems helpful to distinguish between three aspects involved in the stress pathway. This helps to formulate some assumptions how personality may affect work stress and its health-related consequences. The proposed three aspects are: (1) the likelihood of exposure to work-related stressors; (2) the individual perception of a stressor as a threat; (3) the individual reaction and health-related consequences, including coping mechanisms. Personality may have an influence on all three aspects.

First, at the *level of the stress stimulus*, personality could have an impact on the likelihood of exposure as certain personality traits could lead to a self-selection into stressful occupations or stressful situations at work. A number of studies have shown that the likelihood of being exposed to stress at work is linked to factors like the type of occupation, job industry or the occupational position (Wahrendorf et al. 2012). It can be hypothesized that a systematic self-selection into specific occupations or tasks in relation to personality traits may occur. For example, one may assume that an organized and cautious person is less likely to choose a profession with expected higher levels of job insecurity. Furthermore, personality traits may influence career opportunities, such that supervisors could be more likely to promote employees with certain personality traits. For instance, a person with an open personality could have advantages compared to a neurotic person when competing for a management position. Or, personality may influence the decision to maintain working under stressful circumstances. As such, specific personality traits may 'self-select' personality types into specific jobs with high levels of work stress. Similarly, personality may also increase the probability that work stress emerges within an occupation, because the way in which the social environment responds to an individual may depend on personality (Törnroos et al. 2012). As an example, the likelihood for conflicts increases when an individual shows personality traits which are not compatible with the business climate, such as introversion in a team with a preference for extraversion. Taken together, these are a number of plausible examples how the likelihood to be exposed to an adverse psychosocial work environment is related to personality, where personality directly affects the likelihood to choose a stressful job or to experience stressful situations within an existing workplace.

Second, at the *level of the perception* of the stressor, personality factors could affect the appraisal of a situation as threatening or as challenging. This link is rather indirect and refers to the question how different personalities evaluate a given situation. More specifically, the perception of a situation is not exclusively determined by the nature of the stressor but also by an individual process of reasoning. Along these lines, Lazarus and Folkman (1984) argue that there is no uniform reaction towards the same stressor because large inter-individual differences in perceptions exist. Accordingly, an activation of the stress response will only occur when two conditions exists. First, a situation has to be perceived subjectively as potentially threatening. Second, the individual has to perceive that necessary resources to deal with the threat are not available. For example, anxious or neurotic personalities may have a lower threshold for perceiving a situation as threatening and also perceive available resources as insufficient compared to persons with an optimistic and open personality. These latter individuals may even feel excitement, without negative consequences for health. Empirical findings are, however, scarce, and it is often not clearly distinguishable if associations between personality and self-reports of work stress are the consequence of differences in the perception of a situation or to one of the above-mentioned selection processes. Nevertheless, with regard to the likelihood of reporting a subjective high level of work stress in standardized questionnaires measuring work stress, single studies indicate that personality traits are indeed associated with reports of specific stress inducing working conditions (Hintsa et al. 2010; Judge et al. 2002). For example, neuroticism was associated with lower work satisfaction (Judge et al. 2002) or lower financial security (Roberts et al. 2003). Indirect evidence for inter-personal variations in the perception of work as stressful comes from a study which observed a higher risk of reporting symptoms of burnout in employees with a neurotic personality trait (Alarcon et al. 2009). Further, among existing exceptions using Big Five and work stress models (Sutin and Costa 2010; Törnroos et al. 2012, 2013), each personality trait of the Big Five (high neuroticism, low extraversion, low openness, low conscientiousness and low agreeableness) was related to a perceived low control and job strain. Similar associations were documented in case of effort-reward imbalance, with except of openness and conscientiousness (men only) that was not associated with an imbalance between effort and reward (Törnroos et al. 2012). Further support for an association between personality and the demand-control model comes from a US study, where low neuroticism, high extraversion, high conscientiousness and high openness were associated with higher control at work (Sutin and Costa 2010).

Third, personality traits may affect the way individuals *react to existing stress at work*. More specifically, once a situation is appraised as stressful (under the conditions described above), the reaction may differ by personality, including direct physiological body reactions and the selection of coping strategies. For example an insecure and sorrowful person may cope and adapt differently as compared to someone who is rather calm and reasonable, with different physiological reaction as well. Similarly, one may assume that an extraverted individual will choose strategies of problem-solving when experiencing conflict with colleagues at work, while introverted individuals may choose strategies of conflict-avoidance. This reaction may then modify the effect of stress on subsequent health outcomes. In case of coping mechanism, existing studies suggest that extraversion and conscientiousness are related to more problem-solving behaviour and cognitive restructuring whereas neuroticism predicted problematic strategies like wishful thinking, withdrawal and emotion-focused coping (Grant and Langan-Fox 2007). Other examples for associations between coping and personality can be found in other chapters of this book. Another aspect in this respect is the question of resilience of the affected person. Pre-existing behavioural or biomedical risk factors can increase the vulnerability towards the negative health effects of a work-related stress reaction. It has been shown that certain elements of personality like hostility or negative affectivity have negative effects on health or health-damaging behaviours, e.g. smoking or physical inactivity (Wong et al. 2013) . Such comorbidities or risk factors may then increase the vulnerability of the person towards negative effects of work stress.

Despite variations in coping styles and personal vulnerabilities, direct evidence is inconclusive. Studies rather suggest that the health effects of stress occur irrespectively of individuals' personality. More specifically, Grant and Langan-Fox (2007) showed that the Big Five personality does not moderate the association between occupational stressors and health. However, this study again did not use the demand-control model or the effort-reward imbalance model to assess occupational stress.

It can be summarized that existing studies support some of the assumed associations between personality and work stress. There is, for instance, evidence that certain personality traits (e.g. high neuroticism) are associated with higher levels of work stress and are also associated with different coping styles. In contrast, empirical findings suggest that personality does not confound the associations between work stress and health, with similar associations between work stress and health for different personalities. It must also be pointed out that those conclusions must be considered as preliminary as the number of available studies is still too small. Moreover, in existing studies measures of personality and of work stress are rather heterogeneous and often do not refer to established concepts of personality and/or of work stress, with only a few exceptions (Törnroos et al. 2012, 2013). Therefore, results are often not comparable and knowledge is still limited. Thus, conclusions must be drawn carefully, because study designs do not allow clarifying at what stages personality interferes, for example, whether small effect sizes of work stress are rather due to different appraisal or to different coping mechanisms.

Accordingly, there is not only a need to better integrate the concept of personality in common theoretical work stress models it is also important to widen the evidence base. In order to further explore the role of personality in the frame of work stress research, we therefore set out to investigate some possible links between the domains in a longitudinal study design. In particular, we want to analyse if personality traits are related to work stress in a large population sample of the elder working population and if the association between work stress and health varies according to personality. Both questions relate to the assumptions made above and answers should provide us with some new information about the complex interplay between personality, the work environment, stress and health.

Methods

Data for the following analyses were obtained from the US Health and Retirement Study (HRS) (Juster and Suzman 1995). The HRS was developed to examine sociological, economic and health-related topics for Americans over the age of 50. The HRS started in 1992 with ongoing waves of data collection in two-year intervals. The study is based on representative samples and participants were interviewed using Computer Assisted Personal Interviews and self-completion questionnaires. For our analyses we used data from two waves (2008 and 2010). In the case of our first research question, we investigate associations between personality factors and measures of work stress (both assessed in 2008). To study the second question, we excluded men and women that reported increased depressive symptoms in 2008 and tested whether individuals who reported work stress at baseline were more likely to develop increased symptoms at the second wave (2010).

Work stress was assessed by short versions of validated scales taken from questionnaires which assess the demand-control (Karasek et al. 1998) and the effort-reward imbalance (ERI) model (Siegrist et al. 2004). In case of the demand-control model the measure was restricted to control at work, as measured with two Likert-scale items (higher scores indicating lower control at work). In case of effort-reward imbalance, effort was measured with two items and five items for reward, and we calculated the ratio of both sum scores to define an imbalance (adjusted for unequal number of items). The scores of the effort-reward imbalance and the low control scale were dichotomized so that participants in the upper tertile of the score were considered to experience stressful work.

In the HRS the Big Five personality traits were measured with 26 items (Smith et al. 2013). The source of these items is the Midlife Development Inventory (MIDI) personality scale. The participants were asked whether an attribute describes them a lot, some, a little, or not at all. Neuroticism was measured with four attributes (moody, worrying, nervous, calm), Extraversion with five attributes (outgoing, friendly, lively, active, talkative), Agreeableness with five attributes (helpful, warm, caring, softhearted, sympathetic), Conscientiousness with five attributes (organized, responsible, hardworking, careless and thorough) and Openness to Experience with seven attributes (creative, imaginative, intelligent, curious, broadminded, sophisticated, adventurous). The single scales were computed according to the HRS Documentation Report (Smith et al. 2013), with scores ranging from 1 to 4 (higher scores representing higher values for the corresponding personality trait). The personality scales were also dichotomized (median split) and used as a categorical variable.

Depressive symptoms were measured with a short form of the Centre for Epidemiologic Studies Depression scale (CES-D). We use binary indicators to identify employees with elevated depressive symptoms in the years 2008 and 2010. To explore the associations between personality traits and work stress we first show descriptive statistics where we present the percentage of employees with effort-reward imbalance or low control by personality traits (Figure 4.1). Next, we present pairwise correlations between personality traits and the two measures of work stress for men and women separately. Finally, we perform linear regression analyses with the Big Five personality traits predicting work stress levels using two models. In model 1 we adjust for age and gender and in model 2 for age, gender and education. To answer our second research question we perform logistic regression analyses stratified by personality traits. For these analyses we use the dichotomized personality traits to test if the association between work stress and depressive symptoms is more pronounced in persons with certain personality profiles.

Results

Descriptive statistics of the association between the Big Five personality traits and work stress are displayed in Figure 4.1, where we present the percentage of employees with high levels of work stress by personality (e.g. high vs. low neuroticism). For both models of work stress, we see that the group of employees who score high on the neuroticism scale also report higher levels of work stress as compared to those with low neuroticism. However, although significant differences exist it must also be pointed out that a considerable work stress level is measured in persons with low scorings on the neuroticism scale. Further, in case of the remaining four personality traits (extraversion, agreeableness, conscientiousness and openness) those with high levels are less likely to experience stress at work as compared to those with low scores (again for both models of work stress).

These findings are confirmed in Table 4.1 for both men and women, where pairwise correlations between each single personality factor scale and the two work stress measures are presented for both sexes separately. The directions of the correlation coefficients are comparable for men and women, but there is a tendency for higher coefficients in the male sample – with the exception of neuroticism where coefficients are nearly the same.

Results of the linear regression analyses are displayed in Table 4.2. In model 1, where we adjust for gender and age, we find significant associations between the personality traits and the two work stress scales. After including education as a control variable into the model the regression coefficient for the association between openness and effort-reward imbalance diminished and is no longer significant. With regard to the other personality traits we find slightly reduced regression coefficients, but coefficients remain significant.

Our second research question asks if the association between work stress and health differs by personality. An answer is given in Figure 4.2, where we present associations between work stress and depressive symptoms at follow-up by personality (e.g. high vs. low neuroticism). In details, for each personality trait, we estimated logistic regression models for those with high and those with low manifestation. The figure shows that employees who reported effort-reward imbalance or low control are generally more likely to report increased levels of depressive symptoms. However, we do not see substantial differences in the association by personality traits. These findings were confirmed in additional analyses, where we tested for interactions between work stress and each personality trait (results not shown). In other words, our results show that effects of work stress on depressive symptoms do not vary by personality, but have a similar effect regardless of the five personality traits under study.

In summary, our results suggest that personality traits (as measured by the Big Five) are related to levels of work stress, with strongest associations in case of neuroticism. However, while personality was linked to higher levels of work stress, we found no support that the effects upon mental health differ by personality. In other words, personality is related to levels of work stress, but does not confound its health-related consequences.

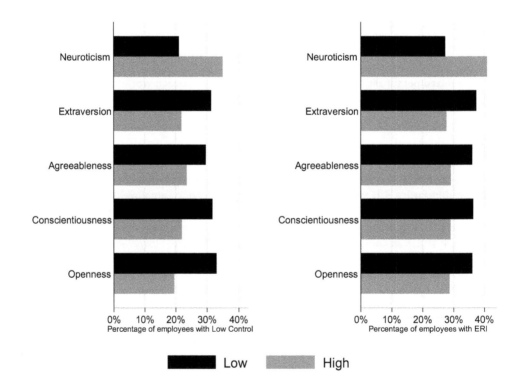

Figure 4.1   **Percentage of employees with low control or effort-reward imbalance (ERI) by Big Five personality factors (dichotomised)**

Table 4.1   Bivariate correlations between Big Five personality traits, effort-reward imbalance (ERI) and low control (men in the lower part and women in the upper part)

Men		Women						
		ERI	Low Control	Neuroticism	Extraversion	Agreeableness	Conscientiousness	Openness
	ERI	1.0	0.5362***	0.2586***	-0.1085***	-0.0769*	-0.0869**	-0.0691*
	Low Control	0.4973***	1.0	0.2248***	-0.1369***	-0.0993**	-0.1468***	-0.1590***
	Neuroticism	0.2448***	0.2499***	1.0	-0.1719***	-0.0892**	-0.2517***	-0.2371***
	Extraversion	-0.1502***	-0.2478***	-0.2202***	1.0	0.4731***	0.2403***	0.5089***
	Agreeableness	-0.1477***	-0.2090***	-0.1704***	0.5773***	1.0	0.3119***	0.2864***
	Conscientiousness	-0.1300***	-0.2329***	-0.3029***	0.2935***	0.3306***	1.0	0.3552***
	Openness	-0.0832*	-0.2480***	-0.1956***	0.4877***	0.3801***	0.3445***	1.0

Notes: *$p \leq 0.05$ **$p \leq 0.01$ ***$p \leq 0.001$.

Table 4.2   Association between Big Five personality traits and work stress (standardized linear regression coefficients and R^2 values)

			Model 1		Model 2	
			β	R^2	β	R^2
Neuroticism	ERI	No (Ref.)				
		Yes	0.2318***	0.09	0.2246***	0.11
	Low Control	No (Ref.)				
		Yes	0.2292***	0.06	0.2189***	0.09
Extraversion	ERI	No (Ref.)				
		Yes	-0.1068***	0.05	-0.1054***	0.07
	Low Control	No (Ref.)				
		Yes	-0.1773***	0.04	-0.1762***	0.07
Agreeableness	ERI	No (Ref.)				
		Yes	-0.0975***	0.05	-0.0966***	0.07
	Low Control	No (Ref.)				
		Yes	-0.1497***	0.03	-0.1499***	0.06
Conscientiousness	ERI	No (Ref.)				
		Yes	-0.0995***	0.05	-0.0865***	0.07
	Low Control	No (Ref.)				
		Yes	-0.1831***	0.04	-0.1651***	0.07
Openness	ERI	No (Ref.)				
		Yes	-0.0707**	0.05	-0.0428	0.06
	Low Control	No (Ref.)				
		Yes	-0.1939***	0.05	-0.1598***	0.07

Note: Model 1 – adjusted for age and gender. Model 2 – adjusted for age, gender and education. *$p \leq 0.05$ **$p \leq 0.01$ ***$p \leq 0.001$.

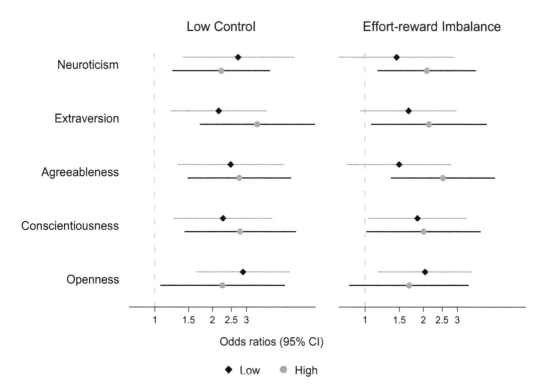

Figure 4.2   **Associations of work stress and elevated depressive symptoms at follow up stratified by personality characteristics (results of logistic regression analyses)**

Conclusion

This chapter investigated how personality is related to work-related stress and its consequences for mental health. To do so, we first described existing concepts of stress in general and of work stress in particular. These served as an important basis to propose a preliminary conceptual framework of how personality affects work-related stress and its impact on health. More specifically, we first assumed that specific personality traits may be related to the likelihood of ending up in jobs with high levels of work stress. Second, we suggested that personality is related to the perception of stress at work. Finally, we assumed that specific personalities may react differently and choose different coping strategies. Thus, personality may either be related to levels of work stress (because of self-selection or different perception) or to its health-related consequences (because of different coping strategies). To shed some light on these questions, we presented first empirical findings based on longitudinal data from the United States.

Although the presented results are clearly preliminary and deserve further analyses, they are in line with existing studies and point at least into two directions. First, we found associations between the five personality traits under study ('Big Five') and average levels of work stress. On the one side this indicates that specific personalities may be more likely to end up in jobs with higher levels of work stress. On the other side, though, this also supports the second mechanism proposed, where the perception of work stress differs by personality. Additional studies are necessary to examine this in more detail. For example, longitudinal studies of young adolescents may investigate the causality between personality and subsequent levels of work stress in more details, or experimental studies could investigate the individual perception of an identical (experimental) stressor in relation to personality. Hence, the results suggest that personality is related to levels of work stress, but also point to the necessity of further studies to investigate if this is rather due to self-selection or to perception.

Second, we found that health-related consequences do not differ by personality. In accordance with previous studies (Bosma et al. 1998) this suggests that personality does not affect the association between work stress and health. However, in order to conclude whether this is due to similar coping strategies or whether these strategies are different (as suggested in the chapter) we clearly need studies that include measures to describe coping styles in their analyses as well. Yet, it is important to note that findings nevertheless support that stress reactions occur independently of an individual's personality, and thus, that workplace interventions aiming at reducing levels of work stress remain important, because health-related consequences of work stress (as measured by the demand-control model and ERI) appear to be similar across all types of personality.

In sum, the results provide some evidence that individuals with specific personality traits are more likely to have higher levels of work stress (e.g. high neuroticism) or, on the contrary, lower levels of work stress (e.g. high extraversion). At the same time, results suggest that the mental health of different personalities suffers similarly under work-related stress. In conclusion, considering personality factors may therefore be an important supplement, in particular helping to understand individual variations of work stress in more detail. A better understanding of links between personality and work stress may also have consequences for the improvement of existing stress management and occupational health interventions. More specifically, while systems of psychosocial risk assessment at work are often restricted to expert ratings or to self-reported stress at work, a supplementary assessment of personality may help to identify groups at higher risk of experiencing work stress and, thus, help to conduct targeted interventions.

Acknowledgements

The HRS (Health and Retirement Study) is sponsored by the National Institute on Aging (grant number NIA U01AG009740) and is conducted by the University of Michigan.

References

Alarcon, G., Eschleman, K.J. and Bowling, N.A. (2009). Relationships between personality variables and burnout: A meta-analysis. *Work Stress* 23(3), 244–63.

Bonde, J.P.E. (2008). Psychosocial factors at work and risk of depression: A systematic review of the epidemiological evidence. *Occup. Environ. Med.* 65, 438–45.

Bosma, H., Stansfeld, S.A. and Marmot, M.G. (1998). Job control, personal characteristics, and heart disease. *J. Occup. Health Psychol.* 3(4), 402–9.

Cartwright, S. and Cooper, C.L. (eds) (2009). *The Oxford Handbook of Organizational Well-being*. Oxford and New York: Oxford University Press.

Chandola, T., Heraclides, A. and Kumari, M. (2010). Psychophysiological biomarkers of workplace stressors. *Neurosci Biobehav Rev* 35(1), 51–7.

Fransson, E.I., Heikkilä, K., Nyberg, S.T., Zins, M., Westerlund, H., Westerholm, P., Väänänen, A., Virtanen, M., Vahtera, J., Theorell, T., Suominen, S., Singh-Manoux, A., Siegrist, J., Sabia, S., Rugulies, R., Pentti, J., Oksanen, T., Nordin, M., Nielsen, M.L., Marmot, M.G., Magnusson Hanson, Linda L., Madsen, Ida E.H., Lunau, T., Leineweber, C., Kumari, M., Kouvonen, A., Koskinen, A., Koskenvuo, M., Knutsson, A., Kittel,

F., Jöckel, K., Joensuu, M., Houtman, I.L., Hooftman, W.E., Goldberg, M., Geuskens, G.A., Ferrie, J.E., Erbel, R., Dragano, N., Bacquer, D. de, Clays, E., Casini, A., Burr, H., Borritz, M., Bonenfant, S., Bjorner, J.B., Alfredsson, L., Hamer, M., Batty, G.D. and Kivimäki, M. (2012). Job strain as a risk factor for leisure-time physical inactivity: An individual-participant meta-analysis of up to 170,000 men and women: The IPD-Work Consortium. *Am. J. Epidemiol.* 176(12), 1078–89.

Gilbert-Ouimet, M., Trudel, X., Brisson, C., Milot, A. and Vézina, M. (2014). Adverse effects of psychosocial work factors on blood pressure: Systematic review of studies on demand-control-support and effort-reward imbalance models. *Scand. J. Work Environ. Health* 40(2), 109–32.

Grant, S. and Langan-Fox, J. (2007). Personality and the occupational stressor-strain relationship: The role of the Big Five. *J. Occup. Health Psychol.* 12(1), 20–33.

Heikkilä, K., Nyberg, S.T., Fransson, E.I., Alfredsson, L., Bacquer, D. de, Bjorner, J.B., Bonenfant, S., Borritz, M., Burr, H., Clays, E., Casini, A., Dragano, N., Erbel, R., Geuskens, G.A., Goldberg, M., Hooftman, W.E., Houtman, I.L., Joensuu, M., Jöckel, K., Kittel, F., Knutsson, A., Koskenvuo, M., Koskinen, A., Kouvonen, A., Leineweber, C., Lunau, T., Madsen, Ida E.H., Magnusson Hanson, Linda L., Marmot, M.G., Nielsen, M.L., Nordin, M., Pentti, J., Salo, P., Rugulies, R., Steptoe, A., Siegrist, J., Suominen, S., Vahtera, J., Virtanen, M., Väänänen, A., Westerholm, P., Westerlund, H., Zins, M., Theorell, T., Hamer, M., Ferrie, J.E., Singh-Manoux, A., Batty, G.D. and Kivimäki, M. (2012). Job strain and tobacco smoking: An individual-participant data meta-analysis of 166,130 adults in 15 European studies. *PLoS ONE* 7(7), e35463.

Hintsa, T., Hintsanen, M., Jokela, M., Pulkki-Råback, L. and Keltikangas-Järvinen, L. (2010). Divergent influence of different type A dimensions on job strain and effort-reward imbalance. *J. Occup. Environ. Med.* 52(1), 1–7.

Jarczok, M.N., Jarczok, M., Mauss, D., Koenig, J., Li, J., Herr, R.M. and Thayer, J.F. (2013). Autonomic nervous system activity and workplace stressors--a systematic review. *Neurosci. Biobehav. Rev.* 37(8), 1810–23.

Judge, T.A., Heller, D. and Mount, M.K. (2002). Five-factor model of personality and job satisfaction: A meta-analysis. *J. Appl. Psychol.* 87(3), 530–41.

Juster, F. and Suzman, R. (1995). An overview of the Health and Retirement Study. *J. Hum. Resour.*, 7–56.

Juvani, A., Oksanen, T., Salo, P., Virtanen, M., Kivimäki, M., Pentti, J. and Vahtera, J. (2014). Effort-reward imbalance as a risk factor for disability pension: The Finnish Public Sector Study. *Scand. J. Work Environ. Health* 40(3), 266–77.

Karasek, R.A. (1979). Job decision latitude, and mental strain: Implications for job redesign. *Adm. Sci. Q.* 24, 285–307.

Karasek, R.A. and Theorell, T. (1990). *Healthy Work: Stress, Productivity and the Reconstruction of Working Life.* Nw York: Basic Books.

Karasek, R., Brisson, C., Kawakami, N., Houtman, I., Bongers, P. and Amick, B. (1998). The Job Content Questionnaire (JCQ): An instrument for internationally comparative assessments of psychosocial job characteristics. *J. Occup. Health Psychol.* 3(4), 322–55.

Kivimaki, M., Nyberg, S.T., Batty, G.D., Fransson, E.I., Heikkila, K., Alfredsson, L., Bjorner, J.B., Borritz, M., Burr, H., Casini, A., Clays, E., Bacquer, D. de, Dragano, N., Ferrie, J.E., Geuskens, G.A., Goldberg, M., Hamer, M., Hooftman, W.E., Houtman, I.L., Joensuu, M., Jokela, M., Kittel, F., Knutsson, A., Koskenvuo, M., Koskinen, A., Kouvonen, A., Kumari, M., Madsen, Ida E.H., Marmot, M.G., Nielsen, M.L., Nordin, M., Oksanen, T., Pentti, J., Rugulies, R., Salo, P., Siegrist, J., Singh-Manoux, A., Suominen, S.B., Vaananen, A., Vahtera, J., Virtanen, M., Westerholm, Peter J.M., Westerlund, H., Zins, M., Steptoe, A. and Theorell, T. (2012). Job strain as a risk factor for coronary heart disease: A collaborative meta-analysis of individual participant data. *Lancet* 380(9852), 1491–7.

Kraatz, S., Lang, J., Kraus, T., Münster, E. and Ochsmann, E. (2013). The incremental effect of psychosocial workplace factors on the development of neck and shoulder disorders: A systematic review of longitudinal studies. *Int. Arch. Occup. Environ. Health* 86(4), 375–95.

Laine, S., Gimeno, D., Virtanen, M., Oksanen, T., Vahtera, J., Elovainio, M., Koskinen, A., Pentti, J. and Kivimäki, M. (2009). Job strain as a predictor of disability pension: The Finnish Public Sector Study. *J. Epidemiol. Community Health* 63(1), 24–30.

Lazarus, R. and Folkman, S. (1984). *Stress, Appraisal, and Coping.* Göttingen: Hogrefe.

Liao, J., Brunner, E.J. and Kumari, M. (2013). Is there an association between work stress and diurnal cortisol patterns? Findings from the Whitehall II study. *PLoS ONE* 8(12), e81020.

McCrae, R. and Costa, P. (1999). A five-factor theory of personality. In Pervin, L. and John, O. (eds), *Handbook of Personality: Theory and Research,* 2nd edn. New York: Gilford Press, 139–53.

Magnusson Hanson, Linda L., Theorell, T., Oxenstierna, G., Hyde, M. and Westerlund, H. (2008). Demand, control and social climate as predictors of emotional exhaustion symptoms in working Swedish men and women. *Scand. J. Public Health* 36(7), 737–43.

Mols, F. and Denollet, J. (2010). Type D personality in the general population: A systematic review of health status, mechanisms of disease, and work-related problems. *Health Qual. Life Outcomes* 8, 9.

Mommersteeg, Paula M.C., Denollet, J. and Martens, E.J. (2012). Type D personality, depressive symptoms and work-related health outcomes. *Scand. J. Public Health* 40(1), 35–42.

Nakata, A. (2012). Psychosocial job stress and immunity: A systematic review. *Methods Mol. Biol.* 934, 39–75.

Ndjaboué, R., Brisson, C., Vézina, M., Blanchette, C. and Bourbonnais, R. (2014). Effort--reward imbalance and medically certified absence for mental health problems: A prospective study of white-collar workers. *Occup. Environ. Med.* 71(1), 40–47.

Netterstrøm, B., Conrad, N., Bech, P., Fink, P., Olsen, O., Rugulies, R. and Stansfeld, S. (2008). The relation between work-related psychosocial factors and the development of depression. *Epidemiol. Rev.* 30, 118–32.

Niedhammer, I., Sultan-Taïeb, H., Chastang, J., Vermeylen, G. and Parent-Thirion, A. (2012). Exposure to psychosocial work factors in 31 European countries. *Occup. Med.* 62(3), 196–202.

Ozer, D.J. and Benet-Martínez, V. (2006). Personality and the prediction of consequential outcomes. *Annu. Rev. Psychol.* 57(1), 401–21.

Roberts, B.W., Caspi, A. and Moffitt, T.E. (2003). Work experiences and personality development in young adulthood. *J. Pers. Soc. Psychol.* 84(3), 582–93.

Siegrist, J. (1996). Adverse health effects of high-effort/low-reward conditions. *J. Occup. Health Psychol.* 1(1), 27–41.

Siegrist, J., Starke, D., Chandola, T., Godin, I., Marmot, M., Niedhammer, I. and Peter, R. (2004). The measurement of effort-reward imbalance at work: European comparisons. *Soc. Sci. Med.* 58(8), 1483–99.

Smith, J., Fisher, G., Ryan, L., Clarke, P., House, J. and Weir, D. (2013). Psychosocial and lifestyle questionnaire, 2006–2010. Documentation Report Core Section LB. Ann Arbor, MI: Survey Research Center, Institute for Social Research, University of Michigan.

Sutin, A.R. and Costa, P.T. (2010). Reciprocal influences of personality and job characteristics across middle adulthood. *J. Pers.* 78(1), 257–88.

Törnroos, M., Hintsanen, M., Hintsa, T., Jokela, M., Pulkki-Råback, L., Hutri-Kähönen, N. and Keltikangas-Järvinen, L. (2013). Associations between five-factor model traits and perceived job strain: A population-based study. *J. Occup. Health Psychol.* 18(4), 492–500.

Törnroos, M., Hintsanen, M., Hintsa, T., Jokela, M., Pulkki-Råback, L., Kivimäki, M., Hutri-Kähönen, N. and Keltikangas-Järvinen, L. (2012). Personality traits of the five-factor model are associated with effort-reward imbalance at work: A population-based study. *J. Occup. Environ. Med.* 54(7), 875–80.

Vearing, A. and Mak, A.S. (2007). Big five personality and effort–reward imbalance factors in employees' depressive symptoms. *Pers. Individ. Dif.* 43(7), 1744–55.

Wahrendorf, M., Dragano, N. and Siegrist, J. (2012). Social position, work stress, and retirement intentions: A study with older employees from 11 European countries. *Eur. Sociol. Rev.* 29, 792–802.

Wong, J.M., Na, B., Regan, M.C. and Whooley, M.A. (2013). Hostility, health behaviors, and risk of recurrent events in patients with stable coronary heart disease: Findings from the Heart and Soul Study. *J. Am. Heart Assoc.* 2(5), e000052.

5

Joint Moderating Effects of Self-Efficacy and Coping on Social Stressor–Psychological Strain Relationships in Greater China: Evidence from Three Subregions

Oi-Ling Siu, Paul E. Spector, Chang-qin Lu and Luo Lu

Introduction

This chapter explores the relationship between two focal social stressors (interpersonal conflict and organizational politics) and psychological strains (job satisfaction and psychological symptoms). We also examine an unexplored mechanism of how self-efficacy and active coping might protect employees from negative effects of social stressors.

We reported a survey which was conducted among 1,032 Chinese employees in Hong Kong, Mainland China and Taipei, representing the three subregions in Greater China. Interpersonal conflict and organizational politics were the two focal social stressors, self-efficacy and active coping were examined as individual difference factors, and job satisfaction and psychological symptoms were outcomes of psychological strains. Results from two-way moderated regression analyses consistently revealed that high self-efficacy exacerbated the relationship between social stressors and psychological strains. Furthermore, three-way moderated regression analyses showed that self-efficacy and active coping displayed a joint moderating effect in reducing the impact of interpersonal conflict or organizational politics on psychological symptoms when both were high. We also found high self-efficacy acted as an exacerbator which amplified the impact of interpersonal conflict or organizational politics on employees' psychological symptoms, when active coping was low.

With the globalization of the world economy, and the rapid development of Southeast Asia economies, the problem of work stress has become relevant particularly for Greater China, encompassing Hong Kong, Taiwan and Mainland China. These three regions are undergoing fundamental transformations of industrial structures from labor-intensive to high-tech, as well as rapid social modernization in both work and nonwork life (e.g., Lu et al. 2011a; Siu et al. 2002). There is more free competition, and urban employees in Hong Kong, the People's Republic of China (PRC) and Taiwan are becoming more exposed to stressful industrialized work situations similar to the West.

Many occupational stress models have suggested that stressors at work lead to psychological strain (e.g., Kahn and Byosiere 1992). Dormann and Zapf (2002) distinguished task stressors from social stressors. Task stressors are related to the task structure and the organization of work, for example, time pressure, work overload, role conflict and role ambiguity, whereas social stressors are related to negative social interactions with colleagues, supervisors and clients, such as social animosities, conflicts with co-workers and supervisors, unfair treatment, and a negative interpersonal climate. As summarized by Spector and Bruk-Lee (2008), occupational stress research has experienced a recent shift in focus from task stressors to social stressors (e.g., interpersonal conflict). However, social stressors have been understudied by occupational stress researchers (Dormann and Zapf 2002; Semmer 2003; Spector and Bruk-Lee 2008).

As Chinese societies place strong emphasis on group harmony, "forbearance" and Guanxi (good relationships) (Farh et al. 1998; Hwang 1997), Chinese employees may be more prone to social stressors such as interpersonal conflicts and organizational politics. In a meta-analysis, Chang et al. (2009) reported the negative impacts of organizational politics on employees' well-being and work-related behaviors. They argued that organizational politics is a relatively less explored stressor, and should be given more attention in future stress research. As expressed by Harris and Kacmar (2005), although a good deal is known about organizational politics in the United States, little is known about the role of organizational politics as a social stressor in Eastern cultures. Furthermore, it is argued that culture is related to interpersonal conflict (e.g., Liu et al. 2008; Triandis et al. 1988) and culture could affect how employees express conflict behaviors (Liu et al. 2007). Yet, relatively, little has been done on social stressors in Greater China.

We therefore investigated the relationship between two focal social stressors (interpersonal conflict and organizational politics) and psychological strains (job satisfaction and psychological symptoms). We also examined an unexplored mechanism of how self-efficacy and active coping might protect employees from negative effects of social stressors.

Interpersonal Conflict, Organizational Politics and Psychological Strains

Interpersonal conflict has been found to be one of the most common social stressors in the workplace in a series of Western (e.g., Keenan and Newton 1985) and cross-cultural (e.g., Liu 2002; Liu et al. 2007, 2008; Lu et al. 2011a) studies. In general, interpersonal conflict at work implies stressful incidents which were caused by social interactions with supervisors, subordinates or colleagues. Thomas's (1992) Process Model of Conflict depicts interpersonal conflict as a process that includes cognitive, affective, motivational and behavioral stages. Interpersonal conflict has been shown to positively correlate with strains and other outcomes, including job dissatisfaction, anxiety/tension, poor job performance and counterproductive work behaviors (Bruk-Lee and Spector 2006; Lu et al. 2011a; Spector and Jex 1998).

Another potential common social stressor in Western societies is organizational politics. It is defined as any activity that "involves actions by individuals which are directed toward the goal of furthering their own self-interests without regard for the well-being of others or their organization" (Kacmar and Baron 1999, p. 4). Organizational politics has recently attracted research attention showing that it relates to job anxiety, strains (such as low job satisfaction and job distress) and aggressive behavior (e.g., Ferris et al. 1996; Harris and Kacmar 2005). Thus organizational politics is operationalized as a stressor in the current study. As advocated by Harris and Kacmar (2005), there is a need to continue to investigate and gain additional insights into the antecedents, moderators and consequences of organizational politics. They further proposed to examine organizational politics more in a cross-cultural context.

There is reason to expect that study of social stressors is particularly relevant in China. People in collectivistic cultures, such as China, tend to be more concerned with group harmony and they pay more attention to interpersonal relationships (Chinese Culture Connection 1987). Furthermore, people in Chinese societies demonstrate a strong preference for uncertainty avoidance (Hofstede 1980) and harmony maintenance (Lu and Yang 2006). Nevertheless, the existence of interpersonal conflict or even covert political behavior can lead to strains. Organizational politics as a stressor is conceptually distinct from interpersonal conflict. The former is frequently used as an upward influence strategy to promote self-interests, such as salary rise or promotion (Porter, Allen and Angle 1981), while the latter mainly refers to conflicts among people involved at work. We examined the impact of these two social stressors on psychological strains in a heterogeneous sample of Chinese employees from all three subregions in Greater China. Psychological strains in this study are conceptualized as job (dis)satisfaction and psychological symptoms. We hypothesized that:

> H1: Social stressors (interpersonal conflict and organizational politics) will be negatively related to job satisfaction and positively related to psychological symptoms.

Role of Self-Efficacy on the Stress–Strain Relationship

Bandura (1997) defined self-efficacy as the extent to which people believe they can perform a behavior to produce a particular desired outcome. According to the cognitive appraisal theory (Lazarus and Folkman 1984), stressors lead to strains only when employees evaluate the stressors as threatening to their well-being, thus self-efficacy can protect people against stressors and reduce strains. For instance, it has been found that self-efficacy is related to job satisfaction and psychological strains in both Western and Chinese societies (e.g., Judge and Bono 2001; Lu et al. 2005; Lu et al. 2011a).

As concluded by Xie and Schaubroeck (2001) in their discussion of organizational research on stress and well-being, individual differences such as self-efficacy might influence the direction and strength of the relationship between job stressors and strains. Some studies have found that self-efficacy exerts a moderating effect on the stressor–strain relationship in both Western and Chinese societies (Jex et al. 2001; Lu et al. 2005; Lu et al. 2011a; Siu et al. 2007). For instance, the results of Siu et al.'s study (2007) verified that self-efficacy plays an important role in employees' well-being in collectivist societies such as China. Recent findings in Taiwan (Lu et al. 2011a) corroborated that self-efficacy not only had direct effect on strains, but also buffered the negative impact of a task stressor (lack of autonomy) on job performance. Therefore self-efficacy is also relevant to collectivistic cultures. As social stressors such as interpersonal conflict may be beyond individuals' control, it is theoretically likely that self-efficacy would have direct and moderating effects on psychological strains. We therefore hypothesized that:

H2: Self-efficacy will be positively related to employees' job satisfaction, but negatively with psychological symptoms.

H3: Self-efficacy beliefs would moderate the relationship between job stressors and job strains such that the negative relationship between job stressors and job satisfaction will be mitigated when the level of self-efficacy is high; and the positive relationships between job stressors and psychological symptoms will also be mitigated when the level of self-efficacy is high.

Role of Active Coping on the Stress–Strain Relationship

Coping has been considered an important element in the stress process because coping strategies can help buffer the effects of stressors on strains (Lazarus and Folkman 1984). According to the transactional stress theory, coping consists of "cognitive and behavioral efforts to master, reduce or tolerate the internal or external demands that are created by the stressful transaction" (Folkman 1984, p. 843). Semmer (2003) advocated that "people differ in the probability of encountering stressors, depending on the social environment but also on their own behavior" (p. 82). Semmer also argued that people differ in their appraisal of stressors thus people differ in their way of coping with them; and there are cultural differences in stress appraisal and coping. He noted that optimistic individuals with more problem-focused coping strategies (a form of active coping) report fewer psychological strains (Semmer 2003). It has been argued that active or problem-focused coping methods are advantageous to employees in Western and Chinese societies (e.g., Carver et al. 1989; Siu et al. 2006). Furthermore, when examining the relationship of coping resources to occupational stress and strain, it was proposed that coping moderated the stress–strain relationship (Osipow and Davis 1988; Osipow and Spokane 1984). Empirically, among a group of senior police officers in Great Britain, coping was found to moderate the relationship between job stress and job satisfaction (Kirkcaldy et al. 1995). A recent study found that coping resources moderated stress–strain and stress–satisfaction relationships in American educational administrators (Thomas et al. 2012). Taking previous theoretical arguments together and combining empirical findings in Western and Chinese societies, we expect Chinese employees who adopt more active coping would tackle social stressors better and would report lower levels of psychological strains. In turn, coping would further influence the stress–strain relationship. Therefore, we hypothesized that:

H4: Use of active coping will be positively related to employees' job satisfaction and negatively with psychological symptoms, and active coping will moderate the relationships between job stressors and strains, such that under high levels of coping the effect of stressors on strains will be reduced.

Joint Role of Self-Efficacy and Active Coping on the Stress–Strain Relationship

As self-efficacy refers to a sense of competence to have control over one's own environment, it is logical to infer that self-efficacy impacts stressor–strain relationships jointly with active coping in the workplace (Jex et al. 2001; Leiter 1992). For instance, Jex et al. (2001) tested three-way interactions and demonstrated that self-efficacy mitigated the effects of low role clarity on strain when active coping was high; but strain levels were lower for participants with high self-efficacy than for participants with lower self-efficacy when workload was low but avoidance coping was high. One earlier study found that Chinese people who adhered to internal locus of control beliefs, a concept closely related to self-efficacy, favored planning (a form of active coping) but not suppression strategies to cope with stress (Lu and Chen 1996). We therefore hypothesized that:

> *H5: There will be a three-way interaction between stressors, self-efficacy and active coping in predicting psychological strains. Specifically, the relationship between stressors and strains will be greater under high self-efficacy and high active coping than any of the other three combinations of self-efficacy and active coping (high self-efficacy, low active coping, or low self-efficacy and either high or low active coping). In other words, high self-efficacy and more frequent use of active coping would mitigate the effects of social stressors on psychological strains.*

Method

SAMPLE AND PROCEDURE

For the Hong Kong sample, a multistage cluster random sampling method was used to recruit employees. A sample of 2% (every 50th company on the list) of the 34,619 available companies in the service sector were randomly drawn from the Census and Statistics Department of Hong Kong government. For each company that agreed to participate, approximately 25% of the employees were invited to participate in the survey. The first author was responsible for distributing the questionnaires and collecting the completed questionnaires in person. A total of 324 employees (132 males, 192 females) were successfully surveyed, the return rate was 100%. The mean age was 32.1 years (SD = 9.4 years) and the mean of current job tenure was 6.3 years (SD = 6.1). For the sample recruited in the PRC, a total of 540 questionnaires were distributed to employees in various service industries in several cities in the PRC, and 402 questionnaires were returned, making a response rate of 74.4%. The PRC sample consisted of 209 males and 182 females (11 unidentified), with a mean age of 31.9 years (SD = 7.4 years). The mean of current job tenure was 4.3 years (SD = 5.2). For the sample recruited in Taiwan, a total of 520 questionnaires were distributed to employees in various service industry settings, and 306 questionnaires were returned, making a response rate of 60%. The Taiwan sample consisted of 134 males and 172 females, with a mean age of 32.9 years (SD = 6.7 years) and mean current job tenure of 6.3 years (SD = 6.3). The third and the fourth authors were responsible for data collection in the PRC and Taiwan respectively. A designated person was invited to distribute and collect the questionnaires. The participants in the three regions were informed about the purpose of the study and participation was on a voluntary basis.

INSTRUMENTS

Social Stressors. Interpersonal conflict was assessed with the Interpersonal Conflict at Work Scale (ICAWS) (four items) (Spector and Jex 1998) (e.g., "How often are people rude to you at work?"), and organizational politics was assessed with three items (one item from Cooper et al. (1988), and two items from Kacmar and Carlson (1997) (e.g., "There has always been an influential group in your department that no one ever crosses")). These two scales were translated into Chinese, used in a previous study using Chinese samples and were found reliable (Siu et al. 2005). The ICAWS was also used in Lu et al. (2011a) and proved reliable ($\alpha = 0.74$) among Taiwan Chinese workers. Each item was given a frequency rating using the response choices "Less than once per month or never" (*1*), "Once or twice per month" (*2*),

"Once or twice per week" (3), "2–3 times per week" (4), "Once or twice per day" (5) to "Several times per day" (6).

Psychological Strains. Two scales were used to measure psychological strains: *Job (dis) satisfaction scale* (three items) (Cammann et al. 1979) (e.g., "All in all, I am satisfied with my job"), and *Psychological Well-being* scale of ASSET (An Organizational Stress Screening Tool) (Cartwright and Cooper 2002) to measure psychological symptoms (10 items). The items are symptoms of stress-induced mental ill-health such as constant tiredness. Each item was scored on a six-point scale with respective high score denoting higher job satisfaction and worse well-being. These scales have been used in Chinese samples and found reliable with respective alpha value as 0.79 and 0.82 (Siu et al. 2006). The job satisfaction scale was also used in Lu et al. (2011a) and proved reliable ($\alpha = 0.86$) among Taiwan Chinese workers.

Self-Efficacy. The Chinese version of the 10-item General Self-efficacy Scale (Schwarzer et al. 1997) was adopted to measure self-efficacy (Siu et al. 2005, 2007). However, the scoring procedure was modified, instead of the original four-point Likert Scale, each item was scored from "Not at all True" (1) to "Exactly True" (6). This version was also used in Lu et al. (2011a) and proved reliable ($\alpha = 0.93$) among Taiwan Chinese workers.

Active Coping. Six items of the Occupational Stress Indicator (Cooper et al. 1988) measuring control coping were used to measure active coping. This scale has been used in Chinese societies and demonstrated acceptable reliability (e.g., Siu et al. 2002). Each item was scored on a six-point scale with a high score indicating high frequency of using an active coping strategy.

A confirmatory factor analysis on the seven items measuring the two social stressors confirmed that they are two distinct stressors ($\chi^2 = 111.20$, $df = 13$, $\chi^2/df = 8.554$, SRMR = 0.031, CFI = 0.97, NFI = 0.97, RMSEA = 0.08). We used LISREL 8.70 to conduct a series of confirmatory factor analysis (CFA) of the items from the interpersonal conflict, organizational politics, self-efficacy, active coping, job satisfaction, and psychological symptoms scales to verify that the items fit their intended scales both within each of the three regions analyzed separately (analysis 1) and the three regions combined (analysis 3). For analysis 1, we conducted three six-factor CFAs, one for each region, placing the items for each of the six scales into a separate factor. We allowed the factors to intercorrelate. In all three regions the fit indices were within the usually accepted values for good fit (see Table 5.1). To verify measurement equivalence of the six scales across the three regions before combining the samples, we conducted multi-group CFA. Table 5.1 shows that the fit index is still acceptable when constraining the factor loading, factor covariance and error terms of corresponding latent variables to be equal across the three regions (Model 4). Given the high degree of measurement equivalence, we combined the data from the three regions and conducted a CFA for the entire sample, finding evidence for good fit ($\chi^2 = 2547.42$, $p < 0.001$, $df = 579$, $\chi^2/df = 4.40$; CFI = 0.96; NNFI = 0.96; SRMR = 0.056; RMSEA = 0.065). All of the above results showed that our measurements were equivalent across the three regions.

Table 5.1   Confirmatory Factor Analysis (CFA) results of the study variables (N=1032)

Model	df	χ^2	SRMR	CFI	NNFI	RMSEA
Beijing (n = 402)	579	1,376.69***	.065	.94	.94	.067
Hong Kong (n = 324)	579	1,433.51***	.079	.94	.93	.071
Taiwan (n = 306)	579	1,214.22***	.055	.96	.96	.063
Multi-group (n = 1032)	1911	5,239.79***	.088	.92	.92	.079

Note: Model 4 means multi-group CFA when constraining the factor loading, factor covariance and error terms of corresponding latent variables to be equal across the three regions. *** p < .001.

Results

Table 5.2 presents the means, standard deviations, Cronbach's alphas of the variables, and intercorrelations among variables for the overall sample. The scales showed acceptable alphas ranging from 0.75 to 0.93. A series of hierarchical regression analyses were conducted to test the hypotheses (see Tables 5.3 and 5.4). As there have been discussions on misuse of statistical control variables (e.g., Spector and Brannick 2011), we ran the regressions without the controls (actually we reran the regressions and found there was not much difference in the results). All predictor variables were centered to minimize multicollinearity among them (Cohen et al. 2003). For testing the hypotheses 1, 2 and 3, interpersonal conflict or organizational politics was entered in the first step, self-efficacy and the interaction term were entered in the second and third step respectively (see Tables 5.3 and 5.4). We found that social stressors positively correlated with psychological symptoms, but negatively with job satisfaction. Therefore Hypothesis 1 was fully supported. We also found that SE positively correlated with job satisfaction and negatively with psychological symptoms. Hence Hypothesis 2 can be fully supported. We find these results are consistent with the correlations depicted in Table 5.2.

Table 5.2   Descriptive statistics, correlations, and reliabilities for variables for overall sample (N=1032)

	1	2	3	4	5	6	7	8	9	10	11
Gender	-										
Age	-.10**	-									
Marital status	.03	-.55**	-								
Tenure(in years)	-.02	.58**	-.31**	-							
Job level	-.11**	-.17**	-.08*	.10**	-						
Job satisfaction	-.02	.19**	.11*	.26**	.06	(.75)					
Psychological symptoms	.03	-.00	-.03	.09*	.04	-.33***	(.93)				
Interpersonal conflict	-.06	.15**	.10**	.19**	.09*	-.27***	.41***	(.88)			
Organizational politics	.05	-.04	.05	-.02	.00	-.36***	.40***	.63***	(.78)		
Self-efficacy	-.11**	.26**	.24**	.15**	.13**	.25***	-.23***	-.10**	-.08*	(.90)	
Active coping	-.03	.14**	.09*	.13**	.01	.18***	-.12***	-.17***	-.12***	.43***	(.82)
Mean	1.54	32.25	1.43	5.53	2.23	12.47	30.42	7.82	6.38	41.64	25.96
Range	1-2	17-65	1-2	0-40	1-6	3-18	10-60	4-24	3-18	10-60	6-36
SD	.50	7.71	.50	5.81	1.42	2.90	9.90	4.27	3.51	7.19	4.35

Note: Gender: 1 = male, 2 = female. Marital status: 1 = married, 2 = single; job level: 1 = non-manager, 2 = first-line supervisor, 3 = junior manager, 4 = middle manager, 5 = senior manager, 6 = top manager.; * p < .05, ** p < .01, *** p < .00.

Table 5.3   Moderated regressions for overall sample with interpersonal conflict as independent variable (N=1032)

	Job Satisfaction		Psychological Symptoms	
	ΔR^2	b	ΔR^2	b
Step 1	.069		.161	
Interpersonal conflict		-.26***		.40***
Step 2	.051		.037	
Self-efficacy		.23***		-.19***
Step 3	.007		.010	
Interpersonal conflict * Self-efficacy		-.08**		.10***
Step 4	.003		.001	
Active coping		.06⁺		.03
Step 5	.002		.008	
Interpersonal conflict * Active coping		-.04		.03
Self-efficacy * Active coping		-.02		-.09**
Step 6	.000		.004	
Interpersonal conflict * Self-efficacy * ctive coping		-.02		-.08*

Note: ⁺ $p < .10$, * $p < .05$, ** $p < .01$, *** $p < .001$.

Table 5.4   Moderated regressions for overall sample with organizational politics as independent variable (N=1032)

	Job Satisfaction		Psychological Symptoms	
	ΔR^2	b	ΔR^2	b
Step 1	.129		.152	
Organizational politics		-.36***		.39***
Step 2	.049		.040	
Self-efficacy		.22***		-.20***
Step 3	.004		.007	
Organizational politics * Self-efficacy		-.07*		.08**
Step 4	.002		.000	
Active coping		.06⁺		.02
Step 5	.001		.008	
Organizational politics * Active coping		-.03		-.01
Self-efficacy * Active coping		-.01		-.09**
Step 6	.000		.004	
Organizational politics * Self-efficacy * Active coping		.01		-.07*

Note: ⁺ $p < .10$, * $p < .05$, ** $p < .01$, *** $p < .001$.

The results presented in Tables 5.3 and 5.4 show that self-efficacy significantly moderated the relationship between interpersonal conflict and psychological strains (job satisfaction and psychological symptoms), and between organizational politics and psychological strains. Separate plots were drawn for individuals whose scores on the moderator (self-efficacy) were one standard deviation below and above the mean (Aiken and West 1991). When the stressor is interpersonal conflict, the simple slopes for both groups were negative and significant for job satisfaction. The simple slope was larger for the high self-efficacy group (b = -0.24, $p < 0.001$) and smaller for the low self-efficacy group (b = -0.11, $p < 0.05$). In other words, the impact of interpersonal conflict is more serious to employees with high self-efficacy than those with low self-efficacy. Moreover, for the high self-efficacy group, the simple slope for psychological symptoms was significantly positive (b = 0.93, $p < 0.001$); for the low self-efficacy group, the simple slope for psychological symptoms was smaller but still significantly positive (b = 0.53, $p < 0.001$). Self-efficacy had the same moderating pattern on the relationship between organizational politics and psychological strains. When the stressor was organizational politics, the simple slopes for both groups were negative and significant for job satisfaction. The simple slope was larger for the high self-efficacy group (b = -0.38, $p < 0.001$) and smaller for the low self-efficacy group (b = -0.25, $p < 0.05$). For the high self-efficacy group, the simple slope for psychological symptoms was significantly positive (b = 1.21, $p < 0.001$). For the low self-efficacy group, the simple slope for psychological symptoms was smaller but still significantly positive (b = 0.69, $p < 0.001$). Hence Hypothesis 3 was only partially supported.

In order to test the joint moderating effects of self-efficacy and active coping (see Tables 5.3 and 5.4), active coping was entered in the fourth step, the two-way interaction term of interpersonal conflict or organizational politics and active coping, self-efficacy and active coping were entered in the fifth step. The three-way interaction term (interpersonal conflict or organizational politics, active coping and self-efficacy) was entered in the sixth step (see Tables 5.3 and 5.4). We found that active coping was only marginally positively correlated with job satisfaction but not related to psychological strains, and did not moderate any of relationships between social stressors and strains. Therefore Hypothesis 4 was only partially supported. We also found the joint moderating effect of self-efficacy and active coping was significant on the relationship between interpersonal conflict and psychological symptoms (see Table 5.3). We calculated the simple slopes based on Aiken and West's (1991) procedures to show the exact effects of interpersonal conflict on psychological symptoms. Figure 5.1 shows that, for employees with high self-efficacy, the impact of interpersonal conflict on psychological symptoms was reduced when their active coping increased. The simple slopes were (b = 4.42, $p < 0.001$) when the active coping level was low, and (b = 3.76, $p < 0.001$) when the active coping level was high. On the contrary, for employees with low self-efficacy, the impact of interpersonal conflict on psychological symptoms was reduced when their active coping decreased. The simple slopes were (b = 2.07, $p < 0.001$) when the active coping level was low, and (b = 3.33, $p < 0.001$) when the active coping level was high. Similar results were obtained with organizational politics as the stressor. Figure 5.2 also shows the same pattern as Figure 5.1. For employees with high self-efficacy, the impact of organizational politics on psychological symptoms was reduced when their active coping increased. We also found high self-efficacy acted as an exacerbator which amplified the impact of organizational politics on employees' psychological symptoms, when active coping was low. Therefore Hypothesis 5 was partially supported.

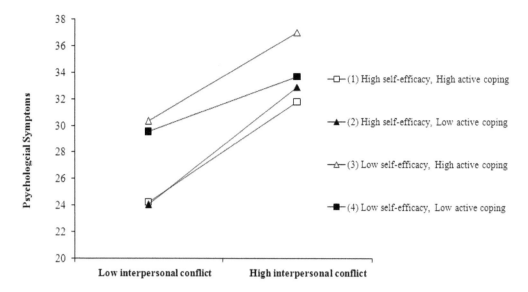

Figure 5.1   Joint moderating effect of self-efficacy and active coping on the relationship between interpersonal conflict and psychological symptoms

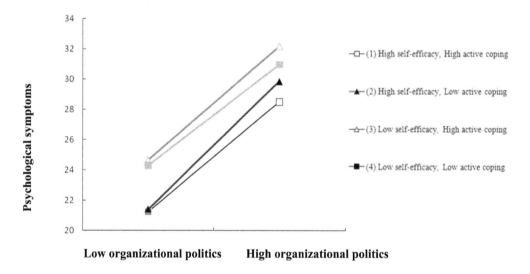

Figure 5.2   Joint moderating effect of self-efficacy and active coping on the relationship between organizational politics and psychological symptoms

Discussion

This chapter aims to examine the relationship between social stressors (interpersonal conflict and organizational politics) and psychological strains (job dissatisfaction and psychological symptoms), and investigate how self-efficacy moderates the relationship between social stressors and psychological strains together with the use of active coping. Based on a study conducted in Greater China, we found direct relationships of self-efficacy with job satisfaction and psychological symptoms, as high self-efficacy was generally associated with better outcomes (lower psychological symptoms and/or higher job satisfaction) than low self-efficacy. These results corroborate previous studies (e.g., Lu et al. 2005; Lu et al. 2011a; Siu et al. 2007). Concerning active coping, we found significant direct relationship with outcomes, with a more frequent use of active coping being associated with higher levels of job satisfaction and fewer psychological symptoms. These results corroborate previous findings (e.g., Siu et al. 2006). The results of the present study also revealed the moderating effect of self-efficacy on the social stressor–strain relationships. These results build onto previous studies in Western and Chinese societies (e.g., Lu et al. 2005; Lu et al. 2011a; Siu et al. 2007) to a certain extent that overall the results suggested an exacerbator effect, but a closer examination showed the exacerbator effect cannot be always found. That is, the impact of interpersonal conflict/organizational politics was more serious to employees with high self-efficacy than those with low self-efficacy. In other words, these social stressors were a greater risk factors for Chinese employees with high than low self-efficacy. It can be explained that employees with high self-efficacy find that social stressors are beyond their control and thus those stressors are more intolerable.

The young Chinese generation in the PRC grew up when China reopened her doors, exposing them to Western influences during a period of rapid globalization (Egri and Ralston 2004). It was concluded from studies on managerial values in Greater China that, due to different political and economic backgrounds, there are both similarities and differences between Hong Kong and the PRC (Cheung and Chow 1999; Chia et al. 2007). However, they also concluded that there are more similarities than differences, particularly among young managers. As the average age of the three current samples ranged 31–32 years, we believe the young employees in Greater China are quite similar and they tend to have increasingly similar values. Maxwell and Siu (2008) also concluded that, due to the fact that we live in a globalized world, there is more convergence in individual behaviors, attitudes and beliefs among Chinese in Hong Kong and outside Hong Kong (including the PRC and Taiwan). Further, because the multiple group analysis shows the fitness of the constrained model is acceptable, hence we combined all three samples in the analyses.

As aforementioned, Chinese societies place strong emphasis on group harmony, "forbearance" and Guanxi (e.g., Farh et al. 1998), so the experience of interpersonal conflict and organizational politics is quite atypical or unfamiliar and that might lead to distress. This kind of distress experience could have more damaging effects for those employees with high self-efficacy because it was out of their expected control. Siu et al. (2007) reported the buffering role of self-efficacy between broadly defined job stressors and mental well-being among Chinese employees; Nauta et al. (2010) found the importance of looking at a particular type of stressor in the stress process because they demonstrated that when the stressor is low autonomy, high self-efficacy may not protect against psychological strains. Indeed, Lu et al. (2011a) found that self-efficacy may be a double-edged sword: it buffered the negative impact of lack of autonomy on job performance (a behavioral outcome), but exacerbated the negative impact of lack of autonomy on job satisfaction (a psychological outcome). Thus, it may also be important to look at a particular indicator of strain in the stress process, and the exact nature of self-efficacy as a moderator for the Chinese needs more fine-grained examination in the future.

We also found support for the beneficial or exacerbating role of self-efficacy depending on the use of coping styles, as initially suggested by Jex et al. (2001). We found a joint moderating effect of self-efficacy and coping on the relationship between interpersonal conflict or organizational politics and psychological symptoms. We found high self-efficacy and high active coping reduced the impact of interpersonal conflict or organizational politics on psychological symptoms. Furthermore, we found self-efficacy might well be an exacerbator which amplifies the impact of interpersonal conflict or organizational politics on employees' psychological symptoms in a context when they refrained from using active coping strategies (see Figures 5.1 and 5.2). This again points to the importance of attending to culture in examinations of stressor–strain relations (Nauta et al. 2010). Inferring from our findings, self-efficacy may have an added value for those who favor the use of active coping among Chinese employees, thus reducing their psychological symptoms regardless of the level of interpersonal conflict or organizational politics; conversely, among those who either did not have the adequate skills of active coping or were unwilling to resort to active coping, self-efficacy beliefs became a vulnerability when the level of interpersonal conflict or organizational politics increased.

As reviewed by Cheng et al. (2010), Chinese are characterized by a greater tendency to use avoidant or emotion-focused coping, not active coping. Hence Chinese employees should be reminded of the potential impact of self-efficacy and/or the use of active coping in the stress processes. Specifically, our results suggested that the disparity between one's general beliefs (e.g., self-efficacy) and inability or unwillingness to take action (e.g., active coping) may be prerequisite for psychological symptoms. Since beliefs and behaviors are seldom examined together in existing occupational stress research, the intricate interplay between personal beliefs, coping skills, and perhaps autonomy (e.g., Nauta et al. 2010) should receive more attention particularly in a cross-cultural context.

Limitations and Future Research

It should be kept in mind that these data came from a cross-sectional study, so we cannot draw causal conclusions about the effects of stressors on strains. The three-way moderating effects were modest. Even though according to Aguinis et al.'s (2005) meta-analysis, the median effect size in published papers for moderated regression analyses indexed by the change in R^2 when the moderator term is added is 0.002, and the effect size of our study is higher ($R^2 =$ 0.004), interpretation of findings should be cautious. Furthermore, the single-source nature of the data raises possibilities of shared biases that may have affected observed relationships. Another limitation is that we did not recruit representative samples in all three cities due to limited time and resources. One cannot conclude that the results obtained are representative of the entire workforce in Greater China. In future research, it would be better to replicate the study adopting a longitudinal design with larger and more representative samples in other Chinese and Western societies. Further, a measure of culture or cultural value should be added.

To conclude, we found the joint moderating effect of self-efficacy and active coping in collectivist societies of Hong Kong, Taipei and Mainland China. Our proposed model was supported specifically with the social stressors of interpersonal conflict and organizational politics. Our discussion in this chapter has provided evidence that bridges the gaps in knowledge about the stress processes. In brief, high self-efficacy is not always a benefit, as some might believe, but it can contribute to increased strains for employees who experience social stressors.

Acknowledgments

This research was fully supported by grants from the Research Grants Council of the Hong Kong Special Administrative Region, China (Project nos.: LU3006/02H, LU3111/04H). We gratefully thank Mr. Wang Hai-jiang for his assistance in preparation of this chapter.

References

Aguinis, H., Beaty, J.C., Boik, R.J. and Pierce, C.A. (2005). Effect size and power in assessing moderating effects of categorical variables using multiple regression: A 30-year review. *Journal of Applied Psychology*, 90, 94–107.

Aiken, L.S. and West, S.G. (1991). *Multiple Regression: Testing and Interpreting Interactions.* Newbury Park: Sage.

Bandura, A. (1997). *Self-Efficacy: The Exercise of Control.* New York: Freeman.

Bruk-Lee, V. and Spector, P.E. (2006). The social stressors-counterproductive work behavior link: Are conflicts with supervisors and coworkers the same? *Journal of Occupational Health Psychology*, 11, 145–56.

Cammann, C., Fichman, M., Jenkins, D. and Klesh, J. (1979). *The Michigan Organizational Assessment Questionnaire.* Unpublished manuscript, University of Michigan, Ann Arbor.

Cartwright, S. and Cooper, C.L. (2002). *ASSET: An Organizational Stress Screening Tool. The Management Guide.* Manchester: RCL Ltd.

Carver, C.S., Scheier, M.F. and Weintraub, J.K. (1989). Assessing coping strategies: A theoretically based approach. *Journal of Personality and Social Psychology*, 56, 267–83.

Chang, C.-H., Rosen, C.C. and Levy, P.E. (2009). The relationship between perceptions of organizational politics and employee attitudes, strain, and behavior: A meta-analytic examination. *Academy of Management Journal*, 52, 779–801.

Cheng, C., Lo, B.C.Y. and Chio, J.H.M. (2010). The Tao (way) of Chinese coping. In M.H. Bond (ed.), *The Oxford Handbook of Chinese Psychology* (pp. 399–419). New York: Oxford University Press.

Cheung, G.W. and Chow, I.H.S. (1999). Subcultures in Greater China: A comparison of managerial values in the People's Republic of China, Hong Kong, and Taiwan. *Asia Pacific Journal of Management*, 16, 369–87.

Chia, H.B., Egri, C., Ralston, D., Fu, P.P., Kuo, M.C., Lee, C., Li, Y. and Moon, Y. (2007). Four tigers and a dragon: Values differences, similarities, and consensus. *Asia Pacific Journal of Management*, 24, 305–20.

Chinese Culture Connection (1987). Chinese values and the search for culture-free dimensions of culture. *Journal of Cross-Cultural Psychology*, 18, 143–74.

Cohen, J., Cohen, P., West, S.G. and Aiken, L.S. (2003). *Applied Multiple Regression/Correlation Analysis for the Behavioral Sciences* (3rd edn). New Jersey: Lawrence Erlbaum Associates.

Cooper, C.L., Sloan, S.J. and Williams, S. (1988). *Occupational Stress Indicator Management Guide.* Windsor: Nfer-Nelson.

Dormann, C. and Zapf, D. (2002). Social stressors at work, irritation, and depressive symptoms: Accounting for unmeasured third variables in a multi-wave study. *Journal of Organizational and Occupational Psychology*, 75, 33–58.

Egri, C.P. and Ralston, D.A. (2004). Generation cohorts and personal values: A comparison of China and the United States. *Organizational Science*, 15, 210–20.

Farh, J.L., Tsui, A.S., Xin, K. and Cheng, B.S. (1998). The influence of relational demography and guanxi: The Chinese case. *Organization Science*, 9, 471–88.

Ferris, G.R., Frink D.D., Galang, M.C., Zhou, J., Kacmar, K.M. and Howard, J.L. (1996). Perceptions of organizational politics: Predictions, stress-related implications, and outcomes. *Human Relations*, 49, 233–66.

Folkman, S. (1984). Personal control and stress and coping processes: A theoretical analysis. *Journal of Personality and Social Psychology*, 46, 839–52.

Harris, K. and Kacmar, K.M. (2005). Organizational politics. In J. Barling, E.K. Kelloway and M.R. Frone (eds), *Handbook of Work Stress* (pp. 353–74). Thousand Oaks: Sage Publications.

Hofstede, G. (1980). *Culture's Consequences: International Differences in Work-Related Values*. Beverly Hills: Sage Publications.

Hwang, K.K. (1997). *Guanxi* and *mientze*: Conflict resolution in Chinese society. *Intercultural Communication Studies*, 7, 17–37.

Jex, S.M., Bliese, P.D., Buzzell, S. and Primeasu, J. (2001). The impact of self-efficacy on stressor-strain relations: Coping style as an exploratory mechanism. *Journal of Applied Psychology*, 86, 401–9.

Judge, T.A. and Bono, J.E. (2001). Relationship of core self-evaluations traits – self-esteem, generalized self-efficacy, locus of control, and emotional stability -with job satisfaction and job performance: A meta-analysis. *Journal of Applied Psychology*, 86, 80–92.

Kacmar, K.M. and Baron, R.A. (1999). Organizational politics: The state of the field, links to related processes, and an agenda for future research. In G.R. Ferris (ed.), *Research in Personnel and Human Resources Management* (Vol. 17, pp. 1–39). Stamford: JAI.

Kacmar, K.M. and Carlson, D.S. (1997). Further validation of the Perceptions of Politics Scale (POPS): A multiple sample investigation. *Journal of Management*, 23, 627–58.

Kahn, R.L. and Byosiere, P.B. (1992). Stress in organizations. In M.D. Dunnette and L.M. Hough (eds), *Handbook of Industrial/Organizational Psychology* (2nd edn, Vol. 3, pp. 571–650). Palo Alto: Consulting Psychologists Press.

Keenan, A. and Newton, T.J. (1985). Stressful events, stressors, and psychological strains in young professional engineers. *Journal of Occupational Behavior*, 6, 151–6.

Kirkcaldy, B.D., Cooper, C.L. and Brown, J.M. (1995). The role of coping in the stress–strain relationship among senior police officers. *International Journal of Stress Management*, 2(2), 69–78.

Lazarus, R.S. and Folkman, S. (1984). *Stress, Appraisal, and Coping*. New York: Springer.

Leiter, M.P. (1992). Burnout as a crisis in self-efficacy: Conceptual and practical implications. *Work and Stress*, 6, 107–15.

Liu, C. (2002). A comparison of job stressors and job strains among employees holding comparable jobs in Western and Eastern societies. USA: Unpublished Ph.D. dissertation, University of South Florida.

Liu, C., Spector, P.E. and Shi, L. (2007). Cross-national job stress: A quantitative and qualitative study. *Journal of Organizational Behavior*, 28, 209–39.

Liu, C., Nauta, M.M., Spector, P.E. and Li, C. (2008). Direct and indirect conflicts at work in China and the US: A cross-cultural comparison. *Work & Stress*, 22, 295–313.

Lu, C.Q., Siu, O.L. and Cooper, C.L. (2005). Managers' occupational stress in China: The role of self-efficacy. *Personality and Individual Differences*, 38, 569–78.

Lu, L. and Chen, C.S. (1996). Correlates of coping behaviours: Internal and external resources. *Counselling Psychology Quarterly*, 9, 297–307.

Lu, L. and Yang, K.S. (2006). The emergence and composition of the traditional-modern bicultural self of people in contemporary Taiwanese societies. *Asian Journal of Social Psychology*, 9, 167–75.

Lu, L., Chang, Y.Y. and Lai, S.Y.L. (2011a). What differentiates success from strain: The moderating effects of self-efficacy. *International Journal of Stress Management*, 396–412.

Lu, L., Kao, S.F., Siu, O.L. and Lu, C.Q. (2011b). Work stress, work values, and work well-being in the Greater China. *The Journal of Social Psychology*, 151, 767–83.

Maxwell, J.P. and Siu, O.L. (2008). The Chinese Coping Strategies Scale: Relationships with aggression, anger, and rumination in a diverse sample of Hong Kong Chinese adults. *Personality and Individual Differences*, 44, 1049–59.

Nauta, M.M., Liu, C. and Li, C. (2010). A cross-national examination of self-efficacy as a moderator of autonomy/job strain relationships. *Applied Psychology: An International Review*, 59, 159–79.

Osipow, S.H. and Davis, A.S. (1988). The relationship of coping resources to occupational stress and strain. *Journal of Vocational Behavior*, 32(1), 1–15.

Osipow, S.H. and Spokane, A.R. (1984). Measuring occupational stress, strain, and coping. *Applied Social Psychology Annual*, 5, 67–86.

Porter, L.W., Allen, R.W. and Angle, H.L. (1981). The politics of upward influence in organizations. In L.L. Cummings and B.M. Staw (eds), *Research in Organizational Behavior* (Vol. 3, pp. 109–49). Greenwich: JAI Press.

Schwarzer, R., Bäßler, J., Kwiatek, P., Schröder, K. and Zhang, J.X. (1997). The assessment of optimistic self-beliefs: Comparison of the German, Spanish, and Chinese versions of the general self-efficacy scale. *Applied Psychology: An International Review*, 46, 69–88.

Semmer, N. (2003). Individual differences, work stress and health. In M.J. Schabracq, J.A.M. Winnubst and C.L. Cooper (eds), *Handbook of Work and Health Psychology* (2nd edn, pp. 83–120). Chichester: John Wiley & Sons, Inc.

Siu, O.L., Lu, C.Q. and Spector, P.E. (2007). Employees' well-being in Greater China: The direct and moderating effects of general self-efficacy. *Applied Psychology: An International Review*, 56, 288–301.

Siu, O.L., Spector, P.E. and Cooper, C.L. (2006). A three-phase study to develop and validate Chinese coping strategies scales in Greater China. *Personality and Individual Differences*, 41, 537–48.

Siu, O.L., Spector, P.E., Cooper, C.L. and Lu, C.Q. (2005). Work stress, self-efficacy, Chinese work values and work well-being in Hong Kong and Beijing. *International Journal of Stress Management*, 12, 274–88.

Siu, O.L., Spector, P.E., Cooper, C.L., Lu, L. and Yu, S.F. (2002). Managerial stress in Greater China: The direct and moderator effects of coping strategies and work locus of control. *Applied Psychology: An International Review*, 51, 608–32.

Spector, P.E. and Bruk-Lee, V. (2008). Conflict, health, and well-being. In C.K.W. De Dreu and M.J. Gelfand (eds), *The Psychology of Conflict and Conflict Management in Organizations* (pp. 267–88). San Francisco: Jossey-Bass.

Spector P.E. and Jex, S.M. (1998). Development of four self-report measures of job stressors and strains: Interpersonal Conflict at Work Scale, Organizational Constraints Scale, Quantitative Workload Inventory, and Physical Symptoms Inventory. *Journal of Occupational Health Psychology*, 3, 356–67.

Thomas, A., Matherne, M.M., Buboltz, W.C., Jr. and Doyle, A.L. (2012). Coping resources moderate stress-strain and stress-satisfaction relationships in educational administrators. *Individual Differences Research*, 10(1), 37–48.

Thomas, K. (1992). Conflict and negotiation processes in organizations. In M.D. Dunette and L.M. Hough (eds), *Handbook of Industrial and Organizational Psychology* (2nd edn, Vol. 3, pp. 651–718). Palo Alto: Consulting Psychological Press.

Triandis, H.C., Bontempo, R., Villareal, M.J. and Asai, M. (1988). Individualism and collectivism: Cross-cultural perspectives on self-group relationships. *Journal of Personality and Social Psychology*, 54, 323–38.

Xie, J.L. and Schaubroeck, J. (2001). Bridges approaches and findings across diverse disciplines to improve job stress research. In P.L. Perrewé and D.C. Ganster (eds), *Research in Occupational Stress and Well Being* (Vol. 1, pp. 1–61). Netherlands: JAI Elsevier.

6

Burnout and the Battle for Your Own Happiness

Edwin A. Locke and Ellen Kenner

Introduction

Janine was exhausted. She had lost all interest in her work and was confused as to why. She had done everything she was supposed to do. From an early age she had been told that it's important to choose a career to help people in need. In her private moments, this puzzled her. Wasn't any honest job a means to helping people? The baker, the dress designer, the actress, the computer tech guy, the architect, the banker, the airline pilot, and the individuals who created her mobile phone—weren't they helping others? What she heard from those around her was that the *good* person helped people in need *and did not expect anything in return*; a one-way trade. Janine recoiled at the idea of being selfish, so she became a psychological counselor even though she secretly had wanted to become a fashion designer. She put her all into her career, working long hours with emotionally troubled clients for five years. Some she helped; others she could not. Some appreciated her efforts, but few said so. Many whined and complained and blamed her for not fixing them.

Janine felt increasingly empty and resentful as time passed. The pay was low, the hours all-consuming, her supervisor was a control freak, and her peers were indifferent or antagonistic to her. Most importantly, she did not even like counseling but felt guilty at the prospect of abandoning her clients. Her private longings to become a designer left her feeling even guiltier. Janine felt psychologically trapped. She kept asking herself, "Is this all there is to life?" And now, after five tedious years, she no longer cares about her clients, her job, or herself. She feels depressed and beaten. Janine has burned out.

What is Burnout?

The term "burnout" originally referred to a rocket's depletion of fuel (Manago 1982). In the 1980s, Herbert Freudenberger (Freudenberger and Richelson 1980) and Christine Maslach (1982) popularized the term *emotional burnout*. What is it?

KEY CHARACTERISTICS OF BURNOUT

Burnout is characterized by *emotional exhaustion*, *depersonalization* (negative, cynical attitudes and emotional detachment from others) and a *diminished sense of personal accomplishment*, as described by Maslach and Jackson (1986, p. 1). This latter characteristic consists of a loss of confidence and a lowered motivation to work with worsening performance. Freudenberger, along with Gail North (Borysenko 2011) described stages of burnout, which include: being driven by your goal/ideal; working like crazy; putting your own needs last; feeling miserable and defeated; clueless as to why you feel so down; becoming defensive; experiencing inner emptiness, emotional and physical exhaustion; and just giving up. Burnout was first studied in relation to people in the helping professions such as nurses, doctors, psychologists, and teachers. In these initial studies, burnout in individuals was ascribed to factors including the nature of the work (intense involvement with the lives of others), personal attributes such as perfectionism, and organizational factors such as bureaucratic rules and lack of autonomy (Kenner 1992; Udovich 1983). In the present chapter, we show that there is a fundamental, deeper cause of burnout.

PREVALENCE AND WIDER IMPLICATIONS OF BURNOUT

Burnout is a widely discussed phenomenon with one book noting there are over 7,200 publications on the subject (Bahrer-Kohler 2013). It is recognized worldwide. In Japan, they even have a word associated with burnout, "karoshi," which means "death by overwork" (Glouberman 2002, p. 9). There are wider implications. For example, in *Banishing Burnout*, the authors state that job stress, which is a correlate of burnout, "is estimated to cost the U.S. economy $300 billion in sick time, long-term disability, and excessive job turnover" (Leiter and Maslach 2005, p. 3). Burnout on the job is a serious concern, for the individuals experiencing it, and for businesses managers concerned with burnout in their employees.

THE SCOPE OF BURNOUT

Initially, burnout was differentiated from other emotional problems such as depression, emotional breakdown, and workaholism (Manago 1982). However, more recent books have expanded the boundaries of burnout. For example, Borysenko (2011) and Glouberman (2002) view burnout as capable of permeating your entire life, from mental and physical health, to marriage, parenting, friendship, and more. One author has described burnout generally as "a motivational problem," which is another way of saying a lack of energy or desire (Borysenko 2011, p. xxviii). Such lack of motivation can occur in any facet of life or in all facets. Borysenko (2011) and Glouberman (2002) include depressed individuals in their many examples of burnout.

However broadly the phenomenon of burnout is conceptualized, none of us want to experience it, or be on the receiving end of the cynicism and depersonalization of a burnt-out spouse, friend, family member, boss, or service provider.

THE EXPERIENCE OF BURNOUT

What is the experience of burnout actually like? How might it permeate your whole life?

> Imagine waking up in the morning, dreading another day at work. You dread even having to get out of bed. You may feel humorless, grumpy, anxious, bitter, or depressed. Perhaps you wish you were sick, so you could avoid work and get some needed rest. You know you're falling behind at work, you have projects that require your attention and phone calls you haven't made, and part of you just doesn't care.

Part of you does though. You feel guilty and exhausted just thinking of facing your boss or your clients. You may no longer care much about their lives and try to force yourself to show interest.

The guilt and shame are weighing you down, and perhaps you notice you've cut yourself off from co-workers, family, and friends. You may have stopped exercising, or dropped out of a hobby you once loved. Physically, you may feel like you're "falling apart," suffering from back pain, headaches, gastritis and just wanting to go back to sleep, or escaping by having yet another drink or popping another pill. You may have no desire to spend time with your spouse, let alone enjoy an intimate moment together. You may find yourself short-tempered and critical, or worse, toward your kids.

Privately you may barrage yourself with seemingly unanswerable queries, also known as negative rhetorical questions: What's wrong with me?! Why can't I get myself going?! Why is the world set against me?! Why me?! You've lost (or perhaps never fully discovered) your personal "rocket fuel," proactive motivation, the energy and enthusiasm in life that builds confidence. Instead, you are swimming in self-doubt. You are at a low point and you may not see a way to rescue yourself.

Burnout symptoms are both psychological and physical, affecting your mind and body. Burnout not only involves cynicism, indifference, and emotional cut-offs from others, but it usually entails intense *self-criticism*. You feel you are not the person you should be. As noted, burnout can happen at work, in a marriage, with parenting, in friendships, in a hobby, or in several (or all) of these areas. If you, or a loved one, are on the road to burnout, you will recognize some of these symptoms, thoughts, and patterns.

Problems with Goal-Setting

Your life is uniquely your own. Simply put: You own your life. Since all life is a process of goal-directed action, your life is a process of identifying your values and then setting and pursuing the goals that will fulfil them. Goals guide many facets of life: education, job/career, romance, art (paintings, literature, movies, music, etc.), sports, hobbies, friendships, family, and more. If you choose well, all else being equal, your life has color. You experience your life as an adventure with ongoing success, despite occasional setbacks. Your days are interesting and fulfilling. By choosing and pursuing your personal goals, *you give your life purpose and meaning. The actual meaning of life is: the values that you choose, pursue, and attain.*

Pause for a moment to think of a personal goal you chose and pursued that has worked (or is working) nicely for you (e.g., earning a college degree, having an interesting career, choosing a romantic partner, achieving skill in parenting, enjoying a hobby and the arts, exercising regularly, having a healthy diet). Such goal-focused action results in a growing sense of pride and accomplishment. It gives a lovely upscale tempo to your life.

The choice and pursuit of goals is not an automatic process. There is no built-in LIFE-GPS that gives us a map to success. We can and do make errors. We can choose poorly. For example, in college we earn a degree in a field that our parents chose for us, but that is not a career path we want. We can choose a romantic partner based on a wrong judgment (becoming infatuated based solely on looks) or based on wrong information (your partner lied about his unfaithful past). We can also choose well, only to be undermined by external causes. For example, we can save for and buy a home, only to have circumstances, a hurricane or flood (natural causes) or eminent domain laws (man-made causes) undermine our success. All of these factors are stressful, and in such circumstances we may feel like we've hit rock bottom with no fuel to continue. When this happens, we may experience burnout.

Burnout can be a consequence of outside factors, but more often it is due to goals gone awry, due to our own errors in setting and pursuing goals. The way we choose and pursue goals greatly affects our motivational fuel. When done right, we build pride, self-esteem, self-confidence, and learn how to nurture ourselves and enjoy life. We also learn how to cope well with setbacks. When done wrong, our goal pursuits bring us self-doubt, anxiety, pain, unhappiness—and burnout.

What can go wrong with setting your goals? There are at least three related, internal causes of unfulfilling goal pursuit:

1. Altruism.
2. Being a second-hander (going by what others think, say, or do, rather than making your own independent decisions.)
3. Setting only one big goal in life.

Let's examine each of these.

1. ALTRUISM VS. EGOISM

The literal meaning of altruism is: other-ism. It means that your highest moral purpose, the justification for your existence, is to sacrifice your life and happiness for others. You may have heard since childhood that altruism is good. (You're a "good kid" if you *share* your brand new toy with the mean kids next door or better yet, give it away. You're a good daughter if you give up your beloved career to care for your abusive father.) The "helping professions" (doctors, nurses, psychologists, teachers) are especially prone to such selflessness. In looking at the "stages" of burnout, Borysenko describes Stage 3 as "Putting Your Own Needs Last." She elaborates on the martyr syndrome with its accompanying negative emotions such as guilt and depression (Borysenko 2011, p. 14). Selfless relationships can occur in all fields and across all aspects of life (e.g., in marriage, friendships, and parenting; with your boss or co-workers).

Altruism is a dead-end street. If person A sacrifices a goal for person B, then B must, according to altruism code, sacrifice for C (to avoid being selfish by accepting A's sacrifice), and then C for D, and so on, ad infinitum. This means that no one in an altruistic cascade ends up achieving the goals they wanted, an absurd outcome. When guided by altruism, relationships become defined by lack of goal attainment. Or put more strongly, under a martyrdom moral code, relationships become a living graveyard of mutual self-sacrifice. Furthermore, no one can actually practice altruism consistently without dying; even eating and breathing are selfish.

A modified version of altruism is that the more productive, successful, and able should sacrifice for the less productive, less successful, and less able. How would (or does) such a policy work out in your own family, with your siblings and relatives? Who would (or does) benefit? Perhaps the family couch-potato, gambler, or alcoholic. Who would lose? The one with the most ambition and sense of responsibility such as the family entrepreneur or the family member who worked to put herself through college? This policy is insidious: the "reward" of any success is guilt followed by giving up the very values one has earned. Who would want to seek any values under these terms?

A third view of altruism is that one should feel happy when sacrificing because one has done a "good" (moral) thing. But why is it moral? If morality is a code of values to guide your life on earth, then altruism harms you. It is a moral inversion. To act on it means to act *against* your own life and your personal happiness. It means the destruction of your *self* (Binswanger 1986, see "Altruism"; Locke and Kenner 2011b, ch. 2; Rand 1943, 1957, 1962, 1982, p. 61).

The tragedy of altruism was poignantly expressed by an art teacher, "Being me and achieving something was tantamount to being selfish while someone else suffered or went without" (Glouberman 2002, p. 97). And Glouberman tells her own story. She wanted to be the "good girl" even into adulthood. She describes trying to be "wonderful to everyone" and how that gave her a "glow." However:

> The glow never lasted too long anyway before I'd be forced to notice that I had ignored someone's need, or that someone else was kinder than me. [...]
>
> I'd go into overdrive [...] to prove I would do anything for anybody and nothing for myself. (Glouberman 2002, pp. 100–101)

You might be thinking: *But altruism is just being kind and benevolent toward others—there is nothing wrong with that.* Altruism *is* often used synonymously with *helping* others (cooperating in some endeavor), showing *goodwill toward others,* and *generosity.* But this is a disastrously wrong package-deal.

Altruism is not the same as *helping others whom you value* (without harming yourself). You may want to help others who are in trouble because you personally value them (relatives, friends, colleagues, neighbors). And you can properly draw a line between those who are honestly striving to help or better themselves versus the outright moochers who want a free ride in life at your expense. The latter will use the code of altruism as a weapon against you. They will try to make you feel guilty for your effort and success, and attempt to make you feel that you are "somehow" responsible for their lack of it.

Altruism is not the same as *goodwill toward others.* You can help an elderly lady put her carry-on luggage in the overhead compartment because you empathize with her frailty—but should not do so if you yourself risk injury due to serious back problems. You can give a stranger directions if you have time because you know they are searching for something they value (a store, a friend's home) and you also enjoy the short, benevolent human connection—but you do not have to spend the whole day trying to help them out. You can donate money to a cause because you love the cause, but in doing so you do not have to sacrifice a special birthday present for your loved one. You can help a co-worker who is trying hard but not at the expense of being unable to do your job.

Nor is *generosity* by nature altruistic. You might help a financially struggling, honest and hardworking student with car repairs, assuming you can afford it. It is altruistic if you do not even like the student and bankrupt yourself and your family in the process.

Altruism is especially devastating in your career, and especially if it is a business career. An honest businessperson wants to make a profit in return for providing a value to customers. For this they are routinely demonized because they do not pay above-market wages and provide their goods and services at a loss (which would cause bankruptcy). Often the smears come from envious people, maybe even some members of your own family.

If you accept the self-sacrificial code of altruism, the more successful you are (assuming you use honest means), the more immoral you will feel. There are pejorative phrases to capture that view, such as "filthy rich" or "big shot." With success, altruism says you are making money that "rightly" belongs to others. So-called "justice" means *not* keeping what you earned. Altruism causes burnout, because the better you do, the more your guilt piles up. You are in a no-win situation. Altruism is anti-happiness (Locke and Kenner 2011a, 2011b).

In contrast, your honest success, seen through the moral code of rational egoism, leaves you feeling accomplished and motivated—fueled by moral pride. Altruism takes away both your money and your spiritual reward: the earned pride that comes with success.

Your moral code matters. Most people have mixed moral codes: they feel some proper egoistic pride for their success, but it is poisoned by altruism—the code that tells them that self-sacrifice is the standard of morality.

Altruism and the "helping professions"

Many people enter the "helping professions" because they want to "help people," even at their own expense. We emphasize: *even at their own expense.* What's wrong here? It is not enough to enter a profession just to help people—this is a vacuous cliché. *Every legitimate career or job offers something to clients or customers.* You are helping people, through trade, when you sell a sandwich or a shirt or therapy. The real issue is:

> *Why do YOU want to enter this profession?*
> *What do YOU personally enjoy about it?*
> *What's in it for YOU?*

Helping people is not a sufficient answer. Obviously everyone wants to feel efficacious, but: why in this way? With this group?

Sometimes people want to help those who suffer, yet it comes at the expense of their own suffering. They may want to help, not out of goodwill, but out of duty. A duty is an unchosen obligation divorced from any benefit, material or spiritual, to you. In perverse cases, some altruists secretly want to feel power over or superior to others. The common element in both cases is: *they need people to suffer in order to feel good about themselves.*

Altruism example

Let's take a deeper look at one person who is beset by inner conflict as a consequence of having altruism (self-sacrifice) as her moral standard. Below are some excerpts from her "burnout diary." This author wanted success, achieved it, and felt guilty because of it. She tried to appease her guilt by giving to everyone without concern for herself (Sue Townsend qtd in Glouberman 2002, pp. 40–48).

> *"I felt nothing about my own welfare."*

> *"I would never have been able to say to someone—'I'm tired, I'm going to lie down now'."*

> *"I was giving hugely to everybody, including my husband–doing everything he asked me to do, becoming the person he wanted me to be—but I obviously couldn't do that wholly. I had my own life going on inside my head."*

> *"I didn't know how to say no. I just obeyed people [...] I had no self-esteem at all–and the more successful I became, the less it seemed I had."*

> *"The glittering prizes of success were within my grasp and I wouldn't quite reach my hand out to take them though I wanted them. I was afraid I'd lose something else–my family and friends, the safe people. I was always very nervous about seeming different. It was to do with people saying—she's getting above herself, she thinks a lot of herself, she's a snob, she's superior. That was massively important to me. And*

I was also loyal to my class. You can't be successful and working-class—I'm the disappeared one–you're immediately promoted to a different class."

This person says she coped by being "ridiculously neglectful" of herself, allowing her body to break down. This was the only way she allowed herself to get rest without guilt. She paid a psychological and physical price for the moral "ideal" of altruism. If you are motivated by altruism, not wanting or taking anything for yourself, eventually you become resentful for not feeling properly rewarded for your work. Worse, you may feel guilty about your own resentment, thinking you should be totally selfless. This often ends in depression, as you gradually become a non-person—a self-*less* person. You feel depleted of the joy in life and become cynical and burnt out.

Now consider egoism. Those promoting altruism work hard to portray egoism as an evil moral code. If your morality "file folder" has been corrupted with a pejorative view of egoism, you're in for some good news. Egoism, *properly understood*, is good, moral and the only path to genuine, unadulterated happiness.

Goal-setting and goal pursuit, if the goals are yours, are egoistic processes—that is, you are choosing and pursuing what you want to do because it contributes to your own happiness. If you do not have your own values and goals, you rob yourself of happiness. You have no personal values to ground your identity in as an individual.

Egoism, if based on reason and respect for others' rights, is benevolent. Under an egoistic moral code, others are not enemies who drains you of all personal desire. You want others to enjoy pursuing their own goals because they have the same right to pursue happiness as you do. Instead of sacrifice, bitterness, resentment, and cynicism, egoism promotes mutual growth and happiness. You enjoy trading with others, both emotionally and with goods and services. It is a *just* system.

If this is so, why does egoism get an undeserved "bad name"? We saw how, from an altruistic framework, self-valuing is considered immoral by definition. But there is another reason why egoism gets an undeserved "bad" name. This is due to lumping it in with narcissism and criminality. Another deadly package deal.

Egoism must be distinguished from narcissism (Locke and Kenner 2011b). The narcissist (a "me-only," a "my-way-or-the-highway" person) is riddled with self-doubt and covers this up with an attitude of entitlement. The world owes him! A narcissist desperately wants other people to work for, sacrifice for, and worship him. He wants self-sacrificing altruists to attend to his neurotic needs. The narcissist is accused of having a big ego, but in reality has no genuine ego at all. He is a puffed up balloon with nothing inside except an emptiness longing to be filled—by others. Without external inflation, the balloon deflates and he is devastated. A narcissist does not possess genuine self-esteem. He is self-destructive; he is his own first victim. Privately, alone in the dark basement of his own mind, he is anxious, empty, and desperate.

A genuine egoist is, in the deepest sense, *self-sufficient*—he has his own sense of identity and his own values. Other people can add to his happiness in profound ways (e.g., romance, friendship), but they do not fill an inner emptiness. Other people cannot create one's self-esteem or happiness *ex nihilo*, because they cannot substitute for a mind that is not functioning properly—a mind that lacks genuine personal values.

As a true egoist, *you pursue your own interests by the use of your own mind*. You experience your own efficacy and pride. You do not need constant "strokes"; you are not fundamentally insecure.

That doesn't mean you don't enjoy *earned visibility* from others, such as respect, recognition, and earned admiration. You want to enjoy what you have earned. You rationally enjoy others' admiration of your good character or accomplishments, however small or large, when you've done something to deserve it.

True egoists, who do their own thinking, are not riddled with guilt or self-doubt. As with anyone, they can have moments of insecurity, such as when entering a new work situation or when asking someone on a date. But this is only due to uncertainty of the situation, or perhaps anticipating the need for some new skills, not a fundamental lack.

As a true egoist, you don't need to boast. You are secure in yourself. You have no desire to use or manipulate people. Goodwill and generosity aside, your only desire is to *trade* with them (economically or spiritually), to mutual benefit, which creates a "win-win" relationship. You deal with others fairly not by begging or exploiting. When you strive to make money, it's not to prove anything or to show off, but primarily because you love the work and want to be justly rewarded for your efforts. Secondarily, you want to buy things for yourself, help your business grow, and provide for your family. As a true egoist, you are an individualist; you are self-contained. You've earned genuine self-esteem.

As to criminality and the like, dishonesty is not a way of earning values, but of stealing them. Nor is mindless indulgence of emotions (feelings, urges) in one's self-interest. Out-of-control drinking, drug abuse, driving recklessly, engaging in indiscriminate, promiscuous sex, assaulting, manipulating, and defrauding, reduces one, in the end, to a sub-human level, the level without a rational mind. This can only end in disaster.

To act in your *true self-interest* requires rational thought and honest introspection. This involves asking yourself questions such as: *What do I really want? Why? What is the best means of making myself able to pursue values through voluntary, honest trade? How can I plan for success longer range? How can I balance my important personal values to make my life fulfilling? What obstacles do I face? How can I overcome each one? How can I best achieve my own happiness?* This brings us to a second way that goals can go awry. *And it is related to altruism.*

2. PSYCHOLOGICAL INDEPENDENCE VS. DEPENDENCE

Many of us choose goals, not based on what we want for ourselves, but to please, appease, impress, or rebel against others. This is other-focused goal-setting, psychological dependence. We hear the pleasing-others strategy in simple phrases such as: "Whatever you want dear. It doesn't matter to me." "I just want to make you happy, so I'll go along with whatever you choose." We lose our voice, our choices, our lives.

In whatever way we do it, when our goals are focused on others in ways that ignore our own values, we are giving up our psychological independence, our autonomy. When we brush aside our own personal wants we end up self-sabotaging and invite burnout.

To the extent that we don't choose and assert our own values, by default we have to get them from others. These others may be parents, spouses, teachers, ministers, friends, or public figures. Others can certainly inspire you, including childhood heroes, and great teachers, and you often get useful advice from others, but in the end you have to decide what you want for yourself. If you are passive, you leave a value vacuum, and there is no alternative but to let others fill it. Ayn Rand calls this *second-hand motivation* (Binswanger 1986, see "Second-Handers"; Rand 1963). Being a second-hander means you have no genuine self (Locke and Kenner 2011b, ch. 6). There are many forms of living second-hand:

- Living for the expectations of others (a spouse, parents).
- Proving to your parents that you are better than they claimed or expected.
- Seeking constant "validation" that you're OK to relieve self-doubt.
- Status seeking: driving big showy cars *just* to "prove" you're important. Seeking titles (e.g., "Vice President") *just* to impress others.

- Celebrity seeking: *Guess who I know! Look at what awards I got!*
- Craving recognition: continually seeking the spotlight.
- Comparing yourself to others and using them as the standard: *I'm never "good enough" so I have to copy what others want and do to be accepted.*
- Wanting success to show off your "position": a politician broadcasting, in an arrogant, disdainful manner, his "control" over multiple districts in his state.
- Showing off your wealth: pompously wearing jewelry that is "over the top" just to impress others, not because you love a particular piece of jewelry; conspicuous consumption.

Goals chosen by such motives are not chosen first-hand, based on what you personally want, but are adopted second-hand, fueled by insecurity, self-doubt, and outside pressure. When these goals are attained they routinely lead to anxiety: *Will I be a big enough big shot? Will I be noticed and envied? What about tomorrow? What if someone is better than me? What if people see through me?*

What is the typical sad ending to second-hand motivation? *When you reach your goal, such as getting a career that your parents or spouse want for you, or that you choose to copy from your peers, or that you chose in order to feel like a big shot, you find yourself feeling empty.* True, you may feel some "happy" relief, but it's only temporary. This is not your personally chosen goal, so the relief you feel in pleasing a parent or spouse is short-lived. Tomorrow you need to start pleasing others and proving yourself all over again. And on and on. You may stay in a career or job you actually hate because of second-hand motivation.

In our personal lives, we've all seen examples of someone (perhaps yourself) who chooses second-hand goals. For example, they work very hard in business; they attain challenging goals and then emotionally crash and burnout—only to be "rescued" by discovering meditation, yoga and some sort of Eastern or Western mysticism, or a "back to nature" lifestyle. Although we're fans of relaxation and exercise (and Dr. Kenner enjoys yoga), and fans of enjoying nature (lovely walks, gardening, listening to the birds), unless you make this your career, these are mainly leisure activities. They don't substitute (except as a temporary respite) for having pursued a productive career based on goals you've chosen for yourself, first-hand goals.

Some second-hand goals may be related to childhood trauma or unreasonable parental expectations. For example, perhaps your parents were hypercritical and repeatedly called you "dumb" or "stupid." It's understandable, but not healthy, to focus your efforts on proving to them (even after they are dead) that you are better than they claim. Or perhaps they wanted you to excel in the career of *their* dreams, not yours. It takes courage to be your own person. You can still love them—but your life belongs to you, not them. You need not prove anything to them, or rebel against them, or meet their unreasonable expectations. Of course, you might selfishly (egoistically) want to enter the family business because it is your interest and not out of guilt, conformity, or duty. The choice to value your own life is yours. Psychological independence is liberating.

Whether or not you set goals, and how you set goals (by first-hand or second-hand motivation) matters greatly! You can set a good course for your life by increasing your psychological independence and consciously setting personal, first-hand goals. Your happiness depends on it.

A word about money. Making money is conventionally treated as low and materialistic—something to be ashamed of. The more you make the more guilt you are supposed to feel. If there is a problem with money, however, the problem is not with money as such—rather with *what it means to you.*

If you are an altruist, having or making money means you are bad, unless you give it away. If you are a second-hander, you are probably using your money to show off, buying things because others are buying them, seeking power over others, all in order to relieve profound self-doubt. This will not work because lack of money is not the cause of the self-doubt. Growing up poor does not cause self-doubt unless you agree, consciously or subconsciously, that poverty proves you are inferior. Your parents' income does not make you either good or bad. What is important is what you do with your life when you grow up.

Consider this bizarre, yet true, story: Jones buys a house in a posh neighborhood. He then realizes that there is a bigger house down the block. This makes him feel inferior, so he demolishes his new home and builds a bigger, more expensive one than that of his neighbor. What has he gained? He gains a temporary respite from self-doubt—temporary because he will have to constantly worry about someone else on the block building a bigger house than his. And what about the houses on the next block? Jones will never be at peace if his neighbors serve as his standard of self-worth.

What would an independent person do in choosing a home? He would ask one, core question: *What kind of a home do I want for myself and my family?* What others on the block have done would be of no relevance (other than providing architectural examples). With such an attitude, the independent person can never be threatened by someone's bigger home, because others are not his frame of reference.

The same principle holds for choosing a job or career. All of your friends are going to law school. So what? Many lawyers hate their profession. *What do you want for yourself? What personally interests you?* You want to be a veterinarian. Lower status than a lawyer? Again, so what? What do you want to be for yourself?

Being desperate for money for reasons of status guarantees burnout. In such situations, you're on a treadmill—there's no escape. Endlessly pursuing values that others have set for you will not have any real meaning.

As we noted earlier, honestly earning money by doing something you personally love and doing it very well, is something to take great pride in. Being successful at anything requires hard work and dedication. If your motivation is egoistic and you chose the work for yourself because it is something you love, then it will yield genuine pleasure. If you selfishly love being a stockbroker, doing well at it (including making good money for your clients and yourself) will give meaning to your life and bring you pleasure. You will not feel burned out because the values you are pursuing are yours. The better you do the happier you will be. (This does not preclude changing careers if, at some point, you lose interest or develop a new interest.)

Repressed hurt or anger may be behind setting your goals. You may want to rebel against your parents, or show them how wrong they were—by becoming successful. You may eagerly long for their warmth and support. But here is the sad part: you cannot relive your childhood; it's gone forever. If, as an adult, you are desperately trying to prove something to your parents, then they are still in charge of your life. Unfortunately, you are still powered by second-hand motivation, even if the cause of your goals is hidden in your subconscious, rather than chosen consciously. In reality, your life does not belong to your parents; it belongs to you.

Sometimes people view independence as *doing whatever I want to do—whatever the consequences.* They act on emotional whim. This is not in your self-interest. A psychologically independent egoist is a responsible person. For example, if you have chosen to marry and have children, and then abandon those chosen responsibilities, you should and will feel guilty. You have shown a lack of integrity. That is when you want to stand back and rethink the appropriate goals for your life. There is not just one perfect model, but children require parenting and spouses require care and affection. If you do not care about them, why did you marry and have children? If you want to be a happy and responsible parent and partner, you want to embrace these goals and values. Of course if your marriage is not working out for other reasons, sometimes it makes sense to get counseling or to part ways. But this is not something to do on a whim. It requires a deep understanding of what went wrong and why it can't be repaired. To understand why romantic love is properly egoistic and requires moral integrity, read *The Selfish Path to Romance: How to love with passion and reason* (Locke and Kenner 2011b).

Some commentators claim that burnout is due to egoism and individualism (Berglas 2001), but this is not true when egoism is properly understood. Quite the opposite; *it is altruism and second-handedness that are most likely to put one at risk of burnout.* Egoism and independent judgment are the antidotes. First-hand motivation is the foundation and the cause, the heart and soul, of genuine self-esteem. First-hand motivation requires that you decide:

> *What do I truly enjoy?*
> *What are my passions?*
> *What do I really want for myself?*
> *What kind of person do I want to be?*

Actively thinking about these questions, considering what will serve your genuine happiness longer range, making specific plans to achieve your goals, and pursuing your passions, is a gift only you can give yourself.

3. ONE BIG SINGLE GOAL—ONLY

A third factor that could lead to burnout involves setting one really important goal in life, but nothing after that (Berglas 2001). Such goals include: to graduate from college, to become a CEO, to make X millions, to get recognized by some national association, to be a tenured professor, to take a rocket to the moon. There is nothing wrong with big goals as such if they are fueled by first-hand motivation (your personal values). Life is a process of goal-directed action but *life does not stop when you reach one big goal.* Thus, when you reach a milestone, you need to identify new goals to continue enjoying your life. It's fine if these goals are smaller, but they need to have some degree of challenge in them or you will be bored to death. Consider the example of figure skater and Olympic gold medalist Dorothy Hamill:

> As strains of "The Star-Spangled Banner" filled the 1976 Winter Olympics stadium in Austria, the smiling 19-year-old stood atop the podium with the gold medal for figure skating hanging from her neck. "I was thrilled and proud to be an American," recalls Hamill, now 51. And then came panic. "I thought, 'Now what do I do?'"
> The Olympic champ – who minted the Hamill camel spin and launched a hairstyle craze with her distinctive wedge cut – experienced an emotional downward spiral after realizing she had no Plan B. "I thought, naively, that I'd win the Olympics, and life would be set," she says. "It was the first really down, depressed time for me." (Tan 2007)

Subsequently, she did make some Plan Bs.

A single big goal is especially risky if it is *fully* second-hand. You've put a lot of energy into something that was not yours (e.g., achieving a career your parents wanted for you but you don't like, selling your soul to become famous). When you make it, you will feel like you've achieved nothing—nothing that is personally your own. Your "big wins" are big wins to please, appease, shock, or impress others. Your goals are guided by the standards of others, not your own first-hand motivation. The bigger the second-hand goals, the bigger the letdown. Happily, Dorothy Hamill seems to have loved skating first-hand, even though there was a harmful second-hand element to her goal (pleasing her difficult mother and feeling the need to be "America's Sweetheart"). It seems to be her first-hand independently chosen value: "The youngest of three children, it was Hamill who had the drive and determination to become a world class figure skater" (CBS News 2007).

Your deepest ideas matter. In *Atlas Shrugged*, Ayn Rand states, "The purpose of morality is to teach you, not to suffer and die, but to enjoy yourself and live." Through her books, *Atlas Shrugged* and *The Virtue of Selfishness*, Ayn Rand has spared many individuals from the psychological death trap of altruism. She advises us all to "check our premises"—especially our core moral code.

In a detailed review on the nature and causes of job satisfaction, Locke (1976) notes, "research indicates that work satisfaction is engendered by work which is varied, allows autonomy, is not physically fatiguing, which is mentally challenging and yet allows the individual to experience success and is personally interesting." How can such work satisfaction be sabotaged—resulting in burnout? Let's consider some additional individual factors that contribute to burnout. You can see how both altruism and second-hand motivation underlie some of these traps.

Individual Problems Causing Susceptibility to Burnout

1. *Unrealistic expectations*: this applies especially to the "helping" professions. Not everyone can be cured or even helped. Not all clients are appreciative. Some do not even want help; they want to be left alone. Not all institutions for helping are well run. Not all managers are competent or trustworthy. Not all coworkers are supportive. This does not leave the provider helpless. There is more than one place to work and the job situation can often be modified.
2. *Irrational perfectionism*: wanting to do really well at your work is admirable, but you can't be omniscient or omnipotent. Your standards need to be your own, and put into a context: what is possible and reasonable in this situation?
3. *Inadequate knowledge or lack of skills*: this is experienced as low self-efficacy (low confidence). Obviously, if you are experiencing this, gain the needed education, skills training, and experience (or change professions).
4. *A strong need for approval from others due to low self-esteem*: if you think you are not fundamentally OK, altruism will not cure this feeling. It will only make it worse by reinforcing your sense of worthlessness: *I am not worthy of anything for myself.* Egoism is the antidote. You need to learn to approve of yourself.
5. *Inadequate resilience*: what makes resilience possible? A determination to improve and a proactive approach to problems. Persistence in the face of difficulty. What you say to yourself when you are under stress really matters. If you say, *I can figure this out* or *I'll find a solution to this*, you're more likely to stay focused and look for reasonable solutions. If you say, *I'll never be able to handle this*, you may make this a self-fulfilling prophecy. Your mind won't search for alternative solutions to the difficulty.

Self-sabotaging "coping" mechanisms (anger, withdrawal, passivity, isolation, substance abuse) make you less resilient and more prone to burnout. If you are struggling with such habits, consider learning alternative coping skills with cognitive therapy. There are many excellent books such as *Mind Over Mood: Change How You Feel by Changing the Way You Think* (Greenberger and Padesky 1995). Other resources are available at the Academy of Cognitive Therapy (academyofct.org). Learn skills to relax your mind enough to focus on healthy solutions. It's well worth the time to practice how to deal with "failure," setbacks, or adversity in a self-respecting manner.

1. *Inadequate social skills*: we are not born knowing how to start conversations, keep them going, listen carefully to one another, disagree without attacking the other person, or express our wants and needs assertively. If you have difficulty connecting or bonding with others, you

can significantly improve this. Dr. Kenner is living proof of this. She used to be quite shy. She's now had a radio show for well over a decade. Don't short change yourself in life by thinking you can't acquire better social skills.

2. *Treating your body as expendable*: perhaps you sit at the computer all day, or are not getting enough sleep, neither eating well nor exercising. Perhaps you are smoking, abusing substances, and not getting proper medical attention. You may think that taking care of yourself is no big deal. Whether we like it or not, our bodies have biological requirements: proper nutrition, restorative sleep, and exercise. In *Restore Yourself*, the author warns: "Beginning in high school, we start treating sleep as though it is 'free' time. We treat time for sleep like a big, nightly bank account that we can borrow from whenever we need some extra time to work, party, or unwind." " We also wear our sleep deprivation as a parental medal of honor or symbol of professional commitment" (Greenblatt et al. 2009, p. 64). If you are not tending to your body, consider changing that. Regular medical check ups are a gift to your self. We have heard this all our lives, but many of us are prone to take our own bodies for granted. It's your only home for life—take good care of it.

Organizational and Situational Factors Contributing to Burnout

1. *Work overload*. The most commonly noted situational cause of burnout is *work overload*—which means: more work than you can handle, or work that takes up too much of your life, even if you can handle it—there is no time for other values (Maslach 2003). For an altruist, the work overload is especially pernicious because you are working endless hours doing something you do not love; you work out of duty—and others' wants are never fully satisfied. Sometimes a heavy workload is necessary to reach an important goal, but we all need to know our own limits in order to avoid working unbearable hours due to altruistic guilt. (We noted earlier that a heavy workload is much less stressful if you are doing something you genuinely love.)

An altruist will have special difficulty saying "no" to requests for his time, effort, and energy. From the "burnout diary" we referred to earlier: "I was afraid people would be angry and upset and disappointed. I felt physical fear, extreme anxiety about saying no" (qtd in Glouberman 2002, p. 42). Setting self-valuing boundaries will rescue you. But that requires rethinking altruistic ideas that make you prone to burnout. In *Banishing Burnout*, the authors describe several "workload problems": too available, not enough time, too much work assigned, and exhaustion (Leiter and Maslach 2005, ch. 4). You can see how altruism sets one up for these problems.

Another type of work overload is *emotional overload*. In the book, *Restore Yourself*, Greenblatt describes "emotional labor" as a "sneaky depleter" leading to burnout. She uses the example of flight attendants who have to smile cheerily regardless of what they think, holding their tongue, so to speak (Greenblatt et al. 2009, p. 78). And interestingly, "cultures of relentless enthusiasm," such as working at a Club Med Resort, can create "self-depletion." If you have to be "up" and super enthusiastic all the time, everyday—you may find yourself burning out. Some people really like the positive interactions involved in customer service and some do not—and sometimes enough is enough. Greenblatt emphasizes the need to learn what uniquely depletes you and what uniquely restores you. That will make you more burnout-resistant (Greenblatt et al. 2009, pp. 85–6).

2. *Lack of reward/recognition*. A second factor is *lack of reward* including recognition. We need rewards, not to boost fake self-esteem, but as a matter of justice. Wanting fair rewards is egoistic. If we do a good job, we've earned and deserve recognition. Such recognition can come in many

forms (money, verbal appreciation, respect, vacation days, awards, presents, promotions, or other privileges). In *Banishing Burnout*, the authors state, "You want key people to notice your contribution and react positively if not enthusiastically. There is an emptiness when this recognition is missing" (Leiter and Maslach 2005, p. 92).

Compounding this desire for positive feedback is altruism. Altruism makes you feel guilty for even wanting a reward. Your sacrifice is a duty. Wanting something for yourself would be selfish. (Improper rewards, of course, can be as upsetting as no reward.) *Lack of reward can make you feel both deprived and guilty at the same time.*

Remember to reward yourself when possible. In *Banishing Burnout*, they recommend keeping track of your major accomplishments and celebrating them (Leiter and Maslach 2005; see also Potter 2005). And remember to acknowledge the accomplishments of others with whom you work. This becomes a win-win situation. (Leiter and Maslach 2005, ch. 6).

3. *Lack of autonomy.* A third factor is *lack of autonomy*, lack of the opportunity to make decisions that are within the scope of your competence. Autonomy not only allows you to use your rational, creative mind, but also allows you to feel more in control of your work—it gives you ownership. Leiter and Maslach put it succinctly: "Micromanagement is a pervasive blight upon the work world. It reflects a misplaced confidence in the wisdom of central control" (2005, p. 72).

4. *Conflict.* A fourth factor is *conflict*: you may experience everyday conflict with others in the organization (supervisors, peers), or with clients. This may be associated with perceived lack of support, e.g., in the form of knowledge and practical help, rudeness, lack of integrity, and more. You may have career conflict with your partner. Conflict fuels stress. You may need to learn conflict management skills through some form of training—or learn how to avoid certain people. (Of course, you may also have conflict within your self about what you want or what you should want.)

5. *Danger.* A fifth factor is *danger*. This obviously applies to soldiers in combat and many need treatment for post-traumatic stress disorders. The danger issue applies to the police and firemen too. In such jobs it's especially important to passionately love your work and to be very well trained.

6. *Dealing with "difficult" people.* It is claimed that there is a sixth factor: *being demoralized by dealing with mentally troubled, or immoral people all the time.* However, there is a wider context. First, if you love doing what you are doing (and are not doing it out of altruism) then there is something positive in principle: you are working to improve lives by using your skills. And the more skills you develop, the better your results can be. You can better help clients improve themselves. Avoid unrealistic standards: you won't be able to "cure" everyone (there is a context to hold). And helping a difficult person get a bit better is still a gain. If you are a policeman, you can take pride in knowing that you are helping keep good people (or your country) safe from harm. If you do not get recognition or positive feedback from clients, make it a point to seek it from your peers (and even your boss). A culture of mutual admiration goes a long way to preventing burnout. And privately, let yourself experience the pride of a job well done.

As emphasized, it is important to set limits on how much you give because the demands may seem infinite. Altruism demands unlimited sacrifice. Egoism is based on trade. This applies to empathy—you can empathize with clients or those you are helping, but taking on their emotions as your own is self-sacrificial.

It is also important to avoid viewing external factors as routinely controlling or determining your life. Why?

a) We usually have the power to choose the situations that we enter (e.g., spouses, jobs, careers). What about parents and assorted relatives—can you choose them? No, but you can choose how much contact you have, what relatives you hang out with, and what "rules of engagement" you agree to.

b) We often have the power to change or re-structure the situations that we're in (e.g., re-design our jobs, change jobs, get divorced).

c) We generally have some power to adapt to situations (e.g., avoid the obnoxious boss 90% of the time).

You need to get pleasure from your work, career, and life and this may require some changes. You may discover that you are in the wrong job or profession, in which case, you want to make an action plan to change course. Value yourself and your own personal happiness—and become more burnout resistant. This is the moral, egoistic battle for your own happiness.

SUMMARY

How can you become more burnout resistant? To replenish your life after a setback? To banish altruism and embrace your own happiness? Here are some summary points:

1. Be a rational egoist: choose a profession and job that you personally love. Don't sacrifice your happiness. Expect to get pleasure and rewards from your work.
2. Choose your values and goals independently. Don't run your life by constantly comparing yourself to others.
3. Treat goal pursuit as a lifelong process.
4. Set limits on how much you will give. Take time for yourself.
5. Constantly develop your knowledge and skills. Grow in your career.
6. Use contextual standards (goals) to judge your performance.
7. Build a support network, if needed.
8. Look for ways to change or restructure your job or job environment if you are unhappy with either.

Conclusion

Does being in the helping professions necessarily make you more vulnerable to burnout? Is it possible to *love* being in the helping profession? We thought you'd enjoy ending on a mostly upbeat note. Dr. Kenner, aka Ellen, will share her story.

***

When I finished my undergraduate work at Brown University, I tried different career possibilities: infant research, secretarial work, handbag design, and I considered entering medical school. My dad would have loved for me to work for him. I tried it and it wasn't a good fit. I helped my husband with secretarial and accounting work, a temporary job, not my forte. Infant research, both at the maternity hospital and at the Brown University Child Study Lab, was interesting, but I was not passionate about it.

After college, I read *The Fountainhead* and *Atlas Shrugged*. My life was forever changed. The heroes and heroines in Ayn Rand's novels were passionate about their careers and their lives. I wanted to feel that way too. *What did I want?* An exciting life, Yes. What stood in the way? My confidence in setting and pursing my dreams. In some subtle way, I felt it was selfish to do something I loved. After reading the novels, I saw the power of self-valuing ideas. And in my own life, I saw that the right ideas made an enormous difference in the way individuals experienced their everyday life. I was deeply moved by the following exchange in *Atlas Shrugged* between Dagny, the heroine, and Cherryl, a lovely young woman losing hope, tormented by the shady characters around her (Rand 1957, pp. 820–21):

> *"Dagny, how did you do it? How did you manage to remain unmangled?"*
> *"By holding to just one rule."*
> *"Which?"*
> *"To place nothing – nothing – above the verdict of my own mind."*
> *"You've taken some terrible beatings ... maybe worse than I did ... worse than any of us. ... What held you through it?"*
> *"The knowledge that my life is the highest of values, too high to give up without a fight."*
> *She saw a look of astonishment, of incredulous recognition on Cherryl's face [...].*
> *"Dagny" – her voice was a whisper – "that's ... that's what I felt when I was a child ... that's what I seem to remember most about myself ... that kind of feeling ... and I never lost it, it's there, it's always been there, but as I grew up, I thought it was something that I must hide. ... I never had any name for it, but just now, when you said it, it struck me that that's what it was. ... Dagny, to feel that way about your own life – is that good?"*
> *"Cherryl, listen to me carefully: that feeling – with everything, which it requires and implies – is the highest, noblest and only good on earth."*
> *"The reason I ask is because I ... I wouldn't have dared to think that. Somehow, people always made me feel as if they thought it was a sin ... as if that were the thing in me which they resented and ... and wanted to destroy."*
> *"It's true. Some people do want to destroy it. And when you learn to understand their motive, you'll know the darkest, ugliest and only evil in the world, but you'll be safely out of its reach."*

I knew that I was Cherryl in the sense of being confused about my fundamental ideas: egoism *vs.* altruism and narcissism. I took Dagny's advice to heart. I gave serious thought to what career I wanted—and it was to become a clinical psychologist. I wanted to learn about the role of ideas, about emotions, about the root cause of genuine happiness, about how my own mind works, and what thinking skills would help me flourish in life and cope with setbacks. I wanted to shed the habit of altruistic self-doubt and self-criticism. I was learning, first-hand, about the source and value of genuine self-esteem.

I studied harder than I ever had in my life in preparation for entering a Ph.D. program. I excelled on tests that I had formerly performed adequately on. I was elated when I received news that I had an interview with my first choice university. My daughter, a tot at the time, warmly recalls my hanging up the phone after receiving the good news, joyously lifting her up and dancing around the kitchen with her—I was exuberant. I enjoyed my university studies, received my degree, and subsequently worked at group practices and at a hospital. I enjoyed the collegial friendships, mutual support and learning with my fellow mental health professionals. I was continually learning, reading self-help books and soaking up classes in Cognitive Therapy and all sorts of therapy interventions. I studied Objectivism, a rational philosophy, in depth.

As a psychologist, I worked with individuals of all ages, including children. My clients suffered from a range of problems: from marital or parenting difficulties to anxiety, depression, eating disorders, borderline personality disorder, sexual abuse, and more. I worked long hours—and loved it. And I didn't burn out. Learning about each client was like opening up a new mystery novel. We worked together to get to the root of their emotional pain with methods uniquely tailored to each one's learning style (e.g., role plays, cognitive therapy exercises, introspective work, relaxation methods, problem solving, and stress management tools). The clients and I collaborated as detectives, which involved information gathering, asking questions, careful listening, making inferences, checking hypothesis, decoding emotions, reading body language, and more.

Giving clients the knowledge that their life is their own, helping them gain the social skills to make friends, helping with career choices, helping them set self-valuing boundaries with others, and arming them against unearned guilt—this was an ideal career for me.

On a deeper level, I saw the efficacy of egoistic ideas that helped me rescue myself, and helped my clients find joy. And I saw benefit of helping them grasp the psychological destructiveness of self-sacrifice. I loved seeing the progress they made; it showed me the efficacy of the right ideas—to see a parent connect better with their child, to see a woman gain the courage to leave an abusive relationship and subsequently find a better partner, to see a mom recover from the unbearable death of her son, find a deeply personal way to grieve the loss, and eventually rediscover some joy in living while retaining the warm memories of her son, to see couples reignite the passion, or part ways rather than trap one another in a loveless marriage, to seeing a student apply herself and get into the college of her choice.

Let's look at a specific example (details changed to protect my clients). Donald is a young adult, living in a strongly religious family—with eight younger siblings. What are the chances that he will feel comfortable pursing his own dreams to become an engineer? His parents, subtly or not so subtly, expect and demand that he take care of all his siblings and their needs. Is it his life or not? Is he their indentured servant? Should he feel forever shackled to his siblings and parents' unending needs? Should he feel guilty going to college to pursue a career he loves? Should he even dare to dream and set personal goals? If he buys into the "moral" code of altruism, he will suffocate his genuine dreams in unrelenting, *unearned* guilt; his dreams will make him feel "selfish"—immoral. Under altruism, he will betray himself; he will most likely resent his siblings (those who dare to pursue their dreams as well as those who do nothing), feel guilty for the resentment, and eventually burn out. Lost dreams and a lost life. Fortunately, Donald chose not to betray himself. He gradually set healthier boundaries with his family while still staying close with them. He is pursuing a career he enjoys.

I am not a fan of lost dreams and lost lives. I like joyous endings. I have had the pleasure of helping such clients liberate themselves from unearned guilt, gradually and assertively setting boundaries with family members, staying lovingly and reasonably connected with some siblings and their parents, while shifting moral gears and pursuing their personal dreams.

Did I sometimes have "failures"—clients who didn't want to change, may not have liked me, or who resented the need for mental effort? Yes, for example, a husband who wanted to continue cheating, a child who wanted to be popular and hang with the wrong crowd rather than look for alternatives, an addict who preferred prostitution and cocaine addiction to reconnecting with her young child, an adolescent who was court-ordered into therapy and defiant, a person on welfare who wanted me to help them milk the system by supporting their "right" to food stamps, "free" housing, "free" healthcare, etc., rather than helping them gain psychological independence and self-esteem. There were those who didn't care to put in the mental effort to improve their lives and preferred to rely on medication only. Any good value in life, especially learning introspective and better thinking skills is effortful. Some individuals wanted quick fixes. But, as the cognitive therapy saying goes, "Pills don't teach skills."

How did I deal with these infrequent situations? I learned from them. I asked myself: *Did I go off base? Could I have reached them in other ways?* If I felt that was the case, I grew in knowledge. If

I was convinced that I couldn't reach them, I reminded myself that their lives are theirs to control (or mess up, if they choose). If they are not invested in therapy, or if they'd prefer a different type of therapist, that is their right. They are in the driver's seat in their own life. This approach turned such "failures" into learning experiences and growth opportunities. Fortunately, I enjoy collaborating with my clients. I can happily look back at many individuals who liberated themselves from the grips of altruism and enjoyed their lives and relationships more.

I grew my career in other directions too—having a radio call-in talk show with my husband, *The Rational Basis of Happiness*, writing a book that Dr. Locke (the first author) and I are proud of: *The Selfish Path to Romance: How to Love with Passion and Reason* (2011b). I also taught psychology classes at the university, and I gave courses at summer conferences—including two with Dr. Locke. I would never have done any of these had I not discovered what we've shared with you in this chapter: that it is good and moral to own your own life (without ever violating anyone else's right to their own life), that I needed to set my own goals and pursue them, that I needed to learn how to cope well with setbacks.

On the home front: my husband and I were passionate about raising our two children and giving them the same philosophical basis (encouraging them to think independently and pursue their dreams). We remain very close with our "kids"—they are grown adults now. And I've enjoyed my delightfully playful, romantic relationship with my husband of many years. I never would have experienced such un-conflicted joy without a rational philosophy, Objectivism. I learned how to comfortably give myself a voice, and make independent decisions. I also pursued my hobbies: my husband and I love ballroom dancing and I'm a regular at the gym—a Zumba and yoga enthusiast (yoga without the mysticism). I have good relations (and proper boundaries) with my siblings, my parents, and my extended family. My life has had that lovely tempo that we want you to have also. I never burned out from being a therapist.

Warning: there is a cultural change that does not bode well for many of us; it is leading to burnout on a massive scale. Information is power and we hope this motivates you to protect yourself, and your loved ones, and fight for a country that respects our rights to life, liberty, and the pursuit of happiness. I wish what follows were not so.

I recently closed my practice. I had not planned on doing so. Over the past 20 years I have loved my career as a therapist. Writing this chapter with Dr. Locke helped me underscore that I never burned out: no emotional exhaustion, no depersonalization, and no sense of diminished personal accomplishment. I was (and still am) passionate about therapy and discovering the power of the right ideas.

But something external happened (situational factors): increasing government controls and Obamacare/ACA are continuing to cannibalize the flourishing landscape of the free market in medicine. Obama preaches altruism, "shared sacrifice" (not shared growth) on a daily basis. He's using the "moral code" of altruism as a weapon against good, productive, motivated, intelligent individuals. Many healthcare professionals feel *unearned* guilt for their virtues: their ambition, integrity, intelligence, and success, yet don't know how to fight the moral battle—to embrace egoism. Obama is creating a culture of unearned guilt, despondency, and cynicism—burnout—causing many, especially those in business or the helping professions, to adopt a foreshortened view of the future. Just as we saw altruism destroying the lives of individuals, when endorsed by a culture, altruism decays the hopes and dreams of its citizens.

Obamacare abruptly ended my career. From several sources, including the insurance companies, State Officials (from our Department of Health), and from my own colleagues, I learned that solo practice and fee-for-service models were an endangered species. I learned of the plans for intensified bureaucratic control—needless rules and regulations that we were being saddled with. I learned that healthcare is to be delivered in a new model, "medical health stations," controlled by the government (The Rhode Island Primary Care Trust 2013). I learned that personal therapy records need to be online—a major violation of privacy. I learned that clinical psychologists, increasingly being corralled into working for the state "for the good of others," had already started growing yet another government union with SEIU (Service Employees International Union).

Needless paperwork, rules and regulations, reduced choices in patients, types of treatment allowed, reduced remuneration, hovering bureaucrats who know little about the profession, looking for you to trip up on their petty controls, and lots more. The upshot? Loss of autonomy, decreased motivation, work overload—imposed by the new state medical model—and with it, emotional overload, more of an entitlement attitude by clients and patients, decreased respect and appreciation of our doctors and healthcare workers, decreased pay, increased cynicism, depersonalization and a diminished sense of personal accomplishment—that is, burnout. A fellow healthcare provider summed it up in two words, "fear and loathing." She was attending a full day seminar on the ongoing changes in healthcare delivery under Obamacare.

State-controlled healthcare was destroying my autonomy, my joy—my clinical practice. Decades ago, I did my dissertation on burnout in clinical psychologists when they lose their autonomy to a state-controlled healthcare system (Kenner 1992). I am keenly aware of the longer-range consequences of the destruction of the best healthcare system in the world. I made the decision to bow out of this nightmare. It is a recipe for doctor (and general) burnout on a massive scale. Leiter and Maslach's comment is worth repeating: "Micromanagement is a pervasive blight upon the work world. It reflects a misplaced confidence in the wisdom of central control" (2005, p. 72).

Ending my practice didn't end my career passions or my goal setting. I enjoy my radio show. I still see an occasional client who is not part of any insurance program. I promote the book that Ed and I wrote on romantic love. And I speak up about the dangers of altruism and burnout.

On a playful note, I continue to enjoy my personal values: my loving relationship with my husband (and ballroom dancing with him), my grown "kids," a tap dancing class with my sisters and niece, good times with friends, yoga, Zumba, and more.

Personal goal-setting in your career and other areas (e.g., hobbies, friendships) is the life-force of happiness—and makes you resistant to burnout. We wish you all a satisfying career, a healthier political climate in which you can pursue your professional goals in a free market ... and genuine happiness in your life.

References

Bahrer-Kohler, S. (2013). *Burnout for Experts*. New York: Springer.

Berglas, S. (2001). *Reclaiming the Fire*. New York: Random House.

Binswanger, Harry (1986). *The Ayn Rand Lexicon: Objectivism from A to Z*. New York: Penguin. Also available at: http://aynrandlexicon.com.

Borysenko, Joan (2011). *Fried: Why you Burn Out and How to Revive*. Carlsbad: Hay House.

CBS News (October 14, 2007). Dorothy Hamill's struggle with depression. Available at: http://www.cbsnews.com/news/dorothy-hamills-struggle-with-depression/, accessed February 2, 2014.

Freudenberger, Herbert J. and Richelson, G. (1980). *Burn-Out: The High Cost of High Achievement*. New York: Anchor Press.

Glouberman, Dina (2002). *The Joy of Burnout: How the End of the World can be a New Beginning*. Isle of Wight: Skyrosbooks.

Greenberger, Dennis and Padesky, Christine (1995). *Mind Over Mood: Change How You Feel by Changing the Way You Think*. New York: Guilford Press.

Greenblatt, Edy, with Michael Allan Kirk and Erin V. Lehman (2009). *Restore Yourself: The Antidote for Professional Exhaustion*. Los Angeles: Execu-Care Press.

Kenner, Ellen (1992). The clinical psychologist practitioner: Job autonomy and burnout. Unpublished doctoral dissertation, University of Rhode Island.

Leiter, Michael P. and Maslach, Christina (2005). *Banishing Burnout: Six Strategies for Improving Your Relationship with Work*. San Francisco: Jossey-Bass.

Locke, Edwin A. (1976). The nature and causes of job satisfaction. In M.D. Dunette (ed.), *Handbook of Industrial and Organizational Psychology* (pp. 1297–349). Chicago: Rand McNally College Publishing Company.

Locke, E.A. and Kenner, E. (2011a). How altruism undermines mental health and happiness. In A.G. Antoniou, C.L. Cooper, G.P. Chrousos, C.D. Spielberger, and M.W. Eysenck (eds), *Handbook of Managerial Behavior and Occupational Health* (pp. 179–92). Cheltenham: Edward Elgar.

Locke, E.A. and Kenner, E. (2011b). *The Selfish Path to Romance: How to Love with Passion and Reason*. PA: Platform Press.

Manago, C. (Author and Producer), Majo, K. (Editor), Freudenberger, H. (Consultant) (1982). *Burnout on the Job*. [Video and accompanying teacher's guide]. New York: Human Relations Media.

Maslach, C. (1982). *Burnout: The Cost of Caring*. New Jersey: Prentice Hall.

Maslach, C. (2003). *Burnout: The Cost of Caring*. CA: Malor (ISHK).

Maslach, C. and Jackson, S. (1986). *Human Services Survey*. Palo Alto: Consulting Psychologists.

Potter, B. (2005). *Burnout: How to Renew Enthusiasm at Work*. Berkeley: Ronin.

Rand, Ayn (1943). *The Fountainhead*. New York: Penguin.

Rand, Ayn (1957). *Atlas Shrugged*. New York: Penguin.

Rand, Ayn (1963). *For The New Intellectual*. New York: New American Library.

Rand, Ayn (1964). *The Virtue of Selfishness*. New York: New American Library.

Rand, Ayn (1982). *Philosophy: Who Needs It*. New York: Bobbs-Merrill.

The Rhode Primary Care Trust (2013). The Rhode Island Department of Health. Available at: http://www.health.ri.gov/publications/briefs/TheRhodeIslandPrimaryCareTrust.pdf, accessed April 4, 2014.

Tan, Michelle (2007, October 8). Skating through the sadness, *People Magazine*. Available at: http://www.people.com/people/archive/article/0,,20161033,00.html, accessed July 25, 2015.

Udovich, S.L. (1983). The effects of work environment and personality in burnout: A study of psychologists. Unpublished doctoral dissertation, United States International University.

7

Striving for a Stress-Free Workplace: Examining the Role of Positive Personality on Coping and Burnout

Nicholas J. Gailey and Tahira M. Probst

Introduction

The field of psychology has historically operated from the perspective of a "disease model" (Seligman 2002) in which researchers were primarily focused on negative aspects of psychological functioning that required a "cure" (e.g., depression, anxiety, schizophrenia). Such an approach focused on the abnormal or pathological in an attempt to repair damage and restore an individual to normalcy. In recent decades, however, the Positive Psychology movement has shifted this focus away from "fixing what is wrong" to "identifying and nurturing" that which is best in ourselves (Seligman 2002, p. 4).

In a similar fashion, industrial-organizational researchers have likewise begun to focus on the study of positive psychology in the workplace (PPW; Mills, Fleck, and Kozikowski 2013) in an effort to build upon employee strengths rather than merely rectify perceived weaknesses or shortcomings. PPW is the study of employees and organizations that are performing at high levels on various tasks and the promotion of strengths within employees and organizations to better enable them to flourish. Incorporating the positive side of the workplace has opened the door to understanding how employees and organizations function at their optimal levels rather than solely raising them up to an average level.

In this chapter, we focus on these positive aspects of employee personality that can better enable employees to cope with the myriad workplace stressors confronting workers today. Although organizations have long focused on the bottom line—"a do more for less" mentality that historically put profits over the welfare of employees (Turner, Barling, and Zacharatos 2002), the growth of technology, globalization, culturally diverse work groups, and changing employee and customer demands have added to the confluence of potential stressors facing employees. Today's employees work more part-time jobs, have multiple careers, work longer and more hours, and have greater work–family conflicts compared to employees from earlier generations

(Turner et al. 2002). Given these conditions, the most proactive organizations not only focus on their bottom line, but also seek to improve employee well-being and their overall experience at work by nurturing positive personality traits that can foster better coping (Mills et al. 2013). Such an increased organizational emphasis on social responsibility offers a unique contribution toward nurturing a healthy society (Cameron, Dutton, and Quinn 2003).

Below, we begin by providing a brief summary of Lazarus and Folkman's (1984) Transactional Model of Stress and Coping. Using this theoretical framework, we will review a number of positive personality traits and the mechanisms they use to influence primary appraisals, secondary appraisals, and coping efforts for workplace stress. Next, we will discuss how organizations can promote these strengths within their employees and evaluate the extent to which organizational interventions to promote these positive personality traits have proven successful. Lastly, we will consider the limitations in the literature and suggest possible directions for future research.

Theoretical Framework Relating Positive Personality Traits to Coping with Job Stress

Most contemporary behavioral science models of stress acknowledge that a complete understanding of the structure and process of stress requires a consideration of both person and environment characteristics (Sulsky and Smith 2005). Such models originally arose from an awareness that purely biological models of stress fail to reliably predict which potential stressors will be perceived as stressful and how this process is influenced by personal and contextual factors. In particular, Lazarus and Folkman's (1984) Transactional Model of Stress and Coping posits that there are few, if any, universal stressors. Rather, the perception of and reactions to a potential stressor will vary within and across individuals and may differ over occasions and time. Whether the potential stressor is perceived to be stressful, therefore, intimately depends on characteristics of the individual (e.g., needs, abilities, personality) and the situation (e.g., demands, resources). In other words, stress is a function of a person to environment transaction. When faced with a potential stressor, individuals first evaluate the situation and what it means to them as a potential threat (primary appraisal). Specifically, primary appraisal is an individual's assessment of the possible effects of the demands and available resources on their well-being. The individual makes judgments about the event (e.g., is it benign, positive, irrelevant, challenging, stressful, and/ or harmful?). A perception of threat triggers the secondary appraisal process, which consists of the individual's evaluation regarding their ability to manage the situation and the availability of resources needed to cope with the threat. In other words, the secondary appraisal process involves determining what coping resources are available and whether these will be effective at contending with the threat. Coping efforts refer to those strategies and resources actually used to combat the potential stressors. Finally, as new information regarding the threat and/or available resources becomes available, reappraisal might occur.

We argue below that a variety of positive personality traits can influence both the primary and secondary appraisal processes, as well as influence the nature and extent of coping resources that employees can bring to bear when faced with workplace stressors. Thus, these personality traits not only may serve to reduce the perception of a stressor, but they may also serve to mitigate the felt threat and offer valuable resources needed to successfully cope with the stressor. As a result, these traits may also ultimately lead to lower levels of burnout as a result.

Following the seminal article on negative affectivity by Watson and Clark (1984), many job stress researchers considered personality characteristics as statistical noise whose influence required partialing out. However, Spector, Zapf, Chen, and Frese (2000) convincingly argued that such characteristics were not something to be statistically controlled for, but rather represented substantive constructs of interest when attempting to understand how employees perceive and react to potential job stressors. Although they were primarily concerned with the construct of negative affectivity, many of their arguments for the roles of disposition in the job stress process are similarly applicable to other traits. Three proposed mechanisms are particularly salient to the current chapter: the perception mechanism, the stressor creation mechanism, and the hyper-responsivity mechanism. First, they argued that personality can influence the primary appraisal process by impacting the extent to which employees perceive their jobs as having high levels of stressors (i.e., the perception mechanism). Second, they argued that personality can influence on-the-job behaviors that might influence objectively higher or lower levels of job stressors such as interpersonal conflict, time management, etc. (i.e., the stressor creation mechanism). Finally, the hyper-responsivity mechanism contends that personality can influence the strain response that employees have to job stressors, i.e., their ability to effectively cope with the stressors.

Although Spector et al. (2000) were primarily concerned with negative affectivity, we argue that these same mechanisms may be at play when considering the potentially beneficial effects of positive personality traits. Specifically, employees with high levels of positive personality traits may create job conditions that are lower in objective stressors. When potential stressors are present, they may be less likely to perceive them as a threat. Finally, when stress is present, they may have more numerous and more effective coping resources to respond to the threat. Below we discuss the evidence for each of these propositions.

Positive Personality Traits and the Stress Appraisal Process

While there are many important personality traits, it is impossible to address all within this short chapter. Therefore, we restrict our review to those traits that have been most researched with respect to the positive role that they can play in creating a stress-free workplace. This includes: positive affectivity, subjective well-being, extraversion, psychological capital, hardiness, and internal locus of control. Below we discuss each in greater detail and describe how these traits can influence the primary and secondary appraisal processes.

POSITIVE AFFECTIVITY

Positive affectivity (PA) refers to a trait that contains the pleasurable engagement with the environment (Rydstedt, Johnsen, Lundh, and Devereux 2013). Individuals high on this dimension experience positive moods and emotions when encountering circumstances that they desire (Lyubomirsky, King, and Diener 2005). Some of the characteristics of PA include happiness, cheerful, enthusiastic, energetic, confident, alert, optimistic, self-efficacy, active, and social (Lyubomirsky et al. 2005; Watson and Naragon 2009). This means that individuals with high PA will view situations with a positive primary appraisal, whereas individuals low on PA will view it with a negative primary appraisal. In other words, individuals that experience more PA could view work situations as nonthreatening or beneficial to their work life, whereas low PA individuals may have a tendency to view them as stressful or potentially harmful events. Also, individuals with high levels of PA could experience more positive secondary appraisals because these individuals are more confident and optimistic about situations that arise compared to individuals with low PA scores. Thus, these individuals may be more likely to perceive a stressful event as something that they can overcome (e.g., a challenge). It is important to note that high PA individuals do not have an absence of negative emotions; rather, they experience more positive emotions than negative emotions. PA has been found to be moderately stable over time and across situations (Naragon and Watson 2009), but that is not to say that individuals cannot increase their PA (as we will later discuss).

SUBJECTIVE WELL-BEING

Subjective well-being (SWB) is the global evaluation of one's life. According to Diener (1984), SWB is composed of an individual's cognitive and affective evaluations of their life. In Diener's work, SWB is considered the same as hedonic well-being, which is the pursuit of happiness and the pleasant life (Chen, Jing, Hayes, and Lee 2013). The cognitive components are the individual's conscious appraisals of conditions in their life (Diener 2000) and a global evaluation of their life's satisfaction as a whole (Diener 1994). The affective component is a hedonic appraisal guided by the individual's emotions; individuals experience more positive emotions than negative emotions in reaction to their lives (Diener 2000). In other words, SWB is experienced when individuals have low levels of negative emotions, high levels of positive emotions, and high evaluations of their life satisfaction as a whole. Individuals that score high on SWB will experience events with a positive primary appraisal compared to individuals that score low on SWB. These individuals would view various work situations and events as benign-positive events, whereas low SWB could view them as threatening or harmful to their well-being.

   This construct has been viewed as the measure for happiness in one's life. Happiness (SWB) is not a product of an individual's age, sex, ethnicity, or income level (Myers and Diener 1995); rather, it is derived from the inner traits that individuals possess. Happy individuals have higher self-esteem, a greater sense of personal control, greater optimism, and lower perceived stress (Myers and Diener 1995; Schiffrin and Nelson 2010). Individuals that are happy like themselves more than people who are not happy, which is the result of higher self-esteem within those individuals (Myers and Diener 1995). Individuals that have personal control feel empowered to do better and live a happier life (Myers and Diener 1995), which leads to greater success and progress toward personal goals. Individuals high on SWB have greater health outcomes (i.e., psychological and physical) and they experience more joy in life. The relationship between SWB and PA is very clear because SWB needs the affective component to create high levels of happiness. Specifically, when individuals experience more PA than negative affectivity and they are satisfied with their life as a whole then these individuals experience higher levels of SWB. As it was with PA, high SWB individuals could experience more positive secondary appraisals as well, because they have greater personal control and they are more optimistic than low SWB individuals. This means that they would evaluate the use of their internal strengths (i.e., optimism and personal control) as something that can be used to overcome the threat.

EXTRAVERSION

This Big Five personality trait is manifested in an outgoing, talkative, energetic individual. Extraversion is related to assertiveness, ambitiousness, dominance, and sociability (Judge, Higgins, Thoresen, and Barrick 1999). Extraverts become energized when around other coworkers. They have a great ability to make small talk and they think when they are talking, unlike introverts who think before they speak. Extraverts view events as a challenge (i.e., a positive primary appraisal), whereas neurotics perceive it as a threat (i.e., a negative primary appraisal) (Gallagher 1990). Although this trait is fairly stable across time, most people have a mix of both extraversion and introversion characteristics.

Although introversion is not a negative personality trait, extraverts have more coworker friends and take on more leadership roles than do introverts (Judge et al. 1999), which creates larger social networks for them to rely upon when exposed to potential job stressors. These individuals seek out social interaction and enjoy being in large social gatherings such as concerts, parties, and community groups. Since extraverts have greater external coping options (i.e., social support), they are more likely to have positive secondary appraisal compared to introverts. Extraverts have additional coping options that introverts do not, which would give them more options to evaluate when making the secondary appraisal.

The relationship between extraversion and SWB is very strong; happy people tend to be extraverted because they are happy alone or with other individuals (Myers and Diener 1995). Extraverts are happy whether they live alone or with others and if they live in a big city or small town (Myers and Diener 1995). In other words, they experience more positive emotions in life situations with or without people compared to introverts. Extraverts experience more happiness, life satisfaction, PA, and quality of life than do introverts (Steel, Schmidt, and Shultz 2008). That being said, the relationship between extraversion and PA is quite clear. Individuals that are extraverted are happier (i.e., SWB) and experience higher levels of PA (Pavot, Diener, and Fujita 1990).

PSYCHOLOGICAL CAPITAL

Psychological Capital (PsyCap) is a multifaceted construct that consists of four positive personality strengths: self-efficacy, hope, resilience, and optimism. The first strength is *self-efficacy*, which is an individual's belief in their ability to succeed in executing the required behavior for the situation (Bandura 1977). People with strong self-efficacy view challenges as tasks that can be mastered. Employees with strong self-efficacy have higher levels of effort and persistence when learning difficult tasks and they have increased performance while on the job (Lunenburg 2011). The second strength is *hope*, which is a trait that is goal-directed thinking in which people perceive that they can find a pathway to desired goals and they have the motivation to use those pathways (Snyder 2000). Hopeful employees overcome adversity easier, and they bounce back with stronger effectiveness (Youssef and Luthans 2007). The third strength is *resilience*, which is the capacity to rebound from adversity, conflict, failure, and increased responsibility (Luthans 2002). Resilient employees recover from workplace adversities and they grow and learn through those challenges (Youssef and Luthans 2007). For example, if a resilient employee were to be demoted, they would learn from the experience rather than allow it to affect their work. On the other hand, an employee that is not resilient might take this event personally and possibly quit. The fourth strength is *optimism*, which is the global generalized tendency to believe that one will experience positive outcomes over negative ones (Scheier and Carver 1985). Optimistic employees have higher workplace performance and retention with their organizations (Luthans, Luthans, and Luthans 2004). Employees that are optimistic do not dwell on the negative side of work; rather, they see the best that work provides them. For example, optimistic employees could view downsizing as a necessary means because of the economy, while other employees would see it as unnecessary and an attack on them.

Individuals with high levels of PsyCap exhibit more evidence of positive secondary appraisals because they view situations as a challenge that can be overcome. These individuals are persistent, motivated, and they have high belief in their own abilities which creates stronger internal coping options during secondary appraisal compared to individuals with lower levels of PsyCap. PsyCap is also associated with desirable employee attitudes, behaviors, and performance (Avey, Reichard, Luthans, and Mhatre 2011). Employees with high PsyCap support organizational and leadership changes (Avey, Luthans, and Wernsing 2008), report higher job satisfaction, and demonstrate greater engagement within their organization (Larson, Norman, Hughes, and Avey 2013). PsyCap is directly related to SWB (Avey, Luthans, Smith, and Palmer 2010) and PA (Avey Coping, Personality and the Workplace al. 2008). In other words, individuals with high PsyCap are happier people and experience more positive emotions than negative emotions. Furthermore, extroverted individuals scored higher on all four dimensions of PsyCap, which means that extraverts exhibit hope, resilience, optimism, and self-efficacy more than introverts (Brandt, Gomes, and Boyanova 2011).

HARDY PERSONALITY

Hardiness consist of three components; control beliefs, commitment, and challenge. It is a resource for resistance against stressful life events that an individual encounters (Parkes 1994). Hardy individuals display commitment or involvement in daily activities, view threats or unexpected changes as a positive challenge, and believe they have control of their lives (Allred and Smith 1989). This means that hardy individuals have a positive secondary appraisal when facing stressors; they believe that they have control over the circumstance and that they will be effective at overcoming the stressful event. They have a strong sense of purpose in life and challenges are seen as something to overcome rather than something stressful. Hardy employees will attack challenges and focus their attention on accomplishing the goal, while other employees may experience stress in response to that same challenge. Hardiness is the individual level pathway that leads to resilient outcomes.

Hardiness is highly correlated with SWB (DeNeve and Cooper 1998), which also includes increased PA. Individuals with high self-efficacy and hardy personality both feel deep commitment to various aspects of their lives. Hardy individuals see challenges as something that will change, however individuals with high self-efficacy see challenge as something stable over time. Hardiness, optimism, and self-efficacy all use some form of goal-directed behaviors, which is used as an internal coping option during the secondary appraisal process. These relationships between components of PsyCap (i.e., optimism and self-efficacy) and hardiness suggest a relationship between the constructs. Extraversion has been found to be positively correlated with hardiness (Parkes and Rendell 1988). In other words, hardy individuals are more likely to be extraverts because they have common characteristics such as stability, flexibility, optimism, sociability, active orientation, and an enjoyment of novelty and challenge (Parkes and Rendell 1988).

INTERNAL LOCUS OF CONTROL

An internal locus of control is a personality characteristic that a person holds about their power, control, and influence over the outcome of various situations (Taylor and Cooper 1989). These individuals believe in their own ability to control themselves and they have a strong belief about their influence over the world around them. In other words, they believe that their future is in their hands and that their hard work and decisions will lead them to success and/or failure. For example, internal locus of control would view being late for work as something internal (e.g., I forgot to set my alarm clock); whereas external locus of control would view being late to work as something external (e.g., the traffic was crazy this morning). "Internals" give more personal effort and ability (Parkes 1994) to personal health and health related behaviors (Taylor and Cooper 1989). Internal locus of control has been found to increase academic performance (Gifford, Briceño-Perriott, and Mianzo 2006) and be related to higher self-motivation and social maturity (Nelson and Mathias 1995). This means that internal locus of control individuals have a positive secondary appraisal when facing stressors; they believe that they have control over the circumstance and that they will be effective at overcoming the stressful event.

Internal locus of control is positively correlated with subjective well-being and positive affectivity (Kulshrestha and Sen 2006). Moreover, extraversion has been shown to have a positive correlation with internal locus of control (Organ 1975). "Internals" are better able to tolerate ambiguous situations, better at resisting coercion; have lower anxiety, less depression, and less helplessness (Singh and Mansi 2009). They experience more positive emotions than negative emotions and have a happier outlook on life than external locus of control individuals. Internal locus of control is also directly correlated with hardiness because they both view events as a challenge and they feel that they are in control of their lives.

Positive Personality Characteristics: Coping with Job Stress and Burnout

How we perceive our work experiences, both negative and positive, can be instrumental in influencing how we interpret potential workplace stressors and how we experience and cope with workplace stress. In addition to influencing the primary and secondary appraisal processes, the positive personality characteristics described above have also been shown to be excellent traits for combating workplace stress and burnout by fostering more effective coping resources and strategies.

POSITIVE AFFECTIVITY AND SUBJECTIVE WELL-BEING

It has been theorized that individuals who cope effectively with stress in part handle stressful situations through their ability to maintain positive emotions (Tugade, Fredrickson, and Barrett 2004). Individuals with high levels of SWB feel more empowered, which in turn should help them to cope better with stress (Myers and Diener 1995). Thus, PA should counteract stressful situations and contribute to greater psychological and physical well-being via more effective coping with challenges and stressful situations (Lyubomirsky et al. 2005). In support of this, Yavas, Karatepe, and Babakus (2011) found that positive affectivity attenuated the adverse effects of interrole conflicts on employee job performance and turnover intentions. Additionally, Zellars, Hochwater, Hoffman, Perrewé, and Ford (2004) found that employees with high PA had lower levels of burnout and perceptions of personal accomplishments. Similarly, Gloria, Faulk, and Steinhardt (2013) found that PA had a direct positive effect on resilience and a direct negative effect on burnout. Indeed, in a meta-analysis conducted by Alarcon, Eschleman, and Bowling (2009), PA was found to have a strong negative association with burnout. Moreover, PA completely mediated the relationship between job stress and resilience indicating that PA functions by enabling more successful adaptation to job stress.

EXTRAVERSION

Extraverts use problem focused coping strategies (e.g., re-appraisal) and adaptive forms of emotion focused coping strategies (e.g., seeking social support and positive thinking) when coping with workplace stressors. Extraverts have been shown to be negatively associated with burnout because they perceive work situations more positively compared to introverts (Alarcon et al.

2009). Additionally, Sur and Ng (2014) proposed that extraversion will lead to lower perceived workplace stress, which could be the result of increased social connections while on the job. Extraverted employees experience lower levels of emotional exhaustion and burnout (Anvari, Kalali, and Gholipour, 2011; Zellars et al. 2004), which may reflect the effectiveness of their coping resources to combat the stressful situations. In addition, extraverted employees have a greater sense of personal accomplishments while on the job because their social network provides feedback and support, which is a coping mechanism they use during stressful on-the-job situations (Zellars et al. 2004).

PSYCHOLOGICAL CAPITAL

Research suggests that PsyCap is associated with reduced perceptions of job stress (Avey, Luthans, and Jensen 2009) and that PsyCap represents a constellation of developable traits. Sur and Ng (2014) propose that increasing self-efficacy (a key construct in PsyCap) will lead to lower perceived workplace stress because the employees will believe in their own ability to complete their tasks and reach their goals. PsyCap has also been found to be negatively associated with burnout in the employees (Mills et al. 2013), suggesting that individuals with higher levels of PsyCap have more effective coping mechanisms to overcome workplace stress before it leads to burnout. Similarly, in Alarcon et al.'s (2009) meta-analysis, they found that optimism and self-efficacy were associated with lower levels of emotional exhaustion, reduced personal accomplishment, and depersonalization (the three key components of burnout). Finally, research indicates individuals high in PsyCap use both problem-focused and emotion-focused coping strategies while dealing with the stressors on the job, have better coping resources, lower perceived job stress, decreased turnover, lower absenteeism, and lower levels of burnout than employees who score lower on PsyCap (Avey et al. 2009; Avey, Patera, and West 2006; Avey et al. 2011).

HARDINESS

Hardy individuals are confident at implement effective solutions when they come across problems. Soderstrom, Dolbier, Leiferman, and Steinhardt (2000) found that hardiness was inversely related to avoidance coping strategies but directly related to approach coping strategies. This means that hardy individuals approach stressful or challenging situations, instead of avoiding them, which gives these individuals the most direct pathway for coping with the stressor head on. Similiarly, Alarcon et al. (2009) found that hardiness was negatively associated with burnout. Other research indicates this relationship is due to more active coping mechanisms (Garrosa, Rainho, Moreno-Jimenez, and Monteiro, 2010). Hardy individuals have the commitment to make it through, the personal control to see it through, and they view stressful events as a challenge which they can overcome (Beasley, Thompson, and Davidson 2003; Kobasa 1979). These approach coping mechanisms drive the hardy individual to be resilient and overcome the stressors in their lives.

LOCUS OF CONTROL

Internals believe that they are in control of their own destiny and their behavior is a direct representation of what they receive. Ng, Sorensen, and Eby (2006) argued that internal locus of control is positively associated with increased job motivation, positive task experiences, and positive social experiences. In other words, they experience different appraisals and view them in a positive light while they continue to be motivated to approach the stressors that do arise. Similarly, internals put in more effort and ability when facing challenges or stressors (Parkes 1994) and they do this with higher self-motivation (Nelson and Mathias 1995). They utilize an approach-focused coping strategy, in which they directly confront the stressor in an effort to find more effective ways to deal with the stressor (e.g., through reappraisal, obtaining more information, generating new productive ways to handle the situation). As a result, not surprisingly, Alarcon et al. (2009) found that internal locus of control was negatively associated with burnout.

Promoting Positive Personality Traits among Employees

The above review indicates that there are numerous beneficial effects associated with positive personality traits with respect to perceiving, responding to, and coping with job stress. Thus, the next question is how employees and organizations can best promote these positive personality strengths. Fortunately, research indicates that there are several promising avenues and that many of these positive strengths and psychological capacities can be developed (Luthans 2002).

Froman (2009) suggests that there are three different strategies that organizations can use to promote human resource resilience. First, organizations should promote a "supportive environment" in that the organization impacts their employee's job satisfaction and commitment positively. Second, organizations should cultivate an "ethical and trustworthy culture" which will seek input from various areas of the organization so that the decision-making process encompasses everyone that is affected by the changes. Lastly, organizations should target training programs that improve employee performance and that push for a competitive edge for the organization as well as organizational designs that push for team work. This will create a supportive and collaborative culture which will promote human resource resilience.

Empirical research suggests that PsyCap resources can be developed through brief training interventions (Luthans, Avey, and Patera 2008; Luthans, Avey, Avolio, Norman, and Combs 2006; Luthans, Avey, Avolio, and Peterson 2010). Moreover, PsyCap resources tend to persist over time (Peterson, Luthans, Avolio, Walumbwa, and Zhang 2011). Web-based PsyCap interventions focus on asking employees to reflect on work circumstances where they have seen PsyCap constructs in the workplace (Mills et al. 2013). Avey et al. (2009) found that PsyCap interventions can be effectively utilized to lower workplace stress and turnover.

Recently, a growing research interest in PPW is the potential utility of appreciative inquiry (AI) interventions. AI is a change management approach that focuses on promoting what is working well for the organization and employees (Cooperrider, Whitney and Stravros 2008). These interventions consist of asking questions that seeks to change the perception that the employee has about the organization in positive ways. It is a four phase process (i.e., discover, dream, design, and destiny) which is the process that individuals take to foster their AI (Mills et al. 2013). Organizations and employees that use these interventions have shown to foster hope, excitement (e.g., PA), and enthusiasm in the employees (Stellnberger 2010). Employees can also promote their own SWB through gratitude interventions. Gratitude interventions increase the individuals SWB (Emmons and McCullough 2003) and increased PA (Kaplan, Bradley-Geist, Ahmad, Anderson, Hargrove, and Lindsey 2013). Furthermore, in a meta-analysis conducted by Mesmer-Magnus, Glew, and Viswesvaran (2012), they found that employee humor is associated with greater satisfaction and coping effectiveness, as well as lower workplace stress and burnout.

A growing body of research also suggests the fruitfulness of creating positive organizational experiences as they have been shown to increase the experience of positive emotions. For example, Gloria et al. (2013) suggest that organizations should create opportunities for positive emotions particularly during times of stressful working conditions as such emotions enable more effective coping and subsequently lower levels of burnout. In support of this, Bono, Glomb, Shen, Kim, and Koch (2012) found that naturally occurring positive work events and a positive reflection intervention were both associated with reduced job stress and improved health outcomes. As such, they concluded that organizations should focus not only on reducing negative events, but also on proactively increasing positive events in order to facilitate positive employee outcomes.

Limitations and Future Directions

Like the field of psychology in general, industrial-organizational research has focused on the negative within organizations for far too long, which has resulted in limited research on the positive development of organizations. Although there is growing interest in PPW, PPW research is still new and many opportunities exist for future substantive exploration, including: AI interventions; gratitude interventions and coping with job stress; pride in the organization and burnout; and positive organizational teams and their effect on job-related stress and burnout. Understanding the most effective ways for employees and organizations to function at optimal levels will help create workforces that have better coping resources for job stress, which will decrease the employees level of burnout and in turn improve the overall well-being of their employees.

In addition to substantive research needs, methodological improvements are needed as well. Longitudinal designs should be implemented to better evaluate the effectiveness of interventions (e.g., PsyCap, gratitude, and AI interventions) on enabling better coping resources, decreasing employee levels of burnout, and increasing their SWB. Perhaps the most serious limitations with the literature are that most of the data is self-reported, which can inflate relationships and cause individuals to respond with social desirability bias. Different studies have also relied on a myriad of different scales to measure ostensibly the same latent trait (e.g., PA measured with Positive and Negative Affect Schedule (PANAS), Satisfaction with Life Scale (SWLS), Subjective Happiness Scale (SHS), and Oxford Happiness Inventory). Such scales could be measuring similar but not entirely the same constructs (Diener, Emmons, Larsen, and Griffin 1985; Hills and Argyle 2002; Lyubomirsky and Lepper 1999; Watson, Clark, and Tellegen 1988). Additional psychometric research may be warranted to ensure that different empirical results across different studies are due to substantive reasons rather than psychometric non-equivalence (cf. Rydstedt et al. 2013, and Zellars et al. 2004 in evaluating the relationship between PA and perceived stress).

Conclusion

The extant literature suggests that there may be stress-free personality characteristics that organizations can promote for their employees to flourish. Although more research still needs to be conducted, it appears that individuals who display more positive emotions, are happier, more extroverted, hardier, and have higher levels of PsyCap, tend to: (1) perceive fewer job stressors; (2) evaluate those stressors as being less threatening; and (3) have more effective coping resources to navigate today's work environment and respond to job stress. Importantly, research indicates that many of these positive personality characteristics are developable suggesting that they are amenable to organizational intervention. Given this, an increased focus by organizational researchers on PPW and positive personality traits may be a fruitful way to increase employee well-being and ultimately improve organizational performance.

References

Alarcon, G., Eschleman, K.J. and Bowling, N.A. (2009). Relationships between personality variables and burnout: A meta-analysis. *Work & Stress*, 23(3), 244–63.

Allred, K.D. and Smith, T.W. (1989). The hardy personality: Cognitive and physiological responses to evaluative threat. *Journal of Personality and Social Psychology*, 56(2), 257–66.

Anvari, M.R.A., Kalali, N.S. and Gholipour, A. (2011). How does personality affect on job burnout? *International Journal of Trade, Economics, and Finance*, 2(2), 115–19.

Avey, J.B., Luthans, F. and Jensen, S. (2009). Psychological capital: A positive resource for combating employee stress and turnover. *Human Resource Management*, 48, 677–93.

Avey, J.B., Luthans, F. and Wernsing, S. (2008). Can positive employees help positive organizational change? Impact of psychological capital and emotions on relevant attitudes and behaviors. *The Journal of Applied Behavioral Science*, 44(1), 48–70.

Avey, J.B., Patera, J.L., and West, B.J. (2006). The implications of positive psychological capital on employee absebteeism. *Journal of Leadership & Organizational Studies*, 13(2), 42–60.

Avey, J.B., Luthans, F., Smith, R.M. and Palmer, N.F. (2010). Impact of positive psychological capital on employee well-being over time. *Journal of Occupational Health Psychology*, 15, 17–28.

Avey, J.B., Reichard, R.J., Luthans, F. and Mhatre, K.H. (2011). Meta-analysis of the impact of positive psychological capital on employee attitudes, behaviors, and performance. *Human Resource Development Quarterly*, 22, 127–52.

Bandura, A. (1977). Self-efficacy: Towards a unifying theory of behavior change. *Psychological Review*, 84, 191–215.

Beasley, M., Thompson, T. and Davidson, J. (2003). Resilience in response to life stress: The effects of coping style and cognitive hardiness. *Personality and Individual Differences*, 34, 77–95.

Bono, J., Glomb, T., Shen, W., Kim, E. and Koch, A. (2012). Building positive resources: Effects of positive events and positive reflection on work-stress and health. *Academy of Management Journal*, amj-2011.

Brandt, T., Gomes, J.F. and Boyanova, D. (2011). Personality and psychological capital as indicators of future job success? *Liiketaloudellinen Aikakauskirja*, 3, 263–89.

Cameron, K., Dutton, J. and Quinn, R.E. (eds) (2003). *Positive Organizational Scholarship: Foundations of a New Discipline*. San Francisco: Berrett-Koehler Publishers.

Chen, F.F., Jing, Y., Hayes, A. and Lee, J.M. (2013). Two concepts or two approaches? A bifactor analysis of psychological and subjective well-being. *Journal of Happiness Studies*, 14(3), 1033–68.

Cooperrider, D.L., Whitney, D. and Stavros, J.M. (2008). *Appreciative Inquiry Handbook: For Leaders of Change* (2nd edn). San Francisco: Berrett-Koehler Publishers.

DeNeve, K.M. and Cooper, H. (1998). The happy personality: A meta-analysis of 137 personality traits and subjective well-being. *Psychological Bulletin*, 124, 197–229.

Diener, E. (1984). Subjective well-being. *Psychological Bulletin*, 95, 542–75.

Diener, E. (1994). Assessing subjective well-being: Progress and opportunities. *Social Indicators Research*, 31, 103–57.

Diener, E. (2000). Subjective well-being: The science of happiness and a proposal for a national index. *The American Psychologist*, 55, 34–43.

Diener, E.D., Emmons, R.A., Larsen, R.J., and Griffin, S. (1985). The satisfaction with life scale. *Journal of Personality Assessment*, 49(1), 71–5.

Emmons, R.A. and McCullough, M.E. (2003). Counting blessings versus burdens: An experimental investigation of gratitude and subjective well-being in daily life. *Journal of Personality and Social Psychology*, 84, 377–89.

Froman, L. (2009). Positive psychology in the workplace. *Journal of Adult Development*, 17, 59–69.

Gallagher, D.J. (1990). Extraversion, neuroticism, and appraisal of stressful academic events. *Personality and Individual Differences*, 2, 1053–7.

Garrosa, E., Rainho, C., Moreno-Jimenez, B. and Monteiro, M.J. (2010). The relationship between job stressors, hardy personality, coping resources and burnout in a sample of nurses: A correlational study at two time points. *International Journal of Nursing Studies*, 47, 205–15.

Gifford, D.D., Briceño-Perriott, J. and Mianzo, F. (2006). Locus of control: Academic achievement and retention in a sample of university first-year students, *Journal of College Admission*, 191, 18–25.

Gloria, C.T., Faulk, K.E. and Steinhardt, M.A. (2013). Positive affectivity predicts successful and unsuccessful adaptation to stress. *Motivation and Emotion*, 37(1), 185–93.

Hills, P. and Argyle, M. (2002). The Oxford Happiness Questionnaire: A compact scale for the measurement of psychological well-being. *Personality and Individual Differences*, 33(7), 1073–82.

Judge, T.A., Higgins, C.A., Thoresen, C.J. and Barrick, M.R. (1999). The big five personality traits, general mental ability, and career success across the life span. *Personnel Psychology*, 52, 621–52.

Kaplan, S., Bradley-Geist, J.C., Ahmad, A., Anderson, A., Hargrove, A.K. and Lindsey, A. (2013). A test of two positive psychology interventions to increase employee well-being. *Journal of Business Psychology*, 29, 367–80.

Kobasa, S.C. (1979). Stressful life events, personality and health: An inquiry into hardiness. *Journal of Personality and Social Psychology*, 37, 1–11.

Kulshrestha, U. and Sen, C. (2006). Subjective well-being in relation to emotional intelligence and locus of control among executives. *Journal of the Indian Academy of Applied Psychology*, 32, 93–8.

Larson, M.D., Norman, S.M., Hughes, L.W. and Avey, J.B. (2013). Psychological capital: A new lens for understanding employee fit and attitudes. *International Journal of Leadership Studies*, 8(1), 28–43.

Lazarus, R. and Folkman, S. (1984). *Stress, Appraisal, and Coping*. New York: Springer Publishing Company.

Lunenburg, F.C. (2011). Self-efficacy in the workplace: Implications for motivation and performance. *International Journal of Management, Business, and Administration*, 14(1), 1–6.

Luthans, F. (2002). The need for and meaning of positive organizational behavior. *Journal of Organizational Behavior*, 23, 695–706.

Luthans, F., Avey, J.B. and Patera, J.L. (2008). Experimental analysis of a web-based training intervention to develop positive psychological capital. *Academy of Management Learning & Education*, 7(2), 209–21.

Luthans, F., Luthans, K.W. and Luthans, B.C. (2004). Positive psychological capital: Beyond human and social capital. *Business Horizons*, 47(1), 45–50.

Luthans, F., Avey, J.B., Avolio, B.J. and Peterson, S.J. (2010). The development and resulting performance impact of positive psychological capital. *Human Resource Development Quarterly*, 21(1), 41–67.

Luthans, F., Avey, J.B., Avolio, B.J., Norman, S.M. and Combs, G.M. (2006). Psychological capital development: Toward a micro-intervention. *Journal of Organizational Behavior*, 27(3), 387–93.

Lyubomirsky, S. and Lepper, H.S. (1999). A measure of subjective happiness: Preliminary reliability and construct validation. *Social Indicators Research*, 46(2), 137–55.

Lyubomirsky, S., King, L. and Diener, E. (2005). The benefits of frequent positive affect: Does happiness lead to success? *Psychology Bulletin*, 131(6), 803–55.

Mesmer-Magnus, J., Glew, D.J. and Viswesvaran, C. (2012). A meta-analysis of positive humor in the workplace. *Journal of Managerial Psychology*, 27(2), 155–90.

Mills, M.J., Fleck, C.R. and Kozikowski, A. (2013). Positive psychology at work: A conceptual review, state-of-practice assessment, and a look ahead. *Journal of Positive Psychology*, 8(2), 153–64.

Myers, D.G. and Diener, E. (1995). Who is happy? *Psychological Science*, 6(1), 10–19.

Naragon, K. and Watson, D. (2009). Positive affectivity. In *The Encyclopedia of Positive Psychology*. Hoboken: Wiley-Blackwell, 707–11.

Nelson, E.S. and Mathias, K.E. (1995). The relationships among college students locus of control, learning styles and self-prediction of grades. *Education Research and Perspectives*, 22, 110–17.

Ng, T.W.H., Sorensen, K.L. and Eby, L.T. (2006). Locus of control at work: A meta-analysis. *Journal of Organizational Behavior*, 27, 1057–87.

Organ, D.W. (1975). Extraversion, locus of control, and individual differences in conditionability in organizations. *Journal of Applied Psychology*, 60(3), 401–4.

Parkes, K.R. (1994). Personality and coping as moderators of work stress process: Models, methods and measures. *Work & Stress*, 8(2), 110–29.

Parkes, K.R. and Rendell, D. (1988). The hardy personality and its relationship to extraversion and neuroticism. *Person Individual Differences*, 9(4), 785–90.

Pavot, W., Diener, E. and Fujita, F. (1990). Extraversion and happiness. *Personality and Individual Differences*, 11(12), 1299–306.

Peterson, S.J., Luthans, F., Avolio, B.J., Walumbwa, F.O. and Zhang, Z. (2011). Psychological capital and employee performance: A latent growth modeling approach. *Personnel Psychology*, 64(2), 427–50.

Rydstedt, L.W., Johnsen, S.A.K., Lundh, M. and Devereux, J.J. (2013). The conceptual roles of negative and positive affectivity in the stressor-strain relationship. *Europe's Journal of Psychology*, 9(1), 93–103.

Scheier, M.F. and Carver, C.S. (1985). Optimism, coping, and health: Assessment and implications of generalized outcome expectancies. *Health Psychology*, 4(3), 219–47.

Schiffrin, H.H. and Nelson, S.K. (2010). Stressed and happy? Investigating the relationship between happiness and perceived stress. *Journal of Happiness Studies*, 11, 33–9.

Seligman, M.E. (2002). Positive psychology, positive prevention, and positive therapy. *Handbook of Positive Psychology*, 2, 3–12.

Singh, S. and Mansi, S. (2009). Psychological capital as predictor of psychological well being. *Journal of the Indian Academy of Applied Psychology*, 35(2), 233–8.

Snyder, C.R. (2000). *Handbook of Hope*. San Diego: Academic Press.

Soderstrom, M., Dolbier, C., Leiferman, J. and Steinhardt, M. (2000). The relationship of hardiness, coping strategies, and perceived stress to symptoms of illness. *Journal of Behavioral Medicine*, 23(3), 311–28.

Spector, P.E., Zapf, D., Chen, P.Y. and Frese, M. (2000). Why negative affectivity should not be controlled in job stress research: Don't throw out the baby with the bath water. *Journal of Organizational Behaviour*, 21(1), 79–95.

Steel, P., Schmidt, J. and Shultz, J. (2008). Refining the relationship between personality and subjective well-being. *Psychological Bulletin*, 134(1), 138–61.

Stellnberger, M. (2010). *Evaluation of Appreciative Inquiry Interventions* (Doctoral dissertation, Victoria University of Wellington).

Sulsky, I. and Smith, C. (2005). *Work Stress*. Belmont: Thomson Wadsworth.

Sur, S. and Ng, E.S. (2014). Extending theory on job stress: The interaction between the "other 3"and "big 5" personality traits on job stress. *Human Resource Development Review*, 13, 79–100.

Taylor, H. and Cooper, C.L. (1989). The stress-prone personality: A review of the research in the context of occupational stress. *Psychology of Stress*, 5, 17–27.

Tugade, M.M., Fredrickson, B.L. and Barrett, L.F. (2004). Psychological resilience and positive emotional granularity: Examining the benefits of positive emotions on coping and health. *Journal of Personality*, 72, 1161–90.

Turner, N., Barling, J. and Zacharatos, A. (2002). Positive psychology at work. *Handbook of Positive Psychology*, 715–28.

Watson, D. and Clark, L.A. (1984). Negative affectivity: The disposition to experience aversive emotional states. *Psychological Bulletin*, 96(3), 465.

Watson, D. and Naragon, K. (2009). *Positive Affectivity: The Disposition to Experience Positive Emotional States*. New York: Oxford University Press.

Watson, D., Clark, L.A. and Tellegen, A. (1988). Development and validation of brief measures of positive and negative affect: The PANAS Scale. *Journal of Personality and Social Psychology*, 54(6), 1063–70.

Yavas, U., Karatepe, O.M. and Babakus, E. (2011). Do customer orientation and job resourcefulness moderate the impact of interrole conflicts on frontline employees' performance? *Tourism and Hospitality Research*, 11(2), 148–59.

Yavas, U., Karatepe, O.M. and Babakus, E. (2012). Interrole conflicts in the hospitality industry: The role of positive affectivity as an antidote. *Hospitality Review*, 29(2), Article 6.

Youssef, C.M. and Luthans, F. (2007). Positive organizational behavior in the workplace: The impact of hope, optimism, and resilience. *Journal of Management*, 33, 774–800.

Zellars, K.L., Hochwater, W.A., Hoffman, N.P., Perrewé, P.L. and Ford, E.W. (2004). Experiencing job burnout: The roles of positive and negative traits and states. *Journal of Applied Social Psychology*, 34(5), 887–911.

8

Perceived Responsiveness, Stress, and Coping in the Workplace

Cameron T. McCabe, Sarah Arpin, and Cynthia D. Mohr

Introduction

The experience of stress is ubiquitous in daily life, the consequences of which are well established in the organizational literature (Ganster and Rosen 2013; Sonnentag and Frese 2012; Taylor 2010). More specifically, the experience of stress and resultant strain may effect physiological and psychological well-being and performance proximally, in that they serve as a significant distraction and are often accompanied by a loss or perceived loss of resources (Hobfoll 1989; Muraven et al. 1998). In addition to health and performance decrements, resource depletion has been linked to increased hostility and aggression (Grandey 2000; Taylor and Kluemper 2012), and unsafe work behaviors that may lead to accidents and injuries (Nahrgang et al. 2011). In efforts to mitigate these risks, and in response to the ever-changing demands of today's workplace, occupational health psychologists have devoted significant attention to uncovering strategies and characteristics of the workplace (e.g., supportive work climate, proactive coping) that may avert or reduce the psychological, physiological, and behavioral consequences of occupational stress.

To date, much of the stress and coping literature within the realm of occupational health has addressed this process from either a physiological and/or cognitive perspective (Ganster and Rosen 2013). In contrast, the present chapter offers a *relational* approach to understanding the interplay between job stress and coping in the workplace. Specifically, while the experience of stress clearly affects the mind and body (from a physiological perspective), researchers such as Haslam and colleagues (2005) posit that stress is just as much a social process, in that it may be mitigated by interpersonal processes and positive social interactions. Previous research has examined the effects of interpersonal processes, such as social support, on the extent to which stress manifests in health outcomes. Moreover, supportive *behaviors* and relationships at work have been shown to be important for reducing conflict between work and family life, positive attitudes and perceptions of one's work, and the perceptions of one's health and well-being (Hammer et al. 2007; Hammer et al. 2009; Kirmeyer and Lin 1987).

The purpose of the present chapter is to propose a theoretical model delineating the importance of perceived responsiveness, the perception that one is genuinely cared for and understood (Reis et al. 2004), as an invaluable resource for managing occupation stress. The authors seek to build on past research and theory by emphasizing perceived responsiveness and other supportive processes in the workplace as central to the development of trust within work relationships. Additionally, we propose perceived responsiveness as one potential mechanism through which social support and supportive behaviors lead to positive outcomes. Perceptions that others are attentive and responsive to one's needs provide a critical resource from which to draw from when experiencing stressful events. Subsequently, we posit the role of perceived responsiveness as a critical determinant of organizational and individual well-being. Additionally, we explore the possible role of responsiveness within various work–relationship contexts, as these processes may unfold differently depending on the distribution of perceived power and authority within the relationship.

Social Support as a Resource

Conservation of resources (COR) theory (Hobfoll 1989) explains that stress arises from an actual or perceived loss of resources (e.g., time, energy, money). Individuals experience situations where the demands of one's job or a given task are perceived to exceed one's available resources. These demands are then perceived as aversive, stressful, and are accompanied by a negative affective state. That social support is an integral part of this process and has implications for stress, coping, and health is now beyond question (see Cohen and Wills 1985). Further, despite criticisms of COR theory's general definition of what may constitute a "resource" (e.g., Halbesleben and Wheeler 2012), social support remains a central component of resource-based models of job stress, such as the Job Demand-Control-Support Model (JDC-S; Karasek and Theorell 1990) and the Job Demands Resources Model (JDR; Demerouti et al. 2001). Indeed, evidence in support of these theories has shown that social support is a key predictor of positive employee and work-related outcomes, including positive affect (PA; Cohen and Wills 1985; Greenglass and Fiksenbaum 2009), health (Ikeda et al. 2008; Toker et al. 2012), lower levels of burnout (Halbesleben 2006; Haslam et al. 2005; Luchman and González-Morales 2013), work–family conflict (Kossek et al. 2011; Selvarajan et al. 2013), and higher levels of job satisfaction and commitment (Randall et al. 1999; Wayne et al. 1997). Support and other resources are thought to facilitate progress toward one's goals, personal growth, and development while also reducing perceived demands and potential consequences (Demerouti et al. 2001). By expanding one's pool of available contacts (i.e., people), social support provides a mechanism through which individuals gain new resources, and replace resources which may have been lost or depleted (Halbesleben 2006). As such, it is not surprising that support remains a fundamental resource in times of stress.

Beyond the inclusion of social support within resource-based models of job stress, perceived support has been thoroughly examined within psychological literatures as vital to individual health and well-being. Generally, social support is conceptualized as taking the form of one or more of the following: (1) instrumental support, (2) esteem or emotional support, (3) informational support, and/or (4) social companionship (Cohen and Wills 1985; Uchino 2004). Instrumental support is most often described as the provision of aid or tangible resources to directly address the problem at hand. When faced with high levels of job demands (e.g., workload, time pressure), instrumental support may take the form of the provision of necessary tools, supplies, or other resources to adequately complete a given task, or direct help and assistance to solve problems. Emotional support is more personalized, involving efforts to make the person feel cared for and acknowledging their experience with the goal of reducing the emotional toll a stressor may have. Informational support involves defining and providing strategies and guidance so that one may successfully navigate a problem. In line with transactional theories of coping (e.g., Lazarus and Folkman 1984), informational support may provide an opportunity to reappraise a stressful situation, thereby facilitating effective coping and emotion-regulation (Dunkel-Schetter et al. 1992).

A fourth resource comes in the form of social companionship, or belongingness support, which involves spending time with others and feeling a sense of community and social connectedness. Traditionally, this form of support has received less attention within the organizational literature; however, we would argue its relevance to fostering a healthy and happy workplace. From a social psychological perspective, social integration and connectedness satisfy basic needs for contact and relatedness (Baumeister and Leary 1995), and evidence has shown that time with close others is fundamental to one's social and physical health and well-being. For example, relative to individuals who work in groups or who interact regularly with other employees, solitary workers (e.g., commercial drivers) who have limited social contact with their coworkers or supervisors may be at risk for negative mental health outcomes (e.g., loneliness, depression, anxiety) and subsequent physical health (e.g., reduced immune functioning, mortality, poor health behaviors) as a function of their experience of isolation at work. Indeed, research examining the negative effects of social isolation and loneliness has revealed that a perceived lack of connectedness to others is predictive of various negative health outcomes, as well as deficits in self-regulation and well-being (i.e., Berkman and Breslow 1983; Cacioppo and Hawkley 2003).

Research examining the effects of social support have uncovered two distinct pathways through which support influences individual health and well-being. Specifically, social support is thought to have a more direct effect on well-being, regardless of one's level of stress (direct effect), as well as a stress-buffering effect by reducing the negative impact of stress on well-being (Cohen and Wills 1985). Considerable efforts have since been made to determine which type of support is most effective in reducing different forms of stress, for whom, and when buffering effects are typically observed. Researchers have concluded that support is most beneficial at low or moderate levels of stress. Further, in order for support to effectively reduce the negative impact of stress, there must be a match between the type of support desired, the type of support provided (Cutrona 1990), and the specific demands of the stressor (de Jonge and Dormann 2006). Additional evidence has pointed toward the domain (e.g., work–family) and source of one's support (e.g., coworker or supervisor support) as being important for individual health and well-being (Halbesleben 2006; Hammer et al. 2011; Karasek et al. 1982). As such, in order to observe the positive benefits that resources such as support provide, it is imperative that they be congruent with the expectations and desires of the recipient, and also the demands of the situational context. To achieve this requires that those providing support be attentive, aware, and responsive to the needs, values, and expectations of the recipients. Additionally, individuals at the receiving end of responsive behavior should perceive this type of interaction as caring, understanding, and validating of the self. Such actions and related perceptions epitomize what researchers and theorists have described as responsiveness (Reis et al. 2004).

Perceived Responsiveness in the Workplace

Drawing from work within the general social support literature, recent research and theory within social psychology has identified perceived responsiveness as an organizing construct in understanding interpersonal processes and interactions within personal relationships. Specifically, perceived responsiveness is defined as the process by which individuals believe that specific others attend to and provide support to defining features of the self (Reis et al. 2004), thus providing a sense of identity, support, and validation of the self. It is through this process that particular relationships are deemed as satisfying and through which an individual's needs in a given relationship are met. As such, relationship theorists argue that responsiveness is a vital aspect of interpersonal relationships yielding benefits for both intrapersonal and interpersonal outcomes (Lemay et al. 2007; Maisel and Gable 2009). Indeed, research has shown that perceived responsiveness is related to increased self-esteem and feelings of self-worth, and that *receiving* responsiveness from others is related to increased well-being, coping (e.g., positive adjustment and reduced distress; Major et al. 1997), goal pursuit, and greater physiological health (Clark and Lemay 2010). Moreover, perceptions of responsiveness are linked with better relationship functioning (Collins and Feeney 2000), trust, and lower levels of conflict (Gable et al. 2004).

Perceived responsiveness within a relationship is distinguished from other forms of social support in that it consists of a broader array of behaviors, and represents an ongoing exchange, whereby one member's responsiveness (or lack thereof) to another facilitates or impedes the likelihood of future disclosure, trust, and liking within the relationship. This dyadic process is most clearly demonstrated by Clark and Lemay's (2010) integrative model of responsiveness, which describes an interactive process involving (1) the provision and receipt of responsive behavior, (2) desiring and seeking responsiveness, and (3) the benefits of responsiveness within a given relationship. For instance, theory and subsequent research have shown that the perceived receipt of responsive behavior predicts support-seeking behavior, and facilitates trust and liking within a relationship. Similarly, past experiences of responsiveness with an interaction partner (e.g., one's supervisor or coworkers) informs one's likelihood to seek support through emotional disclosure, and trust that another will act in a responsive manner.

As demonstrated in Clark and Lemay's (2010) model, responsiveness is a two-way street set in a relational context, where the attitudes, cognitions, and behaviors of all parties involved frame each social interaction. Expectancy confirmation processes (e.g., Darley and Fazio 1980) describe how previous interactions shape our perceptions and provide the interpretive filter through which we view the current situation. For example, if an employee experiences a general lack of support from one of their coworkers, they may anticipate that this coworker is unlikely to be responsive to future requests for support. Rather than seeking support, guidance, or other resources when faced with common job stressors (e.g., heavy workload, time-sensitive deadlines), employees may temper their reactions and choose not to reveal or disclose a problem at all. From the perspective of the coworker, a lack of such disclosure may signify that no problem exists at all, therefore the employee's struggles may go unnoticed and the necessary support will not be provided. Inaction on behalf of the coworker would then confirm the employee's early suspicions, thereby contributing to future perceptions of their coworker as being unresponsive.

RESPONSIVENESS AS A RELATIONSHIP-SPECIFIC CONSTRUCT

Although perceived responsiveness has been primarily examined within close communal relationships, theorists have argued that it likely applies to other types of relationships within a given social network (Reis et al. 2004), including exchange relationships, where the exchange of task-oriented, personal, and tangible resources are based on a mutual expectation of reciprocity (Clark & Mills, 1993). These types of exchange-based relationships are inherent in relationships between employees and their supervisors (Hogg 2010; Sparrowe and Liden 1997).

Due to the dyadic nature of responsiveness, valuable information can be gleaned from the perspectives of both the support seeker as well as the individual providing subsequent support. Such models would be important to explore within the occupational health literature, given the implications for both employee and supervisor behavior and experiences in the workplace (Clark and Lemay 2010). For example, drawing from Clark and Lemay's (2010) model, it is possible that perceived responsiveness serves as a prerequisite for employees engaging in support-seeking behavior in the workplace and within employee–supervisor relationships. More specifically, if an employee perceives that a supervisor is understanding and caring, and validates his/her sense of self, he/she may be more likely to engage in support-seeking behavior at work (e.g., asking for time off to visit a sick family member; requesting more flexible work hours to accommodate child-care needs). As mentioned, responsiveness from one's supervisor may provide benefits for the self (i.e., feeling validated and cared for), but may also influence positive job attitudes, increase satisfaction with one's work and supervisor, and improve work-life balance.

Other evidence suggests that in the initial stages of relationship formation within an organization, such as when one starts a new job or role within an organization, it may be the *employees* who are most responsive to their supervisors. Supervisors and other organizational leaders are incredibly influential in defining the norms, expectations, goals, and culture within an organization (Avolio and Yammarino 2003; Hogg 2010; Kabanoff 1991). Employees, particularly new hires, may be motivated to be increasingly attentive to the needs and expectations of their superiors. By satisfying or exceeding initial job requirements, employees may solidify their position as a "good" and dependable employee. Supervisors and employers who then believe in and rely on their employees may be more apt to give attention, support, and responsiveness to those who are high performers (Wayne et al. 1997).

It is important to note, however, that the benefits of perceived responsiveness and social support in general, are not restricted to hierarchically structured exchange relationships such as those between supervisors and their subordinates. Research has similarly shown coworkers to be significant support resources, providing benefits for strain and organizational outcomes (e.g., Beehr et al. 2000; Luchman and González-Morales 2013). Specifically, peer relationships with one's coworkers act as a form of social capital, and unlike supervisor–employee relationships where a clear power differential exists, these relationships are more likely to flourish among individuals at a similar level of employment. Relationships among coworkers are often based on common goals and mutual interests, thus promoting a feeling of solidarity and shared purpose (Kabanoff 1991). To the extent that one's relationship with a coworker(s) is valued, perceived responsiveness will be similarly beneficial. Moreover, having multiple coworkers with whom one shares a mutually responsive relationship provides additional supportive resources to draw from in times of need. By re-affirming aspects of the self, providing positive regard and caring (Reis et al. 2004), these resources may offset potentially negative consequences of having a non-responsive supervisor. Thus, it is critical to examine perceptions of responsiveness within a broad array of organizational relationships, as these processes may differ drastically. Doing so would provide insight into an important element of support processes in the workplace context.

PERCEIVED RESPONSIVENESS, STRESS, AND COPING

In addition to the benefits that such supportive processes have for organizational, personal, and family-related outcomes, these processes have implications for how individuals manage and cope with stressful situations in the workplace. In the sense that responsiveness is an ongoing process that can fluctuate based on the nature of the relationship and situational context, it is akin to certain theories of leadership, such as leader–member exchange (LMX). Similar to relationships with high levels of responsiveness, high LMX relationships are characterized by feelings of trust, reciprocity, and a mutual sense of commitment. From a leadership perspective, high LMX relationships are associated with reduced role stress (e.g., role conflict and ambiguity) and subsequent burnout (Thomas and Lankau 2009). Harris and Kacmar (2006), however, described a curvilinear relationship between LMX and stress, in the form of job demands. In their study, it was *moderate* LMX relationships that were associated with the lowest levels of stress (Harris and Kacmar 2006). They explained this effect as being a function of the increased demands and expectations placed on employees in high LMX relationships. Leaders tend to invest more energy and attention into developing stronger relationships with their high-performing employees (Wayne et al. 1997), and despite potential benefits of LMX, the norm of reciprocity may place additional burden on the employee to achieve and maintain a high level of performance.

In contrast, perceiving responsiveness from alternative sources, such as one's coworkers, where the relationship is based more on a social, rather than economical exchange may be better suited for navigating one's day-to-day stressors (Halbesleben 2006). Halbesleben and Wheeler (2011) argue that employees may become more economical with how they expend their limited resources when stressed or when they perceive a threat to self. Although this preservation motive may lead people to be more selective in their allocation of resources, they may be more likely to invest additional resources and engage in helping behaviors for other members of their social network as a means of "restocking" and increasing their relational value to others. They explain this effect as a function of desired reciprocity within a relationship (Halbesleben and Wheeler 2011, 2012). Although somewhat counterintuitive, as helping behaviors themselves may be experienced as depleting, this argument makes sense from a responsiveness perspective. One is more likely to invest resources in relationships that are perceived to be more equitable, and the provision of aid to others may indirectly act as a form of support seeking behavior (i.e., I am helping you today, hopefully you will do the same for me tomorrow). Within the realm of responsiveness, research and theory have shown that people are more likely to provide aid, support, and responsiveness to those that have been responsive to them previously (Reis and Shaver 1988).

By facilitating feelings such as liking, trust, and identification, we propose that perceived responsiveness may offset strain in two ways: (1) by promoting the experience of positive emotions, and (2) through the accruement of resources to be used to cope with or even prevent the experience of stress (see Figure 8.1). This view is consistent with the theoretical model proposed by Greenglass and Fiksenbaum (2009), which revealed that social support benefits well-being through the promotion of positive affect, and through proactive coping efforts which similarly promote positive affect.

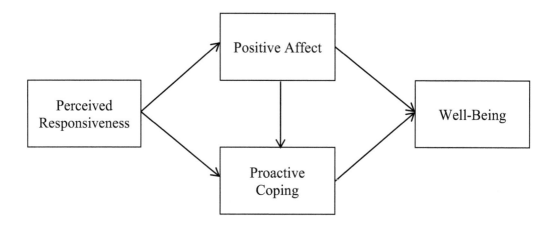

Figure 8.1   Theoretical model of perceived responsiveness, affect, coping, and well-being

According to broaden-and-build theory (Fredrickson 2001), positive emotions and experiences serve to inspire creative and flexible thinking, and to expand one's attention and ability to navigate problems. Moreover, discrete emotions such as happiness, joy, or contentment, may dampen one's physiological reaction following a stressful experience and aid in recovery (Fredrickson and Levenson 2000), while simultaneously promoting effective regulation of competing life demands (Aspinwall 2005), allowing individuals to "bounce back" from aversive experiences. To the extent that perceived responsiveness from others elicits positive emotion and experiences, it may aid in the down-regulation physiological reactivity, having significant implications for long-term physical health (Ganster and Rosen 2013; Melamed et al. 2006; Sonnentag and Frese 2012).

In addition to positive affect, perceptions of responsiveness may increase the likelihood that individuals may be able to offset or even prevent stressful work events from occurring, by adopting proactive coping strategies (Aspinwall and Taylor 1997). Relative to more traditional forms of coping (such as actions made in response to a perceived threat), proactive coping is anticipatory, and is motivated toward the *prevention* of stress rather than a reduction in one's emotional or physiological reaction to stressful events (Aspinwall and Taylor 1997; Greenglass and Fiksenbaum 2009; Taylor 2010).

Greenglass and Fiksenbaum (2009) applied a similar framework in an effort to predict positive well-being outcomes, showing that proactive coping is predictive of positive outcomes (e.g., lower levels of depression and absenteeism from work, greater functional independence) through increases in positive affect (Greenglass and Fiksenbaum 2009). Their model also emphasized the reciprocal influence of social support processes and proactive coping. While their model is based on perceived support (both general support and organizational support), it may also be relevant to the application of responsiveness to relationships within the workplace.

Responsiveness may also alter one's appraisal of forthcoming events. Specifically, perceiving that one has support from responsive others gives one a sense of control and access to additional support resources and perspectives which may alter one's initial appraisal of a stressful work event. The ability to reappraise a situation is particularly beneficial for individuals who tend to engage in proactive coping, who appraise events as challenging, and are thus capable of allocating resources toward facilitating goal-setting and efforts to prevent negative experiences (Greenglass 2005). For example, responsive supervisors are cognizant and aware of the demands placed on their employees. They may be able to anticipate the occurrence of future deadlines, and beyond the instrumental benefits of social support that supervisors provide (e.g., autonomy, control over work time, flexible scheduling), they may be able to provide valuable informational support, clarifying tasks and providing strategies with which their employees can anticipate and even prevent potential threats, thus offsetting potential strain outcomes before they occur (Aspinwall and Taylor 1997). By virtue of being exposed to comparable demands, coworkers and team members are similarly in a position to provide responsiveness in the form of emotional, informational, and instrumental support. In addition to the *intrapersonal* benefits with respect to the prevention of strain outcomes (e.g., burnout; Greenglass 2005; Schwarzer and Taubert 2002), and the promotion of physical health and well-being (Aspinwall 2005; Greenglass et al. 2005), responsive behaviors and personalized attention produce *interpersonal* benefits, such as perceptions of trust, commitment, and satisfaction in one's relationship.

WHO IS RESPONSIVE?

A majority of research within the close relationships literature has emphasized the role of perceptions of responsiveness from close others as being an essential component for satisfaction within a relationship, positive affect, and well-being. However, *provision* of responsiveness and other supportive behaviors are equally important to consider (Reis et al. 2004). This then begs the question of *who* is more likely to be responsive. Moreover, which traits or characteristics are associated with a higher likelihood of being attentive, caring, and responsive to others?

An individual's ability to be responsive depends on many factors including qualities and characteristics of the individuals involved, characteristics of the relationship itself, and past interactions which inform expectations for responsiveness (Clark and Lemay 2010). Though various factors predicting expectations for the provision of responsive behavior have been examined in the close relationships literature (e.g., attachment and caregiving; Collins and Feeney 2000), specific personality traits which relate to responsive behavior have yet to be explored. However, one can glean the characteristics which make someone more or less responsive from the personality literature. Research has shown that relative to other dimensions of the Big Five (Costa and McCrae 1992), high levels of neuroticism (N) are associated with low quality social interactions and relationships. High levels of N are associated with the highest levels of negative affectivity, emotionality, and pessimism, and these individuals are unlikely to engage others on a personal level and are more likely to experience high levels of interpersonal conflict (Bolger and Zuckerman 1995). Moreover, supervisors fitting this profile often shirk their responsibilities as a leader altogether (Bono and Judge 2004). These individuals are less likely to be responsive, as they likely fear that others are similarly unresponsive to them.

Other characteristics, such as proactive personality, may play an important role in determining one's likelihood of being responsive to others, particularly during times of stress. Proactive individuals tend to show initiative, problem-solve and exert control over their surroundings environment (Seibert et al. 1999). These individuals may be more attentive to their environment, thus may be more apt to identify and implement strategies to offset potential challenges. Consistent with Halbesleben and Wheeler (2012), even under stress, proactive individuals may become more responsive to others in their social network, and engage in positive behaviors which benefit others. These actions build social capital and supportive resources which one can draw from in times of need.

Additionally, it is important to acknowledge that the provision of responsive behavior may differ based on power differentials between members of a given relationship (Chen et al. 2001). For example, one might expect to observe lower levels of responsive behavior in relationships characterized purely by economic exchange (relative to social exchange or communal-orientation). In their experimental study, Chen et al. (2001) were able to show that when primed with perceptions of power or authority, individuals who are more exchange-oriented tend to focus more on self-interest and goals, rather than what may benefit others, whereas those who are more communally oriented tended to be more attentive and responsive to the needs and demands of others. This research suggests that within exchange-based relationships which would perhaps benefit most from high levels of responsiveness among its members, those in a position of authority may feel less compelled to attend to the needs of their subordinates, and will prefer to act in a manner which satisfies their own needs. Conversely, more egalitarian and communal relationships, such as those among coworkers, may be more apt to engage in supportive and responsive behavior. Much work is needed to understand who is responsive and when within the workplace context, particularly given the unique nature of different relationships within the workplace.

Implications and Future Directions

Drawing from prior empirical evidence and theory, we have proposed a theoretical model whereby perceptions of responsiveness from others (e.g., supervisors or coworkers) plays a significant role in how people cope with and manage work stress. Given the novelty of this concept within this context, it is not surprising that some questions remain unanswered. For example, is it the case that individuals desire or even expect responsive relationships in the work context? Past research and theory within the close relationships literature suggests that, yes, people desire responsiveness from others, as it makes them feel validated, understood, and cared for (Clark and Lemay 2010). However, the extent to which responsiveness is important in a given relationship depends on individuals' expectations of the relationship, norms within a relationship context, as well as the nature of the relationship as being communal or exchange (Clark and Mills 1993; Reis et al. 2004). Moreover, this process may function differently based on factors such as the cultural context (e.g., independent vs. interdependent cultures; Diener et al. 2003; Markus and Kitayama 1991), and the centrality of the relationship to one's self-concept and identity.

Whether responsiveness is expected or effective also likely differs based on the centrality or relative importance of a given relationship to the self (Clark and Lemay 2010). Relationships which are most central to our identities are those with which we invest the most time, energy, and emotion in cultivating. However, while much research and theory have described the benefits of social integration and connectedness, researchers such as Sani and colleagues (2012) have argued that while support processes such as responsiveness are clearly important for health and well-being (Cohen and Wills 1985), they may have unintended consequences for both the recipient (e.g., reduced sense of autonomy and competence) and the support provider (e.g., resource depletion and fatigue), leading to conflict (Sani 2012). However, to the extent that the relationship is central or important to one's self-concept, the potential consequences of receiving or providing support and responsiveness are likely mitigated (Sani et al. 2012). Future research should explore the role of centrality and identification with one's coworkers and/or supervisor as a potential moderator of responsiveness-stress and well-being outcomes.

Beyond the intra- and interpersonal benefits of responsiveness, a relational approach to understanding stress and coping has further implications for the organization as a whole. Perceptions that one is treated well and cared for is generally considered important to members of their organization as it relates to greater perceptions of justice and fairness. Given strong norms of reciprocity, it is likely that these perceptions will be accompanied by higher levels of performance, lower levels of turnover (Mitchell and Daniels 2003), positive job attitudes (Meyer et al. 2002), and organizational citizenship behaviors, beyond the scope of one's initial job description (Cropanzano et al. 2001). Moreover, to the extent that responsiveness elicits positive emotions, responsiveness may aid in one's recovery from stress (Fredrickson 2001). Over time, reductions in physiological reactivity may offset potential long-term health consequences associated with chronic stress (e.g., cardiocascular disease, hypertension; Ganster and Rosen 2013; Marmot and Wilkinson 2005), thereby reducing potential absenteeism and subsequent healthcare costs.

Conclusions

A stress and coping framework which incorporates perceived responsiveness as a valuable resource would make a significant contribution to the organizational and occupational health literatures. The extant literature on perceived responsiveness reveals this process to be critical for intra- and interpersonal health and well-being within close relationships, as it may facilitate both reactive and proactive forms of coping with stressors. However, this work has yet to be translated to other forms of social relationships typically experienced in the workplace context (e.g., economic and social exchange relationships). Further, this approach provides valuable insight into the perspective of both members of the relationship. Current models of responsiveness, such as Clark and Lemay's (2010) integrative process model of responsiveness, emphasize this as a dyadic process, informed by the characteristics of the individuals involved, the type of relationship in question, and the expectations they both bring with them based on previous interaction experiences (Reis et al. 2004). When examined within this theoretical framework, it is likely that supervisors and coworkers who are attentive and responsive to the needs of others provide critical resources (e.g., flexibility, control and autonomy, alternative perspectives and social support) which yield benefits for the employee (e.g., positive affect, lower levels of stress, improved health and well-being), the relationship (e.g., trust, liking, and identification), and the organization (e.g., commitment, satisfaction, performance).

References

Aspinwall, L.G. (2005). The psychology of future-oriented thinking: From achievement to proactive coping, adaptation, and aging. *Motivation and Emotion*, 29, 203–35.

Aspinwall, L.G. and Taylor, S.E. (1997). A stitch in time: Self-regulation and proactive coping. *Psychological Bulletin*, 121, 417–36.

Avolio, B.J. and Yammarino, F.J. (eds) (2003). *Transformational and Charismatic Leadership: The Road Ahead*. New York: Elsevier.

Baumeister, R.F. and Leary, M.R. (1995). The need to belong: Desire for interpersonal attachments as a fundamental human motivation. *Psychological Bulletin*, 117, 497–529.

Beehr, T.A., Jex, S.M., Stacy, B.A. and Murray, M.A. (2000). Work stressors and coworker support as predictors of individual strain and job performance. *Journal of Organizational Behavior*, 21, 391–405.

Berkman, L.F. and Breslow, L. (1983). *Health and Ways of Living: The Alameda County Study*. New York: Oxford University Press.

Bolger, N. and Zuckerman, A. (1995). A framework for studying personality in the stress process. *Journal of Personality and Social Psychology*, 69, 890–902.

Bono, J.E. and Judge, T.A. (2004). Personality and transformational and transactional leadership: A meta-analysis. *Journal of Applied Psychology*, 89, 901–10.

Cacioppo, J.T. and Hawkley, L.C. (2003). Social isolation and health, with an emphasis on underlying mechanisms. *Perspectives in Biology and Medicine*, 46, S39–52.

Chen, S., Lee-Chai, A.Y. and Bargh, J.A. (2001). Relationship orientation as a moderator of the effects of social power. *Attitudes and Social Cognition*, 80, 173–87.

Clark, M.S. and Lemay, Jr., E.P. (2010). Close relationships. In S.T. Fiske, D.T. Gilbert and G. Lindzey (eds), *Handbook of Social Psychology* (5th edn, Vol. 2, pp. 898–940). New York: Wiley.

Clark, M.S. and Mills, I. (1993). The difference between communal and exchange relationships: What it is and is not. *Personality and Social Psychology Bulletin*, 19, 684–91.

Cohen, S. and Wills, T.A. (1985). Stress, social support, and the buffering hypothesis. *Psychological Bulletin*, 98, 310–57.

Collins, N.L. and Feeney, B.C. (2000). A safe haven: An attachment theory perspective on support seeking and caregiving in intimate relationships. *Journal of Personality and Social Psychology*, 78(6), 1053–73.

Costa, P.T. Jr. and McCrae, R.R. (1992). *NEO-PI-R Professional Manual*. Odessa: Psychological Assessment Resources.

Cropanzano, R., Byrne, Z.S., Bobocel, D.R. and Rupp, D.E. (2001). Moral virtues, fairness heuristics, social entities, and other denizens of organizational justice. *Journal of Vocational Behavior*, 58, 164–209.

Cutrona, C.E. (1990). Stress and social support – In search of optimal matching. *Journal of Social and Clinical Psychology*, 9, 3–14.

Darley, J.M. and Fazio, R.H. (1980). Expectancy confirmation processes arising in the social interaction sequence. *American Psychologist*, 35, 867–81.

de Jonge, J. and Dormann, C. (2006). Stressors, resources and strain at work: A longitudinal test of the triple-match principle. *Journal of Applied Psychology*, 91, 1359–74.

Demerouti, E., Bakker, A.B., Nachreiner, F., and Schaufeli, W.B. (2001). The job demands-resources model of burnout. *Journal of Applied Psychology*, 86(3), 499–512.

Diener, E., Oishi, S., and Lucas, R.E. (2003). Personality, culture, and subjective well-being: Emotional and cognitive evaluations of life. *Annual Review of Psychology*, 54, 403–25.

Dunkel-Schetter, C., Feinstein, L.G., Taylor, S.E., and Falke, R.L. (1992). Patterns of coping with cancer. *Health Psychology*, 11, 79–87.

Fredrickson, B.L. (2001). The role of positive emotions in positive psychology. *American Psychologist*, 56(3), 218–26.

Fredrickson, B.L. and Levenson, R.W. (1998). Positive emotions speed recovery from the cardiovascular sequelae of negative emotions. *Cognition and Emotion*, 12, 191–220.

Gable, S.L., Reis, H.T., Impett, E., and Asher, E.R. (2004). What do you do when things go right? The intrapersonal and interpersonal benefits of sharing positive events. *Journal of Personality and Social Psychology*, 87, 228–45.

Ganster, D.C. and Rosen, C.C. (2013). Work stress and employee health: A multidisciplinary review. *Journal of Management*, 39, 1085–122.

Grandey, A.A. (2000). Emotional regulation in the workplace: A new way to conceptualize emotional labor. *Journal of Occupational Health Psychology*, 5(1), 95–110.

Greenglass, E.R. (2005). Proactive coping, resources and burnout: Implications for occupational stress. In A.G. Antoniou and C.L. Cooper (eds), *Research Companion to Organizational Health Psychology* (pp. 503–15). Northampton, MA: Edward Elgar.

Greenglass, E.R. and Fiksenbaum, L. (2009). Proactive coping, positive affect, and well-being: Testing for mediation using path analysis. *European Psychologist*, 14, 29–39.

Greenglass, E.R., Marques, S., deRidder, M. and Behl, S. (2005). Positive coping and mastery in a rehabilitation setting. *International Journal of Rehabilitation Research*, 28, 331–9.

Halbesleben, J.R.B. (2006). Sources of social support and burnout: A meta-analytic test of the conservation of resources model. *The Journal of Applied Psychology*, 91(5), 1134–45.

Halbesleben, J.R.B. and Wheeler, A.R. (2011). I owe you one: Coworker reciprocity as a moderator of the day-level exhaustion–performance relationship. *Journal of Organizational Behavior*, 32, 608–26.

Halbesleben, J.R.B. and Wheeler, A.R. (2012). To invest or not? The role of coworker support and trust in daily reciprocal gain spirals of helping behavior. *Journal of Management*, DOI: 10.1177/0149206312455246.

Hammer, L.B., Kossek, E.E., Zimmerman, K. and Daniels, R. (2007). Clarifying the construct of family-supportive supervisory behaviors (FSSB): A multilevel perspective. In P.L. Perrewe and D.C. Ganster (eds), *Research in Occupational Stress and Well being: Vol. 6. Exploring the Work and Non-work Interface* (pp. 165–204). Amsterdam: Elsevier.

Hammer, L.B., Kossek, E.E., Anger, W.K., Bodner, T. and Zimmerman, K.L. (2011). Clarifying work-family intervention processes: The roles of work-family conflict and family-supportive supervisor behaviors. *The Journal of Applied Psychology*, 96(1), 134–50.

Hammer, L.B., Kossek, E.E., Yragui, N.L., Bodner, T.E. and Hanson, G.C. (2009). Development and validation of a multidimensional measure of family supportive supervisor behaviors (FSSB). *Journal of Management*, 35, 837–56.

Harris, K.J. and Kacmar, K.M. (2006). Too much of a good thing: The curvilinear effect of leader-member exchange on stress. *The Journal of Social Psychology*, 146, 65–84.

Haslam, S.A., O'Brien, A., Jetten, J., Vormedal, K. and Penna, S. (2005). Taking the strain: Social identity, social support, and the experience of stress. *The British Journal of Social Psychology*, 44, 355–70.

Hobfoll, S.E. (1989). Conservation of resources: A new attempt at conceptualizing stress. *American Psychologist*, 44, 513–24.

Hogg, M.A. (2010). Influence and leadership. In S.T. Fiske, D.T. Gilbert and G. Lindzey (eds), *The Handbook of Social Psychology* (5th edn, Vol. 2, pp. 1166–206). New York: Wiley.

Ikeda, A., Iso, H., Kawachi, I., Yamagishi, K., Inoue, M. and Tsugane, S. (2008). Social support and stroke and coronary heart disease: The JPHC study cohorts II. *Stroke; A Journal of Cerebral Circulation*, 39, 768–75.

Kabanoff, B. (1991). Equity, equality, power, and conflict. *The Academy of Management Review*, 16, 416–41.

Karasek, R. and Theorell, T. (1990). *Healthy Work: Stress, Productivity, and the Reconstruction of Working Life*. New York: Basic Books.

Karasek, R.A., Triantis, K.P. and Chaudry, S.S. (1982). Coworker and supervisor support as moderators of associations between task characteristics. *Journal of Occupational Behavior*, 3, 181–200.

Kirmeyer, S.L. and Lin, T. (1987). Social support: Its relationship to observed communication with peers and superiors. *The Academy of Management Journal*, 30, 138–51.

Kossek, E.E., Pichler, S., Bodner, T. and Hammer, L.B. (2011). Workplace social support and work-family conflict: A meta-analysis clarifying the influence of general and work-family-specific supervisor and organizational support. *Personnel Psychology*, 64(2), 289–313.

Lazarus, R.S. and Folkman, S. (1984). *Stress, Appraisal, and Coping*. New York: Springer.

Lemay, E.P., Jr., Clark, M.S. and Feeney, B.C. (2007). Projection of responsiveness to needs and the construction of satisfying communal relationships. *Journal of Personality and Social Psychology*, 92, 834–53.

Luchman, J.N. and González-Morales, M.G. (2013). Demands, control, and support: A meta-analytic review of work characteristics interrelationships. *Journal of Occupational Health Psychology*, 18(1), 37–52.

Maisel, N.C. and Gable, S.L. (2009). The paradox of received support: The importance of responsiveness. *Psychological Science*, 20, 928–32.

Major, B., Zubek, J.M., Cooper, M.L., Cozzarelli, C. and Richards, C. (1997). Mixed messages: Implications of social conflict and social support within close relationships for adjustment to a stressful life event. *Journal of Personality and Social Psychology*, 72, 1349–63.

Markus, H.R. and Kitayama, S. (1991). Culture and the self: Implications for cognition, emotion, and motivation. *Psychological Review*, 98, 224–53.

Marmot, M. and Wilkinson, R.G. (2005). *Social Determinants of Health* (2nd edn). New York: Oxford University Press.

Melamed, S., Shirom, A., Toker, S., Berliner, S. and Shapira, I. (2006). Burnout and risk of cardiovascular disease: Evidence, possible causal paths, and promising research directions. *Psychological Bulletin*, 132(3), 327–53.

Meyer, J.P., Stanley, D.J., Herscovitch, L. and Topolnytsky, L. (2002). Affective, continuance, and normative commitment to the organization: A meta-analysis of antecedents, correlates, and consequences. *Journal of Vocational Behavior*, 61(1), 20–52.

Mitchell, T.R. and Daniels, D. (2003). Motivation. In W.C. Borman, D.R. Ilgen, and R.J. Klimoski (eds), *Handbook of Psychology, Vol. 12. Industrial Organizational Psychology* (pp. 225–54). New York: Wiley.

Muraven, M., Tice, D.M. and Baumeister, R.F. (1998). Self-control as a limited resource: Regulatory depletion patterns. *Journal of Personality and Social Psychology*, 74, 774–89.

Nahrgang, J.D., Morgeson, F.P. and Hofmann, D.A. (2011). Safety at work: A meta-analytic investigation of the link between job demands, job resources, burnout, engagement, and safety outcomes. *The Journal of Applied Psychology*, 96(1), 71–94.

Randall, M.L., Cropanzano, R., Bormann, C.A. and Birjulin, A. (1999). Organizational politics and organizational support as predictors of work attitudes, job performance, and organizational citizenship behavior. *Journal of Organizational Behavior*, 20, 159–74.

Reis, H.T. and Shaver, P.R. (1988). Intimacy as an interpersonal process. In S. Duck (ed.), *Handbook of Research in Personal Relationships* (pp. 367–89). London: Wiley.

Reis, H.T., Clark, M.S. and Holmes, J.G. (2004). Perceived partner responsiveness as an organizing construct in the study of intimacy and closeness. In D.J. Mashek and A.P. Aron (eds), *Handbook of Closeness and Intimacy* (pp. 201–25). Mahwah: Lawrence Erlbaum Associates.

Sani, F. (2012). Group identity, social relationships, and health. In J. Jetten, C. Haslam and A.S. Haslam (eds), *The Social Cure: Identity, Health, and Well-being*. New York: Psychology Press.

Sani, F., Herrera, M., Wakefield, J.R.H., Boroch, O. and Gulyas, C. (2012). Comparing social contact and group identification as predictors of mental health. *The British Journal of Social Psychology*, 51(4), 781–90.

Schwarzer, R. and Taubert, S. (2002). Tenacious goal pursuits and striving toward personal growth: Proactive coping. In E. Fydenberg (ed.), *Beyond Coping: Meeting Goals, Visions and Challenges* (pp. 19–35). London: Oxford University Press.

Seibert, S.E., Crant, J.M. and Kraimer, M.L. (1999). Proactive personality and career success. *Journal of Applied Psychology*, 84, 416–27.

Selvarajan, T.T., Cloninger, P.A. and Singh, B. (2013). Social support and work-family conflict: A test of an indirect effects model. *Journal of Vocational Behavior*, 83, 486–99.

Sonnentag, S. and Frese, M. (2012). Stress in organizations. In I.B. Weiner, N.B. Schmitt and S. Highhouse (eds), *Handbook of Psychology, Vol. 12. Industrial Organizational Psychology* (2nd edn, pp. 560–92). New York: Wiley.

Sparrowe, R.T. and Liden, R.C. (1997). Process and structure in leader–member exchange. *Academy of Management Review*, 22, 522–52.

Taylor, S.E. (2010). Health. In S.T. Fiske, D.T. Gilbert and G. Lindzey (eds), *Handbook of Social Psychology* (5th edn, Vol. 2, pp. 698–723). New York: Wiley.

Taylor, S.G. and Kluemper, D.H. (2012). Linking perceptions of role stress and incivility to workplace aggression: The moderating role of personality. *Journal of Occupational Health Psychology*, 17(3), 316–29.

Thomas, C.H. and Lankau, M.J. (2009). Preventing burnout, the effects of LMX and mentoring on socialization, role stress, and burnout. *Human Resource Management*, 49, 417–32.

Toker, S., Shirom, A., Melamed, S. and Armon, G. (2012). Work characteristics as predictors of diabetes incidence among apparently healthy employees. *Journal of Occupational Health Psychology*, 17(3), 259–67.

Uchino, B. (2004). *Social Support and Physical Health: Understanding the Health Consequences of Relationships*. New Haven: Yale University Press.

Wayne, S.J., Shore, L.M. and Liden, R.C. (1997). Perceived organizational support and leader-member exchange: A social exchange perspective. *Academy of Management Journal*, 40, 82–111.

PART III
COPING AND THE ROLE OF RESILIENCE

9

The Psychology of Resilience: Defining, Categorizing and Measuring Resilience

Luke Treglown and Adrian Furnham

Introduction

Research on resilience is dramatically on the rise. A growing number of articles in both the print and electronic media, in academic journals, and in books are referencing resilience each year, detailing the different facets of its conceptualization. This chapter seeks to examine different definitions of resilience, different typologies and categories of resilience, and different measures of resilience.

1. What is Resilience?

Resilience is concerned with how well complex systems anticipate, adapt, recover and learn in the contexts of major threats, surprises and disasters. The field has deep roots in child development, clinical sciences and the study of individual differences. Resilience appears most clearly in response to disasters (Masten 2014).

Defining resilience is an important step for progressing with research in the area. As Windle (2010) notes, there is no agreed operationalization of resilience within the literature, causing the research to become incomparable and the conceptualizations to become muddled. Different researchers use a definition that is founded upon the factors they deem most important to building, establishing and maintaining resilience. As a result, research will elicit different factors of resilience as paramount, whilst potentially omitting key attributes of resilience.

In an attempt to cover the multitude of approaches and ideologies on resilience, it is sensible to start at the very beginning. Resilience has its etymological roots within the Latin word *resilire*, meaning 'to leap back' or 'rebound from'. Lexicographers define resilience in two general ways: firstly, referring to objects or materials – being able to recoil or spring back into shape after bending, stretching or compressing; being capable of regaining its original shape after a distortion – and secondly to the resilience of a person – being able to withstand or recover quickly from difficult conditions; recovering easily from misfortune or illness.

Table 9.1   **Resilience definitions**

Focus	Context	Author	Definition	Implication
Stability	Mathematics	Bodin and Wiman (2004)	'The dynamic behaviour of the system as it strives (if at all) to return to equilibrium, i.e., the extent to which, and the speed with which return occurs, can be broadly studied in terms of *resistance, elasticity, trajectory, stability,* and the extension of potential *stability domains*'	Resilience is used synonymously with elasticity. It concerns itself purely with a body returning to its natural state; emphasises a 'bounce-back' definition.
Resilience	Engineering	Pimm (1984)	A measure of the speed at which a system returns to equilibrium following some kind of disturbance.	Within this definition is the presupposition that the body exists near a condition of equilibrium.
Resilience	Ecology	Holling (1973)	'A measure of the persistence of systems and of their ability to absorb change and disturbance and still maintain the same relationships between populations or state variables'	Persistence, adaptiveness, variability, and unpredictability – all attributes embraced and celebrated by those with an evolutionary or developmental perspective. This definition is concerned with the maximum deviation from the norm that can be endured without causing a change to an alternative stable state. 'the amount of disruption the system can cope with before the relationships within the system alter significantly' (Reid and Botterill, 2013: 33) This definition 'envisions ecosystems as constantly changing and focuses on renewal and reorganisation processes rather than on stable states' (Berkes 2007: 286) These definitions emphasise change and adaption rather than focusing on a single equilibrium. The emphasis, however, is on the community as a whole. Whilst the community may have the resilience to carry on after the disturbance, the fate or survival of the individual is not guaranteed.

Term	Field	Author/Year	Definition	Notes
Resilience	Clinical Psychology	Richardson (2002)	The 3 evolutionary steps of the use of resilience in clinical psychology: Concerned with deciphering which attributes aid a person's resilience; How to acquire these attributes; Focus on the concept of resilience itself	The outcome of this evolution was a 'resilience movement' that has deepened the meaning of the term; it has caused 'resilient reintegration' to accommodate faculties of growth and adaption in adversity rather than purely to 'bounce back'. This definition is somewhat different to the ecological definition due to its strong focus upon growth and change. However, it is closer to ecological definitions than those found in equilibrium-centred engineering and mathematical terms.
Resilience	Clinical Psychology	Bonanno (2004)	'Resilience reflects the ability to maintain a stable equilibrium'	Bonanno's work makes a clear distinction between the faculty of resilience and the process of recovery. There is a relationship between the two, but the focus of resilience is on 'bouncing back' rather than moving forward.
Resilience	Clinical Psychology	Masten (2014)	'Resilience can be broadly defined as the capacity of a dynamic system to adapt successfully to disturbances that threaten system function, viability, or development.'	The word resilience has Latin roots, *resilire*, which means 'to rebound'. The concept has been adopted into many fields concerned with how well complex systems anticipate, adapt, recover, and learn in the context of major threats, surprises, and disasters
Community/ Social Resilience	Geography	Adger (2000)	'[Resilience is] an important component of the circumstances under which individuals and social groups adapt to environmental change... [Social resilience] is defined at the community level rather than being a phenomenon pertaining to individuals. Hence it is related to the social capital of societies and communities'	A relationship must exist between the different forms of resilience; individual resilience will impact community resilience, which together will affect ecological resilience.

Table 9.1   Resilience definitions (*continued*)

Stability vs. Resilience	Interdisciplinary	Holling (1973) Gallopin (2006) DeAngelis (1980) Common and Perrings (1992)	'Resilience is the property of the system and persistence or probability of extinction is the result. Stability on the other hand is the ability of a system to return to an equilibrium state after a temporary disturbance; the more rapidly it returns and the less it fluctuates, the more stable it is.' '[Resilience is] measured by the speed at which the system returns to the stable point or trajectory following perturbation' Bodys or ecosystems can exist in multiple and changing stable states, where resilience is a form of relative stability. 'Resilience admits the extinction of some resource stock providing that the extinction does not affect the stability of the system parameters'	Resilience and stability do not mean the same thing, but there is an overlap with common terms. For instance, resilient items can consist of highly unstable parts. In regards to the Gallopin definition, stability is the more important in the topic of ecosystem resilience; this topic is more concerned with bouncing back rather than growth and progress. Common and Perrings' statement reflects a reference to Holling's (1973) definition of resilience, expanding it in a slightly more brutal manner. This definition indicates the prerogative to the system at the expense of the individual component parts. Sometimes, in regards of evolution, remaining stable is not always desirable. If a species remained stable in the face of disruption and adversity, it would never adapt, progress, and evolve.
Resilience vs. Recovery	Interdisciplinary	Bonanno (2004)	Recovering individuals often experience subthreshold symptom levels. Resilient individuals, by contrast, may experience transient perturbations in normal functioning … but generally exhibit a stable trajectory of healthy functioning across time.	Rose sees recovery in contrast to mitigation and as a part of recovery. Bonanno proposes that resilience and recovery are quite different phenomena.
Resilience	Counselling Psychology	Found in Lee et al. (2013)	Resilience is 'the personal qualities and skills that allow for an individual's healthy/successful functioning or adaption within the context of significant adversity or a disruptive life event.'	It is a multidimensional variable consisting of psychological and dispositional attributes, such as competence, external support systems, and personal structure. Individuals who possess a greater number of the attributes that have been associated with resilience are found to more likely successfully adapt to a disruptive even compared to individuals who have fewer.

Resilience as a trait	Counselling Psychology	Found in Lee et al. (2013)	The ability to 'bounce back' being an individual trait that is fixed and stable, referring to 'a personality trait for negotiating, managing, and adapting to significant sources of stress or trauma.'	Some psychoanalysts have defined resilience in terms of 'ego-resilience' - the changing faculty of an individual to regulate their level of ego-control in any direction as a function and response to the adversity of environmental context (Block & Block, 1980). Some feel that resilience can be characterised by three trait types: resilient, over-controlled, and under-controlled. This view fails to account for the dynamic process of adaption that occurs between the individual and the environment.
Resilience as a dynamic process	Counselling Psychology	Found in Lee et al. (2013)	Resilience is not a fixed but dynamic and evolving, dependent upon the individuals' interactions among various factors within the environment.	The concept of resilience within this view allows for the notion of evaluating related variables to change including specific prevention and intervention strategies.
Risk factors	Psychological factors to resilience	Found in Lee et al. (2013)	These are actors that increase the likelihood of maladaptation	People who these factors are found to be less resilient: Depressive symptoms (e.g. Baek et al., 2010) Severe anxiety-related impairments (Norman et al., 2006) High levels of stress (Bruwer et al., 2008) PTSD (Lee et al., 2013)
Protective factors	Psychological factors to resilience	Found in Lee et al. (2013)	These area factors that refer to these characteristics that enhance adaptation.	A positive relationship has been established between resilience and these factors: Life satisfaction (e.g. Beutel et al., 2009) Optimism (e.g. Lamond et al., 2008) Positive affect (e.g. Burns & Anstry, 2010) Self-efficacy (e.g. Gillespie et al., 2007) Self-esteem (e.g. Baek et al., 2010) Social support (e.g. Brown, 2008)

Table 9.1 **Resilience definitions** *(concluded)*

| Organisational Resilience | Organisational Psychology | Found in Mamouni Limnios et al. (2014) | Organisational resilience has been defined as a 'psychological or behavioural attribute, applied at the individual or collective behavioural level, commonly adopting an agency rather than structural approach.' | Organisational resilience therefore "builds on the foundation of the resilience of members of that organisation" (Riolli & Savicki, 2003) It requires "people who can respond quickly and effectively to change while enduring minimal stress" (Mallak, 1998) This approach to resilience is effective in that it leads to a development of social systems of collaboration in order to manifest the ability to respond adequately to change. However, the definition lacks the ability to "link behavioural responses to complex system dynamics" (Moamouni Liminios et al., 2014). |
| Organisational Resilience | Organisational Psychology | Horne (1997) | "Organisational resilience is the ability of a system to withstand the stresses of environmental loading based on the combination/composition of the system pieces, their structural inter-linkages, and the way environmental change is transmitted and spread throughout the entire system. To varying degrees, resilience is a fundamental quality found in individuals, groups, organisations, and systems as a whole. It allows for positive response to significant change that disrupts the expected pattern of events without resulting in regressive/non-productive behaviour.' | Horne goes on to say that if organisations have not taken the required steps in order to withstand intensive changes and cannot rebound to continue to use the assets of the system while it is under pressure to respond in a flexible and creative manner, then it will not matter what the previously attained productive capacity of that organisation was or what it might have become. |

| Adaptability | Organisational Psychology | Sutcliffe & Vogus (2003) | The ability to 'rebound from adversity strengthened and more resourceful.' | A definition that is focused on the development as a result of the adversity, not just the faculty to bounce back. This definition is observed in the literature surround high reliability organisations (HRO). Due to the high potential that failures could cause an escalating issue of wide spread damage, these organisations put a large focus on reliability over efficiency. (Weick, 1987) Examples of these organisations include nuclear power stations, air traffic control systems, and wild-land firefighting crew. (Weick & Sutcliffe, 2001) Exploration in HROs is not an option for organisational learning due to the high cost of failure, which leads to the development of adaptive strategies i.e. decentralising decision making dynamics to allow migration of decisions to find the best qualified individuals for the task. |
| Exploration and Exploitation | Organisational Adaption | Mamouni Limnois et al. (2014) | 'Organisations that balance exploration and exploitation are able to continuously scan their environment and identify the need and opportunity to change when it presents itself, while maintaining and evolving the key organisational capabilities. Such organisations are resilient through a balanced combination of strategic offense and defence, operating in a highly desirable system state.' | Exploitation refers to improving the efficiency of existing skills. Exploration refers to seeking new opportunities for the organisation. |

The general lexicographic definition encompasses a three-stage process to resilience: the subject of the definition is at its current and functioning resting state; force, misfortune and stress is applied to the subject; the subject is able to return to the state which it previously inhabited and carry on.

What is missing from these definitions is the notion of adaptability; progressing as a result of the adversity, and changing the state of the equilibrium as a function of bouncing back from adversity. This is touched upon briefly by Berkes (2007), who notes that some ecological theories 'envision ecosystems as constantly changing and focuses on renewal and reorganisation processes rather than on stable states' (p. 286). Berkes' definition emphasizes something new in that the focus falls away from attempting to reclaim a state lost, but instead on change and adaptation. This theory looks forward to the new organization of the system post-adversity, where the conceptualization of how the system should be formed and function is banished and started afresh in light of the recent events.

Whilst the use of resilience within the psychology literature has not been definitively connected to other disciplines, the definitions remain very similar and appear to have been assimilated by the discipline as a means to explain individual differences in regards to adversity. Earvolino-Ramirez (2007) notes that the origin of resilience within the psychological literature emerged from early psychiatric research investigating those children who appear to be invulnerable to adversity and trauma in their lives, where resilience was used as an interchangeable term for (and later replaced) invulnerability.

The manifestation of the science of resilience was elicited as the result of the progression of developmental psychopathology research. The science first fully came onto the scene in response to the Second World War, where clinicians from a variety of disciplines were called to help children who had been psychologically affected by the war.

The progression of resilience within the clinical psychological discipline has been outlined as evolving in three waves. Firstly, the discipline focused on identifying attributes that would facilitate an individual's resilience. This wave was marked by the work of Norman Garmezey who pioneered the field by investigating stress-resistance children and the factors that may function to protect these children against negative experiences. The second wave marked an investigation by psychologists to ascertain the process by which individuals can acquire and obtain the factors that manifest resilience. Organizations are especially fascinated with this wave, looking constantly to discover how to build a resilient organization and an organization of resilient individuals. Finally, the psychological inquiry has fallen upon (almost philosophically) conceptualizing what resilience is. It is within this wave especially that discord emerges between the differing disciplines and their focus.

One of the biggest names currently in the clinical psychology discipline for resilience is Masten, who stated in a recent paper that 'Resilience can be broadly defined as the capacity of a dynamic system to adapt successfully to disturbances that threaten system function, viability, or development' (p. 6). Masten went on to state that the concept of resilience has been adopted into a multitude of fields that concern themselves with how well complex and intricate systems pre-empt, adjust, recuperate and learn in the context of major threats, surprises and disasters. Lee et al. (2013), however, state that resilience is 'the personal qualities and skills that allow for an individual's healthy/successful functioning or adaption within the context of significant adversity or a disruptive life event' (p. 269).

Resilience is a multidimensional characteristic that comprises of both psychological and dispositional factors: a sense of competence, the existence of an external support systems, and a personal structure. When looking at these sub-facets of resilience, researchers have found that the more of these that an individual is in possession of, the greater the probability of a successful adaptation, compared those individuals with fewer facets, in response to a disruptive event. Resilience becomes a dynamic process; an interaction between the personal faculties and the environmental stress; 'a personality trait for negotiating, managing, and adapting to significant sources of stress or trauma' (Lee et al. 2013, p. 269). Within the clinical perspective, however, what remains unclear is what all the sub-facets of resilience are, which ones are the most important for a successful adaptation, or whether resilience is a faculty that is conceptualized categorically or dimensionally (you either have it or you don't, compared to falling along some scale of resilience).

Developmental psychologists are the majority discipline in researching resilience, investigating it from the viewpoint of children and adolescents who have experience adversity in their life. Masten et al. (1990) deciphered resilience as the faculty to, in the response of a disturbance that poses a threat to the functionality, stability and existence of the system, successfully and efficiently adapt; it is the successful adaptation and progression of an individual despite experiencing misfortune. The view of developmental psychologists is that resilience acts as an innate self-righting mechanism (Werner and Smith 1992) that is present throughout an individual's life.

Masten (2001) defines the process of resilience as experiencing serious adversity and threat to your development, but still adapting in a manner that produces good outcomes. Several things become unclear with this however. Firstly, what constitutes a severe enough threat to derail someone's development? If we use Lazarus' (1982) cognitive appraisal system to a stressor, an individual will primarily cognitively assess the level of the threat, followed by secondarily assessing the inner resources needed to cope with the stressor and whether you have enough to successfully cope. This subjective response to stressors depicts individualistic responses to the same stressor, making it difficult to establish what is worthy to be classified as 'a significant threat to their development' (p. 228). Secondly, Masten's definition does not specify what level of adaptation and subsequent functioning is necessary to be consider 'good'. Some developmental psychologists define good functioning as meeting an observable track record of development as outlined by one's culture and society. Others, however, define good adaption as the avoidance of psychopathology and substance abuse rather than the presence of positive outcomes, such as social or work achievements. What still remains unclear for developmental psychology is whether to define resilience in an outward adaptation manner (e.g. meeting societal norms), inner characteristics and requirements (e.g. the avoidance of psychopathology), or a combination of both.

Closely related to developmental psychology are those psychologists who focus upon context and the *life course* in regards to a person's resilience. This perspective does not consider resilience or adversity to be singular and isolated moments in an individual's life, rather they can be pervasive, constant and actively changing. Windle (2010) notes that in resilience research with children and adolescents, poverty and deprivation are frequently occurring adversity conditions that are investigated. However, life-span investigators are aware of other traumas that can befall an individual when developing as an adult, such as bereavements, unemployment or divorce.

In regards to a longitudinal perspective, resilience is conceptualized as the ability to bounce back from a significant negative event and then carry on with life. One of the key differences about life-span researches is a shift in the population investigated. These theorists focus on adults and the elderly, assessing how an individual handles multiple isolated occurrences or chronic and pervasive adversity yet is able to persevere. Therefore, like the developmental psychologists, this area views resilience as something that manifests and builds with experience; it is something that will develop and aid an individual throughout their lifetime, acting as a self-right mechanism in hardship.

In search of a definition of resilience, the science spans into concepts of environmental resilience, specifically in regards to a community or society. Social resilience has been defined as the ability of groups or communities to cope with external stresses and disturbances as a result of social, political and environmental change (Adger 2000). It is defined at the community level rather than being a phenomenon pertaining to individuals. Hence it is related to the social capital of societies and communities. A relationship must exist between the different forms of resilience; individual resilience will impact community resilience, which together will affect ecological resilience.

2. Typologies and Categories of Resilience

This section of the chapter outlines various attempts by researchers to categorize and classify resilience into subcomponents and factors. As with the previous part, an array of perspectives have been taken into account in order to account for an overarching typology.

Rose (2004) spoke of *Economic Resilience*, referring specifically to the inherent and adaptive reply of individuals and communities to a hazard that allows for minimal losses. Rose stated that economic resilience can take place at three levels: *Microeconomic*: individual behaviour of firms, households or organizations; *Mesoeconomic*: economic sector, individual market, or cooperative group; *Macroeconomic*: all individual units and markets combined, including interactive affects. For Rose, Inherent resilience manifests itself under normal, everyday type circumstances, and represents the ability to reallocate resources in light of unfortunate external circumstances (e.g. reallocating resources in a market as a response to price signals). Adaptive resilience, however, refers to 'the ability in crisis situations to maintain function on the basis of ingenuity or extra effort' (p. 42), such as improving the business' information supply, identifying new suppliers, or a small business increasing the amount of resource substitutions it has available to it in order to respond accordingly and appropriately to the crisis.

Bruneau and his colleagues (2003) researched into earthquakes as a specific form of crisis that impacts millions worldwide and how people, communities and economies cope with this disaster. In defining seismic resilience, Bruneau et al. developed dimensions of resilience which can be thought of in terms of four Rs:

1. *Robustness* – referring to the 'strength, or the ability of elements, systems, and other units of analysis to withstand a given level of stress or demand without suffering degradation or loss of function'.
2. *Redundancy* – 'the extent to which elements, systems, or other units of analysis exist that are substitutable, i.e. capable of satisfying functional requirements in the event of disruption, degradation, or loss of functionality'.
3. *Resourcefulness* – 'the capacity to identify problems, establish priorities, and mobilise resources when condition exist that threaten to disrupt some element, system, or other unit of analysis; resourcefulness can be further conceptualised as consisting of the ability to apply material (i.e. monetary, physical, technological, and informational) and human resources to meet established priorities and achieve goals'.
4. *Rapidity* – 'the capacity to meet priorities and achieve goals in a timely manner in order to contain losses and avoid future disruption' (pp. 737–8).

In their investigation of global environmental change and human sustainability, Dovers and Handmer (1992) designed a typology of societal resilience. It comprised of three types: resilience as resistance and maintenance; as change at the margins; and as openness and adaptability. The *first* type places an avoidance of change and uncertainty as paramount; it is the case that a vast measure of effort and resources can be exhausted in order to maintain an equilibrium or status quo, leading to poor preparation and reaction to unexpected disruptions. The *second* type, resilience as change at the margins, manifests itself in small, gradual changes. These do not rock the boat or disrupt immensely, but can cause a great deal of change in the societal margins.

Table 9.2   Typologies of resilience

Discipline	Author	Outline of typology	Definitions	Additional Comments

Engineering	Bruneau et al. (2003)		In discussing resilience to earthquakes, Bruneau defined:
			
			1. A resilient system - demonstrating 'reduced failure probabilities; reduced consequences from failures, in terms of lives lost, damage, and negative economic and social consequences; reduced time to recovery (restoration of specific system or set of systems to their "normal" level of performance)'
			
			2. Resilience as:
			
			  a) Robustness – referring to the 'strength, or the ability of elements, systems, and other units of analysis to withstand a given level of stress or demand without suffering degradation or loss of function.'
			
			  b) Redundancy – 'the extent to which elements, systems, or other units of analysis exist that are substitutable, i.e. capable of satisfying functional requirements in the event of disruption, degradation, or loss of functionality.'
			
			  c) Resourcefulness – 'the capacity to identify problems, establish priorities, and mobilise resources when condition exist that threaten to disrupt some element, system, or other unit of analysis; resourcefulness can be further conceptualised as consisting of the ability to apply material (i.e. monetary, physical, technological, and informational) and human resources to meet established priorities and achieve goals'
			
			  d) Rapidity – 'the capacity to meet priorities and achieve goals in a timely manner in order to contain losses and avoid future disruption.'
				• This typology is in reference to community resilience rather than institutions or the individual.

Table 9.2   Typologies of resilience (continued)

Discipline	Author	Outline of typology	Definitions	Additional Comments

Economics	Rose (2004)	Economic Resilience (inherent vs. adaptive)	Resilience can take place at three levels:
			
			1. Microeconomic: *individual behaviour of firms, households, or organisations*
			2. Mesoeconomic: *economic sector, individual market, or cooperative group*
			3. Macroeconomic: *all individual units and markets combined, including interactive effects*
			
			Inherent resilience 'refers to the ordinary ability to deal with crises.'
			
			Adaptive resilience refers to 'the ability in crisis situations to maintain function on the basis of ingenuity or extra effort.'
				• Resilience is defined in terms of post-disaster conditions and reaction, which is differentiated from pre-disaster activities that will minimize potential losses through alleviation.
				• Examples of inherent resilience:
				  – A firm's ability to substitute other inputs for those curtailed by an external shock
				  – The ability of markets to reallocate resources in response to price signals.
				• Examples of adaptive resilience:
				  – Increasing input substitution possibilities in individual business operations
				  – Strengthening the market by providing information to match suppliers without customers with customers without suppliers.

	Dovers and Handmer (1992)		1. Resilience as:
			  a) Resistance and maintenance – characterised by a resistance to change.
			  b) Change at the margins – characterised by incremental change
			  c) Openness and adaptability – reduces vulnerability through a high degree of flexibility
				• Proactive resilience assumes high levels of information as well as system and subsystem control in the face of low levels of change
				• Within Reactive resilience, stability is an end in itself; communities will do whatever it takes to guard themselves against change and maintain the equilibrium.

		2. Proactive vs. Reactive resilience
		   a) Proactive is an approach to coping with change and moving towards sustainability based on abandoning the generally fruitless search for stable systems towards evolving resilient systems capable of adaption
		   b) Reactive resilience 'does not adapt to change, but resists change other than at the margins.
			• Openness and adaptability is linked to Dovers and Handmer's second typology in that it is the preparedness to be reactive or proactive given the specific circumstances.
			• This typology is more focused up institutional resilience rather than the resilience of a community.

Organisational Psychology	Mamouni Limnios et al. (2014)	Offensive vs. Defensive	• Offence (adaptive) – the adaptive capacity to react to disturbances by changing its structure, processes and functions in order to increase its ability to persist. • Defence (resistant) – the faculty to resist change and maintain the current status quo (structure and processes) in the face of adversity	• This typology is important in deciphering whether resilience is desirable for an organisation – "resilience is neither desirable in itself nor is it in general a necessary or sufficient condition for sustainable development" (Derissen et al., 2011). • System states that decrease social welfare, such as polluted water supplies and dictatorships, can be highly resilient (Carpenter et al., 2001), but this is not necessarily desirable. • Organisational Psychology Additionally, large organisations that fail to satisfy stakeholders' needs can be very resilient in maintaining an underperforming system state for extended periods of time.

Table 9.2   Typologies of resilience (continued)

Discipline	Author	Outline of typology	Definitions	Additional Comments
Organisational Resilience	Mamouni Limnios et al. (2014)	Resilience Architecture Framework	1. Adaptability Quadrant • High Resilience; High Desirability • These systems enjoy prosperity and exhibit high levels of resilience in the form of adaptive capacity – they hold the ability to adapt, integrate, and reconfigure internal and external organisational skills, resources, and functional competences to match the changing environment. • The business model satisfied the majority of stakeholders' needs through establishing win-win relationships and successful negotiations. • Their structures and processes allow successful assessment of internal and external environment and effectively innovate and adapt through a balance of exploitation and exploration – 'functional momentum' (Miller and Friesen, 1980) • They are ambidextrous organisations – they can simultaneously apply exploration and exploitation. 2. Vulnerability Quadrant • Low Resilience; High Desirability • These companies achieve stakeholder satisfaction, but this is dependent upon certain situations (external, internal, or a combination). This makes them vulnerable to change. • A situational dependence can be caused by underinvesting in exploration – resource rigidity (Gilbert, 2005); the dependency on resources and a necessity of reinvestment incentives. • These organisations are susceptible to external disturbances: government intervention, sociocultural perceptions, change in regulation and natural environment.	• Resilience refers to • Desirability refers to the organisations ability to satisfy stakeholders' needs. • Examples of environmental disturbances in the Vulnerability Quadrant: the introduction of the cassette tape that cause the vinyl industry to become obsolete (Manuel, 1991); climate change on agricultural businesses; the recent credit crunch on the automotive industry where supply and demand became contingent on the availability of credit. • Organisations in the Rigidity Quadrant can survive for long periods of time, but are depicted as 'accidents waiting to happen' (Holling, 2001). Arend (2010) found that these companies continuously slowly decelerate until close to complete failure when they experience a 'death-spiral'.

3. Rigidity Quadrant

- High Resilience; Low Desirability
- These organisations are not satisfying a major proportion of their stakeholders. This is a result of obvious system performance decline, usually taking the forms of decreased sales and profitability with increased customer dissatisfaction and employee turnover.
- The system, however, remains in denial, making it unable to enter phases of change. This can occur in organisations that develop defence mechanisms that maintain current structure and formations, or a lack of sufficient capital to instigate and support a restructure.
- They become caught in a rigidity trap. This occurs by continuously reinforcing successful previous strategies and neglecting information of the changing market; their successes become their downfall. Resilience in these cases is undesirable, exhibiting a 'dysfunction momentum' (Miller and Friesen, 1980). These companies do not accelerate in decline, displaying a resilience to failure.

4. Transience Quadrant

- Low Resilience; Low Desirability
- These organisations face a highly uncertain future, commonly changing structure and procedures to adapt with external disturbances. Whilst these systems are very flexible (as seen in the Adaption Quadrant), they differ in that they are highly unstable and may achieve successful adaptation or fail (ending in destruction or becoming a company of lesser productivity).
- Companies early in life usually pass through this quadrant due to having not yet achieved full stakeholder satisfaction nor resilience.
- Depending on the ability of the change process to minimise the risk of failure and maintain a level of resilience, some organisations may pass through stage for differing periods of time.

Table 9.2   Typologies of resilience (concluded)

Discipline	Author	Outline of typology	Definitions	Additional Comments
Organisational Resilience	Horne (1997)	Strands of developing a sustainable framework for resilience	• Communication of goals, directions, and patterns that relate to change in markets, finances, operations, mission, or vision throughout the entire organisation • Coordination of large and small change efforts throughout the organisations to present a 'whole goal' picture to the workforce • Competencies of individuals, groups, and large segments that are known throughout the entire organisation so they can be interlinked as resources during periods of major change • Commitment by all sectors of the organisation to work together during periods of organisational uncertainty (with a sense of trying) to maintain trust and goodwill • Consideration by organisational leadership that change surround, and creeps into, peoples' lives to such a degree that they may perceive even small shifts in organisational activity as overload • Connections for communication and interaction within the organisation that are focused, functional, and flexible enough to adapt to rapidly-changing needs and conditions • Community perspective that is rooted in converging areas of self-interest by organisational members with regard to training/learning, compensation, work standards, culture and work environment, and future vision.	• Relationships within the organisation and how information flows along these relational paths is a key element in the development of resilience; just as rumours and threats can spread, functional information can be more encouraged to leap across rigid routes to mobilise adaptive responses.

However, the *third* and only type to reduce vulnerability is resilience as openness and adaptability; a high degree of flexibility allows the alterations of basic operation assumptions and structures in order to adopt new ones in times of uncertainty. What is noted, however, is that throughout history societies have rarely done this voluntarily, but have changed slowly and painfully, often out of necessity.

Dovers and Handmer (1992) argued that someone or something's resilience capacity can be conceptualized along a continuum of ignorance, uncertainty and risk. The extremes of this continuum are termed as proactive and reactive resilience. Reactive resilience is very similar to the first type of societal resilience they provided; the focus is on barricading the status quo against any form of disruption, barring it from the possibility of change in 'a quest for constancy and stability' (Handmer and Dovers 1996). At the other end of the continuum, proactive resilience is accepting of the notion and inexorability of change, and will build a system and structure that is capable of flexibility and adaptability.

When it comes to a clinical approach to resilience typography, there are two basic approaches to identifying and testing the resources and protective factors associated with resilience: a person focused approach and a variable focused approach (Masten 2001). The former includes case studies and research on groups of individuals who meet specified criteria for both risk and good adaptation, typically to compare them with other groups of people who share the same level of risk but were maladaptive, and sometimes also others who shared the same positive outcomes but had lower risk. A variable-focused approach, however, relies on multivariate statistical analysis, looking for a main effect or interaction effect between the disruptive event, outcome and potential qualities of an individual or their environment that may act as protective (or compensatory) factors against adversity (Luther, Cicchetti and Becker 2007; Masten 2001).

Within the clinical approach to resilience, researchers often refer to the psychological resources available to an individual and how they ameliorate adversity and foster resilience. The specifics of what factors have been identified is not discussed here, but instead how these factors may come into play. The *Protective Model* outlines that the existence and availability of these resources influences the direction and strength of the adversity in a multitude of ways. The Compensatory component suggests that an individual who has an availability of these resources will respond in a similar pattern to an individual without, but on a higher plane of functioning; that is, the resources provide a higher level of initial functioning which is reduced by the same amount in adversity, but does not fall as far as a result. The *Protective-Stabilizing* component states that the existence of resources elicits overall higher function (as in the compensatory model), but also yields no decrease in functioning, despite the presence of a level of adversity that causes others without sufficient resources to severely decline in functioning. The Protective-Stabilizing model is commonly tested in association with a variable-focused approach; statistical analysis with the inclusion of an interaction term between the risk and protective factor in multiple regression. Finally, the *Protective-Reactive* model states that these resources may present an advantage in situations of low stress. However, as seen with Dovers and Handmer's (1992) first type of societal resilience, when stress is encountered this has a more severe impact on functioning. Whilst the functioning still is not as impeded as those without the resources, the difference in functioning before and during the disruption is far greater.

In contrast to the Protective Model of resilience is the Challenge Model; there is a curvilinear relationship between a risk-factor and an outcome, where there exists an optimal level of exposure to adversity that renders the individual most apt and resilient. At the extremes, too little or too much expose to adversity can leave an individual, society or organization weaker to respond.

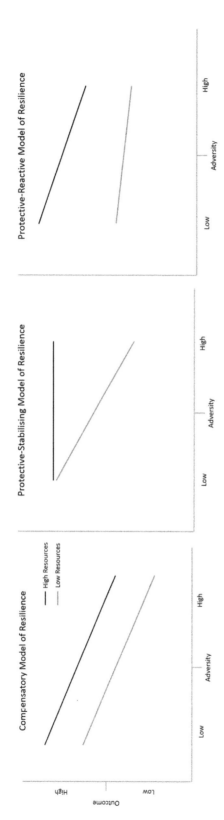

Figure 9.1   The three Protective Models of resources

Coutu (2002) stated that the framework for a resilient individual rests upon three pillars. The first of which is the ability to accept and face reality; resilience does not derive from optimism. Whilst removing the rose-tinted glasses does not necessitate acquiring a cynical and bitter view, it does bring a sense of preparedness; you are aware of what the situation is and what the consequences will be, and you know how to deal with that appropriately when the time comes. Second, Coutu states one needs a strongly held view that life has meaning and a continued search for that meaning. Resilient people devise constructs about their suffering to create some sort of meaning for themselves and others. The dynamic of meaning making is the way resilient people build bridges from present-day hardships to a fuller, better constructed future. Third, Coutu states that the resilient individual possesses *bricolage*, an incredible ability to improvise when needed with only what you have. In her research of concentration camp victims she found that the most resilient people knew to pocket pieces of string or wire as they may later become useful.

A typology proposed by Mamouni Limnios et al. (2014) provides light into deciphering whether resilience is desirable for an organization – 'one may conclude that resilience is neither desirable in itself nor is it in general a necessary or sufficient condition for sustainable development' (Derissen et al. 2011, p. 1122). The desirability of resilience is a factor that is often overlooked in the literature. Mamouni Limnios et al. therefore outline two styles of resilience: offence, which represents an adaptive capacity to react to disturbances by changing structure, processes and functions in order to increase sustainability; and defence, the faculty to resist change and maintain the current status quo in the face of adversity. The defensive resilience, again, appears very similar to Dovers and Handmer's (1992) first type of societal resilience.

Using this distinction, Mamouni Limnios et al. (2014) went on to create the *Resilience Architecture Framework* to determine the resilience magnitude of an organisation. The framework consists of two dimensions; resilience (a continuum from offence as high to defence as low) and desirability (which refers to an organization's ability to satisfy its stakeholders' needs). As a result, four quadrants are formed: the *adaptability quadrant*, where organizations enjoy high prosperity and exhibit high levels of resilience; the *vulnerability quadrant*, where organizations have achieved stakeholder satisfaction but this is contingent on many external factors, making them vulnerable to change; organizations within the *rigidity quadrant* are able to persevere and display high levels of resilience, but are not pleasing a large proportion of their stakeholders; and the *transience quadrant*, in which organizations face a highly uncertain future, commonly changing structure and procedures to adapt to external disturbances.

Horne (1997) developed a sustainable framework for resilience made up of seven relational pathways; the relationships within the organization and how information flows along these relational paths is a key element in the development of resilience. Horne's framework comprised of seven Cs: Communication; Co-ordination; Competencies; Commitment; Consideration; Connections; and Community.

It is clear that there remains a number of interesting and overlapping conceptual distinctions and typologies in this area with no agreement as to which is clearest or has most empirical support.

Table 9.3   Resilience measures

Measure	Authors	Measurement Factors [items]	Internal Consistency	Evaluation
Baruth Protective Factors Inventory	Baruth and Carroll (2002)	Four primary protective factors: Adaptable Personality; Supportive Environments; Fewer Stressors; and Compensating Experiences [16]	Total Cronbach's alpha .83; subscales scored .76 (adaptive personality), .98 (supportive environment), .55 (fewer stressors), .83 (compensating experiences).	Used as a measure to identify resiliency factors in adolescents. Very little published research on the scale. Authors indicate that the validity and reliability 'Fewer Stressors' does not correlate with the other variables, hinting towards the curvilinear model of resilience – optimal level of adversity for maximum resilience
Connor-Davidson Resilience Scale (CD-RISC)	Connor & Davidson (2003)	Five factors: personal competence, high standards, and tenacity; trust in one's instincts, tolerance of negative affect, and strengthening effects against stress; positive acceptance of change and secure relationships; control; and spiritual influences [25]	Alphas of .89 (Connor & Davidson, 2003), and cross-culturally of .89 (Yu et al., 2011), .93 (Baek et al., 2010), .91 (Yu & Zhang, 2010).	Lack of consistency in exploratory factor analysis: differing five factor solutions (Ito et al., 2009; Baek et al., 2010; Yu et al., 2011), four factor solution (Lamond et al., 2008; Singh & Yu, 2010; Bitsika, Sharpley, & Peters, 2010), three factor solutions (Kariarkmak, 2010; Yu & Zhang, 2010), two-factor model (Green et al., 2014), and a uni-dimensional model (Burns & Anstey, 2010).
Resilience Scale for Adults (RSA)	Friborg, Hjemdal, Rosenvinge, & Martinussen (2003)	Intended to measure the protective resources that promote adult resilience: personal competence; social competence; family coherence; social support; and personal structure. [37]	Internal consistency of subscales ranges from .67 to .90.	Studies have repeatedly support the reliability and validity of the five-factor model of the RSA (Friborg et al., 2003; 2005; Friborg, Martinussen, & Rosenvinge, 2006). The scale also displays high levels of convergent validity (Friborg et al., 2005) The scale has been found to load with the Big 5 traits Agreeableness, Conscientiousness, and Emotional Stability (Friborg et al., 2005) It has predicted subjective stress for participants both before and as a main effect during an induced pain condition (Friborg et al., 2006) Issues are that the scale emerged from research outlining the three broad resilience protective factors which were used to define questionnaire items, but from this it is unclear how decisions for item wording was made, or whether the target population piloted and involved in selecting the items used (Windle et al., 2011)

Scale	Description	Reliability	Notes
Adolescent Resilience Scale (ARS) Oshio, Kaneko, Nagamine, & Nakaya (2003)	Comprised of three factors: novelty seeking; emotional regulation; and positive future orientation. [21]	Internal consistency among factors ranges from .72 to .75	Very little theoretical rationale is presented, and it is unclear as to how the psychological characteristics were chosen to represent resilience. Designed for, and piloted with, Japanese adolescents between 18–23 years old. Of the very few clinical applications, it was unsuccessful at predicting dispositional differences between a resilient and clinical sample (Klasen et al., 2010).
Brief Resilient Scale (BRCS) Smith et al., (2008)	Designed to measure tendencies to cope with stress in a highly adaptive manner, and bounce back successfully [6]	Total Cronbach's alpha across four samples yielded an alpha of .86	This scale is unique in that it was developed to have a specific focus on bouncing back from stress. Sinclair and Wallston (2004) state most other scales emphasis examining the resources/protective factors that might facilitate a resilient outcome. The data reduction appears to be based on feedback and piloting of the original list, no empirical validation of the data reduction is reported. Windle et al. (2011) state that this scale could be a useful outcome measure in the context of stress. The scale was found to be related to numerous health-related outcomes, including less negative affect, more positive affect, less perceived stress, and less physical symptoms. Thought that the resilience the scale measures may be an understated personal resource (Smith et al., 2010)
Resilience Scale (RS) Wagnild and Young (1993)	The scale has two factors: personal competence and acceptance of self and life. [25 / 14 in shorter version]	Reliability coefficient of .91	Has been applied to Russian immigrants in Israel (Arorian & Norris, 2000), adolescent mothers (Black & Ford-Gillboe, 2004), Alzheimers family care givers (Garity, 1997), Mexican women and depression (Heilemann, Lee, & Kury, 2002), homeless adolescents (Rew, Taylor-Sheehanfer, & Taylor, 2002), and Chinese cancer patients (Tian & Hong, 2013). Controversy over factor structure: original two-factor model (Wagnild & Young, 1993) has been supported cross-culturally (Tian & Hong, 2013; Heilemann, Lee, & Kury, 2003; Ruiz-Parraga, Lopez-Martinez, and Lydia Gomez-Perez, 2012), but it one-factor (Nishi et al., 2010) and five-factor (Lundman et al., 2007) models have been found.

Table 9.3   Resilience measures *(concluded)*

Measure	Authors	Measurement Factors [items]	Internal Consistency	Evaluation
Dispositional Resilience Scale	Bartone (1991; 1995)	3 dimensions: Commitment; Control; and Challenge. [30; 15]	Alpha score for the 15-item scale has been reported as .82 (Bartone, 1999)	Both the 30- and 15-item version of the scale have been to have good reliability, as well as displaying the appropriate criterion-related and predictive validity in multiple samples (Bartone, 1995; Bartone, 2007) Both versions of the scale have been applied to military samples and displayed success in predictive ability (e.g. Bartone, Ursano, Wright, and Ingraham, 1989; Britt, Adler, & Bartone, 2001; Bartone et al., 2008). Scale has been applied clinically to demonstrate a trait ability that facilitates the adjustment process after the loss of a spouse (Rossi, Bisconti, & Bergeman, 2010). The scale has been successfully translated and applied cross-culturally (Picardi et al., 2012). The scale has often been applied as a measure of hardiness due to its theoretical background and foundation. The scale may assist in measuring resilient response from an individual level, but its fixed view of resilience does not fit well with the literature on resilience as a dynamic process.
The Ego Resiliency 89 (ER89)	Block & Kremen (1996)	1 dimension that represents a stable personality trait [14]		Resilience, as measured by the ER89, is a personal characteristic that reflects how an individual adapts to stress, uncertainty, conflict, and change in their environment (Block & Block, 1980) The research assumes that resilience measured by the ER89 is pre-disposition to resist anxiety and to engage positively with the world. The score created from the ER89 does not depend on risk or adversity. The ER89 measures the personal factor that is a part of the dynamic process in dealing with everyday change. Using the ER89 as an indicator of resilience on its own has been regarded as the incorrect use of the measure. Instead, Ego-resiliency may represent a single facet of the protective process that results in a resilience outcome (Windle et al., 2011). Individuals found to be high on the ER89 are more intellectually flexible and comfortable with a vague interpersonal world. Those with high, raw IQ are efficient in a clear world of structure but are less competent affectively. (Block & Kremlin, 1996) The ER89 has been translated into different languages and successfully applied cross-culturally (Alessandri et al., 2012).

3. How to Measure Resilience

Measuring resilience is an important aspect of the research agenda. With no operationalized definition of resilience, scales measuring it are large in variety and application. A review by Windle et al. (2011) stated there is no 'gold standard' of resilience scale, but there are measures in existence with appropriate and specific application. This section reviews a few of the more prominent scales in the literature.

MEASURES FOR RESILIENCE

The Connor-Davidson Resilience Scale (CD-RISC; Connor and Davidson 2003) comprises 25 items where resilience is viewed as a successful stress-coping ability based on theories of stress, coping and adaptation research. They developed questions to elicit protective factors such as self-efficacy, sense of humour, secure attachments, patience, and thinking of change as a challenge. It is a self-report measure, where respondents indicate responses on a five-point Likert scale, ranging from 0 to 100, where higher scores indicate greater resilience. In their initial investigation, exploratory factor analysis revealed five factors within the CD-RISC: personal competence, high standards and tenacity; trust in one's instincts, tolerance of negative affect, and strengthening effects against stress; positive acceptance of change and secure relationships; control; and spiritual influences.

Cronbach's Alpha scores for the CD-RISC are always found to be high, with alphas of 0.89 (Connor and Davidson 2003), and cross-culturally of 0.89 (Yu et al. 2011), 0.93 (Baek et al. 2010) and 0.91 (Yu and Zhang 2007). An issue with the CD-RISC, however, is that it fails to be consistent in its five-factor model of resilience. Previous studies have supported the five-factor solution of the measure cross-culturally – such as Yu et al. (2011) within Chinese adolescents after the 2008 Sichuan earthquakes – but others have found differing interpretations of the factors; Baek et al. (2010) investigated the Korean version of the CD-RISC, and yielded a slightly altered five-factor solution, where the factors represented hardiness, persistence, optimism, social support and meaningful relationships, and spiritual influence. Furthermore, others have revealed a four-factor solution (e.g. Bitsika et al. 2010; Lamond et al. 2008; Singh and Yu 2010), for example Campbell-Sills and Stein (2007) found the factors to represent hardiness, social support/purpose, faith and persistence.

Researchers using the measure have also yielded a three-factor solution: Yu and Zhang (2007) found with a Chinese sample that the factors represent tenacity, strength and optimism. A recent study with post-9/11 US military veterans revealed that the best fitting model was found from a two-factor solution, representing adaptability and self-efficacy (Green et al. 2014). Burns and Anstey (2010), however, tested the structural validity of the CD-RISC and revealed that 54% of the variance in the measure could be explained by four factors, with most loaded onto the first factor and one or two items cross-loading; 40% of variance was explained by a single factor. The results from their testing did not support the hypothesis that the CD-RISC comprises multiple resilience factors, but instead revealed a one-factor CD-RISC model compromising of a revised 22-item scale.

The Resilience Scale (RS) was developed by Wagnild and Young (1993), and has been acclaimed as one the best measures for resilience (Ahern et al. 2006). The scale is derived from the researchers conducting interviews with 'resilient' individuals, as well as investigating measures of personal attributes that are associated with resilience. The RS is a 25-item scale (although a shorter, 14-item scale has been generated and validated), where participants indicate a response upon a seven-point Likert Scale. The RS views resilience as a personality characteristic that aids and enhances individual adaptation. The RS is comprised of five components: equanimity and remaining composed in adversity, perseverance, self-reliance, meaningfulness, and existential aloneness.

The scale has been applied successfully to a vast amount of contexts: the assessment of Russian immigrants in Israel (Arorian and Norris 2000), adolescent mothers (Black and Ford-Gilboe 2004), Alzheimers family care givers (Garity 1997), Mexican women and depression (Heilemann et al. 2003), homeless adolescents (Rew et al. 2001), and Chinese cancer patients (Tian and Hong 2013). However, there are issues with the RS in regards to its dimensions. The original construction of the scale revealed a two-factor model (Wagnild and Young 1993), comprising of personal competence and acceptance of self and life. This has since been supported cross-culturally with a Chinese (Tian and Hong 2013) and Spanish version (Heilemann et al. 2003; Ruiz-Parraga et al. 2012). Lundman et al. (2007), however, yielded a five-factor solution with a Swedish sample that reflected the five components of resilience originally outlined by Wagnild and Young. Furthermore, an analysis of both the RS and its abridged version yielded a single-factor solution with a Japanese sample (Nishi et al. 2010).

Research into resilience states that there are three broad categories of protective factors in the adult population: positive characteristics and resources; coherent, stable and supportive family environment; and a social network that supports and reinforces adaptive coping. *The Resilience Scale for Adults* (RSA; Friborg et al. 2003) was developed through a need to measure these three resilience aspects. It comprises of five factors: personal strength – which itself is made of positive perception of self and of the future – social competence, structured style, family cohesion, and social resources.

Studies have repeatedly support the reliability and validity of the five-factor model of the RSA (Friborg et al. 2003, 2005, 2006a). The scale also displays high levels of convergent validity, implying that if individuals experienced strong personal strength or social competence, they most probably also experienced a coherent and stable family or good social resources (Friborg et al. 2005). The RSA has also been associated with the Big 5 model of personality, finding that social competence and social resources loaded with Agreeableness, structured style and perceptions of future loaded with Conscientiousness, whilst family cohesion loaded on to Emotional Stability (Friborg et al. 2005).

Feelings of pain and pain related dysfunctions are often augmented by psychopathology, negative and stressful life events, and personality traits such as neuroticism. In one study, the RSA predicted subjective stress for participants both before and as a main effect during an induced pain condition (Friborg et al. 2006b); the RSA reliably distinguished between participants with high and low levels of resilience, and thus resistance to stress and possessing the ability to moderate pain as a corollary. The RSA has previously distinguished between healthy controls and psychiatric patients, and protected against negative life events by increasing adaptability to life stresses. The RSA has shown strong negative correlations with neuroticism and introversion. Results support the predictive validity of the RSA, finding that respondents' scores obtained several days before the experiment could reliably predict individual differences in reported pain and stress.

OTHER MEASURES

Baruth and Carroll (2002) developed the *Baruth Protective Factors Inventory (BPFI)* as a means to identify factors of resilience within individuals. The measure focuses on four types of protective factor: firstly, it looks at how adaptable the individual's personality is; secondly, the supportive nature of the environment; thirdly, whether the individual has low or high amount of stressors; and finally, the compensating experiences that the individual has been through. The scale primarily was created for adults, but it has been used with adolescents as well despite a paucity of research to indicate the appropriateness of this scale and age-group (Bogar 2006).

The Dispositional Resilience Scale (DRS) has been developed and modified multiple times over the lifetime of resilience inquiry. Based upon Maddi and Kobasi's work on hardiness, the DSR was developed into a 45-item scale to reflect resilience as a function of the interrelation of the three hardiness facets: Commitment, Control and Challenge. Resilience is viewed as a fixed trait that allows a successful pattern of adaptive responses to contexts involving severe adversity or risk, as well as acute stress and trauma. The scale has been successfully applied to military samples (e.g. Bartone et al. 1989; Britt et al. 2001); Bartone et al. (2008) found that Dispositional Resilience was significant in predicting which students of Military 'Special Forces' training would succeed and who would fail. The scale has also been shown to demonstrate trait resilience: applied in a clinical sense, finding that dispositional resilience represents a factor that facilitates in the adjustment and bereavement process for widows (Rossi, Bisconti and Bergeman 2007); as well as finding that differences in Dispositional Resilience accounts for variance in daily emotional response to stress (Ong et al. 2006). The scale has also been translated and its psychometric and hierarchical properties found to be reliable and consistent cross-culturally (Hystad et al. 2010; Picardi et al. 2012).

4. Conclusion

Those less familiar with psychological research may express dismay that there seems to be no agreed definition and typology of the concept of resilience or the development of an universally applied and psychometrically proven measure. Yet, most researchers would recognize this as a common, inevitable – if not desirable – state of affairs. The optimist might point to agreement about the fundamental concept and definition and all the good effort put into developing a robust measure; the pessimist to muddle and confusion.

However what is most clear from the above is the amount of inter-disciplinary effort that has been, and remains being, put in to investigate the most important of human characteristics.

References

Adger, W.N. (2000). Social and ecological resilience: Are they related? *Progress in Human Geography*, 24(3), 347–64.

Ahern, N.R., Kiehl, E.M., Sole, M.L. and Byers, J. (2006). A review of instruments measuring resilience. *Issues in Comprehensive Pediatric Nursing*, 29, 103–25.

Aroian, K.J. and Norris, A.E. (2000). Resilience, stress, and depression among Russian immigrants to Israel. *Western Journal of Nursing Research*, 22(1), 54–67.

Baek, H.S., Lee, K.U., Joo, E.J., Lee, M.Y. and Choi, K.S. (2010). Reliability and validity of the Korean version of the Connor-Davidson resilience scale. *Psychiatric Investigation*, 7, 109–15.

Bartone, P.T., Roland, R., Picano, J. and Williams, T. (2008). Psychological hardiness predicts success in US army special forces candidates. *International Journal of Selection and Assessment*, 16, 78–81.

Bartone, P.T., Ursano, R.J., Wright, K.W. and Ingraham, L.H. (1989). The impact of a military air disaster on the health of assistance workers: A prospective study. *Journal of Nervous and Mental Disease*, 177, 317–28.

Baruth, K.E. and Carroll, J.J. (2002). A formal assessment of resilience: The Baruth Protective Factors Inventory. *The Journal of Individual Psychology*, 58, 235–44.

Berkes, F. (2007). Understanding uncertainty and reducing vulnerability: Lessons from resilience thinking. *Natural Hazards*, 41, 283–95.

Bitsika, V., Sharpley, C. and Peters, K. (2010). How is resilience associated with anxiety and depression? Analysis of factor score interactions within a homogeneous sample. *German Journal of Psychiatry*, 13, 9–16.

Black, C. and Ford-Gilboe, M. (2004). Adolescent mothers: Resilience, family health work, and health-promoting practices. *Journal of Advanced Nursing*, 48, 351–60.

Bogar, C.B. (2006). Resiliency determinants and resiliency processes among female adult survivors of childhood sexual abuse. *Journal of Counselling and Development*, 84(3), 318–27.

Britt, T.W., Adler, A.B. and Bartone, P.T. (2001). Deriving benefits from stressful events: The role of engagement in meaningful work and hardiness. *Journal of Occupational Health Psychology*, 6, 53–63.

Bruneau, M., Chang, S.E., Eguchi, R.T., Lee, G.C., O'Rourke, T.D., Reinhorn, A.M., Shinozuka, M., Tierney, K., Wallace, W.A. and von Winterfeldt, D. (2003). A framework to quantitatively assess and enhance the seismic resilience of communities. *Earthquake Spectra*, 19(4), 733–52.

Burns, R.A. and Anstey, K.J. (2010). The Connor-Davidson Resilience Scale (CD-RISC): Testing the invariance of a uni-dimensional resilience measure that is independent of positive and negative affect. *Personality and Individual Differences*, 48, 527–31.

Campbell-Sills, L. and Stein, M.B. (2007) Psychometric analysis and refinement of the Connor-Davidson Resilience Scale (CD-RISC): Validation of a 10-item measure of resilience. *Journal of Trauma and Stress*, 20, 1019–28.

Connor, K.M. and Davidson, J.R.T. (2003). Development of a new resilience scale: The Connor–Davidson Resilience Scale (CD–RISC). *Depression and Anxiety*, 18, 76–82.

Coutu, D.L. (2002). How resilience works. *Harvard Business Review*, 80(5), 46–56.

Derissen, S., Quass, M.F. and Baumgartner, S. (2011). The relationship between resilience and sustainability of ecological-economic systems. *Ecological Economics*, 70(6), 1121–8.

Dovers, S.R. and Handmer, J.W. (1992). Uncertainty, sustainability, and change. *Global Environmental Change*, 2(4), 262–76.

Earvolino-Ramirez, M. (2007). Resilience: A concept analysis. *Nursing Forum*, 42(2), 73–82.

Friborg, O., Martinussen, M. and Rosenvinge, J.H. (2006a). Likert-based vs. semantic differential-based scorings of positive psychological constructs: A psychometric comparison of two versions of a scale measuring resilience. *Personality and Individual Differences*, 40, 873–84.

Friborg, O., Hjemdal, O., Rosenvinge, J.H. and Martinussen, M. (2003). A new rating scale for adult resilience: What are the central protective resources behind healthy adjustment? *International Journal of Methods in Psychiatric Research*, 12(2), 65–76

Friborg, O., Barlaug, D., Rosenvinge, J.H., Martinussen, M. and Hjemdal, O. (2005). Resilience in relation to personality and intelligence. *International Journal of Methods in Psychiatric Research*, 14(1), 29–42.

Friborg, O., Hjemdal, O., Rosenvinge, J.H., Martinussen, M., Aslaksen, P.M. and Flaten, M.A. (2006b). Resilience as a moderator of pain and stress. *Journal of Psychosomatic Research*, 61(2), 213–19.

Garity, J. (1997). Stress, learning style, resilience factors, and ways of coping in Alzheimer family caregivers. *American Journal of Alzheimer's Disease*, 12, 171–8.

Green, K.T., Hayward, L.C., Williams, A.M., Dennis, P.A., Bryan, B.C., Taber, K.H., Davidson, J.R.T., Beckham, J.C. and Calhoun, P.S. (2014). Examining the factor structure of the Connor-Davidson Resilience Scale (CD-RISC) in a post-9/11 U.S. military veteran sample. *Assessment*, 21(4), 443–51.

Handmer, J.W. and Dovers, S.R. (1996). A typology of resilience: Rethinking institutions for sustainabile development. *Organisation and Environment*, 9, 482–511.

Heilemann, M.V., Lee, K.A. and Kury, F.S. (2003). Psychometric properties of the Spanish version of the Resilience Scale. *Journal of Nursing Measurement*, 11, 61–72.

Horne, J.F.I. (1997). The coming age of organizational resilience. *Business Forum*, 22(2/3/4), 24–8.

Hystad, S.W., Eid, J., Johnsen, B.H, Laberg, J.C. and Bartone, P.T. (2010). Psychometric properties of the revised Norwegian dispositional resilience (hardiness) scale. *Scandinavian Journal of Psychology*, 51, 237–54.

Lamond, A.J., Depp, C.A., Allison, M., Langer, R., Reichstadt, J., Moore, D.J., Golshan, S., Ganiats, T.G. and Jeste, D.V. (2008). Measurement and predictors of resilience among community-dwelling older women. *Journal of Psychiatric Research*, 43, 148–54.

Lazarus, R.S. (1982). Thoughts on the relations between emotion and cognition. *American Psychologist*, 37(9), 1019–24.

Lee, J.H., Nam, S.K., Kim, A.-R., Kim, B., Lee, M.Y. and Lee, S.M. (2013). Resilience: A meta-analytic approach. *Journal of Counselling and Development*, 91, 269–79.

Lundman, B., Strandberg, G., Eisemann, M., Gustafson, Y. and Brulin, C. (2007). Psychometric properties of the Swedish version of the resilience scale. *Scandinavian Journal of Caring Sciences*, 21(2), 229–37.

Luther, S.S., Cicchetti, D. and Becker, B. (2007). The construct of resilience: A critical evaluation and guidelines for future work. *Child Development*, 71(3), 543–62.

Mamouni Limnios, E.A., Mazzarol, T., Ghadouani, A. and Schilizzi, S.G.M. (2014). The resilience architecture framework: Four organisational archetypes. *European Management Journal*, 32, 104–16.

Masten, A.S. (2001). Ordinary magic: Resilience processes in development. *American Psychologist*, 56(30), 227–38.

Masten, A.S. (2014). Global perspectives on resilience in children and youth. *Child Development*, 85, 6–20.

Masten, A.S., Best, K.M. and Garmezym, N. (1990). Resilience and development: Contributions from the study of children who overcome adversity. *Developmental Psychopathology*, 2, 425–44.

Nishi, D., Uehara, R., Kondo, M. and Matsuoka, Y. (2010). Reliability and validity of the Japanese version of the Resilience Scale and its short version. *BMC Research Notes*, 3(310), doi: 10.1186/1756–0500–3-310.

Ong, A.D., Bergeman, C.S., Bisconti, T.L. and Wallace, K.A. (2006). Psychological resilience, positive emotions, and successful adaptation to stress in later life. *Personality Processes and Individual Difference*, 91(4), 730–49.

Picardi, A., Bartone, P.T., Querci, R., Bitetti, D., Tarsitani, L., Roselli, V., Maraone, A., Fabi, E., De Michele, F., Gaviano, I., Flynn, B., Ursano, R. and Biondi, M. (2012). Development and validation of the Italian version of the 15-item Dispositional Resilience Scale. *Rivista di psichiatria*, 47(3), 231–7.

Rew, L., Taylor-Sheehafer, M., Thomas, N.Y. and Yockey, S. (2001). Correlates of resilience in homeless adolescents. *Journal of Nursing Scholarship*, 33, 33–40.

Rose, A. (2004). Defining and measuring economic resilience to earthquakes. *Disaster Prevention and Management*, 13, 307–14.

Rossi, N.E., Bisconti, T.L. and Bergeman, C.S. (2007). The role of dispositional resilience in regaining life satisfaction after the loss of a spouse. *Death Studies*, 31, 863–83.

Ruiz-Parraga, G.T., Lopez-Martinez, A.E. and Gomez-Perez, L. (2012). Factor structure and psychometric properties of the resilience scale in a Spanish chronic musculoskeletal pain sample. *The Journal of Pain*, 13(11), 1090–98.

Singh, K. and Yu, X. (2010). Psychometric evaluation of the Connor-Davidson Resilience Scale (CD-RISC) in a sample of Indian students. *Journal of Psychology*, 1, 23–30.

Tian, J. and Hong, J.S. (2013). Validation of the Chinese version of the Resilience Scale and its cutoff score for detecting low resilience in Chinese cancer patients. *Support Care Cancer*, 21, 1497–502.

Wagnild, G.M., and Young, H.M. (1993). Development and psychometric evaluation of the Resilience Scale. *Journal of Nursing Measurement*, 1, 165–78.

Werner, E. and Smith, R. (1992). *Overcoming the Odds: High-risk Children from Birth to Adulthood*. New York: Cornell University Press.

Windle, G. (2010). What is resilience? A review and concept analysis. *Reviews in Clinical Gerontology*, doi:10.1017/S0959259810000420.

Windle, G., Bennett, K.M. and Noyes, J. (2011). A methodological review of resilience measurement scales. *Health and Quality of Life Outcomes*, 9(8), doi:10.1186/1477–7525-9-8.

Yu, X. and Zhang, J. (2007). Factor analysis and psychometric validation of the Connor-Davidson resilience (CD-RISC) with Chinese people. *Social Behaviour and Personality*, 35, 19–30.

Yu, X., Lau, J.F., Mak, W., Zhang, J. and Lui, W. (2011). Factor structure and psychometric properties of the Connor-Davidson Resilience Scale among Chinese adolescents. *Comprehensive Psychiatry*, 52(2), 218–24.

10

Examining Proactive Coping and Resilience within the Context of the Economic Recession

Constance A. Mara and Esther R. Greenglass

Introduction

The financial crisis which began in 2008 and the recession that followed have had a serious and profound impact on economies worldwide. Since its onset, news headlines around the world have reported widespread effects at the individual level, including increased insecurity about the future, soaring unemployment, precarious jobs, increased debt, a decline in quality of life, and deterioration in both physical health and mental well-being (Froman 2010). For example, one report presents research from the United States linking unemployment and job insecurity with increased risk of heart attack (Mozes 2012). Challenges associated with financial insecurity and joblessness can have a significant impact on the mental health of individuals and their families. For example, underemployment and unemployment have been linked with loss of self-esteem, which can lead to depression and anxiety (Froman 2010; Sojo and Guarino 2011). In Canada, a recent report found that the recession is linked to a 24% decline in overall well-being of Canadians (Sun Life Canadian Health Index 2012).

Given the cutbacks both at the government and business levels, millions worldwide have lost their jobs, with the youth in most countries being disproportionately affected (Greenglass 2014). Students face a particularly challenging economic landscape. Many of them have borrowed heavily to finance their education but are finding it difficult to find a job both while in school and after graduation. Since they face the highest rates of unemployment, they experience greater stress due to their inability to repay their student loan debt (Canadian Centre for Policy Alternative 2012). Indeed, some reports indicate that today's young adults may be so affected by the recession because of decreasing employment quality, non-permanent jobs and fewer benefits, that they will never enjoy the comfortable lifestyles of their parents and grandparents (Goar 2012). Across many countries, the unemployment rates among youth are approximately twice the national average. In Canada, for example, the unemployment rate among youth was 13.6% in April 2014, whereas the overall national unemployment rate in Canada was 6.9% during the same period. Youth unemployment in February 2014 in Ireland was 26% (national rate was 11.9%), and in Portugal the youth unemployment rate was 35% in

February 2014, compared to the national rate of 15.3%. Italy and Spain are dealing with youth unemployment rates of 42.3% and 53.6%, respectively, while the overall unemployment rate for these countries is 13% and 25.6%, respectively. More than 75 million young people around the world are unemployed (International Labour Organization 2014) and recent studies reveal that youth jobless rates worldwide will continue to rise through 2016 (International Labour Organization 2014). Despite signs of economic recovery from various reports, this tends to be restricted to certain sectors of the society with the advantages concentrated mainly with those who are already wealthy (Greenglass 2014).

The problem of youth unemployment and underemployment can have severe consequences both for the individuals involved and the nation itself. On the individual level, unemployment can lead to widespread distress and difficulties in the short term, and may have negative long-term effects as well. For example, when individuals experience early unemployment, there are delays in obtaining experience and training that often can lead to increased pay. Prior work experience has a profound effect on future earnings. A 13-week unemployment spell in one year reduces wages the following year by 3.4% or about $900 (in 1993 US dollars) for a full-time employee. In addition to suffering from lower wages, after experiencing an unemployment spell, many individuals also experience an increased likelihood of future unemployment (Mroz and Savage 2001). This can lead to widespread suffering in the short term and may have negative long-term effects on a societal level.

Additional research has shown that concerns about economic matters and financial strain can adversely affect health. For example, Rios and Zautra (2011) report that economic hardship was a moderator of the effects of financial worry on reported daily pain. Challenges and losses related to the economic sphere have also been associated with an increase in psychological stress (Belluck 2009). Given the association between stress and economic hardship, it is important to specify both the causes of the financial stress but also to examine factors that can alleviate the stress.

Stress and Threat

Recent research underlines the perception of one's financial situation as a potential threat (Marjanovic, Greenglass, Fiksenbaum, and Bell 2013). Given that one's financial situation can be stressful, it is possible to determine the predictors of the stress as well as those factors that can alleviate distress. The transactional theory of stress provides a useful theoretical framework to understand how stress responses may differ among individuals (Folkman, Lazarus, Dunkel-Schetter, DeLongis and Gruen 1986). Psychological stress occurs when individuals appraise their environment as taxing or exceeding their resources and endangering their well-being. According to this theory, exposure to a potential stressor triggers an evaluative cognitive process where individuals consider whether or not the stressor is a threat to their well-being, known as primary appraisal. In turn, this process prompts secondary appraisal – an evaluation of options for coping with the perceived stressor. Threat appraisals can be defined as assessing an experience or event's potential for harm or loss in the future (Lazarus and Folkman 1984). If harm or threat is expected, individuals evaluate resources – both internal and external – that are available to them to cope with the stressor. Internal resources include self-esteem, coping style, resilience, for example, and external resources can include factors like social support. Perception of a paucity of resources to adequately cope with the stressor is associated with feeling anxious, depressed, hopeless and exhausted.

There are two important aspects of the transactional theory of stress that are relevant to an understanding of the stress that can emanate from one's financial situation. First, individuals need resources in order to effectively cope with a stressor. Second, individuals need to re-evaluate the threat in light of their resources. For example, individuals may reframe a stressor as positive, or the individual may perceive the stressor as a challenge (that can be overcome) rather than a threat. Through re-appraising a stressor from a threat to a challenge, individuals are less likely to experience anxiety (Greenglass 2006). Recent research findings provide support for conceptualizing economic stress from a stress and coping perspective (Greenglass, Marjanovic and Fiksenbaum 2013). In this study, a comprehensive model was put forth to predict financial well-being, feelings of security and confidence regarding one's financial situation. The model, which was tested using multiple regression, accounted for 43% of the variance in financial well-being scores. Predictors included student debt, economic hardship, financial threat, negative coping such as ruminative brooding (which resulted in less financial well-being), and practical support. Thus, the model incorporated stressors, negative coping, as well as resources (in this case, practical support). It is likely that financial well-being can be achieved if individuals have the resources and coping skills to adequately overcome and manage financial crises.

Coping

There are several ways that individuals can cope with stressors. For example, individuals use positive coping strategies, which are associated with less stress and anxiety, and negative coping, i.e. ruminative brooding, which is related to more stress (see example from Greenglass et al. 2013). In addition, according to Schwarzer (2002), coping may be reactive or proactive. Most research in the coping area has focused primarily on reactive coping which is defined as an effort to deal with a stressful encounter that has already taken place. Since the stressful events have already taken place, coping efforts are directed here to either compensating for a loss or alleviating harm. In contrast, proactive coping is focused more towards the future. With proactive coping, people strive for more resources, desire to maximize gains, and build up resistance factors either to ward off future crises or to grow and cultivate their capabilities for their own sake. This forward time perspective that is characteristic of proactive coping opens new research questions and helps to overcome traditional coping models that overemphasize the reactive nature of coping. It also allows for the study of factors that influence psychological and physical well-being. Proactive coping consists of efforts to build up general resources that facilitate promotion of challenging goals and personal growth, and involves drawing on both internal and external resources that are available in a stressful situation (Greenglass 2002).

Proactive coping is goal management instead of risk management. Individuals are not reactive, but proactive in the sense that they initiate a constructive path of action and create opportunities for growth. Research has shown that proactive coping is associated with higher challenge appraisals and lower on appraisals of threat and loss (Schwarzer and Taubert 2002), less burnout (Schwarzer and Knoll 2003), greater perceived social support (Greenglass and Fiksenbaum 2009), and increased levels of well-being, as assessed by a variety of psychological measures (Greenglass, Schwarzer and Taubert 1999). Proactive coping may be particularly useful when dealing with financial problems given that it enables individuals to plan ahead, accumulate resources and reframe a negative situation in a positive way. Resources may include advice from others, emotional, practical and financial support.

Resilience

Resilience refers to the personal qualities that allow a person to thrive in the face of adversity (Connor and Davidson 2003); it is a process whereby the individual reacts to the environment according to their expectancies, biases, goals, values, affects and competencies (Connor and Davidson 2003). Alternatively, resilience can be defined as a complex phenomenon that refers to the ability to rebound from, and positively adapt to, significant stressors, or an ability to recover from or adjust easily to misfortune or change. Trait resilience goes beyond self-efficacy, which refers to an individual's belief in his or her own ability to achieve desired objectives (Bandura 1977). While individuals who are high in self-efficacy may believe that they are able to achieve a certain goal, those who are high in resilience will also believe that facing obstacles strengthens them, and they generally consider themselves to be strong.

Much of the research on resilience has focused on the question of why some people survive adversity without apparent ill effect and has focused on younger populations, the elderly, or individuals who have experienced/survived extreme circumstances (e.g. major loss, trauma, war, etc.). The previous research on resilience has aimed to identify the characteristics that differentiate individuals who achieve positive outcomes in the face of stress or adversity from those who experience maladaptive outcomes after facing the same stress or adversity. At the same time, there is a paucity of research that has focused on the function of resilience in normal functioning adults in less severe circumstances. Some suggest that resilience is not a trait, but instead is an ability to maintain normative functioning after experiencing stress or adversity (Campbell-Sills, Cohen and Stein, 2006; Richardson 2002). In contrast to the past when it was thought that resilience was an exceptional quality, current researchers in this area argue that resilience can be a common phenomenon (Bonanno 2004; Davis and Asliturk 2011).

Resilience and Coping

There is considerable debate on the relationship between resilience and coping. While some argue that resilience is a type of coping, in fact, these concepts, while overlapping, are quite distinct (Leipold and Greve 2009). Coping involves the use of cognitive, emotional and behavioral resources after a situation has been appraised as threatening or taxing with the intention of managing the situation. In contrast, resilience is conceptualized as the ability to maintain healthy and stable levels of physical and psychological functioning (i.e. adapt), or even grow, in the face of adversity or stress. Resilience is one factor that is related to the way in which an individual appraises stressors and consequently copes with them. Resilience can be defined by the positive outcomes an individual experiences after coping with a stressful or adverse situation (Leipold and Greve 2009). For example, Campbell-Sills et al. (2006) proposed and tested a model where coping predicted resilience in young adults. Leipold and Greve (2009) suggest that the relationship between coping and resilience is hierarchical – coping precedes resilience. Proactive copers evaluate their current situations while deliberating potential situations. This means that they proactively develop their personal and social resources, actively attempt to remove obstacles to future goals, and plan for alternative courses of action (Davis and Asliturk 2011). They also tend to be better prepared for difficulties that may arise and tend to report personal growth (Schwarzer and Taubert 2002). Many of these qualities overlap with the qualities that make an individual resilient. For example, personal growth in the face of adversity, positive adaptation in the face of difficulties and successfully overcoming obstacles are key features that define resilience (Davis and Asliturk 2011; Leipold and Greve 2009). Thus, for many researchers, coping style contributes to resilience (Campbell-Sills et al. 2006), and resilience is the outward expression of successfully coping with adversity (Leipold and Greve 2009). Proactive coping and resilience are also related to several individual difference variables. For example, optimism, self-esteem and perceived sense of control have been found to predict a proactive coping style and are important variables in partially explaining the difference between resilient and non-resilient individuals (Aspinwall and Taylor 1992; Dumont and Provost 1999).

The Present Study

The present study was designed to examine empirically the relationship between proactive coping and resilience in relation to feelings about the recent financial crisis. This follows from reports that financial problems can contribute to a wide array of negative psychosocial outcomes, such as psychological distress and mental illness (Brown, Taylor and Wheatley Price 2005; Fitch, Hamilton, Bassett and Davey 2011). Given the extent of negative outcomes that have been documented related to one's financial situation, we chose to examine three negative feelings: self-reported confusion, depression and fatigue that can be associated with one's financial situation. Our goal was to understand how coping style and resilience are related and how this relationship is related to the negative feelings individuals experience regarding their financial situation. Specifically, we hypothesized that the relationship between proactive coping and negative feelings about one's financial situation would be mediated by resilience. Thus, according to our theoretical formulation, proactive coping should lead to greater resilience which is expected to lead to lower distress regarding one's financial situation. Resilience is seen as a mediator of coping on the psychological distress associated with economic difficulties (see Figure 10.1). In this study, coping and resilience were assessed at Time 1 and psychological distress at Time 2, eight weeks later.

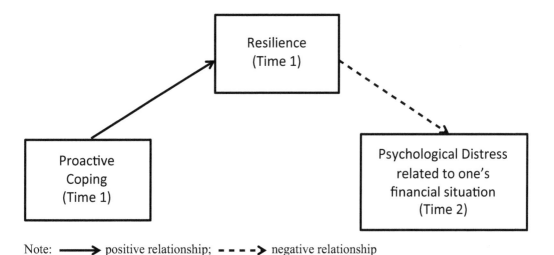

Note: ──▶ positive relationship; ‑ ‑ ‑ ‑▶ negative relationship

Figure 10.1   The hypothesized relationships among proactive coping, resilience and psychological distress

Method

Participants were 283 undergraduate primarily first-year students from a large university in Ontario, Canada who completed an online survey anonymously on the effects of the economic downturn in two waves, eight weeks apart. In the instructions, participants were informed that the study examined how people perceive themselves and their reactions to daily events, including economic ones. The age of the participants ranged from 17 to 47, with a mean age of 20.56 years (SD = 4.97). Average debt associated with one's student status, including tuition, residential fees, books, etc., was $5890.06, SD = 7344.34.

STATISTICAL ANALYSES

The hypothesis stating that resilience mediates proactive coping on psychological distress was tested using a mediation model (see Figure 10.1). Proactive coping (Time 1) was the predictor, resilience (Time 1) was the mediator, and psychological distress related to one's financial situation (a latent variable comprised of self-reported depression, confusion, and fatigue regarding one's financial situation at Time 2) was the outcome. This allowed us to examine Time 1 variables, coping and resilience, as predictors of psychological distress, measured at Time 2.

STUDY VARIABLES

The survey consisted of several psychological and economic measures as well as items assessing various demographics. The Cronbach alphas for each of the measures can be found on the diagonal in Table 10.1 Measures of the following constructs were included in the survey: proactive coping, resilience, confusion, depression, and fatigue.

Table 10.1   Bivariate correlations among the observed variables in the model

Variable	Resilience (Time 1)	Depression (Time 2)	Fatigue (Time 2)	Confusion (Time 2)	Proactive Coping (Time 1)
Resilience (Time 1)	α =.87				
Depression (Time 2)	-.124*	α =.93			
Fatigue (Time 2)	-.151*	.890**	α =.93		
Confusion (Time 2)	-.183**	.909**	.882**	α =.87	
Proactive Coping (Time 1)	.715**	-.065	-.080	-.129*	α =.85

Note: Cronbach alphas (α) are reported on the diagonal. * p < .05 ** p < .01.

Proactive coping. Proactive coping was assessed using the 14-item proactive coping subscale of the Proactive Coping Inventory (PCI; Greenglass et al. 1999). This scale includes items such as, "I always try to find a way to work around obstacles; nothing really stops me." Respondents were presented with four response alternatives: "1 = not at all true," "2 = barely true," "3 = somewhat true," "4 = completely true."

Resilience. Resilience was measured using a 10-item version of the Connor-Davidson Resilience Scale (CD-RISC; Campbell-Sills and Stein 2007), based on the original 25-item CD-RISC (Connor and Davidson 2003). Participants rated whether items such as "I am able to adapt when changes occur" describe them on a five-point scale ranging from (1) "not at all true" to (5) "true nearly all the time."

Psychological Distress – Profile of Mood States (POMS; Shacham 1983). The POMS consists of several subscales that assess the degree to which individuals experience various moods, primarily negative ones. In this study, we modified instructions to the POMS by adding the following directive: "Using the scale below, indicate your recent feelings about your financial situation." Participants responded on a five-point Likert-type scale ranging from "1, not at all" to "5, extremely." Three POMS subscales were included in this study:

Confusion. Confusion was assessed using the confusion/bewilderment subscale of the POMS, consisting of five items. A sample item of this particular subscale is "Bewildered."

Depression. An eight-item depression/dejection subscale of the POMS was employed to assess depression. A sample item of this subscale is "Unhappy."

Fatigue. Fatigue was assessed using the five-item fatigue/inertia subscale of the POMS. A sample item of this subscale is "Worn out."

Results

Most of the sample was female (83.2%), 49.5% were unemployed, with 44.2% stating that they were looking for work. Participants were asked several background questions about their employment and financial situation. For example, participants were asked: "Over the last few years, has your financial situation changed?" with response options that ranged from "greatly worsened" to "greatly improved." 28.2% of the respondents responded that their financial situation had "worsened" or "greatly worsened." In addition, when asked to indicate the degree of financial hardship they experienced, close to two-thirds of the sample (62.8%) reported they had some degree of financial hardship in the past.

Bivariate correlations among model variables were computed and are shown in Table 10.1. As expected, resilience and proactive coping are significantly and positively correlated ($r = 0.72$). In addition, resilience is significantly and negatively correlated with depression, fatigue and confusion. Finally, confusion, depression and fatigue were all highly positively correlated with each other, ranging from $r = 0.88$, to $r = 0.91$.

In order to test the hypothesis that the relationship between proactive coping and psychological distress is mediated by resilience, a mediation model was developed and tested in *Mplus* (Muthen and Muthen 2010) using structural equation modeling. In order to assess model fit, several fit indices were examined. The Comparative Fit Index (CFI) and Tucker Lewis Index (TLI) should be above 0.95 if the proposed model is a good fit to the sample data. A Root Mean Square Error of Approximation (RMSEA) value of less than 0.05 indicates a good-fitting model, and the 90% confidence interval for RMSEA should include values less than 0.05. Additionally, if the p-value for RMSEA is not significant (i.e. > alpha), then it can be concluded that the value of RMSEA is close to 0.05. Finally, the Standardized Root Mean Residual (SRMR) should be less than 0.08 to indicate a good-fitting model (see Browne and Cudeck 1993; Hu and Bentler 1999).

The assumptions for the structural equation model were also evaluated. There were three cases with missing data on the variables of interest, so these cases were deleted. All the variables were linearly related. There was one multivariate outlier, as evaluated by the squared Mahalanobis distance (D^2), so this case was deleted before proceeding with the analysis. There was no excessive kurtosis for any particular variable, however, Mardia's (1970) normalized estimate of multivariate kurtosis indicated that there was slightly excessive positive multivariate kurtosis, z = 8.72 (values greater than 5.00 indicate multivariate non-normality). Thus, the Satorra-Bentler (S-B; 1988) χ^2 statistic was used to evaluate model fit.

The proposed model was a good fit to the data, S-B χ^2 (5) = 5.62, p = 0.35, CFI = 0.99, TLI = 0.99, SRMR = 0.01, RMSEA = 0.02, 90% CI = 0.00, 0.09, p = 0.68 (see Table 10.2). As seen in Figure 10.2, at Time 1, higher proactive coping significantly predicted higher resilience scores. Higher resilience scores significantly predicted lower Time 2 psychological distress symptoms. The indirect effect of proactive coping on psychological distress through resilience was significantly different from zero, p = 0.038, indicating that resilience was a significant mediator of the relationship between proactive coping and psychological distress.

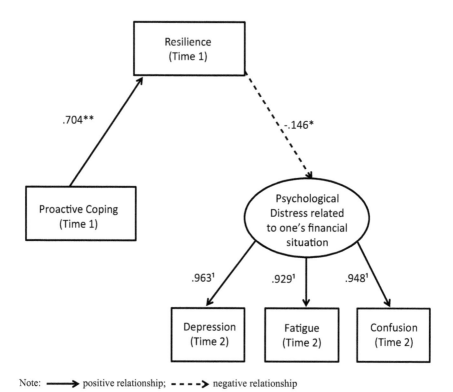

Note: ⟶ positive relationship; ⇢ negative relationship

Figure 10.2   Standardized regression coefficients for the hypothesized model relating proactive coping, resilience, and psychological distress

Notes: ** p < .001 * p < .05. [1] Standardized regression coefficients relating our latent variable "Psychological Distress" to our observed indicators – Depression, Fatigue, and Confusion.

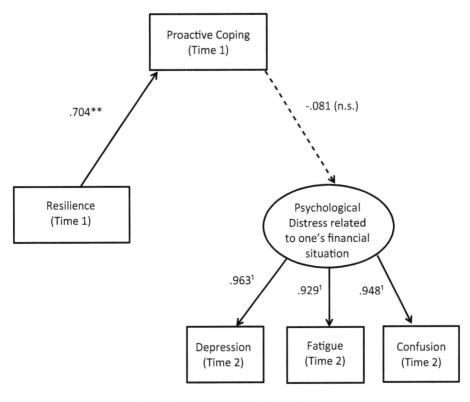

Note: ——→ positive relationship; - - - -> negative relationship

Figure 10.3 Standardized regression coefficients for the alternate model relating proactive coping, resilience, and psychological distress

Notes: ** p < .001 (n.s.) = nonsignificant. [1] Standardized regression coefficients relating our latent variable "Psychological Distress" to our observed indicators – Depression, Fatigue, and Confusion

Given that resilience and proactive coping were measured at the same time (Time 1) it was possible that proactive coping was the mediator between resilience and psychological distress and not the other way round. Thus, an alternate model was tested in which these variables were reversed such that resilience was the predictor, proactive coping was the mediator and psychological distress remained as the outcome (see Figure 10.3). This model was a slightly worse fit than the previous model, but still an acceptable fit to the data, S-B χ^2 (5) = 9.404 p = 0.09, CFI = 0.99, TLI = 0.99, SRMR = 0.04, RMSEA = 0.06, 90% CI = 0.00, 0.11, p = 0.36 (Table 10.2). However, the indirect effect of resilience on psychological distress through proactive coping was not significantly different from zero, p = 0.21, which indicated that proactive coping was *not* a mediator of the relationship between resilience and psychological distress.

Thus, the results demonstrated that proactive coping indirectly reduced psychological distress through resilience. That is, proactive coping leads to greater resilience, which reduces psychological distress symptoms associated with one's financial situation.

Table 10.2   Fit indices for the hypothesized model and the alternate model

	χ^2	df	p-value*	SRMR	CFI	TLI	RMSEA	p-value**
Hypothesized Model	5.62	5	.35	.014	.999	.999	.021	.682
Alternate Model	9.40	5	.09	.035	.996	.992	.056	.361

Notes: df = degrees of freedom for the χ^2 test of model fit; SRMR = Standardized Root Mean Square Residual; CFI = Comparative Fit Index; TLI = Tucker Lewis Index; RMSEA = Root Mean Square Error of Approximation. * p-value for the χ^2 test of model fit ** p-value for the RMSEA statistic.

Discussion

The recent financial crisis has resulted in considerable psychological distress due in part to increasing unemployment, ambiguity and confusion regarding one's future employment and anxiety about the consequences. In the present chapter we developed a conceptual model linking coping, resilience and feelings about one's financial feelings in order to understand how one's personal resources can alleviate some of these negative reactions. The goal of this model is to evaluate empirically the relationship between proactive coping and resilience and their effects on psychological distress within the context of the present financial crisis. To address this goal, we hypothesized that the effects of proactive coping strategies on psychological distress would be facilitated by resilience. Specifically, we expected that resilience could explain *how* proactive coping leads to less psychological distress symptoms in times of hardship. Our results provide new evidence for understanding the relationship between coping and resilience and how these constructs contribute to improved strategies for dealing with the negative outcomes associated with economic hardship. Specifically, it was found that individuals who use proactive coping strategies tended to have higher resilience scores, which lead to less psychological distress symptoms associated with one's financial situation. Previous theoretical work has posited that coping style contributes to resilience and that resilience is the outward expression of successfully coping with adversity (Campbell-Sills et al. 2006; Leipold and Greve 2009). Our results provide empirical support for this theory. Proactive coping contributes to greater resilience, which in turn contributes to less psychological distress. Resilience helps to explain how proactive coping decreases psychological distress symptoms. This conclusion was further supported by additional statistical results reported here. An alternate model was tested in which we substituted proactive coping, as a mediator for resilience. Results of this analysis showed that proactive coping did not mediate the relationship between resilience and psychological distress, thus adding more support for our hypothesis that proactive coping strategies contribute to resilience, as previously theorized in the literature (e.g. Leipold and Greve 2009).

RESILIENCE AND COPING

The results presented in this chapter suggest that resilience is the outcome of successful use of proactive coping strategies, a finding in line with theoretical work in the area. That is, after successful coping strategies have been employed, the individual demonstrates resilience, which lessens the effect of any psychological distress associated with the stressor. These results suggest two conclusions. First, an individual must first successfully employ proactive coping strategies in order to demonstrate resilient qualities. While coping and resilience were assessed at the same time in this study, we cannot state that proactive coping precedes resilience. At the same time, in line with previous theorizing in this area, it is reasonable to suggest that coping could, and often does, precede resilience. For example, recent definitions of resilience suggest that it involves the accumulation of resources and preventative problem solving, both of which are also facets of proactive coping (Davis and Asliturk 2011). In addition, Richardson's (2002) widely cited meta-theory of resilience speculates that resilience can be viewed as a measure of successful stress-coping ability. However, as discussed previously, recent criticisms of Richardson's theory emphasize that it is important to understand that resilience and coping are considered conceptually distinct constructs (Campbell-Sills et al. 2006; Connor and Davidson 2003; Fletcher and Sarkar 2013). Thus, this chapter addressed a limitation of Richardson's theory by examining resilience as an outcome of successful coping, rather than just an alternative measure; resilience and coping are distinct, in that proactive coping often precedes resilience. Related to this point is our second conclusion: resilience is one mechanism that explains *how* proactive coping indirectly affects the emotional response associated with a stressor. Much of the resilience literature has focused on understanding what qualities make individuals more resilient. The view of resilience as a mediator is unique to this research.

These conclusions lead to an interesting possibility: can proactive coping be taught in order to foster resilience in young adults and children? Recent research has shown that proactive coping skills can be taught. For instance, Bode, de Ridder, Kuijer and Bensing (2007) significantly increased proactive coping competencies in a group of middle-aged and older adults. Given the results of the Bode et al. paper, it is possible that interventions could be developed that target younger age groups that instruct these young people to identify and utilize personal resources, engage in social support networks, and create a sense of self-efficacy. Thus, it may be possible to design interventions that consist of teaching skills to young adults to help them cope with economic hardship by building up their self-efficacy and personal resources. By increasing proactive coping, it is possible to increase people's resilience in reaction to financial stressors.

YOUNG ADULTS FACING ECONOMIC CRISIS

These results are of particular value when considering that young adults are most likely to feel the effects of the recent financial crisis (Sun Life Canadian Health Index 2012). Among Canadians aged 18–24, for example, 58% stated that personal or household finances were a major source of stress for them and 49% stated that a major stress was their work life. Greater use of proactive coping strategies could lead to more effective use of resources as well as the development of resilience which could be beneficial in dealing with the economic difficulties that have resulted from the recent downturn. Research has shown that students in particular show significantly higher levels of both somatic and psychological symptoms during a recession than during a boom. Indeed, health among students, and women in particular, is generally poorer during times of economic recession (Novo, Hammarstrom and Janlert 2001). Further, low levels of control, pessimism about the future, and high demands are significantly correlated with ill health during times of economic recession among students (Novo et al. 2001). So why is health poorer among students in times of recession? The effects of unemployment in society on young people's health may be mediated through pessimism about the future, high demands, and financial problems. However, our study found that students in a financial crisis were less likely to feel these negative psychological consequences if they employed proactive coping strategies, which increased their resilience. Proactive coping skills have been associated with feelings of greater control (Aspinwall and Taylor 1992), which may explain why individuals also feel more resilient in times of economic difficulty – they have the resources and preparedness to overcome these difficulties.

It is especially important to help young people deal with the consequences of a financial crisis. While it is not uncommon to find considerable pessimism about the future when economic times are difficult, unabated, there can be negative consequences for health (Novo et al. 2001) and declining aspirations and uncertainty about the future can lead to longer periods of unemployment (Vuolo, Staff and Mortimer 2012). During the recession, youth unemployment has increased disproportionately with respect to the overall unemployment level (Aassve, Cottini and Vitali 2013; Greenglass 2014). Declining earnings and poor employment prospects for young people result in a "failure to launch" into economic independence (Aassve et al. 2013). As the economy struggles and young people are faced with higher unemployment rates, increased risk of poverty, and increased financial difficulties, it also becomes more difficult to gain or maintain their residential independence from the parental home (Aassve et al. 2013), which sets youth even farther behind on their path to adulthood and independence. However, a realistic expectation of one's future resources, such as active job search behaviors, can increase resilience among young people and enable them to successfully navigate the school-to-work transition (Vuolo et al. 2012).

The community can also play a part in helping young people develop the skills and resources they need to compete in the job market. For example, providing young people with the resources and skills needed to weather financial difficulties can enable them to become proactive copers. Specifically, it may be possible to provide seminars and lectures specifically for young people where they can learn how to search for employment that is suitable for them; how to prepare résumés that present their skills in a positive way, and point them to courses that will assist them in developing additional skills that may be needed for certain jobs. In addition, schools can provide courses and presentations on managing finances, saving, and borrowing wisely so young people learn the skills to make smart financial decisions. Thus, there is a role for community support of young people in their search for jobs and managing their finances that will not only provide them with needed knowledge and skills but will also give them a sense of efficacy and optimism as they enter the job market and foster resilience during times of economic uncertainty.

Conclusions

In this chapter, we have focused on the study of positive factors that can empower youth to deal with financial strain in time of economic recession. This is in contrast to much of the extant research that has documented the negative impact of financial difficulties on health (Maclean 2013), increase in suicides (Goldman-Mellor et al. 2014), job prospects (Aassve et al. 2013), unemployment, marital breakdown (Arkes and Shen 2014), for example. While it is important to understand the negative impact of financial crises, researchers must also devote attention to the factors that contribute to individuals successfully weathering financial and economic adversity. This is especially true among young adults who are establishing their careers, seeking financial independence, as well as engaging in strategies to establish their own families. Proactive coping can enable young adults to successfully adapt to and overcome financial challenges by fostering resilience. In the current research, these skills resulted in decreased psychological distress associated with one's financial situation. In future research, it may be possible to examine the role of other coping strategies in the development of resilience and to study their effects on economic stress. In this way, it may be possible to promote psychological well-being in times of economic hardship.

Acknowledgements

We would like to acknowledge the contributions of the Greenglass Lab at York University, including Lisa Fiksenbaum, Zdravko Marjanovic, Joana Katter, Taryn Nepon, Tonia Relkov, Alyssa Counsell, Zohreh Sojudi and Melina Condren. In addition, we would like to thank Dr. Robert Cribbie for his feedback on this work. We would also like to acknowledge the contributions of the Faculty of Health, York University for supporting this research.

References

Aassve, A., Cottini, E. and Vitali, A. (2013). Youth prospects in a time of economic recession. *Demographic Research*, 29, 949–62.

Arkes, J. and Shen, Y.C. (2014). For better or for worse, but how about a recession? *Contemporary Economic Policy*, 32, 275–87.

Aspinwall, L. and Taylor, S. (1992). Modeling cognitive adaptation: A longitudinal investigation of the impact of individual differences and coping on college adjustment and performance. *Journal of Personality and Social Psychology*, 63, 989–1003.

Bandura, A. (1977). Self-efficacy: Toward a unifying theory of behavioral change. *Psychological Review*, 84, 191–215.

Belluck, P. (2009, April 9). Recession anxiety seeps into everyday lives. *New York Times*. Available at: www.nytimes.com/2009/04/09/health/09stress.html. Accessed 11th March 2010.

Bode, C., de Ridder, D.T.D., Kuijer, R.G. and Bensing, J.M. (2007). Effects of an intervention promoting proactive coping competencies in middle and late adulthood. *The Gerontologist*, 47, 42–51.

Bonanno, G.A. (2004). Loss, trauma, and human resilience: Have we underestimated the human capacity to thrive after extremely adverse events? *American Psychologist*, 59, 20–8.

Brown, S., Taylor, K. and Wheatley Price, S. (2005). Debt and distress: Evaluating the psychological cost of credit. *Journal of Economic Psychology*, 26, 642–63.

Browne, M.W. and Cudeck, R. (1993). Alternative ways of assessing model fit. In K.A. Bollen and J.S. Long (eds), *Testing Structural Equation Models* (pp. 45–55). Newbury Park: Sage.

Campbell-Sills, L. and Stein, M.B. (2007). Psychometric analysis and refinement of the Connor-Davidson resilience Scale (CD-RISC): Validation of a 10-item measure of resilience. *Journal of Traumatic Stress*, 20, 1019–28.

Campbell-Sills, L., Cohen, S.L. and Stein, M.B. (2006). Relationship of resilience to personality, coping, and psychiatric symptoms in young adults. *Behaviour Research and Therapy*, 44, 585–99.

Canadian Centre for Policy Alternatives (2012, October 4). Canada's underemployed youth slow to recover in post-recession: Study. Available at: http://www.policyalternatives.ca/newsroom/news-releases/canadas-underemployed-youth-slow-recover-post-recession-study. Accessed October 2014.

Connor, K.M. and Davidson, J.R.T. (2003). Development of a new resilience scale: The Connor-Davidson Reslience Scale (CD-RISC). *Depression and Anxiety*, 18, 76–82.

Davis, C.G. and Asliturk, E. (2011). Toward a positive psychology of coping with anticipated events. *Canadian Psychology*, 52, 101–10.

Dumont, M. and Provost, M.A. (1999). Resilience in adolescents: Protective role of social support, coping strategies, self-esteem, and social activities on experience of stress and depression. *Journal of Youth and Adolescence*, 28, 343–63.

Fitch, C., Hamilton, S., Bassett, P. and Davey, R. (2011). The relationship between personal debt and mental health: A systematic review. *Mental Health Review Journal*, 16, 153–66.

Fletcher, D. and Sarkar, M. (2013). Psychological resilience: A review and critique of definitions, concepts, and theory. *European Psychologist*, 18, 12–23.

Folkman, S., Lazarus, R.S., Dunkel-Schetter, C., DeLongis, A. and Gruen, R.J. (1986). Dynamics of a stressful encounter: Cognitive appraisal, coping, and encounter outcomes. *Journal of Personality and Social Psychology*, 50, 992–1003.

Froman, L. (2010). Positive psychology in the workplace. *Journal of Adult Development*, 17, 59–69.

Goar, C. (2012, October 12). Jobless youth will carry lasting scars. *Toronto Star*, p. A23.

Goldman-Mellor, S.J., Caspi, A., Harrington, H., Hogan, S., Nada-Raja, S., Poulton, R. and Moffitt, T.E. (2014). Suicide attempt in young people: A signal for long-term health care and social needs. *JAMA Psychiatry*, 71, 119–127.

Greenglass, E.R. (2002). Proactive coping. In E. Frydenberg (ed.), *Beyond Coping: Meeting Goals, Vision, and Challenges* (pp. 37–62). London: Oxford University Press.

Greenglass, E.R. (2006). Vitality and vigor: Implications for healthy functioning. In P. Buchwald (ed.), *Stress and Anxiety: Application to Health, Community, Work Place and Education* (pp. 65–86). Newcastle: Cambridge Scholars Press Ltd.

Greenglass, E.R. (2014). The great recession: Stress and coping in difficult economic times. In K. Kaniasty, K.A. Moore, S. Howard and P. Buchwald (eds), *Stress and Anxiety: Applications to Social and Environmental Threats, Psychological Well-being, Occupational Challenges and Developmental Psychology* (pp. 7–16). Berlin: Logos Verlag.

Greenglass, E.R. and Fiksenbaum, L. (2009). Proactive coping, positive affect, and well-being: Testing for mediation using path analysis. *European Psychologist*, 14, 29–39.

Greenglass, E., Marjanovic, Z. and Fiksenbaum, L. (2013). The impact of the recession and its aftermath on individual health and well-being. In A.-S.G. Antoniou and C. Cooper (eds), *The Psychology of the Recession in the Workplace* (pp. 42–58). Cheltenham: Edward Elgar.

Greenglass, E.R., Schwarzer, R. and Taubert, S. (1999). *The Proactive Coping Inventory (PCI): A Multidimensional Research Instrument*. [Online publication]. Available at: http://www.psych.yorku.ca/greenglass/. Accessed November 2010.

Greenglass, E., Antonides, G., Christandl, F., Foster, G., Katter, J.K.Q. and Kaufman, B.E. (2014). The financial crisis and its effects: Perspectives from economics and psychology. *Journal of Behavioral and Experimental Economics*, 50, 10–12.

Hu, L.T. and Bentler, P.M. (1999). Cutoff criteria for fit indexes in covariance structure analysis: Conventional criteria vs. new alternatives. *Structural Equation Modeling*, 6, 1–55.

International Labour Organization (2014, January). Global Employment Trends, 2014: Risk of a jobless recovery? Available at: http://www.ilo.org/wcmsp5/groups/public/---dgreports/---dcomm/---publ/documents/publication/wcms_233953.pdf. Accessed April 2014.

Lazarus, R.S. and Folkman, S. (1984). *Stress, Appraisal and Coping*. New York: Springer.

Leipold, B. and Greve, W. (2009). Resilience: A conceptual bridge between coping and development. *European Psychologist*, 14, 40–50.

Maclean, J.C. (2013). The health effects of leaving school in a bad economy. *Journal of Health Economics*, 32, 951–64.

Mardia, K.V. (1970). Measures of multivariate skewness and kurtosis with applications. *Biometrika*, 57, 519–30.

Marjanovic, Z., Greenglass, E.R., Fiksenbaum, L. and Bell, C.M. (2013). Psychometric evaluation of the Financial Threat Scale (FTS) in the context of the great recession. *Journal of Economic Psychology*, 36, 1–10.

Mozes, A. (2012, November 19). Unemployed at high risk for heart attack? Available at: http://consumer.healthday.com/Article.asp?AID=670830. Accessed April 2014.

Mroz, T.A. and Savage, T.H. (2001). The long term effects of youth unemployment. *Employment Policies Institute, University of North Carolina*, Chapel Hill and Welch Consulting Economists.

Muthen, L.K. and Muthen, B.O. (2010). *Mplus User's Guide* (6th edn). Los Angeles: Authors.

Novo, M., Hammarstrom, A. and Janlert, U. (2001). Do high levels of unemployment influence the health of those who are not unemployed? A gendered comparison of young men and women during boom and recession. *Social Science and Medicine*, 53, 293–303.

Richardson, G.E. (2002). The metatheory of resilience and resiliency. *Journal of Clinical Psychology*, 58, 307–21.

Rios, R. and Zautra, A.J. (2011). Socioeconomic disparities in pain: The role of economic hardship and daily financial worry. *Health Psychology*, 30, 58–66.

Satorra, A. and Bentler, P.M. (1988). Scaling corrections for chi-square statistics in convariance structure analysis. In *1988 American Statistical Association Proceedings of the Business and Economic Section* (pp. 308–13). Alexandria, VA: American Statistical Association.

Schwarzer, R. (2002). Manage stress at work through preventive and proactive coping. In E.A. Locke (ed.), *Basic Principles of Organizational Behavior: A Hand-book* (pp. 342–55). Oxford: Blackwell.

Schwarzer, R. and Knoll, N. (2003). Positive coping: Mastering demands and searching for meaning. In S.J. Lopez and C.R. Snyder (eds), *Positive Psychological Assessment: A Handbook of Models and Measures* (pp. 393–409). Washington, DC: American Psychological Association.

Schwarzer, R. and Taubert, S. (2002). Tenacious goal pursuit and striving towards personal growth: Proactive coping. In E. Frydenberg (ed.), *Beyond Coping: Meeting Goals, Visions, and Challenges* (pp. 19–35). London: Oxford University Press.

Shacham, S. (1983). A shortened version of the Profile of Mood States. *Journal of Personality Assessment*, 47, 305–6.

Sojo, V. and Guarino, L. (2011). Mediated moderation or moderated mediation: Relationship between length of unemployment, resilience, coping, and health. *The Spanish Journal of Psychology*, 14, 272–81.

Sun Life Canadian Health Index (2012). Canadian health index report. Available at: http://cdn.sunlife.com/static/canada/Sponsor/About%20Group%20Benefits/Group%20benefits%20products%20and%20services/Sun%20Life%20Wellness%20Institute/2012%20Canadian%20Health%20Index%20Report%20English.pdf. Accessed October 2012.

Vuolo, M., Staff, J., and Mortimer, J.T. (2012). Weathering the great recession: Psychological and behavioraly trajectories in the transition from school to work. *Developmental Psychology*, 48, 1759–73.

11

Investigating Teachers' Well-Being and the Role of Resilience

Maria Armaou and Alexander-Stamatios Antoniou

Introduction

Teaching is long known to be an occupation with high demands for teachers. For this reason teachers' stress and coping has attracted a lot of attention from researchers in the last decades. Sources of teachers' stress are well-documented and are relatively the same across different educational systems and countries. However, they vary in nature and involve both external causes of stress and individual processes. External sources of stress include student motivation and behavioural problems, role conflicts, time pressures and excessive workload, evaluative environments, managing change, the way the teaching profession is perceived by members of the public, poor work relationships and career obstacles (Howard and Johnson 2004; Kyriacou 2001; Paulik 2012; Roache 2008).

Internal processes involve teacher motivation and coping patterns within the context of the school and classroom, explaining individual differences on responses to external sources of stress (Parker et al. 2012; Vandenberghe and Huberman 1999). Most of the research on teachers' responses to external sources of stress is based on Lazarus and Folkman's (1984) transactional model of stress and coping in order to highlight how situations that are perceived as threatening give rise to coping behaviours that impact on teachers' well-being at work. As there is a 'stable hierarchy of preferred coping strategies' (Frydenberg 1997, p. 40), understanding those processes is paramount for improving teachers' work conditions and ultimately keeping them in the profession.

On the other hand, research into the notion of resilience has its origins in psychiatry and developmental psychology. Masten et al. (1990, p. 425) define resilience as 'the process of, capacity for, or outcome of successful adaptation despite challenging or threatening circumstances'. Early studies within the field of resilience (Benard 1991; Silva and Stanton 1996; Werner and Smith 1982) focused on characteristics and personality traits that enabled some children among 'groups of *at risk* children and adolescents' that had suffered negative life events, to thrive and adapt positively to their environment (e.g. Howard et al. 1999; Waller 2001). Over the last two decades, resilience research has progressed to address positive qualities and strengths (Henderson and Milstein 2003) and underlying protective processes (Luthar et al. 2000). However, researchers also noted that resilience studies still lacked a strong theoretical base (Howard et al. 1999; Luthar et al. 2000) and only some isolated studies had tried to adapt key ideas and language of childhood resilience to describe the adaptive behaviours of various professional groups which experience work-related stress (Gordon and Coscarelli 1996), including teachers (Bobek 2002).

Gu and Day (2007) in discussing their longitudinal findings of teachers' professional lives in relation to teachers' resilience, mention that at the time they were not able to find research on teachers resilience which examined the impact of environmental and life factors upon teacher effectiveness. For this reason, they approach resilience as a psychological construct focusing on the role of positive emotions (Fredrickson 2001, 2004) for teaching (Fried 2001; Nias 1989, 1999; Palmer 1998), and as a multidimensional, socially constructed concept (e.g. Benard 1991, 1995; Gordon 1995; Henderson and Milstein 2003; Luthar et al. 2000). Their research findings are in line with the developing literature in teachers' resilience and constitute a key source of information about the role of supportive factors in teachers' work-lives. Within the area of teacher education, researchers began paying attention to teacher resilience in order to better understand teachers' identity development (e.g. Kirk and Wall 2010), job satisfaction and motivation (e.g. Brunetti 2006; Kitching et al. 2009), teacher burnout and stress (e.g. Howard and Johnson 2004), career decision-making (e.g. Bobek 2002; Tait 2008) and teaching effectiveness (e.g. Day 2008; Gu and Day 2007).

Similar to resilience research conducted by VanBreda (2001) and Masten et al. (1990), Bobek (2002) defined teacher resilience as the ability to adjust to a variety of situations and to increase one's competence in the face of adversity. Tait (2008) argued that self-efficacy is a characteristic of a resilient teacher in that efficacious teachers see stressors as challenges rather than threats; while Pretsch et al. (2012) found that among 170 teachers and 183 non-teaching employees resilience contributed more than neuroticism to the prediction of general perception only for the group of teachers. Finally, Howard and Johnson (2004) noted in their studies that resilient teachers are those that can resist stress through the use of protective factors and learned strategies.

Teachers' Coping Strategies and Well-Being

Coping refers to cognitive and behavioural efforts aiming to reduce the intensity of stressful events and recover one's resources. These can be differentiated into two main categories: problem-focused and emotion-focused (Cooper et al. 2001; Frydenberg and Lewis 2004). The former refers to behaviours geared towards resolving directly challenges or threats, whereas the latter refers to strategies whereby the purpose is to reinterpret or change the meaning of the existing challenges or threats (Folkman et al. 1986). These categories have also been examined among teachers and defined as 'active' and 'palliative' strategies. Active strategies are considered to be problem-oriented, seeking to eliminate the source of stress such as searching for solutions, social support, and time management. On the other hand, 'palliative' strategies are more avoidant in nature as they do not target directly the sources of stress bur rather aim to reduce its negative effects (Austin, Shah and Muncer 2005; Chan 1998; Kyriacou 2001). For example, Chan (1998) demonstrated the mediating role of coping strategies on the effects of stressors in that these direct effects are sizably reduced when coping strategies such as problem solving and seeking support are involved. Researchers have often addressed the relationship between teachers' coping strategies and their well-being as burnout and engagement are phenomena that are considered to be the outcome of individuals' appraisal and coping processes (Maslach et al. 2001; Schaufeli et al. 2008; Vandenberghe and Huberman 1999).

Overall, research findings suggest that active coping strategies tend to lead to more positive outcomes than 'palliative' coping strategies (Cooper et al. 2001; Kyriacou 2001). Such positive outcomes may include higher levels of resilience which in turn leads to greater well-being (e.g. Campbell-Sills et al. 2006; Coifman et al. 2007; Martin and Marsh 2008). For example, the strategy of social support has been associated with greater work satisfaction and lower levels of absenteeism (Brown and Ralph 1998; Cohen and Wills 1985; Pisanti et al. 2003); while avoidance is not favourable to the restoration of a positive psychological state (Austin et al. 2005; Chan 1998). However, what makes a difference to teachers' well-being is the long-term use of active coping strategies over the course of one's career (Martin and Marsh 2003; Sharplin et al. 2011).

Lewis (1999) examined the relationship between discipline and coping among teachers. He examined teachers' estimations of the stress that arises when they are unable to discipline students as they would ideally prefer, and the way in which teachers cope with any stress that arises. Results indicated that teachers who report more stress were those most interested in empowering their students in the decision-making process. Associated with increased concern is a greater use of coping responses such as worry, self-blame, tension reduction, wishful thinking, and keeping concerns to yourself. The most concerned teachers also expressed a greater tendency to get sick as a result of stress. According to Lewis, these findings suggested the need for professional development curricula for teachers, to assist them in effectively sharing power with students and in reflecting upon a range of more productive coping strategies.

In a sample of 515 Australian secondary school teachers, Lewis et al. (2011) examined the relationship between the stress teachers feel as a result of student misbehaviour, the generic coping strategies they use and six classroom management techniques (punishment, reward, involvement, hinting, discussion and aggression). Their results showed that the most common and effective form of coping used by the participants was Social Problem Solving and they sometimes turn to relaxing activities and less frequently engage in passive, emotion-focused, avoidant strategies. Furthermore, their results showed that teachers who are more concerned about student misbehaviour and classroom management use slightly more aggressive classroom management. However, regardless of teachers' levels of concern about misbehaviour, those who perceive their classes to contain more badly behaved students make more use of punishment and aggression. Moreover, teachers who use Avoidant and Passive coping strategies, also, employ more coercions and aggression towards students.

Griffith et al. (1999), in a sample of 780 primary and secondary school teachers in South London, examined the associations between teacher stress (measured by the Teacher Stress Inventory, Borg et al. 1991), dispositional coping (measured by COPE, Carver et al. 1989) and work social support (Unden et al. 1991) taking into consideration negative affectivity (measured using PANAS, Watson et al. 1988). Their results showed that teacher stress levels were greater for respondents who reported low social support at work and higher levels of coping by cognitive and behavioural disengagement, although the measure of social support was not correlated with coping by seeking social support.

Moreover, coping by active planning, suppression of competing activities and seeking support were positively interrelated, and were negatively associated with disengagement; while the results of a multiple regressions analysis showed that workplace social support and psychological coping were associated with ratings of teacher stress independently of negative affect and demographic and school factors. Parker and Martin (2009) in a sample of 515 teachers from 18 schools in Australia explored a model of teacher well-being and engagement (measuring work satisfaction, participation and positive career aspirations (Martin 2007; Martin and Marsh 2008)). Their results confirmed their hypotheses as the 'direct' coping strategies (planning and mastery orientation) positively predicted buoyancy, which in turn was a strong predictor of engagement and well-being, while the opposite was the case with 'palliative' coping strategies (self-handicapping and failure avoidance). Furthermore, the cognitive strategies of mastery orientation and failure avoidance were much stronger predictors of teachers' engagement and well-being.

More recently, Parker et al. (2012), based on the transactional model of stress (Lazarus and Folkman 1984), tested a process model of teachers' goal-orientation, coping behaviour and well-being in a longitudinal sample of 430 Australian teachers, using structural equation modelling (SEM). Their model consisted of three core elements: (1) teachers' goal orientations which underlie the appraisal of threatening obstacles, (2) coping strategies emanating from these orientations, and (3) teacher well-being emanating from the relevant coping strategy. Overall, to a large extent, their results confirmed their hypothesized model and were consistent across the two time waves. In particular, mastery goal orientation was a strong predictor of problem-focused coping, failure avoidance was a strong predictor of both emotion-focused and problem-focused coping, and coping was a strong predictor of teacher engagement. Unexpectedly, though, problem-focused coping negatively predicted burnout at Time 2 and the relationship was weaker than expected perhaps due to the nature of teaching work and the requirement of a high minimum standard of problem-focused copings (e.g. creation and submission of lesson and classroom plans) irrespective of individual coping preferences.

Differences on Stress Appraisal based on Personality Traits, Types of Schools and Subject Experience

Sources of stress in the teaching profession may be similar across diverse educational contexts but not all teachers are equally affected. Some tend to be more susceptible to workplace stressors experiencing higher levels of stress, whereas others are much more resilient. Individual characteristics are often the key to understanding such individual differences on stress appraisal (Burns and Machin 2013; Jepson and Forrest 2006). Furthermore, as we move down the educational ladder there is a greater chance for teachers to perceive higher levels of stress followed by a significant drop in the levels of job satisfaction for more experienced teachers (Borg et al. 1991; Chaplain 1995; Cooper and Kelly 1993).

Carton and Fruchart (2014) examined the degree to which the level of experience affected sources of stress, coping responses and emotional experience in a sample of 125 teachers, working in 11 primary schools, in France. Their research participants were all asked to choose a recent professional stressful situation and to then complete the French version of the Way of Coping Checklist-revised (WCC-R) (Graziani et al. 1998) and the French version of the Differential Emotions Scales (St. Aubin et al. 2010). Their results showed that teachers' sources of stress and coping responses differ significantly depending on their level of experience. In particular, novice teachers are mainly stressed by student behaviour doubting their own ability to handle pupils' misbehaviour, while they seek more often social support. After the first seven years they become more concerned about relations with their pupils' parents, but still they seek again the support and expertise from their colleagues although slightly less often than novice teachers. After 26 years in service teachers tend to become more stressed by the direction of the teaching profession. These teachers still often turn to social support but the use of escape, reappraisal and acceptance as coping strategies are on the increase.

Finally, at the end of their career (36–40 years of experience) their pervasive sources of stress are again their students' behaviour and their reflections on the teaching profession. They more often utilize the strategy of confrontation, and less frequently the strategies of self-control and diplomacy when dealing with stressful events. Even in spontaneous discussions carried out after these teachers had complete their questionnaires, they revealed that they indulged in avoidance behaviours such as sleeping, smoking or eating more when they were stressed. Their results correspond with earlier research findings acknowledging student misbehaviour as the main source of stress (e.g. Gevin 2007; Martin 2006; Pithers 1995), the importance of social support in the beginning of one's career as a teacher (Greenberg 2002; Hayes 2003; Hoy and Spero 2005; Viswesvaran et al. 1999) and the concerns about the teaching profession for more experienced teachers that may feel less in control (Compas et al. 1991; Forsythe and Compas 1987; Huberman 1989).

Burns and Machin (2013) examined the relationship between individual and workplace characteristics and their effects on teacher and school well-being outcomes among 250 Norwegian secondary school teachers from rural, urban and city locations. Their results showed that school location had strong relationships with many school well-being outcomes (measured using the School Organisational Health Questionnaire (Hart et al. 2000)) with rural teachers reporting higher levels of curriculum co-ordination, effective discipline policy, goal congruence, participative decision-making, student orientation, and supportive leadership as well as higher levels of professional interaction role clarity and more positive organizational climates than teachers in urban and city schools. On the other hand, personality characteristics (extraversion and neuroticism) were strongly related to positive and negative affect but had less strong effects on school well-being outcomes.

Jepson and Forrest (2006) performed a multiple regression analysis examining the predictive validity of a range of individual contributors on perceived workplace stress within the teaching profession in a sample of 95 primary and secondary school teachers from the UK. Their results showed occupational commitment, achievement striving, Type A behaviour and type of school were all significant predictors of work-related stress explaining overall 53.6% of the variance. Occupational commitment (defined as 'dedication and loyalty to the teaching profession' and measured by a six-item scale generated from a focus group) had the strongest negative relationship with perceived work-related stress, followed by achievement striving (defined as 'tendency to work hard to achieve goals' and measured by a 10-item scale, also generated from a focus group) and Type A behaviour (measured with Bortner's (1969) scale). Finally, the type of school also had a moderate significant relationship with teachers' levels of stress. This is in line with previous research that has indicated that individuals who exhibit low commitment, motivation to strive for high levels of achievement, and more physiological and emotional activity are in greater danger of experiencing higher levels of stress (Cooper and Kelly 1993; Jex et al. 2002; Siu and Cooper 1998).

Chan (2008) examined the degree to which the personal resources of emotional intelligence (intrapersonal and interpersonal; measured with the Emotional Intelligence Scale; Schutte et al. 1998) and general teacher self-efficacy (measured with General Teacher Self-Efficacy scale; Schwarzer et al. 1999) facilitated active and passive coping (measured with the Chinese Ways of Coping Questionnaire; Chan 1994) in a sample of 273 Chinese prospective and in-service teachers in Hong Kong. The findings of multiple regression analyses showed that only active coping could be significantly predicted by intrapersonal and interpersonal emotional intelligence, while teacher self-efficacy did not emerge as a significant predictor.

Paulik (2013/2014) examined the relation between dispositional optimism, self-confidence and work-related and non-work-related stress among 481 school teachers from primary schools at various locations in the Czech Republic. The results showed a significant relationship between those two personality traits and teachers' perception of both work-related and non-work-related load. Previous research by the same author (Paulik 2012) using samples from various levels of the Czech and Slovak educational systems also showed that personality variables such as hardiness, dispositional optimism, sense of coherence and neuropsychological stability have a positive relationship with stress resistance and mediate the negative relationship between increased workload and teachers' job satisfaction. In an overview of his research to date he concludes that for teachers who stay in the profession, such personality traits seem to counterbalance the negative effects of their profession.

Teachers' Coping and Resilience

Studies of teachers' coping strategies have provided useful insights for our understanding of teachers' resilience. However, the research focus on resilience has allowed researchers to address factors and processes that may count for teachers' resistance to stress and their optimal functioning using a broader range of research methods. Howard and Johnson (2004) conducted a qualitative enquiry using semi-structured interviews in order to examine 'resilient' teachers' strategies for coping with stress in day-to-day teaching among 10 teachers within the context of three very disadvantaged Australian schools. Their thematic analyses reflected the adult equivalents of protective factors found in the authors' earlier work with young people (Howard and Johnson 1999, 2000a, 2000b, 2000c, 2002). A consistent feature of 'resilient' teachers' talk was a strong belief in their ability to control what happens to them and, especially, respond to daily phenomena of aggression and violence towards them. The key strategy mentioned by all 10 teachers was to depersonalize the unpleasant or difficult events. They would do this in various ways such as not seeing the event as their fault, choosing to learn from this, trying to understand the offending parents' and students' motivation, or by using strategies that they have learnt from others. The second most common strategy employed by seven out of 10 participants was their 'moral purpose' which reflected their personal choice to teach in disadvantaged schools and their confidence of 'being able to make a difference' in children's lives. Furthermore, resilient individuals had strong support groups consisting of people that cared for them outside their schools, but they were also able to feel the support from their colleagues and leadership on a daily basis.

Finally, an important protective factor was individuals' pride in their own achievement and pride in areas of personal importance or significance (e.g. due to their competence in behaviour management their students learnt in orderly classrooms). The authors highlight that such protective factors can make a big different in teachers' lives and as they are also easy to organize within a school they represent a number of policy suggestions towards teacher education faculties and policy-making regarding the training, care and management of practising teachers:

1. Depersonalizing stressful incidents is a simple strategy that senior staff and colleagues in any school can teach new teachers, and that students can be taught in their teacher education courses.
2. When principals are at liberty to choose their own staff, they can ensure that new staff actually want the challenge of a difficult school
3. Schools can organize strong and reliable whole-school behaviour management strategies that will support teachers both in everyday and emergency situations.
4. Leadership teams can make staff support a priority for both professional and personal issues.
5. Schools can be organized in such a way as to promote strong peer group support (e.g. work-teams, social activities, supportive rather than competitive school culture). Students in training can be alerted to the importance of developing strong peer support both within and outside of school.
6. Staff achievements should be celebrated and valued.
7. The critical importance of competence in the key areas of behaviour management, program organization, lesson preparation and the effective management of resources can be taught both in teacher education programmes and on the job.

Cole et al. (2013) explored the coping strategies that were used in seven cases by school staff after a crisis. Three measures were used: the WHO (Five) Wellbeing Index (WHO 1998, 2011), the Impact of Event Scale-Revised (Weiss and Marmar 1997), and the Ways of Coping-Revised

(Folkman and Lazarus 1985). Their findings showed that reactions of staff to critical events in school can last for years. For this reason, the authors highlight the importance of having in place mechanisms for social support at schools and making sure that all staff have opportunities to take part in future planning activities. In three of the cases where reactions were strong, intrusion was reported by all as their reaction towards a critical event. Furthermore, in those cases where a low level of well-being was reported, there was also a high level of reported reactions to a critical event. Finally, planful problem solving and seeking social support were the most commonly reported coping strategies; whereas distancing, escape or avoidance were the least common ones.

Maring and Koblinsky (2013), adopting an ecological risk and resilience framework (Bronfenbrenner 1986) examined, through semi-structured interviewing, the challenges, strategies and support needs of 20 teachers from three urban schools near the Washington, DC border that were affected by high levels of community violence. Their perspective allowed them to examine how risk and protective factors at various levels may influence teacher outcomes. The interpretations of their interviews described teachers' challenges, strategies and support needs on various levels of analysis (individual-level, family-level, school-level, community-level) (see Table 11.1).

Table 11.1   Maring and Koblinsky's multi-level framework of risk and protective factors for teachers' challenges, strategies and support needs

Challenges	Strategies	Support needs
Individual		
Lack of training	Praying	Behaviour management training
Fears for personal safety	Emotional withdrawal	
Somatic stress symptoms		
Family		
	Communication with family and friends	
School		
Inadequate school security	Sharing stressful events with teachers	Effective school leadership
	Limiting involvement with difficult students	Improved safety and security
		Peer mediation programmes
	Separating work and personal life	Mental health services
Community		
Neighbourhood violent crime	Professional counselling	Parental support and involvement

These findings are in line with previous research among African American pupils, students and other community members (Bryant-Davis 2005; Farrell et al. 2001; Metlife 2008; Thompson et al. 2004) and also show the importance of developing programmes and policies that can help teachers cope effectively with community violence such as conflict resolution skills training, top-down, comprehensive initiatives to support violence prevention and provide a safe school environment (e.g. clear expectations for student behaviour, enforce disciplinary rules, and ensure adequate safety and security protections), peer mediation programmes and exploring use of professional counsellors to address students' and teachers' violence related trauma.

Analysing narrative interviews of 12 secondary school teachers in England, Mujtaba and Reiss (2013) explored factors that contribute to the development of positive stress and distress based on the quantitative findings of their earlier research (Mujtaba 2013). Eustress was identified as a positive influence that motivates teachers to aim for challenges in their professional life, aids personal and professional growth and pushes teachers to make the necessary changes to their environment in order to reap benefits. In this sense, positive stress is indicative of problem-solving actions and creative solutions to areas of their professional lives that require improvement. On the other hand, distress was characterized by events/stressors that create anxiety, ill-feeling and a negative impact on teachers. Overall, 10 themes emerged describing what constitutes eustress and distress for their interviewees (see Table 11.2).

Table 11.2   Mujtaba and Reiss' analysis of teachers' eustress and distress

Eustress	Distress
Trust	Mistrust
High self-efficacy	Low self-efficacy
Social support	Social isolation
Teachers having their skills affirmed	Teachers having to prove their skills
Autonomy	Lack of autonomy
Reflection	Lack of reflection
Motivation	Lack of motivation
Good leadership and collegiality	Poor leadership and lack of collegiality
Good role model department and school	Lack of a good role model department and school

The findings demonstrate that the use by teachers of appropriate coping mechanisms and seeing stressors as capable of being overcome, can help teachers throughout their career to view stress in a positive, healthy manner and lessen the likelihood of negative long-term effects associated with distress. For example, the way in which teachers appraised a situation was related to the kind of coping strategy that they adopt. The 12 teachers exhibited a mix of different types of coping strategies which helped them to regulate distress and produce positive affect. For all 12 teachers it appeared that many of the issues to do with trust or mistrust lay with senior management; while those teachers who had higher levels of self-efficacy were more resistant to distress and were able to work under stressful conditions. However, not all of the teachers were able to recognize eustress, but for those who did recognize it an indicator of positive stress was positive affect; while teachers of mathematics and science felt that they faced more pressures compared to teachers from other departments, highlighting the negative perceptions of many pupils towards their subject.

Teachers' Resilience and Retention

There has recently been a growing research focus on teachers' resilience and its importance for teachers' retention. This has been fuelled mainly by the increase in teacher shortages in many countries and the limitations of organizational models of attrition that focus on the external assessable result of loss of commitment, rather than upon the ways in which commitment is built (Day and Gu 2009; Doney 2013; Hong 2012).

Hong (2012) provided an insight into new teachers' needs and the challenges that they face by exploring the differences between seven leavers and seven stayers focusing on the transactional process of their resilience and decision-making through their psychological lenses of value, self-efficacy, beliefs and emotions. The findings of this study showed that leavers perceived and interpreted challenges differently than stayers. In particular, when leavers faced the challenges of managing the classroom and handling students' misbehaviours, they often experienced diminished self-efficacy beliefs and they attributed the difficulty to their own personality or characteristics and experienced emotional burnout. Stayers, however, were able to maintain strong self-efficacy beliefs with the help and support of administrators. Additionally, they could strategically set emotional lines or boundaries between themselves and students, so that they would not take negative events personally or become burned out; while leavers held the belief that they were heavily responsible for students' learning, not realizing the students' own role and effort in the learning process.

Doney (2013) examined the resilience-building process of four female novice secondary science teachers in the United States and its links to teacher retention in a qualitative two-year study. For the purposes of this study, a resilience framework was established consisting of three factors: (1) stressors and protective factors in the lives of novice secondary science teachers and provided direction and goals for the research; (2) a case study was developed for each of the four teachers participating in the research in order to emphasize the detailed analysis of factors linked to resilience; (3) cross-case analysis was employed to identify similarities and differences and provide insight into issues concerning the resilience process. The study's results suggest that the interaction between stressors (e.g. personal live vs. career, inexperience, control of decision, extra-curricular activities, control of time, etc.) and protective factors (e.g. creating support systems, using individual skills to problem solving, maintaining self-efficacy and a sense of humour, use palliative and control techniques) act as a primary force in the resilience process and stimulate responses to help counteract negative effects of resulting stress. For this reason, the authors suggest that resilience can be fostered in novice teachers, by revising protective factors in order to address changing stressors as a means to encourage teacher retention.

Sharplin et al. (2011) present the findings from a qualitative longitudinal collective case study of 29 teachers newly appointed to a rural or remote school in Western Australia. Their conceptual framework consisted of the quality of work-life which encompasses a model of person-environment (P-E) including personal attributes (self-efficacy, locus of control), teacher coping strategies, and structures for workplace socialization. The findings of this study showed that all participants experienced stress and responded with direct-action, palliative and avoidant strategies. However, where protective structures and processes existed in environments, teachers employed direct-action problem-solving strategies. Avoidant strategies were more common in young and mature-aged novices, rather than experienced teachers. These authors highlight three critical times that are important for teachers' retention as they support adaptation: first weeks of appointment for information, first semester for assistance, support, feedback for development of competence, and three months before the year-end for stability and certainty.

The VITAE research, 'Variations in Teachers' Work, Lives and Effectiveness' was a mixed method, four-year (2001–2006) study conducted in England with 300 teachers in 100 schools across seven local authorities (Day et al. 2007) through twice yearly semi-structured, face-to-face interviews with teachers. It investigated factors contributing to variations in teachers' effectiveness in different phases of their professional lives showing that teachers' capacities to sustain their commitment and resilience were influenced by their professional life phases and their identities which in turn were mediated by the contexts in which they lived and worked. Those mediating influences had three dimensions: the *personal* (related to their lives outside school); the *situated* (related to their lives in school); and the *professional* (related to their values, beliefs and the interaction between these and external policy agendas). Of the 300 teachers in the study, 76% were able to sustain relatively positive commitment trajectory identities across all professional life phases over the three-year period of the fieldwork.

However, in each phase there were a number who did not and that increased as the professional life phase progressed, especially for those with 24–30 years of experience and those with 31-plus years of experience. Day and Gu (2009) present the stories of three such veteran teachers highlighting the significance of the provision of appropriate and responsive leadership support. They also note that as long as such support is available, veteran teachers are more likely to sustain their commitment and effectiveness and their experiences, values for education and sense of vocation can serve as sources of wisdom and strength which enable them to bounce back from adverse circumstances.

Conclusions

The role of resilience for teachers' well-being is a multi-faceted phenomenon that incorporates diverse factors and processes that take place both inside and outside the school. Quantitative and qualitative research findings equally support the notion that individuals' coping strategies play a significant role for teachers' resilience and their overall well-being at work. However, the development and maintenance of resilience is also influenced by other supportive and non-supportive factors that need to be adequately addressed within the contexts of teachers' work and, when possible, within their teacher education programmes.

Overall, the use of active coping strategies (e.g. active planning, seeking social support, etc.) is associated with higher levels of resistance to stress and greater well-being throughout teachers' careers. On the other hand, employing 'palliative coping strategies' (e.g. worry, self-blame, failure avoidance) is related with low resistance to stress, disengagement and negative well-being outcomes such as getting sick due to stress. However, individual differences among teachers including differences in years of experience, school location and personality characteristics are equally important for our understanding of the role of resilience for teachers' well-being. For example, individual characteristics such as Type A behaviour, emotional intelligence and general self-efficacy are also related to teachers' stress-appraisal process and their resistance to stress.

However, the impact of teachers' sources of stress (e.g. pupil misbehaviour, direction of the teaching profession) varies across the span of their career and so does their choice of coping strategies. Research in teachers' resilience has offered a broader understanding of protective factors in teachers' work-lives that are important for their coping. Such factors can reflect either personal or organizational resources. Personal resources may include a strong belief in individual teachers' ability to control what is happening in their daily work-lives, a sense of 'moral purpose' in teaching, and their self-efficacy; while organizational resources may include school-wide mechanisms for social support, opportunities for staff to take part in future planning activities, behaviour management training, parental support and involvement. Understanding how such factors influence teachers' coping and resilience is imperative for teachers' well-being and their desire to stay in the profession.

References

Austin, V., Shah, S. and Muncer, S. (2005). Teacher stress and coping strategies used to reduce stress. *Occupational Therapy International*, 12(2), 63–80.

Benard, B. (1991). *Fostering Resiliency in Kids: Protective Factors in the Family, School, and Community*. San Francisco: WestEd Regional Educational Laboratory.

Benard, B. (1995). *Fostering Resilience in Children*. ERIC/EECE Digest, EDO-PS-99.

Bobek, B. (2002). Teacher resiliency: A key to career longevity. *Clearing House*, 202–6.

Borg, M.G., Riding, R.J. and Falzon, J.M. (1991). Stress in teaching: A study of occupational stress and its determinants, job satisfaction and career commitment among primary school teachers. *Educational Psychology*, 11(1), 59–74.

Bortner, R.W. (1969). A short rating scale as a potential measure of pattern A behaviour. *Journal of Chronic Diseases*, 22, 87–91.

Bronfenbrenner, U. (1986). Ecology as a context for human development: Research perspectives. *Developmental Psychology*, 22, 723–42.

Brown, P. and Ralph, S. (1998). *Change-linked Stress in British Teachers*. Paper presented to the British Educational Research Association Conference, Queen's University Belfast, September.

Brunetti, G. (2006). Resilience under fire: Perspectives on the work of experienced, inner city high school teachers in the United States. *Teaching and Teacher Education*, 22, 812–25.

Bryant-Davis, T. (2005). Coping strategies of African American adult survivors of childhood violence. *Professional Psychology: Research and Practice*, 36, 409–14.

Burns, R.A. and Machin, M.A. (2013). Employee workplace well-being: A multi-level analysis of teacher personality and organisational climate in Norwegian teachers from rural, urban and city schools. *Scandinavian Journal of Educational Research*, 57(3), 309–24.

Campbell-Sills, L., Cohan, S.L. and Stein, M.B. (2006). Relationship of resilience to personality, coping, and psychiatric symptoms in young adults. *Behaviour Research and Therapy*, 44, 585–99.

Carton, A. and Fruchart, E. (2014). Sources of stress, coping strategies, emotional experience: Effects of the level of experience in primary school teachers in France. *Educational Review*, 66(2), 245–62.

Carver, C.S., Scheier, M.F. and Weintraub, J.K. (1989). Assessing coping strategies: A theoretically based approach. *Journal of Personality and Social Psychology*, 56, 267–83.

Chan, D.W. (1994). The Chinese Ways of Coping Questionnaire: Assessing coping in secondary school teachers and students in Hong Kong. *Psychological Assessment*, 6, 108–16.

Chan, D.W. (1998). Stress, coping strategies, and psychological distress among secondary school teachers in Hong Kong. *American Educational Research Journal*, 35(1), 145–63.

Chan, D.W. (2008). Emotional intelligence, self-efficacy, and coping among Chinese prospective and in-service teachers in Hong-Kong. *Educational Psychology*, 28(4), 397–408.

Chaplain, R.P. (1995). Stress and job satisfaction: A study of English primary school teachers. *Educational Psychology*, 15(4), 473–89.

Cohen, S. and Wills, T.A. (1985). Stress, social support, and the buffering hypothesis. *Psychological Bulletin*, 98, 310–57.

Coifman, K.G., Bonanno, G.A., Ray, R.D. and Gross, J.J. (2007). Does repressive coping promote resilience? Affective-autonomic response discrepancy during bereavement. *Journal of Personality and Social Psychology*, 92, 745–58.

Cole, R., Hayes, B., Jones, D. and Shah, S. (2013). Coping strategies used by school staff after a crisis: A research note. *Journal of Loss and Trauma: International Perspectives on Stress & Coping*, 18, 472–81.

Compas, B.E., Banez, G.A., Malcarne, V. and Worsham, N. (1991). Perceived control and coping with stress: A developmental perspective. *Journal of Social Issues*, 47, 23–34.

Cooper, C.L. and Kelly, M. (1993). Occupational stress in head teachers: A national UK study. *British Journal of Educational Psychology*, 63, 130–43.

Cooper, C.L., Dewe, P. and O'Driscoll, M. (2001). *Organizational Stress: A Review and Critique of Theory, Research, and Applications*. Thousand Oaks: Sage Publications.

Day, C. (2008). Committed for life? Variations in teachers' work, lives and effectiveness. *Journal of Educational Change*, 9, 243–60.

Day, C. and Gu, Q. (2009). Veteran teachers: Commitment, resilience and quality retengion. *Teachers and Teaching: Theory and Practice*, 15(4), 441–57.

Day, C., Sammons, P., Stobart, G., Kington, A. and Gu, Q. (2007). *Teachers Matter*. Maidenhead: McGraw-Hill.

Doney, P.A. (2013). Fostering resilience: A necessary skill for teacher retention. *Journal of Science Teacher Education*, 24, 645–64.

Farrell, A.D., Meyer, A.L. and White, K.S. (2001). Evaluation of Responding in Peaceful and Positive Ways (RIPP): A school-based prevention program for reducing violence among urban adolescents. *Journal of Clinical Child Psychology*, 30(4), 451–63.

Folkman, S. and Lazarus, R.S. (1985). If it changes it must be a process: Study of emotion and coping during three stages of a college examination. *Journal of Personality and Social Psychology*, 48, 150–70.

Folkman, S., Lazarus, R.S., Dunkel-Schetter, C., DeLongis, A. and Gruen, R.J. (1986). Dynamics of a stressful encounter: Cognitive appraisal, coping, and encounter outcomes. *Journal of Personality and Social Psychology*, 50, 992–1003.

Forsythe, C.J. and Compas, B.E. (1987). Interaction of cognitive appraisals of stressful events and coping: Testing the goodness of fit hypothesis. *Cognitive Therapy and Research*, 11, 473–85.

Fredrickson, B.L. (2001). The role of positive emotions in positive psychology: The broaden-and build theory of positive emotions. *American Psychologist*, 56(3), 218–26.

Fredrickson, B.L. (2004). The broaden-and-build theory of positive emotions. *The Royal Society*, 359, 1367–77.

Fried, R. (2001). *The Passionate Teacher: A Practical Guide* (2nd edn). Boston: Beacon Press.

Frydenberg, E. (1997). *Adolescent Coping: Theoretical and Research Perspectives*. New York: Routledge.

Frydenberg, E. and Lewis, R. (2004). Adolescents least able to cope: How do they respond to their stresses? *British Journal of Guidance & Counselling*, 32, 25–37.

Gevin, A. (2007). Identifying the types of student and teacher behaviours associated with teacher stress. *Teaching and Teacher Education*, 23(5), 624–40.

Gordon, K.A. (1995). The self-concept and motivational patterns of resilient African American high school students. *Journal of Black Psychology*, 21, 239–55.

Gordon, K. and Coscarelli, W. (1996). Recognising and fostering resilience. *Performance Improvement*, 35(9), 14–17.

Graziani, P., Rusinek, S., Servant, D., Hautekeete-Sence, D. and Hautekeete M. (1998). Validation française du questionnaire de Coping 'Way of Coping Check-List-Revised' (W.C.C-R.) et analyse des événements stressants du quotidien. *Journal de Thérapie Comportementale et Cognitive*, 8(3), 100–112.

Greenberg, L.S. (2002). *Emotion-focused Therapy: Coaching Clients to Work through Their Feelings*. Washington, DC: American Psychology Association Press.

Griffith, J., Steptoe, A. and Cropley, M. (1999). An investigation of coping strategies associated with job stress in teachers. *British Journal of Educational Psychology*, 69, 517–31.

Gu, Q. and Day, C. (2007). Teachers' resilience: A necessary condition for effectiveness. *Teaching and Teacher Education*, 23, 1302–16.

Hart, P.M. (2000). *Understanding Organizational Health: Benchmarking and Improvement in Victoria Schools*. Melbourne: Department of Education, Employment and Training.

Hart, P.M., Wearing, A.J., Cohn, M., Carter, M., Carter, N.L. and Dingle, R.K. (2000). Development of the School Organisational Health Questionnaire: A measure for assessing teacher morale and school organisational climate. *British Journal of Educational Psychology*, 70(2), 211–28.

Hayes, D. (2003). Emotional preparation for teaching: A case study about trainee teachers in England. *Teacher Development*, 7(2), 153–71.

Henderson, N. and Milstein, M. (2003). *Resiliency in Schools: Making it Happen for Students and Educators*. Thousand Oaks: Corwin Press.

Hong, J.Y. (2012). Why do some beginning teacher leave the school, and others stay? Understanding teacher resilience through psychological lenses. *Teachers and Teaching: Theory and Practice*, 18(4), 417–40.

Howard, S. and Johnson, B. (1999). Tracking student resilience. *Children Australia*, 24(3), 14–23.

Howard, S. and Johnson, B. (2000a). What makes the difference? Children and teachers talk about resilient outcomes for students at risk. *Educational Studies*, 26(3), 321–7.

Howard, S. and Johnson, B. (2000b). *An Investigation of the Role of Resiliency-promoting Factors in Preventing Adverse Life Outcomes during Adolescence*. A Report to the Criminology Research Council of Australia, Adelaide, University of S.A.

Howard, S. and Johnson, B. (2000c). Resilient and non-resilient behaviour in adolescents. *Trends and Issues in Crime and Criminal Justice*, 183, 1–6.

Howard, S.M. and Johnson, B.J. (2002). Participation and involvement: Resilience-promoting factors for young adolescents. In M. Gollop and J. McCormack (eds), *Children and Young People's Environments* (pp. 113–28). Dunedin: Children's Issues Centre.

Howard, S. and Johnson, B. (2004). Resilient teachers: Resisting stress and burnout. *Social Psychology of Education*, 7, 399–420.

Howard, S., Dryden, J. and Johnson, B. (1999). Childhood resilience: Review and critique of literature. *Oxford Review of Education*, 25(3), 307–23.

Hoy, A.W. and Spero, R.B. (2005). Changes in teacher efficacy during the early years of teaching: A comparison of four measures. *Teaching and Teacher Education*, 21, 343–56.

Huberman, M. (1989). *La vie des enseignants. Evolution et Bilan d'une Profession*. Lonay: Ed Delachaux et Niestlé.

Jepson, E. and Forrest, S. (2006). Individual contributory factors in teacher stress: The role of achievement striving and occupational commitment. *British Journal of Educational Psychology*, 76, 183–97.

Jex, M., Adams, G.A., Elacqua, T.C. and Bachrach, D.G. (2002). Type A as a moderator of stressors and job complexity: A comparison of achievement strivings and impatience-irritability. *Journal of Applied Social Psychology*, 32(5), 977–96.

Kirk, J. and Wall, C. (2010). Resilience and loss in work identities: A narrative analysis of some retired teachers' work-life histories. *British Educational Research Journal*, 36(4), 627–41.

Kitching, K., Morgan, M. and O'Leary, M. (2009). It's the little things: Exploring the importance of commonplace events for early career teachers' motivation. *Teachers and Teaching: Theory into Practice*, 15(1), 43–58.

Kyriacou, C. (2001). Teacher stress: Directions for future research. *Educational Review*, 53, 27–35.

Lazarus, R. and Folkman, S. (1984). *Stress, Appraisal, and Coping*. New York: Springer Publishing Company.

Lewis, R. (1999). Teachers coping with the stress of classroom discipline. *Social Psychology of Education*, 3, 155–71.

Lewis, R., Roache, J. and Romi, S. (2011). Coping styles of teachers' classroom management techniques. *Research in Education*, 85, 53–68.

Luthar, S.S., Cicchetti, D. and Becker, B. (2000). The construct of resilience: A critical evaluation and guidelines for future work. *Child Development*, 71(3), 543–62.

Maring, E. and Koblinsky, S.A. (2013). Teachers' challenges, strategies, and support needs in schools affected by community violence: A qualitative study. *Journal of School Health*, 83(6), 379–88.

Martin, A.J. (2006). The relationship between teachers' perceptions of student motivation and engagement and teachers' enjoyment of and confidence in teaching. *Asia-Pacific Journal of Teacher Education*, 34, 73–93.

Martin, A.J. (2007). Examining a multidimensional model of student motivation and engagement using a construct validation approach. *British Journal of Educational Psychology*, 77, 413–40.

Martin, A.J. and Marsh, H.W. (2003). Fear of failure: Friend or foe? *Australian Psychologist*, 38, 31–8.

Martin, A.J. and Marsh, H.W. (2008). Workplace and academic buoyancy: Psychometric assessment and construct validity amongst school personnel and students. *Journal of Psychoeducational Assessment*, 26, 168–84.

Maslach, C., Schaufeli, W.B. and Leiter, M.P. (2001). Job burnout. *Annual Review of Psychology*, 52, 397–422.

Masten, A.S., Best, K.M. and Garmezy, N. (1990). Resilience and development: Contributions from the study of children who overcome adversity. *Development and Psychopathology*, 2, 425–44.

Metlife, Inc. (2008). The Metlife survey of the American teacher. 2008. Available at: http://www.eric.ed.gov/PDFS/ED504457.pdf.

Mujtaba, T. (2013). The role of self-efficacy, motivation and professional factors in the development of positive and negative stress in primary teachers, and secondary school teachers of mathematics and English. *International Journal of Quantitative Research in Education*, 1(1), 103–19.

Mujtaba, T. and Reiss, M. (2013). Factors that lead to positive or negative stress in secondary school teachers of mathematics and science. *Oxford Review of Education*, 39(5), 627–48.

Nias, J. (1989). *Primary Teachers Talking*. London: Routledge.

Nias, J. (1999). Teachers' moral purposes: Stress, vulnerability, and strength. In R. Vandenberghe and A.M. Huberman (eds), *Understanding and Preventing Teacher Burnout: A Sourcebook of International Research and Practice* (pp. 223–37). Cambridge: Cambridge University Press.

Palmer, P.J. (1998). *The Courage to Teach: Exploring the Inner Landscapes of a Teacher's Life*. San Francisco: Jossey-Bass.

Parker, P.D. and Martin, A.J. (2009). Coping and buoyancy in the workplace: Understanding their effects on teachers' work-related well-being and engagement. *Teaching and Teacher Education*, 25, 68–75.

Parker, P.D., Martin, A.J., Colmar, S. and Liem, G.A. (2012). Teachers' workplace well-being: Exploring a process model of goal orientation, coping behavior, engagement, and burnout. *Teaching and Teacher Education*, 28(4), 503–13.

Paulik, K. (2012). Job satisfaction and stress among teachers. *The Educational Review*, 30(4), 138–49.

Paulik, K. (2013/2014). *Optimism, Self-confidence and Perception of Workload among Teachers*, 3rd International e-conference on Optimization, Education and Data Mining in Science, Engineering and Risk Management (OEDM SERM 2013/2014).

Pisanti, R., Garliardi, M.P., Raziino, S. and Bertini, M. (2003). Occupational stress and wellness among Italian secondary school teachers. *Psychology and Health*, 18, 523–36.

Pithers, R.T. (1995). Teacher stress research: Problems and progress. *British Journal of Educational Psychology*, 65, 387–92.

Pretsch, J., Flunger, B. and Schmitt, M. (2012). Resilience predicts well-being in teacher, but not in non-teaching employees. *Social Psychology of Education*, 15, 321–36.

Roache, J. (2008). Strategies to ameliorate teacher stress. *Leadership in Focus*, 12, 38–41.

Schaufeli, W.B., Taris, T. and van Rhenen, W. (2008). Workaholism, burnout, and work engagement: Three of a kind or three different kinds of employee well-being? *Applied Psychology*, 57, 173–203.

Schutte, N.S., Malouff, J.M., Hall, L.E., Haggerty, D.J., Cooper, J.T., Golden, C.J. and Dornheim, L. (1998). Development and validation of a measure of emotional intelligence. *Personality and Individual Differences*, 25, 167–77.

Schwarzer, R., Schmitz, G.S. and Daytner, G.T. (1999). *The Teacher Self-Efficacy scale* [online publication]. Available at: http://www.fu-berlin.de/gesund/skalen/ t_se.htm.

Sharplin, E., Neill, M. and Chapman, A. (2011). Coping strategies for adaptation to new teacher appointments: Intervention for retention. *Teaching and Teacher Education*, 27, 136–46.

Silva, P. and Stanton, W. (eds) (1996). *From Child to Adult: The Dunedin Multidisciplinary Health and Development Study*. Auckland: Oxford University Press.

Siu, O.-L. and Cooper, C.L. (1998). A study of occupational stress, job satisfaction and quitting intention in Hong Kong firms: The role of locus of control and organizational commitment. *Stress and Health*, 14(1), 55–66.

St Aubin, R., Philippe, F.L., Beaulieu-Pelletier, G. and Lecours, S. (2010). Validation francophone de l'Echelle des émotions différentielles IV (EED-IV). *Revue Européenne de Psychologie Appliquée*, 60, 41–53.

Tait, M. (2008). Resilience as a contributor to novice teacher success, commitment, and retention. *Teacher Education Quarterly*, 35(4), 57–75.

Thompson, V.L.S., Bazile, A. and Akbar, M. (2004). African Americans' perception of psychotherapy and psychotherapists. *Professional Psychology: Research and Practice*, 35(1), 19–16.

Unden, A.L., Orth-Gomer, K. and Elfosson, S. (1991). Cardiovascular effects of social support in the work place: Twenty-four-hour ECG monitoring of men and women. *Psychosomatic Medicine*, 53, 50–60.

VanBreda, A.D. (2001). *Resilience Theory: A Literature Review with Special Chapters on Deployment Resilience in Military Families & Resilience Theory in Social Work*. Pretoria: South African Military Health Service, Military Psychological Institute, Social Work Research and Development.

Vandenberghe, R. and Huberman, A.M. (1999). *Understanding and Preventing Teacher Burnout.* Cambridge: Cambridge University Press.

Viswesvaran, C.L., Sanchez, J.L. and Fisher, J. (1999). The role of social support in the process of work stress: A meta-analysis. *Journal of Vocational Behavior,* 54, 314–34.

Waller, M. (2001). Resilience in ecosystemic context: Evolution of the concept. *American Journal of Orthopsychiatry,* 7(3), 290–97.

Watson, D., Clark, L.A. and Tellegen, A. (1988). Development and validation of brief measures of positive and negative affect: The PANAS scales. *Journal of Personality and Social Psychology,* 54, 1063–70.

Weiss, D.S. and Marmar, C.R. (1997). The impact of event scale-revised. In J.P. Wilson and T.M. Keane (eds), *Assessing Psychological Trauma and PTSD* (pp. 399–411). New York: Guilford Press.

Werner, E. and Smith, R. (1982). *Vulnerable but Invincible: A Study of Resilient Children.* New York: McGraw-Hill.

World Health Organization (1998). *Wellbeing Measures in Primary Health Care: The Depcare Project.* Copenhagen: World Health Organization.

World Health Organization (2011). WHO-Five Well-being Index (WHO-5) 2011. Available at: https://www.psykiatri-regionh.dk/who-5/Documents/WHO5_English.pdf. Accessed June 2015.

PART IV
PERSONALITY AND COPING IN EDUCATIONAL SETTINGS

The Role of Personality Traits in the Perception of Occupational Stress and the Coping Style of Teachers: A Few Points to Consider

Alexander-Stamatios Antoniou and Antigoni Garyfallaki

Introduction

Educators' occupational stress and wellbeing are increasingly becoming a crucial issue among researchers. Teaching has been suggested to be among the most stressful occupations (Johnson et al. 2005), as the nature of the job encompasses high levels of stress and professional exhaustion, broadly referred to as 'burnout' (Jalongo and Heider 2006). Surveys report rates ranging from 5% up to 30% of teachers suffering from burnout symptoms (Rudow 1999; Schaufeli, Daamen and Van Mierlo 1994) as well as an increasing number of referrals of teachers to occupational therapists with stress-related disorders (Austin, Shah and Muncer 2005). The alarming rates of teachers experiencing psychological and occupational strain have been observed both in Eastern (Chan 1998; Gaziel 1993; Shen 2009; Yang, Ge, Hu, Chi and Wang 2009; Yang, Wang, Ge, Hu and Chi 2011) and Western societies (Austin et al. 2005; Johnson et al. 2005; Laugaa, Rascle and Bruchon-Schweitzer 2008; Lewis 1999; Parker, Martin, Colmar and Liem 2012).

Therefore, occupational stress and the ways in which teachers cope with this are of great interest to researchers. It is widely suggested that a better understanding of the factors influencing occupational stress as well as the factors determining response to psychological strain, may enable occupational therapists and policy makers to effectively help teachers build resilience and prevent negative outcomes, namely low performance, burnout and poor wellbeing. In this chapter the emphasis is upon teachers' work-related stress, ways of coping with stressful situations at the workplace as well as the influential role of personality in selecting coping strategies.

Coping with Stress

Initially coping was conceptualized as a psychodynamic defence mechanism, which was stable, influencing perceptions of events and dictated adaptive and maladaptive responses. Many theorists conceived coping as unconscious and involuntary responses (Eisenberg, Fabes and Guthrie 1997). Contrary to this definition, Lazarus and Folkman (1984) introduced the *transactional model of coping*. In this model coping is defined as a conscious, intentional, goal-directed response, tailored to the specific demands of a stressor (Lazarus and Folkman 1984). The processes used in order to respond to a stressor and minimize the effect on the individual are called *coping strategies* (Lazarus 1996) and are widely defined as the specific efforts, both behavioural and cognitive, that people employ to master, tolerate, reduce or minimize the internal and external demands resulting from the interaction between the individual and the environment. What is of central importance in this theoretical framework is that coping becomes activated after the individual's appraisal of the demands as taxing his personal resources, and being at risk (Folkman, Lazarus, Gruen and DeLongis 1986). Thus, the emphasis is shifted from the subconscious or non-conscious strategies (e.g. defence mechanisms) towards more adaptive or constructive coping strategies (i.e. strategies that reduce stress levels) (Connor-Smith and Flachsbart 2007).

Many researchers have attempted to address and categorize different ways of coping in order to bridge the general conceptual definitions and the actual responses of the individuals when they deal with psychological distress (Skinner and Wellborn 1994). The most widely used categorization is that of the *Problem-focused* and *Emotion-focused coping*. Problem-focused coping is conceptualized as an action-centred response aiming towards the direct resolve of challenges. On the contrary, emotion-focused coping refers to an active attempt to manage, reinterpret and alter the meaning of challenges as well as the associated emotions (Folkman et al. 1986; Lazarus and Folkman 1984). Problem-focused coping involves, among others, the rationalization of the stressful situation and positive thinking of self, while emotion-focused coping encompasses strategies such as escape and avoidance of the stressful situation, distraction and turning to religion (Carver and Connor-Smith 2010; Connor-Smith and Flachsbart 2007; Folkman et al. 1986; Lazarus and Folkman 1984). Although this dichotomy has been used in numerous studies across the decades, it has been critiqued for failing to incorporate the entire range of coping strategies. Specifically, researchers argue that this categorization neglects the role of the engagement–disengagement dimension and incorporates strategies to overly broad categories (Compas, Connor-Smith, Saltzman, Thomsen and Wadsworth 2001; Skinner, Edge, Altman and Sherwood 2003).

Apart from problem-/emotion-focused coping, numerous taxonomic approaches have been proposed. These approaches place the emphasis on the extent to which the individual becomes activated and is oriented towards confronting the problem, and strategies that call for an effort in order to minimize or eliminate strain by avoiding dealing with the problem (Moos and Billings 1982). Latack (1986) went a step further by combining the control/escape dimension with the level of action (cognitive/behavioural) yielding four types of coping strategies: active behavioural; active cognitive; inactive behavioural; and inactive cognitive coping strategies. A critique cited upon this issue is that researchers failed to reach a consensus regarding the necessary number and kind of coping strategies that should be used (Carver, Scheier and Weintraub, 1989; Skinner and Wellborn 1994).

Beyond these classifications, recent reviews and meta-analysis (Connor-Smith and Flachsbart 2007; Skinner et al. 2003) mention that over 100 coping categorization schemes and scoring systems for common coping measures have been reported, which makes the aggregation across studies a difficult task. Hence, using factor analyses a more complex model of coping was proposed based on a hierarchical structure. The highest level of categorization is *engagement* (approach, active) coping and *disengagement* (avoidant) coping. At the second level of the hierarchy, engagement coping is furthered distinguished in *primary control and secondary control*, a distinguish focusing on the coping goals. That is, primary control is used towards the stressor and the related emotions while the secondary control refers to the adaptation to stress.

Each of these coping dimensions involves three specific strategies. Primary control engagement coping involves *problem solving, instrumental support* and *emotion regulation/support*, while for secondary control engagement coping, *distraction, cognitive restructuring, acceptance* and *religious coping* are involved. On the other side of categorization, there is the disengagement dimension which involves strategies such as *avoidance, denial, wishful thinking, withdrawal and substance use* (Figure 12.1) (Connor-Smith and Flachsbart 2007).

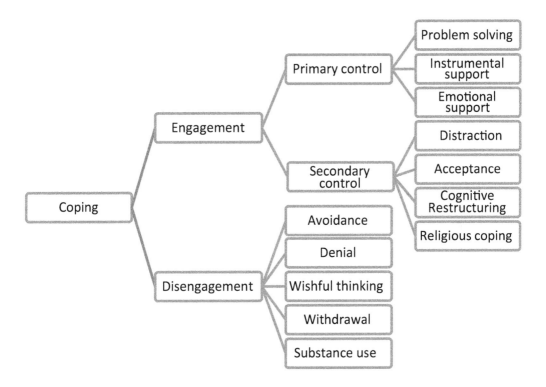

Figure 12.1   Hierarchical structure of coping
Source: Connor-Smith and Flachsbart, 2007.

What is crucial within the coping research is the differentiation between coping strategies and its consequences. Albeit, early theories attempted to define coping by its outcomes ('All responses to stressful events or episodes', Compas 1987, p. 393), later theorists suggested that coping must be regarded independently of its outcomes and its effectiveness (Lazarus and Folkman 1984). Yet the taxonomic approach followed by most researchers results from factor analysis of open-ended questions concerning the individual's response during a recent stressful event. This dimensionalization fails to recognize the coping's independence from coping resources and outcomes (Skinner and Wellborn 1994). However, it would be naïve if we assumed that the outcomes play no role in the selection of a coping strategy later in life. That is, an effective coping method might reinforce the individual to reselect the strategy used before.

The criticism of the taxonomies of coping strategies have gone a step further by arguing that the dimensionalization of strategies based on their nature and the level of function is not sufficient, and more finely designed models, incorporating the factors that lead to the individual's selection of certain strategies, on a longitudinal basis, should be used (Macrodimitris and Endler 2001; Parker et al. 2012). Parker and his colleagues (Parker et al. 2012) in investigating coping in teacher populations attempted to construct a model of coping by combining the transactional model (Lazarus and Folkman 1984), self-worth and goal-orientation theories and the outcomes of coping strategies (engagement or burnout). In this sense, self-worth is a motivating drive which is evaluated, maintained or threatened by achievement domains.

In the occupational field, work-related stress, work conditions and job nature as well as achievement domains, might pose threats to self-worth and, in turn, might affect the appraisals of stressful events. Simultaneously, goal orientation is a key factor regarding individuals' efforts to protect their sense of identity in order to preserve conceptions of self-results (Nias 1999, in Parker et al. 2012). Goal orientation provides two components; mastery (orientation to seek out challenges, define goals and engage tasks for their intrinsic value) and failure avoidance (orientation towards reducing the chances to failure). Adaptive behaviours, such as problem-focused coping, were suggested to be direct outcomes of a mastery orientation, whereas palliative behaviours (emotion-focused coping and short-term avoidant strategies) were associated with failure avoidance oriented individuals which result in engagement behaviours in the first case and burnout in the latter one (Figure 12.2).

Regarding the effectiveness of coping strategies, cumulative research findings suggest that active coping aiming to confront and change the stressful situation (positive thinking, planning, positive reinterpretation, etc.) is concerned with adaptive ways of coping and is associated with individuals' well-being and lower stress levels. While denial, behavioural and mental disengagement are negative coping strategies and are linked to burnout and poorer mental health (Austin et al. 2005; Compas et al. 2001; Shen 2009). However, the notion of positive/adaptive and negative/maladaptive coping has been recently criticized. Positive and negative coping, although opposites, are relative concepts. It has been argued that a person can effectively cope with stress when selected strategies are compatible with the stressful event and stress stage (Lazarus 2000). That is to say, a perceived negative coping strategy (e.g. turning to religion) may be functional in minimizing the psychological strain at an initial coping stage, and may strengthen the individual's ability to cope with the problem. However, in the long-term this might impede the coping process (Austin et al. 2005; Carver et al. 1989; Shen 2009).

Further support for the above notions emerges from researchers claiming that coping, although targeting stress reduction, is not universally beneficial (Compas et al. 2001). Some strategies are shown to be effective for some individuals, while for others such strategies could be non-effective or even harmful (Connor-Smith and Flachsbart 2007). Thus, concerning the influencing factors of coping, there is an ongoing debate. Some researchers claim that individual (i.e. personality) and situational differences (i.e. work conditions) determine coping selection

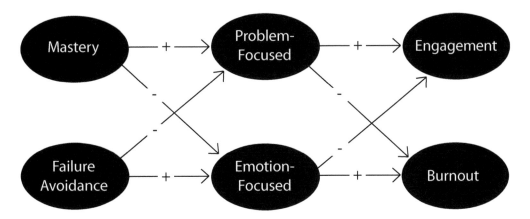

Figure 12.2   Process model of goal orientation, coping, engagement and burnout
Source: Parker et al., 2012.

(Carver et al. 1989; Lazarus and Folkman 1984), whilst others argue that coping styles are stable and should be conceived as dispositions brought about by people in every stressful situation that they encounter (McCrae 1984). In the following section, the link between personality and coping will be discussed.

Personality and Coping

Personality is generally defined as characteristic patterns of thoughts, feelings and behaviours over time and across situations, influenced by both biological predispositions (temperament) and environmental factors (Connor-Smith and Flachsbart 2007). Studying personality, researchers aim to understand human nature by defining basic similarities among individuals (e.g. humans are biological creatures, self-protective, etc.) as well as differences that make individuals unique (e.g. five-factor model of personality traits) (Carver and Connor-Smith 2010).

Coping, on the other hand, has been described as 'personality in action under stress' (Bolger 1990, p. 525) and it has been argued that coping should be redefined as a personality process. This notion gained support on a theoretical basis as Lazarus and Folkman (1984) suggested that individuals' personality traits may influence the appraisal process and therefore the selection of coping strategies. Apart from the theoretical basis, empirical evidence links personality to coping strategies (Bolger 1990; Kato and Pedersen 2005; Mosher 2006).

It has been proposed that personality affects coping in both direct and indirect ways (Connor-Smith and Flachsbart 2007). At a biological level, it is suggested that responses to stressful situations result from temperament based systems which either make the individual approach (active/engagement coping) or avoid (disengagement coping) the threat (Skinner and Zimmer-Gembeck 2007) and thus affect coping selection throughout the lifespan (Connor-Smith and Flachsbart 2007). Moreover, taking into account that the coping process is generated and reinforced by stress exposure and that personality affects whether each individual experiences a situation as stressful (intensity and frequency), we could assume the association between coping processes and personality traits. Thus, people who perceive more situations as negative and stressful and experience more negative feelings, are also more prone to disengage in order to buffer and regulate their intense emotions. On the other hand, people who are low in stress reactivity and have more positive appraisals towards adversities are more likely to make use of active/engagement coping strategies (Carver and Connor-Smith 2010; Connor-Smith and Flachsbart 2007).

As mentioned above, empirical evidence suggests that certain coping strategies may prove beneficial for some individuals and less effective or even harmful for others with different personality traits (Connor-Smith and Flachsbart 2007). Although a coping strategy (e.g. problem solving) might have beneficial long-term outcomes, the short-term costs and benefits might have a more crucial role in selecting future coping strategies. For instance, the short-term benefits of disengagement may reinforce a person with high levels of stress reactivity to continue selecting strategies with poor long-term outcomes (Connor-Smith and Flachsbart 2007).

Research into personality and coping is relatively diverse. In their effort to define the individual differences that make certain strategies optimal for some individuals and harmful for others, as well as to investigate the strategy selection process, researchers have proposed several models. In this chapter we review the well-established five-factor model, the role of self-efficacy feelings as well as the role of locus of control of a stressful situation.

THE FIVE-FACTOR MODEL

The five-factor model, being a well-established construct, offers a useful set of individual differences measures which have been found to be relatively stable across age cohorts and cultures (McCrae and John 1992). In order to investigate the role of personality in coping with stress and its consequences, namely burnout, numerous studies have used the 'Big Five' model (Bolger 1990; Carver and Connor-Smith 2010; Connor-Smith and Flachsbart 2007; Grant and Langan-Fox 2006; McCrae and Costa 1986; Swider and Zimmerman 2010). A recent meta-analysis of 165 samples (Connor-Smith and Flachsbart 2007) has linked each personality trait to certain coping strategies.

Extraversion has its roots in the approach temperament system and is characterized by sensitivity to reward, positive emotions, sociability and assertiveness (McCrae and John 1992). Empirical evidence links this trait to more frequent use of engagement coping, namely problem solving, seeking social support and cognitive restructuring, and less frequently to disengagement coping, such as wishful thinking and withdrawal (Connor-Smith and Flachsbart 2007).

On the other hand, *Neuroticism*, deriving from an avoidance temperament system, reflects a trend towards vulnerability to fear, sadness and distressful experiences, that is frequent negative affectivity, negative emotionality and behavioural inhibition (McCrae and John 1992). Consequently, neuroticism has been associated to less engagement coping, mainly to distraction and social support and more strongly related to disengagement (wishful thinking and withdrawal) and emotion-focused coping (expression of negative emotions).

Conscientiousness involves self-discipline, organization, goal-orientation, persistence and planful properties (Lengua et al. 1999; Vollrath 2001) leading to the association towards engagement coping strategies such as problem solving and cognitive restructuring rather than seeking social support and disengagement strategies (denial and substance use). Moreover, conscientiousness is negatively related to expression of negative emotions.

Openness to experiences entails creativity, imagination, curiosity, flexibility and tendency towards intellectual and innovative activities (McCrae and John 1992). Possessing these characteristics, individuals high in openness are more likely to engage with stressful situations through problem solving and cognitive restructuring from negative thinking to positive activities and thoughts. Yet it is also possible for these people to disengage, by selecting wishful thinking and using their fantasy and imagination (Connor-Smith and Flachsbart 2007).

Last but not least, *Agreeableness* suggests altruism, compliance and concern for others (Caspi et al. 2005; McCrae and John 1992). People high in agreeableness often have a strong social network, which in turn leads them to rely on their social contacts during stressful situations. Similar to conscientiousness, agreeableness negatively predicts expression of negative emotions (Carver and Connor-Smith 2010; Connor-Smith and Flachsbart 2007).

Meta-analytic findings suggest that although individual studies provide correlations between personality traits and coping of strong effect size, when it comes to summarizing the studies, the magnitude of the relationship is modest (Connor-Smith and Flachsbart 2007). This is partially explained by the diversity of samples and measures of variables. Notwithstanding, the effect of such a link in everyday life remains significant, taking into account that personality affects every stressor an individual encounters, resulting in shaping his/her coping style over time. Moreover, authors argued that relationships were more interesting when specific coping strategies were under examination, rather than broad categories. They also proposed that in the future researchers should address specific facets of each personality trait in order to further the insight of the mechanisms that underlie the relationship between personality and coping.

SELF-EFFICACY

Self-efficacy is a crucial component in the Social Cognitive Theory (Bandura 1997). Self-efficacy refers to individuals' beliefs about their capabilities to successfully carry out a particular course of action, and overcome barriers by investing effort and strategies. According to Bandura (1997), there are four sources of self-efficacy beliefs: *enactive mastery experiences*; *vicarious experiences*; *verbal persuasion*; and *personal physiological and affective states* from which people judge whether or not they are capable of accomplishing a task or confronting a situation. Efficacy beliefs determine the way individuals perceive events as opportunities or obstacles (Bandura 2006). Hence self-efficacy influences the choice of tasks undertaken, the effort put into these, and the extent to which the individual will persist in confronting a problem (Skaalvik and Skaalvik 2010). Given this framework, we could assume the important role of self-efficacy in the coping process.

Reviewing the literature from research within the the occupational psychology field, self-efficacy beliefs seem to affect individuals' wellbeing in both a direct and indirect way. To begin with, a sizeable amount of studies have revealed an inverse relationship between teachers' self-efficacy and burnout (Betoret 2006, 2009; Fives, Hamman and Olivarez 2007; Shen 2009; Skaalvik and Skaalvik 2010; Tschannen-Moran and Hoy 2007). High levels of self-efficacy in teachers were significantly and negatively associated with work-related stressors and in turn negatively linked to burnout dimensions (Betoret 2009; Fives et al. 2007).

Moreover, self-efficacy has been directly linked to job satisfaction, commitment to profession, good cooperation with colleagues and supervisors (Caprara, Barbaranelli, Steca and Malone 2006; Skaalvik and Skaalvik 2010) as well as positive relationships with parents (Skaalvik and Skaalvik 2010), better classroom management (Martin, Sass and Schmitt 2012) and greater motivation and performance (Tschannen-Moran and Woolfolk 2001). Therefore, self-efficacy seems to play an important role in the promotion of a rich and stimulating learning environment, which in turn limits certain environmental stressors related with the teaching occupation (student misbehaviour, fear of losing control), thus promoting occupational wellbeing and preventing teachers from burnout.

In addition, the concept of self-efficacy has been directly associated with positive coping of stress (Devonport et al. 2003; Devonport, Lane, City, Campus and Road, 2006; Lane et al. 2002; Laugaa et al. 2008; Shen 2009). More specifically, self-efficacy is conceptualized as a key factor in cognitive evaluation of a stressful situation. Hence, teachers with high levels of self-efficacy feel more empowered to act on the stressor instead of avoiding it. There is empirical evidence linking teachers' high self-efficacy to problem-focused coping strategies (problem solving, positive reinterpretation, planning and acceptance), whereas low self-efficacy predicted emotion-focused disengagement coping strategies, such as denial, turning to religion and behavioural disengagement (Shen 2009).

Furthermore, the relationship between coping strategies and self-efficacy seems to be reciprocal. This is illustrated by the fact that research evidence suggests that self-efficacy predicts active coping strategies, while simultaneously it is argued that problem-focused coping behaviours derive from mastery and tend to reinforce self-worth attributes, such as self-efficacy and competence. This in turn provides the individual with resources for successful confrontation of stressful situations, resulting in increased achievements and consequently improved self-worth and competence feelings (Parker et al. 2012).

However, the relation between self-efficacy and coping does not remain intact by mediating factors, such as control of situations. Researchers suggest that although high self-efficacy is linked to adaptive coping strategies, where there is greater stress intensity whereby individuals have limited control over the situation, active, problem-focused coping tends to be replaced by emotion-focused strategies (Shen 2009). Locus of control has been suggested to act as a mediating factor influencing the relationship between work-related sources of stress and mental wellbeing. Traits such as hardiness (a component of internal locus of control) may buffer the effects of stress and have been associated with lower levels of stress and better performance. These individuals, who have a greater sense of internal control, prefer active coping strategies aiming to alter the stressful situation. Contrary to internal locus of control, there is also the external locus of control, where individuals select palliative coping strategies in order to regulate their emotional arousal. Recent empirical evidence support this theoretical framework, suggesting that people who manifest higher levels of stress also exhibit higher levels of illness, and are more likely to perceive control as external and to have lower levels of self-efficacy (Roddenberry and Renk 2010).

Coping with Occupational Stress in Educational Workplaces

As mentioned in the introduction section of this chapter, considerable interest has been given to research into teachers' stress, due to alarming rates of them dropping out of the profession (Martin et al. 2012) and increased symptoms of occupational stress and burnout (Austin et al. 2005; Parker et al. 2012; Shen 2009). Researchers aim to identify the elements that make teaching a stressful profession, by defining the main stressors that teachers encounter on a daily basis. Numerous studies both in mainstream educational settings (Antoniou, Polychroni and Vlachakis 2006; Austin et al. 2005; Forlin 2001; Pithers and Fogarty 1995) and special educational settings (Antoniou and Polychroni 2000; Jennett, Harris and Mesibov 2003) have identified the main stressors for teachers. Individual studies have highlighted work-related stress including excessive caseload, administration of lesson preparation, parental involvement, hours worked overtime (Austin et al. 2005; Pithers and Fogarty 1995; Yang et al. 2011), poor work conditions (Gaziel 1993; Yang et al. 2011), student misbehaviour (Boyle et al. 1995), lack of support, school policies, time and funds (Austin et al. 2005) as well as the discrediting of the profession (Laugaa et al. 2008) to be among the major job stressors for teachers.

Recent studies however have attempted to classify all of these factors into three broad clusters; that is, stressors that *directly refer to the teaching profession* (i.e. class structure, student misbehaviour, class heterogeneity, work overload), *personal factors* (i.e. individual differences concerning age, gender, years of experience, personality traits) and *administrative factors* (i.e. limited government support, deficient training, excessive demands from school administration, continuous changes in the curriculum and communication with parents) (Antoniou et al. 2006; Forlin 2001). However, there is still no consensus when it comes to defining the main stressors, as inconsistencies emerge among research findings, underlining the dynamic nature of stressors which change over time and across different cultures and educational systems (Betoret 2009).

Nevertheless, an understanding of what causes teachers to become stressed will accommodate the discussion with regard to their coping strategies towards stressful situations. Research in teacher populations suggests that active/engagement coping, either behavioural or cognitive, is associated with relatively low stress levels, while palliative strategies, such as emotional expressive strategies, increase teachers' urge to escape, and decrease their involvement in the problem (Austin et al. 2005).

More precisely, problem-focused coping, involving strategies such as putting problems into perspective, rationalizing and analysing the situation, being coherent in the relationship with students and self-management and regulation, has been found to have positive and useful effects on confronting stress within the educational setting (Antoniou, Ploumpi and Ntalla 2013; Austin et al. 2005; Chan 1998; Martin 2008; Mattern and Bauer 2014; Shen 2009). Moreover, active coping was found to be the most frequent strategy used among Chinese teachers (Shen 2009). Problem-oriented coping has predicted higher levels of personal accomplishment, inversely linking active coping strategies to teachers' burnout (Antoniou et al. 2013; Betoret and Artiga 2010).

Other problem-focused strategies have also been suggested as positively relating to stress confrontation. For example, seeking social support and job control were found to actively contribute to teachers' wellbeing (Pisanti, Gagliardi, Razzino and Bertini 2003). Seeking social support has been linked with reduced burnout dimensions such as depersonalization (Chan and Hui 1995), which implies that by relying on seeking support from social contacts (colleagues, family, friends) teachers manage to reduce a negative attitude towards their students and colleagues, leading to a more positive climate within their workplace. Yet individual differences such as years of experience are moderating factors, as novice teachers were found to use such strategies less frequently, possibly due to difficulties in becoming integrated into an already well-established team during the first years of teaching (Laugaa et al. 2008).

On the contrary, palliative and emotion-focused coping strategies have been associated with higher perceived stress, low self-efficacy and limited social support among teachers (Austin et al. 2005; Chan and Hui 1995; Shen 2009). In addition, disengagement strategies, including escape, avoidance and denial were positively associated with distress and had a direct positive predictive effect on teachers' burnout components of emotional exhaustion and depersonalization (Antoniou et al. 2013; Austin et al. 2005; Chan and Hui 1995; Laugaa et al. 2008). That is to say, by denying or escaping the stressful situation without attempting to change it, teachers may become ineffective in overcoming problems and the demands of their profession, which inevitably results in their emotional exhaustion and affect their relationships with students, colleagues and supervisors.

Moreover, other maladaptive strategies, such as turning to religion (Shen 2009), uncontrolled aggressiveness (Austin et al. 2005) and adopting a traditional teaching style (Laugaa et al. 2008), have also been examined. Although the frequency with which teachers selected such strategies was significantly lower than for problem-focused ones, such coping styles were positively linked to subjective stress, that is highly stressed teachers tended to select them more frequently (Austin et al. 2005; Shen 2009). Additionally, maladaptive strategies predicting negative outcomes in teachers' wellbeing were negatively associated with teachers' self-efficacy (Austin et al. 2005; Shen 2009), while positively related to emotional exhaustion, depersonalization and reduced professional accomplishment (Laugaa et al. 2008).

Nonetheless, research studies on occupational stress and coping strategies have received important criticism regarding methodological as well as general concept and theoretical issues. To begin with, the vast majority of the research studies have adopted correlational, cross-sectional designs. Such methodologies fail to provide direction of the relationship between occupational stress and coping strategies, and also make it difficult to understand the role of moderating factors. Consequently, it is not clear in a given possible positive correlation between subjective stress, disengagement strategies and low self-efficacy whether personality predisposes people to appraise situations as stressful and select certain coping strategies leading to negative outcomes, or certain strategies boost distress and negative feelings, affecting self-efficacy. Recently, however, the need for more complicated models rather than linear relation between variables, as well as a reciprocal relationship among factors, have been proposed (Betoret 2009).

Moreover, self-reports and retrospective responses are the main measures in the research literature (Antoniou et al. 2013; Betoret 2009; Betoret and Artiga 2010; Carver and Connor-Smith 2010; Connor-Smith and Flachsbart 2007; Parker et al. 2012) using principally dispositional coping. These studies fail to consider other factors, such as the combination of strategies, duration and order (Carver and Connor-Smith 2010). Hence, successive assessment and longitudinal designs as well as more objective measures, namely observations triangulated with multiple informant approaches, are needed (Compas et al. 2001; Skinner et al. 2003).

Finally, the coping process should not be considered as independent of the nature of the stressor and the context of assessment (Carver and Connor-Smith 2010; Prokopčáková 2004). Perceived intensity of stressful stimuli might moderate the relationship between personality and coping strategies (Shen 2009). Furthermore, different professions have profound effects on employees that might affect their resilience or vulnerability towards stress. In particular, teaching as a job enquires certain planning skills as most teachers are required by their supervisors to submit lesson plans beforehand. Additionally, cultural context plays an important role, given that the professional status and hence the expectations of the teachers change across different cultures (Gaziel 1993). Also, different educational systems and national policies may affect the stressful situations that teachers confront and in turn impact on their response to it (Laugaa et al. 2008).

Implications

The practical implications for teachers, and educators in general, concerning stress and consequently burnout as well as teachers' attrition phenomenon are of significant importance (Parker et al. 2012). Pithers and Fogarty (1995) have drawn attention to the fact that in order to reduce work-related stress in teachers, a greater change at a whole educational system level is essential. Moreover, given the associations between teachers' stress, personality, coping strategies and psychological and professional outcomes, it has been suggested that apart from coping itself, an emphasis upon cognitions that generate coping behaviour and context in which coping takes place would be of greater utility (Parker et al. 2012). However, it would be naïve to believe that reducing stress and ill-being of teachers is solely a matter of optimizing their coping strategies. What is equally important is reducing the major stressors and improving the working conditions (Laugaa et al. 2008).

Consequently, intervention programmes of multiple levels seem to be the optimal way of dealing with occupational stress in educational workplace. Laugaa and colleagues (2008) presented an integrated programme consisting of three stages. More specifically, early prevention of work stress encompasses interventions implemented at the early stages of a teacher's career intensifying the personal resources of the professional through information programmes on job stress and effective ways of coping as well as teaching ways of identifying stressful situations and building up self-esteem and self-efficacy beliefs.

Moreover, prevention entails a great change at an organizational level by improving working conditions and modifying government and school policies, considering the major stressors (e.g. workload outside working hours, demands from parents, discredit by society, etc.). On a secondary level, interventions aiming to improve coping skills by focusing on problem solving instead of discharging emotions, through cognitive and behavioural approaches and peer support groups, are being suggested in order for teachers to function effectively under stressful conditions. Simultaneously, promoting lifelong learning at all teaching levels could empower teachers and boost their competence and self-efficacy beliefs. Last but not least, intervention in crisis, when burnout symptoms are manifested, constitutes the third level of the programme. In this case, occupational therapists and human resources specialists should play a crucial role in diagnosing and treating burnout as well as offering alternative options to the teachers.

Nevertheless, coping is a complex process and generalized methods are not relatively effective. Considering individual differences, namely personality and years of experience and contexts, it has been proposed that professional development programmes should be tailored to teachers' career stages (novice teachers may need general skills while experienced teachers may make greater use of more specific skills) (Klassen and Chiu 2010). Individual interventions may seem practically impossible to be designed and implemented. Hence, schools staffed with specialized personnel (i.e. psychologists and/or counsellors) may be of great use for teachers, as well as their supervisors and students (Betoret 2009).

Conclusion

This chapter focused on the role of personality on perceiving occupational stress and teachers' coping strategies. Research has shown that personality plays an important role in conceiving occupational stress as it affects the way a person interprets a situation. Thus, individuals with low self-efficacy feelings and high stress reactivity (high neuroticism) are more likely to perceive a difficult situation as stressful. In turn, exposure to stress affects individuals' responses. Thus, individuals who tend to experience greater stress are more likely to respond by selecting a coping strategy that will discharge intense emotions rather than focusing on the problem and finding a solution.

On the contrary, individuals with higher self-efficacy, mastery oriented with greater social network (high agreeableness) and persistence (conscientiousness) are more likely to perceive a stressful situation as challenging and try to alter the problem by channelling their negative emotions in a more positive direction. Although research evidence reports small effect sizes of relations between personality and coping, the impact on individuals' lives is still of significance.

Nevertheless, coping is a complex process with numerous mediating factors. Hence, the educational context, which is reviewed here, provides a fertile ground for research as teachers encounter numerous stressors at multiple levels and on a daily basis. Ranging from the organizational level (government and school policies) to class level (class management, student misbehaviour) and personal level (personality traits, self-efficacy beliefs, relationships with parents) stressors and moderating factors work together to form the background of coping process for teachers.

In line with general research on coping, problem-focused strategies are suggested as being more efficient than avoidant and palliative coping styles, helping teachers to confront stressful situations, building up resilience and avoiding burnout symptoms. However, the relationship between personality, stress and coping strategies in teachers is not yet clear, with methodological gaps limiting the value of empirical evidence. As such, further research is needed in order to enhance our insight and implement findings at a practical level, through finely designed interventions.

References

Antoniou, A.-S. and Polychroni, F. (2000). Sources of stress and professional burnout of teachers of special educational needs in Greece – ISEC 2000. In International Conference of Special Education, ISEC 2000. Manchester.

Antoniou, A.-S., Ploumpi, A. and Ntalla, M. (2013). Occupational stress and professional burnout in teachers of primary and secondary education: The role of coping strategies. *Psychology*, 4(3), 349–55.

Antoniou, A.-S., Polychroni, F. and Vlachakis, A.N. (2006). Gender and age differences in occupational stress and professional burnout between primary and high-school teachers in Greece. *Journal of Managerial Psychology*, 21(7), 682–90.

Austin, V., Shah, S. and Muncer, S. (2005). Teacher stress and coping strategies used to reduce stress. *Occupational Therapy International*, 12(2), 63–80.

Bandura, A. (1997). *Self-efficacy: The Exercise of Control*. New York: Freeman.

Bandura, A. (2006). Guide for constructing self-efficacy scales. In F. Pajares and T. Urdan (eds), *Self-efficacy Beliefs of Adolescents* (pp. 307–37). Greenwich, CT: Information Age Publishing.

Betoret, F.D. (2006). Stressors, self-efficacy, coping resources, and burnout among secondary school teachers in Spain. *Educational Psychology*, 26(4), 519–39.

Betoret, F.D. (2009). Self-efficacy, school resources, job stressors and burnout among Spanish primary and secondary school teachers: A structural equation approach. *Educational Psychology*, 29(1), 45–68.

Betoret, F.D. and Artiga, A.G. (2010). Barriers perceived by teachers at work, coping strategies, self-efficacy and burnout. *The Spanish Journal of Psychology*, 13(2), 637–54.

Bolger, N. (1990). Coping as a personality process: A prospective study. *Journal of Personality and Social Psychology*, 59(3), 525–37.

Boyle, G.J., Borg, M.G., Falzon, J.M. and Baglioni, A.J. (1995). A structural model of the dimensions of teacher stress. *British Journal of Educational Psychology*, 65, 49–56.

Caprara, G.V., Barbaranelli, C., Steca, P. and Malone, P.S. (2006). Teachers' self-efficacy beliefs as determinants of job satisfaction and students' academic achievement: A study at the school level. *Journal of School Psychology*, 44(6), 473–90.

Carver, C.S. and Connor-Smith, J. (2010). Personality and coping. *Annual Review of Psychology*, 61, 679–704.

Carver, C.S., Scheier, M.F. and Weintraub, J.K. (1989). Assessing coping strategies: A theoretically based approach. *Journal of Personality and Social Psychology*, 56(2), 267–83.

Caspi, A., Moffitt, E.T., Cannon, M., McClay, J., Murray, R., Harrington, H., Craig, I.W. et al. (2005). Moderation of the effect of adolescent-onset cannabis use on adult psychosis by a functional polymorphism in the catechol-o-methyltransferase gene: Longitudinal evidence of a Gene X environment interraction. *Biological Psychiatry*, 57(10), 1117–277.

Chan, D.W. (1998). Stress, coping strategies, and psychological distress among secondary school teachers in Hong Kong. *American Educational Research Journal*, 35(1), 145–63.

Chan, D.W. and Hui, E.K. (1995). Burnout and coping among Chinese secondary school teachers in Hong Kong. *The British Journal of Educational Psychology*, 65 (Pt 1), 15–25.

Compas, B.E. (1987). Coping with stress during childhood and adolescence. *Psychological Bulletin*, 101(3), 393–403.

Compas, B.E., Connor-Smith, J.K., Saltzman, H., Thomsen, A.H. and Wadsworth, M.E. (2001). Coping with stress during childhood and adolescence: Problems, progress, and potential in theory and research. *Psychological Bulletin*, 127(1), 87–127.

Connor-Smith, J.K. and Flachsbart, C. (2007). Relations between personality and coping: A meta-analysis. *Journal of Personality and Social Psychology*, 93(6), 1080–107.

Devonport, T.D., Lane, A.M., Milton, K.E. and Williams, L. (2003). *Self-efficacy as a Predictor of Strategies used to Cope with Dissertation Stress*. Paper presented at the Annual Conference of the British Psychological Society, Bournemouth.

Devonport, T.J., Lane, A.M., City, I., Campus, W. and Road, G. (2006). Relationships between self-efficacy, coping and student retention. *Social Behaviour and Personality*, 34(2), 127–38.

Eisenberg, N., Fabes, R.A. and Guthrie, I.K. (1997). Coping with stress: The roles of regulation and development. In S.A. Wolchik and I.N. Sandler (eds), *Handbook of Children's Coping: Linking Theory and Intervention. Issues in Clinical Child Psychology* (pp. 41–70). New York: Plenum Press.

Fives, H., Hamman, D. and Olivarez, A. (2007). Does burnout begin with student-teaching? Analyzing efficacy, burnout, and support during the student-teaching semester. *Teaching and Teacher Education*, 23(6), 916–34.

Folkman, S., Lazarus, R.S., Gruen, R.J. and DeLongis, A. (1986). Appraisal, coping, health status, and psychological symptoms. *Journal of Personality and Social Psychology*, 50(3), 571–9.

Forlin, C. (2001). Inclusion: Identifying potential stressors for regular class teachers. *Educational Research*, 43(3), 235–45.

Gaziel, H.H. (1993). Coping with occupational stress among teachers: A cross-cultural study. *Comparative Education*, 29(1), 67–79.

Grant, S. and Langan-Fox, J. (2006). Occupational stress, coping and strain: The combined/interactive effect of the Big Five traits. *Personality and Individual Differences*, 41(4), 719–32.

Jalongo, M.R. and Heider, K. (2006). Editorial teacher attrition: An issue of national concern. *Early Childhood Education Journal*, 33(6), 379–80.

Jennett, H.K., Harris, S.L. and Mesibov, G.B. (2003). Commitment to philosophy, teacher efficacy, and burnout among teachers of children with autism. *Journal of Autism and Developmental Disorders*, 33(6), 583–93.

Johnson, S., Cooper, C., Cartwright, S., Donald, I., Taylor, P. and Millet, C. (2005). The experience of work-related stress across occupations. *Journal of Managerial Psychology*, 20(2), 178–87.

Kato, K. and Pedersen, N.L. (2005). Personality and coping: A study of twins reared apart and twins reared together. *Behavior Genetics*, 35(2), 147–58.

Klassen, R.M. and Chiu, M.M. (2010). Effects on teachers' self-efficacy and job satisfaction: Teacher gender, years of experience, and job stress. *Journal of Educational Psychology*, 102(3), 741–56.

Lane, A.M., Jones, L. and Stevens, M. (2002). Coping with failure: The effects of self-esteem and coping on changes in self-efficacy. *Journal of Sport Behavior*, 25, 331–45.

Latack, J.C. (1986). Coping with job stress: Measures and future directions for scale development. *Journal of Applied Psychology*, 71(3), 377–85.

Laugaa, D., Rascle, N. and Bruchon-Schweitzer, M. (2008). Stress and burnout among French elementary school teachers: A transactional approach. *Revue Européenne de Psychologie Appliquée/European Review of Applied Psychology*, 58(4), 241–51.

Lazarus, R.S. (1996). The role of coping in the emotions and how coping changes over the life course. In C. Magai and S.H. McFadden (eds), *Handbook of Emotion, Adult Development, and Aging* (pp. 289–306). California: Academic Press.

Lazarus, R.S. (2000). How emotions influence performance in competitive sports. *The Sport Psychologist*, 14, 229–52.

Lazarus, R.S. and Folkman, S. (1984). *Stress, Appraisal, and Coping*. New York: Springer Publishing Company.

Lengua, L.J., Sandler, I.N., West, S.G., Wolchik, S.A. and Curran, P.J. (1999). Emotionality and self-regulation, threat appraisal, and coping in children of divorce. *Development and Psychopathology*, 11, 15–37.

Lewis, R. (1999). Teachers coping with the stress of classroom discipline. *Social Psychology and Education*, 3(3), 155–71.

Macrodimitris, S.D. and Endler, N.S. (2001). Coping, control, and adjustment in type 2 diabetes. *Health Psychlogy*, 20(3), 208–16.

Martin, A.J. (2008). Motivation and engagement in the workplace: Examining a multidimensional framework and instrument from a measurement and evaluation perspective. *Measurement and Evaluation in Counseling and Development*, 41(4), 223–43.

Martin, N.K., Sass, D.A. and Schmitt, T.A. (2012). Teacher efficacy in student engagement, instructional management, student stressors, and burnout: A theoretical model using in-class variables to predict teachers' intent-to-leave. *Teaching and Teacher Education*, 28(4), 546–59.

Mattern, J. and Bauer, J. (2014). Does teachers' cognitive self-regulation increase their occupational well-being? The structure and role of self-regulation in the teaching context. *Teaching and Teacher Education*, 43, 58–68.

McCrae, R.R. (1984). Situational determinants of coping responses: Loss, threat, and challenge. *Journal of Personality and Social Psychology*, 46(4), 919–28.

McCrae, R.R. and Costa, P.T. (1986). Personality, coping, and coping effectiveness in an adult sample. *Journal of Personality*, 54, 385–405.

McCrae, R.R. and John, O.P. (1992). An introduction to the five-factor model and its applications. *Journal of Personality*, 60(2), 175–215.

Moos, R.H. and Billings, A.G. (1982). Conceptualizing and measuring coping resources and processes. In L. Goldberger and S. Breznitz (eds), *Handbook of Stress: Theoretical and Clinical Aspects* (pp. 212–30). New York: Free Press.

Mosher, C.E. (2006). Coping and social support as mediators of the relation of optimism to depressive symptoms among black college students. *Journal of Black Psychology*, 32(1), 72–86.

Parker, P.D., Martin, A.J., Colmar, S. and Liem, G. (2012). Teachers' workplace well-being: Exploring a process model of goal orientation, coping behavior, engagement, and burnout. *Teaching and Teacher Education*, 28(4), 503–13.

Pisanti, R., Gagliardi, M.P.I.A., Razzino, S. and Bertini, M. (2003). Occupational stress and wellness among Italian secondary school teachers. *Psychology and Health*, 18(4), 523–36.

Pithers, R.T. and Fogarty, G.J. (1995). Occupational stress among vocational teachers. *The British Journal of Educational Psychology*, 65(1), 3–14.

Prokopčáková, A. (2004). Choice of coping strategies in the interaction: Anxiety and type of a demanding life situation (A research probe). *Studia Psychologica*, 46(3), 235–8.

Roddenberry, A. and Renk, K. (2010). Locus of control and self-efficacy: Potential mediators of stress, illness, and utilization of health services in college students. *Child Psychiatry and Human Development*, 41(4), 353–70.

Rudow, B. (1999). Stress and burnout in the teaching profession: European studies, issues, and research perspectives. In R. Vandenberghe and A.M. Huberman (eds), *Understanding and Preventing Teacher Burnout* (pp. 38–58). New York: Cambridge University Press.

Schaufeli, W.B., Daamen, J. and Van Mierlo, H. (1994). Burnout among Dutch teachers: An mbi-validity study. *Educational and Psychological Measurement*, 54(3), 803–12.

Shen, Y.E. (2009). Relationships between self-efficacy, social support and stress coping strategies in Chinese primary and secondary school teachers. *Stress and Health*, 25(2), 129–38.

Skaalvik, E.M. and Skaalvik, S. (2010). Teacher self-efficacy and teacher burnout: A study of relations. *Teaching and Teacher Education*, 26(4), 1059–69.

Skinner, E.A. and Wellborn, J.G. (1994). Coping during childhood and adolescence: A motivational perspective. In D. Featherman, R. Lerner and M. Perlmutter (eds), *Life-span Development and Behavior* (pp. 91–133). Hillsdale: Erlbaum.

Skinner, E.A., Edge, K., Altman, J. and Sherwood, H. (2003). Searching for the structure of coping: A review and critique of category systems for classifying ways of coping. *Psychological Bulletin*, 129(2), 216–69.

Swider, B.W. and Zimmerman, R.D. (2010). Born to burnout: A meta-analytic path model of personality, job burnout, and work outcomes. *Journal of Vocational Behavior*, 76(3), 487–506.

Tschannen-Moran, M. and Hoy, A.W. (2007). The differential antecedents of self-efficacy beliefs of novice and experienced teachers. *Teaching and Teacher Education*, 23(6), 944–56.

Tschannen-Moran, M. and Woolfolk, A. (2001). Teacher efficacy: Capturing an elusive construct, *Teaching and Teacher Education*, 17(7), 783–805.

Vollrath, M. (2001). Personality and stress. *Scandinavian Journal of Psychology*, 42(4), 335–47.

Yang, X., Ge, C., Hu, B., Chi, T. and Wang, L. (2009). Relationship between quality of life and occupational stress among teachers. *Public Health*, 123(11), 750–5.

Yang, X., Wang, L., Ge, C., Hu, B. and Chi, T. (2011). Factors associated with occupational strain among Chinese teachers: A cross-sectional study. *Public Health*, 125(2), 106–13.

13

Stress, Coping and Drug Abuse of High Achieving Students: The Role of Personality Traits

Marina Dalla and Alexander-Stamatios Antoniou

Introduction

The use and abuse of drugs by adolescents has become one of the most disturbing short and long-term health related phenomena in many parts of the world (Kaminer and Tarter 2004). Five-year trends are showing significant increases in past-year and past-month (current) marijuana use and stimulants across all three grades as well as increases in lifetime and daily marijuana use among 10th graders in the United States (National Institute on Drug Abuse 2013). By the time these adolescents become seniors, almost 70% of high school students will have tried alcohol, half will have taken an illegal drug, nearly 40% will have smoked a cigarette, and more than 20% will have used a prescription drug for a nonmedical purpose (National Institute on Drug Abuse 2014). Lifetime prevalence levels of cannabis use of between 13% and 25% are reported by 15 countries of the European Union (EMCDDA 2011). Collectively, one in every two European adolescents is engaged in maladaptive use of cannabis. Approximately 15% of youths between 15 and 17 years of age in Greece have used marijuana and 3% have tried other illegal drugs (EKTEPN 2014).

There is frequent evidence that school failure is a risk factor for the emergence of drug use problems, especially during the high school years (Anthony and Chen 2004; Luthar 2003; National Institute on Drug Abuse 2003; Zimmerman and Schmeelk-Cone 2003). However, significant problems of drug abuse have been seen at the other end of academic performance, among high achieving (Dalla, Matsa, Antoniou and Prapas 2012) and gifted students (Peairs, Eichen, Putallaz, Costanzo and Grimes 2010) or youth in wealthy, ultra-achievement oriented communities (Luthar and Barkin 2012). High alcohol use, binge drinking and marijuana use were found to be a common occurrence amongst youths in areas with mostly educated, high income, white, two-parent families.

These trends escalate through college, where full-time students were two and a half times more likely to meet diagnostic criteria of substance abuse or dependence (23% versus 9%) and half of all full-time college students reported binge drinking and abuse of illegal or prescription drugs (Luthar, Barkin and Crossman 2013). Data collected in treatment settings by EKTEPN (2011) in Greece indicated that 9.1% of people affected by drug dependence have completed university or postgraduate studies. A clinical study in the Open Therapeutic Setting of 18 ANO at the State Psychiatry Hospital of Attica in Athens indicated that one in 10 drug abusers who came for treatment had university and post-university education. They admitted that their first experience of drugs was in adolescence. Good and high achievement in adolescence was one of the common characteristics of drug abusers (Dalla et al. 2012).

From a developmental perspective, the passage from adolescence into adulthood is considered a critical developmental transition that is related to new developmental tasks which all play critical roles in some experimentation with alcohol and drugs among young people (Masten, Faden, Zucker and Spear 2008; Schulenberg, O'Malley, Bachman and Johnston 2005). The experimentation can lead to drug abuse and dependence when people experience multiple transitions and developmental tasks that sometimes overwhelm coping capabilities. Alcohol and drug use may serve as an alternative coping strategy (Schulenberg and Maggs 2002) at the age of identity exploration in love and work (Arnett 2005), and also at the individualization stage when adolescents move away and separate from parent images (Blos 1967). It is the age of instability in terms of love partners, career and educational status; it is the age when adolescents experience the feeling of being 'in-between', of being neither adolescent nor adult; it is the age of possibilities in the sense that these young people have the opportunity to make dramatic changes in their lives; the expectations are so high that they may not recognize the negative consequences that can result from alcohol and drug use (Arnett 2005).

The motivational theories look to drinking motives, such as coping, conformity, enhancement and social motives (Read, Wood, Kahler, Maddock and Palfai 2003) as major components in the establishment and continuation of substance abuse through which different distal factors such as personality traits operate and exert their influence (Tragesser, Sher, Trull and Park 2007). Coping motives involve drinking to ameliorate or to reduce the experience of negative emotions, such as depression, anxiety and dysphoria (Stewart and Devine 2000). Characteristically, deficiencies in coping skills lead people to use alcohol and drugs as a coping device to avoid negative states (Read et al. 2003).

Conformity motives involve drinking as a result of implicit or explicit social pressure (Neighbors, Larimer, Geisner and Knee 2004), while enhancement motives are driven by beliefs that alcohol and drug use can induce, increase or maintain positive effect (MacLatchy-Gaudet and Stewart 2001). Enhancement motives are linked to impulsivity, sensation and enjoyment seeking that reflects a dispositional need for a high level of stimulation and reward seeking (Read et al. 2003). Among people with enhancement motives, there may be great expectations of positive consequences and low expectations regarding negative consequences of heavy drinking (Katz, Fromme and D'Amico 2000). Social motives involve drinking to achieve positive social outcomes for fulfilling affiliate needs and the desire of socialization in different situations (Stewart and Devine 2000). Most people desire social contact for reducing uncertainty and receiving emotional support, other are concerned with the desire to obtain attention from others or to be stimulated by social interaction. Some studies indicated that high social goals among first-year students was associated with increased alcohol use while high academic/occupational goals was related to reduced alcohol use (Rhoades and Maggs 2006).

Stress theories study the relationship between external demands named stressors, bodily processes and coping as the cognitive and behavioural efforts made by people to master, tolerate or reduce external and internal demands and conflicts (Lazarus 1966). Clinical data suggest that stressful events and chronically stressful conditions increase alcohol and drug intake and the risk of relapse by enhancing craving (Soderpalm and De 2002). In such conditions drugs may be used as self-medication for stress-related disorders such as anxiety (Zimmerman et al. 2003). The longitudinal study of adolescents and young adults showed that those with certain anxiety disorders (social phobia and panic attacks) were more likely to develop substance abuse or dependence prospectively over four years.

Findings regarding the cumulative stress–alcohol relationship indicated that drinkers who had six or more stressful events reported a daily alcohol intake and frequency of drinking three times that of those respondents who endorsed no stressful events (Dawson, Grant and Ruan 2005). Stressors experienced early in life may also have a bearing on alcohol and drug use: reports of death of parents or relatives, parental divorce, parents with mental health issues and being bullied at school are associated with heavy drinking in early adulthood among men (Kestila, Rahkonen, Martelin, Lahti-Koski and Koskinen 2009). A significant positive relationship is reported, across time, between the number of cumulative adversities and risk for alcohol and drug dependence after a lapse of over two years (Dawson et al. 2005).

The stress model focuses on the presence of negative effect as a precipitant of alcohol and drug use; however, recent psychological theories focus on coping as the cognitive and behavioural efforts made by individuals to master, tolerate or reduce external and internal demands and conflicts (Lazarus and Folkman 1984). People who use a problem-focused approach of coping tend to change a stressful situation or the cause of the stress, cognitively or behaviourally, by dealing directly with it using different strategies such as planning, seeking information about possible choices, social support, positive cognitive restructuring of the situation, acceptance, seeking emotional social support, and focusing on and venting of emotions (Lazarus and Folkman 1984).

The emotion-focused approach includes passive coping strategies that contribute to evasiveness, trying to avoid thinking about or confronting a stressful situation. Such strategies are behavioural distancing, self-distraction, self-blame, humour and escape/avoidance. Given the relation between coping style and alcohol use and abuse, researchers have proposed that coping styles may moderate the relations between stressors and negative effect and drug use and abuse is strongly related to passive strategies of coping such as avoidance and denial of stressful situations (Cooper, Frone, Russell and Mudar 1995). Emotion-focused coping tends to be related to deficits in the ability to organize, integrate the interplay among emotions and thoughts (Hien and Miele 2003).

The socioecological theory indicates the changes that the adolescent period has experienced over the past 50 years, encountering many revolutions in education, family and the advent of the home computer, etc. (Luthar and Sexton 2004). Cohort comparison of personal aspirations between new generations (coming of age during the 1990s and 2000s) and earlier generations indicated significant differences. The development of a meaningful philosophy of life was rated by college students as an essential life goal by 86% of respondents in 1967 versus 42% in 2004. To be financially secure and independent was rated by 45% of students in 1967 versus 74% in 2004. 'Having a lots of money' was rated as very important by twice as many in 1990 versus 1970, and expectations of attaining prestigious, professional jobs changed from 42% to 70% across the decades (Twenge 2006, cited in Luthar et al. 2013). Generation shifts are found regarding internalizing symptoms, when the average college student in the 1990s was more anxious and overwhelmed than in the previous decades. Furthermore, feelings of narcissism and externalizing problems increased in 2006 compared to the 1980s. External locus of control beliefs has risen as well, with youth seeing their success as depending largely on luck, rather than effort. Believing that success is determined by luck indicates despair or helplessness, and is also associated with impulsive actions.

Regarding coping strategies, there is an increasing tendency of parents to solve the problems of their children exclusively which does not allow them to acquire and practice everyday life and coping skills. The lack of coping skills is associated with uncertainty, fear and anxiety among college students. Worries were less about academic achievement than about how they handle everyday life problems, such as dealing with a difficult roommate or providing food, for example (Luthar et al. 2013). There are new trends in connecting with friends. New technologies have enabled connections with friends online, when in fact they are disconnecting from friends in real life (Akhtar 2011). The problems of initiation, use, abuse and drug dependence by many high-achieving students are a cause for concern, because drug abuse is also widely assumed to be problem of low achievement and school-related variables such as grades, low school motivation, and leaving school before graduation (Bergena, Martina, Roegerb and Allisonb 2005; Zimmerman and Schmeelk-Cone 2003).

The purpose of this study is the understanding of the issue of substance abuse among academically achieving people. The first part of the study presents information about the prevalence of illicit drug abuse among academically achieving students that have graduate or postgraduate education compared to that of low-achievers. The data collection method used in this study involved structured interviews with the subjects, incorporating procedures that would be likely to increase respondents' cooperation and willingness to report honestly about their illicit drug use behaviour. The interviews considered personal and demographic information regarding age, education in years, living status (stable or unstable accommodation), employment status, health status (HIV/AIDS), criminal and deviant behaviours, as well as information relating to a lifetime's use of illicit substances. The interviews were conducted following the subject's decision to participate in the programme of drug rehabilitation.

The second part of the study examines the nature of drug abuse among achieving students based on data from clinical records of focus groups and current literature.

Drug Abuse among High and Low Achievers: Experience from 18 ANO

The 18 ANO Dependent Treatment Unit of Psychiatric Hospital of Attica in Athens operates under the auspices of the Ministry of Health and implements programmes of internal residence and external supervision for a general adult population in drug-free abuse treatment. It has developed and integrated a psychosocial therapeutic model consisting of sensitization (0–3 months), psychological recovery (main treatment about 6–8 months) and social reintegration (8–12 months) of drug dependent people. The therapeutic team consists of specialized personnel such as psychologists, psychiatrists, social workers and nurses, for instance who, through psychoanalytic and behavioural approaches, psychodrama and educational activities, support rehabilitation and recovery process of people seeking admission to the 18 ANO Dependence Unit.

This study presents information on the prevalence of illicit drug use among 117 males and 23 females aged 19 or older (M=34.37, S.D.=7.97). Most people were high school graduates (59.3%), followed by primary or lower secondary education graduates (22.9%), and university and postgraduates accounted for 17.9%. Estimates for drug abusers are based on data collected during the period 2013–2014 from adults on the Open Supervision Program of the Drug Dependence Unit-State 18 ANO Psychiatry Hospital of Attica.

HOW DIFFERENT ARE HIGH-ACHIEVING DRUG ABUSERS?

Age at first substance use and length of involvement in substance abuse. There are no significant differences between groups regarding affiliation with drug using and the length of involvement with drug abuse (Table 13.1). The age of initiation into drug using ranged from 15.4 to 17.3 years of age. The length of involvement in drug using was from 16.5 (primary or secondary education) to 13.5 (high achievers) years.

Table 13.1   Means and standard deviation of age at first substance use and length of involvement in substance use and dependence

	Target Group					
	Primary or secondary education		High school		High achievers – university or postgraduate education	
	M	S.D.	M	S.D.	M	S.D.
Age at first development	15.4	3.1	16.5	3.8	17.3	2.1
Length of involvement – years	16.7	9.9	13.2	6.8	13.5	7.8

The path to drug addiction. The path to drug addiction begins with the act of taking hashish or marijuana for about 80.7% of the responders. About 4.3% of responders began by using alcohol, 3.6% by using heroin and the rest by other types of substances. There were no significant differences between groups.

Drug-related crimes. Mean of drug law offences (prior arrest, imprisonment, etc.) accompanying the dependence seemed to be higher among primary or secondary graduates (M=2.4) and lower among high achievers (M=0.8). The mean of high school graduates was lower than the mean of high achievers but higher compared to primary or secondary graduates (M=1.8) $F(2,139)=4.26$, $p<0.05$ (see Figure 13.1).

Infectious diseases. Overall HIV prevalence among all the sample was 4.4% while Hepatitis virus prevalence was 24.4%. Furthermore, about 10% of drug abusers have no information about AIDS and Hepatitis infection. There were no significant differences between the groups.

Mental disorders associated with drug abuse. Some common disorders associated with drug abuse are, for example, generalized anxiety and mood disorders, temporary psychotic states, suicidal ideation. According to crosstab analysis, anxiety disorders are found to co-occur in 40.4% of cases, depression in 37.2% of cases, psychotic states in 20.6% of cases and suicidal ideation in 19.7% of cases. The relationship between mental health and educational status is not significant (Table 13.2).

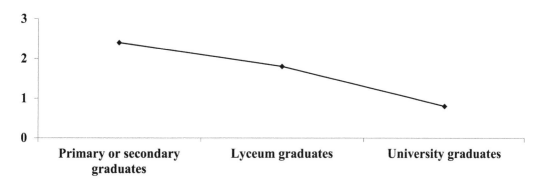

Figure 13.1   Mean of drug-related crimes according to education status

Table 13.2   Disorders associated with chronic drug abuse according to educational status

	Target group					
	Primary or secondary education		High school		High achievers – university or postgraduate education	
	f	%	f	%	f	%
Anxiety disorders	14	48.3	33	40.2	8	32
Mood disorders	13	44.8	30	36.1	8	32
Temporary psychotic states	6	20.7	16	19.5	6	24
Suicidal ideation	8	27.6	13	15.7	6	24

On balance, the results suggest that not only low-achieving students are at risk of using drugs. Increasingly, significant problems of drug abuse are occurring at the other end of the educational spectrum, among youths who qualify as high achievers. These are adolescents distinguished by high achievement, high scores that approach university and post-university standards in study. The age at first substance use indicates that adolescence is the critical period when the use of drugs is first recognized among all groups, including high-achieving students. The path to drug addiction, the length of involvement in substance use and dependence is the same for all groups of people. A number of infectious diseases and psychiatric disorders are commonly associated with substance abuse among all groups.

The main difference among high-achievement and low-achievement groups is the deviant and crime related behaviour. Substance use refers to two very different profiles of adolescent substance users (Peairs et al. 2010). The first group consists of sociable and self-confident individuals, whereas the other group consists of aggressive and emotionally insecure young people, who are more involved in deviant risk behaviour. High-achieving and gifted adolescents who try and finally use drugs seem to fit the first group and, as such, may be less at risk of the negative crime related behaviour associated with using substances. However, it is important for future research to focus on these differences between groups.

WHY MIGHT HIGH-ACHIEVING ADOLESCENTS BE TROUBLED AND ENGAGE IN DRUG ABUSE?

In exploring pathways to drug abuse in high-achieving students, we considered case studies and clinical reports of some drug abusers in the previous study. The intention is to provide an overview for some personality and interpersonal (family and peer groups) factors associated with initiation of substance abuse of high-achieving students in adolescence. *Individual factors* included personality traits such as poor self-concept, loneliness and coping behaviour. The first case study encompasses *personality factors*, feelings of being inadequate, and coping strategies associated with the drug abuse, although she has been identified as an excellent student in primary school through high school. The second case study includes *interpersonal factors* such as relationship with parents, and the academic pressure brought to bear in this respect.

The Case of Maria

Maria began treatment at the age of 28, after one month's hospitalization due to a psychotic state. She seemed a rather pleasant girl, but obviously shocked and silent. She described herself as a quiet child who followed the wishes of her mother. At school, she excelled in all classes. She referred to several incidents when, after finishing her allotted studies, her mother then asked her to continue studying to anticipate the workload of the next few days of the week. Her mother criticized Maria harshly; she was never satisfied with her daughter's performance which in all probability had implications concerning her low self-concept. At the same time, she attended language courses and ballet. She had particular girlfriends amongst a wider circle of friends, but she was jealous of them despite being an excellent student. Overall, she felt deficient.

Maria reported use of marijuana at the time as starting studies at university. At 19 she met Peter at a 'get-together'. She had difficulty making relationships and marijuana helped to reduce the stress. As she met more drug-using friends, the frequency of her drug use progressively increased. Upon completing her postgraduate studies she found the 'perfect partner' user, and they lived together for two years. These two years are characterized by the daily use of large quantities of hashish, and the onset of psychotic episodes which, as indicated by Maria, were witnessed by her friend who believed as well as she did that, in fact, she could 'fly'.

The etiology of Maria's substance abuse will be conceptualized from a developmental perspective of adolescence. Neurotic perfectionism (Nugent 2000), and pressures from her mother left Maria with feelings of never being good enough, of emptiness and dissatisfaction with herself. Maria believed that her parents, especially her mother disproportionally, valued success over receiving the filial love and respect of their daughter. For her, perceived parents' love rests largely on achieving and maintaining the status of high achievement. According to Luthar and Latendresse (2005), perceived parental criticism and disparaging words show stronger association with diverse adjustment as compared to family indices of positive attachment.

Furthermore, in the course of her identity exploration and establishing relationships with the opposite sex, marijuana was used as an alternative strategy for coping and reducing stress of embarrassment, for achieving harmony with other people (Stewart and Devine 2000). According to Muisener (1994), adolescent drug use includes either experimental use, wherein adolescents first experiment with the mood swing, or social use, wherein adolescents seek the mood swing in social contexts, or operational use, wherein adolescents are preoccupied with the mood swing whether it is to seek euphoria or to avoid pain. Furthermore, dependent use emerges wherein adolescents must resort to drugs to feel normal. Other researchers refer to conformity motives which consider drug abuse as a result of implicit or explicit social pressure (Neighbors et al. 2004).

The stress model theorists (Hien and Miele 2003) proposed that drug abuse is strongly related to passive strategies of coping such as avoidance and denial of stressful situations. Emotion-focused coping tends to be related to deficiencies in the ability to organize and integrate the interplay among emotions and thoughts. A consensus of opinion amongst other studies concluded that there are differences in individuals who use problem-focused strategies versus emotion-focused strategies. Compared with people with problem-focused strategies, people with problematic alcohol use practise avoidant coping because other more adaptive ways of coping are unavailable (Cooper et al. 1995). If an individual experiences negative effect and approaches a successful coping strategy, such as well-planned problem-solving and positive reappraisal, then he or she does not need to turn to drug abuse in response to negative effect. In contrast, if an individual uses avoidant styles or distancing to cope with the negative effect, he or she is more likely to use drugs in order to deal with the stressor.

INTERPERSONAL FACTORS REFERRED TO FAMILY RELATIONSHIPS AND STRESS OF NEGATIVE LIFE EVENTS

The case of Maria indicated that her poor self-concept of being less than adequate, in concert with conformity to both family pressure and social conformity, are associated with drug abuse and dependence. In the second case study, we intend to refer to interpersonal mechanisms of risk and vulnerability among high-achieving students. An important factor is academic pressure; the pressure to do well in school and earn a place at college.

The Case of Kosta

Kosta was 15 years old when he started to use drugs. He was an excellent student and his parents had high expectations of him. Indeed, his mother decided on the accelerated placement of her son, first through early entrance to school and later the whole-grade acceleration when he was 13 years old (Colangelo, Assouline and Gross 2004). At 15, Kosta was left at home alone for many hours each week, while his parents believed that this promoted self-sufficiency in their son. His parents worked hard and were preoccupied with their professional careers. Achievement pressure, low levels of parental monitoring and the negligible amount of time parents spent in the family home were risk factors as a source of loss of control, and led to the initiation into drug abuse which occurred when Kosta met up with some new acquaintances at a 'get-together' and joined in smoking marijuana.

Studies indicate that high achievers when pressured to further excel became a risk factor related to drug abuse and which, in general, may have a negative influence in personal adjustment (Ansary and Luthar 2009). The sense of pressure, criticism and overly high expectations correlated with distress or loneliness and low connectedness with parents all play an important role in the onset of drug abuse. Academic pressure leads to high levels of academic anxiety and therefore drug abuse may be a mechanism to reduce apprehension of academic performance (Kieffer, Cronin and Gawet 2006). Emotional closeness to both parents together with a simple family routine was linked not only to positive adjustment in children, but also to their good performance at school (Luthar and Latendresse 2005).

Pressure to excel and the commitment to high achievement leave little time to pursue rewards such as friendships and emotional intimacy which in adolescence is greater with friends than with parents. This remains or becomes stronger during emerging adulthood, especially for those who are isolated from their parents. Peer groups sometimes lead to greater involvement with alcohol through different mechanisms, such as social learning, peer group influence, modelling and social facilitation (Sher, Grekin and Williams 2005). It seems that sometimes friends may act as a source of loss of control, especially when young adults seek affiliation with peers who display similar patterns of substance use or deviant behaviour. It has been found that adolescents and emerging adults who have a proclivity for substance abuse tend to select their peers with respect to that very substance use (Arnett 2005).

The Case of Fani

Fani has an excellent degree and brilliant studies in the field of fine arts. He approached the treatment programme at the age of 40, after 24 years of using alcohol first and then cocaine and heroin. His responses to the structured diagnostic interview indicated that he met the criteria not only for substance dependence, but also for major depressive disorder.

The first child of a single-parent family, Fani lived with his mother and his father died when Fani was 20 years old. The 'abandonment' of the family by the father made their relations difficult, a love–hate–dependence relationship associated with the need of the son for constant confirmation. He 'hated' his father a lot when he left home. But later Fani realized that the father was not to blame for the breakup. His father was, as Fani mentioned, a respected and generous man. For his mother, Fani was "her son" with the "perfect" resume, who could not find work despite his qualifications. She did everything to support him financially, while expressing fears of his death or self-destruction, as he had already planned to commit suicide during his studies. She called him five or six times a day, shaped her daily routine according to the needs of her son over the weekend, shopping, cooking and packaging his meals for the entire week.

The etiology of substance use and Fani's depression will be conceptualized from the perspective of parent–child conflict and negative family life events, although other personality factors may have influenced his behaviour. Fani described himself as 'novelty seeking' or 'sensation seeking', trying to engage in new experiences (Moss and Dyer 2010), seeking enjoyment that reflects a dispositional need for a high level of stimulation and reward (Read et al. 2003). The stress coping model suggests that some adolescents use drugs to cope with stressful life events and as a way of self-regulating emotions (Hien and Miele 2003), such as anxiety, sadness or loneliness (Woodward and Fergusson 2001). The substance abuse is considered as a kind of self-medication (Reimuller, Shadur and Hussong 2011), especially when high levels of emotional distress are associated with unsuccessful coping strategies, resulting in maladaptive outcomes (Cooper, Wood, Orcutt and Albino 2003).

Parental divorce (Burt, Barnes, McGue and Iacono 2008) and negative bonding with family can act as a risk factors, predicting delinquency and other externalizing behaviours during childhood and adolescence. Stress theories indicate that such negative life events are out of the control of children and adolescents, and divorce or the loss of parent has a negative effect on development due to the loss of attachment to the parent. However, the post-disruption trajectory is considered most important for producing delinquency and drug abuse among children and adolescents (Farrington 2009). Although Fani did very well academically, he engaged in drug abuse, because he didn't feel attachment to important adults in his live.

Conclusion

On the whole, high-achieving adolescents are not always found to be at low risk. In contrast to the enhanced attention to low-achieving young people, there is no research concerning those at the other end of the achievement status, that is to say, those with high achievement. Our interest emerged from the work in 18 ANO Dependent Treatment Unit of Psychiatric Hospital of Attica in Athens. These studies indicate some important personal and interpersonal factors related to initiation into drug use and dependence. Striving for high achievement, valuing it more than personal development in adolescents, passive coping skills, lack of parental emotional closeness and relations with drug users are referred to as being some risk factors for future research in the field of the psychology of addiction among high-achieving students.

References

Akhtar, S. (2011). *The Electrified Mind: Development, Psychopathology, and Treatment in the Era of Cell Phones and the Internet*. Lanham: Jason Aronson.

Ansary, N.A. and Luthar, S.S. (2009). Distress and academic achievement among adolescents of affluence: A study of externalizing and internalizing problem behaviors and school performance. *Development and Psychopathology*, 21, 319–41.

Anthony, J.C. and Chen, C.Y. (2004). Epidemiology of drug dependence. In M. Galanter and H.D. Kleber (eds), *Textbook of Substance Abuse Treatment* (3rd edn, pp. 55–73). Washington, DC: American Psychiatric Publishing, Inc.

Arnett, J.J. (2005). The developmental context of substance abuse in emerging adulthood. *Journal of Drug Issues*, 35(2), 235–54.

Bergena, H.A., Martina, G., Roegerb, L. and Allisonb, S. (2005). Perceived academic performance and alcohol, tobacco and marijuana use: Longitudinal relationships in young community adolescents. *Addictive Behaviors*, 30(8), 1563–73.

Blos, P. (1967). The second individuation process of adolescence. *Psychoanalytic Studies of the Child*, 22, 162–86.

Burt, S.A., Barnes, A.R., McGue, M. and Iacono, W.G. (2008). Parental divorce and adolescent delinquency: Ruling out the impact of common genes. *Developmental Psychology*, 44(6), 1668–77.

Colangelo, N., Assouline, S. and Gross, M.U.M. (2004). *A Nation Deceived: How Schools Hold Back America's Brightest Students* (vols 1–2). Iowa City: University of Iowa, The Connie Belin and Jacqueline N. Blank International Center for Gifted Education and Talent Development.

Cooper, M.L., Frone, M.R., Russell, M. and Mudar, P. (1995). Drinking to regulate positive and negative emotions: A motivational model of alcohol use. *Journal of Personality and Social Psychology*, 69(5), 990–1005.

Cooper, M.L., Wood, P.K., Orcutt, H.K. and Albino, A. (2003). Personality and the predisposition to engage in risky or problem behaviors during adolescence. *Journal of Personality and Social Psychology*, 84(2), 390–410.

Dalla, M., Matsa, K., Antoniou, A.-S. and Prapas, C. (2012). High achieved students, narcissistic contract and drug abuse in adolescence (in Greek). *Tetradia Psychiatrikis*, 120, 58–68.

Dawson, D.A., Grant, B.F. and Ruan, W.J. (2005). The association between stress and drinking: Modifying effects of gender and vulnerability. *Alcohol & Alcoholism*, 40(5), 453–60.

EKTEPN (2011). *The State of Drugs and Alcohol Problem in Greece*. Annual Report 2011. Athens: EKTEPN (in Greek).

EKTEPN (2014). *The State of Drugs and Alcohol Problem in Greece*. Annual Report 2013. Athens: EKTEPN (in Greek).

EMCDDA (2011). *Annual Report 2011: The State of Drugs Problem in Europe*. European Monitor Centre for Drugs and Drug Addiction.

Farrington, D.P. (2009). Conduct disorder, aggression, and delinquency. In R.M. Lerner and L. Steinberg (eds), *Handbook of Adolescent Psychology: Vol. 1. Individual Bases of Adolescent Development* (3rd edn, pp. 683–722). Hoboken: John Wiley & Sons.

Hien, D.A. and Miele, G.M. (2003). Emotion-focused coping as a mediator of maternal cocaine abuse and antisocial behavior. *Psychology of Addictive Behaviors*, 17(1), 49–55.

Kaminer, Y. and Tarter, R.E. (2004). Adolescent substance abuse. In M. Galanter and H.D. Kleber (eds), *Textbook of Substance Abuse Treatment* (3rd edn, pp. 505–19). Washington, DC: American Psychiatric Publishing, Inc.

Katz, E.C., Fromme, K. and D'Amico, E.J. (2000). Effects of outcome expectancies and personality on young adults' illicit drug use, heavy drinking, and risky sexual behavior. *Cognitive Therapy and Research*, 24(1), 1–22.

Kestila, L., Rahkonen, O., Martelin, T., Lahti-Koski, M. and Koskinen, S. (2009). Do childhood social circumstances affect overweight and obesity in early adulthood? *Scandinavian Journal of Public Health*, 37(2), 206–19.

Kieffer, K.M., Cronin, C. and Gawet, D.L. (2006). Test and study worry and emotionality in the prediction of college students' reasons for drinking: An exploratory investigation. *Journal of Alcohol & Drug Education*, 50(1), 57–81.

Lazarus, R.S. (1966). *Psychological Stress and the Coping Process*. New York: McGraw-Hill.

Lazarus, R.S. and Folkman, S. (1984). *Stress, Appraisal, and Coping*. New York: Springer.

Luthar, S.S. (ed.) (2003). *Resilience and Vulnerability: Adaptation in the Context of Childhood Adversities*. Cambridge: Cambridge University Press.

Luthar, S.S. and Barkin, S.H. (2012). Are affluent youth truly 'at risk'? Vulnerability and resilience across three diverse samples. *Development and Psychopathology*, 24, 429–49.

Luthar, S.S. and Latendresse, S.J. (2005). Children of the affluent: Challenges to well-being. *Current Directions in Psychological Science*, 14, 49–53.

Luthar, S.S. and Sexton, C. (2004). The high price of affluence. In R.V. Kail (ed.), *Advances in Child Development* (pp. 126–62). San Diego: Academic Press.

Luthar, S.S., Barkin, S.H. and Crossman, E.J. (2013). 'I can, therefore I must': Fragility in the upper-middle classes. *Development and Psychopathology, 25th Anniversary Special Issue*, 25, 1529–49.

MacLatchy-Gaudet, H.A. and Stewart, S.H. (2001). The context-specific positive alcohol outcome expectancies of university women. *Addictive Behaviors*, 26(1), 31–49.

Masten, A.S., Faden, V.B., Zucker, R.A. and Spear, L.P. (2008). A developmental perspective on underage alcohol use. *Alcohol Research and Health*, 32(1), 3–15.

Moss, A.C. and Dyer, K.R. (2010). *Psychology of Addictive Behaviour*. London: Palgrave Macmillan.

Muisener, P.P. (1994). *Understanding and Treating Adolescent Substance Abuse*. London: Sage Publications.

National Institute on Drug Abuse (2003). *Preventing Drug Abuse among Children and Adolescents. A Research-based Guide for Parents, Educators and Community Leaders* (2nd edn). U.S. Department of Health and Human Services. National Institute of Health.

National Institute on Drug Abuse (2014). *Principles of Adolescent Substance Use Disorder Treatment: A Research-based Guide*. NIH: National Institute on Drug Abuse.

Neighbors, C., Larimer, M.E., Geisner, I.M. and Knee, C.R. (2004). Feeling controlled and drinking motives among college students: Contingent self-esteem as a mediator. *Self and Identity*, 3(3), 207–24.

Nugent, S.A. (2000). Perfectionism: Its manifestation and classroom-based interventions. *The Journal of Secondary Gifted Education*, XI(4), 215–21.

Peairs, K., Eichen, D., Putallaz, M., Costanzo, P. and Grimes, C. (2010). Academic giftedness and alcohol use in early adolescence. *Gifted Child Quarterly*, 55(2), 95–110.

Read, J.P., Wood, M.D., Kahler, C.W., Maddock, J.E. and Palfai, T.P. (2003). Examining the role of drinking motives in college student alcohol use and problems. *Psychology of Addictive Behaviors*, 17(1), 13–23.

Reimuller, A., Shadur, J. and Hussong, A.M. (2011). Parental social support as a moderator of self-medication in adolescents. *Addictive Behaviors*, 36, 203–8.

Rhoades, B.L. and Maggs, J.L. (2006). Do academic and social goals predict planned alcohol use among college-bound high school graduates? *Journal of Youth and Adolescence*, 35(6), 913–23.

Schulenberg, J.E. and Maggs, J.L. (2002). A developmental perspective on alcohol use and heavy drinking during adolescence and the transition to young adulthood. *Journal of Studies on Alcohol*, 63, 54–70.

Schulenberg, J., O'Malley, P.M., Bachman, J.G. and Johnston, L.D. (2005). Early adult transitions and their relation to well-being and substance use. In R.A.J. Settersten, F.F.J. Furstenberg and R.G. Rumbaut (eds), *On the Frontier of Adulthood: Theory, Research, and Public Policy* (pp. 417–53). Chicago: University of Chicago Press.

Sher, K.J., Grekin, E.R. and Williams, N.A. (2005). The development of alcohol use disorders. *Annual Review of Clinical Psychology*, 1, 493–523.

Soderpalm, A.H. and De, W.H. (2002). Effects of stress and alcohol on subjective state in humans. *Alcoholism: Clinical and Experimental Research*, 26(6), 818–26.

Stewart, S.H. and Devine, H. (2000). Relations between personality and drinking motives in young adults. *Personality and Individual Differences*, 29(1), 495–511.

Tragesser, S.L., Sher, J.S., Trull, T.T. and Park, A. (2007). Personality disorders symptoms, drinking motives, and alcohol use and consequences. *Experimental Clinical Psychopharmacology*, 15(3), 282–92.

Twenge, J. M. (2006). *Generation Me: Why Today's Young Americans are More Confident, Assertive, Entitled and More Miserable Than Ever Before*. New York: Free Press.

Woodward, L.J. and Fergusson, D.M. (2001). Life course outcomes of young people with anxiety disorders in adolescence. *Journal of the American Academy of Child and Adolescent Psychiatry*, 40(9), 1086–93.

Zimmerman, M.A. and Schmeelk-Cone, K.H. (2003). A longitudinal analysis of adolescent substance use and school motivation among african american youth. *Journal of Research on Adolescence*, 13(2), 185–210.

Zimmerman, P., Wittchen, H.U., Hofler, M., Pfister, H., Kessler, R.C. and Lieb, R. (2003). Primary anxiety disorders and the development of subsequent alcohol use disorders: A 4-year community study of adolescents and young adults. *Psychological Medicine*, 33(7), 1211–22.

14

Coping Strategies and Personality Dimensions of Teachers in Primary and Secondary Education

Alexander-Stamatios Antoniou and Eftychia Mitsopoulou

Introduction

During the last decades, there has been a shift of research in occupational and organizational psychology that is focused on the work conditions that affect the organizational environment of employees, as well as the factors that either facilitate or hamper their performance. The success of an organization may depend, in part, on whether employees feel engaged and committed to their profession, if they are satisfied with what they are doing, if this satisfaction derives from their sense of belonging and if the service that they are offering is appreciated. Nevertheless, there are some professions that are considered quite stressful for those who practice them and these employees may not perceive their profession as a satisfying part of their lives. As such, their profession may leave them feeling frustrated and disappointed. Among these professions, teaching is considered to be one of the most demanding and challenging.

According to Thornton, Peltier and Hill (2005) 50% of new teachers in Great Britain leave their profession within the first five years. This alarming rate may raise questions as to the reasons for this turnover. It seems that teaching is considered to be a 'high stress' profession, with approximately one-quarter of schoolteachers finding their work extremely stressful (Kyriacou 2001). It is not difficult to imagine the scenario of children wandering around in class, and a desperate teacher trying to calm them down. But, is this what constitutes a key source of stress for a teacher, or do other sources occur? Do the same sources of stress apply to all teachers indifferently or is it a matter of personality? What coping strategies do teachers use in order to overcome the burdens they face in their everyday professional life? These questions form the subject matter of the current chapter.

Stress and Burnout among Teachers

On a global scale, teachers struggle on a daily basis with a variety of problems and challenges in their profession. Students with special needs, pressure from parents, workload, low salary, classroom management, student absenteeism, lack of support from peers, administration, state, etc. are some examples of the problems faced by teachers. Their job is challenging, multifaceted and diverse. As the society changes, so do the responsibilities teachers have. Teachers have a multidimensional role in schools: they are professionals, listeners, practitioners, colleagues, subordinates, experts and so on. They have to combine a variety of skills in order to respond to the differential needs of their students, and to balance between what they can do and what others expect them to do. The above places a heavy load onto them, which can in turn result in stress and, in some cases, professional burnout. According to Markham (2000) it is necessary to identify the factors that are stressful to teachers and try to alleviate some of these factors, in order to prevent talented teachers from abandoning their career and pursuing an occupation that is less stressful, as high levels of stress can disrupt teachers' homeostasis (Gloria, Faulk and Steinhardt 2013).

While stress refers to the temporary adaptation process that is accompanied by mental and physical symptoms, when the individual is imbalanced between job demands and his/her response capability, burnout is a final stage in a breakdown in adaptation that results from the long-term imbalance of demands and resources and is accompanied by chronic malfunctioning at work (Storm and Rothman 2003). Both stress and burnout include emotional elements of work including face-to-face or voice-to-voice interaction. This is why employees who have occupations that involve display of emotion are likely to be more vulnerable than employees whose occupations do not require this type of emotional openness (Johnson, Cooper, Cartwright, Donald, Taylor and Millet 2005).

Burnout has been identified as a type of chronic response to the cumulative and long-term negative impact of work (Tatar 2009). Teachers' burnout is characterized by three interrelated components: emotional exhaustion, depersonalization and reduced personal accomplishment (Maslach, Jackson and Leiter 1996). Emotional exhaustion occurs when the individual reports overwhelming feelings, frustration, irritability and emotional strain. Depersonalization is described as feeling cynical and negative towards others (Gloria, Faulk and Steinhardt 2013), while reduced personal accomplishment is the feeling that the person cannot respond to the expectations of others, and experiences a decline in feelings of being competent, thus feeling defeated and incapable.

Burnout and related stress are correlated with emotional exhaustion and depersonalization, as well as feelings of little professional accomplishment (Lambert, McCarthy, O'Donell and Wang 2009; Stoeber and Rennert 2008). Stress is a situation that is more common among teachers, than burnout, which is a much more extreme form, when frustration reaches a final end and the person feels that they have no more to offer, they cannot struggle on anymore and they feel that they have nothing to invest in their professional life. Stress at work is associated with unpleasant experiences such as anger and depression (Hamama, Ronen, Shachar and Rosenbaum 2013), while long-term stress may affect teachers' health, both physically and mentally, leading to them showing signs of depression, feelings of resignation and inferiority, as well as helplessness (Wisniewski and Garguilo 1997).

Forlin, Hattie and Douglas (1996) and Forlin (2001) made a distinction between stressors among teachers and classified these into three general clusters: (1) administrative; (2) classroom-based; and (3) personal. Administrative stressors include heavy workload and time resources, while classroom-based stressors refer to classroom management and climate and lack of support. Lastly, some personal stressors are low salary, low professional and unsuccessful collaboration and relations with colleagues and administration. The above distinction is detectable in many studies, such as Tatar's (2009) who, in a study with 281 teachers in Israel, found that they reported various concerns in their work, such as the emotional difficulties of their students, discipline issues and misbehaviour, learning and social problems of the students, didactic and pedagogical topics and curriculum issues.

Heavy workload is considered to be an administrative issue and serves as a predictor of stress (Boyle, Borg, Falzon and Baglioni 1995), while it is positively correlated with burnout, as workload at home for teachers may result in cynicism, emotional exhaustion and depersonalization of students (Lewis, Roache and Romi 2011). Another administrative challenge for teachers includes demands such as testing and paperwork (Lambert et al. 2009). Teachers devote many hours, on a daily basis, preparing for the next day and this is considered not only time-consuming, but also something that affects their personal lives.

Moreover, concomitant poor quality relationships between teachers and students may contribute to teacher stress (Mintz 2007), while disciplinary problems in the classroom predict higher emotional exhaustion (Klusmann, Kunter, Trautwein, Lüdtke and Baumert 2008). According to Brenner (1985) it is the daily interaction with students in the classroom that determines the flow of teacher stress. Teachers' collective efficacy as a means of affecting group performance and influencing students is positively related to job satisfaction (Spilt, Koomen and Thijs 2011), while coping with threatening or uncontrollable classroom events and students' interactions sets the level of strain or misfit. If these problems are mastered, they may become controllable but if control over the situation is lost then it is quite impossible to improve the situation.

With this in mind, these authors suggest that it is within the first months of the school year that all key work should be addressed. If the start of the school year sets the tone for the rest of the school year, then experience of the teachers is highly significant. Nevertheless, although higher levels of stress may be expected in new teachers, it seems that this is not always the case, as data show that experienced teachers often report more stress. However, experienced teachers have higher levels of self-efficacy to help them to cope with this stress (Akpochafo 2014).

Problems occurring among students, such as bullying and aggression, may become overwhelming for new teachers who are not sufficiently trained to deal with this type of behaviour and who may perceive such behaviour as an additional stressor for them (Kahn, Jones and Wieland 2012). Students who exhibit disruptive behaviour or academic and emotional needs are likely to increase distress for a teacher, as well as frustration and sense of incompetence over time, as this behaviour requires significant time and attention from the teacher (Lhospital and Gregory 2009). When conflicts are encountered in schools, the teacher is the person who can direct treatment of conflict situations into a culture of discussion (Maslovaty 2000) and if he/she permits stress to intervene then there will be no ease of the conflict.

For some teachers, the social character of their profession, including communication with parents, may be quite stressful for them. Stoeber and Rennert (2008) in a study with 80 German teachers found that these teachers perceived the highest pressure to derive mainly from parents of the students, rather than from colleagues or students. Dealing with parents, such as contacting them through phone or email and being questioned by them as to how their children were assessed in the behavioural and academic field was a significant concern for novice teachers (Rieg, Paquette and Chen 2007). Perhaps, however, this may not be the case for experienced teachers who have established relationships with parents throughout the years and who know how to evaluate, assess and communicate their ideas about the students. Moreover, anxiety for children to do well in tests due to the fact that student performance is a reflection of the teaching has also been reported (Rieg et al. 2007), while teachers felt pressure from parents who wanted their children to get better grades and excel academically (Hung 2011).

Rieg et al. (2007) identified four themes in connection with concerns regarding self among pre-student teachers. These were: content knowledge, pedagogy, workload and relationships. Content knowledge was concerned with the feeling that they were not fully capable to teach in class as they thought students would know more than them. Some of them were also afraid that they could not manage the classroom effectively, they would not succeed in discipline, while they questioned their abilities to apply and implement their lessons and pedagogical theory with success. Workload was related to time, changing requirements, having professors adding to their workload, and activities leading to lack of sleep. Lastly, relationships were concerned with the type of relationships that they may have with their students, and whether they would be liked and at the same time respected.

While the pressure from parents may be quite high for the majority of teachers, this is not always the case when children with disabilities are involved. Forlin, Keen and Barrett (2008) found that contact with parents was not a major issue of concern among Special Educational Needs (SEN) teachers even when they had excessive meetings with them. Rather, the inadequate social skills of the child appeared to place more pressure on them, as issues such as poor communication skills and limited speech seemed to be of high concern. According to these researchers most teachers thought they had insufficient pre-service training to cater adequately for a child with an intellectual disability within the classroom and this introduced a further obstacle to the teaching process, as they felt they had a reduced ability to teach all students in an effective way and they were unable to effectively monitor all students at the same time. Furthermore, depersonalization was found to be higher among teachers of special education compared to elementary and secondary teachers who work in mainstream schools, something which led to less satisfaction from their work and, thus, acting neutral or with apathy (Antoniou and Ntalla 2010).

Children with problem behaviours are also considered a challenge for teachers (Lambert et al. 2009). Pupil misbehaviour may serve as a stressor for a teacher, while the way this stressor is appraised may even lead to the selection of coping strategies that are sub-optimal, e.g. the adoption of an aggressive or over-dominant classroom management approach (Mintz 2007). Teachers working in special schools, which included students who had dropped out of or were expelled from other educational day or residential frameworks within the community, felt fear, anger, guilt and stress and at the same time they felt happiness, energy and joy (Hamama et al. 2013). These contradictory feelings may be due to the fact that these teachers were facing many challenges with these types of students and although they were perhaps poorly trained, they felt at the same time that they had been given the opportunity to make a difference in the lives of these children.

Teaching may also be stressful for English as a Second Language (ESL) teachers. In a study by Markham (2000) ESL teachers mentioned how stressful it was to work with Limited-English Proficient (LEP) students who were struggling with many subject matter areas. In addition, other stressors included: serving too many LEP students, not having the support of non-ESL faculty and administrators and not coordinating with non-ESL teachers and administrators. Another concern for elementary teachers is students who come from diverse backgrounds, e.g. ethnic, religious, racial, etc. (Rieg et al. 2007).

The age of the teacher as well as type of class within which he/she teaches represents another variable for stress. Forlin et al. (2008) found that teaching a student with an intellectual disability was a concern for teachers who were 36–45 years old, while those who taught older classes were less concerned about classroom issues compared to those who taught kindergarten, 1st, 2nd and 3rd grade. Klusmann et al. (2008) found that teachers who were older were less engaged than their younger colleagues. Furthermore, primary teachers seem to have higher levels of perceived stress than their secondary colleagues (Jepson and Forrest 2006), while married individuals report low levels of burnout as compared to their single colleagues (Kantas 1996). These findings are quite interesting as for some teachers family may serve as a way of relaxation from the everyday stress.

Gender also plays an important role, although studies seem to reach contradictory results. In some studies, male teachers were more stressed than their female counterparts, less engaged and more emotionally exhausted (Akpochafo 2014; Klusmann et al. 2008), while, in others, females reported greater work stress (Antoniou, Ploumpi and Ntalla 2013; Gloria, Faulk and Steinhardt 2013). There are also studies reporting no significant differences in stress between men and women (Jepson and Forrest 2006), which, according to Eichinger (2000), may be attributed to the fact that it is not the biological differences that have an effect on job stress and satisfaction, but, rather, the social role orientation of both genders.

Further interesting research includes that of Miller and Travers (2005) who found that minority ethnic teachers in the UK experienced stress due to ethnic discrimination, believing that they worked within an environment with signs of institutional racism and this is a field of research that would provide very helpful information in the future if studied thoroughly. What is of major importance in this study, according to its authors, is the poor mental well-being of these teachers, with a large number of both female and male teachers experiencing high-to-severe mental distress.

Data reveal that some teachers feel stressed due to the low status of the teaching profession (Litt and Turk 1985), while it is held in low public esteem compared to other professions (Jarvis 2002). This may lead to reduced personal accomplishment which includes feelings of ineffectiveness and a lack of productivity and achievement at work (Gloria, Faulk and Steinhardt 2013). Poor salary, poor opportunities for advancement and role overload, such as too much work or too little time to accomplish, are issues of concern for teachers (Litt and Turk 1985; Miller and Travers 2005), with a lot of them leaving teaching due to dissatisfaction. It is possible that these teachers do not feel that they are paid according to their skills, knowledge and role, and that in the public view teaching is not considered a profession with status, compared to professions such as doctors or lawyers. Still, those teachers who feel that what they are offering is appreciated, for example, when they receive awards, report greater positive affect, greater resilience and less burnout (Gloria et al. 2013).

In many countries teacher surplus serves as a stressor, due to the fact that teachers are afraid that they will lose their jobs. For example, in a study in Taiwan, due to teacher surplus, teachers mentioned being stressed and that this stress derived from their increased teaching load as well as from educational policy reform (Hung 2011). This finding has many implications, because if teachers constantly feel threatened that they will lose their job, then they may not be committed to their profession and to their responsibilities. Occupational commitment is negatively correlated with perceived stress, something that shows that teachers who are committed to their profession may face less stress (Jepson and Forrest 2006) and vice versa.

As far as head teachers are concerned, there is little research concerning them. In a study by Cooper and Kelly (1993) it was found that British male head teachers had significantly higher mental ill health scores than the normative population, while work overload and handling relationships among staff proved to be dominant stressors for them, thus, causing them to make use of palliative coping strategies such as smoking and drinking. However, female head teachers used diversionary coping strategies, such as exercising and engaging in relaxation techniques. Apart from workload, work–life imbalance is also identified as a main stressor for head teachers, with female head teachers being significantly more stressed than males by overload and control issues (Phillips, Sen and McNamee 2007). On the other hand, there is data showing that compared to head teachers and teaching assistants, teachers experience higher stress levels and lower job satisfaction levels (Johnson et al. 2005). According to these authors, this may be due to various reasons such as the fact that teachers work very closely with children, while head teachers and teaching assistants do not take charge of the class for a long period of time, if at all, and head teachers engage in a more managerial position.

As far as head teachers in special educational settings are concerned, data provide evidence that they feel less personal accomplishment than special school teachers and display high depersonalization, but, nevertheless, they appear to have higher job satisfaction than their teacher colleagues (Sari 2004). In general, it seems that declared sources of job satisfaction for head teachers are the quality of relationships within school, enjoying the support of colleagues and a shared focus (Chaplain 2001). Lastly, early retirement of school principals seems to be associated with prychiatric/psychosomatic disorders, such as depression, exhaustion, cardiovascular diseases and muscular/skeletal diseases (Weber, Weltle and Lederer 2005). Health issues among head teachers are not thoroughly studied, thus leaving a lot of unanswered questions as to which factors may lead them to face different types of disorders.

Teachers' Coping Strategies

In order for individuals to try and restrain the factors that lead them to stress and, in some cases, burnout, they use a variety of coping techniques. This is also the case for professionals whose stress factors undermine their performance. 'Coping is typically referred to as the cognitive and affective responses used by an individual to deal with problems encountered in everyday life' (Lewis et al. 2011, p. 55) while Lazarus and Folkman (1984) defined coping as 'constantly changing cognitive and behavioral efforts to manage specific external and/or internal demands that are appraised as taxing or exceeding the resources of a person' (p. 141).

Usually coping is multifaceted and versatile. When the stressful situation occurs, the individual attempts to evaluate the problem, to appraise and implement possible courses of action, and, lastly, to regulate emotional responses (Parker 1986). Due to the fact that stress has to do with feelings, the individual must be able to monitor, discriminate among them and label them accurately, in order to employ strategies that will alter these feelings, as well as find ways to evaluate if these strategies are effective or need alteration (Brackett, Palomera, Mojsa-Kaja, Reyes and Salovey 2010). According to Endler and Parker's (1999) Coping Inventory for Stressful Situations (CISS), there exist three styles of coping: task-oriented, emotion-oriented and avoidant. Task-oriented coping is characterized by an active problem-solving approach to stressful situations, while emotion-oriented coping is characterized by use of maladaptive, ruminative or emotional reactions in response to stressful situations. Lastly, avoidant coping is characterized by behaviours aimed at avoiding the stressful situation.

Each person uses different ways of coping that adjust according to the conditions, but at the same time derive from their personality traits. According to Lazarus (2000) people can cope with stress in an effective manner if they use suitable strategies which are adjusted to different situations and stress stages. Coping style is a significant construct for understanding individual differences in vulnerability to mental and physical health problems, and this also applies in the case of teachers (Jang, Thordarson, Stein, Cohan and Taylor 2007).

According to the 'Transactional Model of Stress and Coping' of Lazarus (1991) and Lazarus and Folkman (1984), an individual reacts to stress according to his/her subjective interpretation or appraisal of an external stressor which asks for an emotional response. Whether the stimulus is judged as threatening or challenging will be appreciated by the individual. If the incident that is happening is closely connected to the person's goals, needs and values then it is considered relevant. Otherwise, it may lead to the person feeling fear or anger.

Coping behaviour that is interpreted as signalling an emotionally stable and conscientious person is beneficial at a large grade to the individual's social functioning, mainly because such an impression signals reliability and mastery (Geisler, Wiedig-Allison and Weber 2009). We can assume from this how important it is for teachers to cope with stressful events in school, in order to establish positive social interactions with others. Two very important studies on teachers' coping strategies were those of Kyriacou (2001) and Tatar (2009). According to Kyriacou (2001) coping strategies among teachers are dichotomized into direct action and palliative techniques. Direct action refers to strategies teachers use in order to eliminate sources of stress, while palliative techniques focus in reducing the feelings the person has when the stress occurs. Direct actions techniques aim to rule out the source where stress comes from such as seeking support from colleagues and prioritizing work tasks, while palliative techniques are concerned with finding ways to reduce the impact of the stressor, such as avoiding the fact or drinking (Howard and Johnson 2004).

Tatar (2009) suggested mapping teachers' coping strategies into three broad realms:

1. Individual coping strategies. With these strategies teachers try to empower themselves in order to overcome difficulties by acquiring and assimilating the necessary skills.
2. Group-mediated strategies. These are used by teachers in order to reduce their feelings of isolation by discussing their problems in professional life and exchanging ideas about arising issues with colleagues through support groups.
3. Turning for help strategies. These refer to the individual's attempts to seek help from teacher colleagues, school counsellors or psychologists, principals, etc.

One coping strategy used by some teachers is denial. In a study by Kahn, Jones and Wieland (2012), preservice teachers who dealt with incidents of bullying refused to believe the stressor occurred, denied the fact when they encountered problems with bullying among students and were less likely to report that relational aggression involving boys required teacher intervention. Others blamed themselves for the incident, and, probably, underestimated the role of the student during the incident. Apart from denial, self-blame is another way for a teacher to cope with a stressful event (Lewis 1999), while keeping others from knowing how bad thing really are has proven to be a non-helpful technique (Forlin et al. 2008). Denial, self-blame and keeping others from knowing how difficult a situation is, could be considered maladaptive strategies, mainly due to the fact that the individual does not let others engage in the problem and help. This is also the case with suppression and rumination, as they reduce an individual's capacity to process incoming events (Brackett et al. 2010).

When teachers are open to discussion with others and ask for support, then their stress is lessened. Schonfeld (1990) found that teachers in primary and secondary education showed higher levels of job satisfaction and increased motivation to remain in the profession, due to the use of advice seeking, positive comparisons and direct action as means of coping and, thus, showed lower levels of stress. Collaboration with colleagues or professional personnel as well as receiving support from peers or leadership facilitates teachers to engage in discussions with pupils when a dilemma is encountered (Forlin et al. 2008; Maslovaty 2000). This serves as a way to relax the stressor. Moreover, when at a school there is a strong sense of collegiality and good communication among staff, then teachers feel more committed, are more satisfied with their job and express lower levels of stress (Kyriacou 2001), and they are even more engaged when they have a supportive principal (Klusmann et al. 2008).

Lastly, lower work engagement is indirectly associated with poor job resources, such as job control, social climate and innovativeness (Hakanen, Bakker and Schaufeli 2006). It seems that when teachers have feelings of belongingness, they are work engaged and satisfied with their job, then they are not motivated to leave the teaching profession (Skaalvik and Skaalvik 2011), as job burnout and intention to quit are negatively related to work engagement (Høigaard, Giske and Sundsli 2012).

Social support including peer support works as a moderator for stress and negative emotions, as this support, mainly from peers, whether this is instrumental, appraisal, emotional or informative, may increase their positive affect and life satisfaction (Hamama et al. 2013). Still, teacher burnout is negatively correlated with turning for help to internal sources of support, e.g. colleagues, which may be attributed to the fact that these teachers may be pessimistic or frustrated, something that impedes them from making any attempt to seek help (Tatar 2009). On the other hand, maintaining a sense of humour is crucial for a teacher to overcome stressful situations (Forlin et al. 2008), as perceiving life and work optimistically may lessen concerns of any kind.

In a study by Antoniou, Polychroni and Kotroni (2009) with 158 Greek teachers who worked in special needs classrooms and experienced potential sources of stress, it was found that these teachers used coping strategies which were loading onto the involvement factor (i.e. finding ways to make the job more interesting), the task strategies factor (i.e. setting priorities in their duties) and the social support factor (i.e. maintaining stable relationships). The social support factor may craft coherence in schools, and, due to the fact that strong coherence has a protective effect and is correlated with average levels of coping (Brown, Howcroft and Jacobs 2009), then the reduction of stress is feasible.

Middle school teachers who worked in schools with incidents of community violence used a variety of coping strategies, including the following: praying, emotional withdrawal, professional counselling, sharing stressful events with teachers, communicating with family and friends and separating work and personal life (Maring and Koblinski 2013). According to these researchers, such strategies helped teachers to somehow reduce stress but they did not equip them to implement problem-focused solutions.

From the above study, praying proved to be a very important source of emotional balance for these teachers. Praying as a coping strategy among teachers is infrequently identified in the literature, and it was interesting to see that some teachers used this type of strategy in order to face problems within schools. Religion as a coping resource is not studied in reference to teachers, and, turning to God is a positive religious coping strategy that may result in beneficial outcomes, and is clearly differentiated from negative religious coping such as disconnecting with God (Schottenbauer, Rodriguez, Glass and Arnkoff 2006).

As far as gender differences are concerned, it seems that female teachers turn more frequently for help to both internal resources (within the school), e.g. teacher colleagues, school counsellors and psychologists for consultation, and external resources (out-of-school), e.g. web-based resources, than their male colleagues (Tatar 2009). According to Tatar (2009) 'the consultation strategy has been found to be very productive in school systems: it allows teachers to apply (and generalise) the fundamentals learned in the process behind the specific case and to broaden their knowledge and professional behavioural repertoire when dealing with psychological and didactic problems' (p. 110). In a study by Stoeber and Rennert (2008) female teachers showed higher levels of active coping, such as planning, than their male counterparts, while Akpochafo (2014) also found that female teachers had higher levels of self-efficacy than their male colleagues. Finally, Antoniou et al. (2009) found that while female SEN primary school teachers used predominantly social support as a coping method, their male colleagues looked for ways to make their work more interesting, while, in another study, males reported feeling less satisfied, more depersonalized and lower levels of personal accomplishment than their female counterparts (Antoniou and Ntalla 2010).

Personality and its Relation to Coping

According to Hambrick and McCord (2010) personality is fundamental to helping us understand coping ability. If coping differentiates individuals then this means that each person uses coping strategies that are not universal. In most studies that examine the correlation between coping and personality, the Five Factor Personality Traits model (McCrae and Costa 1987), commonly referred to as the 'Big Five', is used, as this model, for many reasons, serves as a fruitful basis to examine job satisfaction (Judge, Heller and Mount 2002). In a meta-analysis by Connor-Smith and Flachsbart (2007) concerning personality as indicated by the 'Big Five', it was found that

Extraversion, Conscientiousness, Openness to Experience and Agreeableness were positively associated with coping strategies, such as problem solving, while Neuroticism was positively related with coping behaviours that were considered as disengagement, mainly withdrawal.

Fontana and Abouserie (1993) who studied teachers in Wales found that there was a positive correlation between levels of teacher stress and neuroticism, introversion and psychoticism. Teachers with high scores in conscientiousness and extraversion and low scores in neuroticism are more likely to feel increased personal accomplishment and therefore low burnout, while they are highly motivated to achieve and accordingly obtain gains of performance.

Individuals who are open to experience might be expected to be effective copers (Folkman, Lazarus, Gruen and DeLongis 1986), while people who are emotionally stable rather than neurotic, extraverted, open to experience and conscientious use constructive coping strategies, such as problem-solving and seeking social support, while they accept the stressor and reinterpret a stressful situation (Storm and Rothman 2003). O'Brien and DeLongis (1996) found that those individuals who scored higher on agreeableness were seeking support and were less confronted than those who scored lower, while those higher on conscientiousness used less escape-avoidance and less self-blaming strategies in coping when faced with stressful situations and engaged in problem-solving than those who were lower on this trait.

Using the Lazarus and Folkman (1984) ways of coping with students and prospective teachers, Baloglu (2008) found that teachers dealt with stressful situations using an emotion-focused coping strategy, by exhibiting a helpless approach to stress. On the contrary, a person with a strong character who implements strengths of his/her character in his/her profession will be much more satisfied and happy, than someone who does not invest his/her signature strengths in such tasks, and, accordingly may experience burnout and lowered job satisfaction (McGovern and Miller 2008).

Personality dispositions seem to influence choice of coping and, in this case, dispositions such as hope and optimism are significantly differentiated from pessimism and anxiety (Schottenbauer, Rodriguez, Glass and Arnkoff 2006). This is also the case with positive and negative affect, as higher levels of stress are correlated with higher levels of negative affect (Hamama et al. 2013).

Another personality trait that characterizes teachers is perfectionism. For perfectionists striving for flawlessness, trying to excel and setting high performance standards is stress correlated, as perfectionists feel the pressure to excel because they feel that they have to live up both to their standards and those set by others (Stoeber and Rennert 2008). Workers who tend to have more expectations from themselves may be prone to professional burnout, as perfectionism and extreme confidence as personality traits may cause unpleasant impacts to their professional and personal life (Antoniou and Ntalla 2010).

Ngidi and Sibaya (2002) performed research based on the Big Five personality traits among 444 black teachers from South Africa and found that those teachers who were introverted were susceptible to stress caused by changes in the education system, while those who were extraverted were not influenced by that. Moreover, teachers who manifested a tendency towards neuroticism and were pressured by time, pupil misbehaviour and administrative problems, were more prone to stress.

Conclusion

Reaching the end of this chapter the most important thing to conclude is the fact that teachers do not experience stress in a similar way and that the level of stress that a teacher experiences will depend mainly on the stressors he/she faces, e.g. class management, workload, pupil misbehaviour, etc., and his/her personality traits. Stress is not a generalized concept, due to the fact that it is an individual process, it may vary from one individual to another. The way people react to life situations or social conditions depends upon the way in which they attribute meaning to these experiences, they way they appraise them (Jepson and Forrest 2006), the way they value them. Although researchers are knowledgeable about teachers' stressors, it is not useful to assume that there is a universal formula to prevent these stressors from occurring, as, according to Antoniou, Ploumpi and Ntalla (2013) the sources of stress experienced by teachers are unique to each individual and depend on the interaction between personality, values and skills.

Personality is pivotal to help us understand why working in the same environment and facing similar stress and demands, does not necessarily mean that all individuals will suffer the same levels of stress (Furnham 1992). According to Jang et al. (2007), 'a clearer understanding of personality and coping style is essential because it will impact the approach taken to interventions for stress-related disorders' (p. 18). Insight into teachers' well-being is crucial as it adds to the understanding of teachers' careers, thus, knowing what factors are of concern for teachers helps in creating school contexts that prevent teachers' dropout and foster their commitment to their job (Spilt et al. 2011). Investigating teachers' feelings while teaching is very important as teachers who experience high rates of stress and burnout may not be as capable as they should be in order to create a supportive and positive social environment for children, particularly when they feel emotionally exhausted and perceive their students as objects, thus, becoming role models for negative social behaviours (Lambert et al. 2009).

Environmental factors also play a significant role in coping, due to the fact that the nature of the environment in which a particular stressful episode occurs may influence the types of coping used, as it can be regarded as a potential source (Parker 1986). This has many implications in schools as the work environment may either be supportive or the opposite. According to Jepson and Forrest (2006) individual differences play a significant role in understanding teachers' stress, due to the fact that although teachers are exposed to similar environmental stressors as well as intrinsic job factors, still, not everyone suffers high levels of stress, as some teachers are more susceptible than others and only a small percentage reach the burnout stage.

In a study by Battle and Looney (2014), involving secondary school teachers in the United States, it was found that the teachers' intention to continue working and remain in teaching was positively correlated with how much they felt enjoyment, found their job interesting, viewed it as useful and saw it as a salient aspect of their self concepts, while only their perceived psychological and financial costs were reasons to quit. It is, according to Hargreaves (2000), the relationship with students that serves as a source of enjoyment and motivation to teachers both in elementary and secondary education. Teachers attach value to personal relationships with students in their classroom and this illustrates how their professional and personal well-being is threatened by conflictual or alienated relationships (Spilt et al. 2011).

The percentage of teachers who do not experience symptoms of burnout, rather, they adapt to stressful situations and due to their positive affect prove to be more resilient than expected, thus, coping with adversity and balancing their needs and desires with those of their students (Gloria, Faulk and Steinhardt 2013), is an issue that is not thoroughly investigated. Some teachers adapt to stressful situations in a successful manner and they do not perceive them as threats, but rather as challenges (Brunetti 2006). This is the case of proactive coping as proposed by Schwarzer and Taubert (2002) where people, instead of viewing stressors as setbacks, are motivated to succeed. Thus, people who consistently cope in a proactive manner are likely to be endowed with personality traits that allow successful coping, while they prevent their emotional distress when encountered with a stressful situation (Hambrick and McCord 2010). Further research is needed in the relationship between coping and personality as boosters of resilience among teachers.

According to Curtis (2012), 'the illusion of what teaching entails is drastically different than what teachers find when they step into the classroom' (p. 787). That is why it is important for teachers to have the sense of belonging, as this is positively correlated with job satisfaction and negatively correlated with emotional exhaustion and motivation to leave the teaching profession (Skaalvik and Skaalvik 2011). Being a teacher is not an easy task, but it can be one of the most inspiring, and it would be sad if teachers' needs and aspirations were not considered and no measures were taken in order to prevent the turnover of this part of the population that shapes the consciences of children all over the world.

References

Akpochafo, O.G. (2014). Self efficacy and some demographic variables as predictors of occupational stress among primary school teachers in Delta State on Nigeria. *Education*, 134, 457–64.

Antoniou, A.-S. and Ntalla, M. (2010). Επαγγελματική εξουθένωση και ικανοποίηση από το επάγγελμα Ελλήνων δασκάλων (ειδικής και γενικής αγωγής) και καθηγητών δευτεροβάθμιας εκπαίδευσης: Συγκριτική Μελέτη. [Professional burnout and job satisfaction among Greek teachers of elementary (special and mainstream) and secondary education: A comparative study]. Στο Χ. Καρακιουλάφη and Μ. Σπυριδάκη (*Επιμ.*). *Εργασία και Κοινωνία* (σσ. 365–99). Αθήνα: Διόνικος.

Antoniou, A.-S., Ploumpi, A. and Ntalla, M. (2013). Occupational stress and professional burnout in teachers of primary and secondary education: The role of coping strategies. *Psychology*, 4, 349–55.

Antoniou, A.-S., Polychroni, F. and Kotroni, C. (2009). Working with students with special educational needs in Greece: Teachers' stressors and coping strategies. *International Journal of Special Education*, 24, 100–111.

Baloglu, N. (2008). The relationship between prospective teachers' strategies for coping with stress and their perceptions of student control. *Social Behaviour and Personality*, 36, 903–10.

Battle, A.A. and Looney, L. (2014). Teachers' intentions to stay in teaching: The role of values and knowledge of adolescent development. *Education*, 134, 369–79.

Boyle, J.G., Borg, G.M., Falzon, M.J. and Baglioni, J.A. Jr. (1995). A structural model of the dimensions of teacher stress. *British Journal of Educational Psychology*, 65, 49–67.

Brackett, A.M., Palomera, R., Mojsa-Kaja, J., Reyes, R.M. and Salovey, P. (2010). Emotion-regulation ability, burnout, and job satisfaction among British secondary-school teachers. *Psychology in the Schools*, 47, 406–17.

Brenner, S.-O. (1985). The stress chain: A longitudinal confirmatory study of teacher stress, coping and social support. *Journal of Occupational Psychology*, 58, 1–13.

Brown, O., Howcroft, G. and Jacobs, T. (2009). The coping orientation and resources of teachers educating learners with intellectual abilities. *South African Journal of Psychology*, 39, 448–59.

Brunetti, G.J. (2006). Resilience under fire: Perspectives on the work of experienced, inner city high school teachers in the United States. *Teaching and Teacher Education*, 22, 812–25.

Chaplain, P.R. (2001). Stress and job satisfaction among primary headteachers: A question of balance? *Educational Management & Administration*, 29, 197–215.

Connor-Smith, J.K. and Flachsbart, C. (2007). Relations between personality and coping: A meta-analysis. *Journal of Personality and Social Psychology*, 93, 1080–107.

Cooper, L.C. and Kelly, M. (1993). Occupational stress in head teachers: A national UK study. *British Journal of Educational Psychology*, 63, 130–43.

Curtis, C. (2012). Why do they choose to teach-and why do they leave? A study of middle school and high school mathematics teachers. *Education*, 132, 779–88.

Eichinger, J. (2000). Job stress and satisfaction among special education teachers: Effects of gender and social role orientation. *International Journal of Disability, Development and Education*, 47, 397–412.

Endler, N.S. and Parker, J.D.A. (1999). *CISS: Coping Inventory for Stressful Situations manual*. Toronto: Multi-Health Systems.

Folkman, S., Lazarus, R.S., Gruen, R.J. and DeLongis, A. (1986). Appraisal, coping, health status, and psychological symptoms. *Journal of Personality and Social Psychology*, 50, 571–9.

Fontana, D. and Abouserie, R. (1993). Stress levels, gender and personality factors in teachers. *British Journal of Educational Psychology*, 63, 261–70.

Forlin, C. (2001). Inclusion: Identifying potential stressors for regular class teachers. *Educational Research*, 43, 235–45.

Forlin, C., Hattie, J. and Douglas, G. (1996). Inclusion: Is it stressful for teachers? *Journal of Intellectual and Developmental Disability*, 21, 199–217.

Forlin, C., Keen, M. and Barrett, E. (2008). The concerns of mainstream teachers: Coping with inclusivity in an Australian context. *International Journal of Disability, Development and Education*, 55, 251–64.

Furnham, A. (1992). *Personality at Work: The Role of Individual Differences in the Workplace*. London: Routledge.

Geisler, M.C.F., Wiedig-Allison, M. and Weber, H. (2009). What coping tells about personality. *European Journal of Personality*, 23, 289–306.

Gloria, T.C., Faulk, E.K. and Steinhardt, A.M. (2013). Positive affectivity predicts successful and unsuccessful adaptation to stress. *Journal of Motivation and Emotion*, 37, 185–93.

Hakanen, J.J., Bakker, B.A. and Schaufeli, B.W. (2006). Burnout and work engagement among teachers. *Journal of School Psychology*, 43, 295–513.

Hamama, L., Ronen, T., Shachar, K. and Rosenbaum, M. (2013). Links between stress, positive and negative affect, and life satisfaction among teachers in special education schools. *Journal of Happiness Studies*, 14, 731–51.

Hambrick, P.E. and McCord, M.D. (2010). Proactive coping and its relation to the five-factor model of personality. *Individual Differences Research*, 8, 67–77.

Hargreaves, A. (2000). Mixed emotions: Teachers' perceptions of their interactions with students. *Teaching and Teacher Education*, 16, 811–26.

Høigaard, R., Giske, R. and Sundsli, K. (2012). Newly qualified teachers' work engagement and teacher efficacy influences on job satisfaction, burnout, and the intention to quit. *European Journal of Teacher Education*, 35, 347–57.

Howard, S. and Johnson, B. (2004). Resilient teachers: Resisting stress and burnout. *Social Psychology of Education*, 7, 399–420.

Hung, C.-L. (2011). Coping strategies of primary school teachers in Taiwan experiencing stress because of teacher surplus. *Social Behaviour and Personality*, 39, 1161–74.

Jang, L.K., Thordarson, S.D., Stein, B.M., Cohan, L.S. and Taylor, S. (2007). Coping styles and personality: A biometric analysis. *Anxiety, Stress, and Coping*, 20, 17–24.

Jarvis, M. (2002). Teacher stress: A critical review of recent findings and suggestions for future research directions. *Stress News: The UK Journal of the International Stress Management Association*, 14, 12–16.

Jepson, E. and Forrest, S. (2006). Individual contributory factors in teacher stress: The role of achievement striving and occupational commitment. *British Journal of Educational Psychology*, 76, 183–97.

Johnson, S., Cooper, C., Cartwright, S., Donald, I., Taylor, P. and Millet, C. (2005). The experience of work-related stress across occupations. *Journal of Managerial Psychology*, 20, 178–87.

Judge, A.T., Heller, D. and Mount, K.M. (2002). Five-factor model of personality and job satisfaction: A meta-analysis. *Journal of Applied Psychology*, 87, 530–41.

Kahn, H.J., Jones, L.J. and Wieland, L.A. (2012). Preservice teachers' coping styles and their responses to bullying. *Psychology in the Schools*, 49, 784–93.

Kantas, A. (1996). Το σύνδρομο της επαγγελματικής εξουθένωσης στους εκπαιδευτικούς και στα επαγγέλματα υγείας και πρόνοιας [Burnout syndrome in teachers and in health and social care employees]. *Ψυχολογία*, 3, 71–85.

Klusmann, U., Kunter, M., Trautwein, U., Lüdtke, O. and Baumert, J. (2008). Engagement and emotional exhaustion in teachers: Does the school context make a difference? *Applied Psychology: An International Review*, 57, 127–51.

Kyriacou, C. (2001). Teacher stress: Directions for future research. *Educational Review*, 53, 27–35.

Lambert, G.R., McCarthy, C., O'Donell, M. and Wang, C. (2009). Measuring elementary teachers stress and coping in the classroom: Validity evidence for the classroom appraisal of resources and demands. *Psychology in Schools*, 46, 973–88.

Lazarus, R.S. (1991). Progress on a cognitive–motivational–relational theory of emotion. *American Psychologist*, 46, 819–34.

Lazarus, R.S. (2000). Toward better research on stress and coping. *American Psychologist*, 55, 665–73.

Lazarus, R.S. and Folkman, S. (1984). *Stress, Appraisal and Coping*. New York: Springer.

Lewis, R. (1999). Teachers coping with the stress of classroom discipline. *Social Psychology of Education*, 3, 155–71.

Lewis, R., Roache, J. and Romi, S. (2011). Coping styles as mediators of teachers' classroom management techniques. *Research in Education*, 85, 53–68.

Lhospital, S.A. and Gregory, A. (2009). Changes in teacher stress through participation in pre-referral intervention teams. *Psychology in Schools*, 46, 1098–112.

Litt, D.M. and Turk, C.D. (1985). Sources of stress and dissatisfaction in experienced high school teachers. *Journal of Educational Research*, 78, 178–85.

Maring, F.E. and Koblinski, A.A. (2013). Teachers' challenges, strategies, and support needs in schools affected by community violence: A qualitative study. *Journal of School Health*, 83, 379–88.

Markham, L.P. (2000). Stressors and coping strategies of ESL teachers. *Journal of Instructional Psychology*, 26, 268–79.

Maslach, C., Jackson, SE. and Leiter, M.P. (1996). *Maslach Burnout Inventory Manual*. Palo Alto: Consulting Psychologists Press.

Maslovaty, N. (2000). Teachers' choice of teaching strategies for dealing with socio-moral dilemmas in the elementary school. *Journal of Moral Education*, 29, 429–44.

McCrae, R.R. and Costa, P.T. (1987). Validation of the five-factor model of personality across instruments and observers. *Journal of Personality and Social Psychology*, 52, 81–90.

McGovern, V.T. and Miller, L.S. (2008). Integrating teacher behaviours with character strengths and virtues for faculty development. *Teaching of Psychology*, 35, 278–85.

Miller, F.V.G. and Travers, J. (2005). Ethnicity and the experience of work: Job stress and satisfaction of minority ethnic teachers in the UK. *International Review of Psychiatry*, 17, 317–27.

Mintz, J. (2007). Psychodynamic perspectives in teacher stress. *Psychodynamic Practice*, 13, 153–66.

Ngidi, P.D. and Sibaya, T.P. (2002). Black teachers' personality dimensions and work-related stress factors. *South African Journal of Psychology*, 32, 7–15.

O'Brien, T.B. and DeLongis, A. (1996). The interactional context of problem-, emotion-, and relationship-focused coping: The role of the big five personality factors. *Journal of Personality*, 64, 775–813.

Parker, R.K. (1986). Coping in stressful episodes: The role of individual differences, environmental factors, and situational characteristics. *Journal of Personality and Social Psychology*, 51, 1277–92.

Phillips, S., Sen, D. and McNamee, R. (2007). Prevalence and causes of self-reported work-related stress in head teachers. *Occupational Medicine*, 57, 367–76.

Platsidou, M. and Agaliotis, I. (2008). Burnout, job satisfaction and instructional assignment-related sources of stress in Greek special education teachers. *International Journal of Disability, Development and Education*, 55, 61–76.

Rieg, A.S., Paquette, R.K. and Chen, Y. (2007). Coping with stress: An investigation of novice teachers' stressors in the elementary classroom. *Education*, 128, 211–26.

Sari, H. (2004). An analysis of burnout and job satisfaction among Turkish special school headteachers and teachers, and the factors effecting their burnout and job satisfaction. *Educational Studies*, 30, 291–306.

Schonfeld, S.I. (1990). Coping with job-related stress: The case of teachers. *Journal of Occupational Psychology*, 63, 141–9.

Schottenbauer, A.M., Rodriguez, F.B., Glass, R.C. and Arnkoff, B.D. (2006). Religious coping research and contemporary personality theory: An exploration of Endler's (1997) integrative personality theory. *British Journal of Psychology*, 97, 499–519.

Schwarzer, R. and Taubert, S. (2002). Tenacious goal pursuits and striving toward personal growth: Proactive coping. In E. Frydenberg (ed.), *Beyond Coping: Meeting Goals, Visions, and Challenges* (pp. 20–35). London: Oxford University Press.

Skaalvik, M.E. and Skaalvik, S. (2011). Teachers' feeling of belonging, exhaustion, and job satisfaction: The role of school goal structure and value consonance. *Anxiety, Stress, & Coping*, 24, 369–85.

Spilt, L.J., Koomen, Y.M.H. and Thijs, T.J. (2011). Teacher wellbeing: The importance of teacher-student relationships. *Educational Psychology Review*, 23, 457–77.

Stoeber, J. and Rennert, D. (2008). Perfectionism in school teachers: Relations with stress appraisals, coping styles, and burnout. *Anxiety, Stress, & Coping*, 21, 37–53.

Storm, K. and Rothman, S. (2003). The relationship between burnout, personality traits and coping strategies in a corporate pharmaceutical group. *SA Journal of Industrial Psychology*, 29, 35–42.

Tatar, M. (2009). Teachers turning for help to school counsellors and colleagues: Toward a mapping of relevant predictors. *British Journal of Guidance & Counselling*, 37, 107–27.

Thornton, B., Peltier, G. and Hill, G. (2005). Do future teachers choose wisely: A study of pre-service teachers' personality preference profiles. *College Student Journal*, 39, 480–96.

Weber, A., Weltle, D. and Lederer, P. (2005). Ill health and early retirement among school principals in Bavaria. *International Archives of Occupational and Environmental Health*, 78, 325–31.

Wisniewski, L. and Garguilo, R.M. (1997). Occupational stress and burnout among special educators: A review of the literature. *Journal of Special Education*, 31, 325–47.

PART V
PERSONALITY AND
COPING WITH JOB LOSS

15

The Role of Personality in Coping with Job Loss and Job Insecurity

Tahira M. Probst and Jesse L. Byrd

Introduction

Given the focus of this edited volume on the role that personality plays in responding to psychological crises and critical events, it would be incomplete without a consideration of the role of personality in coping with economic stressors. According to Voydanoff (1990), economic stress refers to aspects of economic life that are potential stressors for employees and their families and consists of both objective and subjective components reflecting the employment and income dimensions of the worker-earner role. Objective indicators of economic stress include employment instability (e.g., the frequency and length of unemployment versus employment) whereas employment uncertainty (i.e., job insecurity) is considered to be a subjective indicator of economic stress (Kinnunen and Pulkkinen 1998).

As early as 1967, Holmes and Rahe proposed that the loss of one's job was one of the top 10 life stressors one could face; not surprisingly, recent research (Spurgeon, Jackson, and Beach 2001) has confirmed the significance of unemployment as a major life stressor. Similarly, research also suggests that job insecurity is one of the most significant organizational stressors encountered by employees (Ironson 1992) with devastating physical health consequences on par with the health effects of a serious illness (Burgard, Brand, and House 2009). *Thus, together, these two phenomena represent critical events that can potentially lead to psychological crisis.*

Although the Great Recession of 2007–2009 has officially receded into the past, this widespread economic downturn had devastating long-term consequences for millions of individuals around the globe with lingering effects still felt by the millions of laid-off workers as well as those whose job security was (and perhaps still is) threatened. One key feature of the recession in the United States was the unusually large number of individuals who were out of work for more than six months, i.e., the long-term unemployed; for many of these individuals, the recession is not over. For those who are currently employed or re-employed, the fear of job loss has become a persistent and common stressor. Indeed, in a survey conducted by the American Psychological Association (2010), 49% of US respondents reported worrying about the future stability of their job. In another recent study of workers in several European countries, the percentage of workers who were worried about their job security ranged from 28% in the Netherlands to 46% in Spain (Muñoz de Bustillo and De Pedraza 2010).

The purpose of the current chapter is to ask and begin to answer a series of questions related to the role of personality in coping with the economic stressors of job insecurity and job loss. In particular, we review the state of the literature in addressing the following questions:

- How does personality relate to the stress appraisal process and coping with job loss and insecurity?
- To what extent are certain personality traits protective in coping with economic stress? In other words, do personality characteristics explain the mismatch between objective stressful circumstances and the resulting level of subjective distress felt by a person?
- To the extent that certain individual differences are potentially malleable and thus open to development, can we teach people more effective coping strategies? Can coping interventions tailored to personality traits be successful?

Before delving into these questions, we begin with a brief review of the literature documenting the overwhelmingly negative outcomes of job loss and job insecurity, as well as major theories of coping with job loss.

Outcomes of Job Loss and Job Insecurity

To do nothing may be to be nothing for many Americans. (Judge and Hulin 1993, p. 413)

Although the above quote was directed to the US context, research suggests that it may be widely applicable in understanding why the outcomes of job loss and insecurity are so adverse. According to Warr's (1987) vitamin model of work and unemployment, individuals require nine environmental "vitamins" in order to maintain their psychological health: opportunity for control, opportunity for skill use, externally generated goals, variety, environmental clarity, availability of money, physical security, opportunity for interpersonal contact, and valued social position. Many of these vitamins are threatened or compromised under conditions of job loss and job insecurity. For example, unemployed individuals have lost control over their employment status; their skills are no longer being utilized. The external structure and opportunities for social interaction that work provided are gone, and a loss of income and valued social position accompany job loss. A loss of control over one's employment security, low environmental clarity, and an anticipation of a loss of income accompany employee job insecurity. Based on Warr's (1987) model, one would expect that the consequences of economic stress would be extensive and overwhelmingly negative as a result of these vitamin needs being compromised.

Indeed, research has found that individuals faced with unemployment or job insecurity experience strikingly similar outcomes that fall into one of three primary categories: individual outcomes, family and social outcomes, and job-related outcomes.

Individual outcomes. Virtually every study of the consequences of unemployment documents negative psychological and physical outcomes for the affected individual (see Hanisch 1999 and McKee-Ryan et al. 2005 for comprehensive reviews). The unemployed exhibit increases in hostility, depression, anxiety, psychiatric illness, worry, strain, stress, suicide attempts, alcohol abuse, violent behavior, anger, fear, paranoia, loneliness, pessimism, despair, and social isolation. In addition, individuals affected by unemployment exhibit decreases in self-esteem, positive affect, life satisfaction, perceptions of competence, feelings of mastery, aspiration level, and social identity (Hanisch 1999; McKee-Ryan et al. 2005). There are also multiple negative physical health effects that accompany unemployment. Unemployed individuals suffer from more headaches, stomach aches, sleep problems, lack of energy, and death from stroke, heart, and kidney disease than individuals who are employed. In addition, unemployment is associated with an increase in disability, hypertension, ulcers, vision problems, cholesterol levels, and other doctor-diagnosed illnesses (Hanisch 1999; McKee-Ryan et al. 2005).

With respect to job insecurity, research from as early as the 1970s suggests that this economic stressor can have a detrimental effect on employee health outcomes. Cobb (1974) found that the stress of possible job termination was associated with significant increases in norepinephrine excretion, serum creatinine, serum uric acid, and serum cholesterol. Research since then has supported the finding that employees with low job security report a greater incidence of physical health conditions (Cottington, Matthews, Talbot, and Kuller 1986; Dooley, Rook, and Catalano 1987; Kuhnert, Sims, and Lahey 1989; Probst 2000, 2002, 2003; Roskies and Louis-Guerin 1990) when compared with employees with secure jobs. Moreover, in a four-wave longitudinal study of employees facing an organizational restructuring, Pollard (2001) found that job insecurity and role ambiguity significantly predicted higher blood pressure and cholesterol levels.

Job insecurity has also been associated with higher levels of general psychological distress (Dekker and Schaufeli 1995; Probst 2000, 2002, 2003) and with increased medical consultations for psychological distress (Catalano, Rook, and Dooley 1986). Roskies and Louis-Guerin (1990) reported that job insecurity among managers was related to an increase in anxiety, depression, and general distress. Finally, Kuhnert et al. (1989) found that job insecurity was related to overall increases in somatization, depression, anxiety, and hostility.

Family and social outcomes. In addition to affecting the workers themselves, the phenomena of job loss and insecurity have spillover effects on the families of affected employees. Research on unemployment has documented increases in spousal abuse, marital stress and dissolution, wife battering, and spousal depression and psychiatric disorders (Hanisch 1999). At the same time, decreases in spousal well-being and spousal contact with friends have also been reported (Hanisch 1999). In addition, there is a growing body of research that suggests the children of unemployed workers are also negatively affected. Increases in family conflict, child abuse, family violence, and aggression and hostility toward children have been documented, as well as decreases in family cohesion and the physical and mental well-being of children. Finally, research indicates that children of unemployed individuals act out more frequently, exhibit greater cognitive difficulties, and achieve lower levels of academic performance than children of employed individuals (Harland, Reijneveld, Brugman, Verloove-Vanhorick and Verhulst, 2002) and are at increased risk of accidents (Ström 2002).

Similar findings have been seen for the effects of job insecurity on family and other social relationships. Work and family research clearly suggests that these two spheres of life do not operate independently of each other. Therefore, it is not surprising that research has found that the economic worries of one member of a couple cross over to predict the job security of the other partner (Mauno and Kinnunen 2002). In their study of job insecurity and the crossover of burnout among married couples, Westman, Etzion, and Danon (2001) found that job insecurity was related to burnout and that the burnout experienced by one member of the couple influenced the burnout reported by the other member. More importantly, couples who were experiencing job insecurity exhibited higher levels of both given and received social undermining toward one another. Larson, Wilson, and Beley (1994) found that the stress of job insecurity was predictive of marital and family dysfunction. Similar findings were reported by Burke and Greenglass (1999) who found that organizational restructuring predicted work–family conflict.

Children of parents who are experiencing job insecurity at work are not immune from its negative effects. Barling, Dupre, and Hepburn (1998) found that children's perceptions of work, work beliefs, and work attitudes are influenced by their parents' job insecurity. Furthermore, student grades were negatively associated with perceptions of their parent's job insecurity (Barling and Mendelson 1997). In an exploration of those findings, Barling, Zacharatos, and Hepburn

(1999) report that this relationship is mediated by children's cognitive difficulties. This series of relationships is particularly alarming as it suggests a potential negative cyclical relationship whereby parental job insecurity is related to lower academic performance and potentially fewer and/or lower quality employment opportunities for their children.

Job-related outcomes. Extensive research has been conducted on the job-related outcomes associated with job insecurity. Two meta-analyses (Cheng and Chan 2008; Sverke, Hellgren, and Näswall 2002) summarizing the effects of job insecurity reported that insecure employees experience decreased job satisfaction, are less involved in their jobs, are less committed to the organization and more likely to quit their jobs, place less trust in management, and have lower levels of performance than workers with more job security. Other studies not reviewed in the meta-analysis report significantly higher levels of job-related stress (Tombaugh and White 1990), more work withdrawal behaviors such as absenteeism, tardiness, and work task avoidance (Probst 1998), and lower levels of creativity (Probst, Stewart, Gruys, and Tierney 2007) among less secure workers. Finally, recent research also suggests that worker safety can be compromised as a result of job insecurity and the threat of job loss (Landsbergis, Cahill and Schnall 1999; Probst and Brubaker 2001; Probst, Barbaranelli, and Petitta 2013), resulting in decreased safety compliance, more injuries and workplace accidents, as well as a greater underreporting of such experienced accidents.

The experience of unemployment itself also has long-term negative job-related outcomes. In particular, the longer a person remains unemployed, the lower their chances of finding re-employment are, due to the loss of current job-skills, motivation, and job-related networks (Aaronson, Mazumder, and Schechter 2010), as well as to societal stigmas associated with unemployment (Gallie and Russell 1998; Heslin, Bell, and Fletcher 2012; Vishwanath 1989).

Given the wide and pervasive set of negative outcomes of job insecurity and job loss, theoretical and empirical insight into variables that can mitigate these outcomes can be extremely valuable. Below we discuss theories of coping with job loss and uncertainty in order to provide a theoretical framework for our assertion that a variety of personality-related constructs might facilitate (or alternatively, inhibit) such coping.

Theories of Coping with Job Loss

There are numerous theories that can help explain the negative impact of job loss and job insecurity on reduced employee well-being and more negative employee behaviors. This includes Lazarus and Folkman's transactional model of stress and coping; Karasek's (1979) demands-control model; French and colleagues' P-E fit model (French, Caplan, and Van Harrison 1982, Van Harrison 1978); and Demerouti, Bakker, Nachreiner, and Schaufeli's (2001) Job Demands-Resources model. However, in this chapter, we focus on two theories we believe provide particular insight into the potentially beneficial and/or adverse role of personality in coping with job loss and insecurity: Hobfoll's (1989, 2001) Conservation of Resources theory and Fredrickson's (2001) Broaden-and-Build theory.

PERSONALITY AS A RESOURCE

Hobfoll's (1989, 2001) Conservation of Resources (COR) theory provides an excellent and intuitive explanation for explaining what causes job insecurity and why it often (but not always) leads to adverse outcomes. COR posits that people strive to obtain, build, and protect that which they value (e.g., resources). When these resources are lost or threatened with loss, psychological stress occurs. Job insecurity, of course, inherently implies a threat of resource loss in the form of lost employment and income or loss of valued aspects of one's job. Moreover, in the context of unemployment, such resource loss is no longer potential, but rather has in fact occurred.

COR also predicts that individuals with greater resources are more capable of resource gain and those with limited or fewer resources are more susceptible to resource loss. Thus, a lack of resources can not only cause stress, but access to resources can potentially buffer the stressor–strain relationship. While such resources may accrue from the individual, organizational, and/or socioeconomic levels to moderate the effects of job loss and insecurity on employee outcomes, we are most interested in those individual-level resources that occur as a function of one's personal traits. Indeed, in Hobfoll and Lilly's (1993) COR-E scale, several characteristics are explicitly noted that reflect personality traits such as self-efficacy, hope, endurance, resilience, optimism, and a sense of control. Notably, COR's focus on resource investment also suggests that these personal traits may be amenable to development and enrichment in order to ameliorate the adverse effects of insecurity or job loss. Thus, resources are not static, but can be invested and built upon.

In a similar vein as Hobfoll's COR theory, Fredrickson's (2001, 2003) Broaden-and-Build theory would also imply that one can build a reservoir of psychological resources. Broaden-and-Build theory contends that an individual's capacity to experience positive emotions is central to understanding whether one flourishes in the face of challenge. In particular, positive emotions are thought to broaden one's momentary thought-action repertoire. Moreover, this enlarged set of resources serves as a pool that can be drawn from when later facing stressors that require coping by fueling psychological resiliency, optimism, and openness to new experience.

In summary, personality is thought to potentially influence how individuals cope with the stressors of job insecurity and job loss via two primary mechanisms. First, personality can influence how individuals initially appraise the stressors and their potential impact for their future well-being. For example, employees might reframe a challenging situation as an opportunity rather than as a threat using a process of cognitive reappraisal (Latack 1986). Second, personality can influence how individuals respond to the stressor itself and whether they select adaptive vs. maladaptive mechanisms of coping with the situation. Below we consider a variety of personality constructs thought to interface with the transactional process of stress and coping.

Personality Constructs Potentially Influencing Coping with Job Loss and Insecurity

Given the theoretical basis for personality and personal traits as potentially valuable resources in coping with stress, there is value in identifying which of these individual-differences characteristics might facilitate or alternatively hinder individual coping with job insecurity and potential job loss, as well as review the extent to which these characteristics can be developed. Toward that end, it is important to note that we use the term "personality" to broadly include constructs that range the spectrum from trait-like stable characteristics (e.g., Big Five personality dimensions) to more malleable resources (e.g., psychological capital such as resilience, hope, and optimism). Although both represent structures and propensities that explain individual patterns of thought, emotion, and behavior, the former may be useful in helping to identify individuals who may be more vulnerable to the threat of job loss, whereas the latter offers opportunities for intervention to better assist individuals with coping with job insecurity and/or eventual job loss. Below, we explore the empirical evidence for these propositions beginning with more stable enduring traits and ending with aspects of personality that might be more amenable to intervention

244 COPING, PERSONALITY AND THE WORKPLACE

and development. Where empirical investigation is scant, this may represent areas for future research opportunities.

CULTURAL VALUES

Although not personality characteristics per se, cultural values can influence the development of people's personality traits, as well as how those traits are manifested in daily interactions. Perhaps the most well-known and best studied dimension of cultural difference is that of individualism and collectivism (Hofstede 1980; Kagitcibasi and Berry 1989; Triandis 1995). According to Triandis (1995), collectivism may be defined as a cultural syndrome where individuals "see themselves as parts of one or more collectives (family, co-workers, tribe, nation); are primarily motivated by the norms of, and duties imposed by, those collectives ... and emphasize their connectedness to members of these collectives" (p. 2).

Based on the theory of individualism and collectivism, Probst and Lawler (2006) proposed that collectivists would react more negatively to the threat of job loss than individualists due to their greater emphasis on group ties, greater need for affiliation, and higher value placed upon security. In two separate studies – one examining cultural values at the national level and a second at the individual level of analysis – they found that cultural values held by employees were related to the manner in which employees reacted to organizational announcements of downsizing, their job attitudes, levels of job-related stress, and future turnover intentions. Specifically, collectivist employees had more negative reactions to job insecurity than their individualistic counterparts.

In a multilevel study of 15,200 employees from 24 countries, Debus, Probst, König, and Kleinmann (2012) found that another commonly studied cultural value, uncertainty avoidance, influenced employee appraisals of job insecurity. Specifically, greater enacted uncertainty avoidance at the societal level (evidenced by more laws and regulations protecting employment security and the social safety net) buffered the negative relationships between job insecurity and job satisfaction and organizational commitment.

Although values vary significantly within and between cultures, they tend to be quite intra-personally stable (e.g., Schwartz et al. 2001). Thus, the primary significance in the research on cultural values as a moderator of reactions to job insecurity may be to help identify those individuals at greater risk for such negative reactions.

SPIRITUALITY

According to Zinnbauer et al. (1997), spirituality is a function of four dimensions: the search for personal or existential meaning; the degree to which one feels the presence of a higher being; a sense of interconnectedness with other living things; and participation in activities designed to promote spiritual growth. Although prior research (e.g., Chen and Koenig 2006; Pargament, Smith, Koenig, and Perez 1998) examined the role of spirituality in coping with life stressors, Probst and Strand (2010) first developed theoretical propositions regarding how spirituality might influence the appraisal of and responses to job insecurity and suggested it might have multiple points of interaction. First, spirituality might influence the initial appraisal of the stressor itself, as individuals with a highly developed sense of spirituality might appraise insecurity or the threat of job loss as less threatening to their sense of self. Alternatively, spirituality might potentially exacerbate the consequences of job insecurity, if one views one's job in the context of a sacred calling or vocation. Second, highly spiritual individuals might also be more likely to interpret job insecurity or eventual job loss as a "sent opportunity" for future growth and development.

Finally, spirituality might serve as a resource or source of strength to draw upon. Thus, even if the appraisal of insecurity is a negative one, spirituality might operate to buffer the adverse consequences by offering additional coping resources.

Despite this theorizing, scant empirical research has been published and results are somewhat inconsistent. Safaria, bin Othman, and Abdul Wahab (2010) found that religious coping significantly moderated the effect of job insecurity on job stress. Specifically, under conditions of low job insecurity, the use of religious coping had no impact on self-reported job stress levels. However, at high levels of job insecurity, greater use of religious coping attenuated the negative relationship between insecurity and stress levels, suggesting that religion serves as a positive coping resource.

In a more nuanced approach, Lucero (2013) considered both the use of positive (e.g., "tried to see how God might be trying to strengthen me in this situation") and negative (e.g., "wondered if God allowed this event to happen to me because of my sins") religious coping in responding to job insecurity. That study found that negative coping exacerbated the relationships between insecurity, psychological distress and health, whereas the use of positive religious coping exhibited no significant moderating effects.

Schreuers, van Emmerik, De Cuyper, Probst, van den Heuvel, and Demerouti (2014) posited that religiousness could operate as either a job demand or resource when employees are faced with the threat of job loss. However, their results were largely consistent with the "religion as a demand" hypothesis, since the adverse impact of job insecurity was stronger for highly religious employees than for employees with low levels of religiousness. They suggested that these results indicate religion might serve to influence the importance of work in an individual's self-concept, and that for religious people job insecurity undermines an individual's most salient role-identities.

Clearly, the relationship between religion, spirituality, and coping with job insecurity is a complex one that warrants further examination in order to determine the conditions under which these variables might foster more positive outcomes. Moreover, spirituality is linked to positive affectivity, the benefits of which are discussed below.

POSITIVE AND NEGATIVE AFFECTIVITY

Negative affectivity (NA) consists of a constellation of personality traits including high levels of neuroticism, low self-esteem, and frequent negative emotionality (Watson and Clark 1984). It is associated with a predisposition to focus on the negative aspects of oneself, others, and life in general. Individuals high in NA are more likely to experience distress and report strain outcomes (Burke, Brief, and George 1993; Fogarty, Machin, Albion, Sutherland, Lalor, and Revitt 1999; Parkes 1990; Spector, and O'Connell 1994; Watson and Pennebaker 1989). On the other hand, positive affectivity (PA) reflects stable individual differences in the tendency to experience positive emotional states such as cheerfulness, enthusiasm, and energy (Watson and Naragon 2012) and has been shown to be related to lower levels of perceived stress and greater coping skills (Fogarty et al. 1999).

Despite the attention paid to NA and PA in the stress literature, surprisingly little research has examined their influence with respect to the stressors of job insecurity or job loss. Moreover, some research treats affectivity as a control variable, rather than a construct of interest (e.g., Hellgren, Sverke, and Isaksson 1999). In one of the first studies to focus on affectivity as a substantive construct of interest, Roskies, Louis-Guerin, and Fournier (1993) found that negative affectivity exacerbated the relationship between job insecurity and mental health complaints. In a later study, Mak and Mueller (2000) found similar exacerbating effects of negative affectivity on physical strain. Similarly, Bosman, Rothmann, and Buitendach (2005) found that NA also interacted with job insecurity to influence burnout and work engagement. On the other hand, two recent studies found no support for the moderating effects of affectivity in either perceiving (Debus, König, and Kleinmann 2014) or responding (Näswall, Sverke, and Hellgren 2005) to job insecurity.

Research on negative affectivity and unemployment has primarily examined NA as an outcome, rather than a moderator variable. However, one recent study examined how positive affectivity might facilitate a successful job search. Côté, Saks, and Zikic (2006) found that job seekers high in positive affectivity were more likely to secure a job because PA was related to greater job search clarity and intensity. Additionally, Crossley and Stanton (2005) found that NA was negatively related to job search success.

BIG FIVE PERSONALITY TRAITS

Although historical estimates of the meaningful number of personality traits have varied greatly, contemporary research has largely coalesced around a taxonomy consisting of five personality traits (Digman 1990). These include: *extraversion* (e.g., being communicative, talkative, outgoing, and sociable); *agreeableness* (e.g., having a forgiving nature, being considerate and kind to others); *conscientiousness* (e.g., exhibiting high levels of thoughtfulness and goal-directed behaviors; being efficient and effective); *neuroticism* (e.g., having a tendency toward getting nervous easily, worrying, being irritable); and *openness to experience* (e.g., having an active imagination, valuing artistic experience and a broad range of interests). Although it is generally accepted that these traits are intra-personally quite stable (e.g., Costa and McCrae 1988; McCrae and Costa 1994), there is also some evidence that suggests these personality traits can change over one's life cycle (Srivastava, John, Gosling, and Potter 2003). Nevertheless, their primary interest to economic stress researchers may be in understanding how they influence employee appraisals of and reactions to economic stressors such as job insecurity or unemployment rather than as points of interventions.

In a study investigating the relationship between personality and unemployment duration, Uysal and Pohlmeier (2011) posited that the intensity of one's job search would be largely influenced by personality traits and resultant propensity for motivation and discipline. Indeed, prior research (Schmit, Amel, and Ryan 1993; Kanfer, Wanberg, and Kantrowitz 2001) found that conscientiousness, extraversion, and openness were positively correlated with effective job search behaviors, whereas neuroticism was negatively correlated. Uysal and Pohlmeier's (2011) results were largely consistent in that individuals higher in conscientiousness and openness were more likely to find a new job faster, while neuroticism appeared to hinder job opportunities. They interpreted these results as a function of conscientious individuals being more organized and efficient job searchers. On the other hand, they speculated that individuals high in neuroticism do not fare well in the face of challenging stressful situations such as unemployment. In support of this, Langens and Mose (2006) found that neuroticism significantly predicted greater use of more non-productive coping methods during unemployment (e.g., denial, venting of emotions, substance abuse, behavioral disengagement, and self-blame) which in turn predicted greater somatic complaints.

Interestingly, Uysal and Pohlmeier (2011) found that the relationships between personality traits and job search success were more pronounced for blue-collar workers compared to white-collar workers. They posited that this may be a function of the greater weight placed on cognitive skills of white-collar workers rather than their personality traits. Additionally, they found that personality was a better predictor of unemployment duration than employment duration. In other words, personality may have a larger effect on how quickly one can land a job than on how long one can retain a job.

Personality also appears to influence how one copes with the strain of unemployment. Jahoda's (1982) latent deprivation model posited that employment provides several latent benefits in addition to more tangible manifest ones such as income. One such latent benefit is the provision of structure to one's day. Meta-analytic research indicates that this ability to maintain time structure during periods of unemployment is related to higher psychological well-being (McKee-Ryan et al. 2005). Van Hoye and Lootens (2013) found that the personality traits of conscientiousness and neuroticism most strongly related to the various facets of time structure, such that individuals high in conscientiousness reported a greater sense of purpose, more structured daily routine, more effective organization, and greater persistence, whereas neuroticism was negatively related to sense of purpose and present orientation.

Together, these results suggest that extraversion and conscientiousness are beneficial personality traits when faced with economic stress, whereas neuroticism may serve to exacerbate the adverse experience of economic stress. Further, Vakola, Tsaousis, and Nikolaou (2004) found that openness, extraversion, conscientiousness, and agreeableness were related to more positive attitudes toward impending organizational change, whereas neuroticism was negatively related to such attitudes. Using these results, they proposed that one could construct a profile of the "positive to organizational change" employee: one "who is an extrovert, open to new experiences, agreeable and conscientious" (p. 103).

EMOTIONAL INTELLIGENCE

Another variable that has been theorized to buffer the effects of job insecurity on employee outcomes is emotional intelligence (EI), i.e., the ability to express and control one's own emotions, as well as to understand, interpret, and appropriately respond to the emotions of others. Jordan, Ashkanasy, and Hartel (2002) argue that because emotional intelligence regulates the way in which individuals manage emotions, it will moderate the effects of job insecurity on emotional reactions and behaviors. Specifically, they predict that low emotional intelligence employees will be more likely to experience negative emotional reactions to job insecurity and utilize more negative coping strategies than high emotional intelligence employees. Moreover, because researchers have found that EI is a developable trait and competency (Dulewicz and Higgs 2000; Steiner and Perry 1997), this suggests it might be a fruitful avenue for organizational intervention.

In a longitudinal test of Jordan et al'.s (2002) propositions, Cheng, Huang, Lee, and Ren (2012) found that EI significantly moderated the relationship between job insecurity and later somatic complaints suggesting that the ability to perceive the emotions of others and appropriately manage one's own emotions may be an important protective resource during times of job uncertainty. Similarly, Vakola et al. (2004) found that EI predicted incremental variance in attitudes toward organizational change over and above the use of Big Five personality traits, such that individuals high in EI were more positive about the impending changes.

Although Jordan et al. (2002) did not make predictions regarding unemployment, by extension, one would predict similar relationships for low emotional intelligence individuals experiencing unemployment. Unfortunately, to date, no empirical research has tested these propositions.

LOCUS OF CONTROL

Locus of control (Rotter 1966) refers to an individual's tendency to perceive life events as being within one's control (internal LOC) or beyond one's control (external LOC). With respect to job insecurity and unemployment, this would reflect the extent to which individuals perceive that their behavior can influence or control whether their jobs are insecure or if they become unemployed. For example, high internal LOC employees might believe that they can protect their job security by proactively taking steps to increase their value to the organization (Ito and Brotheridge 2007). Indeed, LOC has been shown to impact how individuals deal with stress with internal LOC related to increased use of proactive problem-solving strategies (Parkes 1994).

In perhaps the first study to examine the moderating role of LOC in coping with job insecurity, Orpen (1994) found that Australian employees high in external LOC exhibited more negative psychological well-being in response to job insecurity compared to their internal LOC counterparts.

Näswall et al. (2005) found a similar interaction effect of job insecurity and external LOC on mental health complaints. They concluded that individuals high in external LOC would benefit from additional organizational support during periods of organizational uncertainty in order to prevent and alleviate strain in this group. More recently, König, Debus, Häusler, Lendenmann, and Kleinmann (2010) investigated the impact of LOC (specifically work LOC) and found that internal LOC was only related to greater self-rated task performance under conditions of job security. However, when perceived security was low, this beneficial impact of an internal LOC disappeared.

In addition to its moderating effects, locus of control has also been examined as both an antecedent and a consequence of job insecurity and unemployment. For example, a recent meta-analysis by Keim, Landis, Pierce, and Earnest (2014) found that individuals with an internal locus of control were less likely to perceive their jobs as insecure. On the other hand, Patton and Noller (1984) and Layton (1987) both found that becoming unemployed was related to an increase in external locus of control perceptions, suggesting that intrapersonal levels of LOC can change over time in response to job threats.

Based on the above findings, it appears that LOC interfaces with the experience of job loss and insecurity in numerous ways: as an antecedent influencing the initial appraisal of the threat, as a consequence of these stressors, and as a potential (albeit inconsistent) moderator attenuating the harmful effects of insecurity. Unlike cultural values, spirituality, and personality traits such as the Big Five which tend to be quite stable, interventions to foster greater internal LOC might be a fruitful endeavor in helping employees cope during times of organizational change and upheaval. Below we consider additional protective constructs that may be more malleable and open to development.

PSYCHOLOGICAL CAPITAL: HOPE, EFFICACY, RESILIENCE, AND OPTIMISM

According to Luthans (2002b), positive organizational behavior (POB) consists of "positively oriented human resource strengths and psychological capacities that can be measured, developed, and effectively managed" (p. 59). Within the study of POB, Luthans (2002a) suggests that four psychological constructs are of particular interest: hope, efficacy, resilience, and optimism; further, the psychological capacity generated by the interaction of these four constructs is synergistically greater than would be predicted by each construct alone (Luthans, Avolio, Avey, and Norman 2007). This set of psychological capacities form a higher order construct known as psychological capital (PsyCap) and serve as resources that – unlike many of the earlier discussed personality traits – are capable of being learned and thus further developed. Indeed, empirical research suggests that PsyCap resources can be developed through brief training interventions (Luthans, Luthans, and Avey 2014; Luthans, Avey, Avolio, and Peterson 2010; Luthans, Avey, Avolio, Norman, and Combs 2006). Moreover, PsyCap resources tend to persist over time (Peterson, Luthans, Avolio, Walumbwa, and Zhang 2011). Researchers have argued (e.g., Peterson et al. 2011) that this balance between stability and potential for further development renders PsyCap an optimal resource for workplace development.

Given the prevalence of economic stress in today's workplace, the potential of PsyCap in attenuating its negative effects is ripe for exploration, particularly given that the underlying commonality amongst these constructs is the tendency for individuals to form positive appraisals of past, present, and future events. For example, Avey, Luthans, and Jensen (2009) found that individuals with higher PsyCap reported fewer symptoms of job stress, providing support for the contention that PsyCap partially operates by influencing the primary appraisal of potential stressors. PsyCap also appears to predict adaptive behaviors in the context of unemployment. For example, Chen and Lim (2012) proposed and found that PsyCap influences eventual re-employment by primarily affecting the amount of coping resources (specifically, perceived employability) displaced employees possess which indirectly predicted both preparatory and active job search behaviors. A recent dissertation conducted by Oglensky (2014) subsequently found that while PsyCap did not predict preparatory job search behaviors, it was predictive of active job search behaviors. A second dissertation (Millard, 2011) proposed that the resources provided by PsyCap might offset so-called "psychological debt" (consisting of emotional labor, job insecurity, job stress, job deviance, and stigmatic injustice) resulting in a certain level of psychological net worth. Given that very little research has been conducted to date on the higher-order construct of PsyCap in relation to job loss or insecurity specifically, we consider below the empirical evidence for each of these constructs separately.

Hope has been defined as "a positive motivational state that is based on an interactively derived sense of successful (1) agency (goal-directed energy) and (2) pathways (planning to meet goals)" (Snyder, Irving, and Anderson 1991, p. 287). Thus, it includes not just willpower, i.e., determination to achieve one's goals, but also "waypower," i.e., planned pathways to meet one's goals. Higher levels of hope foster goal achievement by proactively dealing with obstacles and engaging in contingency planning (Snyder 2000). As a result, hope would presumably be an effective aid to coping with the threat and/or experience of losing one's job in that high-hope employees would be more likely to proactively make contingency plans for the possibility of job loss.

Although little research has specifically focused on the positive role that hope might have on coping with job insecurity or unemployment, a recent dissertation (Schalk 2013) used a qualitative approach to examine coping strategies used by couples experiencing unemployment. Thematic analysis indicated that hope was one coping strategy used by the partner of the unemployed individual. Thus, future research could benefit from examining whether this is also related to more successful job search strategies and eventual re-employment. Additionally, because research indicates that hope is state-like and developable (Snyder 2000; Snyder, Sympson, Ybasco, Borders, Babyak, and Higgins 1996), interventions to increase hope during times of job uncertainty could prove valuable.

Self-efficacy is defined as the belief in one's ability to successfully "organize and execute courses of action required to attain designated types of performance" (Bandura 1986, p. 391). As with other PsyCap variables, research indicates that self-efficacy can be developed via mastery experiences, vicarious learning/modeling, social persuasion, and physiological and psychological arousal (Bandura 1997). According to COR theory (Hobfoll 1989), self-efficacy can be considered an important personal resource in coping with stress by affecting how people react when confronted with potential resource loss. Specifically, high self-efficacy may buffer the negative effects of job insecurity, since individuals high in self-efficacy may perceive that they have the capacity to successfully cope with the potential challenges of job loss.

In a test of this, Probst (2007) predicted that self-efficacy would serve to buffer the stress of working in an organization undergoing a major transition, but only when the employee's outcome expectancy was positive. Results indicated that high self-efficacy was associated with more positive attitudinal and behavioral job-related outcomes. However, the positive effects of self-efficacy were attenuated when outcome expectancies (i.e., perceptions of job security) were low. Thus, to attenuate the effects of economic stress associated with organizational change, her results suggest that organizations should increase communication during times of organizational transition to improve the accuracy of job security perceptions and to increase the extent to which employees feel capable of handling pending organizational changes.

A second study conducted by Lau and Knardahl (2008) found that job insecurity (measured as confidence in having a good job in two years) was predictive of mental distress and that this effect was strongest among respondents with low self-efficacy. However, they also acknowledged that causality could run in the opposite direction, such that among low self-efficacy individuals, poor mental health might be related to less confidence in obtaining a job in the future.

Although there is scant research on self-efficacy as a moderator of coping with job insecurity, ample evidence indicates that self-efficacy is a key and positive predictor of job search behaviors, job search intensity, job offers, and eventual re-employment (Eden and Aviram 1993; Kanfer and Hulin 1985; Saks 2006; Saks and Ashforth 2000; Wanberg et al. 1999).

Resilience is the positive psychological capacity to "rebound or bounce back from adversity, conflict, and failure or even positive events, progress, and increased responsibility" (Luthans 2002a, p. 702). Unlike the other sub-facets of PsyCap, resilience in the face of economic stress would primarily be expected to operate as a reactive aid to coping, rather than also influencing the primary appraisal of the stressor itself. However, like the other sub-facets of PsyCap, resilience has been found to be developable (Masten 2001; Masten, Cutuli, Herbers, and Reed 2009) and, therefore, would be a potentially valuable target for intervention.

Resilient employees may be better equipped to deal with the threats of job insecurity and potential job loss as they tend to be more open to new experiences, flexible in the face of changing demands, and have demonstrated more emotional stability when faced with adversity (Tugade and Fredrickson 2004). Additionally, research also indicates that resilient individuals are better able to deal with large-scale corporate downsizing (e.g., Maddi 1987).

Optimism consists of a generalized expectation of positive outcomes (Carver, Scheier, Miller, and Fulford 2009) coupled with an attributional style (Seligman 1998) whereby individuals view adversity as an externally-driven, challenging, and temporary setback. Optimism can serve to attenuate the impact of stress due to the tendency for optimists to view obstacles to goal accomplishment as resolvable, as well as their differential use of avoidance coping strategies (Scheier, Weintraub, and Carver 1986). Specifically, Scheier et al. (1986) found that optimism was associated with greater use of problem-focused coping, social support, and emphasis on positive aspects of the stressful situation, whereas pessimism was associated with greater use of avoidance coping strategies such as denial and distancing, a greater emphasis on one's stressful feelings, and with disengagement from goal attainment. Like the other PsyCap constructs, optimism has been demonstrated to be something that can be learned and developed (Seligman 1998).

Evidence suggests that optimism is positively related to the psychological health of the unemployed (Leana and Feldman 1995; Wanberg 1997) as well as predictive of eventual re-employment (Leana and Feldman 1995). Optimism also appears to operate as a moderator of reactions to economic stress. In a study comparing employed and unemployed women, Lai and Wong (1998) found that optimism moderated the relation between employment status and psychiatric morbidity. Moreover, in a longitudinal study of managers during and following a major organizational downsizing, Armstrong-Stassen and Schlosser (2008) found that optimism measured 18 months prior to the downsizing positively predicted managerial cognitions, attitudes, job performance, and self-reported coping effectiveness 12 months following the downsizing.

ADAPTABILITY

Adaptability refers to one's willingness and ability to change personal factors – knowledge, skills, abilities, dispositions, behaviors, feelings, and thoughts – either in response to environmental demands or proactively in anticipation of such demands (Ashford and Taylor 1990; Chan 2000; Fugate, Kinicki, and Ashforth 2004). Thus, while the constructs of PsyCap described above are ones that *can* be developed and changed, adaptability refers to the extent to which an individual is *willing and able* to change. This ability and willingness to proactively adapt may be increasingly important due to changing psychological contracts from a focus on life-time employment to life-time employability in exchange for hard work (Hall 1996, 2004; Kanter 1989; Kluytmans and Ott 1999). Thus, they are potentially quite pertinent to employees' attempts to cope with the economic stressors of job insecurity and/or job loss.

Researchers (e.g., Bateman and Crant 1993; Fugate et al. 2004; Seibert, Crant, and Kraimer 1999) argue that adaptable proactive individuals are actively engaged in influencing their employment situation to fulfill their desired career outcomes; moreover, they will alter their own cognitions and behaviors as needed to optimize employment opportunities. As such, highly adaptable employees may be less vulnerable to job insecurity or job loss due to their proactive management of their employability (Berntson and Marklund 2007; Berntson, Bernhard-Oettel, and De Cuyper 2007). Indeed, DeCuyper et al. (2009) found that employability (a higher-order construct encompassing adaptability, social and human capital, and career identity; Fugate et al. 2004) was predictive of lower levels of perceived job insecurity. Thus, the evidence to date appears to suggest that adaptability primarily operates by influencing the appraisal of potential economic stressors. However, no research has yet explicitly examined whether adaptability might also serve as a moderator that attenuates adverse reactions to economic stress, i.e., that helps employees better cope with the experience of job loss and/or job insecurity.

Conclusion

This chapter reviewed a number of different personality constructs ranging from relatively stable trait-like dispositional variables to state-like variables that are more amenable to modification or intervention. While many of these variables have been found to predict the experience of economic stress and/or assist individuals with coping with these stressors, there still remains much more to be explored. For example, much of the reviewed research has been correlational in nature. While such research provides foundational evidence of important relationships between these personality constructs and economic stress, it does not indicate whether attempts to intervene will successfully alter appraisals of these stressors or improve employee attempts to cope with them. Nevertheless, some of the most promising avenues for future research involve those personality characteristics that prior research has shown to be open to development via interventions. This includes, but is not necessarily limited to, those comprising psychological capital.

Not surprisingly, the field of job insecurity and economic stress has largely focused on the negative – the negative outcomes of such economic stress and conditions that further exacerbate these outcomes. However, little research has considered job insecurity and potential job loss through the lens of positive psychology as a potential opportunity for future growth a development. As demonstrated by our initial review at the beginning of the chapter, job insecurity and unemployment are adverse experiences with overwhelmingly negative consequences for the affected individuals and their loved ones. However, if there are opportunities to develop psychological capacities that would allow employees not just to survive these experiences but also to thrive as a result of having experienced them, these provide economic stress researchers with the opportunity to truly make a positive difference in the millions of today's workers faced with the threats of job insecurity and job loss.

References

Aaronson, D., Mazumder, B. and Schechter, S. (2010). What is behind the rise in long-term unemployment? *Economic Perspectives*, 34(2), 28–51.

American Psychological Association (2010). *Stress in America Findings*. Washington, DC: APA.

Armstrong-Stassen, M. and Schlosser, F. (2008). Taking a positive approach to organizational downsizing. *Canadian Journal of Administration Sciences*, 25, 93–106.

Ashford, S.J. and Taylor, M.S. (1990). Adaptation to work transitions: An integrative approach. In G.R. Ferris and K.M. Rowland (eds), *Research in Personnel and Human Resources Management* (vol. 8, pp. 1–39). Greenwich, CT: JAI Press.

Avey, J.B., Luthans, F. and Jensen, S.M. (2009). Psychological capital: A positive resource for combating employee stress and turnover. *Human Resource Management*, 48(5), 677–93.

Bandura, A. (1986). *Social Foundations of Thought and Action: A Social Cognitive Theory*. Englewood Cliffs: Prentice-Hall.

Bandura, A. (1997). *Self-efficacy: The Exercise of Control*. New York: W.H. Freeman.

Barling, J. and Mendelson, M.B. (1997). Parents' job insecurity affects children's grade performance through the indirect effects of beliefs in an unjust world and negative mood. *Journal of Occupational Health Psychology*, 4, 347–55.

Barling, J., Dupre, K.E. and Hepburn, C.G. (1998). Effects of parents' job insecurity on children's work beliefs and attitudes. *Journal of Applied Psychology*, 83, 112–18.

Barling, J., Zacharatos, A. and Hepburn, C.G. (1999). Parents' job insecurity affects children's academic performance through cognitive difficulties. *The Journal of Applied Psychology*, 84(3), 437–44.

Bateman, T.S. and Crant, J.M. (1993). The proactive component of organizational behavior: A measure and correlates. *Journal of Organizational Behavior*, 14(2), 103–18.

Berntson, E. and Marklund, S. (2007). The relationship between perceived employability and subsequent health. *Work & Stress*, 21(3), 279–92.

Berntson E., Bernhard-Oettel, C. and De Cuyper, N. (2007). The moderating role of employability in the relationship between organizational changes and job insecurity. Paper presented at the XIIIth European Congress of Work and Organizational Psychology, Stockholm, 9–12 May.

Borghans, L. and National Bureau of Economic Research (2008). *The Economics and Psychology of Personal Traits*. Cambridge, MA: National Bureau of Economic Research.

Bosman, J., Rothmann, S. and Buitendach, J.H. (2005). Job insecurity, burnout and work engagement: The impact of positive and negative effectivity. *SA Journal of Industrial Psychology*, 31(4), 48.

Burgard, S.A., Brand, J.E. and House, J.S. (2009). Perceived job insecurity and worker health in the United States. *Social Science & Medicine*, 69, 777–85.

Burke, M.J., Brief, A.P. and George, J.M. (1993). The role of negative affectivity in understanding relations between self-reports of stressors and strains: A comment on the applied psychology literature. *Journal of Applied Psychology*, 78(3), 402–12.

Burke, R.J. and Greenglass, E.R. (1999). Work-family conflict, spouse support, and nursing staff well-being during organizational restructuring. *Journal of Occupational Health Psychology*, 4(4), 327–36.

Carver, C.S., Scheier, M.F., Miller, C.J. and Fulford, D. (2009). Optimism. In S.J. Lopez and C.R. Snyder (eds), *Oxford Handbook of Positive Psychology* (2nd edn, pp. 303–11). Oxford: Oxford University Press.

Catalano, R., Rook, K.S. and Dooley, D. (1986). Labor markets and help-seeking: A test of the employment security hypothesis. *Journal of Health and Social Behavior*, 27, 277–87.

Chan, D. (2000). Understanding adaptation to changes in the work environment: Integrating individual difference and learning perspectives. *Research in Personnel and Human Resources Management*, 18, 1–42.

Chen, D.J.Q. and Lim, V.K.G. (2012). Strength in adversity: The influence of psychological capital on job search. *Journal of Organizational Behavior*, 33(6), 811–39.

Chen, Y. and Koenig, H. (2006). Traumatic stress and religion: Is there a relationship? A review of empirical findings. *Journal of Religion and Health*, 45(3), 371–81.

Cheng, G.H.-L. and Chan, D.K.-S. (2008). Who suffers more from job insecurity? A meta-analytic review. *Applied Psychology*, 57(2), 272–303.

Cheng, T., Huang, G., Lee, C. and Ren, X. (2012). Longitudinal effects of job insecurity on employee outcomes: The moderating role of emotional intelligence and the leader-member exchange. *Asia Pacific Journal of Management*, 29(3), 709–28.

Cobb, S. (1974). Physiologic changes in men whose jobs were abolished. *Journal of Psychosomatic Research*, 18, 245–58.

Costa, P.T.J. and McCrae, R.R. (1988). Personality in adulthood: A six-year longitudinal study of self-reports and spouse ratings on the NEO Personality Inventory. *Journal of Personality and Social Psychology*, 54(5), 853–63.

Côté, S., Saks, A.M. and Zikic, J. (2006). Trait affect and job search outcomes. *Journal of Vocational Behavior*, 68(2), 233–52.

Cottington, E.M., Matthews, K.A., Talbott, E. and Kuller, L.H. (January 1, 1986). Occupational stress, suppressed anger, and hypertension. *Psychosomatic Medicine*, 48.

Crossley, C.D. and Stanton, J.M. (2005). Negative affect and job search: Further examination of the reverse causation hypothesis. *Journal of Vocational Behavior*, 66, 549–60.

Debus, M.E., König, C.J. and Kleinmann, M. (2014). The building blocks of job insecurity: The impact of environmental and person-related variables on job insecurity perceptions. *Journal of Occupational and Organizational Psychology*, 87(2), 329–51.

Debus, M.E., Probst, T.M., König, C.J. and Kleinmann, M. (2012). Catch me if I fall! Enacted uncertainty avoidance and the social safety net as country-level moderators of the job insecurity-job attitudes link. *Journal of Applied Psychology*, 97, 690–98.

De Cuyper, N., Notelaers, G. and De Witte, H. (2009) Job insecurity and employability in fixed-term contractors, agency workers, and permanent workers: Associations with job satisfaction and affective organizational commitment. *Journal of Occupational Health Psychology*, 14(2), 193–205.

Dekker, S.W.A. and Schaufeli, W.B. (1995). The effects of job insecurity on psychological health and withdrawal: A longitudinal study. *Australian Psychologist*, 30, 57–63.

Demerouti, E., Bakker, A.B., Nachreiner, F. and Schaufeli, W.B. (2001). The job demands-resources model of burnout. *The Journal of Applied Psychology*, 86(3), 499–512.

Digman, J.M. (1990). Personality structure: Emergence of the five factor model. *Annual Review of Psychology*, 41, 417–40.

Dooley, D., Rook, K. and Catalano, R. (1987). Job and non-job stressors and their moderators. *Journal of Occupational Psychology*, 60, 115–32.

Dulewicz, V. and Higgs, M. (January 1, 2000). Emotional intelligence: A review and evaluation study. *Journal of Managerial Psychology*, 15(4), 341–72.

Eden, D. and Aviram, A. (1993). Self-efficacy training to speed reemployment: Helping people to help themselves. *Journal of Applied Psychology*, 78(3), 352–60.

Fogarty, G.J., Machin, M.A., Albion, M.J., Sutherland, L.F., Lalor, G.I. and Revitt, S. (1999). Predicting occupational strain and job satisfaction: The role of stress, coping, personality, and affectivity variables. *Journal of Vocational Behavior*, 54, 429–52.

Fredrickson, B.L. (2001). The role of positive emotions in positive psychology: The broaden-and-build theory of positive emotions. *American Psychologist*, 56(3), 218.

Fredrickson, B.L. (2003). Positive emotions and upward spirals in organizations. In K.S. Cameron, J.E. Dutton and R.E. Quinn (eds), *Positive Organizational Scholarship* (pp. 63–175). San Francisco: Berrett-Koehler.

French, J.R.P., Caplan, R.D. and Van Harrison, R. (1982). *The Mechanisms of Job Stress and Strain.* Chichester: Wiley.

Fugate, M., Kinicki, A.J. and Ashforth, B.E. (2004). Employability: A psycho-social construct, its dimensions and applications. *Journal of Vocational Behavior*, 65, 14–38.

Gallie, D. and Russell, H. (1998). Unemployment and life satisfaction: A cross-cultural comparison. *European Journal of Sociology*, 39(2), 248–80.

Hall, D.T. (1996). Protean careers of the 21st century. *The Academy of Management Executive*, 10(4), 8–16.

Hall, D. (2004). The protean career: A quater-century journey. *Journal of Vocational Behaviour*, 65(1), 1–13.

Hanisch, K. (1999). Job loss and unemployment research from 1994 to 1998: A review and recommendations for research and intervention. *Journal of Vocational Behavior*, 55, 188–220.

Harland, P., Reijneveld, S.A., Brugman, E., Verloove-Vanhorick, S.P. and Verhulst, F.C. (January 1, 2002). Family factors and life events as risk factors for behavioural and emotional problems in children. *European Child & Adolescent Psychiatry*, 11(4), 176–84.

Hellgren, J., Sverke, M. and Isaksson, K. (1999). A two-dimensional approach to job insecurity: Consequences for employee attitudes and well-being. *European Journal of Work and Organizational Psychology*, 8(2), 179–95.

Heslin, P.A., Bell, M.P. and Fletcher, P.O. (2012). The devil without and within: A conceptual model of social cognitive processes whereby discrimination leads stigmatized minorities to become discouraged workers. *Journal of Organizational Behavior*, 33(6), 840–62.

Hobfoll, S.E. (1989). Conservation of resources: A new attempt at conceptualizing stress. *The American Psychologist*, 44(3), 513–24.

Hobfoll, S.E. (2001). The influence of culture, community, and the nested-self in the stress process: Advancing conservation of resources theory. *Applied Psychology*, 50(3), 337–421.

Hobfoll, S.E. and Lilly, R.S. (1993). Resource conservation as a strategy for community psychology. *Journal of Community Psychology*, 21(2), 128–48.

Hofstede, G. (1980). *Culture's Consequences: International Differences in Work-related Values.* Beverly Hills: Sage.

Holmes, T.H. and Rahe, R.H. (1967). The social readjustment rating scale. *Journal of Psychosomatic Research*, 11(2), 213–18.

Ironson, G.H. (1992). Job stress and health. In C.J. Cranny, P.C. Smith, and E.F. Stone (eds), *Job Satisfaction: How People Feel about Their Jobs and How it Affects Their Performance.* New York: Lexington Books, 219–39.

Ito, J.K. and Brotheridge, C.M. (2007). Exploring the predictors and consequences of job insecurity's components. *Journal of Managerial Psychology*, 22, 40–64.

Jahoda, M. (1982). Work, employment, and unemployment: Values, theories, and approaches in social research. *American Psychologist*, 36, 184–91.

Jordan, P.J., Ashkanasy, N.M., and Hartel, C.E.J. (2002). Emotional intelligence as a moderator of emotional and behavioral reactions to job insecurity. *Academy of Management Review*, 27, 61–372.

Judge, T. and Hulin, C.L. (1993). Job satisfaction as a reflection of disposition: A multiple source causal analysis. *Organizational Behavior and Human Decision Processes*, 56, 388–421.

Kagitcibasi, C. and Berry, J.W. (1989). Cross-cultural psychology: Current research and trends. *Annual Review of Psychology*, 40(1), 493–531.

Kanfer, R. and Hulin, C.L. (1985). Individual differences in successful job searches following lay-off. *Personnel Psychology*, 38(4), 835–47.

Kanfer, R., Wanberg, C.R., and Kantrowitz, T.M. (2001). A personality-motivational analysis and meta-analytic review. *Journal of Applied Psychology*, 86, 837–55.

Kanter, R.M. (1989). *When Giants Learn to Dance: Mastering the Challenges of Strategy, Management and Careers in the 1990s.* New York: Basic Books.

Karasek, R.A. (1979). Job demands, job decision latitude, and mental strain: Implications for job redesign. *Administrative Science Quarterly*, 24(2), 285–308.

Keim, A.C., Landis, R.S., Pierce, C.A. and Earnest, D.R. (2014). Why do employees worry about their jobs? A meta-analytic review of predictors of job insecurity. *Journal of Occupational Health Psychology*, 19(3), 269–90.

Kinnunen, U. and Pulkkinen, L. (January 1, 1998). Linking economic stress to marital quality among Finnish marital couples: Mediator effects. *Journal of Family Issues*, 19(6), 705–24.

Kluytmans, F. and Ott, M. (1999). The management of employability in the Netherlands. *European Journal of Work and Organizational Psychology*, 8, 261–72.

König, C.J., Debus, M.E., Häusler, S., Lendenmann, N. and Kleinmann, M. (2010). Examining occupational self-efficacy, work locus of control and communication as moderators of the job insecurity relationship -job performance. *Economic and Industrial Democracy*, 31(2), 231–47.

Kuhnert, K.W., Sims, R.R. and Lahey, M.A. (1989). The relationship between job insecurity and employee health. *Groups and Organization Studies*, 14, 399–410.

Lai, J.C.L. and Wong, W.S. (1998). Optimism and coping with unemployment among Hong Kong Chinese women. *Journal of Research in Personality*, 32(4), 454–79.

Landsbergis, P.A., Cahill, J. and Schnall, P. (1999). The impact of lean production and related new systems of work organization on worker health. *Journal of Occupational Health Psychology*, 4(2), 108–30.

Langens, T.A. and Mose, E. (2006). Coping with unemployment: Relationships between duration of unemployment, coping styles, and subjective well-being. *Journal of Applied Biobehavioral Research*, 11(3–4), 189–208.

Larson, J.H., Wilson, S.M. and Beley, R. (1994). The impact of job insecurity on marital and family relationships. *Family Relations: An Interdisciplinary Journal of Applied Family Studies*, 43(2), 138–43.

Latack, J.C. 1986. Coping with job stress: Measures and future directions for scale development. *Journal of Applied Psychology*, 71, 377–85.

Lau, B. and Knardahl, S. (2008). Perceived job insecurity, job predictability, personality, and health. *Journal of Occupational and Environmental Medicine / American College of Occupational and Environmental Medicine*, 50(2), 172–81.

Layton, C. (1987). Externality and unemployment: Change score analyses on Rotter's locus of control scale for male school-leavers and men facing redundancy. *Personality and Individual Differences*, 8(1), 149–52.

Leana, C.R. and Feldman, D.C. (1995). Finding new jobs after a plant closing: Antecedents and outcomes of the occurrence and quality of reemployment. *Human Relations*, 48(12), 1381–401.

Lucero, S.M. (2013). *Job Insecurity and Religious/Spiritual Coping: Sacred Resources for Employment Uncertainty*. Unpublished doctoral dissertation.

Luthans, B.C., Luthans, K.W. and Avey, J.B. (2014). Building the leaders of tomorrow: The development of academic psychological capital. *Journal of Leadership & Organizational Studies*, 21(2), 191–9.

Luthans, F. (2002a). The need for and meaning of positive organizational behavior. *Journal of Organizational Behavior*, 23, 695–706.

Luthans, F. (2002b). Positive organizational behavior: Developing and managing psychological strengths. *Academy of Management Executive*, 16(1), 57–72.

Luthans, F., Avey, J.B., Avolio, B.J. and Peterson, S.J. (2010). The development and resulting performance impact of positive psychological capital. *Human Resource Development Quarterly*, 21(1), 41–67.

Luthans, F., Avolio, B.J., Avey, J.B. and Norman, S.M. (2007). Positive psychological capital: Measurement and relationship with performance and satisfaction. *Personnel Psychology*, 60(3), 541–72.

Luthans, F., Avey, J.B., Avolio, B.J., Norman, S.M. and Combs, G.M. (2006). Psychological capital development: Toward a micro-intervention. *Journal of Organizational Behavior*, 27(3), 387–93.

Maddi, S.R. (1987). Hardiness training at Illinois Bell Telephone. In P. Opatz (ed.), *Health Promotion Evaluation* (pp. 101–15). Stevens Point: National Wellness Institute.

Mak, A. and Mueller, J. (October 1, 2000). Job insecurity, coping resources and personality dispositions in occupational strain. *Work & Stress*, 14(4), 312–28.

Masten, A.S. (2001). Ordinary magic: Resilience processes in development. *American Psychologist*, 56, 227–39.

Masten, A.S., Cutuli, J.J., Herbers, J.E. and Reed, M.-G.J. (2009). Resilience in development. In C.R. Snyder and S.J. Lopez (eds), *Oxford Handbook of Positive Psychology* (2nd edn). Oxford: Oxford University Press, 117–31.

Mauno, S. and Kinnunen, U. (2002). Perceived job insecurity among dual-earner couples: Do its antecedents vary according to gender, economic sector and the measure used? *Journal of Occupational and Organizational Psychology*, 75(3), 295–314.

McCrae, R.R. and Costa, P.T. (1994). The stability of personality: Observations and evaluations. *Current Directions in Psychological Science*, 3(6), 173–5.

McKee-Ryan, F.M., Song, Z., Wanberg, C.R. and Kinicki, A.J. (2005). Psychological and physical well-being during unemployment: A meta-analytic study. *Journal of Applied Psychology*, 90, 53–76.

Millard, M.L. (2011). Psychological net worth: Finding the balance between psychological capital and psychological debt. *Theses, Dissertations, & Student Scholarship: Agricultural Leadership, Education & Communication Department.* Paper 29. Available at: http://digitalcommons.unl.edu/aglecdiss/29. Accessed 16th December 2014.

Muñoz de Bustillo, R. and De Pedraza, P. (2010). Determinants of job insecurity in 5 European countries. *European Journal of Industrial Relations*, 16, 5–20.

Näswall, K., Sverke, M. and Hellgren, J. (2005). The moderating role of personality characteristics on the relationship between job insecurity and strain. *Work & Stress*, 19(1), 37–49.

Oglensky, M.I. (2014). *A Quantitative Study of the Correlational Impact of Psychological Capital on Job Search Intensity as Measured by Job Search Behaviors.* Doctoral disseration. Retrieved from ProQuest Dissertations and Theses (Accession Order No. AAI3588173).

Orpen, C. (1994). The effects of self-esteem and personal control on the relationship between job insecurity and psychological well-being. *Social Behavior and Personality: An International Journal*, 22(1), 53–5.

Pargament, K.I., Smith, B.W., Koenig, H.G. and Perez, L. (1998). Patterns of positive and negative religious coping with major life stressors. *Journal for the Scientific Study of Religion*, 37, 710–24.

Parkes, K.R. (1990). Coping, negative affectivity, and the work environment: Additive and interactive predictors of mental health. *The Journal of Applied Psychology*, 75(4), 399–409.

Parkes, K.R. (1994). Personality and coping as moderators of work stress processes: Models, methods and measures. *Work and Stress*, 8(2), 110.

Patton, W. and Noller, P. (1984). Unemployment and youth: A longitudinal study. *Australian Journal of Psychology*, 36(3), 399–413.

Peterson, S.J., Luthans, F., Avolio, B., Walumbwa, F. and Zhang, Z. (2011). Psychological capital and employee performance: A latent growth modeling approach. *Personnel Psychology*, 64, 427–50.

Pollard, T.M. (2001). Changes in mental well-being, blood pressure and total cholesterol levels during workplace reorganization: The impact of uncertainty. *Work and Stress*, 15, 14–28.

Probst, T.M. (1998). *Antecedents and Consequences of Job Security: Development and Test of an Integrated Model.* Unpublished doctoral dissertation. University of Illinois at Urbana-Champaign.

Probst, T.M. (2000). Wedded to the job: Moderating effects of job involvement on the consequences of job insecurity. *Journal of Occupational Health Psychology*, 5, 63–73.

Probst, T.M. (2002). The impact of job insecurity on employee work attitudes, job adaptation, and organizational withdrawal behaviors. In J.M. Brett and F. Drasgow (eds), *The Psychology of Work: Theoretically Based Empirical Research* (pp. 141–68). Hillsdale: Lawrence Erlbaum.

Probst, T.M. (2003). Exploring employee outcomes of organizational restructuring: A Solomon four-group study. *Group & Organization Management*, 28, 416–39.

Probst, T.M. (2007). Self-efficacy for adapting to organizational transitions: It helps, but only when the prospects are bright. In M. Pearle (ed.), *Industrial Psychology Research Trends* (pp. 9–21). Hauppauge: Nova Science Publishers.

Probst, T.M. and Brubaker, T.L. (2001). The effects of job insecurity on employee safety outcomes: Cross-sectional and longitudinal explorations. *Journal of Occupational Health Psychology*, 6(2), 139–59.

Probst, T.M. and Lawler, J. (2006). Cultural values as moderators of the outcomes of job insecurity: The role of individualism and collectivism. *Applied Psychology: An International Review*, 55, 234–54.

Probst, T.M. and Strand, P. (2010). Perceiving and responding to job insecurity: A workplace spirituality perspective. *Journal of Management, Spirituality and Religion*, 7, 135–56.

Probst, T.M., Barbaranelli, C. and Petitta, L. (2013). The relationship between job insecurity and accident under-reporting: A test in two countries. *Work & Stress*, 27(4), 383–402.

Probst, T.M., Stewart, S., Gruys, M.L. and Tierney, B.W. (2007). Productivity, counterproductivity, and creativity: The ups and downs of job insecurity. *Journal of Occupational and Organizational Psychology*, 80, 479–97.

Roskies, E. and Louis-Guerin, C. (1990). Job insecurity in managers: Antecedents and consequences. *Journal of Organizational Behavior*, 11, 345–59.

Roskies, E., Louis-Guerin, C. and Fournier, C. (1993). Coping with job insecurity: How does personality make a difference? *Journal of Organizational Behavior*, 14, 617–30.

Rotter, J.B. (1966). Generalized expectancies for internal versus external control of reinforcement. *Psychological Monographs*, 80(1), 1–28.

Safaria, T., bin Othman, A. and Abdul Wahab, M.N. (2010). Religious coping, job insecurity and job stress among Javanese academic staff: A moderated regression analysis. *International Journal of Psychological Studies*, 2(2), 159–69.

Saks, A.M. (2006). Multiple predictors and criteria of job search success. *Journal of Vocational Behavior*, 68(3), 400–415.

Saks, A.M. and Ashforth, B.E. (2000). Change in job search behavior and employment outcomes. *Journal of Vocational Behavior*, 56, 277–87.

Schalk, K. (2013). *Job Loss and the Couple Experience: An Exploration of Coping within the Marital Context*. Doctoral dissertation. Retrieved from ProQuest Dissertations and Theses (Accession Order No. AAINR83544).

Scheier, M.F, Weintraub, J.K. and Carver, C.S. (1986). Coping with stress: Divergent strategies of optimists and pessimists. *Journal of Personality and Social Psychology*, 51, 1257–64.

Schmit, M.J., Amel, E.L. and Ryan, A.M. (1993). Self-reported assertive job-seeking behaviors of minimally educated job hunters. *Personnel Psychology*, 46, 105–24.

Schreurs, B.H.J., van Emmerik, H., De Cuyper, N., Probst, T.M., van den Heuvel, M. and Demerouti, E. (2014). Faith at work: Does religion buffer or exacerbate the negative effects of job insecurity? *Career Development International*, 19(7), 755–78.

Schwartz, S.H., Melech, G., Lehmann, A., Burgess, S., Harris, M. and Owens, V. (2001). Extending the cross-cultural validity of the theory of basic human values with a different method of measurement. *Journal of Cross-Cultural Psychology*, 32(5), 519–42.

Seibert, S.E., Crant, J.M., and Kraimer, M.L. (1999). Proactive personality and career success. *Journal of Applied Psychology*, 84, 416–27.

Seligman, M.E.P. (1998). *Learned Optimism: How to Change Your Mind and Your Life* (2nd edn). New York: Pocket Books.

Snyder, C.R. (2000). The past and possible futures of hope. *Journal of Social and Clinical Psychology*, 19, 11–28.

Snyder, C.R., Irving, L. and Anderson, J.R. (1991). Hope and health: Measuring the will and the ways. In C.R. Snyder and D.R. Forsyth (eds.), *Handbook of Social and Clinical Psychology: The Health Perspective*. Elmsford: Pergamon Press, 285–305.

Snyder, C.R., Sympson, S.C., Ybasco, F.C., Borders, T.F., Babyak, M.A. and Higgins, R.L. (1996). Development and validation of the State Hope Scale. *Journal of Personality and Social Psychology*, 70(2), 321–35.

Spector, P.E. and O'Connell, B.J. (1994). The contribution of personality traits, negative affectivity, locus of control and Type A to the subsequent reports of job stressors and job strains. *Journal of Occupational and Organizational Psychology*, 67(1), 1–12.

Spurgeon, A., Jackson, C.A. and Beach, J.R. (2001). The Life Events Inventory: Re-scaling based on an occupational sample. *Occupational Medicine*, 51(4), 287–93.

Srivastava, S., John, O.P., Gosling, S.D. and Potter, J. (2003). Development of personality in early and middle adulthood: Set like plaster or persistent change? *Journal of Personality and Social Psychology*, 84, 1041–53.

Steiner, C. and Perry, P. (1997). *Achieving Emotional Literacy: A Personal Program to Increase Your Emotional Intelligence*. New York: Avon Books.

Ström, S. (2002). Unemployment and gendered divisions of domestic labor. *Acta Sociologica*, 45, 89–104.

Sverke, M., Hellgren, J. and Näswall, K. (January 1, 2002). No security: A meta-analysis and review of job insecurity and its consequences. *Journal of Occupational Health Psychology*, 7(3), 242–64.

Tombaugh, J.R. and White, L.P. (1990). Downsizing: An empirical assessment of survivors' perceptions in a post-layoff environment. *Organization Development*, 8(2), 32–43.

Triandis, H.C. (1995). *Individualism & Collectivism*. Boulder: Westview Press.

Tugade, M.M. and Fredrickson, B.L. (2004). Resilient individuals use positive emotions to bounce back from negative emotional experiences. *Journal of Personality and Social Psychology*, 86(2), 320–33.

Uysal, S.D., and Pohlmeier, W. (2011). Unemployment duration and personality. *Journal of Economic Psychology*, 32, 980–92.

Vakola, M., Tsaousis, I. and Nikolaou, I. (2004). The role of emotional intelligence and personality variables on attitudes toward organisational change. *Journal of Managerial Psychology*, 19(2), 88–110.

Van Harrison, R. (1978). Person-environment fit and job stress. In C.L. Cooper and R. Payne (eds), *Stress at Work* (pp. 175–205). New York: Wiley.

Van Hoye, G. and Lootens, H. (2013). Coping with unemployment: Personality, role demands, and time structure. *Journal of Vocational Behavior*, 82(2), 85–95.

Vishwanath, T. (1989). Job search, stigma effect, and escape rate from unemployment. *Journal of Labor Economics*, 7(4), 487–502.

Voydanoff, P. (1990). Economic distress and family relations: A review of the eighties. *Journal of Marriage and the Family*, 52(4), 1099–115.

Wanberg, C.R. (1997). Antecedents and outcomes of coping behaviors among unemployed and reemployed individuals. *Journal of Applied Psychology*, 82(5), 731.

Wanberg, C.R., Kanfer, R. and Rotundo, M. (1999). Unemployed individuals: Motives, job-search competencies, and job-search constraints as predictors of job seeking and reemployment. *Journal of Applied Psychology*, 84(6), 897–910.

Warr, P.B. (1987). *Work, Unemployment, and Mental Health*. Oxford: Clarendon Press.

Watson, D. and Clark, L.A. (1984). Negative affectivity: The disposition to experience aversive emotional states. *Psychological Bulletin*, 96, 465–90.

Watson, D. and Naragon, K. (2012). Positive affectivity: The disposition to experience positive emotional states. *Oxford Handbooks Online*. Available at: http://www.oxfordhandbooks.com/view/10.1093/oxfordhb/9780195187243.001.0001/oxfordhb-9780195187243-e-019. Accessed 11th July 2014.

Watson, D. and Pennebaker, J.W. (1989). Health complaints, stress, and distress: Exploring the central role of negative affectivity. *Psychological Review*, 96(2), 234–54.

Westman, M., Etzion, D. and Danon, E. (2001). Job insecurity and crossover of burnout in married couples. *Journal of Organizational Behavior*, 22, 467–81.

Zinnbauer, B.J., Pargament, K.I., Cole, B., Rye, M.S., Butter, E.M., Belavich, T.G., Hipp, K.M., Scott, A.B. and Kadar, J.L. (1997). Religion and spirituality: Unfuzzying the fuzzy. *Journal for the Scientific Study of Religion*, 36(4), 549–64.

16

Coping after Job Loss: Impact of Unemployment on Work Attitudes of the Reemployed

Tabea Scheel and Kathleen Otto

Introduction

There is overwhelming evidence in the literature to date that unemployment alters people's lives (Wanberg 2012); it can affect their leisure activities, their engagement in long-lasting relationships and even their family development (e.g., Eckert-Jaffe and Solaz 2001; Jahoda 1997). Undoubtedly though, most of the profound research on unemployment is concerned with its detrimental effects on physical and mental health (e.g., McKee-Ryan, Song, Wanberg and Kinicki 2005; Murphy and Athanasou 1999; Paul and Moser 2009), but also on future employment prospects related to job search behavior (e.g., Kanfer, Wanberg and Kantrowitz 2001). However, little systematic research has been conducted on the attitudes toward work and work behavior of people who have more or less successfully coped with former unemployment, i.e., the reemployed. Additionally, the findings that exist are heterogeneous or deal only with very specific aspects (e.g., people with mental illness), questioning its generalizability and calling for future research.

The aim of this chapter is to summarize and integrate the most substantial findings on the impact of unemployment on work attitudes and behavior. In particular, the chapter was guided by the research question, whether unemployment affects coping abilities and strategies (e.g., seeking social support) and related variables. According to Conservation of Resources (COR) theory (Hobfoll 1989), individuals strive to obtain, retain, foster and protect those things in life they centrally value – such as a secure and satisfying job. In order to avoid stress, individuals strive to gain resources, and then try to conserve and guard these resources (Hobfoll and Shirom 2001). Stress accrues if (a) individuals are threatened by a loss of resources, if (b) they actually lose resources, or if (c) the gaining of resources fails (Hobfoll 1989). If a person lost his or her job in the past – as is the case for reemployed – this person had to cope with this stress-provoking situation by searching for other resources. Particularly social support symbolizes a resource at the meta-level as it benefits employees by enhancing intra-individual resources on external capacities. Granovetter (1974) could demonstrate that those who successfully re-entered the labour market were those with more of those social ties (Brown 2000; Zippay

1990). As these findings exemplify it seems to be logical to assume that also coping with a new job (i.e., in case of reemployment) with respect to work attitudes and work behavior might be affected by prior unemployment experiences.

Unemployment has become an ever-present phenomenon across all countries. The financial crisis in 2007 led to high unemployment figures worldwide, the likes of which were last reported during the time of the Great Depression (i.e., the 1930s). Overall, 210 million people were registered as unemployed in the third quarter of 2010 reflecting an increase of 30 million since the financial crisis started (International Monetary Fund and International Labour Organization 2010). If more people experience unemployment, the number of reemployed people subsequently rises – thus, whether and how their future work attitudes and behavior are affected becomes of greater importance at a personal and organizational level. Prejudices exist against unemployed people in relation to performance; employers are reluctant to employ formerly unemployed individuals as they are assumed to perform worse than their employed counterparts – otherwise they would surely be employed (e.g., Oberholzer-Gee 2008). Kugler and Saint-Paul (2004) state that "firms increasingly prefer hiring employed workers, who are less likely to be lemons" (p. 553). But is it really the case that reemployed people have worse work attitudes and show more negative work behavior? This question remains unanswered to date. Our chapter provides initial evidence of impaired work attitudes and behavior of the reemployed but further studies with a suitable design are nevertheless warranted.

Influence of Unemployment on Work Attitudes and Work Behavior of the Reemployed

How much evidence can be found in the literature for declined employability? Specifically, the review of the evidence for loss of competency during unemployment time is drawn on; this section deals with the consequences of unemployment in connection to work attitudes and behavior once reemployed. Unemployment itself is commonly associated with stigmas (Kulik 2001), such as laziness and apathy, or is even seen as a "contagious disease" (Letkemann 2002). Accordingly, the psychological consequences of unemployment are regularly considered to be accompanied by reduced performance, for example due to outdating of human capital or learned helplessness (e.g., Cole, Daly and Mak 2009). As Jackson (1999) pointed out, unemployed individuals have fewer opportunities to use their skills than employed individuals. In today's working world, these skills include not only having expert knowledge but also other abilities such as working in teams, solving conflicts, thinking flexibly (which might also be relevant to "survive" in job interviews), etc. Research from the field of developmental psychology suggests that competencies which cannot be practiced diminish over time. Hence, in line with the so-called "disuse hypothesis" (e.g., Berkowitz and Green 1965), being unable to advance one's skills and use one's competencies regularly could possibly lead to a shattered self-efficacy, which consequently impacts work attitude and behavior. Note that the term "work behavior" consists of dimensions such as work engagement, proactivity or creativity. We expect that the experience of (repeated) unemployment will have an influence on such motivational or emotional aspects of work behavior.

While findings show that unemployment indeed affects work attitudes and work behavior, for most of the reemployed negative effects of unemployment seem to vanish within a short period of time. Most studies in this field deal with psychological consequences such as (1) self-confidence and coping, (2) employability, (3) networking, (4) work attitudes (satisfaction, commitment, trust, work values) and (5) mental health.

Self-Confidence and Coping

Self-confidence and coping behavior were shown to be important for mental health and to be relevant for the reemployed (Wanberg 1997). In a longitudinal study, Waters and Moore (2002) compared employed, unemployed and reemployed individuals. The latter were unemployed at the first measure and reemployed at the second measure (after six months). In comparison with their unemployment phase, the reemployed had higher self-confidence, felt less deprived and showed a stronger solution-oriented coping behavior. However, findings pointed to selection processes, since the future reemployed already differed from the continuously unemployed when they were unemployed: future reemployed already indicated better cognitive appraisal of their situation, e.g., lower latent deprivation (i.e., corresponding with basic human needs and thus sustaining well-being and mental health; Paul and Batinic 2010) at the first measure and a less affective or more solution-oriented coping strategy than the continuously unemployed. Career decision-making and career confidence positively predicted reemployment quality (Koen, Klehe, Van Vianen, Zikic and Nauta 2010). Waters and Moore (2002), however, did not find any differences in self-confidence between future reemployed and continuously unemployed. Since employability, or "work specific (pro)active adaptability" (Fugate, Kinicki and Ashforth 2004, p. 14), partially predicts self-confidence during unemployment (McArdle, Waters, Briscoe and Hall 2007), a comparable employability of continuously unemployed and future reemployed could be suggested.

Employability

In a study with Australian unemployed individuals, employability was operationalized with the dimensions adaptation ability, career identity and social capital (McArdle et al. 2007). In this context, adaptation ability can be described as a pro-social personality and flexible mentality, career identity as one's consciousness of one's own identity and self-efficacy related to the formation of one's own employment biography, and social capital as networking and the use of social support. In the study by McArdle et al. (2007), employability did not only partially explain self-confidence, but was also relevant for predicting job search intensity and reemployment: unemployed people with higher employability were reemployed faster. Employability explained 16% of the variance in relation to reemployment in a longitudinal design and 39% in relation to job search behavior indicating that the employability of the unemployed influenced the probability of reemployment. Interestingly, job search activities were not related to reemployment success. In contrast, Koen et al. (2010) found that the use of a focused and exploratory strategy in job search contributed to the number of job offers, but also that the use of an exploratory strategy reduced the quality of reemployment eight months later.

However, Koen, Klehe and Van Vianen (2013) showed that employability fosters job search and the chance on finding reemployment among long-term unemployed people (i.e., the facets human capital, social capital and career identity), and reemployment interventions helped to develop people's employability (though effects were small). Thus, employability is significant in the reemployment process and interventions targeted at employability might be beneficial even among long-term unemployed. Though Koen et al. (2013) demonstrated that gain of competency (=employability/human capital) is connected to finding reemployment above and beyond possible barriers, those studied barriers are personal (e.g., physical problems) and situational factors (e.g., lack of transportation to work or job interviews; Koen et al. 2013) and do not include stigmatization by employers and/or society.

Networking

Networking, as an aspect of social capital, showed no longitudinal association with reemployment or job search intensity of unemployed Australian individuals in the study mentioned above (McArdle et al. 2007). The authors concluded that the advantages of networking supposedly tapped its full potential after about six months, since longer unemployment comes with social withdrawal (McArdle et al. 2007). The authors concluded that support with networking is an important intervention goal. However, Wanberg, Kanfer and Banas (2000) did not find incremental prediction by networking intensity of reemployment or reemployment speed when intensity of use of other job-search methods was considered – and the sample had a mean of only 61 days unemployed. Thus, networking may be beneficial for well-being during times of unemployment, but it does not generally seem crucial for gaining reemployment.

Work Attitudes

Life and job satisfaction. Satisfaction, especially with work, is one of the most often examined work attitudes, and its association with work behavior and work attitudes is well proven (see meta-analyses: Bruk-Lee, Khoury, Nixon, Goh and Spector 2009; Judge and Bono 2001). Since unemployed people – due to lack of employment – cannot state their current job satisfaction, the related construct of life satisfaction is often used to compare the respondents' phases of unemployment and reemployment. Additionally, because of spillover effects (e.g., Heller, Judge and Watson 2002), job and life satisfaction are positively correlated (Wanberg, Carmichael and Downey 1999).

Life satisfaction of most unemployed people increases with re-entry into employment. But it is also related to the quality of reemployment. The lack of latent (subjective) functions of work impairs life satisfaction (Grün, Hauser and Rhein 2010). Grün et al. (2010) examined the influence of the change of unemployment to full-time employment on life satisfaction under consideration of the job quality (self-reported job satisfaction, income, kind of contract, fit of person and work demands) within West German data of the Socioeconomic Panel. Over 20% of the respondents felt worse after being reemployed, whereas over 50% felt better. For most of the reemployed people, life satisfaction was still higher after two years in comparison to life satisfaction of the continuously unemployed, even if work was badly paid or terminated. However, this did not apply to reemployed people with low job satisfaction and for those who had a worse job than before. Based on those findings, the authors proposed a threshold model predicting that there will not be a positive effect of reemployment on life satisfaction if at least four of six quality aspects (kind of activity, earnings, advancement possibilities, workload, working hours' regulations, use of professional knowledge) are rated as worse in comparison to the prior job.

Impaired quality of reemployment decreases job satisfaction. Feldman, Leana and Bolino (2002) reported lower job satisfaction in alternative jobs for dismissed managers with higher levels of underemployment (meaning lower pay, working at lower levels of the organizational hierarchy, less opportunities to use one's own abilities and competencies). Thus, subjective underemployment was negatively associated with satisfaction with the new job after one year (McKee-Ryan, Virick, Prussia, Harvey and Lilly 2009).

Interestingly, job satisfaction with former employment influenced the perception of unemployment and showed that favorable conditions can persist (Wanberg et al. 1999). However, it has to be acknowledged that optimism was a better variable for explaining unemployment perceptions. Further, high job satisfaction prior to unemployment did not lead to more negative reactions toward unemployment than lower job satisfaction (Wanberg et al. 1999).

Commitment and trust. Commitment, another central work attitude, was included in studies with a focus on underemployment. The main problem associated with underemployment is the under-use of an individual's own acquired abilities, with the implications of risking deteriorating competencies. In a cross-sectional study of Feldman et al. (2002), dismissed managers not only indicated lower job satisfaction in alternative jobs with underemployment but indicated worse job attitudes more generally: the fewer the opportunities to use one's own skills and abilities (loss of competency), the less commitment and trust that was shown by prior managers and the higher their ongoing job search behavior and career striving. Whereas imminent loss of competencies correlated negatively with all work attitudes due to a lack of possibilities of applying one's own abilities, a position in the hierarchy at a lower level than previous to the dismissal was only connected with less commitment. The level of underemployment was also related to relative deprivation (i.e., wanting more and having the feeling of deserving more), which was, in turn, associated with work attitudes: thus, relative deprivation mediated the relationship between underemployment and work attitudes.

The conditions (subjective appraisal as well as voluntariness of dismissals) under which people become unemployed determined employment success (e.g., commitment, intention to quit, trust) and employment quality (McKee-Ryan et al. 2009; Waters 2007). McKee-Ryan et al. (2009), in a longitudinal study over one year, differentiated between objective (e.g., lower income) and subjective (relative deprivation, see Feldman et al. 2002) underemployment. Subjective underemployment after one year was not only negatively related to satisfaction with the new job but it was also associated with less affective commitment and higher intention to quit. Subjective underemployment therefore mediated the relationship between objective underemployment and employment success (affective organizational commitment, intention to quit).

The voluntariness of dismissals also has implications for the level of commitment: results of a longitudinal study by Waters (2007) showed that of those who were reemployed three months later, the involuntarily dismissed had a lower organizational commitment in comparison to the voluntarily dismissed. The author discussed the lower quality of reemployment for the involuntarily dismissed as a reason for their lower commitment as compared to those who were voluntarily dismissed. Alternatively, broken trust may explain the relation between voluntariness of dismissal and commitment.

Work values. Changes in central work values (work centrality, work involvement and the right to work) due to unemployment experiences were examined in a longitudinal study lasting 15 months (Isaksson, Johansson, Bellaagh and Sjöberg 2004). No specific effects of a change in employment status (e.g., from unemployment into employment) on work values were found, for women or for men (Isaksson et al. 2004).

Mental Health

Mental health plays an important role in the successful handling of work demands. Unemployment is connected to a worsening of mental health (Paul and Moser 2009), but good mental health is important to have any chance in the application process (e.g., Paul and Moser 2009; Vinokur and Schul 2002) and is therefore presumed to be a relevant criterion for reemployment. Overall, successful re-entry into employment seemed to enhance mental health (Schuring, Mackenbach, Voorham and Burdorf 2011). It should be considered, though, that this direct relationship depends on appraisal and voluntariness of prior dismissal, on the one hand, and on the quality of reemployment, on the other hand (McKee-Ryan et al. 2009; Waters 2007).

Whereas the level of work involvement did not influence the well-being of unemployed people, employment status turned out to be relevant: men indicated more psychic and psychosomatic complaints when they were unemployed than when they were employed (Isaksson et al. 2004). Health (physical functioning, but not mental health) influenced the probability of reemployment for employable welfare recipients in a follow-up examination after six months (Schuring et al. 2011): concordant with expectations, worse health led to a higher risk of remaining unemployed. Reemployment overall improved perceived health status (general psychological functions, social functions, vitality, physical pain, role limitations through emotional as well as physical problems), but this effect was particularly true in the case of mental health and less so in the case of functionality. The study provided evidence that reemployment can change self-reported health within a very short timeframe.

According to a study by McKee-Ryan et al. (2009), dismissed employees might even react with symptoms of posttraumatic stress disorder. The perceived (un-)fairness of dismissal and the (negative) appraisal of dismissals determined the respective clinical pathology. Waters (2007) also showed that individuals who were voluntarily dismissed experience lower depressive symptoms than involuntarily dismissed (when controlling for self-confidence). Of those reemployed three months later, the involuntarily dismissed were more depressed and indicated lower quality of reemployment. In contrast, while the depression values of the voluntarily dismissed decreased, those of the involuntarily dismissed did not. Wanberg (1997) examined the relationship of self-confidence, perceived control of the situation (chances of reemployment) and optimism on short-term and long-term mental health as well as on the probability of reemployment, whereas appraisal behavior (proactive search, non-work organization, positive self-assessment, distancing from loss, work devaluation) was analyzed as a mediating variable. For people with a lower control of situation (i.e., lower chance of reemployment) proactive job search behavior was negatively related to mental health and devaluation of loss was related to lower probability of reemployment. Devaluation of loss with high control of the situation, however, had beneficial coping effects in connection to reemployment. Only self-confidence, not control of situation, was positively related to short-term mental health. Both mental health at time 1, as well as reemployment, were significant predictors for mental health at time 2.

However, the effects of unemployment on mental health seem to depend on moderators such as the overall economic situation of the respective labor markets. A recent study in a very favorable labor market (Luxembourg, in terms of economic development, equality of revenue, level of protection through social security, unemployment rate, rate of job creation) did not confirm negative changes of mental health after six and 12 months of unemployment (Houssemand and Meyers 2011). Furthermore, mental health (i.e., self-esteem, psychological distress, perceived stress, depressive symptoms) did not predict employment status six and 12 months after becoming unemployed. Thus, selection and causality processes likewise are not supported, however, specific contexts of labor markets urgently need to be investigated. For instance, Skärlund, Ahs and Westerling (2012) report a mediating role of social and economic factors for the negative relationship between general subjective mental distress and rate of reemployment amongst newly unemployed individuals.

Thus, if social and economic context is favorable and associated with a high level of social protection, mental health seems less jeopardized by unemployment.

Discussion

With regards to the consequences of unemployment for work attitudes and work behavior it can generally be concluded, on the one hand, that unemployed individuals with more beneficial starting positions (like being healthier) were more likely to be reemployed at the second point of measurement. On the other hand, reemployment itself led to a (further) improvement in central job and organizational attitudes (e.g., job satisfaction, commitment) and health variables (e.g., depression, physical symptoms).

While there is only little evidence that unemployment leads to worsened work attitudes and behaviors in case of reemployment, the circumstances seem to have major impact on future work attitudes and behavior – loss of competency seems to be a minor aspect, given the many relevant situational factors. Thus, the nature of the prior dismissal (voluntariness, fairness), as well as the quality of reemployment (underemployment), have to be considered when judging work attitudes. Also, the economic situation of the labor market may have influences on the magnitude of the impact of unemployment on work attitudes and behaviors.

Unemployment experiences damage future employment biographies – due to a decline of employability? Based on assumptions of social identity theory (Tajfel 1974), individuals favor the perceptions, evaluations and behavior of individuals in their in-group than those perceived to be in their out-group. Hence, employers as well as the non-unemployed public might have a tendency to devaluate the out-group, i.e., "the unemployed" by stigmatizing them as being "lazy," for example (Letkemann 2002). Some evidence is in line with stigmatization processes, like the preference of employers hiring (still) employed as compared to (long-term) unemployed people (Oberholzer-Gee 2008). Also, unemployed people are in a low-status group and have highly negative attitudes toward their own group. Thus, their own favoritism of the out-group may be one reason why unemployed people do not have a strong lobby for representing their interests in society (Wahl, Pollai and Kirchler 2013). If stigmatization is a major reason for impaired employment biographies due to episodes of unemployment, the point of competency training is challenged. Rather than action focusing on single unemployed individuals, elucidation at a broad societal level is required, flanked by social-political schemes for an even stronger encouragement of reemployment of unemployed people.

Studies focusing on individual job search training and coping usually disregard the stigmatization effects. Situational focus on learning goals was found to be beneficial for the job search process, leading to more search intentions, more search behavior and higher reemployment probabilities (Van Hooft and Noordzij 2009). The importance of goals in moving from a quantitative orientation of job search to a more qualitative approach is taken up by Van Hooft, Wanberg and van Hoye (2013). Planning of goal establishment, goal pursuit and goal striving (and reflection) are important processes of the "cyclical self-regulatory model of job search process quality" (Van Hooft et al. 2013). However, in their model of antecedents and outcomes of job search quality and potential moderators in these relationships, only "social context" among the situational factors might resemble the stigmatization – but is actually operationalized as social support.

Empirical evidence for personal-circumstantial barriers for long-term unemployed to work is provided not only in terms of stigma but also other physical and psychological barriers to work (e.g., Lindsay 2002; Wanberg, Hough and Song 2002). Based on interviews with 115 job-seekers in a labor market with a low unemployment rate, Lindsay (2002) characterized an "employability gap" as a combination of personal and circumstantial barriers to work. Among these are the lack of sufficiently well paid opportunities or of appropriate opportunities or of information about opportunities, inadequate assistance from public agencies, problems associated with losing benefits, costs related to starting work, lack of access to private transport, costs related to looking for work, health problems, lack access to/cost of public transportation, and lack of access to childcare. Though this supplements the findings by Koen et al.'s study (2013) on impacts of barriers and employability on reemployment, all barriers are self-reported and do not include stigmatization as a broader, situational barrier. The same holds true for the study of Wanberg et al. (2002), reporting multiple factors (barriers) of reemployment success. These factors only explained low variance, leaving room for a possible impact of stigmatization.

Conclusion: Where to Go From Here?

Unemployment seems to be damaging to the work attitudes and work behavior of individuals formerly unemployed by reducing self-confidence and coping ability (e.g., Waters and Moore 2002), impairing life satisfaction (e.g., Grün et al. 2010) and mental health (e.g., Paul and Moser 2009), while central work values seem unaffected (Isaksson et al. 2004). Reemployment depends on employability (e.g., McArdle et al. 2007), and if reemployment leads to underemployment, reductions in commitment and trust are likely (Feldman et al. 2002). Though in most cases only *determinants* of real work behavior are assessed, the pattern suggests an unfavorable impact of unemployment on future work performance.

Besides considering the circumstances surrounding becoming unemployed (e.g., fairness, McKee-Ryan et al. 2009), the activities conducted during unemployment are of interest. A study by Zikic and Klehe (2006) even suggests potentially positive outcomes of job loss for an individual's future career: focusing on specific career adaptability activities, their study found career planning and career exploration influenced reemployment quality. Original evidence of broad sector differences was reported by Dieckhoff (2011), i.e., a lower unemployment risk in the public as compared to the private sector. Details on differences between specific industries are still lacking. Also, cross-cultural differences are at play which need consideration, illustrated by the way part-time employment increases the risk of becoming unemployed in Spain and decreases the same risk in Austria, while employment duration seems to be a protective factor across countries (Dieckhoff 2011). It is possible that the unemployment duration is a more powerful predictor compared to the frequency, as research indicated that the long-term unemployed are at a higher risk of mental health problems, reflected in a higher mortality risk, than continuously employed and short-term unemployed individuals (Grobe 2006).

A subsequent question related to the stigmatization topic is *how others will evaluate formerly unemployed individuals*. It seems to be a fruitful research avenue to explore how others – i.e., employers, direct supervisors and colleagues – evaluate the work attitudes and behavior of the formerly unemployed. Some authors describe that the social network becomes smaller with ongoing unemployment (Jackson 1988; Jones 1991). Whether this decline is due to stigmatization processes needs to be explored.

Note that the introduced findings are partially based on longitudinal studies or a representative population poll (e.g., Socioeconomic Panel), giving some support to the validity of relationships. Still, the findings show that the majority of relevant variables still need further examination to explain the work attitudes and behavior of people with prior unemployment experiences (e.g., performance, involvement, autonomy, motivation, coping, willingness for working overtime). Consequently, future research investigating the justification of stigmatization via relations between unemployment and subsequent work attitudes and work behavior should take into account more direct variables measuring work attitudes and behavior, like overtime, presenteeism, absenteeism, work engagement and performance. Also, a direct comparison of people who have several times, once or never been unemployed is highly recommended. However, if differences regarding work behavior are found between both groups, whether willingness or ability is the reason remains to be assessed. Thus, coping is necessary with regard to employability, but may not always be sufficient, especially when it comes to stigmatization processes.

References

Berkowitz, B. and Green, R.E. (1965). Changes in intellect with age V. Differential changes as functions of time interval and original score. *Journal of Genetic Psychology*, 107, 179–92.

Brown, D.W. (2000). Job searching in a labyrinth of opportunity: The strategies, the contacts, the outcomes. *Journal of Social Behavior and Personality*, 15, 227–42.

Bruk-Lee, V., Khoury, H.A., Nixon, A.E., Goh, A. and Spector, P.E. (2009). Replicating and extending past personality/job satisfaction meta-analyses. *Human Performance*, 22, 156–89.

Cole, K., Daly, A. and Mak, A., (2009). Good for the soul: The relationship between work, wellbeing and psychological capital. *The Journal of Socio-Economics*, 38, 464–74.

Dieckhoff, M. (2011). The effect of unemployment on sebsequent job quality in Europe: A comparative study of four countries. *Acta Sociologica*, 54, 233–49.

Eckert-Jaffe, O. and Solaz, A. (2001). Unemployment, marriage and cohabitation in France. *Journal of Socio-Economics*, 30, 75–98.

Feldman, D.C., Leana, C.R. and Bolino, M.C. (2002). Underemployment and relative deprivation among re-employed executives. *Journal of Occupational and Organizational Psychology*, 75, 453–71.

Fugate, M., Kinicki, A.J. and Ashforth, B.E. (2004). Employability: A psycho-social construct, its dimensions, and applications. *Journal of Vocational Behavior*, 65, 14–68.

Granovetter, M. (1974). *Getting a Job*. Cambridge, MA: Cambridge University Press.

Grobe, T. (2006). Sterben Arbeitslose früher? [Do unemployed people die earlier?] In A. Hollederer, and H. Brand (eds), *Arbeitslosigkeit, Gesundheit und Krankheit* [Unemployment, health and disease] (pp. 75–83). Bern: Huber.

Grün, C., Hauser, W. and Rhein, T. (2010). Is any job better than no job? Life satisfaction and re-employment. *Journal of Labour Research*, 31, 285–306.

Heller, D., Judge, T.A. and Watson, D. (2002). The confounding role of personality and trait affectivity in the relationship between job and life satisfaction. *Journal of Organizational Behavior*, 23, 815–53.

Hobfoll, S.E. (1989). Conservation of resources: A new attempt at conceptualizing stress. *American Psychologist*, 44, 513–24.

Hobfoll, S.E. and Shirom, A. (2001). Conservation of resources theory: Applications to stress and management in the workplace. In R.T. Golembiewski (ed.), *Handbook of organizational behavior* (pp. 57–80). New York: Dekker.

Houssemand, C. and Meyers, R. (2011). Unemployment and mental health in a favorable labor market. *International Journal of Psychology*, 46, 377–85.

International Monetary Fund and International Labour Organization (2010). *The challenges of growth, employment and social cohesion*. Available at: http://www.osloconference2010.org/node/636. Accessed 18th March 2014.

Isaksson, K., Johansson, G., Bellaagh, K. and Sjöberg, A. (2004). Work values among the unemployed: Changes over time and some gender differences. *Scandinavian Journal of Psychology*, 45, 207–14.

Jackson, P.R. (1988). Personal networks, support mobilization and unemployment. *Psychological Medicine*, 18, 397–404.

Jackson, T. (1999). Differences in psychosocial experiences of employed, unemployed, and student samples of young adults. *The Journal of Psychology*, 133, 49–60.

Jahoda, M. (1997). Manifest and latent functions. In N. Nicholson (ed.), *The Blackwell Encyclopedic Dictionary of Organizational Psychology* (pp. 317–18). Oxford: Blackwell.

Jones, L.P. (1991). Unemployment: The effect on social networks, depression, and reemployment opportunities. *Journal of Social Service Research*, 15, 1–22.

Judge, T.A. and Bono, J.E. (2001). Relationship of core self-evaluations traits – self-esteem, generalized self-efficacy, locus of control, and emotional stability – with job satisfaction and job performance: A meta-analysis. *Journal of Applied Psychology*, 86, 80–92.

Kanfer, R., Wanberg, C.R. and Kantrowitz, T.M. (2001). Job search and employment: A personality-motivational analysis and meta-analytic review. *Journal of Applied Psychology*, 86, 837–55.

Koen, J., Klehe, U.-C. and Van Vianen, A.E.M. (2013). Employability among the long-term unemployed: A futile quest or worth the effort? *Journal of Vocational Behavior*, 82, 37–48.

Koen, J., Klehe, U.-C., Van Vianen, A.E.M., Zikic, J. and Nauta, A. (2010). Job-search strategies and reemployment quality: The impact of career adaptability. *Journal of Vocational Behavior*, 77, 126–39.

Kugler, A. and Saint-Paul, G. (2004). How do firing costs affect worker flows in a world with adverse selection? *Journal of Labor Economics*, 22, 553–84.

Kulik, L. (2001). Assessing job search intensity and unemployment-related attitudes among young adults: Intergender differences. *Journal of Career Assessment*, 9, 153–67.

Letkemann, P. (2002). Unemployed professionals, stigma management, and derivative stigmata. *Work, Employment & Society*, 16, 511–22.

Lindsay, C. (2002). Long-term unemployment and the "employability gap": Priorities for renewing Britain's New Deal. *Journal of European Industrial Training*, 26, 411–19.

McArdle, S., Waters, L., Briscoe, J.P. and Hall, D.T. (2007). Employability during unemployment: Adaptability, career identity and human and social capital. *Journal of Vocational Behavior*, 71, 247–64.

McKee-Ryan, F.M., Song, Z., Wanberg, C.R. and Kinicki, A.J. (2005). Psychological and physical well-being during unemployment. A meta-analytic study. *Journal of Applied Psychology*, 90, 53–76.

McKee-Ryan, F.M., Virick, M., Prussia, G.E., Harvey, J. and Lilly, J.D. (2009). Life after the layoff: Getting a job worth keeping. *Journal of Organizational Behavior*, 30, 561–80.

Murphy, C.M. and Athanasou, J.A. (1999). The effect of unemployment on mental health. *Journal of Occupational and Organizational Psychology*, 72, 83–99.

Oberholzer-Gee, F. (2008). Nonemployment stigma as rational herding: A field experiment. *Journal of Economic Behavior & Organization*, 65, 30–40.

Paul, K.I. and Batinic, B. (2010). The need for work: Jahoda's latent functions of employment in a representative sample of the German population. *Journal of Organizational Behavior*, 31, 45–64.

Paul, K.I. and Moser, K. (2009). Unemployment impairs mental health: Meta-analyses. *Journal of Vocational Behavior*, 74, 264–82.

Schuring, M., Mackenbach, J., Voorham, T. and Burdorf, A. (2011). The effect of re-employment on perceived health. *Journal of Epidemiology and Community Health*, 65, 639–44.

Skärlund, M., Ahs, A. and Westerling, R. (2012). Health-related and social factors predicting non-reemployment amongst newly unemployed. *BMC Public Health*, 12, 893–903.

Tajfel, H. (1974). Social identity and intergroup behavior. *Social Science Information*, 13, 65–93.

Van Hooft, E.A.J. and Noordzij, G. (2009). The effects of goal orientation on job search and reemployment: A field experiment among unemployed job seekers. *Journal of Applied Psychology*, 94, 1581–90.

Van Hooft, E.A.J., Wanberg, C.R. and van Hoye, G. (2013). Moving beyond job search quantity: Towards a conceptualization and self-regulatory framework of job seach quality. *Organizational Psychology Review*, 3, 3–40.

Vinokur, A.D. and Schul, Y. (2002). The web of coping resources and pathways to reemployment following a job loss. *Journal of Occupational Health Psychology*, 7, 68–83.

Wahl, I., Pollai, M. and Kirchler, E. (2013). Status, identification and in-group favoritism of the unemployed compared to other social categories. *The Journal of Socio-Economics*, 43, 37–43.

Wanberg, C.R. (1997). Antecedents and outcomes of coping behaviors among unemployed and reemployed individuals. *Journal of Applied Psychology*, 82, 731–44.

Wanberg, C.R. (2012). The individual experience of unemployment. *Annual Review of Psychology*, 63, 369–96.

Wanberg, C.R., Carmichael, H.D. and Downey, R.G. (1999). Satisfaction at last job and unemployment: A new look. *Journal of Organizational Behavior*, 20, 121–31.

Wanberg, C.R., Hough, L.M. and Song, Z. (2002). Predictive validity of a multidisciplinary model of reemployment success. *Journal of Applied Psychology*, 87, 1100–120.

Wanberg, C.R., Kanfer, R. and Banas, J.T. (2000). Predictors and outcomes of networking intensity among unemployed job seekers. *Journal of Applied Psychology*, 85, 491–503.

Waters, L. (2007). Experiential differences between voluntary and involuntary job redundancy on depression, job-search activity, affective employee outcomes and re-employment quality. *Journal of Occupational and Organizational Psychology*, 80, 279–99.

Waters, L.E. and Moore, K.A. (2002). Self-esteem, appraisal and coping: A comparison of unemployed and re-employed people. *Journal of Organizational Behavior*, 23, 593–604.

Zikic, J. and Klehe, U.-C. (2006). Job loss as a blessing in disguise: The role of career exploration and career planning in predicting reemployment quality. *Journal of Vocational Behavior*, 69, 391–409.

Zippay, A. (1990). The limits of intimates: Social networks and economic status among displaced industrial workers. *Journal of Applied Social Sciences*, 15, 75–95.

PART VI
SPECIFIC ISSUES ON PERSONALITY TRAITS AND COPING MECHANISMS

17

Applying Attachment Styles to Workplace Incivility

Michael P. Leiter

Introduction

This chapter explores the potential of attachment theory to contribute to explaining individual variations among members of workgroups in their perception of and reaction to workplace incivility. Attachment anxiety describes an approach to social relationships characterized by low levels of self-confidence. It is proposed that insecure feelings about one's self-worth have the potential to create greater sensitivity to signs of disrespect from others. Attachment avoidance has the potential to weaken employees' participation in workplace social networks, limiting their capacity to participate fully as team members and to benefit from the resources inherent in other members of the workgroup. The potential interaction of attachment styles with workgroup conditions are explored. Recommendations for measurement and future research are explored.

> *Communication: the successful bridging of subjectivities. (Graedon 2014)*

Social dynamics of workgroups make a difference. Organizations, such as hospitals, address complex, multifaceted problems by bringing together people of diverse expertise and capabilities. Ideally, the group establishes an open flow of clear information that members use to address the group's core mission: diagnosing and treating the problem before them.

Most groups appear to work well. They do their work while maintaining a reasonable level of professional demeanor in their social exchanges. Members share information in a matter-of-fact manner with little concern about the risks of unpleasant social exchange. However, some groups encounter persistent difficulties in their social exchanges.

When workgroups encounter problems, the strains are not experienced equally. Individuals report widely different experiences of the social environment of their workgroups. Some member report a high level of civility while other members of the same workgroup report encountering frequency encounters characterized by incivility and disrespect (Leiter, Laschinger, Day, and Gilin-Oore 2011). This study found an average frequency of 0.78 when participants rated on a 0 (never) to 6 (daily) scale the frequency of coworker incivility over the past month. This rating is equivalent to less than one incident per person over the previous month. The frequencies were highly clustered with some individuals reporting many uncivil encounters and others reporting none.

A model of the social context of worklife would be more complete with constructs that explained these variations in members' evaluation of the group's social climate.

Attachment theory proposes attachment styles as persistent approaches to social relationships (Bowlby 1969). People perceive and participate in their social context in accordance with expectations regarding their potential to fulfill innate motivations to find comfort from others (Mikulincer and Florian 1995). On the basis of life-long experience, some develop secure attachment styles that incline them to expect success. In contrast, other people perceive social relationships as fraught with peril.

According to attachment theory, people depart from secure attachment in two ways. One outcome is an anxious attachment style in which people feel insecure about themselves, have a compulsive desire for closeness to others, and have constant concerns about rejection (Mikulincer and Florian 1995). Another resolution is an avoidant attachment style view other people as untrustworthy or deserving of their attention. They maintain emotional distance, preferring relationships with no expectation for intimacy. They have accommodated to a life that provides few opportunities for fulfilling their innate motivation to seek closeness (Miller 2007).

Attachment Styles at Work

It has been proposed that attachment styles often persist through a lifetime, in part because of their self-fulfilling nature (Fraley 2002). By avoiding social contact with others, people with avoidant attachment forego opportunities to experience supportive, trusting relationships (Collins and Read 1990). Experiencing and expressing social anxiety when with others prevents people with anxious attachment styles to develop secure, mutually beneficial relationships (Mikulincer and Florian 1995). In contrast, people with secure attachment styles participate in fulfilling, trusting relationships that confirm their view of the world.

For the most part attachment theory has focused on intimate relationships, but the concepts have been applied to work relationships as well. Hazan and Shaver (1990) applied attachment concepts following Kets de Vries (1991) who argued for the utility of clinical constructs as a means of making sense of some of the irrational qualities of workplaces. That is, through his consulting work Kets de Vries (1991) noted that interactions among managers or between managers and employees at times appeared to operate contrary to pursuing a coherent mission. He proposed that personal dynamics of individuals may interfere with individuals' capacity to work together constructively.

The diversion of the group mission has implications for productivity for the workgroup, its members, and the larger organization. Ideally, the workgroup provides a powerful and expensive resource for pursuing the group's mission. Members of workgroups are expected to interact with one another in a professional manner in accordance with workplace norms for behavior (Pearson, Andersson, and Wegner 2001). When behaving outside of these norms, employees pursue goals that are distinct from and often incompatible with the workgroup's mission. By avoiding appropriate social interaction, they are underutilizing a powerful resource; by behaving uncivilly towards colleagues, they are actively undermining that resource's capacity to operate.

In their initial research Hazan and Shaver (1990) confirmed that securely attached people had a more fulfilling and constructive worklife, reporting greater satisfaction and confirmation from their encounters at work. Securely attached people were healthier and reported better collegial relationships. In contrast, people with anxious attachment reported less pleasant experiences at work. They were more likely to report feeling unfairly evaluated. They reported more disrespect and rejection from colleagues.

PERVASIVENESS OF ATTACHMENT STYLES

An important question is whether attachment styles remain consistent across contexts. That is, do people who behave according to an anxious attachment style in their intimate relationships necessarily behave according to an anxious attachment style at work? Fraley and Shaver (2008) note the relevance of the CAPS (cognitive – affective processing system) approach that posits an "if-then" conditional perspective. Regarding attachment, people may operate according to a conditional rule (if in intimate relationships then people are worthy of trust but if in a work relationship people are untrustworthy). The greater tendency toward avoidance among first-line managers in contrast to their staff members is consistent with advice to maintain an emotional distance from subordinates (e.g., Davidhizar and Farabaugh 1986). Margaret Mead (1978) more colorfully prosed that contemporary workplaces needed incest taboos to restrict the degree of intimacy within the workplace (Case 2008).

MEASURING ATTACHMENT STYLES AT WORK

Both interview and self-report questionnaires have been used to measure attachment styles among adults for many years. One measure is the Adult Attachment Interview (Main, Kaplan, and Cassidy 1985); another measure is the Relationships Questionnaire (Bartholomew and Horowitz 1991). The Experiences in Close Relationships Questionnaire was revised more recently (Fraley, Waller, and Brennan 2000; Wei, Russell, Mallinckrodt, and Vogel 2007) to clarify the two-dimensional structure that underlies attachment theory. These measures focus on personal relationships, consistent with their primary focus as tools to assess attachment styles in family life and romantic relationships (Fraley et al. 2000; Main et al. 1985). This format worked well for the primary focus of attachment research that primarily informed a clinical perspective that had direct application in psychotherapy, especially marital therapy.

Bringing those measures into organizational research encounters important caveats. First, employees who agree to participate in workplace surveys may not intend their agreement to do so to mean that they consent to discussing their personal relationships outside of work. Second, the dynamics that pertain to personal, family, and romantic relationships may be distinct from the dynamics that concern employees' workplace relationships. Although authority relationships at work share some qualities with authority relationships in a family context, they also have clear distinctions in their emotional tone and in the expectations for the relationship. The distinct nature of these feelings and ideas about the limits of workplace relationships in contrast to personal relationships could have a considerable impact on responses to an attachment style questionnaire. Previous measures of attachment styles made little or no reference to workplace relationships, leaving a noticeable gap in assessment tools.

The Short Workplace Attachment Measure (SWAM; Leiter, Price, and Day 2013) was developed to address this gap in workplace attachment styles. This measure specifically addresses workplace attachment in its consistent reference to work relationships. Further, the measure was designed to comprise a small number of items. There are five items for each of the two subscales: anxiety and avoidance. Further, the items are short, direct statements to which respondents respond on a five-point scale from 1 (not at all like me) to 5 (very much like me).

These qualities not only keep the content of the measure within the workplace domain, they follow the standard format that is widely used in workplace surveys. The intention in designing the questionnaire was that it would fit seamlessly into a workplace questionnaire.

Leiter et al. (2013) reported on an application of the scale to 2,045 health care providers. The 10 items divided as expected into two factors that provided a score for each of the two attachment dimensions. The two factors were uncorrelated (r = 0.03, n.s.) and had acceptable internal consistency: Anxiety, α = 0.775; Avoidance, α = 0.783. The two subscales differed in their distribution with the Anxiety scale skewed toward the left with most respondents indicating that the items were not very much like them. In contrast, the avoidance scale had a more normal distribution. The differences in the distributions may reflect the perception among respondents that avoidance is a more acceptable and practical means of managing workplace relationships. That is, maintaining an emotional distance from other people at work is considered acceptable to a point and even a desirable characteristic to a certain extent.

Leiter, Price, and Day (2015) evaluated the validity of the SWAM by examining its association with the quality of workplace relationships reported by participants in a hospital study (N = 1,781). Both attachment anxiety and attachment avoidance were significantly and positively correlated with the frequency of incivility from both supervisors and coworkers. They reported that attachment anxiety was more strongly correlated with both supervisor and coworker incivility than was attachment avoidance. Both attachment anxiety and attachment avoidance were negatively correlated with civility and with psychological safety. These correlations did not differ significantly between attachment anxiety and attachment avoidance.

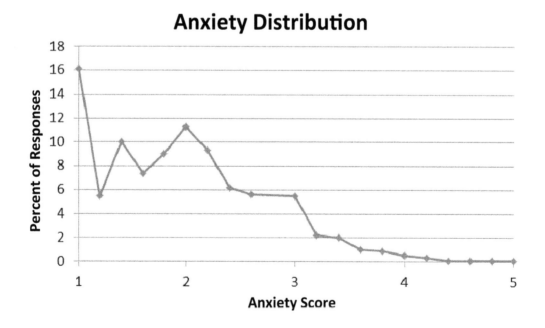

Figure 17.1   Distribution of anxiety on the Short Workplace Attachment Measure

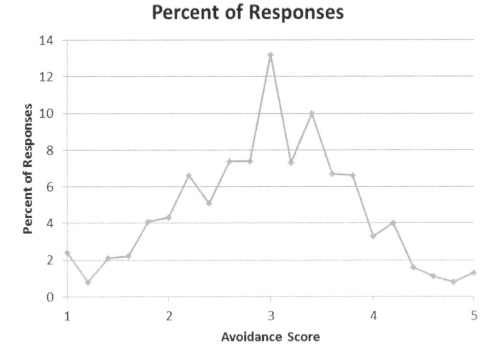

Figure 17.2   Distribution of avoidance on the Short Workplace Attachment Measure

ATTACHMENT STYLES AND PSYCHOLOGICAL SAFETY

One way in which personal characteristics contribute to furthering knowledge in organizational psychology is through moderating the relationship of other constructs. As noted at the beginning of this chapter, a persistent question is research on civility and incivility among members of workgroups is explaining the variation in experiences within workgroups. Although some of the variability among workgroup members on their ratings of workgroup civility and incivility may reflect their distinct participation in the social network, some variability may reflect personal qualities of the individuals. That is, some individuals may encounter more coworker incivility because they are not part of the dominant clique within the workgroup while others report lower levels of incivility because they are generally well regarded. To that extent part of the differences observed among individuals reflect actual differences in the sorts of social encounters they experience day to day. However, part of that variability may reflect personal differences in how individuals perceive and interpret the social behavior of other workgroup members. Differences in social perception may influence the frequency with which individuals perceive incivility but, more importantly, it may influence the extent to which incidents of incivility have an emotional impact on the recipient of these behaviors. That form of moderating effect would point towards the processes that underlie members' experience of their workgroups.

Leiter, Price, and Day (2015) demonstrated the moderating effect of attachment anxiety on the relationship of coworker incivility with psychological safety. The shape of this interaction (see Figure 17.3) is that while low psychological safety is clearly associated with greater coworker incivility, this relationship is especially strong for employees who are high on attachment anxiety.

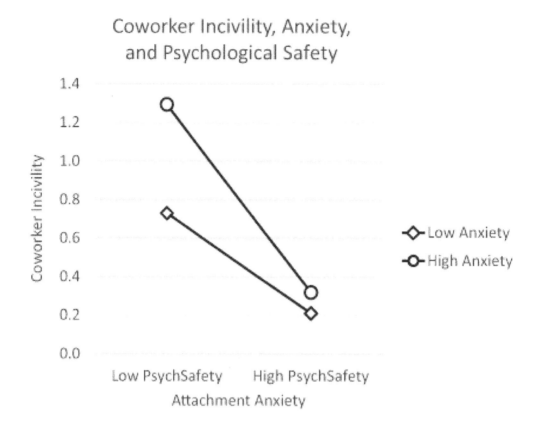

Figure 17.3   **Interaction of attachment anxiety on the relationship of psychological safety and coworker incivility**

This finding is one step towards identifying ways in which personal characteristics interact with social contexts to shape employees' interpretation of events. Incivility is not an absolute quality. Defining a behavior as uncivil requires an interpretation. This feature is especially relevant when people define the absence of behavior – failure to invite to a group discussion or to respond to a greeting – as uncivil or disrespectful. Regarding explicit behaviors, the recipient makes a judgment of whether the behavior is in violation of workplace norms. Not only do people vary in their understanding of relevant workplace norms, they also vary in the relative importance to assign to each of those norms. One person may attribute an inappropriate behavior as uncivil while a colleague may view the same behavior as a trivial lapse not worthy of notice.

The interaction effect displayed in Figure 17.3 supports the proposition that attachment anxiety may be a personal quality that interacts with situational dynamics (psychological safety) to shape an employee's judgment of the frequency or importance of coworker incivility. It is not surprising that coworker incivility occurs less frequently in psychologically safe work environments. What is noteworthy is that within psychologically unsafe work environments, attachment anxiety is associated with significantly different levels of coworker incivility.

One point that remains to be explored is whether attachment anxiety is associated with strikingly different patterns of social encounters during the workday or whether attachment anxiety is associated with strikingly different interpretations of the social encounters that do occur. It may be that people scoring high on attachment anxiety produce social behavior that is quite different from that of people low on attachment anxiety. Alternatively, their social encounters appear very much the same but their interpretations of those similar encounters differ considerably. Observational research is one method for differentiating these interpretations.

Risk

Social encounters are risky. That is, social encounters may evolve in a variety of ways that cannot be entirely predicted at the beginning of an encounter. People have a huge repertoire of social behaviors from which they may choose to respond to a social overture. Social convention narrows the range of responses somewhat, but even when behaving conventionally, people have room for creative or personalized responses. For example, the usual response to "how are you" is to say "fine, thank you," or one may respond "terrible!" if the response is delivered with some humor or with a genuine plea for sympathy. Social encounters have greater uncertainty when people are willing to go outside of convention. For example, "how are you" may be met with a hostile response: "that is none of your business, and I don't think you have any right to ask me anything at all!" Although such an outcome is unlikely, it is not entirely outside the range of possibility. The point is that the outcome of a social exchange is not entirely predictable.

Risk need not be negative. The primary quality of risk is uncertainty, not simply that bad things can happen. Beneficial outcomes are also uncertain. One could encounter a strikingly positive response to "how are you." The other may respond with genuine gratitude that someone cared enough to ask. The conventional overture could then lead to a fascinating conversation and an exceptionally pleasant social encounter. The overall point is that social encounters are risky in both positive and negative directions. While much of social convention constrains responses within a narrow range, those limits may be exceeded.

Workplace norms for proper behavior or professional comportment define those limits for the workgroup context. For example, while recognizing that people have the prerogative to shout in some contexts, shouting at work is inappropriate. Some of these norms may apply broadly across the workplace while other norms are specific to a local workgroup. One element of becoming acculturated to a workplace is becoming aware of these norms and exercising sufficient self-management to behave within these constraints. Workplace norms do not eliminate risk: people may deliberately or inadvertently violate these norms.

People vary in how they manage risk. Research on investment behavior has identified ways in which people misread the risk/reward contingencies of financial investments (Byrne 2005). As Riddles (2001) pointed out, investors are especially concerned with downside risk: the capacity to lose; they attend less closely to upside risk. Investors who cannot tolerate any downside risk are reluctant to act. The same inaction that prevents downside risks also require them to forego opportunities for gain (upside risks). After a major market crash, such as the financial crisis of 2008, many people liquidated their stock holdings and refused to participate in such investing subsequently. In doing so, they controlled the potential downside risk of losing even more money than had already occurred in the initial phase of the crisis. The immediate term evidence was that stocks can lose their value abruptly. Their behavior was not influenced by the potential upside risk of the stocks recovering their value. Although long-term evidence supported an eventual recovery of all of the lost value (as did occur in the subsequent years). The upside risk was that liquidating their positions would relinquish the potential to recover what they have already lost. Both risks represented considerable uncertainty in 2008 because the stock markets were behaving out of the constraints of their usual behavior.

In a parallel fashion people vary in their management of social risks. Inherent in attachment anxiety may be a strong sensitivity to the downside risks of social contact. The most salient risks for attachment anxiety are those associated with desertion, betrayal and humiliation. However, without the capacity for independence, people with attachment anxiety feel compelled to maintain close contact with others. The uncertainty of the situation results in experiencing chronic anxiety. The proximity gives a semblance of belonging, but the constant concern with the risks of rejection and humiliation leaves them unable to feel confident that they truly belong.

Attachment avoidance has a more straightforward response to risk. From the perspective of mistrusting others – the risks of rejection are unacceptable – they minimize their contact with others. It is essentially a trade-off in which they relinquish the upside risk of fulfilling their sense of belonging to prevent the downside risk of betrayal, humiliation or desertion. An avoidance approach to social relationships limits not only the capacity for individuals to find fulfillment, it also limits the capacity of the workgroup to operate a full effectiveness. Groups are more effective at accomplishing a shared mission when they operate with a free flow of information (Cason, Sheremeta, and Zhang 2012; Clampitt and Downs 1993). The knowledge and expertise residing in the various group members becomes shared among the other members of the group to construct a shared and deeper understanding of the work that they are to accomplish. When group members are reluctant to participate in the social exchanges with other members of their workgroup, the capacity of the group overall diminishes.

Personal Fulfillment at Work

Self Determination Theory (SDT) proposes three core social motives: belonging, autonomy, and efficacy (Deci and Ryan 1991). These motives are not drive-based: they do not directly pertain to a physiological deficit. Instead, these motives reflect self-initiated behaviors that arise out of interest or the pleasure intrinsic to the activity itself. To be most effective, intrinsically motivating behaviors are optimally challenging (Csikszentmihalyi 1975) such that they remain within the range of a person's capabilities while stretching that range incrementally.

SDT considers personal integration as directly connect to responsiveness to one's social context. "The development of self involves an organismic integration process through which intrinsic interests and capacities become elaborated and refined. One develops a set of flexible, unified regulatory processes and values that allow one to engaged more willingly in socially prompted and emotionally motivated activities, while feeling both self-determined and connected with others" (Deci and Ryan 1991, p. 260).

BELONGING

A sense of belonging is incompatible with anxiety and mistrust. Attachment anxiety prevents belonging in two ways. First, anxiety about the reliability and goodwill of other people inhibits the extent to which people can establish a level of intimacy that brings a sense of belonging. People experiencing attachment anxiety feel highly dependent on the goodwill of others, preventing them from confidently participating in a social group (Bartholomew and Horowitz 1991). Second, an excessive concern with others' acceptance of oneself introduces persistent doubt about being accepted into their community. Attachment anxiety creates dependency on others but also undermines confidence in acceptance by others. That lack of confidence in others' acceptance is incompatible with a sense of belonging.

Attachment avoidance maintains emotional distance from others based on mistrust. People with attachment avoidance share mistrust with those with attachment anxiety but lack the dependency that encourages proximity (Bartholomew and Horowitz 1991). In this way attachment avoidance interferes with employees finding fulfillment in social relationships with coworkers. Their avoidance of close working relationships does not reflect a lack of social motivation but an incapacity to fulfill that motive because of mistrust (Leary, Twenge, and Quinlivan 2006). Baumeister and Tice (1990) argue that fear of social exclusion and the accompanying frustration of social motives constitute a fundamental foundation for anxiety generally. From this perspective, foregoing participation in groups at work necessarily entails frustration. It also has implications for the other two social motives in the SDT framework.

AUTONOMY

Within SDT, autonomy connotes a sense of agency rather than absolute freedom to act independently of others. At work, a sense of agency arises from latitude to select tasks and to have prerogatives regarding how to pursue those tasks. Agency implies the power to create at work (Elder 1997; O'Meara and Campbell 2011). As Miller (2003) argues, social constraints to act in accordance with others' expectations or a sense of obligation to others runs contrary to confirming a sense of agency.

Obtaining and retaining autonomy at work requires the capacity to develop trusting relationships (Baumeister and Tice 1990). Mistrust tends to prompt reciprocal mistrust (Lewicki, McAllister, and Bies 1998). Both the dependency and lack of confidence evident in the social behavior associated with attachment anxiety and the emotional distance evident in the social behavior associated with attachment avoidance fail to inspire trust in colleagues. Lack of mutual trust encourages close monitoring of workplace behavior that works directly contrary to developing a sense of agency or control (Kramer 1999).

EFFICACY

Through their work people have opportunities to refine and to practice their expertise. The process of working itself provides one channel for a sense of efficacy; reactions of coworkers and supervisors provide an additional channel for confirming efficacy (Bandura 2001).

Attachment anxiety works directly counter to confirming a sense of efficacy. One of the definitive qualities of attachment anxiety is the propensity to interpret social cues in negative ways (Dickerson and Kemeny 2004; Ledley and Heimberg 2006). Attachment anxiety predisposes people to a combination of self-criticism, shame, and perceived criticism from others that in turn intensify experiences of anxiety (Shahar 2013). To the extent that attachment anxiety influences employees' perceptions of social cues, attachment anxiety will predispose people to experience a greater proportion of negative evaluations. This attributed criticism from colleagues amplifies self-criticism to reduce the potential of workplace experiences to confirm a sense of efficacy through their work.

Attachment avoidance also interferes with efficacy experiences, especially in team-based work that characterizes many occupations in post-industrialized economies. First, attachment avoidance is based on mistrust of others (Ravitz, Maunder, and McBride 2008). Without trust, people are unlikely to value or give credence to the opinions of others. That is, attachment avoidance will incline people to discount positive feedback from others, because others are perceived as unreliable sources of evaluation. Second, attachment avoidance reduces the amount of time spent with others at work and the level of intimacy associated with collaborative work. Avoidance work patterns provide fewer opportunities for others to witness one's work or to have a basis for making an evaluation.

Together, these considerations identify multiple ways in which attachment anxiety and attachment avoidance work in ways that are incompatible with fulfilling core social motives identified by SDT (Deci and Ryan 1991) at work.

Propositions

First, a secure attachment style is more reality based than attachment based on anxiety, avoidance, or both. Anxious or avoidant attachment imposes a filter on the way people perceive other people, introducing elements that arise more from the perceivers' attitudes and preconceptions than from the immediate situation.

These qualities of attachment anxiety and avoidance lead to the following propositions.

1. People with secure attachment styles encounter greater success in fulfilling core social motives at work.

A secure attachment style has a greater alignment with accurate social perception. This proposition builds from an assumption that anxious and avoidant attachment styles distort the person's perception of and response to social situations.

2. People with anxious attachment will encounter and initiative more social mistreatment at work.

Success in contemporary workplaces entails a sophisticated capacity to perceive social situations and to manage one's behavior to accommodate the expectations of the workplace. An anxious attachment style entails a lack of confidence in one's capacity to thrive in settings that require collaboration. An anxious attachment style is incompatible with effective participation in social exchanges at work. One potential dynamic is that a lack of self-confidence may interfere with the capacity to engender confidence from others in one's abilities and potential contribution. This dynamic could prompt a greater frequency of disrespectful exchanges with others at work. A second potential dynamic is that an anxious attachment style would incline employees to be more likely to interpret certain behaviors as uncivil or disrespectful. That is, their social exchanges may not appear to differ greatly from the exchanges among other members of the workgroup, but employees with an anxious attachment style would interpret a wider range of those behaviors as uncivil.

3. Avoidant attachment will be associated with less access to resources at work.

In a manner parallel with anxious attachment, avoidant attachment departs from a reality-based perception of social encounters at work. The persistent mistrust of others at the heart of avoidance attachment is not based upon an objective evaluation of the other party's competence or reliability, but arises from a deep-seated disinclination to trust anyone.

4. The anxiety and avoidance will interact such that the combination of high anxiety and high avoidance will be associated with more negative experiences than would be expected on the basis of anxiety and avoidance main effects alone.

The interaction of person qualities with contextual factors provides a means of advancing knowledge regarding the incidence and impact of workplace incivility. Conditional constructs that place the person in context points towards the range of accommodation necessary in intervention programs designed to enhance workplace civility. Evaluations of the CREW intervention program (Leiter et al. 2011) have argued for a flexible approach that adapts to the distinct definitions of workplace social norms among participating workgroups. Variations within workgroups among members may be another important dimension to consider when designing interventions.

Conclusion

This chapter explored attachment styles as a personal quality that could clarify part of the variation among members of workgroups in their evaluation of their workgroup's civility. The central proposition is that attachment styles impose a filter over employees' perceptions of social encounters and their subsequent participation in the social life of their workgroup. Attachment styles may influence social participation in two ways. First, they can increase the frequency with which employees experience workplace incivility. Second, they can increase the intensity of employees' emotional reaction to incivility when it occurs. The development of a short measure of workplace attachment styles opens possibilities for research on the interaction of person and situation in the occurrence of incivility in contemporary workplaces.

References

Bandura, A. (2001). Social cognitive theory: An agentic perspective. *Annual Review of Psychology*, 52, 1–26.

Bartholomew, K. and Horowitz, L.M. (1991). Attachment styles among young adults: A test of a four-category model. *Journal of Personality and Social Psychology*, 61, 226.

Baumeister, R.F. and Tice, D.M. (1990). Point-counterpoints: Anxiety and social exclusion. *Journal of Social and Clinical Psychology*, 9, 165–95.

Bowlby, J. (1969). *Attachment and Loss: Vol. 1. Attachment*. New York: Basic Books.

Byrne, K. (2005). How do consumers evaluate risk in financial products? *Journal of Financial Services Marketing*, 10(1), 21–36.

Case, M.A. (2008). Few words in favor of cultivating an incest taboo in the workplace. *Vermont Law Review*, 33, 551.

Cason, T.N., Sheremeta, R.M., and Zhang, J. (2012). Communication and efficiency in competitive coordination games. *Games and Economic Behavior*, 76(1), 26–43.

Clampitt, P.G. and Downs, C.W. (1993). Employee perceptions of the relationship between communication and productivity: A field study. *Journal of Business Communication*, 30, 5–28.

Collins, N.L. and Read, S.J. (1990). Adult attachment, working models, and relationship quality in dating couples. *Journal of Personality and Social Psychology*, 58, 644–63.

Csikszentmihalyi, M. (1975). *Beyond Boredom and Anxiety*. San Francisco: Jossey-Bass.

Davidhizar, R. and Farabaugh, N. (1986). Finding and keeping proper emotional distance between manager and subordinate is a vital step in assuming a new position. *Nursing Management*, 17(4), 43–9.

Deci, E.L. and Ryan, R.M. (1991). A motivational approach to self: Integration in personality. *Nebraska Symposium on Motivation*, 38, 237–88.

Dickerson, S.S. and Kemeny, M.E. (2004). Acute stressors and cortisol responses: A theoretical integration and synthesis of laboratory research. *Psychological Bulletin*, 130, 355.

Elder, G.H. (1997). The life course and human development. In W. Damon and R.M. Lerner (eds), *Handbook of Child Psychology* (5th edn, pp. 939–91). New York: Wiley.

Fraley, R.C. (2002). Attachment stability from infancy to adulthood: Meta-analysis and dynamic modeling of developmental mechanisms. *Personality and Social Psychology Review*, 6, 123–51.

Fraley, R.C. and Shaver, P.R. (2008). Attachment theory and its place in contemporary personality theory and research. In O.P. Joh, R.W. Robins, and L.A. Pervin (eds), *Handbook of Personality: Theory and Research*. New York: The Guilford Press.

Fraley, R.C., Waller, N.G. and Brennan, K.A. (2000). An item response theory analysis of self-report measures of adult attachment. *Journal of Personality and Social Psychology*, 78, 350–65.

Graedon, A. (2014). *The Word Exchange*. New York: Random House.

Hazan, C. and Shaver, P.R. (1990). Love and work: An attachment-theoretical perspective. *Journal of Personality and Social Psychology*, 59(2), 270–80.

Kets de Vries, M.F.R. (1991). Introduction: Exploding the myth that organizations and executives are rational. In M.F.R. Kets de Vries et al. (eds), *Organizations on the Couch* (pp. 1–21). Jossey-Bass.

Kramer, R.M. (1999). Trust and distrust in organizations: Emerging perspectives, enduring questions. *Annual Review of Psychology*, 50, 569–98.

Leary, M.R., Twenge, J.M., and Quinlivan, E. (2006). Interpersonal rejection as a determinant of anger and aggression. *Personality and Social Psychology Review*, 10, 111–32.

Ledley, D.R. and Heimberg, R.G. (2006). Cognitive vulnerability to social anxiety. *Journal of Social and Clinical Psychology*, 25, 755–78.

Leiter, M.P., Day, A., and Price, L. (2014, May). *Attachment Styles at Work: Measurement, Collegial Relationships, and Burnout*. Presentation at the conference Work, Stress, and Health. Atlanta, GA.

Leiter, M.P., Price, L., and Day, A. (2013). *Short Work Attachment Measure Manual*. Technical Document: Centre for Organizational Research, Acadia University.

Leiter, M.P., Price, L. and Day, A. (2015). Attachment styles at work: Measurement, collegial relationships, and burnout. *Burnout Research*, 2, 25–35.

Leiter, M.P., Laschinger, H.K.S., Day, A., and Gilin-Oore, D. (2011). The impact of civility interventions on employee social behavior, distress, and attitudes. *Journal of Applied Psychology*, 96, 1258–74.

Lewicki, R.J., McAllister, D.J., and Bies, R.J. (1998). Trust and distrust: New relationships and realities. *Academy of Management Review*, 23, 438–58.

Main, M., Kaplan, N., and Cassidy, J. (1985). Security in infancy, childhood, and adulthood: A move to the level of representation. *Monographs of the Society for Research in Child Development*, 66–104.

Mead, M. (1978). A proposal: We need taboos on sex at work. *Redbook*, April. Reprinted in *Sexuality and Organizations: Romantic and Coercive Behaviors at Work* 53, 54.

Mikulincer, M. and Florian, V. (1995). Appraisal of and coping with a real-life stressful situation: The contribution of attachment styles. *Personality and Social Psychology Bulletin*, 21, 406–14.

Miller, J.G. (2003, January). Culture and agency: Implications for psychological theories of motivation and social development. *Nebraska Symposium on Motivation*, 49, 59–100.

Miller, R.S. (2007). *Intimate Relationships*. New York: McGraw-Hill.

O'Meara, K. and Campbell, C.M. (2011). Faculty sense of agency in decisions about work and family. *The Review of Higher Education*, 34, 447–76.

Pearson, C.M., Andersson, L.M., and Wegner, J.W. (2001). When workers flout convention: A study of workplace incivility. *Human Relations*, 54, 1387–419.

Ravitz, P., Maunder, R. and McBride, C. (2008). Attachment, contemporary interpersonal theory and IPT: An integration of theoretical, clinical, and empirical perspectives. *Journal of Contemporary Psychotherapy*, 38, 11–21.

Riddles, N. (2001). A portfolio manager's view of downside risk. *Managing Downside Risk in Financial Markets*. UK: Butterworth-Heinemann.

Shahar, B. (2013). Emotion-focused therapy for the treatment of social anxiety: An overview of the model and a case description. *Clinical Psychology & Psychotherapy*, 21, 536–47.

Wei, M., Russell, D.W., Mallinckrodt, B. and Vogel, D.L. (2007). The experiences in close relationship scale (ECR)-short form: Reliability, validity, and factor structure. *Journal of Personality Assessment*, 88(2), 187–204.

18

Economic Crisis and Business Distress

Panagiotis E. Petrakis

Introduction

The workplace has many features that may affect both the physical and psychological condition of the employees. Personality represents those characteristics of an individual that explain consistent types of his emotions, thinking and behavior. Personality traits reflect trends in behavior, while their formation and management manner vary, making each personality unique, since each individual is characterized by a particular portfolio of personality traits.

Personality development plays an imperative role at the workplace as it decides the way an individual interacts with his fellow employees and responds to various situations. The path of this relationship between personality and workplace starts from the characteristics of human personality, which in turn form the organizational culture and, finally, determine job performance.

This chapter aims to analyze to what extent the workplace and the changes observed in this affect the personality traits of people in the workplace and their levels of productivity. It is also interesting to identify the factors that form labor productivity and job performance in general.

Under conditions of business distress, human personality and the general behavior of the workforce usually suffer a negative shock. Certainly, there is evidence for reverse impact too, so the negative conditions are becoming a motivating factor for "a leap forward." But herein, we mainly deal with the first aspect of the phenomenon, namely the negative impact.

Business distress is considered a crisis that threatens the viability of an enterprise, which may result from both the business itself and the conditions of the external environment. Such a situation leads people to differentiate their attitude in making their own efforts. Consequently, productivity under business distress receives a great blow. This creates a vicious circle, which the organization cannot easily escape from.

This chapter firstly presents the notion of personality traits in the workplace and the role of the connection between organizational culture and the personal traits of the workforce for effective business operation. Thereafter, the relationship between personality traits and productivity is presented, as well as whether personality traits change after conditions of economic crisis and business distress.

1. Personality Traits and Organizational Structure

1.1 PERSONALITY TRAITS IN THE WORKPLACE

Personality psychology is dominated by the trait approach, in which individual differences in enduring dispositions are assessed. Trait psychology can be traced back to the ancient Greeks (e.g. Theophrastus, circa 300 BC) and has been a continuing presence in personality psychology (Hofstede and McCrae 2004). Indeed, in the early 1930s, McDougall (1932) made the first attempt to organize the concept of personality in a coherent structure. McDougall (1932) identified five factors to which personality can be adequately attributed and are distinguishable but separable and highly complex factors at the same time and each comprises many variables: intellect, character, temperament, disposition and temper.

Since then, there has been a large attempt in the literature to identify the factors and characteristics which form people's personality traits. Typical attempts for configuring systems capturing personality traits are Cattell's System (Cattell 1956), Eysenck's System (Eysenck 1970), Guilford's System (Guilford 1975), Murray's Need System (Borkenau and Ostendorf 1989; Costa and McCrae 1988), the Interpersonal Circle (Leary 1957) and linguistic analyses (Goldberg 1981; Osgood, Suci and Tannenbaum 1957). All these attempts result in five or six – and very rarely more – personality traits.

However, the underlying assumption formed on the basic personality traits is that of the "Big Five" personality traits (Digman 1990), whether regarding the personality of an individual in general or his personality in the workplace. These are five broad domains or dimensions of personality, which are based on the five-factor model (FFM) (Costa and McCrae 1992), which attempt to describe human personality. These five factors – in the workplace – are the following (Digman 1990):

1. Openness, which is the distinction between inventive/curious and consistent/cautious traits. The concept refers to the extent that an individual is characterized by intellectual curiosity, creativity, preference for novelty and variety, imagination, independence, and a personal preference for a variety of activities over a strict routine. At the same time, individuals characterized by this personality trait show appreciation for art, emotion, adventure, unusual ideas and curiosity.

2. Conscientiousness is the distinction between efficient/organized and easy-going/careless traits. The concept of conscientiousness refers to the extent that an individual is characterized as well-organized and dependable, responsible, self-disciplined, dutiful, hard-working, achievement oriented, and prefers planned rather than spontaneous behavior.

3. Extraversion, which is the distinction between outgoing/energetic and solitary/reserved traits. The concept of extraversion is defined as an orientation toward the outer world and refers to the extent that an individual is characterized by energy, positive emotions, warmth, gregariousness, assertiveness, activity and excitement seeking, assertiveness, sociability and the tendency to seek stimulation in the company of others, and talkativeness.

4. Agreeableness, the distinction between friendly/compassionate and analytical/detached traits. The concept of agreeableness refers to the extent that an individual is characterized as compassionate, cooperative, trusting the people around him and the people with whom he works, is helpful in nature and is generally good-tempered. Furthermore, it is associated with compliance, modesty and sympathy.

5. Neuroticism, the distinction between sensitive/nervous and secure/confident traits. The concept of neuroticism refers to the extent that an individual is characterized by the ability to overcome difficult situations with relative ease and whether a person is characterized

by emotional stability and impulse control. In other words, it indicates whether there are emotional changes or not. Common facets associated with this trait include being anxious, irritable, depressed, worried and insecure. This concept is very close to that of self-consciousness, the extent to which a person is sensitive to what others think about him or her.

The main reasons for using these factors widely as underlying factors of personality are that: (a) they describe the different traits in personality without overlapping; and (b) they are features which seem to be found across a wide range of participants of different ages and of different cultures. These five factors seem to provide a rich conceptual framework for integrating all the research findings and theory in personality psychology, and represent the basic structure of all personality traits (O'Connor 2002).

All personality traits have two opposite poles, and each individual is characterized by a portfolio of personality traits consisting to a greater or lesser extent of each personality trait. It could therefore be argued that each person is characterized by both poles of all personality traits, but what differentiates each individual from the rest is the degree of convergence with one of the two poles of each trait.

External conditions alter the proportions of bipolar relationships, thus a different prevailing portfolio of personality traits is formed.

1.2 ORGANIZATIONAL CULTURE AND PERSONALITY TRAITS

The characteristics of an individual's personality traits are transferred to the workplace where they are employed or in their professional behavior in general. For this purpose – and in order for employees to be more efficient and productive (see Part 2) – it is fair to assess the degree of cultural match between an individual personality and an organizational culture. In the context of a particular cultural dimension, a personality trait at work should enable the person to feel comfortable in his workplace, to feel motivated and be able to deliver the expected results of the work undertaken.

The organizational culture of a company or organization to a large extent is formed by the personality traits of its employees. Organizational culture can be defined as the collective programming of the mind that distinguishes the members of one organization from others (Hofstede 1980). As defined Hofstede, Hofstede and Minkov (2010),[1] the dimensions that reflect the organizational culture are the following:

1. Process-oriented versus results-oriented. This dimension is closely connected with the effectiveness of the organization. Individuals are distinguished by their attitude toward risk and uncertainty, their effort at work and whether they love the changes or the routine.
2. Employee-oriented versus job-oriented. This dimension captures the management philosophy of an organization and concerns whether the organization is taking into account employees' personal problems, whether or not they are taking responsibility for them and whether important decisions of the organization are taken by groups or committees.
3. Parochial versus professional opposes units in which employees derive their identity largely from the organization (parochial) to units in which people identify with their type of job (professional).

---

1   Whether the score of a unit on a dimension should be interpreted as good or bad depends entirely on where the people responsible for managing the unit wanted it to go.

4. Open system versus closed system relates to the accessibility of an organization. It depends on whether individuals consider all organization members open to newcomers and outsiders, believe that everyone could fit into the organization and in whether newcomers are characterized by adaptability.

5. Loose versus tight control. This dimension refers to the amount of internal structuring in the organization. In loose control cultures, no one is thinking of cost, meeting times are only kept approximately, and jokes about the organization and the job are frequent. In contrast, in tight control cultures, the work environment is cost-conscious, meeting times are kept punctually, and jokes about the company and/or the job are rare.

6. Normative versus pragmatic. This situation refers to the extent that the organization is customer-oriented or not. Pragmatic cultures are market-driven. In contrast, in normative cultures, people perceive their task in relation to the outside world as the implementation of inviolable rules.

Hence, the performance of an organization significantly depends on the degree of convergence between the personality traits of its workforce and organizational culture dimensions that characterize an organization.

From the above description of the "Big Five" personality traits and organizational culture dimensions is found that there is significant convergence between traits and dimensions. For example, there is a close relationship of openness and conscientiousness personality traits with process orientation organizational cultural dimension, extraversion personality trait with employee orientation and open system organizational cultural dimensions, and agreeableness personality trait with professionalism and tight control organizational cultural dimensions.

2. Personality Traits and Productivity

Productivity is directly associated with the company's viability in a highly competitive environment. Labor productivity is the amount of goods and services that a worker produces in a given amount of time.

The purpose of any business should be the best possible use of the available resources. Since the company is a living organism that is constantly evolving, it should be able to adapt to new conditions. This is because the basic component of any business, i.e. workforce, is characterized by a series of cognitive and non-cognitive skills. For example, the level of education as a cognitive skill is a factor in increasing labor productivity (Barro 1991; Baumol, Bakey Blackman and Wolf 1989; Mankiw, Romer and Weil 1992). However, a number of non-cognitive skills such as personality traits affect labor productivity.

A large part of the literature focus on cognitive skills in order to explain the differences in job performance (Cawley, Heckman and Vytlacil 2001; Heckman, Stixrud and Urzua 2006). However, cognitive skills alone fail to fully interpret the wage inequality (Blau and Kahn 2005) and hence productivity differences. By focusing on both cognitive skills and factors, which are related to particular characteristics of the human mentality at the same time, a clearer view of wage inequalities can be formed (Bowles, Gintis and Osborne 2001). These characteristics include, among others, self-control, self-motivation, emotionally secure, ambitious, sociable, etc. The importance given to the personality traits by many researchers is equivalent to that of cognitive skills (Mueller and Plug 2006). The relationship between workplace attitudes and behavior continues to be a dominant theme for examination (Harrison, Newman and Roth 2006; Schleicher, Watt and Greguras 2004).

Trying to identify the key factors that affect the formation of productivity, we will focus on the personality traits of the workforce. In this way, we escape the narrow limits of economics while giving a deeper dimension to the issue by adding social and psychological factors.

More specifically, by focusing on the "Big Five" personality traits, we draw useful conclusions about the way in which human personality affects job performance and labor productivity (Heckman et al. 2006). Recent studies identify strong correlation (positive, negative or both) of openness, conscientiousness, extraversion, agreeableness and neuroticism with productivity (Fletcher 2013).

Investigating the relationship between productivity and personal traits is of special interest for two main reasons. On the one hand, knowledge of the specific characteristics of an individual's personality helps managers to better manage the company's workforce and, on the other hand, offers the opportunity for policy interventions.

A better understanding of the specific characteristics of the company's workforce enables managers to gain flexibility in particularly difficult conditions for the company (Bowles et al. 2001; Green, Machin and Wilkinson 1998). Such a possibility forms a specific organizational culture that boosts efficiency whereas the firm gains competitive advantage. Simultaneously, policy-makers can improve the economic performance of disadvantaged groups and increase social mobility (Cubel, Nuevo-Chiquero, Sanchez-Pages and Vidal-Fernandez 2014).

According to the literature, among the "Big Five" personality traits, conscientiousness is strongly correlated with job performance, while for other traits the result depends on some specific factors that concern occupation or particular job aspect (Cubel et al. 2014). Non-cognitive skills such as self-control and self-esteem contribute to the formation of financial results (Borghans, Duckworth, Heckman and Weel Bas ter 2008; Cobb-Clark and Tan 2011).

Based on the "Big Five" personality traits we may understand the effects of personality in the workplace.

Neuroticism is associated with lower stress levels and less negative thinking. Consequently, this makes people more satisfied with their work and therefore more efficient. Thus, we can assume that high neuroticism levels tend to correlate with low performance.

Extraversion is associated with higher performance, enhanced leadership and job satisfaction. Extraversion may have a negative effect on productivity, but the outcome may depend on the nature of the task (Cubel et al. 2014).

Openness contributes to higher training performance, enhanced leadership and at the same time helps people to be more receptive to any change. Although openness is associated with creativity and imagination, its results are ambiguous. While openness can be constructive for some occupations, it might not have similar effects on some others. Muller and Schwieren (2012) find that openness has a negative impact on performance.

Agreeableness helps people to show team spirit, thereby achieving better results through collaboration. Teamwork in the workplace very often helps to create new ideas and effectively solve complex problems. However, cooperation with other people may have a negative impact on productivity. Collaboration may create intense anxiety and stress for people, resulting in reduced efficiency regarding tasks which are undertaken. Agreeableness, as well as extraversion, is associated with cooperative behavior. However, it is not necessary that these characteristics improve job performance as it is associated concurrently with cognitive skills.

Finally, conscientiousness, which relates to time scheduling and planning, leads to higher performance given that it increases accuracy in the tasks. Being careful and concentrated in the task, an employee could increase his efficiency.

The empirical evidences for those personality traits broadly confirm these assumptions. Nyhus and Pons (2005) find a negative relationship between neuroticism and wages and a negative relationship between agreeableness and wages for the case of female employees. Mueller and Plug

(2006) reach the same conclusion by focusing on the differentiation between the two genders. Viinikainen, Kokko, Pulkkinen and Pehkonen (2010), based on the case of Finland, study the influence of personal traits on wages. Higher conscientiousness and lower agreeableness and lower neuroticism are associated with better results in terms of earnings, job performance and employment (Almlund, Duckworth, Heckman and Kautz 2011; Uysal and Pohlmeier 2011).

To sum up, the existing literature argues that neuroticism and agreeableness are associated with lower compensation of employees. As for conscientiousness, it is consistent with better job performance. The effect of cognitive skills and personality traits are the same. Therefore, by focusing on both human personality and cognitive skills, such as education, we can obtain a better view of the productivity differences within the labor force.

Another significant factor that is related to human behavior and the human personality, regards job satisfaction. The relationship between job performance and job satisfaction has been at the center of organizational psychology since the 1970s (Judge, Thoresen, Bono and Patton 2001). Job satisfaction is valuable due to the fact that it is related with productivity increase (Hunter and Hunter 1984). More precisely, it is a complex mental process through which employees evaluate different working conditions aspects, verbalizing those with individual incentives and preferences. Thus, there is a grid of incentives and behaviors that motivates the employees to become more efficient and to make a greater effort (Depedri, Tortia and Carpita 2010).

Last but not least, the code of ethics for each company matters. Companies that follow a code of ethics tend to perform better (Verschoor 1999). Workers in companies without a code of ethics are less generous and less productive (Flynn 2003).

3. Change and Crisis:
Can Attitudes, Beliefs and Personality Traits be Modified?

In the literature there are many factors presented as external and internal potential triggers for societal changes, even if these changes regard culture or personality traits. Such factors may include macro events, i.e. strong external forces like wars (Barker, Halman and Vloet 1992; Hofstede 2001), major economic changes (Inglehart 2008; Rotondo, Carlson and Nicholson 1997), regime effects (Barker et al. 1992), diffusion and intercultural contact (Berry 2008; Ferraro 1994), socio-demographic effects (Barker et al. 1992; Ester, Braun and Mohler 2006) and changes in economic incentives and opportunities in technology and in institutions (Gruber and Hungerman 2008; Fehr 2009).

While these factors are intuitively appealing, there also exist empirical studies suggesting that societies may preserve their cultures even in the presence of strong external forces (Adams 2003). For instance, Hofstede (2001) argues that a period of 50 to 100 years is needed for a measurable change on cultural characteristics. The values, attitudes and beliefs are deeply rooted in the societies and evolve very slowly over time (Guiso, Sapienza and Zingales 2006; Roland 2004). No matter what the triggering factor, cultures do not change in the short-run and present stability through time (Petrakis and Kostis 2014). The social stereotypes forming the cultural and personal traits may be characterized as long-lasting, as the forces that have shaped the construction of the stereotypes are considered exogenous (e.g. climate and environment) (Schwatrz 2009). In general, cultural stereotypes present a great resistance towards change and to their own redefinition (Johnston 1996). Williams (1979) argued that changes in the social environment do not necessarily result in the sudden abrogation of a particular value, but rather lead to a shift in emphasis in its orientation.

Thus, does the financial and economic crisis represent an external force strong enough to trigger culture and personality change? The recent financial crisis has affected almost all economies worldwide. However, apart from the economies it appears to also have societal consequences, more specifically affecting the culture and the personality traits of members of societies (Magee, Miller and Heaven 2013). The global financial crisis, and the resultant financial strain, have likely contributed to considerable stress and hardship for many individuals (Sargent-Cox, Butterworth and Anstey 2011). The global financial crisis has shrunk the resources of households and has direct implications on cultural habits and consumption (Inkei 2010).

However, deep crises can be seen as a great opportunity for improvement, due to the fact that people and institutions are fully conscious of their potential for change (Bonet and Donato 2011). Thus, an economic crisis could be seen as an opportunity for a cultural change in a society or a change in the personality traits of individuals. A deep economic crisis can push people to evolve and take economic depression as a chance to reorganize some things and break down barriers, resulting in self-improvement.

We argue that changes are responsible for the transformation of a system under study. Change is analyzed in four major aspects: intrusive events, intra-system activity, trans-systems activity and cultural environment (Harrison and McKinnon 1986). In the framework of Harrison and McKinnon (1986) the trans-systems activity provides the critical, associational link between culture and the system under study, while the systems change is the product of both the intrusion of events and the continuous interactions among other systems and the system under study (Choi 2002).

A key feature of human behavior is its response to external environment conditions. Therefore, business distress directly affects the beliefs, attitudes and behavior of the workforce (Deal and Kennedy 1982). Such a condition, however, has a direct impact on the business itself. For example, older adults who have retired, or are nearing retirement, are a particularly vulnerable population to increased economic stress and uncertainty as result of disruptions to their financial preparations (Kelly 2009). Also, the effects of increased neuroticism on life satisfaction arise when negative emotions outweigh the experience of positive emotions (Schimmack, Radhakrishnan, Oishi, Dzokoto and Ahadi 2002).

But there are not only direct effects of economic crisis and business distress on beliefs and personal traits but also indirect effects which may emerge, for instance due to the economic policy applied in order to confront the crisis. More precisely, Aghion, Algan and Cahuc (2008) investigate whether public policy can affect culture, such as beliefs and norms of cooperation, evaluating how state regulation of minimum wage interacts with unionization behavior and social dialogue. They argue that – in contrast to countries with highly cooperative labor relations and high unionization rates – in countries with strong state regulation of the minimum wage, incentives for social dialogue are low and so is union density, as strong state regulation of the minimum wage crowds out social experimentation and learning about cooperation. This crowding out effect progressively undermines cooperation and leads economies toward steady-state equilibria with bad labor relations and high minimum wage regulations.

Similar to the effects of a crisis on all members of a society is the manifestation of a crisis within an organization – a business distress – which may be due to either systemic factors (such as a general crisis in the business activity sector, labor's digital displacement, etc.), or internal factors (such as poor management). Results of a crisis may be lay-offs, wage cuts, the risk of bankruptcy, etc. Whatever the cause of the outbreak of a crisis in the workplace, the results may significantly affect the working conditions and thus the behavior of employees (Prince and Lawler 1986; Stajkovic and Luthans 1997).

At the same time, given the influence of personality traits on job performance, it is important to know how much they can change. What changes in terms of personality traits because of business distress is not obtaining new personality traits or removing others, but a change in the composition of the personality traits portfolio. Therefore, the result of a business distress in the workplace concerns alteration in the scores that people get on the "Big Five" personality traits. For example, a person who is characterized by the following personality traits: inventive/curious, efficient/organized, outgoing/energetic, friendly/compassionate and secure/confident, after a business distress might present the following personality traits: consistent/cautious, easy-going/careless, solitary/reserved, analytical/detached and sensitive/nervous, because usually a business distress pushes to the surface the negative side of personality traits (although this cannot be an absolute claim for all traits).

The biggest changes in the personality of a person occur during adolescence (Borghans et al. 2008). However, changes in traits appear, even to a lesser extent, later in life. More often, they appear under shock conditions. People over the years become increasingly more socially dominant, conscientious and emotionally stable. Social vitality and openness to experience rise early in life and then fall in old ages (Roberts, Walton and Viechtbauer 2006). Le, Donnellan and Conger (2014) provide indications that personality traits are prospectively associated with workplace conditions and that workplace conditions are associated with personality changes during the transition from adolescence to adulthood. It seems as if personality characteristics help shape an individual's work-related circumstances, and such contextual conditions, in turn, seem to contribute to personality development in young adulthood.

In addition, business distress may indirectly alter the organizational culture of an organization. Due to the fact that organizational culture is an aggregation of beliefs and values of the organization, it is directly linked to the notion of organization performance (Brooks 2006; Kotter 2012). For example, an organization which has been characterized as employee-oriented but had recently been in economic trouble accompanied by collective lay-offs, now tends to be job-oriented, even if its operation is balanced right now and there are no further lay-offs.

The outbreak of the global financial crisis was a main factor that contributed to the dramatic wage cuts and the increase in unemployment. This resulted in a condition in which wages became relatively cheap compared to capital investments and investments in new technologies (Pessoa and Van Reenen 2014). Thus, enterprises have had incentives to modify their production process to more labor-intensive and less capital-intensive. These developments contribute to declining productivity in the countries that were more hurt by the crisis. Trying to identify the reasons why productivity is affected by a situation of business distress, it would be interesting to focus on a specific dimension – that of efficiency through which enterprises combine the benefits of innovation with labor and other productive factors (Cardarelli and Lusinyan 2014).

It is interesting in this crisis to assess developments in productivity. Given that productivity is the product per employee, during an economic crisis or business distress, productivity is expected to grow. This happens as the labor force is severely reduced without a corresponding reduction in production. During the global financial crisis it has generally been observed that the rate of decline in employment is higher than the rate of decline in production, at least in economies that suffered the highest pressure (e.g. South Europe). Nevertheless, productivity growth in many countries remains weak (Hughes and Saleheen 2012). This fact suggests that the performance of employees is subject to a decreasing effect due to stress conditions. This matter requires more research and analysis as it involves issues of changes in technology, investment, etc.

References

Adams, M. (2003). *Fire and Ice: The United States, Canada and the Myth of Converging Values*. Toronto: Penguin Canada.

Aghion, P., Algan, Y. and Cahuc, P. (2008). Can policy interact with culture? Minimum wage and the quality of labor relations. *IZA Discussion Papers*, 3680.

Almlund, M., Duckworth, A.L., Heckman, J. and Kautz, T. (2011). Personality psychology in economics. *IZA Discussion Paper No. 5500*.

Barker, D., Halman, L. and Vloet, A. (1992). *The European Values Study 1981–1990*. Aberdeen: Gordon Cook Foundation.

Barro, R. (1991). Economic growth in a cross section of countries. *Quarterly Journal of Economics*, CVI(2), 407–43.

Baumol, W., Batey Blackman, S.A. and Wolf, E. (1989). *Productivity and American Leadership: The Long View*. Cambridge, MA: MIT Press.

Berry, J.W. (2008). Globalization and acculturation. *International Journal of Intercultural Relations*, 32, 328–36.

Blau, F.D. and Kahn, L.M. (2005). Do cognitive test scores explain higher US wage inequality? *Review of Economics and Statistics*, 87(1), 184–93.

Bonet, L. and Donato, F. (2011). The Financial Crisis and its impact on the current models of governance and management on the cultural sector in Europe. *Encat Journal of Cultural Management Policy*, 1, 4–11.

Borghans, L., Duckworth, A.L., Heckman, J.J. and ter Weel, B. (2008). The economics and psychology of personality traits. *IZA Discussion Paper*, No. 3333, February.

Borkenau, P. and Ostendorf, F. (1989). A confirmatory factor analysis of the five-factor model of personality. *Mult. Behav. Res.*

Bowles, S., Gintis, H. and Osborne, M. (2001). Incentive-enhancing preferences: Personality, behavior, and earnings. *The American Economic Review*, 91(2), 155–8.

Brooks, I. (2006). *Organizational Behavior: Individuals, Groups and Organization*. Essex: Pearson Education Limited.

Cardarelli, R. and Lusinyan, L. (2014). A tale of two states-bringing back U.S. productivity growth. IMF direct. Available at: http://blog-imfdirect.imf.org/2014/09/25/a-tale-of-two-states-bringing-back-u-s-productivity-growth/. Accessed 20th October 2014.

Cattell, R.B. (1956). Second-order personality factors. *J. Consult. Psychol.*, 20(4), 11–18.

Cawley, J., Heckman, J. and Vytlacil, E. (2001). Three observations on wages and measured cognitive ability. *Labour Economics*, 8(4), 419–42.

Choi, J.S. (2002). Financial crisis and accounting reform: A cultural perspective. *Journal of Accounting and Finance*, 1, 71–93.

Cobb-Clark, D.A. and Tan, M. (2011). Noncognitive skills, occupational attainment, and relative wages. *Labour Economics*, 18(1), 1–13.

Costa, P.T. Jr. and McCrae, R.R. (1988). From catalog to classification: Murray's needs and the five factor model. *J. Pers. Soc. Psychol.*, 55, 258–65.

Costa, P.T. Jr. and McCrae, R.R. (1992). *Revised NEO Personality Inventory (NEO-PI-R) and NEO Five-Factor Inventory (NEO-FFI) Manual*. Odessa: Psychological Assessment Resources.

Cubel, M., Nuevo-Chiquero, A., Sanchez-Pages, S. and Vidal-Fernandez, M. (2014). Do personality traits affect productivity? *Evidence from the Lab (July 21, 2014)*. IEB Working Paper N. 2014/28. Available at SSRN: http://ssrn.com/abstract=2471066.

Deal, T.E. and Kennedy, A.A. (1982). *Corporate Cultures: The Rites and Rituals of Corporate Life*. Reading, MA: Addison-Wesley Publishing Co.

Depedri, S., Tortia, E. and Carpita, M. (2010). Incentives' job satisfaction and performance: Empirical evidence in Italian social enterprises. *Euricse Working Papers*, 12(10).

Digman, J.M. (1990). Personality structure: Emergence of the five-factor model. *Annual Review of Psychology*, 41, 417–40.

Ester, P., Braun, M. and Mohler, P. (eds) (2006). *Globalization, Value Change, and Generations*. Leiden: Brill.

Eysenck, H.J. (1970). *The Structure of Human Personality*, 3rd edn. London: Methuen.

Fehr, E. (2009). On the economics and biology of trust. *Journal of the European Economic Association*, 7(2–3), 235–66.

Ferraro, G.P. (1994). *The Cultural Dimension of International Business*, 2nd edn. Englewood Cliffs: Prentice Hall.

Fletcher, J.M. (2013). The effects of personality traits on adult labor market outcomes: Evidence from siblings. *Journal of Economic Behavior & Organization*, 89, 122–35.

Flynn, F.J. (2003) How much should I give and how often? The effects of generosity and frequency of favor exchange on social status and productivity. *The Academy of Management Journal*, 46(5), 539–53.

Goldberg, L.R. (1981). Language and individual differences: The search for universals in personality lexicons. In L. Wheeler (ed.), *Review of Personality and Social Psychology* (pp. 141–65). Beverly Hills: Sage.

Green, F., Machin, S. and Wilkinson, D. (1998). The meaning and determinants of skills shortages. *Oxford Bulletin of Economics and Statistics*, 60(2), 165–87.

Gruber, J. and Hungerman, D.M. (2008). The church versus the mall: What happens when religion faces increased secular competition? *Quarterly Journal of Economics*, 123(2), 831–62.

Guilford, J.P. (1975). Factors and factors of personality. *Psychol. Bull*, 82, 802–14.

Guiso, L., Sapienza, P. and Zingales, L. (2006). Does culture affect economic outcomes? *Journal of Economic Perspectives*, 20(2), 23–48.

Harrison, D.A., Newman, D.A. and Roth, P.L. (2006). How important are job attitudes? Meta-analytic comparison of integrative behavioral outcomes and time sequences. *Academy of Management Journal*, 49, 305–25.

Harrison, G.L. and McKinnon, J.L. (1986). Culture and accounting change: A new perspective on corporate reporting regulation and accounting policy formulation. *Accounting Organizations and Society*, 11(3), 233–52.

Heckman, J.J., Stixrud, J. and Urzua, S. (2006). The effects of cognitive and noncognitive abilities on labor market outcomes and social behavior. *Journal of Labor Economics*, 24(3), 411–82.

Hofstede, G. (1980). *Culture's Consequences*. Beverly Hills: Sage.

Hofstede, G. (2001). *Culture's Consequences: Comparing Values, Behaviors, Institutions, and Organizations across Nations*, 2nd edn. Thousand Oaks: Sage.

Hofstede, G. and McCrae, R.R. (2004). Personality and culture revisited: Linking traits and dimensions of culture. *Cross-Cultural Research*, 38(52), 52–88.

Hofstede, G., Hofstede, G.J. and Minkov, M. (2010). *Cultures and Organizations: Software of the Mind, Intercultural Cooperation and its Importance for Survival*. London: McGraw-Hill.

Hughes, A. and Saleheen, J. (2012). UK labour productivity before and after the crisis – an international and historical perspective, *Bank of England Quarterly Bulletin*, 52(2), 138–46.

Hunter, J.E. and Hunter, R.F. (1984). Validity and utility of alternative predictors of job performance. *Psychological Bulletin*, 96, 72–98.

Inglehart, R. (2008). Changing values among western publics from 1970 to 2006. *West European Politics*, 31(1–2), 130–46.

Inkei, P. (2010). The effects of the economic crisis on culture. Paper presented in the Culture Watch Europe Conference, Culture and the Policies of Change, EESC Headquarters, Brussels, September 6–7.

Johnston, L. (1996). Resisting change: Information-seeking and stereotype change. *European Journal of Social Psychology*, 26, 799–825.

Judge, T.A. Thoresen, C.J., Bono, J.E. and Patton, G.K. (2001). The job satisfaction–job performance relationship: A qualitative and quantitative review. *Psychological Bulletin*, 127, 376–407.

Kelly, S. (2009). *Don't Stop Thinking about Tomorrow: The Changing Face of Retirement – The Past, the Present and the Future*. Sydney: AMP. NATSEM.

Kotter, J. (2012). *Corporate Culture and Performance*. New York: Free Press.

Le, K., Donnellan, M.B. and Conger, R. (2014). Personality development at work: Workplace conditions, personality changes, and the corresponsive principle. *Journal of Personality*, 82(1), 44–56.

Leary, T. (1957). *Interpersonal Diagnosis of Personality*. New York: Ronald Press.

Magee, C.A., Miller, L.M. and Heaven P.C.L. (2013). Personality trait change and life satisfaction in adults: The roles of age and hedonic balance. *Personality and Individual Differences*, 55(6), 694–8.

Mankiw, G., Romer, D. and Weil, D. (1992). A contribution to the empirics of economic growth. *Quarterly Journal of Economics*, 407–37.

McDougall, W. (1932). Of the words character and personality. *Character Pers.*, 1, 3–16.

Mueller, G. and Plug, E. (2006). Estimating the effect of personality on male and female earnings. *Industrial and Labor Relations Review*, 60(1), 3–22.

Muller, J. and Schwieren, C. (2012). Can personality explain what is underlying womens unwillingness to compete? *Journal of Economic Psychology*, 33(3), 448–60.

Nyhus, E.K. and Pons, E. (2005). The effects of personality on earnings. *Journal of Economic Psychology*, 26(3), 363–84.

O'Connor, B. (2002). A quantitative review of the comprehensiveness of the five-factor model in relation to popular personality inventories. *Assessment*, 9(2), 188–203.

Osgood, C.E., Suci, G.J. and Tannenbaum, P.H. (1957). *The Measurement of Meaning*. Urbana: University of Illinois Pres.

Pessoa, J.P. and Van Reenen, J. (2014). The UK productivity and jobs puzzle: Does the answer lie in wage flexibility? *Economic Journal*, 124, 433–52.

Petrakis, P.E. and Kostis, P.C. (2014). Medium term effects of culture, transactions and institutions on opportunity entrepreneurship. *Journal of Innovation and Entrepreneurship*, 3(11).

Prince, J.B. and Lawler, E.E. (1986). Does salary discussion hurt the developmental performance appraisal? *Organizational Behavior and Human Decision Processes*, 37, 357–76.

Roberts, B.W., Walton, K.E. and Viechtbauer, W. (2006). Patterns of mean-level change in personality traits across the life course: A metaanalysis of longitudinal studies. *Psychological Bulletin*, 132, 3–27.

Roland, G. (2004). Understanding institutional change: Fast-moving and slow-moving institutions. *Studies in Comparative International Development*, 38(4), 109–31.

Rotondo, F.D., Carlson, D.S., Stepina, L.P. and Nicholson, J.D. (1997). Hofstede's country classification 25 years later. *The Journal of Social Psychology*, 137(1), 43–54.

Sargent-Cox, K., Butterworth, P. and Anstey, K.J. (2011). The global financial crisis and psychological health in a sample of Australian older adults: A longitudinal study. *Social Science and Medicine*, 73, 1105–12.

Schimmack, U., Radhakrishnan, P., Oishi, S., Dzokoto, V. and Ahadi, S. (2002). Culture, personality, and subjective well-being: Integrating process models of life satisfaction. *Journal of Personality and Social Psychology*, 82(4), 582–93.

Schleicher, D.J., Watt, J.D. and Greguras, G.J. (2004). Reexamining the job satisfaction-performance relationship: The complexity of attitudes. *Journal of Applied Psychology*, 89, 165–77.

Schwatrz, S.H. (2009). Culture matters: National value cultures, sources and consequences. In R.S. Wyer, C.Y. Chiu and Y.Y. Hong (eds), *Understanding Culture: Theory, Research and Application* (pp. 127–50). New York: Psychology Press.

Stajkovic, A.D. and Luthans, F. (1997). A meta-analysis of the effects of organizational behavior modification on task performance, 1975–1995. *Academy of Management Journal*, 40, 1122–49.

Uysal, S.D. and Pohlmeier, W. (2011). Unemployment duration and personality. *Journal of Economic Psychology*, 32, 980–92.

Verschoor, C.-C. (1999). Corporate performance is closely linked to a strong ethical commitment. *Business and Society Review*, 100(4), 407–15.

Viinikainen, J., Kokko, K., Pulkkinen, L. and Pehkonen, J. (2010). Personality and labour market income: Evidence from longitudinal data. *Labour*, 24(2), 201–20.

Williams, R.M. (1979). Change and stability in values and value systems: A sociological perspective. In M. Rokeach (ed.), *Understanding Human Values: Individual and Societal* (pp. 15–46). New York: Free Press.

19

From Soldier to Citizen: Examining the Role of Political Skill in Veterans' Experiences in the Civilian Workplace

Kaylee J. Hackney, Charn P. McAllister, Jeremy D. Mackey, Joshua C. Palmer and Pamela L. Perrewé

Introduction

The US Census Bureau reports that there were 21,230,865 veterans in the United States as of 2012. Of these veterans, 11,659,939 were between the ages of 18 to 64 and 8,727,120, or roughly 74.8%, of veterans between the ages of 18–64 are currently employed in the civilian labor force (U.S. Census Bureau 2012). Unfortunately, military veterans have a number of problems maintaining their jobs in the civilian workforce (Bureau of Labor Statistics 2013). Some of this difficulty assimilating into the civilian workforce may be attributed to elevated rates of posttraumatic stress disorder (PTSD) among veterans. According to the US Department of Veteran Affairs 11–20% of veterans from the Iraq and Afghanistan wars, 10% of Desert Storm veterans, and 30% of Vietnam veterans experience some form of PTSD, as opposed to 7–8% of the general US population (2013). However, other factors may also contribute to the ability of veterans to transition to the civilian workforce. Research by Overman and Leonard has shown that many veterans experience difficulty translating their military job skills to the civilian workforce (2010). Our intent in this chapter is to determine which skills contribute to an increased fit between military veterans and civilian organizations.

Although veterans may have numerous relevant work experiences and skills (e.g., leadership, team work), they may not understand how their skills transfer well into addressing their job duties in civilian organizations. Given the research linking political skill to important work outcomes (e.g., lower job stress and higher performance; Ferris, Treadway, Perrewé, Brouer, Douglas, and Lux 2007), we focus on the role of veterans' political skill in the relationship between job skill transfer and person-environment (P-E) fit. Political skill refers to an individual's ability to understand others and themselves at work, and the capacity to influence others in order to achieve both personal and organizational goals (Ferris et al. 2007).

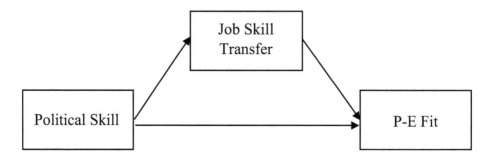

Figure 19.1   The role of political skill and job skill transfer on person-environment fit

Thus far, research on political skill has focused primarily on the general workforce and has not examined veterans as a specific subset of the workforce population. This research examines the role of veterans' political skill on their experiences in the civilian workforce. Figure 19.1 presents the model guiding this research.

Theoretical Foundations and Hypothesis Development

POLITICAL SKILL

Research has consistently demonstrated the predictive ability of political skill and provided evidence of its position as one of the most important social effectiveness constructs (Ferris et al. 2005b). Specifically, political skill is defined as "the ability to effectively understand others at work, and to use such knowledge to influence others to act in ways that enhance one's personal and/or organizational objectives" (Ferris et al. 2005b, p. 127). Individuals with high levels of political skill are capable of understanding situations, reading others, and adapting their behavior to achieve desirable outcomes for themselves and their organizations (Momm, Blickle, and Liu 2013). The political skill construct is made up of four dimensions: social astuteness, interpersonal influence, networking ability, and apparent sincerity (Ferris, Davidson, and Perrewé 2005a).

Individuals who are socially astute are perceptive and are skilled at understanding situations and people well (Momm et al. 2013). Rather than simply accepting the outcomes of social interactions, socially astute individuals are able to interpret the social and environmental cues that result in pertinent outcomes. Likewise, these individuals generally possess a great degree of self-awareness (Ferris et al. 2005a). This sense of awareness allows individuals to know when and if they should contribute to a social situation. Interpersonal influence refers to the ability to exert influence on other members of the organization in order to bring about the desired response of the influencer (Ferris et al. 2007). Individuals who score highly on interpersonal influence are flexible and tend to alter their behavior as interactions develop in order to subtly elicit the desired response (Ferris et al. 2005a). Thus, if used effectively, this skill enables influencers to bring about desired change through subtle and targeted means, instead of trying to overtly overpower co-workers or supervisors.

The networking ability dimension of political skill measures the skill with which individuals establish networks that can then be leveraged for personal or organizational benefit (Ferris et al. 2005a). The ability to foster close relationships with others is advantageous because it increases both individuals' and their organizations' social capital by expanding their networks and potentially stockpiling favors that could benefit the organization. The final dimension of political skill is apparent sincerity; individuals skilled in this dimension generally "are, or appear to be, honest, open, and genuine" (Lvina et al. 2012, p. 173) These individuals are able to present themselves as such due to their ability to "come across as possessing high levels of integrity, authenticity, and sincerity" (Lvina et al. 2012, p. 173) and are capable of convincing their target that they are indeed sincerely engaged and interested in the interaction for altruistic reasons rather than ulterior motives (Jones 1990).

Political skill is a key social effectiveness construct with many practical implications for success in the workforce. Political skill has been shown to facilitate individuals' perceptions of opportunities to perform varying behaviors of value to their organizations and their co-workers (Jawahar, Meurs, Ferris, and Hochwarter 2008). Similarly, politically skilled individuals are able to self-monitor effectively and to pick up on subtle cues that allow them to enhance their own success (Ferris, Treadway, Brouer, and Munyon 2012). Political skill has also been associated with higher job performance ratings from supervisors, more career success, team performance, and less experienced stress (Ferris et al. 2005a; Perrewé, Zellars, Ferris, Rossi, Kacmar, and Ralston 2004). In the following sections, we examine the role of political skill on P-E fit and perceptions of how well veterans' previously acquired job skills will transfer into civilian organizations.

PERSON-ENVIRONMENT FIT

P-E fit research dates back more than 100 years (Kristof-Brown, Zimmerman, and Johnson 2005; Parsons 1909). P-E fit, also referred to as perceived similarity or prototypicality, can be defined as "a person's subjective assessment of the degree to which he or she is a prototypical member of the group" (Ashmore, Deaux, and McLaughlin-Volpe 2004, p. 83). Thus, organizational P-E fit can be defined as the congruence or similarity between the employees and their work environment (Edwards 2008). Edwards (2008) examined Parsons' (1909) early work and how it underscored the importance of good P-E fit by suggesting that an occupation out of harmony with workers' skills and abilities results in inefficiencies and a lack of enthusiasm, whereas an occupation in harmony with workers' skills and abilities results in enthusiasm and passion for work.

In a meta-analysis of the outcomes of P-E fit, Kristof-Brown et al. (2005) found that good P-E fit has been associated with a variety of positive outcomes, such as increased job satisfaction, organizational commitment, satisfaction with one's co-workers and supervisors, and improved performance. Good P-E fit also has been associated with decreased intentions to quit, strain, and perceptions of a political environment (Kristof-Brown et al. 2005). Unfortunately, very little research has examined antecedents of P-E fit. Given the desirability of the above-mentioned outcomes associated with P-E fit, it is important for managers to understand the antecedents of P-E fit so that they encourage and help to develop the P-E fit of their current employees.

POLITICAL SKILL AND P-E FIT

In the present study, P-E fit reflects the extent to which veterans perceive they fit in with the other members of their civilian organizations. Individuals possessing high levels of political skill believe that they are in control of their situation and fully capable of navigating their social environment at work. Conversely, individuals lacking in political skill tend to feel "out of control" and often are unable to pick up on important social cues. One potential reason for this difference is that politically skilled individuals are confident in their ability to adjust their behavior to fit in with their co-workers and their organization. Thus, it is expected that highly politically skilled individuals are more likely to appropriately read social situations, determine the appropriate behaviors to use when engaging with others in the workplace, and ultimately perceive higher levels of P-E fit with the organization than individuals with low levels of political skill. Therefore, we hypothesize:

Hypothesis 1: Political skill will be positively related to P-E fit.

JOB SKILL TRANSFER AND POLITICAL SKILL

Job skill transfer has been defined as "the continuous use of acquired knowledge and abilities when moving from one job to another" (Fine 1957, p. 938). In this chapter, we specifically are interested in the transfer of skills veterans learned in the military to the civilian workplace. Previous research has shown that a key predictor of cross-job skill transfer is inter-job similarity (Lance, Mayfied, and Gould 1993). The greater the similarity between the two jobs, the greater the skill transfer. Lance, Kavanaugh, and Gould (1993) broke inter-job similarity down even further into two categories: job learning difficulty and aptitude requirements. They found that skills are more transferable from jobs that are more difficult to learn and across jobs that draw upon similar aptitudes (e.g., verbal or quantitative abilities) than skills that are easier to learn or draw upon different aptitudes. Although inter-job similarity is a good starting point for the study of transferability, prior research seems to focus on explicit job skills and leaves out a major part of every job – the social environment.

In the training literature, Chiaburu and Marinova (2005) identified three factors that contribute to successful skill transfer from training to the job: individual characteristics, work environment, and training design. Political skill, as an individual characteristic that allows individuals to feel in control of their environment, may be an antecedent to perceptions of P-E fit. This is particularly likely if individuals are attempting to determine whether the skills they acquired while in the military will transfer to the civilian work environment.

Political skill is a type of social self-efficacy that aids individuals attempting to navigate their environment. Chiaburu and Marinova (2005) found that the individual characteristic of self-efficacy, which is the "self-belief in one's capabilities to exercise control over events to accomplish desired goals" (Wood and Bandura 1989, p. 364) was related to skill transfer. Highly politically skilled individuals believe that they can successfully navigate their environment and are aware of their interpersonal skills, know how to use them, and are confident that they will be able to succeed. This awareness suggests that highly politically skilled individuals not only focus on the transfer of explicit skills they learned on the job in the military, but also recognize the importance of their social skills they may have gained in the service (e.g., leadership, networking, and teamwork). Thus, we argue that highly politically skilled individuals will perceive higher levels of job skill transfer than individuals with low levels of political skill because they take into consideration all applicable skills, both explicit and social.

Interestingly, Chiaburu and Marinova (2005) found that peer support was related to skill transfer. The amount of peer support individuals receive depends greatly on how those individuals interact with the people around them. Given that individuals with high political skill have high levels of interpersonal skills, it is logical that they will be able to receive more peer support than individuals with low political skill, leading to better job skill transfer. Based on earlier research on political skill, we argue that individuals who are high in political skill (e.g., they are socially astute and excel at networking) are more likely to perceive opportunities and to generate options when determining how to handle work situations (Zellars, Perrewé, Rossi, Tepper, and Ferris 2008). Thus, individuals high in political skill experience feelings of control over their work environment resulting in higher levels of self-efficacy and confidence. Based on the argument above, we hypothesize:

Hypothesis 2: Political skill will be positively related to job skill transfer.

JOB SKILL TRANSFER AND P-E FIT

One type of P-E fit covered in previous research is the fit between individuals' abilities or skills and the demands of their environment (Edwards 1996; McGrath 1976). If individuals believe they have the necessary skills to succeed, they will perceive themselves to have good P-E fit. This idea is highlighted in Dawis and Lofquist's (1984) theory of work adjustment in which they examined the correspondence between individuals' ability sets and the ability requirements of their jobs. Correspondence can be defined as "a harmonious relationship between individual and environment, suitability of the individual to the environment and of the environment to the individual, consonance or agreement between individual and environment, and a reciprocal and complementary relationship between the individual and environment" (p. 54). Correspondence between individuals' abilities and their job demands leads to satisfactoriness, which is the evaluation of employees' successful fulfillment of the job demands by sources other than the worker. This level of satisfactoriness is then linked to several outcomes, such as retention, promotion, transferring, and firing (Dawis and Lofquist 1984).

Based on the importance placed on individuals' ability sets in the theory of work adjustment (Dawis and Lofquist 1984), it is logical to connect individuals' perceived job skill transfer and P-E fit. If veterans are confident that the skills they obtained in the military and during their lifetime will allow them to meet their job demands (i.e., ability set – ability requirement correspondence), they are likely to perceive high levels of P-E fit with the people around them. Therefore, we hypothesize that job skill transfer will be positively related to P-E fit. Furthermore, based on the connections between political skill and job skill transfer, as well as the relationship between job skill transfer and P-E fit, we argue that job skill transfer will mediate the relationship between political skill and P-E fit.

Hypothesis 3: Job skill transfer will be related positively to P-E fit.
Hypothesis 4: Job skill transfer will mediate the relationship between political skill and P-E fit.

Method

SAMPLE AND PROCEDURES

Participants were 251 veterans recruited through the use of social media sites and personal emails who represented each of the four branches of the US military: Army (84%), Navy (6%), Air Force (7%), and Coast Guard (1%). Specifically, we posted invitations to an online survey on several veterans' group pages on various social media sites (e.g., Facebook, LinkedIn) in order to ensure we reached our target population. All surveys remained open for two months from the time of their original posting to ensure that those who did not log into their accounts very often had the opportunity to see it. The final sample respondents averaged approximately 49 years of age ($M = 49.1$, $SD = 11.5$), 48 hours worked per week ($M = 48.2$, $SD = 11.4$), nine years of organizational tenure ($M = 8.6$, $SD = 9.5$), served in the military for 18 years ($M = 17.8$, $SD = 9.3$), and spent almost two years in combat zones ($M = 1.8$, $SD = 3.6$). The sample was comprised of 59% officers versus 41% enlisted, 90% of which were male.

MEASURES

The following construct measures were rated along an agreement scale (i.e., 1 = "Strongly Disagree," 7 = "Strongly Agree"), unless otherwise noted.

Political skill. We used the 18-item measure of political skill created by Ferris et al. (2005b) that included items such as "I spend a lot of time and effort at work networking with others" and "I am good at building relationships with influential people at work" ($\alpha = 0.91$).

Job skill transfer. We used one item to measure job skill transfer (i.e., "The job skills I utilized in the military transfer well into civilian life"). Prior measurements of job skill transfer amongst veterans have utilized matching individuals' military job with their civilian occupation (i.e., if they match, a successful skill transfer is recorded; Mangum and Ball 1989) or a multi-item measure that resulted in high correlations (i.e., 0.74) between items, which suggested that a single-item measure may be more effective (Spiegel and Shultz 2003).

Person-environment fit. We used the four-item measure of goodness-of-fit from Stoner, Perrewé, and Hofacker's (2011) multidimensional identity scale to examine P-E fit. The measure included items such as "I am like other members of my organization" and "I have attributes, traits, features, and behaviors that are normal for a member of my organization" ($\alpha = 0.92$).

CONTROL VARIABLES

Demographic control variables. One-item measures were used to capture age (i.e., "What is your age (in years)?"), gender (0 = male, 1 = female; "What is your gender?"), hours worked per week (i.e., "On average, how many hours do you work per week?"), and organizational tenure (in years; "How many years and months have you worked at the same organization?"). Age, gender, hours worked per week, and organizational tenure were used as demographic control variables, given their relationships with the mediator (i.e., job skill transfer) and dependent variable (i.e., P-E fit; O'Reilly III, Chatman, and Caldwell 1991).

Time in military. We used one item to measure the number of years respondents served in the military (i.e., "How many years and months were you in the military?").

Time since military service. We used one item to measure the number of years since respondents had served in the military (i.e., "How long has it been since you were last considered on full-time active duty?").

Combat experience. The relationship between stress and experience in combat is well-documented (Grinker and Speigel 1945; Solomon, Mikulincer, and Hofboll 1987). We expected that some variation in veterans' P-E fit would be due to the amount of time they spent deployed to a combat zone. Combat experience was measured by using a single item that asked respondents to report the number of years they were deployed to a designated combat zone (i.e., "How much time [if any] did you spend in a combat zone while you were on active duty in the military?").

Rank. We asked respondents to report their highest rank attained while in the military. Using military convention, we dichotomized responses into two groups: enlisted service members (0) and officers (1).

ANALYSIS

We conducted a simple mediation analysis using Hayes' (2013) PROCESS extension in the SPSS 22.0 statistical package (http://afhayes.com/introduction-to-mediation-moderation-and-conditional-process-analysis.html). Researchers have noted that earlier mediation techniques, such as Baron and Kenny's (1986) methodology, are no longer considered optimal when compared to other readily available alternatives (LeBreton, Wu, and Bing 2009), such as Hayes' PROCESS procedure. Hayes' extension overcomes several problems associated with the Baron and Kenny (1986) method, particularly in that it allows researchers to include more than three variables (e.g., covariates), to review both the direct and indirect effects of the independent variables and the mediator, as well as incorporate bootstrapping to facilitate a single-step mediation analysis. Hayes' (2013) PROCESS extension reports unstandardized effect sizes. We report unstandardized and standardized effect sizes. We calculated standardized effect sizes by multiplying the unstandardized effect sizes by the quotient of the standard deviations for the independent (X) and dependent (Y) variables (i.e., $B * [\sigma_x/\sigma_y]$). Prior to conducting the analysis, the responses for each measure were summed and then the average was taken to provide a mean score for each respondent. To conduct the actual analysis, we used model 4 (i.e., simple mediation) as outlined in Hayes' (2013) templates document. Variables included in the analysis consisted of X = political skill, M = job skill transfer, Y = P-E fit, and covariates (i.e., control variables) = age, gender, hours worked per week, organizational tenure, time in military, time since military service, time in combat, and rank (i.e., officer versus enlisted).

Results

DESCRIPTIVE STATISTICS AND CORRELATIONS

Means, standard deviations, and zero-order correlations among study variables are shown in Table 19.1. The correlations demonstrate that political skill ($r = 0.16$, $p < 0.05$) and job skill transfer ($r = 0.23$, $p < 0.01$) were both related to P-E fit in the hypothesized direction. Also, the time in military ($r = 0.13$, $p < 0.05$) and rank ($r = 0.14$, $p < 0.05$) variables demonstrated significant and positive relationships with the dependent variable.

Table 19.1   Means, standard deviations, and intercorrelations among study variables

	Variable	Mean	s.d.	1	2	3	4	5	6	7	8	9	10	11
1.	Political Skill	5.39	.78	-										
2.	Job Skill Transfer	5.18	1.70	.19**	-									
3.	Person-Environment Fit	4.43	1.53	.16*	.23**	-								
4.	Age	49.12	11.48	.06	.27**	.10	-							
5.	Gender	.10	.29	-.08	-.10	-.07	-.21**	-						
6.	Hours Worked Per Week	48.18	11.35	.08	.07	.01	-.08	-.01	-					
7.	Organizational Tenure	8.56	9.47	.08	.14*	.03	.31**	-.04	.07	-				
8.	Time in Military	17.83	9.29	.06	.25**	.13*	.55**	-.18**	-.14*	.15*	-			
9.	Time Since Military	10.86	10.21	.05	.07	.01	.55**	-.08	-.02	.20**	-.20**	-		
10.	Time in Combat Zone	1.80	3.74	.08	.02	.02	.14*	-.05	.00	-.01	.10	-.16*	-	
11.	Rank	.59	0.49	.11	.31**	.14*	.25**	-.06	.10	-.01	.24**	.03	.04	-

Notes: N = 251. * p<.05 **=p<.01 (all significance tests are 2-tailed). Gender: male = 0, female = 1. Rank: enlisted = 0, officer = 1.

HYPOTHESIZED MODEL

Table 19.2 presents the results of the mediation analysis that tests our four main hypotheses. The results provided support for Hypothesis 1, which predicted that political skill would have a positive relationship with P-E fit ($B = 0.23$, $\beta = 0.12$, $p < 0.05$). Hypothesis 2, which predicted that political skill would have a positive effect on job skill transfer, was also supported ($B = 0.30$, $\beta = 0.14$, $p < 0.05$). The results also supported Hypothesis 3, which predicted that job skill transfer would directly affect P-E fit ($B = 0.16$, $\beta = 0.18$, $p < 0.05$). Overall, the model explained 17% of the variance (i.e., $R^2 = 0.17$) in job skill transfer and 8% of the variance in P-E fit (i.e., $R^2 = 0.08$).

Hypothesis 4 predicted that job skill transfer would mediate the relationship between political skill and P-E fit. Hypothesis 4 was supported because zero was not present in the 95% confidence interval for the indirect effect of political skill on P-E fit through job skill transfer (LLCI = 0.003, ULCI = 0.132, $p < 0.05$). The direct effect of political skill on P-E fit was significant, however when the mediator was included in the model, it was no longer significant ($p > 0.05$). The change in significance due to the addition of the mediator (i.e., job skill transfer) suggested the presence of full mediation. In sum, the results provided support for all four of the hypotheses, suggesting that job skill transfer is an important mediating variable within the political skill – P-E fit relationship.

Table 19.2   Regression results for indirect effect of political skill on Person-Environment fit

Predictor		B	SE	t	p
	Mediator Model (Job Skill Transfer)				
Constant		1.32	.99	1.33	.184
Age		.02	.02	.97	.334
Gender		-.15	.35	-.44	.657
Hours Worked Per Week		.01	.01	1.01	.316
Organizational Tenure		.00	.00	1.07	.287
Time in Military		.00	.00	1.02	.309
Time Since Military		.00	.00	-.08	.939
Time in Combat Zone		.00	.00	-.50	.619
Rank (enlisted/officer)		.80	.21	3.71	< .001
Political Skill		.30	.13	2.29	.023
	Dependent Variable Model				
	(Person-Environment Fit)				
Constant		2.26	.95	2.39	.018
Age		.00	.02	-.02	.986
Gender		-.16	.33	-.47	.638
Hours Worked Per Week		.00	.01	-.24	.814
Organizational Tenure		.00	.00	-.16	.874
Time in Military		.00	.00	.49	.622
Time Since Military		.00	.00	-.02	.981
Time in Combat Zone		.00	.00	-.13	.898
Rank (enlisted/officer)		.19	.21	.88	.380
Political Skill		.23	.13	1.81	.072
Job Skill Transfer		.16	.06	2.56	.011
	Effect	LLCI	ULCI	C.I.	p
	Indirect Effect of Political Skill on Person-Environment Fit				
Indirect Effect	.047	.003	.132	95%	< .05

Notes: N = 251. Unstandardized regression coefficients are reported. Age, organizational tenure, time in military, time since military, and time in combat zone measured in years. Gender: male = 0, female = 1. Rank: enlisted = 0, officer = 1.

Discussion

CONTRIBUTIONS TO THEORY AND RESEARCH

Due to the important outcomes associated with good P-E fit (e.g., increased job satisfaction, increased organizational commitment, and decreased intent to quit) and the current influx of veterans entering civilian life, the purpose of this study was to examine the factors that might impact veterans' levels of P-E fit. In doing so, we investigated the relationships between political skill, job skill transfer, and P-E fit. The results indicated that political skill was positively related to P-E fit such that veterans who perceived they had high political skill reported good P-E fit with their civilian organizations. Furthermore, this relationship was fully mediated by job skill transfer. This suggests that veterans with high political skill better understood how the skills they learned in the military, and throughout their lifetime, transferred to their civilian organization, allowing them to better fit in with their organization than veterans with low political skill.

This study makes two main contributions to research and theory. First, very little research has been conducted on the antecedents of P-E fit. The vast majority of previous research treats P-E fit as a predictor variable and examines the outcomes associated with good fit. Second, the role of political skill has not been examined with veterans as a subpopulation of the workforce. Our results indicated that political skill is an antecedent to good P-E fit. This is an important finding because political skill is not an innate trait or skill; it can be learned and developed (Ferris, et al. 2005a). This suggests that interventions can be developed to help increase veterans' levels of political skill, and ultimately perceptions of P-E fit, when entering the civilian workforce.

STRENGTHS AND LIMITATIONS

The primary strength of this study is its usage of a prevalent and increasingly important population: US military veterans. After over a decade of war that required total troop numbers to soar, the United States is now downsizing all four branches of the military. Consequently, this has led to an ever-increasing population of veterans that will need to transition from military to civilian life. Roughly 44% of the veterans who have served since the September 11, 2001 terrorist attacks have reportedly struggled making this transition (Morin 2011). Our study endeavors to diagnose what causes veterans to experience difficulty during their transition, as well as to provide possible interventions (e.g., political skill training) that may reduce veterans' struggles. Through an examination of factors that affect P-E fit veterans experience in civilian organizations, we believe that an important first step toward providing this unique population some transition guidance has been taken and can be strengthened and developed by future research. A methodological strength of this study was the ability to provide support for the hypothesized relationships even when controlling for several potentially confounding variables (i.e., age, gender, hours worked per week, organizational tenure, time in military, time since military, time in combat zones, and rank).

As with all research, this study has limitations. Although respondents represented all four branches of the military, the sample was comprised of predominantly Army personnel (84%), and 90% of respondents were males. Nonetheless, our sample demographics resemble the male to female ratio of the Army. Furthermore, our sample consists only of employed veterans. There is, perhaps, an even greater need to help our unemployed veterans. Also, our mediating variable, job skill transfer, was based on a single-item measure. In addition, our results relied solely upon self-reported measures. Due to this, common method variance was a concern. However, the likelihood of common method bias was limited by taking the recommended procedural actions for survey design (e.g., protecting respondents' anonymity, offsetting question order to avoid priming effects; Podsakoff, MacKenzie, and Podsakoff 2012; Podsakoff, MacKenzie, Lee, and Podsakoff 2003). Furthermore, the correlations among the variables were low-to-moderate in strength, suggesting that CMV likely was not a major issue.

DIRECTIONS FOR FUTURE RESEARCH

Many of this study's limitations provide opportunities for future research. First of all, given that our sample was comprised of mostly Army personnel, future research on this topic could focus more on the other branches of the military and examine whether responses differ among them. Due to differences in each military branch's purpose, it may be that certain branches train their service members in more readily transferrable job skills than others. Additionally, it would be interesting to examine whether female veterans respond differently than male veterans. Given our small sample of female veterans, we were not able to examine gender differences in this study.

As with much research, future research on veterans' transitions into the civilian workforce should take a longitudinal approach. This type of research design would enable researchers to examine soldiers' levels of political skill when they entered the military, the types of job skills they gained during their service, and how well they perceive these skills transferring into the civilian workplace upon returning home. Given the overarching goal of this study, which was to help veterans transition more successfully from military to civilian life, perhaps the most important direction for future research would be to examine unemployed veterans. By definition, these are the individuals who did not transition well from military to civilian life. In order to help future soldiers transition, it is imperative that we find out why these individuals did not make successful transitions and what the military and/or managers can do to help.

PRACTICAL IMPLICATIONS

Given the abundance of veterans who seek civilian employment after military service, there are a multitude of economic and cultural benefits to examining the factors that facilitate smooth transitions. If veterans are able to successfully assimilate into the civilian workforce, they may provide the workforce with a unique set of skills, experiences, and increased diversity within the workforce. For these reasons, it is critical that the military and civilian organizations ensure that they are providing veterans with proper training to help them become acclimated to the civilian workforce.

We found that political skill is particularly important for smooth transitions from the military to the civilian workforce. Veterans with political skill can use impression management techniques effectively, which can enhance others' evaluations of them (Stone and Stone, 2015). This will not only help improve veterans' performance, but also the extent to which veterans perceive they belong and are connected with others in the organization. Future research on this topic may also be of interest to the US military as they are already providing transition training to individuals leaving military service. Determining the most critical and trainable skills (e.g., political skill) that the military can impart to those transitioning out of the military will ensure the military is giving veterans the necessary skills and guidance to successfully transition to civilian life. This knowledge could be used to develop new training programs designed to ensure veterans receive the proper training in political skill that will help reincorporate them into the workforce after their military careers. Similarly, organizations can use these findings to create workshops and training programs to help facilitate smooth transitions. Although this may have costs for organizations up-front, these costs may be offset by veterans' improved productivity and efficiency, as well as cutting costs associated with failed military to civilian transitions.

Conclusion

We examined and confirmed the important role of veterans' political skill on their perceptions of job skill transferability and P-E fit with their civilian organizations. Military veterans have a multitude of reasons for joining the military, and they provide a vital structure that enables society and business to function in the United States. Due to these contributions, it is critical that we ensure that they are given a fair opportunity to obtain skills which enable them to move on to successful careers after the service. Based on our empirical findings, we argue that political skill is important for a smooth transition from serving in the military to successfully working in the civilian workforce.

References

Ashmore, R.D., Deaux, K. and McLaughlin-Volpe, T. (2004). An organizing framework for collective identity: Articulation and significance of multidimensionality. *Psychological Bulletin*, 130(1), 80.

Baron, R.M., and Kenny, D.A. (1986). The moderator-mediator variable distinction in social psychological research: Conceptual, strategic, and statistical considerations. *Journal of Personality and Social Psychology*, 51(6), 1173–82.

Bureau of Labor Statistics (2013). *U.S. Department of Labor, The Editor's Desk, Unemployment among veterans of the U.S. Armed Forces declines in 2012*. Available at: http://www.bls.gov/opub/ted/2013/ted_20130322.htm, accessed July 7, 2014.

Chiaburu, D.S. and Marinova, S.V. (2005). What predicts skill transfer? An exploratory study of goal orientation, training self-efficacy and organizational supports. *International Journal of Training and Development*, 9(2), 110–23.

Dawis, R.V. and Lofquist, L.H. (1984). *A Psychological Theory of Work Adjustment*. Minneapolis: University of Minnesota Press.

Edwards, J.R. (1996). An examination of competing versions of the person-environment fit approach to stress. *Academy of Management Journal*, 39(2), 292–339.

Edwards, J.R. (2008). Person–environment fit in organizations: An assessment of theoretical progress. *The Academy of Management Annals*, 2(1), 167–230.

Ferris, G.R., Davidson, S.L. and Perrewé, P.L. (2005a). *Political Skill at Work: Impact on Work Effectiveness*. Mountain View: Davies-Black Publishing.

Ferris, G.R., Treadway, D.C., Brouer, R.L. and Munyon, T.P. (2012). Political skill in the organizational sciences. In G.R. Ferris and D.C. Treadway (eds), *Politics in organizations: Theory and research considerations* (pp. 487–528). New York: Routledge/Taylor & Francis.

Ferris, G.R., Treadway, D.C., Perrewé, P.L., Brouer, R.L., Douglas, C. and Lux, S. (2007). Political skill in organizations. *Journal of Management*, 33, 290–320.

Ferris, G.R. Treadway, D.C., Kolodinsky, R.W., Hochwarter, W.A., Kacmar, C.J., Douglas, C. and Frink, D.D. (2005b). Development and validation of the political skill inventory. *Journal of Management*, 31, 126–52.

Fine, S.A. (1957). A reexamination of "transferability of skills" – Part II. *Monthly Labor Review*, 80, 938–48.

Grinker, R.R. and Spiegel, J.P. (1945). *Men under Stress*. Philadelphia: Blakiston.

Hayes, A.F. (2013). *Introduction to Mediation, Moderation, and Conditional Process Analysis: A Regression-based Approach*. New York: Guilford Press.

Jawahar, I.M., Meurs, J.A., Ferris, G.R. and Hochwarter, W.A. (2008). Self-efficacy and political skill as comparative predictors of task and contextual performance: A two study constructive replication. *Human Performance*, 21, 1–20.

Jones, E.E. (1990). *Interpersonal Perception*. New York: W.H. Freeman.

Kristof-Brown, A.L., Zimmerman, R.D. and Johnson, E.C. (2005). Consequences of individuals' fit at work: A meta-analysis of person-job, person-organization, person-group, and person-supervisor fit. *Personnel Psychology*, 58(2), 281–342.

Lance, C.E., Kavanagh, M.J. and Gould, R.B. (1993a). Development and convergent validation of a methodology for estimating cross-job retraining times. *Journal of Business and Psychology*, 8(1), 67–90.

Lance, C.E., Mayfield, D.L. and Gould, R.B. (1993b). A postdictive validation of cross-job retraining time estimates for 43 US Air Force enlisted specialties. *Military Psychology*, 5(3), 173.

LeBreton, J.M., Wu, J. and Bing, M.N. (2009). The truth(s) on testing for mediation in the social and organizational sciences. In C.E. Lance and R.J. Vandenberg (eds), *Statistical and Methodological Myths and Urban Legends* (pp. 107–42). New York: Routledge.

Lvina, E., Johns, G., Treadway, D. C., Blickle, G., Liu, L., Liu, J., Atay, S., Zettler, I., Solga, J., Noethen, D. and Ferris, G.R. (2012). Measure invariance of the political skill inventory (PSI) across five cultures. *International Journal of Cross Cultural Management*, 12(2), 171–91.

Mangum, S.L. and Ball, D.E. (1989). The transferability of military-provided occupational training in the post-draft era. *Industrial and Labor Relations Review*, 42(2), 230–45.

McGrath, J.E. (1976). Stress and behavior in organizations. In M. Dunnette (ed.), *Handbook of Industrial and Organizational Psychology* (pp. 1351–95). Chicago: Rand McNally.

Momm, T.S., Blickle, G. and Liu, Y. (2013). Political skill and emotional cue learning via voices: A training study. *Journal of Applied Social Psychology*, 43(11), 2307–17.

Morin, R. (2011). *The Difficult Transition from Military to Civilian Life*. Washington, DC: Pew Research Center. Available at: www.pewsocialtrends.org/2011/12/08/the-difficult-transition-from-military-to-civilian-life/, accessed December 14, 2013.

O'Reilly, C.A., Chatman, J. and Caldwell, D.F. (1991). People and organizational culture: A profile comparison approach to assessing person-organization fit. *Academy of Management Journal*, 34(3), 487–516.

Overman, S. and Leonard, B. (2010). Translating talent from military to civilian jobs. *Society for Human Resource Management*. Available at: http://www.shrm.org/about/news/pages/militarytocivilianjobs.aspx, accessed July 26, 2014.

Parsons, F. (1909). *Choosing a Vocation*. Boston: Houghton Mifflin.

Perrewé, P.L., Zellars, K.L., Ferris, G.R., Rossi, A.M., Kacmar, C.J., and Ralston, D.A. (2004). Neutralizing job stressors: Political skill as an antidote to the dysfunctional consequences of role conflict stressors. *Academy of Management Journal*, 47, 141–52.

Podsakoff, P.M., MacKenzie, S.B. and Podsakoff, N.P. (2012). Sources of method bias in social science research and recommendations on how to control it. *Annual Review of Psychology*, 63, 539–69.

Podsakoff, P.M., MacKenzie, S.B., Lee, J.-Y. and Podsakoff, N.P. (2003). Common method biases in behavioral research: A critical review of the literature and recommended remedies. *Journal of Applied Psychology*, 88(5), 879–903.

Solomon, Z., Mikulincer, M. and Hobfoll, S.E. (1987). Objective versus subjective measurement of stress and social support: Combat-related reactions. *Journal of Consulting and Clinical Psychology*, 55(4), 577–83.

Spiegel, P.E. and Shultz, K.S. (2003). The influence of preretirement planning and transferability of skills on naval officers' retirement satisfaction and adjustment. *Military Psychology*, 15(4), 285–307.

Stone, C. and Stone, D.L. (2015). Factors affecting hiring decisions about veterans. *Human Resource Management Review*, 25(1), 68–79.

Stoner, J., Perrewé, P.L. and Hofacker, C. (2011). The development and validation of the multi-dimensional identification scale (MDIS). *Journal of Applied Social Psychology*, 41(7), 1632–58.

U.S. Census Bureau (2012). *Veteran Status* (2012 American Community Survey). Washington, DC: U.S. Government Printing Office. Available at: http://factfinder2.census.gov/faces/tableservices/jsf/pages/productview.xhtml?pid=ACS_12_1YR_S2101&prodType=table, accessed July 7, 2014.

U.S. Department of Veteran Affairs (2013). *How Common is PTSD?* Available at: http://www.ptsd.va.gov/public/PTSD-overview/basics/how-common-is-ptsd.asp, accessed July 26, 2014.

Wood, R.E. and Bandura, A. (1989). Social cognitive theory of organizational management. *Academy of Management Review*, 14, 361–84.

Zellars, K.L., Perrewé, P.L., Rossi, A.M., Tepper, B.T. and Ferris, G.R. (2008). Moderating effects of political skill, perceived control, and job-related self efficacy on the relationship between negative affectivity and physiological strain. *Journal of Organizational Behavior*, 29, 549–71.

20

Morbidity and Mortality in Popular Musicians: An Examination by Era, Sex and Music Genre

Dianna T. Kenny

Introduction

Much of the literature on stressful workplaces, occupationally inspired psychological crises and critical incidents has focused on the dangerous or human service professions such as the military, policing, fire-fighting, emergency work, nursing and teaching. Few of us would count among these stressful occupations classical or popular music, or consider that musical workplaces – the symphony orchestra or pop band – to be a source of occupational stress or, worse, psychological trauma and early death. On the contrary, my work with musicians has shown that a significant minority of musicians can be so traumatized by the demands of their occupations that they do indeed experience symptoms of traumatic stress. Some turn to substances to assist their coping efforts. Others engage in suicidal and parasuicidal behaviours, including extreme risk-taking and profound lack of self-care that often results in early death, either intentional or accidental. In the pop music world, it is understood, almost as a *sine qua non*, that there will be sex, drugs, rock'n'roll, risk-taking and early death. In this chapter, I interrogate this proposition by exploring several markers of occupational stress inherent in the death records of popular musicians – shortened life expectancy, suicide, homicide, accidental (non-intentional) death, and increased morbidity throughout the lifespan. Sex differences and differences by music genre membership were also examined. Results indicated that death by suicide, homicide, accident and other health morbidities were significantly more likely in popular musicians compared with age- and sex- matched US populations in musicians surviving beyond 30 years. Musicians dying younger than 31 years mirrored population patterns. Health impacts differed by music genre membership. Metal and punk musicians were most at risk of accidental death and suicide, rap and hip hop musicians were significantly more likely to be murdered, rock musicians were more vulnerable to accidental death, folk and jazz musicians were more likely to die from cancer and blues musicians were more likely to die from heart-related causes. Gospel musicians had the lowest suicide rates, perhaps protected by their religious beliefs.

Introduction

Art is a cry of distress from those who live out within themselves the destiny of humanity ... Inside them turns the movement of the world; only an echo of it leaks out – the work of art. (Schoenberg 1910, p. 12)

Hector Berlioz, a French composer from the late Romantic period once exclaimed, 'Music – What a noble art, what a terrible profession'. (Evans 1994, p. 137). This comment was prompted, no doubt, by the fact that he received very little recognition in his native France during his lifetime for his now universally acclaimed musical compositions. When attention was forthcoming, it came in the form of harsh criticism from contemporaneous French music critics like Hans Gal (1969) and Pierre Scudo, who accused Berlioz of being devoid of melodic ideas and lacking in inspiration. According to Scudo, Berlioz created music that was

sterile algebra ... [with an] incommensurable chaos of a sonority that irritates and shatters the listener without satisfying him ... There is nothing in these strange compositions but noise, disorder ... he behaves like a demon disinherited of divine grace who wants to scale the heavens by force of pride and will. (in Slonimsky 1965, p. 58)

Berlioz scarcely received a better reception overseas, except in Russia, where he was lauded. The *Boston Daily Advertiser* of 29 October 1874, for example, described Berlioz as:

the least respectable of the composers of the new school ... [with] no breath of inspiration and no spark of creative genius ... Knowledge of the principles of composition will no more make a composer than an acquaintance with etymology a poet ... It needs no gift of prophecy to predict that he will be utterly unknown a hundred years hence to everybody but the encyclopaedists and the antiquarians. (Slonimsky 1965, p. 59)

Today's music critics are hardly less brutal. The difference is that everyone who can use a computer, an iPad, an iPhone, a tablet or email is an instant music critic. Some of these media protect critics' identities, allowing them wider scope for the free expression of their vitriol. Justin Bieber discussed his reaction to reading hate mail on Google with Ronson (2010): 'You're so stupid ... your song sucks ... you're gay ... When I like a video I don't waste my time commenting. But people who hate you – they're going to take time to hate you'.

When Justin turned 18, Margary (2012) sketched out his possible futures:

Justin Bieber is now 18 years old. And when you're a teen superstar who has just turned 18, there are really only two options for where you can go next: You can mature into a 'real' artist, or you can swan-dive straight onto the pop-cultural scrap heap with all the other reality stars and drug addicts. [My italics]

Sadly, the 'pop-cultural scrap heap' is piled high with the dead or broken bodies of young musicians whose personal and musical aspirations collided with the aspirations of a commercial machinery that grew up around them, dehumanizing, commodifying and eventually engulfing them. Raeburn (1999, 2000) has noted the rampant substance abuse and large number of premature deaths among popular musicians. She suggested that for psychologically vulnerable musicians who have difficulty with self-esteem and self-regulation, their work culture contributes to early death because it reinforces risk-taking behaviour and treats musicians like income-generating commodities whose role is to satisfy capricious and ever changing consumer demands. Many of these musicians end up feeling suffocated, caged and possessed by their minders, exploiters and fans. Justin Bieber said that while he was on tour, he started to feel like 'a robot ... you're not even yourself. It's weird'. He has become uncertain as to who is trustworthy: 'I keep my guard up a lot, because ... you can't trust anyone in this business ... That's what's sad. You can't trust anybody. I learned that the hard way' (in Ronson 2010). Troubled words indeed from a boy of 18! A year later, Brooker (2013) noticed that Bieber was no longer flying high. He commented that:

> His performances now consist of him quietly begging the audience to leave so he can have some time to himself. But they can't hear his pleas because they're too busy screaming, and they can't see his tears because they're watching his performance while filming it on their Samsungs and he's too far away for the weeping to be visible onscreen. Caught in a trap of his own making, he is the loneliest man in the world.

A recent article on the pop singer, Robbie Williams, began with the sentence: 'After finding fame at 16 with *Take That*, Robbie Williams followed *a classic rock'n'roll script: sex, drugs, rehab and bitterness*' (Hooten 2014, p. 10; my italics). In similar vein, Katel (2010), a blogger for the *Miami New Times* wrote: 'Dead rock stars are a dime a dozen. They usually drink themselves to death, overdose on narcotics, crash cars, or get on faulty aircraft with drunk pilots on drugs who crash cars.' An anonymous biographer left the following comment on the *npr music* website in 2004:

> Singer Dinah Washington, the Grammy-winning 'Queen of the Jukeboxes', left her turbulent life behind at the tender age of 39. In that short period, a volatile mix of undeniable talent and deep-rooted insecurity took her to the heights of fame and the depths of self-doubt. [My italics]

And yet, as the rock guitarist, Mark Volman, observed: 'The music business has a way of making you feel like you're exempt [from] the real world ... there is a kind of false security ... it's impossible to consider that you could die' (in Cody 2007).

Has the path of popular musicians become a 'classic script', and if so, why? Could those observations on Dinah Washington hold the key to a better understanding of this apparently predictable path to desolation, destitution and drug-fuelled destruction to which so many talented popular artists succumb? Does the combination of deep insecurity and uncommon talent that exposes young people to the glare of public scrutiny, criticism and exploitation create a lethal mix for those who are exposed too early?

Justin Bieber appears to be following this 'classic script'. He was born to an 18-year-old mother, who raised him as a single parent after his father abandoned them when Justin was three. Justin told Ronson, 'My mom wasn't the greatest person ... she made mistakes. She drank. She ... did drugs ... she told me about it because she said she did enough bad stuff for the both of us'. Added to personal vulnerabilities are the vagaries of the pop music industry – the loss of boundaries that accrues to the demands of performing and touring that result in dislocation from family, friends and a regular lifestyle, with its constant circadian rhythms and other predictabilities lost through irregular hours, sub-cultural lifestyles and the abuse of alcohol and other substances.

The rock scene is a volatile mix of danger and rebellion. Metal bands evince these qualities in abundance. The thrash metal band, Gwar, is a quintessential exemplar. Founded by Dave Brockie, also known as Oderus Urungus, who recently died of a heroin overdose, aged 51, this band was distinguished by its grotesque costumes, obscenely irreverent lyrics infused with shameless scatological, violent and taboo themes. Brockie and his band described their stage show as 'a microcosm of the human condition' (in Overell 2014). Forever pushing the boundaries of decency and decorum, such bands create moral panic that results in vilification in mainstream media. In 1990, Gwar's British tour was cancelled because it contained simulations of bestiality that were considered too offensive for the public gaze. Indeed, some historians consider metal music partly responsible for the decline of Western civilization. Spheeris's (1988) documentary film exposed the excesses of the metal scene, with its celebration of a profligate lifestyle of drugs, promiscuity, misogyny and valorization of early death. I have long speculated that genres like heavy metal are manifestations of band members' psychological states, which express their rage, impotence and despair, and provide a medium through which vulnerable musicians can project these feelings onto receptive audiences and detractors alike.

Given the inherent hazards of the pop music scene, and the taken-for-granted assumptions that pop musicians will live dangerously, abuse substances and die early, it is concerning that so few systematic attempts have been made to assess the extent of the problem. One old study (Tucker, Faulkner and Horvath 1971) that examined age at death of a small group of musicians who died between 1959 and 1967 found that they had a decreased life expectancy (54 years) compared with the contemporaneous population life expectancy of 69 years. The study also reported higher rates of heart disease among musicians. However, the flawed methods used in this study make the conclusions unreliable. There are, however, three recent studies that describe a profession in crisis.

The first study (Bellis, Hennell, Lushey, Hughes, Tocque and Ashton 2007) showed that pop musicians achieving recent fame or notoriety suffered earlier death compared with population data, and that this finding was robust when age, sex, ethnicity and nationality were controlled. Inclusion criteria were pop musicians who performed on any album in the All-Time Top 1,000 albums (Larkin 2000) from five modern popular music genres (i.e. rock, punk, rap, R&B, electronica). Country, blues, jazz, Celtic, folk and bluegrass were excluded. All of these genres were included in the current study to permit the first comparison of morbidity and mortality between the older and newer genres of popular music. This study calculated total years of musician survival since becoming famous, the date of which was determined by the earliest date of first chart success. In this sample of 1,064 popular musicians, post-fame mortality was 1.7 times greater than demographically matched populations in the United States and United Kingdom. Median age of death for the North American musicians was 35.18 years. Mortality five years post-fame was 2.4%. Chronic drug or alcohol abuse or overdose accounted for one-quarter of the 100 deaths documented in the specified time frame. Pop star survival always fell below that of the matched populations in every year post-fame up to 25 years. In the period two to 25 years post-fame, this sample of popular musicians experienced two to three times the risk of mortality compared with comparable general populations.

The second study (Bellis, Hughes, Sharples, Hennell and Hardcastle 2012) examined the hypothesis that the popular music industry is, as is often claimed in the media, more strongly associated with risk-taking, substance abuse and early death than comparable general populations and that the prevalence of these factors differ by type of performer (solo artist vs band member), nationality (North American vs European) and the experience of childhood adversity. This study investigated these questions using a sample of 1,489 rock and pop musicians who achieved fame between 1956 and 2006. The median age of death for the North American musicians was 45.2 years, compared with 39.6 years for the European musicians. Like the earlier study reported above, musician mortality increased with time since fame and exceeded comparable population death rates for the same time period. Death was strongly associated with substance abuse and risk-taking and, importantly, the experience of childhood adversity. Half of the musicians who died from substance abuse or risk-taking had experienced childhood adversity, compared with a third who died of the same causes but had no childhood adversity recorded. The greater the number of childhood adversities, the more likely a musician was to die of substance abuse or risk-taking. Clinical and epidemiological studies (e.g., Anda et al. 2006; Felitti et al. 1998) have repeatedly identified a strong association between childhood adversity, substance abuse and risk-taking in later life. Post-fame mortality was significantly lower compared with matched general populations – 99.3% in the first year post-fame and 87.6% 40 years post-fame. Solo performers had twice the mortality rate (22.8%) compared with band members (10.2%). Survival improved after 1980 but was still lower than comparable general populations.

The third study (Wolkewitz, Allignol, Graves and Barnett 2011), in the course of investigating whether the age of 27 was a high risk age for death in popular musicians, found that the risk of death for 'famous' musicians aged 20–30 years was two to three times higher than the general UK population. The smoothed death rate showed a peak at 32 years with greatly increased risk of death after age 60.

Most other studies on pop musicians have been interview-based studies with small, non-representative samples that do not address the issues related to life expectancy and cause of death in the pop music population. Notwithstanding, interview studies do give us clues about the occupational stressors experienced by musicians and most of these studies concur with respect to the primary stressors. Sternbach (1995) identified three categories of stressors in the lives of musicians – environmental, inter- and intrapersonal factors, and 'stress factors unique and intrinsic to the lives of performing artists' (p. 4). Cooper and Wills (1989) reported on the outcomes of interviews aimed at understanding the most frequent sources of stress experienced in 70 British male popular musicians. The interviews painted a sobering picture of an occupational group who suffered significant distress, uncertainty, performance anxiety, financial insecurity, and anger at the excessive demands of the music industry, its callous disregard for musician well-being and the absence of a caring social network. Musicians also discussed their irregular work hours, work overload, non-standard hours, lack of sleep, and work underload – periods when they had to play at boring gigs that were not artistically challenging to earn a living. Many commented on the stress of maintaining good relationships with band members and their entourage – promoters, producers, sound engineers – on whom they depended for their work. Family life was also affected, due to irregular work hours, the necessity to travel and the long separations from significant others that this entailed.

Raeburn's (2007) study identified similar sources of stress to those reported in Cooper and Wills (1989), but with several additions. These included the increased exposure and easy access to alcohol and drugs; engaging in depersonalized sex while on tour; increased exposure to pathogenic beliefs about creativity requiring self-destructive or extreme behaviours; and increased exposure to audience, critics, and cultural projections and objectification; conflicts between career and family roles; concerns related to aging in a youth-oriented market; and ongoing issues with the tension between artistic identity and commercial acceptability.

Other researchers have used biographical analysis or psychological autopsy as methods of ascertaining psychiatric diagnoses in musicians, a method that has been criticized on a number of grounds (see, for example, Schlesinger 2004). For example, Wills (2003) formed psychiatric diagnoses of jazz musicians active between 1945 and 1960 and concluded that 29% had an affective disorder, 28% had alcohol-related psychological disorders, and 53% had substance abuse (mostly heroin) disorders. These conclusions have since been challenged, but the method used to critique Wills (2003) – convenience sampling – is also fraught with methodological problems. One study using a convenience sample (Raeburn, Hipple, Delaney and Chesky 2003) reported rates of substance abuse to be as low as 10–16%. This figure may reflect the methodological problems with the study and not the true rate of substance abuse in this population. Dobson (2011) provided a summary of the research to date on popular musicians, but this was also based on an interview study with a very small sample comprising nine jazz and nine classical musicians aged 21 to 34. Other sources of information about the mental and physical health of musicians has come from media and ubiquitous anecdotes that are generalized to much wider segments of the pop music community than might be justified.

Currently, we understand very little about the characteristics of the popular musician population because there have been very few population studies undertaken, in the manner of such studies in the classical musician population (see, for example, Ackermann, Kenny, O'Brien and Driscoll, 2014; Kenny and Ackerman 2015; Kenny, Driscoll and Ackermann 2014). The aim of this study was to assemble a comprehensive dataset representing a strictly defined population of popular musicians who died between 1950 and 2014. Data on gender, year born, age at birth, age at death, decade of death, cause of death and music genre membership were compiled for all musicians who met inclusion criteria. The effects of age of death, sex, music genre and decade of death on the cause of death were assessed in order to identify vulnerable groups within this population. Where possible, comparisons were made with age- and sex-matched data from the US population. I took an inclusive approach to the population. I was interested in all popular musicians, not just those who had achieved fame or 'hit' albums. This study posed some major challenges, which I discuss in detail in the following section.

Method

DEFINING THE POPULATION: POPULAR MUSIC, POPULAR MUSICIANS AND POP STARS

Popular music is defined as any music that does not belong to the classical music genre. Popular musicians perform popular music. They are either singers, instrumentalists or both. Popular genres include African, ballad, bluegrass, blues, Cajun, calypso, Christian pop, conjunto, country, doo-wop, electroclash, folk, funk, gospel, hard rock, hip hop, honky tonk, indie, jazz, Latin, metal (all forms – atmospheric, avant-garde, black, dark, death, extreme, glam, heavy, melodic, thrash), new wave, polka, pop, psychedelic, punk, punk-electronic, rock (including shock rock, glam rock, etc.), rap, reggae, rhythm and blues, rock and roll, rockabilly, ska, soul, swamp, swing, techno (includes electronic and experimental), western and world music (Borthwick and Moy 2004). Those performers who reach a pinnacle of 'stardom' in popular music as defined by fan followings, sales of electronic media containing their songs, international tours and sell-out concerts are called 'pop stars'.

There is no reliable way to assess the number of musicians in the US population or any other population. This is because it is difficult to define a musician. Unlike teachers, lawyers and doctors, who must pass board certified examinations and be registered to practice in their professions, which makes them easy to count, musicians who earn a living at their craft have no equivalent requirements for minimal qualifications, certification, accreditation or society membership. The US Bureau of Labor Statistics (BLS 2013) provides some indication of the size of the population that earns income from music, but does not distinguish between music genres and also excludes self-employed musicians, which would result in a significant underestimate of the musician population as the majority of performing popular musicians are self-employed. In May 2013, the BLS reported that there were 39,260 musicians in the United States, a decrease from 42,530 in May 2011. The US Census codes musicians under the category 'musical groups and artists'. Like the BLS, US Census data shows a decrease in musicians from 45,200 in 1999 to 34,600 in 2012.

Although some musicians belong to unions or other music professional groups, there is no one organization that represents all musicians. Performance rights organizations are not helpful in pursuit of an answer to this question because most define the term 'musician' very broadly to include composers, songwriters and music publishers. Even if we could access a large sample of individuals who earn a living from some aspect of music participation, what inclusion and exclusion criteria would apply? For example, should only professional (as opposed to amateur or hobby) musicians be included? I will discuss this and a great many other issues in depth in the next section.

KEY SOURCES OF DATA AND INCLUSION/EXCLUSION CRITERIA

Data on the age, circumstances and manner of death of popular musicians since 1950 used for this study were accessed from more than 200 sources. The primary sources included Nick Talevski's (2010) *Knocking on Heaven's Door: Rock Obituaries*, Komara's (2006) *Blues Encyclopaedia*; The Dead Rock Stars' Club website; Pop star mortality; (R.I.P.) Encyclopaedia Metallicum; Voices from the Dark Side for Dead Metal Musicians; Hip hop database Wiki; Hip Hop deaths; Rate your Music; Hip Hop Obituaries; Wikipedia's List of Dead Hip Hop Artists; other rapper death websites; Those we have lost in music – Soul and R&B; Dead Punk Stars; Maximum Ink Music Magazine; The Rock n' Roll Death List; BIZARRE!!! The Dead, the Criminals and the Strange Tales related to Music and Musicians; Drugs and Roll; and Cause of death-Suicide.[1]

While the Dead Rock Stars' Club and Talevski (2010) were comprehensive, the listings were far too inclusive and needed careful culling to create a sample that met inclusion criteria. In the first stage of defining the population, performers in the following musical styles were excluded: classical vocal and instrumental music, including chamber groups and symphony orchestras, opera, oratorio, operetta, music theatre, musicals, choirs, big bands, dance bands and jazz orchestras. Musicians who played exclusively in large bands or in large ensembles or orchestras for film music were also not considered to be pop musicians according to the definition used here and were not included in the sample.

Some artists in rock star lists, including those relied upon in this study, are billed as actors, comedians, music theatre/musical performers, TV personalities or TV hosts. To be included, artists needed to have been part of a live performance pop group for a significant period of their careers. Performers who included singing as part of their comedy routine were excluded. Jeff Astle and Carrie Hamilton are examples of exclusion in this category. TV hosts, like Alan Dale, who had his own TV show and starred in films, even though he had done some solo pop singing, were also excluded. Betty Williams Boyd, who was a pianist and singer, was not considered a pop artist, even though she played in a Dixieland band because it was not her primary occupation (she was an antique dealer). There are other exceptional individuals who pursued other professions and played music 'on the side'. None of these were included in the current sample. Examples include Stan Wheeler, a professor of law at Yale Law School, who was also a trumpeter with the Yale Jazz Ensemble. Dr Robert Good, an obstetrician who delivered over 3,000 babies, also played saxophone, piano and flute with the Glenn Miller Orchestra. His exclusion was two-fold – he was a big band musician and also a 'hobby' musician. Similarly, Vice Vukov, a politician in the Croatian parliament, moonlighted as a pop singer, and Bruce Stovel, a Canadian professor of English, who was also a blues musician, were not included in the sample.

---

1   A complete listing of all websites accessed for this study is available upon request from the author.

Other exclusions included promoters, managers, composers, arrangers, lyricists and song writers who did not perform, record producers, record executives, DJs, talent scouts, booking agents, nightclub proprietors, music critics, musicologists, music teachers, sound engineers, instrument makers, roadies, music artists (e.g. CD cover designers) and photographers. For example, Brian Epstein, the manager of the Beatles, frequents lists of rock stars. However, Brian did not perform in front of audiences, and was therefore not included in this sample.

Studio or session musicians were also excluded because they are not subject to the same intense exposure and stresses experienced by pop musicians who front or are members of (small) pop groups. Examples of exclusions include Jesse Ed Davis and Big Jim Sullivan (session guitarists), Jules Chaikin and Calvin Owens (session trumpeters), and Tony Bell (session keyboardist and guitarist), who was also a songwriter, singer, arranger and engineer. Similarly, Dante DiThomas, a film studio musician, who worked on more than 200 films leading the Dante DiThomas Orchestra, while an outstanding musician, did not meet inclusion criteria for this study. Musicians whose primary role was to lead orchestras, big bands and dance bands were not included. Examples of exclusions in this category include Don Beamsley, who worked primarily with the Warner Brothers' Studio orchestra and as an organist at Dodger Stadium, and Gordon Tetley, who was a big band, dance band and Dixieland band man. Nathan Kaproff, who was a session musician and musical contractor for many films, including *Edward Scissorhands*, *Indecent Proposal* and *Rocky*, was likewise not a member of the population of interest. Similarly, Uan Rasey was primarily a studio trumpet player for the MGM film studios orchestra from 1949 until the early 1970s. For the same reasons, playback singers were also excluded from this sample. A playback singer sings pre-recorded songs for movies and soundtracks, and for actors to lip-sync the songs for camera; the playback singer does not appear on stage or screen.

When an artist was given several attributions, such as, for example, singer, pianist, songwriter, composer and arranger, their principal occupation as performer, either as a vocalist or instrumentalist in a popular style, determined their inclusion. Those with dual, triple or multiple attributions who were not principally singers, instrumentalists or band or group members, or had been inducted into a songwriters' hall of fame, not a singers', vocal groups', or musical style hall of fame, were not included in this sample. For example, Roy Orbison, who has been characterized as a singer, songwriter and guitarist, was, in equal measure, a singer (performer) (inducted into the Rock and Roll Hall of Fame) and songwriter (inducted into the Songwriters' Hall of Fame) and was therefore included in the sample. Professor Longhair (Henry Roeland 'Roy' Byrd), sometimes characterized as 'the grandfather of rock'n'roll' was a piano player, singer and songwriter. He was a member of a number of pop groups including The Mid-Drifs, Professor Longhair and the Four Hairs, Professor Longhair And His Shuffling Hungarians and The Blues Jumpers. He had been inducted into the Louisiana Blues Hall of Fame and Rock and Roll Hall of Fame, and was therefore included. By contrast, songwriters included in the 'Dead Rock Stars' Club' list who did not perform, like Linda Creed, Vic McAlpin, Harold Adamson and Hamish Henderson, were not included.

It was particularly difficult to determine inclusion/exclusion for older musicians. The concept of the rock star is very much a post-Second World War phenomenon, after which time modes of communication, travel and technology transformed the universe into a global community. Many of the older musicians identified could not be characterized as 'rock stars' according to its modern definition. Most did not travel internationally; they performed in one location or region for the majority of their musical careers. Joe Birchfield, born in 1912, was an old time fiddler who played dance music primarily in bands comprising members of his family at festivals and celebrations between Washington and Nashville. Is he a pop musician according to the contemporary definition? The fact that he was a dance musician excluded him, so other factors did not need to be considered. Others, possibly by dint of their longevity, spent many years in the latter stages of their lives either teaching or performing a service to community music. Ray Alexander, born in 1925, was a jazz musician who spent the early years of his life travelling, playing piano with some big names in popular music such as George Shearing, Mel Torme, Martin Denny, Mel Lewis and The Dorsey Brothers. However, for the last 20 years of his life, he was a teacher, church organist at his community church, and an accompanist for local high school choirs. Is he a pop musician? Sergeant Charles Corrado is listed as a rock star in the 'Dead Rock Stars' Club'. At the time of his death in 2004, aged 64, he had served 45 years as a member of the US Marine Band; for 41 of those years, he was based at the White House. Similarly, Ivor Cutler was primarily a writer, teacher, poet, songwriter and humourist who appeared on radio, television and in films. He was also a singer who played harmonium and piano and who made several recordings. I concluded that they did not fit the definition of a 'popular musician' used in this study, and were excluded. Another example of exclusion of older musicians is Mervyn Edward Griffin Jr. who died in 2007 aged 83. He was a multi-tasker who was billed as a singer, pianist, entertainer, TV talk show host and showbiz mogul who also created, produced and wrote music for TV's *Jeopardy* and *Wheel Of Fortune*. Many of the older musicians had several simultaneous occupations. Since this study aimed to capture the population of musicians who were primarily devoted to creating and performing music in pop groups (many were also songwriters), those who presented with profiles similar to those just described above were not included.

Additionally, application of the inclusion criteria was sometimes hindered by another problem with older musicians – the scarcity of accurate information. Finally, these older musicians were not part of a popular music culture as we currently understand that culture today. For example, international travel was much slower and more difficult; the frenetic international touring that is part of the current pop scene was not part of the experience of musicians from an older generation. Technology for sound recording was more primitive and the mass production of recordings was not possible in the way that multimedia reproductions are achieved today. Finally, even the most illustrious older musicians, with a few exceptions, did not have the pop paparazzi and fan clubs stalking them at concerts or in cyberspace, or the media frenzy that demands to know all the intricacies of the personal lives of contemporary pop idols – the boundary between public and private was more firmly drawn in previous eras. Inclusions of older musicians were, therefore, necessarily conservative.

DETERMINING CAUSE OF DEATH

The cause of death was verified, if possible, from at least two independent sources. Sources included obituaries, death records, pop musician websites, biographies, newspaper or magazine articles and blogs. A significant number of deaths were listed as 'illness', 'short illness' or 'long illness'. Attempts were made to ascertain the nature of the illness, but this proved impossible in many cases. These cases were included in 'All other causes' of death in the analysis. Similarly, deaths listed as due to 'natural causes' often could not be improved upon, but indicated that the death was probably not due to accident, suicide or homicide. Although it is likely that many of these deaths, particularly in young people (18–44 years) were due to substance abuse, overdose, or acute drug toxicity that resulted in irreversible heart arrhythmias, these cases were also included in 'All other illnesses'. It is often the case that the media are told that the cause of death was 'unknown' or 'natural' to hide the actual cause of death, particularly in the event of suicide, overdose or AIDS. Gram Parsons is an example. After a prolonged stint of poly-substance and alcohol abuse, Gram Parsons stopped breathing. He was revived by a friend and went to sleep. His breathing became laboured and despite attempts to revive him a second time, he could not be resuscitated. The cause of death given to the press at the time was 'natural causes' because his heart stopped beating as he lay sleeping, but the coroner later ruled that the death had been the result of drug toxicity and long-term poly-drug use. Parsons and other similar cases were coded as 'accidental death' in this study.

In the case of suicide, only those deaths that were specifically designated death by suicide were coded into this category, that is, only if the word 'suicide' had been explicitly listed as the cause, or in cases where other clear indicators that suicide was the cause of the death were given, for example, 'shot himself', 'hanged himself', 'jumped in front of a train', 'jumped from a high balcony', 'suicide by overdose' or 'death by carbon monoxide poisoning'. When the cause of death was attributed to 'overdose' without elaboration of the circumstances, these deaths were coded as accidental. There is no doubt that many suicides by overdose have not been classified as such due to lack of evidence or reluctance on the part of family and friends to accept that the death was intentional. This coding rule has no doubt resulted in an underestimation of the suicide rate in this population because many of the deaths designated 'overdose' or 'accidental' are highly likely to have constituted suicidal behaviour (if not conscious suicidal intent).

Michael Hutchence and Amy Winehouse are exemplars of the grey area between suicide and unintentional death. Both Michael and Amy had been engaging in extremely high risk (even parasuicidal) behaviour such as drinking very large amounts of alcohol immediately prior to their deaths, and both had tried unsuccessfully to reach important support people in the hours before their deaths. Although, according to his wife, Paula Yates, Michael Hutchence most likely died as a result of auto-erotic strangulation, and not deliberate suicide, the coroner brought down a verdict of suicide by asphyxiation. On the other hand, Amy Winehouse had been given a dire warning by her physician on the day of her death that she was at imminent risk of death from alcohol poisoning if she persisted with her binge-drinking. This is exactly what she did – she drank herself to death. However, her family and associates defensively insist that she did not intend to kill herself. In this study, I have coded her cause of death as liver-related (due to alcohol poisoning).

Murder was defined as the intentional act of unlawfully killing another when the act was not self-defence. Although most of the murder cases in this dataset were uncontroversial, some required special consideration. For example, 28 musicians were killed by police. Coding in these cases was assessed on a case by case basis. If the musician was shot and killed by police while unarmed, the case was coded as murder. A sad example is that of the 19-year-old rock musician, Jaime Paulo Camilo, also known as Max Love, who was killed by a governor's guard while on the roof of a lorry working a sound-system as part of election celebrations in Mozambique (Hanlon 2013). His case was coded as murder. Don Myrick, a jazz saxophonist aged 53 years, was shot by police after they knocked at his door to serve a search warrant during a narcotics investigation. Myrick answered the door with a butane cigarette lighter in his hand and was fatally shot in the chest at close range by a police officer. His family successfully defended a wrongful death suit and received $400,000 (Katel 2010). His death was coded as murder. The three young men killed in action (during war) were coded as accidental deaths, in view of the fact that, although they were intentionally killed by others, the act during war is not unlawful and is constituted as a form of self-defence.

Accidental death was coded for any death by injury or misadventure that was not caused by self or as a deliberate act of a second party. Three categories were coded – accidental death by overdose, accidental death – vehicular, and accidental death – all other causes. These and other categories for most frequently occurring causes of death are also presented in Table 20.1. Categories were designed to be directly comparable with ICD-10 classifications, in particular those used by the US Center for Disease Control.

Table 20.1   Cause of death categories and exemplars for each category

Cause of death	Includes
*Accidental death – overdose	cocaine, heroin, morphine, painkillers, prescription drugs, speedball (intravenous cocaine with heroin or morphine), Valium, drug toxicity
*Accidental death – vehicular	Boat, bus, car, helicopter, hit-and-run, motorbike, plane, taxi, tour bus, train, van
*Accidental death – other	Choking, drowning, falling from height, fall down stairs, house or nightclub fire, killed in action (war), lost at sea, Russian roulette, skiing accident, strangulation
Cancer	All malignant neoplasms
Liver-related death	Alcohol poisoning, chronic liver disease, cirrhosis
Heart-related death	Acute myocardial infarction, atherosclerosis, cardiomyopathy, cardiovascular disease, congenital heart disease, coronary heart disease, heart attack, heart disease, heart failure, hypertensive heart disease, rheumatic heart disease, pulmonary oedema
Respiratory failure	Asthma, bronchitis, bronchiectasis, COPD, influenza, pulmonary embolism, pulmonary fibrosis, pneumonia, tracheitis
Cerebrovascular	Aneurysm, cerebrovascular disease, cerebral haemorrhage, stroke
All other illnesses	Examples include Alzheimer's disease, Crohn's disease, cystic fibrosis, dementia, diabetes, died in childbirth, epilepsy, septicaemia, multiple sclerosis, motor neurone disease, sudden adult death syndrome, gastrointestinal disorders (ulcers, gastric haemorrhages, colitis, dysentery), obesity-related disorders, peritonitis, swine flu, syphilis, and illnesses (not specified), 'natural causes', 'died in sleep', 'found dead', 'died on stage'

Note: *All accidental deaths in these three groupings were coded as accidental deaths in this study.

DEFINING MUSIC GENRES

Music genres were grouped as shown in Table 20.3. These groupings were based on the identification of distinctive and dominant musical styles. Earlier derivations of the dominant style or contemporaneous variations of the dominant style were grouped together. The groupings were as follows: Blues; Country/Country and Western/Boogie Woogie/Honky Tonk/Bluegrass; Gospel/Spiritual/Christian Rock; Experimental/Electronic/Techno/Disco/Funk; Folk/Ballad/Polka; Hip Hop; Jazz/Bebop/Dixieland; Metal; Pop; Punk; Rap; Rhythm and Blues/Doo Wop/Soul; Rock/Rockabilly; and World Music. Truncated genre styles are presented in the tables for ease of presentation.

Results

DEMOGRAPHICS

Of the total sample of deceased popular musicians (n=12,803), 11,554 (90.3%) were male and 1,249 (9.7%) were female. The distribution of deaths by decade and sex are shown in Table 20.2.

Table 20.2   Decade of death by sex

Decade of death	Male	% Male	Female	% Female	Total	% Decade
1950	186	1.6%	21	1.7%	207	1.6%
1960	376	3.3%	28	2.2%	404	3.2%
1970	612	5.3%	73	5.9%	685	5.4%
1980	973	8.4%	106	8.5%	1,079	8.5%
1990	1,506	13.1%	164	13.2%	1,670	13.1%
2000	4,555	39.5%	457	36.6%	5,012	39.3%
2010–Dec. 2014	3,314	28.8%	398	31.9%	3,712	29.1%
Total	11,522	100%	1,247	100%	12,769	100%

One way analysis of variance (ANOVA) indicated that the average age of death for male and female popular musicians did not differ significantly for the four decades between 1950 and 1980. For the three subsequent decades, male musicians died at significantly younger ages than female musicians [for 1990, ($F_{(1, 1287)}$=9.91, p=0.002); for 2000 ($F_{(1, 4318)}$ =19.89, p=0.001); and for 2010 ($F_{(1, 3462)}$=15.09, p=0.001)]. These sex differences in musician longevity are reflected in male and female life expectancies for the US population for the decades 1990, 2000 and 2010 but not for the earlier decades, in which women also had higher longevity than men.

The frequency distribution of deaths by genre and decade are presented in Table 20.3, which also highlights the significant changes in prevalence of the different genres over the seven decades from 1950 (as reflected in the proportion of deaths by decade for each genre).

Table 20.4 presents numbers per genre, average age of birth, average age of death, age range of death, and maximum age to 2014 for male musicians by music genre. These data are compared with life expectancy for US males who were born in the same year as the average age of birth for each genre.

Table 20.3   Genre by decade of death

Decade	Blues	World	Country	Folk	Gospel	Hip Hop	Jazz	Metal	Pop	Punk	R&B	Rap	Rock	Electronic	Total
N genre	873	919	835	491	413	258	2,044	2,010	696	338	925	157	2,676	155	12,790
% genre	6.8	7.2	6.5	3.8	3.2	2.0	16.0	15.7	5.4	2.6	7.2	1.2	20.9	1.2	100%
1950	5.5%	0.8%	2.5%	0.4%	2.9%	–	3.3%	0.3%	2.4%	–	2.2%	–	0.3%	–	1.6%
1960	7.8%	1.0%	4.7%	1.8%	4.1%	–	6.7%	0.1%	4.2%	–	3.9%	–	2.2%	–	3.2%
1970	13.2%	1.5%	7.3%	3.5%	8.0%	0.4%	6.7%	0.1%	8.1%	1.8%	9.8%	–	5.6%	1.9%	5.4%
1980	13.3%	3.7%	8.5%	9.2%	7.7%	0.4%	10.1%	3.5%	12.9%	5.6%	13.1%	1.3%	9.6%	8.4%	8.5%
1990	12.6%	9.0%	8.5%	10.2%	6.5%	16.3%	7.2%	18.0%	13.8%	17.2%	15.6%	21.7%	15.7%	18.7%	13.1%
2000	28.9%	40.4%	43.1%	45.2%	43.1%	45.7%	41.6%	40.6%	34.5%	45.7%	33.1%	52.2%	37.8%	35.5%	39.2%
2010	18.8%	43.6%	25.4%	29.7%	27.6%	37.2%	24.3%	37.4%	24.0%	29.7%	22.4%	24.8%	28.9%	35.5%	29.1%
TOTAL	100%	100%	100%	100%	100%	100%	100%	100%	100%	100%	100%	100%	100%	100%	100%

Table 20.4 Number, average age of birth, average age of death, and maximum age to 2014 for male musicians and life expectancy (US males)

Music genre	Number	Av Yr birth	Av Age death	Age Range	Max Av Age to 2014	LE (US Males)*
Blues	752	1930	61.7	21–100	84.0	55.8
Jazz	1769	1931	65.6	17–100	82.7	59.4
Country	716	1934	64.1	19–104	80.4	59.3
Gospel/Spiritual/Christian Rock	306	1935	63.3	13–104	78.9	56.6
R&B/Doo Wop/Soul	796	1938	58.0	18–104	76.0	62.1
Pop	455	1941	55.7	11–100	73.0	64.7
Folk/Ballad/Polka	385	1944	58.3	18–94	69.9	62.4
World Music/Reggae	741	1948	56.8	13–100	66.0	64.4
Rock/Rockabilly	2,251	1953	48.4	15–93	60.9	66.0
Electronic/Disco/Funk	131	1956	49.9	17–76	58.0	66.7
Punk	279	1964	40.3	18–79	50.0	66.6
Metal	1,079	1972	35.5	15–74	42.5	67.4
Rap	139	1975	29.2	16–77	38.9	68.8
Hip Hop	180	1976	29.5	14–78	38.0	69.1
TOTAL	**9,979**					

Source: http://demog.berkeley.edu/~andrew/1918/figure2.html.

Figure 20.1 presents the average age of death for popular musicians by genre and sex against Life Expectancy (LE) for US males and females born in the same years as the average year of birth of musicians from each genre.

Musicians from the older genres – blues, jazz (includes bebop and Dixieland), country (includes country and western, boogie woogie, honky tonk and bluegrass), and gospel (includes spiritual and Christian rock) – enjoyed, on average, a normal lifespan when compared with the lifespan of the US populations from the same year of birth. The next group – R&B, pop, folk and world music – have lower life expectancies compared with the US population, even though they have had the opportunity, on average, to live beyond the life expectancy of the US population. Thereafter, there is an increasing and precipitous reduction in the average age of death for the more recent genres – rock, electronic, punk, metal, rap and hip hop.

These figures reflect, to some extent, a confound in the data – that is, musicians who are dying youngest belong to newer genres (hip hop, metal, punk, rap) that have not existed as long as genres such as jazz, country, gospel and blues. The average year of birth for the oldest (i.e. blues) musicians in this sample was 1930; the average year of birth for the youngest (i.e. hip hop) musicians was 1976. The maximum age in 2014 based on average age at birth for someone born in 1930 was 84; the maximum age for a hip hop musician was 38 years. All things being equal, the majority of those born after 1950 should still be alive. However, we have no way of knowing what proportion of musicians from recent genres has died, as it has not been possible to assemble a reliable database of living popular musicians; that is, most researchers in this field have been hampered by difficulties in estimating or deriving appropriate population denominators.

A second issue making it difficult to assess the differential risk and manner of death in popular musicians is the possible existence of selection effects that would make the population of musicians different in some way from the general population with which it is being compared.

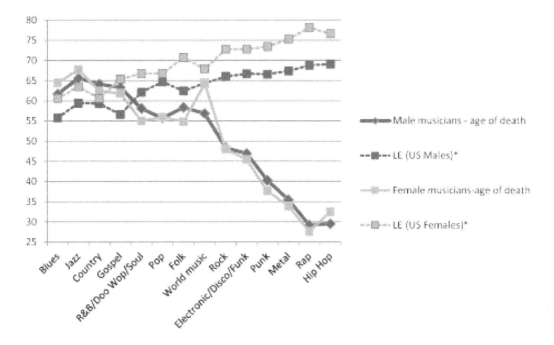

Figure 20.1   Average age of death by genre and sex plotted against Life Expectancy (LE) for US males and females for average year of birth by music genre

Source: *Ref: http://demog.berkeley.edu/~andrew/1918/figure2.html.

An obvious candidate is the relative growth in numbers of popular musicians over time. If the proportion of popular musicians is growing faster than the general population over time, and this is likely given the greatly increased rates of death available in more recent decades, as demonstrated in Table 20.3 (although this could also represent an artefact of better record keeping), the sample of musician deaths will contain more young people and hence average age at death will be younger.

In addition, the deaths of young musicians, particularly if they have achieved fame or notoriety, or died under tragic circumstances are more likely to be widely reported than deaths of older musicians who may have retired long ago from the music industry, which would tend to create an impression of pervasive premature death in the popular music industry. Nonetheless, the data search strategy identified a significant number of older musicians as indicated by the age ranges presented in Table 20.1.

Finally, although great care was taken to include all musicians meeting inclusion criteria, I have no way of knowing which musicians or how many were excluded from the sample on which this study was based, either because their death statistics were never recorded or were not found or retrievable.

COMPARISONS OF DEATH RATES FOR MALE AND FEMALE MUSICIANS WITH US MALE AND FEMALE AGE-MATCHED POPULATION DATA

Given that the youngest average age of death was 29.5 years, the sample was divided into two age groups – those dying before age 30 and those dying after age 30. This division makes a comparison with population data possible because it reduces to some extent the confounds and biases in the data described above. The outcome of this analysis is presented in Table 20.5 and in Figures 20.2 and 20.3 for male musicians.

Table 20.5   Cause of death for male musicians by age group compared with US males

Cause of death	Male musicians 14–30y		US males 14–30y	Male musicians 31=85+		US males 31–85+
	N	%	%	N	%	%
Accidental death	518	47.3	45.6	890	12.5*	3.59
Suicide	155	14.1	16.0	315	4.4*	1.56
Liver-related death	14	1.3*	0.6	306	4.3*	1.51
Homicide	207	18.9	19.3	250	3.5*	0.75
Heart-related death	48	4.4	3.6	1,526	21.4**	35.24
Respiratory diseases	19	1.7*	1.20	350	4.9**	7.79
Cancer	59	5.4	5.60	1,936	27.1*	24.69
All other illnesses	68	6.2	7.2	1,354	19.0	19.20
Cerebrovascular	8	0.7	0.7	217	3.2**	5.66
Total	1,096	100%	N=817,307	7,144	100%	N=16,764,878

Source: http://webappa.cdc.gov/sasweb/ncipc/leadcaus9.html.
Notes: *p<0.001, ** rates significantly lower than US population.

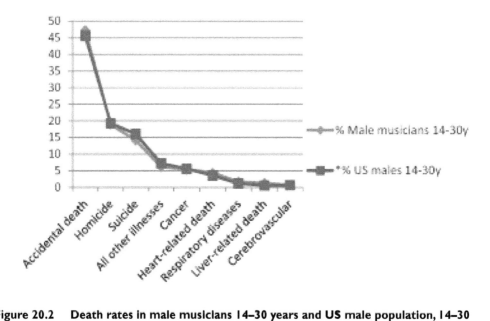

Figure 20.2   Death rates in male musicians 14–30 years and US male population, 14–30 years by cause of death

Source: *Ref: http://webappa.cdc.gov/sasweb/ncipc/leadcaus9.html.

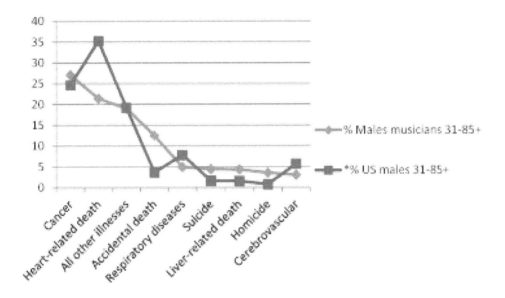

Figure 20.3   Death rates in male musicians 31–85+ years and US male population, 31–85+ years by cause of death

Source: *Ref: http://webappa.cdc.gov/sasweb/ncipc/leadcaus9.html.

Tests of the significance of differences between two independent proportions were conducted for each cause of death in younger and older male musicians and these were compared with the US male population. Male musician deaths in the younger age group closely mirrored the death rates by cause of death found in the same-aged US male population with two exceptions. Young male musicians were more likely to die from liver-related causes (z=3.55; p=0.0004) and from respiratory illnesses (z=3.85; <0.0002). For the older group of male musicians, there were significant differences between the musicians and the US male population in death rates by cause of death for all categories of cause of death except 'all other illnesses' in which the proportions were the same (19.0% vs 19.2%) for both groups. The difference in death rate for accidental death between male musicians and males in the US population (12.6% vs 3.6%) was significant (z=38.9, p<0.0002, two-tailed). Differences were also significant for homicide (3.4% vs 0.75%); (z=24.7, p<0.0002, two-tailed); suicide (4.4% vs 1.6%) (z=18.14, p<0.0002, two-tailed), liver-related deaths (4.17% vs 1.5%) (z=16.16, p<0.0002, two-tailed) and cancer (27.1% vs 24.7%) (z=3.50, p<0.0005, two-tailed) with male musicians between three and four times more likely to die by accident, homicide, suicide and liver-related death than same-aged males in the US population. Musicians were significantly less likely to die of heart-related conditions (20.5% vs 35.2%) (z=-36.12; p<0.0002, two-tailed) or cerebrovascular causes (3.2% vs 5.7%) (z=-9.41, p<0.0002, two-tailed) compared with age-matched males in the US population.

The same comparisons for females produced very similar results. In the 14–30 year age-group, female musicians and same-aged females in the US population showed very similar death rates for cause of death as the male musicians and the US same-aged male population. For all four groups, the leading causes of death were accidental death, homicide and suicide. However, female musicians were significantly more likely to die an accidental death (51.3% vs 41%) (z=2.24, p<0.03, two-tailed) or from liver-related causes than their female population counterparts (4.3% vs 0.9%) (z=3.9, p<0.0002, two-tailed). In the older females (31–85+), female musicians were significantly more likely to die of all of the identified causes of death compared with the same-aged female population except for heart-related deaths (14.8% vs 41.2%) (z=-15.96, <0.0002) and deaths from cerebrovascular causes (4.6% vs 10.32%) (z=-5.569, <0.0002).

SEX DIFFERENCES WITHIN THE POPULAR MUSICIAN POPULATION

There were few sex differences for major causes of death (Figure 20.4).

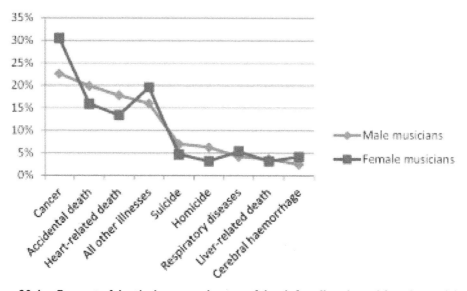

Figure 20.4   Percent of deaths by sex and cause of death for all male and female musicians

There were no sex differences in proportions of male and female musicians dying of particular causes of death for the younger age-group (14–30) (Figure 20.5).

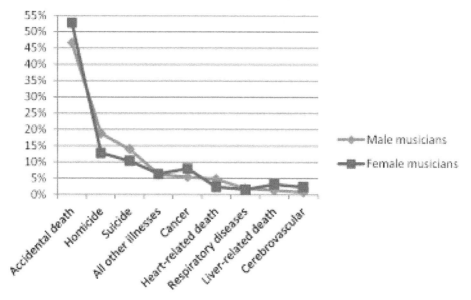

Figure 20.5   Cause of death for male and female popular musicians aged 14–30 years at age of death

Table 20.6 Cause of death (%) in musicians by genre

MALE

Cause of death	N (Cause of death)	Blues	World	Country	Folk	Gospel	Hip Hop	Jazz	Metal	Pop	Punk	R&B	Rap	Rock	Disco	TOTAL
N in genre		609	724	610	373	249	222	1,405	1,391	414	293	669	146	2,315	130	9,550
Cancer	2,156	23.5%	19.1%	25.1%	31.6%	24.1%	5.9%	29.5%	14.2%	24.2%	18.1%	26.9%	8.2%	23.8%	17.7%	22.6%
Accidental death	1,905	9.0%	13.5%	15.7%	16.6%	12.9%	18.5%	11.1%	35.9%	18.8%	29.7%	11.1%	15.8%	25.2%	15.4%	19.9%
Heart-related death	1,700	27.9%	18.0%	23.8%	17.4%	17.7%	6.3%	21.6%	11.1%	20.0%	13.3%	23.9%	6.8%	15.5%	18.5%	17.8%
All other illnesses	1,530	20.4%	22.2%	15.7%	15.0%	29.3%	7.7%	20.7%	7.5%	18.8%	9.6%	20.9%	7.5%	14.0%	20.0%	16.0%
Suicide	672	1.8%	3.5%	4.6%	5.6%	0.8%	7.2%	2.6%	19.6%	5.6%	11.3%	1.5%	6.2%	7.6%	7.7%	7.0%
Homicide	599	3.6%	10.2%	1.5%	4.6%	4.4%	51.8%	2.1%	5.8%	2.9%	6.8%	5.1%	51.4%	3.8%	8.5%	6.3%
Respiratory diseases	401	7.1%	6.4%	6.2%	3.5%	4.0%	1.4%	5.6%	1.5%	4.8%	2.7%	4.5%	2.7%	3.4%	6.2%	4.2%
Liver-related death	351	4.4%	2.6%	4.9%	2.9%	3.2%	0.5%	3.8%	3.3%	2.9%	5.1%	2.7%	0.7%	4.5%	4.6%	3.7%
Cerebrovascular	236	2.3%	4.6%	2.5%	2.7%	3.6%	0.9%	3.0%	1.1%	1.9%	3.4%	3.4%	0.7%	2.2%	1.5%	2.5%
TOTAL	9,550	100%	100%	100%	100%	100%	100%	100%	100%	100%	100%	100%	100%	100%	100%	100%

FEMALE

Cause of death	N (Cause of death)	Blues	World	Country	Folk	Gospel	Hip Hop	Jazz	Metal	Pop	Punk	R&B	Rap	Rock	Disco	TOTAL
N in genre		59	113	71	72	88	5	180	39	184	33	73	5	137	16	1,075
Cancer	328	27.1%	26.5%	28.2%	38.9%	20.5%		38.3%	12.8%	32.1%	21.2%	28.8%		35.0%	43.8%	30.5%
All other illnesses	211	22.0%	30.1%	14.1%	13.9%	21.6%	20.0%	26.1%	12.8%	19.0%	6.1%	21.9%		13.9%	18.8%	19.6%
Accidental death	171	11.9%	8.0%	14.1%	18.1%	15.9%	40.0%	6.7%	46.2%	18.5%	33.3%	9.6%	40.0%	21.2%	18.8%	15.9%
Heart-related death	144	20.3%	16.8%	22.5%	6.9%	19.3%		13.3%	7.7%	9.2%		17.8%		11.7%	12.5%	13.4%
Respiratory diseases	58	1.7%	7.1%	8.5%	5.6%	11.4%	20.0%	3.9%	2.6%	4.9%	12.1%	6.8%	20.0%	2.9%	12.5%	5.4%
Suicide	50	1.7%	2.7%	4.2%	6.9%	1.1%		3.9%	7.7%	8.2%	6.1%	1.4%		4.4%		4.7%
Cerebrovascular	45	6.8%	2.7%	4.2%	4.2%	8.0%	20.0%	4.4%	2.6%	3.3%	6.1%	4.1%	20.0%	2.2%	6.3%	4.2%
Liver-related death	34	5.1%	1.8%	1.4%	2.8%	1.1%		2.8%	2.6%	2.2%	3.0%	5.5%		7.3%		3.2%
Homicide	34	3.4%	4.4%	2.8%	2.8%	1.1%	20.0%	0.6%	5.1%	2.7%	18.2%	4.1%	20.0%	1.5%	6.3%	3.2%
TOTAL	1,075	100%	100%	100%	100%	100%	100%	100%	100%	100%	100%	100%	100%	100%	100%	100%

DIFFERENCES BY GENRE FOR CAUSE OF DEATH IN MALE MUSICIANS

Table 20.6 presents the cause of death by music genre for male musicians (there were too few female musicians to provide adequate cell sizes in some comparisons).

This table highlights the different patterns in cause of death by genre; that is, some genres had significant risk of death from a particular cause that significantly exceeded the mean percentage of deaths for each cause across all genres. For example, the mean percentage of deaths accounted for by cancer was 22.6%. Folk (32%) and jazz (30%) musicians had higher risk of death from cancer than other genres. Similarly, accidental death accounted for 20% of all deaths, yet 35% of deaths in metal musicians, 30% in punk musicians and 25% in rock musicians were accidental. Suicide accounted for 7% of all deaths in the total sample, yet 20% of metal musicians and 11% of punk musicians died by suicide. Although homicide accounted for 6.3% of deaths across the sample, 52% of all deaths in hip hop musicians and 51% of all deaths in rap musicians were from homicide, many of which were drug-related, associated with the commission of crimes like robberies, home invasions, and altercations with police, or occurred during so-called 'crimes of passion', many of which, no doubt, were committed under the influence of substances. Members of these genres do not live long enough to develop heart- and liver-related illnesses causing death and consequently had the lowest rates of death in these categories. In contrast, heart-related deaths accounted for 18% of all deaths, but 28% blues musicians died of heart-related causes, probably due to the fact that they had the highest longevity. Gospel musicians had the lowest suicide rate of all the genres studied, suggesting a protective effect of their religious beliefs.

Discussion

In conducting this study, a number of difficult methodological issues had to be resolved. First, defining the sample involved a number of crucial decisions. Inclusion and exclusion criteria had to be established, as did the timeframe for the study and the classification of popular genres into a manageable number of unique musical styles. Determining the cause of death was also challenging because early abuse of substances and risk-taking, if survived in the earlier part of the lifespan, may exert longer term impacts on health in the form of some cancers, heart disease, cirrhosis and mental health (suicidality) that are not coded on death certificates, in obituaries or other sources. Some of these impacts can be directly responsible for early death even if substance abuse or other risky behaviours reduced or ceased in middle age. Finally, the most problematic element was the inability to estimate or derive appropriate population denominators because there are no reliable repositories of living musicians.

This study has highlighted the very different health and mortality profiles of musicians belonging to different genres of popular music. While there were few differences between the younger male musicians and the same-aged US male population in causes of death (liver-related death and respiratory diseases were the exceptions), there were very marked differences in older musicians. The morbidity and mortality of younger musicians reflected population trends that highlight the increased risk of early death in all young males, not just young musicians at this vulnerable age in which testosterone, risk-taking and substance abuse create a volatile environment to which many young people succumb. Of note, also, was the similarity in profiles of young female musicians with their male counterparts. This suggests that once a young person joins the popular music industry, sex effects in morbidity and mortality are no longer relevant. Both males and females respond to music industry stressors similarly.

The results for older musicians infer a significant level of psychological vulnerability by dint of their elevated suicide, homicide, accidental death, and liver-related death rates compared with the same-aged US population. This was also evident in the Bellis et al. (2012) study that showed that the mortality gap between popular musicians and the general population increased with increasing years (and age) since first becoming famous.

What aspects of the popular music scene are so pathological as to be associated with such disturbing patterns in morbidity and mortality, despair so profound as to result in risk of death by suicide that follows popular musicians into old age, and rage so uncontainable as to result in either the commission of or becoming a victim of homicide? Because this was a quantitative study of dead musicians, whose aim was to gather population data to establish a baseline of the extent and outcome of the occupational hazards in the pop music world, I can only speculate here about the candidate causes of these results. It is likely to be a combination of the factors in the popular music industry and the vulnerability that many young musicians bring with them into their profession from early adverse childhood experiences (Bellis et al. 2012).

I have already canvassed the usual suspects identified in occupational health research in the introduction, and indeed, many of these do apply to the high-octane, peripatetic lifestyle of musicians. A critical destructive aspect of this lifestyle is the ubiquitous presence of alcohol and substances of addiction, which are rendered accessible by the increased disposable income that accrues to a chart success, often after months or years of living in penury and working second and third jobs to pay the rent. Alcohol and substances also have psychological as well as material and physical valences. These include their use to facilitate group cohesion and bonding, to celebrate a successful concert, to wind down after the sustained adrenaline rush of a show, to mask depression, anxiety and other worries, to manage a psychiatric illness, and to chill out, among others. These substances and the practices in which they take centre stage (e.g. as pre-show anxiolytics, at after-parties, as part of sexual encounters, or as morning uppers) become normative and because pop groups are communities of peers, there is no 'adult' oversight, no boundary-makers to curb behaviour that inevitably gets increasingly out-of-control.

We must therefore turn elsewhere for understanding. An examination of the patterns in cause of death by music genre is most instructive; in particular, high rates of suicide and accidental death in metal and punk musicians, and very high rates of homicide in hip hop and rap musicians. One-third of jazz musicians in the current study died of cancer. They accounted for 19.5% of all deaths from cancer (n=2484), and 22.8% of the 335 cases of death by lung cancer. Most jazz musicians were heavy smokers and spent much of their professional lives in smoke-filled clubs. Herer (2000) also found that cancer was the most frequent cause of death in jazz musicians, followed by heart-related causes. Despite this, both studies observed that jazz musicians lived a normal life span. These very different patterns among musical styles indicate that music genre is a lifestyle, not just a type of music.

In addition to distinct mortality patterns in the different genres, the content of the lyrics and the life stories of some of popular music exponents provide further insight that could be subjected to further scrutiny and research. In many of the artists who met tragic, untimely deaths, the clues to their psychological anguish are contained in their songs. For example, Elvis begged an idealized other to 'make the world go away, get it off my shoulders'; to 'walk a mile in my shoes … before you abuse, criticise and accuse'; he was the 'loneliest guy in the crowd'.

Let us return, by way of example, to the heavy metal genre that I discussed in the introduction. There has been a great deal of contention regarding the naming of this particular genre (Weinstein 2013). Notwithstanding, we are left in no doubt as to its central message, cogently expressed by the erudite and colourful music critic, Lester Bangs (1978):

Heavy Metal music in its finest flower had one central, obvious message: There is no hope. Whatever you do, you can't win. The world is run by war pigs who have turned you into human dogs and you must accept your fate as ignominiously as you possibly can. It was, in America at least, more or less the residue of Vietnam ... but it was really a worldwide sentiment, and in that sense obviously the Heavy Metal Cassandras of bombast differed from the punks, who may scream of no future but at least are determined to go out kicking and flailing. Heavy Metal freaks just wanted to forget the whole fucking mess, man; they were, in a word, passive. [My italics]

Bangs's entry for 'Heavy Metal' in *The Rolling Stone Illustrated History of Rock and Roll* 10 years after his original scathing critique, states:

heavy-metal rock is nothing more than a bunch of noise; it is not music, it is distortion – and that is precisely why its adherents find it appealing. Of all contemporary rock, it is the genre most closely identified with violence and aggression, rapine and carnage. Heavy metal orchestrates technological nihilism.(1980, p. 332; my italics)

Another rock music critic, Mike Saunders (1970), expressed a similar opinion, describing the music of the band, Humble Pie, as '27th rate heavy metal crap'. He stated that if the members of Humble Pie had to listen to themselves 'they would probably vomit' and he exhorted them to spare themselves and others, including God, that 'torture'. Alice Cooper, a hard rock/heavy metal musician crowned the 'godfather of shock rock', whose stage shows featured guillotines, electric chairs, (fake) blood, boa constrictors and bizarre makeup and costumes, stated:

We were into fun, sex, death and money when everybody was into peace and love. We wanted to see what was next. It turned out we were next, and we drove a stake through the heart of the Love Generation. (in Furek, 2008, p. 62)

Did they also drive a stake through their own hearts? Do these nihilistic genres attract nihilistic young people, many of whom are suffering the ravages of ruptured attachment experiences in early life (see Kenny 2013), who are cut adrift from mainstream society, who don't fit in, achieve and progress according to normative social expectations? For the shortest time, they find solace and like-mindedness in these crazy bands that simultaneously embrace them while inadvertently nurturing the expression of their final act of self-destruction? Consider a selection of the words of a song (*Doornails*) intended as a tribute to dead rockers by the band, NOFX, on their album *Wolves in Wolves' Clothing* (2006).[2]

... You know, suicide isn't painless
When you leave everyone in pain ...
Sedated, flagellated
You were the one most loved and hated ...
This bowl is for my mom
For drinking more than I did
For posting bail for me in New York
And in Hollywood that first time
And that joint we smoked was the worst time
Cause doing drugs with parents is just wrong
... This song is for winning losers

---

2   Released through Fat Wreck Chords, *Copyright*: Lyrics © OBO APRA/AMCOS.

It's for lucky substance abusers
The ones who left their black marks on us all.

This song expresses the grief and rage felt at the loss of friends through suicide, alcoholism and drug overdoses. Many of the lines not quoted here name lost bandmates and the ways in which they died. The reference to 'winning losers' and 'lucky substance abusers' suggests ambivalence about being left behind to experience the pain of another suicide. I am particularly interested in the songwriter's ambivalence towards his mother, who posted bail for him when he was in trouble but who was also an alcoholic who set him a bad example. He identifies the worst time in his life as the occasion in which he shared a joint with his mother, which he experienced as abandonment. He recognized that doing drugs with parents is 'just wrong'. Spiralling out of control, he looked to his mother to contain him, but she colluded, which resulted in an escalation of his dangerous behaviour.

The ethos of the popular music scene generally is like this songwriter's mother; it not only fails to set boundaries and to model and expect acceptable behaviour, it actually does the reverse – it valorizes outrageous behaviour, the acting out of aggressive, sexual and destructive impulses that most of us dare only live out in fantasy (if at all). A recent example is the award of 'Ultimate Hellraiser' to Ozzy Osbourne in May 2014 by the radio program Planet Rock, purportedly 'where rock lives'. Twenty rockers were honoured on a top 20 list of hellraisers that included Keith Moon, Jim Morrison, Alice Cooper and Keith Richards.

There is ample evidence within the pop music industry that indicates that some of the young men and women who inhabit it are deeply disturbed. Two particularly sad examples are the R&B singer, Houston (Houston Summers IV) and rapper Christ Bearer. In 2005, Houston gouged out one of his eyes, explaining that the 'devil made me do it'. He told his body guard that he 'had to get the devil off his back' and gouging his eye was the only way. His publicist issued a statement that Houston 'found himself in the midst of a spiritual battle against the evil that runs rampant in the entertainment industry' (AAP 2012). A fellow rapper, Bushwick Bill, sent commiserations, stating 'Fame will make you crazy'. He was in a position to know; he had at one time convinced his girlfriend to assist him in suicide, which she eventually did, shooting him in the eye! Christ Bearer (Andre Johnson) cut off his penis and leaped off a two-story balcony because he had been denied access to his two young daughters (Antimusic 2014). All of these young men miraculously survived their physical injuries, so they did not find their way onto my dead musician database.

Conclusions

This study has highlighted the very different morbidity and mortality profiles of musicians belonging to different genres of popular music and cautions against treating the population of popular musicians as homogeneous. Music genre was much more discriminative than sex or age. This suggests that once a young person joins the popular music industry, effects of sex and age are no longer relevant. Both males and females succumb equally to music industry stressors.

Popular musicians are more likely to die of non-natural causes than comparable general populations but these differences do not become evident until after the 'danger' years (i.e. >30 years) in which US population patterns closely align with the much more public patterns evident in young popular musicians. The results for older musicians infer a significant level of continuing psychological vulnerability by dint of their elevated rates of suicide, accidental death, homicide and liver-related death compared with the US population.

It is probable that many pop, rock, metal, electronic, punk, hip hop and rap musicians will simply never live long enough to acquire the illnesses of middle and old age. Subsequent research decades hence, when these newer genres have matured sufficiently to contain members with ages spanning population life expectancies, may further clarify the tentative conclusions drawn from this study.

Acknowledgements

I am indebted to A/Professor Anthony Asher who suggested the analysis presented in Table 20.5 and who calculated the adjusted US population proportions presented therein. Sincere thanks to Dr Roger Adams and Dr Robert Heard for their statistical advice, to A/Professor Leonie Tickle, Professor John Kaldor, and Dr Nic Price for their actuarial and epidemiological perspectives, and to my research assistant, Maria Katelaris, for her assistance in compiling the database on which this study was based.

References

AAP (2012). The devil made him do it. Available at: http://www.today.com/id/6915656#. U3QWs1fN3TA. Accessed 4 July 2013.

Abramson, J.H. (2011). WINPEPI updated: Computer programs for epidemiologists, and their teaching potential. *Epidemiologic Perspectives & Innovations*, 8(1). Available at: http://www.epi-perspectives.com/content/8/1/1. Accessed 8 June 2013.

Ackermann, B.J., Kenny, D.T., O'Brien, I. and Driscoll, T.R. (2014). Sound Practice: Improving occupational health and safety for professional orchestral musicians in Australia. Frontiers in Psychology, 5, 1–11.

Anda, R.F., Felitti, V.J., Bremner, J.D., Walker, J.D., Whitfield, C., Perry, B.D., Dube, S.R. and Giles, W.H. (2006). The enduring effects of abuse and related adverse experiences in childhood: A convergence of evidence from neurobiology and epidemiology. *Eur. Arch. Psychiatry Clin. Neurosci.*, 256, 174–86.

Antimusic (2014). Rapper addresses cutting off penis. Available at: http://www.antimusic.com/news/14/May/14Rapper_Addresses_Cutting_Off_Penis.shtml#.U3QfEIfN3TA. Accessed 5th May 2014.

Bangs, L. (1978). Heavy metal: The final solution. *Hit Parader*, 36–9, 57.

Bangs, L. (1980). Heavy metal. In Jim Miller (ed.), *The Rolling Stone Illustrated History of Rock and Roll* (pp. 332–5). New York: Rolling Stone Press/Random House.

Bellis, M.A., Hughes, K., Sharples, O., Hennell, T. and Hardcastle, K.A. (2012). Dying to be famous: Retrospective cohort study of rock and pop star mortality and its association with adverse childhood experiences. *BMJ Open*, 2:e002089.

Bellis, M.A., Hennell, T., Lushey, C., Hughes, K., Tocque, K. and Ashton, J.R. (2007). Elvis to Eminem: Quantifying the price of fame through early mortality of European and North American rock and pop stars. *J. Epidemiol. Community Health*, 61, 896–901.

BIZARRE. (2000–2015). The dead, the criminals and the strange tales related to music and musicians. Available at: http://rateyourmusic.com/list/Goregirl/bizarre_the_dead_the_criminals_and_the_strange_tales_related_to_music_and_musicians/10/. Accessed 15 September 2013.

Black Sabbath (1970). *Paranoid*. Available at: http://mapofmetal.com/#/home. Accessed 26 February 2014.

Borthwick, S. and Moy, R. (2004). *Popular Music Genres: An Introduction*. Edinburgh: Edinburgh University Press.

Brooker, C. (2013). Justin Bieber: Teen pop idols never die – they're gradually unfollowed. *Guardian*, 28 January. Available at: http://www.theguardian.com/commentisfree/2013/jan/27/justin-bieber-pop-idols-never-die. Accessed 8th April 2014.

Bureau of Labor Statistics (BLS) (2013). United States Department of Labor. Available at: http://www.bls.gov/oes/current/oes272042.htm. Accessed 26 April 2014.

Cause of death-Suicide. (2012).Available at: http://www.nndb.com/lists/287/000069080/. Accessed 7 September 2013.

Cloud, D. (2014). Way of life literature. *The Rapper Deathstyle*. Available at: http://www.wayoflife.org/index_files/rapper_deathstyle.html. Accessed 15 April 2015.

Cody, J. (2007). The tragedy – and triumph – of Judee Sill. Available at: http://canadianchristianity.com/bc/bccn/0607/22sill.html. Accessed 14 June 2013.

Cooper, C.L. and Wills, G.I. (1989). Popular musicians under pressure. *Psychology of Music*, 17(1), 22–36.

Dead Punk Stars. (2009).Available at: http://www.deadpunkstars.com/. Accessed 11 January 2012.

The Dead Rock Stars' Club. (est. 1998). http://thedeadrockstarsclub.com/deadrock.html. Accessed 2 February 2013–7 June 2015.

Dobson, M.C. (2011). Insecurity, professional sociability, and alcohol: Young freelance musicians' perspectives on work and life in the music profession. *Psychology of Music*, 39(2), 240–60.

Dolenko, E. (2003). *Hector Berlioz as reflected in the Russian press of his time*. Available at: http://www.hberlioz.com/Special/edolenko.htm?zoom_highlight=music+as+a+profession#3+. Accessed 8th April 2014.

Drugs and Roll. (2002–2015). Available at: http://www.oocities.org/tomberry992003/bloodyhistory.html. Accessed 2 February 2013–7 June 2015.

Encyclopaedia Metallicum. (2002–2015). Available at: http://www.metal-archives.com/artist/rip. Accessed 2 February 2013–7 June 2015.

Evans, A. (1994). *The Secrets of Musical Confidence: How to Maximize Your Performance Potential*. Sydney: HarperCollins.

Felitti, V.J., Anda, R.F., Nordenberg, D., Williamson, D.F., Spitz, A.M., Edwards, V., Koss, M.P., James, S. and Marks, J.S. (1998). Relationship of childhood abuse and household dysfunction to many of the leading causes of death in adults. The Adverse Childhood Experiences (ACE) Study. *Am. J. Prev. Med.*, 14, 245–58.

Furek, M.W. (2008). *The Death Proclamation of Generation X: A Self-fulfilling Prophesy of Goth, Grunge and Heroin*. i-Universe.

Gal, H. (1969). Preface. In Marion Linton, *Hector Berlioz. Exhibition Drawn from the Cecil Hopkinson Berlioz Collection*. Edinburgh: National Library of Scotland.

Hanlon, J. (2013). Police kill MDM celebrator and declare ban on demonstrations in Quelimane. *Mozambique Political Process Bulletin* (bit.ly/MozEl13), No. 52, November. Available at: http://www.open.ac.uk/technology/mozambique/sites/www.open.ac.uk.technology.mozambique/files/files/Local_Elections_Bulletin_52–23Nov2013.pdf. Accessed 10 February 2014.

Herer, B. (2000). The longevity and causes of death of jazz musicians, 1990–1999. *Medical Problems of Performing Artists*, September, 119–22.

Hip hop database Wiki. Available at: http://hiphopdatabase.wikia.com/wiki/List_of_Dead_rappers. Accessed 2 February 2013–7 June 2015.

Hip Hop deaths. (2012).Available at: http://sites.lib.uh.edu/hiphop/djscrew/index.html. Accessed 2 February 2013–7 June 2015.

Hooten, H. (2014). Better man. *SMH-Good Weekend*, 19–20 April, 10, 12.

Jones, D.J., Podolsky, S.H. and Greene, J.A. (2012). The burden of disease and the changing task of medicine. *The New England Journal of Medicine*, 366, 2333–8.

Katel, J. (2010). Top 10 murdered musicians you've never heard of. Miami NewTimes Blogs. Available at: http://blogs.miaminewtimes.com/crossfade/2010/09/top_10_murdered_musicians.php. Accessed 23rd July 2014.

Kenny, D.T. (2013). *Bringing up Baby: The Psychoanalytic Infant Comes of Age*. London: Karnac.

Kenny, D.T. and Ackermann, B. (2015). Performance related musculoskeletal pain and depression in professional orchestral musicians. *Psychology of Music*, 43, 43–60.

Kenny, D.T., Driscoll, T. and Ackermann, B. (2014). Psychological well-being in professional orchestral musicians in Australia: A descriptive population study. *Psychology of Music*, 42(2), 210–32.

Komara, E. (ed.) (2006). *The Encyclopaedia of the Blues*. Available at: http://www.routledgeonline.com/music/ Login.aspx?ReturnUrl=%2fmusic%2fBook.aspx%3fid%3dw327&id=w327. Accessed 19 November 2013.

Larkin, C. (2000). *All-time Top 1000 Albums*, 3rd edn. London: Virgin Publishing.

The Living Tradition. Available at: http://www.folkmusic.net/htmfiles/inart486.htm. Accessed 2 February 2013–7 June 2015.

Loudwire. (1999). Available at: http://loudwire.com/. Accessed 4th–18th April 2014.

Margary, D. (2012). Man up, Bieber. *GQ Entertainment*. Available at: http://www.gq.com/entertainment/ celebrities/201206/justin-bieber-gq-june-2012-interview. Accessed 26 May 2015.

Maximum Ink Music Magazine. Available at: http://www.maximumink.com/. Accessed 2 February 2013–7 June 2015.

National Vital Statistics Reports (NVSS) (2014). 62(7). Available at: http://www.cdc.gov/nchs/data/nvsr/nvsr62/ nvsr62_07.pdf. Accessed 2 February 2013–7 June 2015.

NOFX (2006). *Doornails* from album *Wolves in Wolves' Clothing*. Available at: http://songmeanings.com/songs/ view/3530822107858588382/. Accessed 29 March 2013.

nprmusic (2004). Dinah Washington: A queen in turmoil. Available at: http://www.npr.org/templates/story/ story.php?storyId=3872390. Accessed 22nd April 2014.

Overell, R. (2014). Gwar is over? The subcultural politics of thrash metal. *The Conversation*, March 26. Available at: https://theconversation.com/gwar-is-over-the-subcultural-politics-of-thrash-metal-24789. Accessed 19 June 2014.

Planet Rock (2014). Ozzy Osbourne declared Ultimate Hellraiser. Available at: http://www.antimusic.com/ news/14/May/14Ozzy_Osbourne_Declared_Ultimate_Hellraiser.shtml#.U3QemFfN3TA. Accessed 5th May 2014.

Raeburn, S.D. (1999). Psychological issues and treatment strategies in popular musicians: A review, part 1. *Medical Problems of Performing Artists*, 14, 171–9.

Raeburn, S.D. (2000). Psychological issues and treatment strategies in popular musicians: A review, part 2. *Medical Problems of Performing Artists*, 15, 6–16.

Raeburn, S.D. (2007). The ring of fire: Shame, fame and rock 'n' roll (Johnny Cash's drug addiction). *Medical Problems of Performing Artists*, 22(1), 3–9.

Raeburn, S.D., Hipple, J., Delaney, W. and Chesky, K. (2003). Surveying popular musicians' health status using convenience samples. *Medical Problems of Performing Artists*, 18, 113–19.

Rate your Music: Hip Hop Obituaries. (2000–2015). Available at: http://rateyourmusic.com/list/Hiighwire/_ the_hip_hop_obituary_/1/. Accessed 2 February 2013–7 June 2015.

R.I.P. Encyclopaedia Metallicum. (2002–2015). Available at: http://www.metal-archives.com/artist/rip. Accessed 2 February 2013–7 June 2015.

The Rock n' Roll Death List. Available at: http://www.biblebelievers.com/RockDeaths.html. Accessed 2 February 2013–7 June 2015.

Ronson, J. (2010). Justin Bieber: One day with the most Googled name on the planet. *Guardian*, 13 November. Available at: http://www.theguardian.com/music/2010/nov/13/justin-bieber-interview. Accessed 8th April 2014.

Saunders, M. (1970). Review of 'Town and Country, Humble Pie, As Safe As Yesterday Is, Humble Pie'. *Rolling Stone*, 12 November.

Schlesinger, J. (2004). Creativity and mental health. *British Journal of Psychiatry*, 184, 184–5.

Schoenberg, Arnold (1910). Aphorismen. In Willi Reich (ed.) (1964). *Schopferische Konfessionem*. Zurich: Peter Schiffferli.

Slonimsky, N. (ed.) (1965). *Lexicon of Musical Invective*. New York: Coleman-Ross.

Spheeris, D. (1988). *The Decline of Western Civilization Part II: The Metal Years*. Documentary film. Available at: http://www.declinemovies.com/. Accessed 12 November 2014.

Sternbach, D.J. (1995). Musicians: A neglected working population in crisis. In Steven L. Sauter and Lawrence R. Murphy (eds), *Organizational Risk Factors for Job Stress* (pp. 283–302). Washington, DC: American Psychological Association.

Talevski, N. (2010). *Knocking on Heaven's Door: Rock Obituaries*. London: Omnibus Press.

T-weaponz: The arsenal of art in everything (2009). Available at: http://tweaponz.blogspot.com.au/2009/11/list-of-all-rappers-who-have-died.html. Accessed 17 March 2014.

Those we have lost in music – Soul and R&B. Available at: http://wolfco.freeiz.com/soul-r-and-b.htm. Accessed 18 May 2014.

Tucker, A., Faulkner, M.E. and Horvath, S. (1971). Electrocardiography and lung function in brass instrument players. *Archives of Environmental Health*, 23, 327–34.

Ultimate Classic Rock. Available at: http://ultimateclassicrock.com/. Accessed 2 February 2013–7 June 2015

University of Berkeley (UB). *Life Expectancy in the USA, 1900–98*. Berkeley: Author. Available at: http://demog.berkeley.edu/~andrew/1918/figure2.html. Accessed 10th April 2014.

U.S. Department of Health and Human Services (2011). *Health, United States*. Available at: http://www.cdc.gov/nchs/data/hus/hus11.pdf#fig32. Accessed 2 February 2013–7 June 2015.

U.S. Department of Health and Human Services (2013). *Health, United States*. Available at: http://www.cdc.gov/nchs/hus/contents2012.htm#fig03. Accessed 2 February 2013–7 June 2015.

Voices from the Dark Side. (2000–2011). Available at: http://www.voicesfromthedarkside.de/index.php. Accessed 4 May 2014.

Weinstein, D. (2013). Just so stories: How heavy metal got its name – A cautionary tale. *Rock Music Studies*. Published online 12 November 2013. Available at: http://www.tandfonline.com/doi/pdf/10.1080/19401159.2013.846655. Accessed 11 July 2014.

World Health Organization (WHO) (2013). List of countries by life expectancies. Available at: http://en.wikipedia.org/wiki/List_of_countries_by_life_expectancy. Accessed 8th August 2014.

Wikipedia: List of Dead Hip Hop Artists. (updated 2015). Available at: http://en.wikipedia.org/wiki/List_of_deceased_hip_hop_artists. Accessed 2 February 2013–7 June 2015.

Wikipedia participants to website (updated 29 March 2014). Available at: http://en.wikipedia.org/wiki/List_of_deaths_in_rock_and_roll found at http://en.wikipedia.org/wiki/Category:WikiProject_Lists_participants. Accessed 2 February 2013–7 June 2015.

Wills, G. I. (2003). Forty lives in the bebop business: Mental health in a group of eminent jazz musicians. *British Journal of Psychiatry*, 183(3), 255–9.

Wolkewitz, M., Allignol, A., Graves, N. and Barnett, A.G. (2011). Is 27 really a dangerous age for famous musicians? Retrospective cohort study. *British Medical Journal*, 343:d7799. doi:10.1136/bmj.d7799.

PART VII
CHALLENGES IN THE COPING PROCESS

21

A Scheme for Workaholism Intervention Including Cognitive, Affective and Behavioural Techniques

Bruce David Kirkcaldy, Diana Malinowska Sabina Staszczyk and Aleksandra Tokarz

> *In dwelling, live close to the ground. In thinking, keep to the simple. In conflict, be fair and generous. In governing, don't try to control. In work, do what you enjoy. In family life, be completely present.*
>
> *Laozi*

Introduction

Many scholars and clinicians have recognized the downside of workaholism and its potentially detrimental consequences for an individual's health and personal and work life. Research has found that workaholism is associated with emotional burnout, fatigue, neglect, generally aberrant behaviour in the workplace, and a low level of life satisfaction (Burke 2000a, 2000b; Galperin and Burke 2006; Garson 2005; Gini 1998; Johnstone and Johnston 2005; Spence and Robbins 1992). However, caution should be applied before prematurely adhering to a 'deficit'-oriented model of excessive work. For example, Furnham (2013) asserts that:

> *Psychological concepts, like workaholism, tend to go through phases. Once the initial discovery is made, some effort is spent on clarification which may reveal subtypes or causative factors, culminating in measurement issues and model building. The research on workaholism is no exception. The literature is now 40 years old and has evolved with an increased methodological sophistication, which means that we are now much clearer about the components and antecedents of workaholism. Perhaps the greatest change is to see some of the positive sides of what was erstwhile thought of as exclusively negative. Spending a long time at work can be seen as positive and possess many beneficial psychological consequences. (pp. 240–41)*

Accordingly, it would be valuable to critically review potential interventions that have been described elsewhere in the literature and to analyse how workaholism is conceptualized in these interventions, the status of their recommendations, and the phase of intervention they address. Although there are some guidelines for coping with workaholism, practical implications remain inadequately addressed, or are restricted to focusing on 'alternative' maladaptive behaviour patterns that are commonly associated with addictive disorders, such as alcoholism and the constructs of frenetic, aggressive and dominant features of Type A behaviour. Therefore, the aim of the current chapter is not only to identify and critically review interventions pertaining to workaholism, but also to focus more on detailed clinically relevant material to support mental health professionals in their provision of treatment for such ailments.

In the first section, we define workaholism and illustrate its cognitive, emotional and behavioural symptoms by using two clinical case studies. We then present an analysis of possible interventions, including a description of the main assumptions of cognitive behavioural therapy (CBT) and rational emotive behaviour therapy (REBT). We also give some examples of cognitive, emotional and behavioural techniques that can be applied in the treatment of workaholism, by adopting some of the features of a multimodal therapy. In the concluding sections, we propose a therapy regimen relating to the workaholism symptoms and make some suggestions on how this may be further developed.

Definition of Workaholism

The term workaholism was first introduced into the scientific community by Oates in 1971, and it remains a useful construct, as stressed by Griffiths (2005, p. 97). However, there still is no meaningful consensus among researchers on either the nature and/or psychological function of this phenomenon. After examining various definitions and conceptualizations of workaholism (e.g., Malinowska 2010a; Malinowska, Trzebińska, Tokarz and Kirkcaldy 2013; Taris, Schaufeli and Schimazu 2010), three basic approaches to this phenomenon are proposed: (1) workaholism as a *negative addiction*, (2) workaholism as a *positive behavioural pattern*, and (3) workaholism as either a *negative or positive behavioural pattern*, depending on *type*. The first two are obviously competing and exclusive approaches, whereas the third can be seen as a way to reconcile them.

Of these three approaches, the third view has been endorsed, namely, that workaholism (depending on type) has many facets, both negative and positive (e.g. Furnham 2013; Naughton 1987; Scott, Moore and Miceli 1997; Spence and Robbins 1992). As Burke and Fiskenbaum (2011) emphasize: 'Workaholism, and long working hours have positive connotations such as dedication, commitment and organizational citizenship behaviour as well as negative connotations such as ill-health and damaged family relationships (Killinger, 1991)' (p. 90).

Consistent with this third 'model', which is well supported by research (Burke 1999; Spence and Robbins 1992; van Beek, Taris and Schaufeli 2011) and buttressed by theoretical conceptualizations (Ng, Sorensen and Feldman 2007), it seems unlikely that people with different *patterns* of workaholic components can be grouped into a single category. Rather, it is desirable to categorize them according to specific patterns of workaholic elements (e.g. drive to work, work engagement, work–life imbalance, work enjoyment, etc.), as well as the degree of workaholism expressed, not as a type but on a linear scale. For instance, McMillan and O'Driscoll (2006) extracted five conceptually overlapping categories associated with workaholism: (1) a personal reluctance to disengage from work (*obsessive personal style* linked with addiction and inadequate control); (2) *driven to work*; (3) *high enjoyment (passion)*; (4) a tendency to work or think about work; (5) and an inclination to work anytime and anywhere (*failure to demarcate work and leisure domains*). The authors concluded that: 'Perhaps researchers should abandon the unitary workaholism construct … [and] focus instead on studying enjoyment, drives and hours worked as separate constructs, albeit interrelated' (p. 103). In other words, workaholism is clearly a multidimensional construct.

Indeed, it appears useful to consider three principal types of 'psychological' processes or dimensions, namely, *cognition* (thoughts), *emotions* and *behaviour* described in the workaholism conceptualization of Ng et al. (2007). By selecting two specific cases of health professionals perceived to be under extreme stress with work-related issues, we attempt to focus on these three facets associated with workaholism.

First, as stated by Ng et al. (2007), 'the cognitive dimension reflects those intellectual processes that propel workaholics to work excessively' (p. 115). It includes 'demand to meet the approval of others', 'subjectively perceived "mediocre" performance' (Case 1) or thinking about themselves as 'a coper, a person who rolls her sleeves up and gets on with things' and about their profession: 'no room for people like that, who are weak and not able to stand the pressure' (Case 2). Probably, the most important cognitive indicator mentioned in many other conceptualizations of workaholism (e.g. McMillan, Brady, O'Driscoll and Marsh 2002; Spence and Robbins 1992) is an inner urge or drive to work hard, which is manifested as 'an urgent sensation of pressure to perform' (Case 2).

Second, the affective workaholism dimension is created by both positive feelings, e.g. 'the passion towards excellence' (Case 1), 'I felt like a master wheel' (Case 2), as well as negative ones: e.g. 'constantly drained', 'weepy, frustrated, aggressive, and angry', 'disappointed at myself for being so weak' (Case 2). Ng et al. (2007) underscore the value of identifying negative emotions, such as guilt and anxiety, when a person is deprived of work. However, other research has shown that workaholics can be found among those employees who enjoy their work, as well as among those who feel dissatisfied with it (Spence and Robbins 1992).

Third, the behavioural dimension of workaholism appears largely to represent genuinely excessive involvement in one's work. It infers that a person will 'experience greater effort', 'strive for recognition and praise', 'improve the quality of performance' and 'pursue perfectionistic strivings' (Case 1), or 'increases the activity', 'take on more and more tasks' and 'double-check everything' (Case 2). Moreover, the behavioural dimension manifests itself in excessive intrusion of work into personal life, that is, a work–life imbalance, which is expressed in the notion, 'my whole life revolved around work' (Case 2).

CASE 1

A clinical and health psychologist with over 30 years of clinical experience describes his feelings associated with attitudes towards work: 'My earliest memories of school were coupled with an urgent sensation of pressure to perform … a chronic sense of feeling a need to apologize for my inadequacies … demand to meet the approval of others, striving for recognition and praise … love and acceptance were intimately linked to conditional demands'. Decades later, he had recurrent nightmare-like dreams connected with scholarly performance, such as a focus on bodily cues of heightened arousal, a wildly fluctuating heart rate, profuse sweating with cold moist hands, and a strange feeling of alienation and dizziness … a distinct compulsive quality, a dire need to impress, and pursuit of perfectionistic strivings. He felt that greater effort was required to attain subjectively perceived 'mediocre' performance … a stage of continual benchmarking, a never-ending dress rehearsal. Such achievement-oriented attitudes may be conducive to long-term benefits, propelling one to improved quality of performance, which are attributes that define performing artists, dancers, singers, actors and no doubt top athletes, facilitating their passion for excellence, yet it would seem to be a fine balancing act with risks of a dramatic fall, which could lead, perhaps, to paralysis of the creative process.

CASE 2

A 50-year-old head nurse on a gynaecology and obstetrics unit in a semi-private, semi-state owned hospital, described nursing as her life. However, this changed a few years ago; she said after being mobbed (or bullied) by one of her superiors, she felt that: … 'everything shut down … like a blown fuse – there was no spark left in me at all. I was an empty shell, felt like a Zombie and when I looked in the mirror, I couldn't recognize this pale-faced, lifeless creature (lacking in motivation) who stared back at me. Even getting washed and dressed in the morning was too much to face. I have always been a coper, a person who rolls her sleeves up and gets on with things. No challenge has ever beaten me before. A born leader and not a follower. Who was this weakling I was looking at? The more my boss demanded, the more I did (increased activity), rising to the challenge like someone demented, taking on more and more tasks and not trusting anyone to do anything so I was sure it was done properly. I checked and double-checked everything … I felt like a master wheel, and one day rolled into the next in a blur. My whole life revolved around work … constantly drained, and yet not able to relax and calm down. My batteries were not able to charge themselves up. I couldn't laugh, cry or feel anything (unable to express emotions). There is a stigma to such (mental) illnesses, and in the caring profession, no room for people like that, who are weak and not able to stand the pressure. I couldn't sleep at all – thoughts running around in my head over and over again like checklists which I had to go through, until it made me feel sick. My appetite waned and eating was at the bottom of my to-do list. I started neglecting myself and my home … Life on a daily basis became a battle for survival, leaving me weepy, frustrated, aggressive, and angry, and at the same time disappointed at myself for being so weak and not being able to cope. Then one day it stopped. I couldn't get out of bed and just couldn't face another day (withdrawal, alienation and inactive). I was catatonic and my body wasn't able to do any of the normal things humans do'.

It should be noted that Ng et al. (2007) propose that in order to be classified as workaholics, employees should have high scores on each of the three workaholism dimensions, although they do not distinguish *explicit* types of workaholic. Conversely, there is a lack of clarity concerning the positive relationships among these dimensions because the affective dimension contains both positive and negative emotions. As demonstrated by Spence and Robbins (1992), the correlation between 'drive to work' (which is a cognitive indicator) and 'work enjoyment' (an affective indicator) is negative for 'unenthusiastic' workaholics, whereas the correlation between these two variables is positive for 'enthusiastic' (presumably well-adjusted) workaholics. As research on emotive aspects of workaholism is still developing (currently, cognitive and behavioural indicators predominant in analysing workaholism), the three-dimensional framework seems preferable for analysing different workaholism indicators, and this framework accommodates the possibility that combinations thereof can result in different workaholic types.

In light of numerous studies in which positive relationships between workaholism and burnout have been observed (Andreassen, Ursin and Eriksen 2007; Guglielmi, Simbula, Schaufeli and Depolo 2012; Schaufeli, Shimazu and Taris 2009; Schaufeli, Taris and van Rhenen 2008; Taris, Schaufeli and Verhoven 2005; van Beek et al. 2011; van Beek, Hu, Schaufeli, Taris and Schreurs 2012) it is well established that workaholics can occasionally display burnout symptoms. Moreover, there are differences in the intensity of burnout among types of workaholics (van Beek et al. 2011). The presence of some burnout indicators can be easily observed in the above case study describing the nurse (consistent with findings from Demerouti, Bakker, Nachreiner and Schaufeli 2001; Maslach 2000). These indicators include physical exhaustion, e.g. 'my batteries were not able to charge themselves up', 'I couldn't get out of bed', 'not being able to cope', 'couldn't face another day (withdrawal, alienation and inactive)' and emotional exhaustion, e.g. 'I couldn't laugh, cry or feel anything (unable to express emotions)', 'weepy, frustrated, aggressive, and angry'.

The cases presented above are only two examples of a wide diversity of existing workaholic types and their coping styles described in the literature (Fassel 1990; Naughton 1987; Peiperl and Jones 2001; Rohrlich 1981; Scott et al. 1997; Spence and Robbins 1992). Although it is evident that workaholics can present more positive symptoms, focus has been on those individuals suffering from high physical and emotional stress in addition to burnout. Not surprisingly, those are people who, being aware of their problems (albeit often delayed), are more likely to seek professional help by themselves or with the support of their families.

As can be seen from the two examples of workaholics presented, the diagnosis and treatment of workaholism ought to be based on a number of symptoms, belonging to the three dimensions, which contribute to one's psychological well-being (Burke 1999; Malinowska 2010a, 2010b). If we look at the many elements of this syndrome, which in combination constitute a specific type and/or an individual case, this may offer a basis for better and more effective interventions. However, before elaborating on the proposition of changing the way the workaholic thinks, feels and behaves, we briefly critically review the workaholic interventions that have been reported in recent psychological literature.

Comments on Workaholism Interventions

As the first step in this analysis, we conducted a search on the Academic Search complete database using the search term 'workaholism', along with 'intervention' or 'treatment' or 'therapy' or 'counselling'. The findings suggested five distinct topical domains: (1) *conceptualization* of workaholism, (2) *types of resources* that were dealt with under interventions, (3) *status* of intervention, (4) *phase* of intervention, and (5) *level* of intervention (intra- vs. inter-individual).

I. CONCEPTUALIZATION OF WORKAHOLISM

The tendency to construe workaholism as either functional or dysfunctional is evident in assumptions and concepts, as well as in empirical models. Some researchers consider workaholism to be an illness, defining its causes and consequences in terms of disorders and dysfunctions. Others perceive workaholism as a healthy, albeit intensive, involvement in work, and consequently explore reasons for this excessive involvement in work and its potential benefits for the individual. Therefore, the accepted conceptualization determines which outcomes are appropriate and desirable. Of course, it can be both, depending on the *type* of workaholism. For example, Spence and Robbins' (1992) conceptualization of workaholism focused on promoting 'pleasure' in work (Andreassen, Hetland and Pallesen 2010), whereas those defining workaholism as working excessively and compulsively (Schaufeli et al. 2009) were inclined to focus on 'decreasing the (undesirable) habitual component' (e.g. van den Broeck, Schreurs, de Witte, Vansteenkiste, Germeys and Schaufeli 2011).

Moreover, accepting a salutogenic or pathogenetic paradigm (Antonovsky 1979) specifically suggests that attention be directed towards treatments that build on positive emotions, strengths, resources and meaning or, on the contrary, to the deficits and disorder related aspects of an individual's life. From the perspective of workaholism treatment, the pathogenetic paradigm has useful sources that have been adopted from interventions originally developed for other 'addictive' disorders, e.g. alcoholism and obsessive compulsive disorder. That approach can be justified if workaholism is considered an addiction 'that share[s] many similarities to other more traditional addictions' (Griffiths 2011, p. 740), e.g. alcoholism (see also: Griffiths 2005; Killinger

1991; Oates 1971; Robinson 1989). Examples of interventions taken from alcoholism treatments include references to Workaholics Anonymous (Burke 2006; Robinson 1996; van Wijhe, Schaufeli and Peeters 2010), rewarding workaholics for non-work activities (Oates 1971), and identifying what reinforces workaholic behaviour (Chamberlin and Zhang 2009; Robinson and Kelley 1998; Seybold and Salomone 1994).

2. TYPE OF RESOURCES ADDRESSED IN INTERVENTIONS

Some interventions for workaholism commonly encompass recommendations for enhancing personal, social and organizational resources. The inclusion of resources into treatment was first postulated by Antonovsky (1979) and it is currently supported by schools of positive psychotherapy that do not focus exclusively on the reduction of negative symptoms. This augments the definition of resources developed by Hobfoll (1986). By analysing workaholism interventions in terms of the resources they address, it is helpful to scrutinize the literature for 'objects, circumstances, personality traits, and energetic potentials that directly or indirectly better enable people to survive in situations of stress', in which they acquire and maintain (Heszen and Sęk 2008, p. 61). As regards personal resources, emphasis has been placed on self-esteem (Seybold and Salomone 1994), time-management skills (Aziz, Adkins, Walker and Wuensch 2010; Piotrowski and Vodanovich 2008; van Wijhe et al. 2010), assertiveness (van Wijhe et al. 2010), work enjoyment (Andreassen et al. 2010), work satisfaction (Burke 2000a), interests (Oates 1971; Piotrowski and Vodanovich 2008; Seybold and Salomone 1994) and health (Burke 2000a; Chamberlin and Zhang 2009; van Wijhe et al. 2010). Among social resources, both social support and work–life balance have been identified as workaholism interventions (Seybold and Salomone 1994). However, most interventions focus on enhancing job resources such as autonomy (Gagné and Deci 2005; van Beek et al. 2012), meaningful feedback (Gagné and Deci 2005; van Beek et al. 2011), rewards (Burke 2000a; Chamberlin and Zhang 2009), and managerial and collegial support (Johnstone and Johnston 2005).

Although research has investigated the use of resources (e.g. job control; van den Broeck et al. 2011), there seem to be no purposeful resource-based interventions regarding workaholism, other than occasional suggestions for decreasing workaholism through the provision of different, predominantly non-specific resources. For example, Piotrowski and Vodanovich (2008) proposed some actions which indirectly focus on each type of resources: establishing organizational values and cultures that support work–life balance (*organizational resources*), learning stress management strategies (*person resources*), providing group and/or family counselling (*social resources*). However, this framework does not link a single step in the intervention process to a particular resource or demand. In contrast, resource-based interventions require a set of strategies that focus on the mobilization and acquisition of resources (Mott 2005). However, interventions should consider the use of resources that can counteract specific demands that lead to a deterioration of employee well-being (Cutrona and Russell 1990). As Seligman, Rashid and Parks (2006) suggest: 'It is possible that directly building these positive resources may successfully counteract negative symptoms and may also buffer against future occurrence' (p. 774).

3. STATUS OF RECOMMENDATIONS

In our database search, we found a wide range of proposed interventions that include purposeful action(s) to promote changes in workaholics. Therefore, the interventions found have ranged from occasional suggestions for changing only one workaholism factor, to comprehensive workaholism treatments aimed at introducing changes to all aspects of this phenomenon (cf.

Ballou 1995). Most of our search results consisted of research studies that proposed hypotheses regarding influencing factors, which in those particular studies, proved to be significant in predicting workaholism, e.g. driven aspects of work style (Burke 2000a) and perfectionism (Piotrowski and Vodanovich 2008). Some studies were limited to recognizing the need to change the factor, e.g. work enjoyment (Aziz et al. 2010) in order to decrease workaholism. Others were rich with suggestions on how to elicit the desired effect. However, such proposals appear beyond the scope of workaholism treatment, directed more towards organizational changes (e.g. Andreassen et al. 2010; Hetland and Sandal 2003).

Fortunately, there are some comprehensive descriptions of therapeutic techniques for specifically combating workaholism. One of the most comprehensive interventions has been developed by Burwell and Chen (2002). This model (presented in Table 21.1) integrates a range of techniques that help to reframe irrational beliefs, to change self-defeating emotions, and to behave in a more balanced way, in opposition to the workaholic's irrational beliefs. However, regardless of the status of such proposals, there has been scarce empirical evidence of their effectiveness in decreasing workaholism per se.

Table 21.1   Techniques used in rational emotive behaviour therapy (REBT) for workaholism treatment

Type of technique	Description
Cognitive intervention	Confronting a client's irrational beliefs, disputing them through questioning and replacing them with novel attitudes and views.
Emotive intervention	Helping a client practice unconditional self-acceptance by accepting the self when being judged by others, or by using shame-attacking exercises (intentionally performing an activity that is disapproved of by others).
Behavioural intervention	Teaching a client to learn new and more effective ways of performing, such as delegating tasks to others, limiting working hours, taking leisure time.

Source: Authors' elaboration based on Burwell and Chen (2002).

4. PHASE OF INTERVENTION

It is useful to classify workaholism interventions into primary, secondary and tertiary prevention and treatment (van Wijhe et al. 2010). It is then possible to select a method that is applicable to the phase which an individual is currently experiencing.

Primary preventions are intended to reduce the risk of workaholism among non-workaholics. It can be directed towards children, e.g. providing unconditional regard for them (Robinson and Kelley 1998) or adult employees, e.g. rewarding them more highly for performing their duties than for extra-role behaviours (van Wijhe et al. 2010).

Secondary preventions aim to assist employees who are at risk of workaholism by attempting to control risk factors. For instance, individuals can be taught relaxation techniques (Robinson and Kelley 1998; van Wijhe et al. 2010), time management (Piotrowski and Vodanovich 2008) and/or ways of improving family life (Robinson 2001; Robinson, Carroll and Flowers 2001).

Tertiary-level actions aim at preventing the consequences of workaholism through early detection and treatment, so these measures frequently overlap with the treatment itself (van Wijhe et al. 2010). Unfortunately, longitudinal studies on workaholism are scarce, so the development phases of workaholism are not readily identifiable, which makes it difficult to distinguish those actions which are either tertiary preventive actions or treatment actions.

Finally, among the examples of actions related to secondary and tertiary interventions are self-care plans focused on balancing personal and occupational life (Robinson 1996, 2000a), employee assistance programmes (Brady, Vodanovich and Rotunda 2008), education about the positive consequences of leisure activities (Chamberlin and Zhang 2009), Workaholics Anonymous (Robinson 1996), cognitive-behavioural intervention strategies (e.g. REBT, Burwell and Chen 2002), therapy addressing feelings of insecurity and worthlessness (Seybold and Salomone 1994), and family approaches examining the origins of workaholism and reducing its reinforcement (Chamberlin and Zhang 2009; Robinson 1996).

5. LEVEL OF INTERVENTION (INTRA- VS. INTER-INDIVIDUAL)

It is possible to differentiate between interventions for workaholism according to the *level* on which they operate. Some are *intra-individual*-level interventions that focus on reframing irrational beliefs (Burwell and Chen 2002), on changing the proportion of time spent on different life domains (Robinson 2000a), on regulating emotions (Robinson and Kelley 1998) and/or on motivation (van Beek et al. 2011, 2012). Others are *inter-individual*-level interventions that focus on implementing social support in the workplace (Johnstone and Johnston 2005; van den Broeck et al. 2011), and/or in the family (Burke 2000a; Shifron and Reysen 2011). Nevertheless, various authors recommend adopting a broader approach that encompasses both intra-individual and inter-individual levels of intervention (e.g. Chamberlin and Zhang 2009; Piotrowski and Vodanovich 2008).

In this respect, the challenges facing researchers are, first, that the chosen intervention should be consistent with the broad definition of workaholism, distinguishing its cognitive, behavioural and emotional indicators. Second, the interventions should offer a comprehensive description of what changes are desired and how these goals can best be achieved. Providing researchers and practitioners with an array of established techniques for interventions is the first step towards establishing a standardized approach, which can enable wider implementation of these techniques in practice and evaluation of their effectiveness. Although useful sources of workaholism interventions have been identified, this area still requires further exploration. As a starting point, it seems promising to look for ideas proven to be effective in decreasing Type A behaviour, or in enhancing work engagement, and to evaluate their usefulness in helping workaholics.

Some authors (Dudek 2008; Furnham 2013; Malinowska, Jochymek and Tokarz 2011) argue that the types of workaholics can reflect the different phases of addiction development, which suggests that therapeutic goals should be matched to specific types of workaholism (Naughton 1987; Robinson 2000a). Finally, a comprehensive intervention may encompass actions focused not only on workaholics themselves, but also on their 'social environment', e.g. work setting and relationships with significant others (van Wijhe et al. 2010).

Cognitive Behavioural Therapy and its Application in Workaholism Treatment

Overall, cognitive behavioural therapy, which pertains to the three principal dimensions of workaholism syndrome, offers a viable starting point in designing effective workaholism interventions. Cognitive behavioural therapy is a system of treatment that addresses the interactions between how we think (cognitions), behave (behaviours/acts) and feel (affective/ emotions). Hazlett-Stevens and Craske (2002) underscore the value of focusing on cognition (thinking), which can lead to behavioural change, or directly on behaviour, which may ultimately change negative beliefs and thought patterns into positive (rational) ones: 'In some forms of therapy the interventions may have very little to do with cognitive appraisals and evaluations but be heavily dependent on client action and behaviour change' (p. 6). Recognizing that cognitions, behaviours and emotions can reinforce each other, not only behavioural and cognitive, but also emotional changes are used as indicators of change in CBT, which is especially useful for emotional disturbances (e.g. anxiety and depressive disorders).

Cognitive behavioural therapy has been applied to a wide range of psychological disorders and problems (Hollon and Beck 2004; Roth and Fonagy 2005; Salkoskis 1996) and its administration and development has been heavily guided by research. A review and meta-analysis by Butler, Chapman, Forman and Beck (2006) reported that there have been over 325 published studies on the outcomes of cognitive-behavioural interventions. Its high efficacy has been widely demonstrated in relation to adult unipolar depression, adolescent unipolar depression, generalized anxiety disorder, panic disorder (with or without agoraphobia), social phobia, PTSD, and childhood depressive and anxiety disorders (Butler et al. 2006; Cartwright-Hatton, Roberts, Chitsabesan, Fothergill and Harrington 2004).

Furthermore, CBT has been adapted and applied for use within the organizational context. The work-focused CBT intervention (W-CBT), which incorporates gradual exposure to the workplace, has been successful for employees who have been on prolonged sick leave due to common mental disorders (depression, anxiety, adjustment disorder; Lagerveld, Blonk, Brenninkmeijer, Wijngaards-de Meij and Schaufeli 2012).

A number of treatment approaches and techniques exist within the scope of CBT, which the American Psychiatric Association suggests should be divided into two broad groups (Wright, Basco, Thase and Gabbard 2006): *cognitive* (e.g. restructuring, identifying cognitive errors, thought change recording) and *behavioural* techniques (e.g. self-monitoring, relaxation training, graded task assignments). In light of the variety of existing approaches, therapists should not limit themselves by strict methodological adherence to any single technique (Goldfried and Davison 1994), but should adopt experimental orientations. This approach features close cooperation between the therapist and the client, with the mutual understanding that the therapist has the expertise in theory and techniques, whereas the client is the expert on him- or herself, and is able to identify his or her problems (Kirkcaldy and Siefen 2012; Newman and Greenway 1997).

The effectiveness of CBT applications in treating workaholism seem to be promising. Previous research has revealed its success in alleviating obsessive compulsive personality disorder tendencies (OCPD; Aziz, Uhrich, Wuensch and Swords 2013). Both concepts, OCPD and workaholism, share some similarities when taking into account the positive correlation between inner drive to work (the main feature of workaholism in each of the theoretical conceptualizations) and obsession, as well as compulsion ($r = 0.51$ and 0.37, respectively; McMillan, O'Driscoll, Marsh and Brady 2001). Moreover, the usefulness of cognitive and behavioural techniques has been demonstrated to be helpful for other behavioural addictions such as compulsive shopping (Mueller et al. 2007) or gambling, even at one-year follow-up (Ladouceur et al. 2001). Chen (2006) emphasizes that techniques designed to change behaviour should be used at the beginning of workaholism treatment, especially cue response techniques, such as imagery desensitization with muscle relaxation techniques.

The combined use of cognitive, behavioural and emotional techniques *for workaholics* derived from the rational emotive behaviour therapy (REBT) – a form of CBT (Beck 2014) that was pioneered by Ellis (1995, 2000) – has been empirically supported by other authors (e.g. Burwell and Chen, 2002). The core techniques included in this psychotherapeutic model are presented and described in Table 21.1. The combination of these three types of technique supports the overall change and it is expected to be durable, but only if a client changes outlook and self-defeating emotions, and applies newly acquired rational beliefs in real-life situations (Neenan and Dryden 2000).

A Novel Multimodal Scheme for Workaholism Interventions

Burwell and Chen (2002) suggest that this threefold treatment can be successfully implemented to modify the affective (emotional), cognitive (thoughts) and behavioural facets of workaholism. Indeed, to a large extent it also meets the assumptions mentioned above in the summary of comments on workaholism interventions. Nonetheless, the crucial *improvement* that should be suggested is to include actions focusing not only on the person, but also on the environment (e.g. family interactions and work setting).

There seems to be a need for an elaboration, driven by and based on clinical experience and the myriad of published research on the CBT therapeutic model, as suggested by Lazarus's Multimodal Therapy (1995). Lazarus (1995) focused on seven dimensions or modalities of a person's functioning, namely, behaviour, physiology, cognition, interpersonal relationships, sensation, imagery and affect. This elaborated model grew out of an observation that the long-term effects of CBT were characterized by a relatively high relapse rate. He argued for a broader spectrum of treatment domains. Clinicians have emphasized the need to extend the spectrum of treatment beyond actions and thoughts to psychosocial functioning by incorporating the significance of imagery, sensory, interpersonal and biological areas. For example, Kirkcaldy (2014) suggests that the initial session(s) – anywhere between 1 to 3 sessions, each 50 minutes in duration – should document the client's biography. First, responses to questions relating to family and childhood history should be gathered that describe, e.g. the temperament and prevailing characteristics of the patient's father and mother; the quality of the marital relationship between parents; parents' main methods of coping with stress; core beliefs underlying their child-rearing practices, number of siblings (their age and gender) and birth order. Next, the inquiry should progress onto questions about childhood illness and problems; attitudes towards primary and secondary school, including relationship with teachers; favourite school subjects and hobbies; influence of peer groups; and details about how puberty and adolescence were experienced. Then, in the final stage of this data collection process, therapists can focus on aspects of the problem that brought the client into therapy, the emotions and physical symptoms which are currently being manifested, and the subjective evaluation of the reasons for these problems. In the early course of therapy, provided the client has agreed, a family member (e.g. spouse) can be invited into therapy to highlight his or her observations of the influences on family functioning. In subsequent sessions, it is necessary to identify the behavioural correlates of the patient's problems or, in other words, to 'translate psychological disorders' into the language of behaviour (asking what behaviours are shown in difficult situations?). Finally, it is possible to detect the concerns (cognitions) which are troubling the individual, and may have an effect on their emotional state. For instance, Case 1 disclosed 'I have to succeed in order to gain approval and acceptance of significant persons such as parents and teachers'; 'I feel sorry and apologize that I disappoint others nearest me'; 'I must strive for credit and praise'; 'I experience guilt when I am unable to meet standards and expectations others place on me!'

When going through this treatment plan, the client and therapist are likely to actively filter out elements contextually related to workaholic attitudes such as perfectionism, competitiveness, hostility, denial, controlling compulsive behaviour, addictive tendencies, achievement orientation, self-defeating attitude (low self-esteem), anxiety (somatic), inadequate leisure time, etc. This is best illustrated by Figure 21.1, which shows the features associated with workaholism. Several of these subcomponents overlap theoretically.

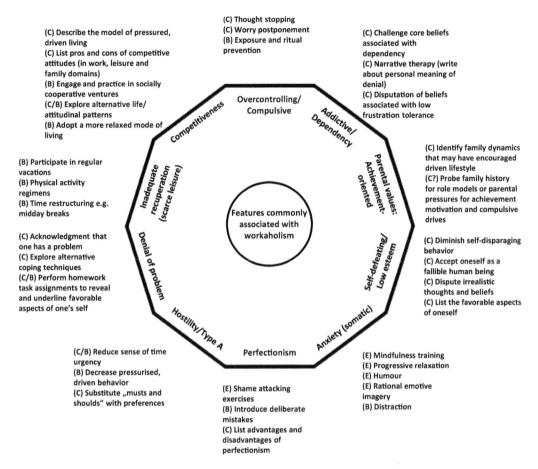

Figure 21.1   Features commonly associated with workaholism and the proposition of behavioral (B), cognitive (C) and emotional (E) techniques to address them

Source: Interventions adapted from Borscherdt, 1989; Jongsma and Petersen, 1999; Kirkcaldy, 2014.

In determining workaholism interventions, one of our recommendations – based on our analysis of the literature – is to identify and incorporate ideas proven to be effective in diminishing disorders associated with workaholism. For example, a leading practitioner of rational emotive therapy, Borcherdt (1989), provides specific advice for counteracting one personal characteristic that is closely aligned to workaholism, that of 'perfectionism'. This involves admitting one has a problem; accepting oneself with the problem (reducing self-negating attitudes); disputing irrational, unrealistic ideas and beliefs; deliberately practising and intentionally introducing errors in one's (working) life; being transparent (revealing, openly to others, your fallible nature); using effective coping statements (listing anti-perfectionistic thoughts); referencing (listing the pros and cons of adopting flexibility and acceptance vs. rigidity and exactness); and performing validity task assignments which serve to uncover and highlight the favourable aspects of oneself and others.

Similarly, in their treatment planning, Jongsma and Petersen (1999) proposed focusing on the frenetic and hostile aspects of Type A behaviour, aspects which correlate with workaholism. Some of the descriptions of this behaviour include patterns of pressurizing oneself and others to over-accomplish because there is often insufficient time; a powerful compulsion to win irrespective of the costs and the nature of the activity or the competitor; and a state of continual impatience and intolerance with any form of waiting, delays or interruptions. This can result in the formation of a series of long-term goals, to, for example, *lessen the sense of time urgency, free-floating anxiety and self-disparaging behaviour; formulate and implement an 'alternative' life/attitudinal pattern, facilitating a more relaxed pattern of living; and achieve an overall decrease in pressured, driven behaviour.* Jongsma and Petersen also provide specific short-term goals (and interventions) such as identifying family of origin dynamics that may foster a driven lifestyle and describing the model of pressured, driven living (e.g. by asking the patient to provide examples of his or her pressured lifestyle; probing family history for role models or parental pressures for high achievement motivation and compulsive drives).

Moreover, elaborate proposals for counteracting perfectionism have been suggested by the Centre for Clinical Interventions (2013). It lists such interventions as identifying the unhelpful 'rule' or underlying assumption (unrealistic core beliefs); pinpointing its origin and its manner of development; establishing if this belief/rule is realistic and achievable; listing the adverse effects, that is, the disadvantages of maintaining this rule; establishing or generating a more constructive and helpful set of rules; and structuring a daily plan of how one could act differently to practise this novel assumption. By means of rehearsing alternative ways of construing and interpreting, as well as challenging traditional belief patterns, the client can capitalize on making steps towards a more realistic way of living.

Conclusions

In this chapter we have argued that effective workaholism interventions should take into account, from the theoretical point of view, that workaholism appears to be a syndrome 'cluster' comprising several different indicators (Ng et al. 2007; Snir and Harpaz 2012). As we can see from the two case studies presented earlier, there is a complexity of overlapping symptoms, which may result in tenuous diagnoses. Workaholism is still an insufficiently explained phenomenon (Malinowska and Tokarz 2014), and research in this area is still at the descriptive level, so therapists generally have not been provided with succinct, well-designed and reliable workaholism indicators (which also applies to burnout syndrome). The actual manifestations of disturbed functioning are much more multifaceted and richer than conventional models suggest. The validity of such 'quasi' psychiatric diagnoses may be challenged, as by Frances (2013), who states:

> We should not be surprised that psychiatric diagnosis has always been, and still is, so faddish ... The good news is that fashions come and fashions go. A century ago, the world was awash in neurasthenia, conversion hysteria, and multiple personality disorder. Then, all three suddenly and mysteriously disappeared. The psychiatric fads that now seem so entrenched are less robust than meets the eye and will also wilt with time as people come to understand their risks. [Yet] most epidemics in the past were isolated, local, and self-limited. Our new fads are globalized, monetized, and becoming part of the societal infrastructure. (p. 137)

Based on our understanding of cognitive behavioural, rational emotive, and multimodal therapies, we have presented a preliminary proposition that could be a first step in promoting the development of a complementary workaholism intervention that includes cognitive, affective and behavioural techniques. It follows that the next step in the development of this model would be to extend it to include motivational factors that have been intentionally omitted because there are very few proposals, and scarce studies, about how to adapt them for workaholism treatment (Jochymek, Malinowska and Tokarz 2013). Nevertheless, there is a strongly justified need to address this category of factors as it is suggestive of a deeper mechanism of intense commitment to work, and can potentially clarify the occurrence of the presented symptoms. This has been confirmed in studies that demonstrate the relationships between workaholism and values, value crisis, and type of motivation (cf. Malinowska 2010a; van Beek et al. 2011; van den Broeck et al. 2011).

First, it should be emphasized that changes within these fundamental personality processes, which strongly determine motivation, occur gradually over the course of maturation and personal development. These processes are not 'easily' susceptible to treatment, but rather, to other indirect actions, e.g. coaching, because they are primarily dependent on self-knowledge/self-awareness (Kozielecki 1986), and on the work of a person on their own development. These influences should be more susceptible to the indirect approach to the practice of psychology, which derives from Rogers' conception that assumes the activity of the patient, assisted by the therapist, can lead to improved well-being and functioning (Rogers 1951).

Second, another potential way to affect the domain of personality and motivation is to stimulate intrinsic motivation (McCombs 1994; Ryan 1995). In its developmentally advanced form (intrinsic regulation and integrated regulation) motivation is substantially integrated with the self and system of values, and determines that undertaking the tasks and challenges comply with them and with the competencies of a person (Deci and Ryan 2000).

Third, not only the developmental phases of workaholism (which are reflected indirectly in the types of intervention) should be taken into account, but also those of a person's life (Erikson 1968; McAdams 1994). It is likely that an individual's personal development can be successful or disturbed precisely because of motivational processes, as emphasized by Burke and Fiskenbaum (2008). The authors discuss Porter's (2001) dichotomy of motivation for doing long working hours, which is, 'a constructive, highly committed achievement-oriented style of workaholism. This expenditure of time results in achievement ... A person can also put in long hours in a compulsive, perfectionistic fashion, driven to achieve perfectionistic standards' (p. 26). Such an approach also indicates the need for the development of the person through changes in his or her personality, value system and motivation (Gałdowa 1992, 2005; Gałdowa and Nelicki 1993; McCombs 1994; Ryan 1995).

Acknowledgements

Our thanks and appreciation goes to Terence Martin (Belfast) and Adrian Furnham (University College London) who provided useful corrections to a draft version of this manuscript.

References

Andreassen, C.S., Hetland, J. and Pallesen, S. (2010). The relationship between 'workaholism', basic needs satisfaction at work and personality. *European Journal of Personality*, 24(1), 3–17.

Andreassen, C.S., Ursin, H. and Eriksen, H.R. (2007). The relationship between strong motivation to work, 'workaholism' and health. *Psychology and Health*, 22(5), 615–29.

Antonovsky, A. (1979). *Health, Stress and Coping: New Perspectives on Mental and Physical Well-being*. San Fransisco: Jossey-Bass.

Aziz, S., Wuensch, K.L. and Brandon, H.R. (2010). A comparison among worker types using a composites approach and median splits. *The Psychological Record*, 60, 627–42.

Aziz, S., Adkins, C.T., Walker, A.G. and Wuensch, K.L. (2010). Workaholism and work–life imbalance: Does cultural origin influence the relationship? *International Journal of Psychology*, 45(1), 72–9.

Aziz, S., Uhrich, B., Wuensch, K.L and Swords, B. (2013). The Workaholism Analysis Questionnaire: Emphasizing work-life imbalance and addiction in the measurement of workaholism. *Journal of Behavioral and Applied Management*, 14, 71–86.

Ballou, M. (ed.) (1995). *Psychological Strategies: Guide to Interventions*. Westport: Praeger.

Beck, A. (2014). The past and future of cognitive therapy. *Journal of Psychotherapy Practice and Research*, 6(4), 276–84.

Borcherdt, B. (1989). *Think Straight! Feel Great! 21 Guides to Emotional Self-control*. Florida: Professional Resource Exchange.

Brady, B.R., Vodanovich, S.J. and Rotunda, R. (2008). The impact of workaholism on work-family conflict, job satisfaction, and perception of leisure activities. *Psychologist Manager Journal*, 11, 241–63.

Burke, R.J. (1999). It's not how hard you work but how you work hard: Evaluating workaholism components. *International Journal of Stress Management*, 6, 225–40.

Burke, R.J. (2000a). Workaholism and extra-work satisfaction. *International Journal of Organizational Analysis*, 7, 352–64.

Burke, R.J. (2000b). Workaholism in organizations: Concepts, results and future research directions. *International Journal of Management Reviews*, 2(1), 1–16.

Burke, R.J. (2006). Workaholic types: It's not how hard you work but why and how you work hard. In R.J. Burke (ed.), *Research Companion to Working Time and Work Addiction* (pp. 173–92). Northampton, MA: Edward Elgar.

Burke, R.J. and Fiskenbaum, L. (2008). Work hours, work intensity and work addictions: Costs and benefits. In R. Burke and C.L. Cooper (eds), *The Long Work Hours Culture: Causes, Consequences and Choices* (pp. 3–37). Yorkshire: Emerald.

Burke, R.J. and Fiskenbaum, L. (2011). Work hours, work intensity and work addiction: Costs and benefits. In A.S. Antoniou and C.L. Cooper (eds), *New Directions in Organizational Psychology and Behavioral Medicine* (pp. 79–106). Surrey: Elgar.

Burwell, R. and Chen, C.P. (2002). Applying REBT to workaholic clients. *Counselling Psychology Quarterly*, 15, 219–28.

Butler, A.C., Chapman, J.E., Forman, E.M. and Beck, A.T. (2006). The empirical status of cognitive-behavioral therapy: A review of meta-analysis. *Clinical Psychology Review*, 26, 17–31.

Cartwright-Hatton, S., Roberts, C., Chitsabesan, P., Fothergill, C. and Harrington, R. (2004). Systematic review of the efficacy of cognitive behaviour therapies for childhood and adolescent anxiety disorders. *British Journal of Clinical Psychology*, 43(4), 421–36.

Centre for Clinical Interventions (CCI) (2013) *Counteracting Perfectionism*. Module 7. 14th November. Available at: http://www.cci.health.wa.gov.au/resources/infopax.cfm?Info_ID=52. Accessed 21 August 2015.

Chamberlin, C.M. and Zhang, N. (2009). Workaholism, health, and self-acceptance. *Journal of Counseling & Development*, 87, 159–69.

Chen, C. (2006). Improving work-life balance: REBT for workaholic treatment. In R.J. Burke (ed.), *Research Companion to Working Time and Work Addiction* (pp. 310–30). Cheltenham: Edward Elgar.

Cutrona, C.E. and Russell, D. (1990). Type of social support and specific stress: Toward a theory of optimal matching. In I.G. Sarason, B.R. Sarason and G.R. Pierce (eds), *Social Support: An Interactional View* (pp. 319–66). New York: Wiley.

Deci, E.L. and Ryan, R.M. (2000). Self-determination theory and the facilitation of intrinsic motivation, social development and well-being. *American Psychologist*, 55(1), 68–78.

Demerouti, E., Bakker, A.B., Nachreiner, F. and Schaufeli, W.B. (2001). The job demands-resources model of burnout. *Journal of Applied Psychology*, 86(3), 499–512.

Dudek, B. (2008). Pracoholizm – szkodliwy skutek nadmiernego zaangażowania w pracę [Workaholism – a negative consequence of excessive work engagement]. *Medycyna Pracy*, 59(3), 247–54.

Ellis, A. (1995). Changing rational-emotive therapy (RET) to rational emotive behavior therapy (REBT). *Journal of Rational- Emotive and Cognitive-Behavior Therapy*, 13, 85–9.

Ellis, A. (2000). Can Rational Emotive Behavior Therapy (REBT) be effectively used with people who have devout beliefs in God and religion? *Professional Psychology: Research and Practice*, 31, 29–33.

Erikson, E.H. (1968). *Identity, Youth and Crisis*. New York: Norton.

Fassel, D. (1990). *Working Ourselves to Death: The High Cost of Workaholism, the Rewards of Recovery*. San Francisco: HarperCollins.

Frances, A. (2013). *Saving Normal: An Insider's Revolt against Out-of-Control Psychiatric Diagnosis, DSM-5, Big Pharma, and the Medicalization of Ordinary Life*. New York: HarperCollins.

Furnham, A. (2013). Workaholism. In B.D. Kirkcaldy (ed.), *Chimes of Time: Wounded Health Professionals Essays on Recovery* (pp. 229–43). Leiden: Sidestone.

Gagné, M. and Deci, E.L. (2005). Self-determination theory as a new framework for understanding organizational behavior. *Journal of Organizational Behavior*, 26, 331–62.

Gałdowa, A. (1992) *Powszechność i wyjątek. Rozwój osobowości człowieka dorosłego*. [Universality and exception. Adult person development]. Kraków: Platan.

Gałdowa, A. (2005). Rozwój i kryteria dojrzałości osobowej [Development and criteria of personal maturity]. In A. Gałdowa (ed.), *Psychologiczne i egzystencjalne problemy człowieka dorosłego* (pp. 41–56). Kraków: Wydawnictwo Uniwersytetu Jagiellońskiego.

Gałdowa, A. and Nelicki, A. (1993). On the possibility and conditions of being creative from the perspective of the axiological theory of personality. In T. Marek (ed.), *Psychological Mechanisms of Human Creativity: The Temptation for Reassessment* (pp. 147–64). Delft: Eburon.

Galperin, B.L. and Burke, R.J. (2006). Uncovering the relationship between workaholism and workplace destructive and constructive deviance: An exploratory study. *International Journal of Human Resource Management*, 17(2), 331–47.

Garson, B. (2005). Work addiction in the age of information technology: An analysis. *IIMB Management Review*, 17(1), 15–21.

Gini, A. (1998). Work, identity and self: How we are formed by the work we do. *Journal of Business Ethics*, 17, 707–14.

Goldfried, M.R. and Davison, G.C. (1994). *Clinical Behavior Therapy* (2nd edn). New York: John Wiley.

Griffiths, M.D. (2005). Workaholism is still a useful construct. *Addiction Research and Theory*, 13(2), 97–100.

Griffiths, M. (2011). Workaholism – a 21st century addiction. *The Psychologist*, 24, 740–4.

Guglielmi, D., Simbula, S., Schaufeli, W.B. and Depolo, M. (2012). Self-efficacy and workaholism as initiators of the job demands-resources model. *Career Development International*, 17(4), 375–89.

Hazlett-Stevens, H. and Craske, M.G. (2002). Brief cognitive-behavioral therapy: Definition and scientific foundations. In F.W. Bond and W. Dryden (eds), *Handbook of Brief Cognitive Behavior Therapy* (pp. 1–20). West Sussex: John Wiley and Sons, Ltd.

Heszen, I. and Sęk, H. (2008). Zdrowie i stres [Health and stress]. In J. Strelau and D. Doliński (eds), *Psychologia. Podręcznik akademicki* (vol. 2, pp. 682–734). Gdańsk: GWP.

Hetland, H. and Sandal, G.M. (2003). Transformational leadership in Norway: Outcomes and personality correlates. *European Journal of Work and Organizational Psychology*, 12(2), 147–70.

Hobfoll, S.E. (ed.) (1986). *Stress, Social Support, and Women*. Washington, DC: Hemisphere.

Hollon, S.D. and Beck, A.T. (2004). Cognitive and cognitive behavioral therapies. In M.J. Lambert (ed.), *Garfield and Bergin's Handbook of Psychotherapy and Behavior Change: An Empirical Analysis* (5th edn, pp. 447–92). New York: John Wiley & Sons, Inc.

Jochymek, S., Malinowska, D. and Tokarz, A. (2013, July). A review of workaholism interventions: Setting the basis for successful treatment focused on Self-Determination Theory. Paper presented at EAWOP Small Group Meeting, Heidelberg.

Johnstone, A. and Johnston, L. (2005). The relationship between organizational climate, occupational type and workaholism. *New Zealand Journal of Psychology*, 34(3), 181–8.

Jongsma, A.E. and Petersen, L.M. (1999). *The Complete Adult Psychotherapy Treatment Planner*, 2nd edn. Chichester and New York: John Wiley.

Killinger, B. (1991). *Workaholics: The respectable addicts*. New York: Simon & Schuster.

Kirkcaldy, B.D. (2014) Therapeutic interventions among persons with compulsive work habits. Unpublished manuscript, ICSOMH, Düsseldorf.

Kirkcaldy, B.D. and Siefen, G. (2012). Subjective models of psychological disorders: Mental health professionals. *Asian Journal of Psychiatry*, 5(4), 319–26.

Kozielecki, J. (1986). *Psychologiczna teoria samowiedzy* [Psychological theory of self-knowledge]. Warszawa: PWN.

Ladouceur, R., Sylvain, C., Boutin, C., Lachance, S., Doucet, C., Leblond, J. and Jacques, C. (2001). Cognitive treatment of pathological gambling. *Journal of Nervous and Mental Disease*, 189, 766–73.

Lagerveld, S.E., Blonk, R.W.B., Brenninkmeijer, V., Wijngaards-de Meij, L.D.N.V. and Schaufeli, W.B. (2012). Work-focused treatment of common mental disorders and return to work: A comparative outcome study. *Journal of Occupational Health Psychology*, 17, 220–34.

Lazarus, A. (1995). *The practice of multimodal therapy – Systematic, comprehensive and effective psychotherapy*. New York: McGraw-Hill.

Malinowska, D. (2010a). *Wybrane motywacyjne i osobowościowe uwarunkowania różnych postaci pracoholizmu* [Selected motivational and personality determinants of workaholism types]. Unpublished doctoral dissertation. Jagiellonian University, Cracow.

Malinowska, D. (2010b, September). *Workaholism: Its structure and types*. Paper presented at Second EAWOP Early Career Summer School, Ghandia.

Malinowska, D. and Tokarz, A. (2014). Psychologiczna charakterystyka osób pracujących nadmiernie: różne postaci zaangażowania w pracę [Psychological characteristics of overworked employees: different types of work engagement]. *Studia Humanistyczne AGH*, 13(1), 79–99.

Malinowska, D., Jochymek, S. and Tokarz, A. (2011). *Is work-life conflict a first step to work addiction? An exploration of workaholism's types and its changes over time*. Paper presented at 15th EAWOP Congress, Maastricht.

Malinowska, D., Trzebińska, M., Tokarz, A. and Kirkcaldy, B. (2013). Workaholism and psychosocial functioning: Individual, family and workplace perspectives. In C. Cooper and A.S. Antoniou (eds), *The psychology of the recession on the workplace* (pp. 59–88). Cheltenham, UK and Northampton, MA: Edward Elgar.

Maslach, C. (2000). Wypalenie w perspektywie wielowymiarowej. In H. Sęk (ed.), *Wypalenie zawodowe. Przyczyny. Mechanizmy. Zapobieganie* [Burnout: Antecedents, mechanism, prevention] (pp. 13–31). Warszawa: PWN.

McAdams, D.P. (1994). Can personality change? Levels of stability and growth in personality across the life span. In T.F. Heatherton and J.L. Weinberger (eds), *Can Personality Change?* (pp. 299–313). Washington, DC: American Psychological Association.

McCombs, B.L. (1994). Strategies for assessing and enhancing motivation: Keys to promoting self-regulated learning and performance. In H.F. O'Neil Jr. and M. Drillings (eds), *Motivation: Theory and Research* (pp. 49–69). Hillsdale: Lawrence Erlbaum Associates.

McMillan, L.H.W. and O'Driscoll, M.P. (2006). Exploring new frontiers to generate an integrated definition of workaholism. In R.J. Burke (eds), *Research Companion to Working Time and Work Addiction* (pp. 89–107). Cheltenham: Edward Elgar.

McMillan, L.H.W., Brady, E.C., O'Driscoll, M.P. and Marsh, N.V. (2002). A multifaceted validation study of Spence and Robbins' (1992) Workaholism Battery. *Journal of Occupational and Organizational Psychology*, 75, 357–68.

McMillan, L.H.W., O'Driscoll, M.P., Marsh, N.V. and Brady E.C. (2001). Understanding workaholism: Data synthesis, theoretical critique and future design strategies. *International Journal of Stress Management*, 8(2), 69–91.

Mott, D.W. (2005). Characteristics and consequences of resource-based intervention practices. *CASEmakers*, 1(5), 1–4.

Mueller, A., Mueller, U., Albert, C., Mertens, C., Silbermann, A., Mitchell, J.E. and de Zwaan, M. (2007). Hoarding in a compulsive buying sample. *Behavior Research and Therapy*, 45(11), 2754–63.

Naughton, T.J. (1987). A conceptual view of workaholism and implications for career counseling and research. *The Career Development Quarterly*, 180–7.

Neenan, M. and Dryden, W. (2000). *Essential rational emotive behaviour therapy*. London: Whurr.

Newman, M.L. and Greenway, P. (1997). Therapeutic effects of providing MMPI-2 test feedback to clients at a university counseling service: A collaborative approach. *Psychological Assessment*, 9(2), 122–31.

Ng, W.H., Sorensen, K.L. and Feldman, D.C. (2007). Dimensions, antecedents, and consequences of workaholism: A conceptual integration and extension. *Journal of Organizational Behavior*, 28(1), 111–36.

Oates, W. (1971). *Confessions of a workaholic: The facts about work addiction*. New York: World Publishing.

Peiperl, M. and Jones, B. (2001). Workaholics and overworkers: Productivity orpathology? *Group and Organization Management*, 26, 369–93.

Piotrowski, C. and Vodanovich, S.J. (2008). *Journal of Instructional Psychology*, 35, 103–5.

Porter, G. (2001). Workaholic tendencies and the high potential for stress among co-workers. *International Journal of Stress Management*, 8(2), 147–64.

Robinson, B.E. (1989). *Work addiction*. Deerfield Beach: Health Communications.

Robinson, B.E. (1996). The psychosocial and familial dimensions of work addiction: Preliminary. *Journal of Counseling and Development*, 74, 446–52.

Robinson, B.E. (2000a). Adult children of workaholics: Clinical and empirical research with implications for family therapists. *Journal of Family Psychotherapy*, 11, 15–26.

Robinson, B.E. (2000b). A typology of workaholics with implications for counseling. *Journal of Addictions and Offender Counseling*, 21, 34–48.

Robinson, B.E. (2001). Workaholism and family functioning: A profile of familial relationships, psychological outcomes, and research considerations. *Contemporary Family Research*, 23, 123–35.

Robinson, B.E. and Kelley, L. (1998). Adult children of workaholics: Self-concept, anxiety, depression, and locus of control. *American Journal of Family Therapy*, 26, 35–50.

Robinson, B.E., Carroll, J.J. and Flowers, C. (2001). Marital estrangement, positive affect, and locus of control among spouses of workaholics and spouses of nonworkaholics: A national study. *The American Journal of Family Therapy*, 29, 397–410.

Rogers, C.R. (1951). *Client-centered Therapy: Its Current Practice, Implications and Theory*. Boston: Houghton Mifflin.

Rohrlich, J.B. (1981). The dynamics of work addiction. *The Israel Journal of Psychiatry and Related Sciences*, 18, 147–56.

Roth, A.D. and Fonagy, P. (2005) *What Works for Whom: A Critical Review of Psychotherapy Research*. New York: Guilford Press.

Ryan, R.M. (1995). Psychological needs and the facilitation of integrative processes. *Journal of Personality*, 63, 397–427.

Salkoskis, P.M. (1996). *Trends in Cognitive and Behavioural Therapies*. Chichester: Wiley.

Schaufeli, W.B., Shimazu, A. and Taris, T.W. (2009). Being driven to work excessively hard: The evaluation of a two-factor measure of workaholism in the Netherlands and Japan. *Cross-Cultural Research*, 43, 320–48.

Schaufeli, W.B., Taris, T.W. and van Rhenen, W. (2008). Workaholism, burnout, and work engagement: Three of a kind or three different kinds of employee well-being? *Applied Psychology: An International Review*, 57(2), 173–203.

Scott, K.S., Moore, K.S. and Miceli, M.P. (1997). An exploration of the meaning and consequences of workaholism. *Human Relations*, 50, 287–314.

Seligman, E.P., Rashid, T. and Parks, A.A. (2006). Positive psychology. *American Psychologist*, 61, 774–88.

Seybold, K.C. and Salomone, P.R. (1994). Understanding workaholism: A review of causes and counseling approaches. *Journal of Counseling and Development*, 73, 4–9.

Shifron, R. and Reysen, R.R. (2011). Workaholism: Addiction to work. *Journal of Individual Psychology*, 67(2), 136–46.

Snir, R. and Harpaz, I. (2012). Beyond workaholism: Towards a general model of heavy work investment. *Human Resource Management Review*, 22(3), 232–43.

Spence, J.T. and Robbins, A.S. (1992). Workaholism: Definition, measurement, and preliminary results. *Journal of Personality Assessment*, 58(1), 160–78.

Taris, T.W., Schaufeli, W.B. and Schimazu, A. (2010). The push and pull of work: About the differences between workaholism and work engagement. In A.B. Bakker and M.P. Leiter (eds), *Work Engagement: A Handbook of Essential Theory and Research* (pp. 39–53). New York: Psychology Press.

Taris, T.W, Schaufeli, W.B. and Verhoeven, L.C. (2005). Workaholism in the Netherlands: Measurement and implications for job strain and work-non-work conflict. *Applied Psychology: An International Review*, 54, 37–60.

van Beek, I., Taris, T.W. and Schaufeli, W.B. (2011). Workaholic and work engaged employees: Dead ringers or worlds apart? *Journal of Occupational Health Psychology*, 16(4), 468–82.

van Beek, I., Hu, Q., Schaufeli, W.B., Taris, T.W. and Schreurs, B.H.J. (2012). For fun, love, or money: What drives workaholic, engaged, and burned-out employees at work? *Applied Psychology*, 61(1), 30–55.

van den Broeck, A., Schreurs, B., De Witte, H., Vansteenkiste, M., Germeys, F. and Schaufeli, W. (2011). Understanding workaholics' motivations: A self-determination perspective. *Applied Psychology: An International Review*, 60(4), 600–621.

van Wijhe, C.I., Schaufeli, W.B. and Peeters, M.C.W. (2010). Understanding and treating workaholism: Setting the stage for successful interventions. In R.J. Burke and C. Cooper (eds), *Psychological, Physical and Financial Costs of High Risk Behavior in Organizations* (pp. 107–34). Farnham: Gower Publishing.

Wright, J.H., Basco, M.R., Thase, M.E. and Gabbard, G.O. (eds) (2006). *Learning Cognitive-behavior Therapy: An Illustrated Guide*. Arlington: APA.

22

Effects of Contextual and Personal Resources on Work–Family Interface

Ewelina Smoktunowicz, Magdalena Lesnierowska, Roman Cieslak and Charles C. Benight

Introduction

EFFECTS OF CONTEXTUAL AND PERSONAL RESOURCES ON
WORK–FAMILY INTERFACE

Work–family interface is a topic that generates high interest both among academics and laymen. The former group continuously encounters research questions that are yet to be answered, whereas for the latter group this is the topic that they relate to in their everyday lives. The research in this area has gone a long way from identifying that major life domains such as work and family/home are often incompatible (Greenhaus and Beutell 1985) to demonstrating that they might actually enrich each other (Greenhouse and Powell 2006).

In this chapter we review the demands that can potentially trigger the negative side of work–family interface (i.e., work–family and family–work conflict) and the resources that contribute to its positive side (i.e., work–family and family–work enrichment). From a resource perspective, we focus specifically on personal resources because they are the ones over which individuals have the most control. Finally we attempt to identify those areas that – if enhanced – have the potential to buffer the work–family and family–work conflict and protect individuals from negative consequences as well as contribute to domain enrichment.

Work–Family Interface: Concepts and Definitions

Work–family interface refers to the constellation of two major life domains: work and family. The latter domain encapsulates a broad area from parenthood and housework to friendship. Under the umbrella term of work–family interface there is a number of specific concepts related either to its negative or positive side. In this chapter we will focus on work–family and family–work conflict on one end and work–family and family–work enrichment and facilitation on the other (for review on clarification of concepts see: Wayne 2009).

Work–family conflict is commonly described as "a form of interrole conflict in which the role pressures from the work and family domains are mutually incompatible in some respect. That is, participation in the work (family) role is made more difficult by virtue of participation in the family (work) role" (Greenhaus and Beutell 1985, p. 77). We distinguish two directions of the conflict: from work to family domain (work–family conflict, WFC) and from family to work domain (family–work conflict, FWC). Hence, this bidirectional conflict is often called an interrole conflict.

Work–family enrichment is also bidirectional suggesting that experience in one role can improve one's experience in the other role and vice versa (Greenhouse and Powell 2006). As Wayne (2009) points out, the crucial aspect of the enrichment concept is that it refers not only to the transfer of resources from one domain to another (a process known as positive spillover), but to the actual improvement in the target domain that can be attributed to this transfer. *Work–family facilitation* differs from work–family enrichment in a sense that the former refers to the improvement on the system level and the latter to the improvement on the individual level (Wayne 2009).

Interrole conflict and enrichment/facilitation are not mutually exclusive; it is possible for employees to experience both the negative and positive sides of being engaged in at least two major life domains (Demerouti, Martinez-Corts and Boz 2013).

Antecedents and Consequences of Work–Family Interface

Research has attempted to identify important predictors and outcomes related to the work–family interface. Origins of WFC and FWC are usually explained by the matching hypothesis according to which WFC originates in work domain and FWC originates in family domain. This assumption has been confirmed first by the meta-analysis by Byron (2005) and then, a few years later, by another meta-analysis which included more studies and more precise conceptualization of both the antecedents and the conflicts themselves (Michel, Kotrba, Mitchelson, Clark and Baltes 2011). Results of both studies indicated that though there were cross-domain relationships (i.e., job demands with FWC and family demands with WFC), they were usually smaller than the within-domain relationships (i.e., job demands with WFC and family demands with FWC).

Meta-analysis by Michel and colleagues (2011) found the largest relationships of WFC with global job stressors and work overload. The remaining identified antecedents of WFC were work role conflict, work time demands (both moderately related) and work ambiguity (small effect). Additionally, the authors found that WFC was positively related to being involved in one's job. Family–work conflict on the other hand was predicted by global family stressors, family role conflict, family role overload (moderate effects) and by role ambiguity, family time demands, parental demands, and number of children/dependents (small effects). The authors also reported cross-domain relationships between WFC and global family stressors and family role conflict, ambiguity, and overload and FWC and global job stressors, work role conflict, ambiguity, and overload. However, none of these effects were large.

Consequences of work–family and family–work conflicts are explained by either matching/within-domain hypothesis (i.e., consequences of the conflict are in the same domain as its origin) or cross-domain hypothesis (i.e., consequences of the conflict impact a different domain than its origin). The latter view has dominated the literature (Peeters, ten Brummelhuis and Steenbergen 2013), but the meta-analysis by Amstad, Meier, Fasel, Elfering and Semmer (2011) indicated that the relationship between the direction of the conflict and its consequences is more in line with the matching hypothesis than with the cross-domain one. The effects were found for both hypotheses but the correlations were stronger between the work–family conflict and the work-related outcomes than for the family-related outcomes, and stronger between the family–work conflict and the family-related outcomes than for the work-related outcomes. Peeters and colleagues (2013) proposed that social exchange theory offers explanation as to why the within-domain relationships are more logical. According to the authors, people tend to associate the benefits or challenges with the source domain (work or family) and then reciprocate. When there are benefits people respond with work engagement or job/family satisfaction, respectively to the domain where they get benefits from. When there are barriers within a domain, people might face adversity in the form of job burnout or marital dissatisfaction, etc., but again most likely within a domain where they met barriers.

Resources and Their Impact on Work–Family Interface

Work–family interface is also predicted by the resources. In his Conservation of Resources theory (COR), Hobfoll (1989) defines resources as objects (e.g., job or home equipment), conditions (job position, job/family stability), personal characteristics (e.g., self-esteem, self-efficacy, skills), or energies (e.g., money, time, knowledge) that are valuable for individuals. Resources are also a crucial part of Job Demands–Resources model (JD–R; Demerouti, Nachreiner, Bakker, and Schaufeli 2001) where they are defined as those physical, organizational or social elements at workplace "that may help individuals to meet job demands, may thus reduce the associated physiological and/or psychological costs, while at the same time stimulating personal growth and development" (Demerouti, Peeters and van der Heijden 2012, p. 244). According to the authors resources are engaged in two psychological processes: (1) health impairment, when resources are too weak to balance high demands; (2) motivational process, when resources facilitate achieving work goals.

In the context of work–family interface employees are exposed to the specific constellation of work and family conditions (job demands/resources and family demands/resources) that determine to what extent individuals experience interrole conflict or enrichment (Greenhaus and Beutell 1985; Greenhaus and Powell 2006). Low job resources, contributing to negative work-related outcomes, may affect family domain, triggering WFC (Demerouti et al. 2012). On the other hand, resources may be transferred from work into the family domain, leading to work–family enrichment (analogous to the family–work direction; Demerouti et al. 2012).

How do resources contribute to the work–family interface? There are several theoretical approaches that help to understand that process. The conflict perspective, based on the role strain theory (Goode 1960), implicates multiple role involvement leading to deterioration of individual resources and impairing functioning in the aftermath (e.g., extensive time investment in the work domain may lead to time deficiency in the family domain). Work–family conflict may be considered a chronic stress condition (Braunstein-Bercovitz, Frish-Burstein and Benjamin 2012) and thus – in line with COR theory (Hobfoll 1989) – be perceived as a consequence of actual loss of resources, threat of losing or of not gaining resources in two critical life domains (Hobfoll 1998). Indeed, a number of studies indicate that the availability of resources predict lower level of WFC (see: Kossek, Pichler, Bodner and Hammer 2011 for review).

Resources play a crucial role in predicting work–family/family–work enrichment as well. Greenhaus and Powell (2006) identified five major groups of work and family resources that promote beneficial exchange of experiences between roles: (1) skills (e.g., cognitive skills, interpersonal skills) and perspectives (e.g., understanding other people's problems, expanded worldview); (2) psychological and physical resources (e.g., self–efficacy, self–esteem, optimism and hope, physical health); (3) social capital resources (e.g., influence and information derived from relationships in work and family domains); (4) flexibility (e.g., flexible time, task organization); (5)

material resources (e.g., money or anything of material value gained as a result of fulfilling work and family roles).

A number of studies demonstrated that engaging in multiple roles might be a resource itself and produce beneficial outcomes. Kulik and Liberman (2013) tested whether "role set density" (defined as the number of roles performed simultaneously) was related to distress in work and family. Their findings showed that performing numerous roles did not elicit higher level of work–family conflict. These findings are in line with the role expansion theory (Marks 1977) which indicates that engagement in multiple roles is beneficial for the individuals through the increase in the resources – personal (e.g., self–esteem), social (social support) or economic (e.g., income) and that those resources can be applied to other life domains.

According to Hobfoll (1998), individuals are able to manage their resources to maintain health and stimulate development. In the next section of this chapter we will review existing studies that included types of resources: *work and family contextual resources* and *personal (dispositional) resources*.

Contextual Resources

Contextual resources are those elements derived from work and family contexts that facilitate managing the demands, protect from interrole conflict and enhance satisfaction and well-being in both domains (Demerouti et al. 2012). On the basis of existing literature, we distinguished two general categories of contextual resources, which were most extensively studied in the context of work–family interface: *job* and *family resources* (e.g., autonomy and job control, flexibility, time resources, and family stabilization) and *social support resources* both in work and family domains.

Job and family resources. Job and family resources are those environmental and social factors in the work and family domains respectively that facilitate coping with the demands and contribute to work–family enrichment (Demerouti et al. 2012). Among job resources there are: perceived job control, participation in decision–making, performance feedback or task diversity; whereas the examples of family resources are: perceived family stability, developmental possibilities, domestic help or spouse support.

Grzywacz and Butler (2005) tested the relationship between job resources and work–family facilitation. They found that a resource-rich work environment fostered work–family facilitation and the effect was significant especially for high autonomy at work, job control, authority and required skills. The authors suggested that job autonomy, control and authority might be related to employees' perceptions of job flexibility, which in turn helps to reconcile interrole demands. An alternative mechanism would be the direct transfer of resources. For example, ability to manage multiple priorities related to job tasks may be transferred and become beneficial for managing family tasks.

Perceived job control may also play a protecting role against work–family conflict. Thomas and Ganster (1995) carried out a study among US healthcare professionals and found a relationship between higher control perceptions and lower WFC. The authors suggested that perception of control – defined as "the belief that one can exert some influence over the environment, either directly or indirectly, so that the environment becomes more rewarding than threatening" (Thomas and Ganster 1995, p. 7) – may be the key resource mediating the relationship between organization practices and WFC. These findings are in line with the Job Demands-Control model (Karasek 1979) and the Demands-Control-Support model (Johnson and Hall 1988), which both assume that highly demanding jobs lead to strain when perceived control is low.

The relationship between perceived control, job flexibility and work–family conflict appeared to be a cross-cultural phenomenon. Hill, Yang, Hawkins and Ferris (2004) found in their study conducted in 48 countries that flexibility (especially the location and timing of work) significantly reduced WFC. However, this relationship seems to be more complex. Parasuraman and Simmers (2001) found significant differences between self-employed and organizationally-employed individuals. Employees who ran their own businesses scored higher on job flexibility and job satisfaction than the organizationally employed individuals, but they also reported greater WFC and lower family satisfaction. These results might be attributed to higher emotional involvement in work role among the self-employed group which in turn is associated with more difficulties in combining work and family roles (Parasuraman and Simmers 2001).

Contrary to those results, Butler, Grzywacz, Bass and Linney (2005) found in their daily diary study among non-professional employees that those who perceived both high job demands and high level of job control experienced grater daily interrole conflict. The authors suggested that employees with high job control tend to work more at home which leads to interrole conflict (Butler et al. 2005).

Another frequently studied contextual resource is the amount of time available to allocate into different life domains (e.g., Greenhaus and Beutell 1985; Hughes and Parkes 2007; Marks 1977). Individuals who due to their demanding jobs cannot spend as much time with their family as they wish may experience work–family strain (see Amstad et al. 2011 for review). Hughes and Parkes (2007) in the study conducted among UK female employees in the public sector tested whether work–family conflict would mediate the relationship between work hours and measures of well-being (psychological distress and family satisfaction). The mediation hypothesis was partially supported with interrole conflict significantly mediating the effect of work hours on family satisfaction. Thus, employees who spent more time at work experienced greater strain leading to WFC, which, in turn, was negatively related to family satisfaction. Authors tested also the moderating role of perceived time control on the relationship between work time and WFC. They found that employees' perceptions of higher control over work hours buffered the negative impact of longer work hours on WFC. Authors suggested that flexible work schedules might decrease the risk of conflict between employees' work and home life (Hughes and Parkes 2007).

Family resources contribute to work–family interface as well. DiRenzo, Greenhaus and Weer (2011) investigated the effect of family-related resources (e.g., working spouse, house ownership and family support) on work–family conflict among lower-level and higher-level employees. Having a working spouse and owning a house negatively related to FWC but only for lower-level employees. Post-hoc analyses did not show higher home-based demands among employees at lower levels than among those at higher levels so these results might indicate that among lower-level employees perceived life stabilization is a key factor in decreasing the risk of WFC (DiRenzo et al. 2011).

Social support resources. Numerous studies have focused on the relationship between social support and work–family interface (see Kossek et al. 2011 for review). In the context of work–family interface workplace support may be "content general" or "content specific" (Kossek et al. 2011). *General support* (e.g., instrumental, emotional) affects employees' global well–being. *Content-specific support* meets particular demands, for example family–specific support refers to supervisors caring for employees' family life. The relationship between work–related support and work–family conflict was studied by Kossek et al. (2011). The authors found that family–specific work support from the organization and from supervisors was negatively related to WFC. These findings suggest that effective work–related support should be family–specific to help protect from WFC.

Considerable research suggests that women and men have fundamentally different work–family experiences. Greenglass and Burke (1988) found that female teachers experienced greater role conflict and only among women this role conflict was associated with job burnout, whereas among male teachers the main predictors of job burnout were job–related (e.g., lack of supervisor support, doubts about job competence). Higher social support predicted lower job burnout only among women. Therefore, as long as women carry the majority of responsibility for family domain (e.g., parenting, housework) they are at greater risk than men to experience role conflict and its outcomes such as job burnout.

At the same time, women made more effective use of social resources (Greenglass and Burke 1988) and that observation might help to explain why in many studies there are no gender differences in levels of work–family interface variables. In fact, the results of a meta–analysis conducted by Byron (2005), which included 61 studies, indicated that gender is a weak predictor of WFC. Nevertheless, male employees seemed to experience slightly more WFC and female employees FWC (Byron 2005).

Michel, Mitchelson, Pichler and Cullen (2010) attempted to clarify the relationship between social support and interrole conflict. In their meta–analytic review of 129 studies, three separate models were tested: (1) independence model in which social support was conceptualized as an independent antecedent of WFC; (2) a mediation model where social support was conceptualized as a mediating variable between the stressor and WFC relationship; and (3) antecedent model, in which social support was conceptualized as an antecedent of WFC via role stressors. The overall results supported only the antecedent model of social support indicating that social support in one domain (e.g., work) predicts same–domain role stressors, which in turn contribute to cross–domain WFC. In other words, both work and family social support may play a role in the reduction of same–domain role stressors and cross–domain conflict in the aftermath.

Beyond contextual resources, personal resources might be also crucial for the work–family interface as they enable resources' cross–domain transfer and facilitate performance in different roles (ten Brummelhuis and Bakker 2012).

Personal Resources

According to Hobfoll (1989), personal resources are those individually valued traits and skills that foster stress resistance, enhance coping and resiliency to various sources of strain. Individuals who dispose of the greater pool of resources are less negatively impacted by stressful life circumstances (Hobfoll 1998). The Job Demands–Resources model (Demerouti et al. 2001) was also expanded with the category of personal resources. A study by Xanthopoulou, Bakker, Demerouti and Schaufeli (2007) indicated three personal resources: self–efficacy, organizational–based self–esteem, and optimism as core elements of the extended JDR model. These personal resources are defined as "unitary resiliency construct that plays a decisive role in employees' functioning at work" (Xanthopoulou et al. 2007, p. 124). Authors suggest that personal resources may play several roles in the relationship between environmental demands and well–being outcomes. First, similar to the other resources in the original JDR model, personal resources may act as a buffer in the health impairment process: employees with high levels of personal resources are better at managing job demands and demonstrate less negative strain–related outcomes. Second, personal resources may mediate the motivational process linking job resources with work engagement and growth. Resourceful environment mobilizes employees' personal resources so they feel in control of dealing with their job demands and, in turn, become more engaged and satisfied with their job (Xanthopoulou et al. 2007).

Personal resources are crucial for life–work balance and work– and family–related well–being (Braunstein-Bercovitz et al. 2012). As discussed above, work and family resources are important to meet within–domain and cross–domain demands. However, perhaps most importantly, contextual resources may increase personal resources which in turn become beneficial for improving home and work outcomes. In other words, "personal resources are the linking pins between the work and home domains" (ten Brummelhuis and Bakker 2012, p. 549) and they may be even stronger determinants of work–family interface than contextual demands (Allen et al. 2012).

Ten Brummelhuis and Bakker (2012) proposed the Work–Home Resources model (W–HR) that highlights the central role of personal resources in the work–family interface. They defined work– family conflict as "a process whereby demands in one domain deplete personal resources and impede accomplishments in the other domain" (ten Brummelhuis and Bakker 2012, p. 545) and work–family enrichment as "a process whereby contextual resources from the home and work domains lead to the development of personal resources. The personal resources developed in each domain subsequently facilitate performance in the other domain" (ten Brummelhuis and Bakker 2012, p. 549). The W–HR model indicates that conflict and enrichment processes originate from demands and resources in the work or home domain and lead to changes in personal resources which in turn influence important outcomes in both domains.

The role of personal resources in the work–family interface research field has been largely neglected. One reason for that was that traditionally the research was based on conflict theories, such as Goode's role strain theory (1960). The later theories of work–family enrichment, such as the W–HR model, shed light on personal resources because the degree to which individuals experienced enrichment was likely to be attributed to their personal resources (Wayne, Musisca and Fleeson 2004). Greenhaus and Powell (2006) suggested two main paths between work–family enrichment and personal resources: instrumental path and affective path. Instrumental path illustrates the direct transfer of resources from one domain to the other which leads to improvement in role performance. For example, core self–evaluations (i.e., self–efficacy, self–esteem) gained at work can be beneficial in the family domain (Erez and Judge 2001). In line with the affective path, resources generated in one domain increase positive affect which subsequently influences and facilitates performance in other domains. For example, positive mood gained from one's family enhances functioning in other roles such as one's work (Greenhaus and Powell 2006).

Core self–evaluations (CSE) are in fact considered important predictors of work–family interface. They are defined as "fundamental, bottom–line evaluations that individuals hold about themselves, the world, and others" (Erez and Judge 2001, p. 6). The indicators of CSE are: self–esteem, neuroticism, locus of control, and general self–efficacy. Boyar and Mosley (2007) investigated the role of CSE in the context of work–family interface. The results of their study indicated that CSE predict interrole conflict, but not interrole enrichment. More specifically, self–esteem was a negative predictor of interrole conflict: individuals who scored high on self–esteem perceived low level of interrole conflict. Authors suggested that these results might indicate that positive self–evaluations are used mainly to minimize or avoid negative situations and in that way be further related to lower interrole conflict.

PERSONALITY TRAITS AS PERSONAL RESOURCES

Personality traits are a separate set of resource variables which – although they do not meet definitional criteria of personal resources provided by the JD–R model or the COR theory – are extensively investigated as dispositional predictors of work–family interface (Wayne et al. 2004). In a nutshell, research results indicated that personality traits play a crucial role in predicting work–family interface and in moderating the effects of other variables on interrole conflict and enrichment (Greenhaus and Powell 2006; Grzywacz and Marks 2000).

The Five Factor model of personality (Costa Jr and McCrae 1992) has been the most often applied framework in research that aims to link personality and work–family interface (e.g.,

Wayne et al. 2004). According to meta–analysis by Allen et al. (2012), neuroticism has been the most frequently studied dispositional variable within the work–family literature and was found to be a stronger direct determinant of work–family conflict than contextual variables. The meta–analytic review by Michel, Clark and Jaramillo (2011) analyzed the overall role of personality traits from the Five Factor model in the perception of work–family interface. Authors found that extraversion, agreeableness, conscientiousness and neuroticism were related to work–family and family–work conflict; extraversion, agreeableness, conscientiousness and openness to experience were related to work–family and family–work enrichment. Moreover, Kinnunen, Vermulst, Gerris and Mäkikangas (2003) indicated a buffering role for personal traits in the relationship between WFC and well–being by demonstrating that emotional stability (low neuroticism) moderated the relationships between WFC and negative outcomes such as job exhaustion and depression. Thus, emotionally stable employees are better protected from potential negative conflict–related outcomes not only in work environment (job exhaustion), but also in other life domains (depression).

SELF-EFFICACY

Self–efficacy is a crucial personal resource and considered to be highly influential on individuals' performance in various life domains. The concept of self–efficacy, rooted in Social Cognitive Theory (Bandura 1997), reflects people's beliefs about their capabilities to perform competently and have influence over events that affect their lives. These beliefs determine how people feel, think and behave (Bandura 1997). Self–efficacy appraisals enhance one's functioning by influencing task accomplishment related to important personal goals. Self–efficacy perceptions also are important during times of stress influencing the ability to manage both internal (emotional challenges) and external (environmental stressors) demands (Benight and Bandura 2004). Numerous studies have discussed the predictive role of self–efficacy on coping abilities while facing various stressors, such as job stress (e.g., Xanthopoulou et al. 2007), family stress (e.g., Dunning and Giallo 2012), disease and health impairment (Korpershoek, van der Bijl and Hafsteinsdóttir 2011), traumatic events (e.g., Benight and Bandura 2004; Cieslak, Benight and Lehman, 2008).

In the context of work–family interface, coping with demands in both domains may be considered as chronic stress (Braunstein-Bercovitz et al. 2012) and thus coping should be related to one's self–efficacy beliefs. Although there are limited studies on self–efficacy in the work–family context the aim of the current review is to highlight the key findings from this promising line of research.

The concept of self–efficacy is multi–faceted: *general self–efficacy*, which reflects the basic belief in one's ability to cope with various challenging demands (Luszczynska, Scholz and Schwarzer 2005); *process–specific self–efficacy*, such as coping self–efficacy, defined as confidence in one's ability to manage specific stressful situational demands and cope with one's own emotional reactions (Benight and Bandura 2004); *domain–specific self–efficacy*, such as work, family or work–family self–efficacy, which reflects one's perceptions of successful performing in a specific life domain (Houle, Chiocchio, Favreau and Villeneuve 2012) and, finally, *task–specific self–efficacy* (e.g., job tasks or parental self–efficacy; Erdwins, Buffardi, Casper and O'Brien 2001).

According to Judge and Bono (2001), generalized self–efficacy – defined as "estimate of one's fundamental ability to cope, perform, and be successful" (Judge and Bono 2001, p. 80) – is one of the core self–evaluations. High general self–efficacy may contribute to perceiving aspects of work and family domains more positively. Boyar and Mosley (2007) investigated a relationship between general self–efficacy and work–family interface and its relationship with work and family well–being via work–family interface. Authors hypothesized that general self–efficacy, along with other core self–evaluations, would negatively predict interrole conflict and positively predict interrole facilitation. The results indicated that while core self–evaluations such as self-esteem, neuroticism and locus of control predicted both WFC and FWC (but not work–family/family–work facilitation), self–efficacy was associated with neither the interrole conflict nor the facilitation (Boyar and Mosley 2007).

Why was self–efficacy not recognized as a significant predictor of work–family interface? One explanation refers to the distinction between general and task–specific or domain–specific self–efficacy. Michel, Clark and Jaramillo (2011) conducted a meta–analytic review of the relationship between dispositional variables and perceptions of work–family interface. The authors compared the predictive role of general self–efficacy and work–family self–efficacy (perceptions of one's ability to cope with both work and family demands). The results revealed that the predictive role of work–family self–efficacy on work–family interface was approximately twice as strong as the general self–efficacy perception (Michel et al. 2011).

Houle et al. (2012) investigated the predictive role of interaction between work–specific and family–specific self–efficacy, social support (from supervisor and life partner) and gender on work–family interface. They hypothesized that social support and gender would moderate the relationship between domain–specific self–efficacy and work–family conflict. Self–efficacy was the strongest predictor of WFC and FWC. This supported the findings from other studies according to which high self–efficacy – both work– and family–related – is as a key protective personal resource in the context of interrole conflict. Moreover, a three–way interaction between gender, self–efficacy and social support indicated that among men with low levels of self–efficacy, social support plays a significant role in reducing FWC. However, among women the pattern of interaction was different. When self–efficacy was low, a high level of social support contributed to a high level of FWC. The authors suggested that for low self–efficacious women receiving support may lead to feelings of guilt and dependency which, in turn, may decrease their ability to cope with family and work demands. These results indicate that the self-efficacy level in the context of work–family interface may affect the ability to gain or maintain other resources (e.g., social resources) which in turn influences the coping process.

Erdwins et al.' (2001) investigated the mediational role of two task–specific self–efficacy variables, namely job tasks self–efficacy and parental self–efficacy, in the relationship between social support from different sources (supervisor, organization and spouse) and work–family conflict. The sample consisted of married, employed women with at least one preschool–aged child. Results confirmed only one relationship: between organizational support and WFC via job self–efficacy. Organizational support appeared to strengthen employees' perceptions of their job efficacy which in turn decreased the WFC. These results support the concept of the enabling hypothesis (Schwarzer and Knoll 2007) which suggests that self–efficacy beliefs are bolstered by positive social resources.

Beyond one's work–family conflict, beliefs of being efficacious may also play a key role in work–family enrichment. To elucidate the mechanism of self–efficacy–related enrichment, Wayne, Grzywacz, Carlson and Kacmar (2007) proposed a concept of the Resource–Gain–Development (RGD). The RGD perspective is rooted in COR theory (Hobfoll 1989) and assumes that "individuals have natural tendencies to grow, develop, and achieve the highest levels of functioning for themselves and the systems in which they participate including families and organizations" (Wayne et al. 2007, p. 66). According to the RGD, there are two main groups of resources that enable facilitation: personal characteristics and environmental resources. Self–efficacy is considered the key personal characteristic that enables the enrichment process as it promotes other resource gains (e.g., skill development and learning). The authors indicated that high self–efficacy is related to the sense of confidence that enhances the ability to acquire knowledge and new skills as well as positive mood. This state of confidence and individual resource development then fosters the gaining of other resources (Wayne et al. 2007).

How do people gain their beliefs about self–efficacy? According to Social Cognitive Theory (Bandura 1997), there are four main sources. The first one – mastery experiences – is when successful performance (for example at work or in the family domain) enhances one's efficacy and the sense of failure decreases it. The second source is named modeling; an individual gains beliefs of efficacy by observing successful performance of other people that are somehow similar to them. The third way of gaining efficacy beliefs is through social persuasion where a trusted source advocates that one is capable to perform competently. The fourth source of self–efficacy is based on one's somatic and emotional states that give a clue about the level of one's performance and, in turn, indicate personal strengths and vulnerabilities. One important value of self–efficacy is that it may be gained, strengthen and trained during one's lifetime which provides an opportunity to enhance performance and a sense of success (Bandura, 1997). In the context of work–family interface self–efficacy might be one of the core resources involved in gaining other resources that promote work–family and family–work enrichment.

In line with Social Cognitive Theory (Bandura 1997) individuals' behaviors are shaped by past thoughts, perceptions and attitudes. Perceived self–efficacy reflects prospective beliefs in one's competence to perform adequately in order to reach desired goals (Luszczynska et al. 2005). Cinamon (2010), unlike most researches investigating the field of work–family interface, conducted a study among unmarried students with the focus on not actual but the anticipated work–family conflict. Anticipated WFC was defined as the expected incompatible pressures from future work and future family roles (Cinamon 2006, 2010). Participants were categorized based on four attributions of the importance of work and family roles: work–oriented, family–oriented, dual–oriented, and no orientation. This division was based on Greenhaus and Beutell's (1985) idea that work–family conflict arises when work domain, family domain or both are salient and require high time and energy investments, allowing less time and energy for other domains. The self–efficacy concept reflected participants' ability to manage future potential WFC. Results indicated that students who attributed high future work importance and low family importance anticipated higher levels of work–family conflict compared to family–oriented, dual–oriented, and participants with no specific orientation. Work–oriented students also demonstrated the lowest self–efficacy to manage this conflict. In comparison, the family–oriented participants anticipated the lowest levels of conflict and reported high efficacy to manage it. Interestingly, those who attributed high importance to both roles reported the highest efficacy to manage conflicts and expected a relatively low level of conflict. These results were consistent with earlier research by Cinamon (2006) where gender differences in perceived self–efficacy were revealed: women expected higher level of anticipated WFC and FWC, and scored lower on self–efficacy in managing conflict than men.

The significance of self-efficacy as a protective and facilitating resource in the work–family interface was confirmed also by Allen et al. (2012) in their meta–analytic review. An overall medium effect size was found for self–efficacy and both the work–family and the family–work conflict. According to the authors, this result indicates that a high level of self–efficacy may contribute to the development of the coping skills necessary to manage competing work and family demands. As self–efficacy seems to be a crucial personal resource in the context of work–family interface, more research is still needed to elucidate its antecedents and outcomes and to understand process through which self-efficacy influences work–home interface and possibly vice versa.

Conclusion

Despite the extensive research in the field of work–family interface there are still considerable gaps. Whereas the role of job and family demands are rather straightforward, the role of resources requires further research. Indeed, resource enhancement may be crucial from a prevention and intervention perspective. Strengthening resources might buffer the negative impact of challenging demands (which is in line with the Job Demands–Resources model) and thus prevent the interrole conflict or – in cases where the conflict has already happened – prevent the negative outcomes of that conflict. Enhancing contextual resources is difficult from employees' perspectives because those resources are often outside (completely or partially) of their control. This is particularly salient in the case of work resources. Personal resources, on the other hand, as the name suggests, belong to the person and in some cases are more vulnerable to change. Self–efficacy is one of these resources. Its quality as a personal resource is that it can be strengthened and enhanced. This has been documented in numerous studies in various disciplines from promoting health behaviors (Warner et al. 2014) to coping with secondary traumatic stress (Cieslak et al. 2013), or recovering after a devastating stroke (Korpershoek et al. 2011). A few studies that have tested the role of self-efficacy in the context of work–family interface provide initial support to suggest that this direction of research is worth pursuing.

References

Allen, T.D., Johnson, R.C., Saboe, K.N., Cho, E., Dumani, S. and Evans, S. (2012). Dispositional variables and work–family conflict: A meta–analysis. *Journal of Vocational Behavior*, 80, 17–26.

Amstad, F.T., Meier, L.L., Fasel, U., Elfering, A. and Semmer, N.K. (2011). A meta–analysis of work–family conflict and various outcomes with a special emphasis on cross–domain versus matching–domain relations. *Journal of Occupational Health Psychology*, 16, 151–69.

Bandura, A. (1997). Self–efficacy. *Harvard Mental Health Letter*, 13, 4–6.

Benight, C.C. and Bandura, A. (2004). Social cognitive theory of posttraumatic recovery: The role of perceived self–efficacy. *Behaviour Research and Therapy*, 42, 1129–48.

Boyar, S.L. and Mosley Jr., D.C. (2007). The relationship between core self-evaluations and work and family satisfaction: The mediating role of work–family conflict and facilitation. *Journal of Vocational Behavior*, 71, 265–81.

Braunstein-Bercovitz, H., Frish-Burstein, S. and Benjamin, B.A. (2012). The role of personal resources in work–family conflict: Implications for young mothers' well-being. *Journal of Vocational Behavior*, 80, 317–25.

Butler, A.B., Grzywacz, J.G., Bass, B.L. and Linney, K.D. (2005). Extending the Demands–Control model: A daily diary study of job characteristics, work–family conflict and work–family facilitation. *Journal of Occupational & Organizational Psychology*, 78, 155–69.

Byron, K. (2005). A meta-analytic review of work–family conflict and its antecedents. *Journal of Vocational Behavior*, 67, 169–98.

Cieslak, R., Benight, C.C. and Lehman, V.C. (2008). Coping self–efficacy mediates the effects of negative cognitions on posttraumatic distress. *Behaviour Research and Therapy*, 46, 788–98.

Cieslak, R., Shoji, K., Luszczynska, A., Taylor, S., Rogala, A. and Benight, C.C. (2013). Secondary trauma self–efficacy: Concept and its measurement. *Psychological Assessment*, 25, 917–28.

Cinamon, R.G. (2006). Anticipated work–family conflict: Effects of gender, self-efficacy, and family background. *Career Development Quarterly*, 54, 202–15.

Cinamon, R.G. (2010). Anticipated work–family conflict: Effects of role salience and self-efficacy. *British Journal of Guidance & Counselling*, 38, 83–99.

Costa Jr, P.T., and McCrae, R.R. (1992). Four ways five factors are basic. *Personality and Individual Differences*, 13, 653–65.

Demerouti, E., Martinez-Corts, I. and Boz, M. (2013). A closer look at key concepts of the work–nonwork interface. In J.G. Grzywacz and E. Demerouti (eds), *New Frontiers in Work and Family Research* (pp. 34–53). New York: Psychology Press.

Demerouti, E., Peeters, M.C.W., and van der Heijden, B.I.J.M. (2012). Work–family interface from a life and career stage perspective: The role of demands and resources. *International Journal of Psychology*, 47, 241–58.

Demerouti, E., Nachreiner, F. Bakker, A.B. and Schaufeli, W.B. (2001). The Job Demands–Resources model of burnout. *Journal of Applied Psychology*, 86, 499–512.

DiRenzo, M.S., Greenhaus, J.H. and Weer, C.H. (2011). Job level, demands, and resources as antecedents of work–family conflict. *Journal of Vocational Behavior*, 78, 305–14.

Dunning, M.J. and Giallo, R. (2012). Fatigue, parenting stress, self–efficacy and satisfaction in mothers of infants and young children. *Journal of Reproductive & Infant Psychology*, 30, 145–59.

Erdwins, C.J., Buffardi, L.C., Casper, W.J. and O'Brien, A.S. (2001). The relationship of women's role strain to social support, role satisfaction, and self–efficacy. *Family Relations*, 50, 230–8.

Erez, A. and Judge, T.A. (2001). Relationship of core self–evaluations to goal setting, motivation, and performance. *Journal of Applied Psychology*, 86, 1270–9.

Goode, W.J. (1960). A theory of role strain. *American Sociological Review*, 25, 483.

Greenglass, E.R. and Burke, R.J. (1988). Work and family precursors of burnout in teachers: Sex differences. *Sex Roles*, 18, 215–29.

Greenhaus, J.H. and Beutell, N.J. (1985). Sources of conflict between work and family roles. *Academy of Management Review*, 10, 76–88.

Greenhaus, J.H. and Powell, G.N. (2006). When work and family are allies: A theory of work–family enrichment. *Academy of Management Review*, 31, 72–92.

Grzywacz, J.G. and Butler, A.B. (2005). The impact of job characteristics on work-to-family facilitation: Testing a theory and distinguishing a construct. *Journal of Occupational Health Psychology*, 10, 97–109.

Grzywacz, J.G. and Marks, N.F. (2000). Reconceptualizing the work–family interface: An ecological perspective on the correlates of positive and negative spillover between work and family. *Journal of Occupational Health Psychology*, 5, 111–26.

Hill, J. E., Yang, C., Hawkins, A.J. and Ferris, M. (2004). A cross–cultural test of the work–family interface in 48 countries. *Journal of Marriage & Family*, 66, 1300–316.

Hobfoll, S.E. (1989). Conservation of Resources: A new attempt at conceptualizing stress. *American Psychologist*, 44, 513–24.

Hobfoll, S.E. (1998). *Stress, Culture, and Community: The Psychology and Philosophy of Stress*. New York: Plenum Press.

Houle, L., Chiocchio, F., Favreau, O.E. and Villeneuve, M. (2012). Role conflict and self–efficacy among employed parents: Examining complex statistical interactions. *Gender, Work & Organization*, 19, 592–614.

Hughes, E.L. and Parkes, K.R. (2007). Work hours and well–being: The roles of work–time control and work–family interference. *Work & Stress*, 21, 264–78.

Johnson, J.V. and Hall, E.M. (1988). Job strain, work place social support, and cardiovascular disease: A cross-sectional study of a random sample of the Swedish working population. *American Journal of Public Health*, 78, 1336–42.

Judge, T.A. and Bono, J.E. (2001). Relationship of core self–evaluations traits—self–esteem, generalized self–efficacy, locus of control, and emotional stability—with job satisfaction and job performance: A meta-analysis. *The Journal of Applied Psychology*, 86, 80–92.

Karasek, R.A. (1979). Job demands, job decision latitude, and mental strain: Implications for job redesign. *Administrative Science Quarterly*, 24, 285–308.

Kinnunen, U., Vermulst, A., Gerris, J. and Mäkikangas, A. (2003). Work–family conflict and its relations to well–being: The role of personality as a moderating factor. *Personality and Individual Differences*, 35, 1669–83.

Korpershoek, C., van der Bijl, J. and Hafsteinsdóttir, T.B. (2011). Self–efficacy and its influence on recovery of patients with stroke: A systematic review. *Journal of Advanced Nursing*, 67, 1876–94.

Kossek, E.E., Pichler, S., Bodner, T. and Hammer, L.B. (2011). Workplace social support and work–family conflict: A meta–analysis clarifying the influence of general and work–family–specific supervisor and organizational support. *Personnel Psychology*, 64, 289–313.

Kulik, L. and Liberman, G. (2013). Work–family conflict, resources, and role set density: Assessing their effects on distress among working mothers. *Journal of Career Development*, 40, 445–65.

Luszczynska, A., Scholz, U. and Schwarzer, R. (2005). The general self–efficacy scale: Multicultural validation studies. *Journal of Psychology*, 139, 439–57.

Marks, S.R. (1977). Multiple roles and role strain: Some notes on human energy, time and commitment. *American Sociological Review*, 42, 921–36.

Michel, J.S., Clark, M.A. and Jaramillo, D. (2011). The role of the Five Factor Model of personality in the perceptions of negative and positive forms of work–nonwork spillover: A meta–analytic review. *Journal of Vocational Behavior*, 79, 191–203.

Michel, J.S., Mitchelson, J.K., Pichler, S. and Cullen, K.L. (2010). Clarifying relationships among work and family social support, stressors, and work–family conflict. *Journal of Vocational Behavior*, 76, 91–104.

Michel, J.S., Kotrba, L.M., Mitchelson, J.K., Clark, M.A. and Baltes, B.B. (2011). Antecedents of work–family conflict: A meta–analytic review. *Journal of Organizational Behavior*, 32, 689–725.

Parasuraman, S. and Simmers, C. (2001). Type of employment, work–family conflict and well–being: A comparative study. *Journal of Organizational Behavior*, 22, 551–68.

Peeters, M.C.W., ten Brummelhuis, L. and Steenbergen, E.F. (2013). Consequences of combining work and family roles: A closer look at cross–domain versus within–domain relations. In J.G. Grzywacz and E. Demerouti (eds), *New Frontiers in Work and Family Research* (pp. 93–109). New York: Psychology Press.

Schwarzer, R. and Knoll, N. (2007). Functional roles of social support within the stress and coping process: A theoretical and empirical overview. *International Journal of Psychology*, 42, 243–52.

ten Brummelhuis, L.L. and Bakker, A.B. (2012). A resource perspective on the work–home interface: The work–home resources model. *American Psychologist*, 67, 545–56.

Thomas, L.T. and Ganster, D.C. (1995). Impact of family–supportive work variables on work–family conflict and strain: A control perspective. *Journal of Applied Psychology*, 80, 6–15.

Warner, L.M., Schuz, B., Wolff, J.K., Parschau, L., Wurm, S. and Schwarzer, R. (2014). Sources of self–efficacy for physical activity. *Health Psychology*. Advance online publication. doi:10.1037/hea0000085

Wayne, J.H. (2009). Reducing conceptual confusion: Clarifying the positive side of work and family. In D.R. Crane and J. Hill (eds), *Handbook of Families and Work: Interdisciplinary Perspectives* (pp. 105–40). Lanham: University Press of America.

Wayne, J.H., Musisca, N. and Fleeson, W. (2004). Considering the role of personality in the work–family experience: Relationships of the Big Five to work–family conflict and facilitation. *Journal of Vocational Behavior*, 64, 108–30.

Wayne, J.H., Grzywacz, J.G., Carlson, D.S. and Kacmar, K.M. (2007). Work–family facilitation: A theoretical explanation and model of primary antecedents and consequences. *Human Resource Management Review*, 17, 63–76.

Xanthopoulou, D., Bakker, A.B., Demerouti, E. and Schaufeli, W.B. (2007). The role of personal resources in the Job Demands–Resources model. *International Journal of Stress Management*, 14, 121–41.

23

Scrambling:
An Ability and a Process

Jennifer K. Dimoff, Lenora A. Collins, and E. Kevin Kelloway

Introduction

It is a scene from every World War II movie – as enemy fighter planes approach, the defending squadron "scrambles," drawing on all available resources to respond to an immediate crisis. In more contemporary terms, the threat of air attack from missiles or terrorism results in jet fighters scrambling to meet an imminent threat. In our personal lives, we scramble to meet more mundane challenges – the car that won't start in the morning, an unexpected weather event, the cancellation of child-care services. All of these crises require us to scramble – to activate or draw on our resources to meet an immediate challenge.

We suggest that this notion of scrambling to meet the immediate demands of a crisis situation has been largely overlooked in the stress literature. Researchers have examined coping as a means of dealing with chronic or ongoing stressors (Folkman, Lazarus, Gruen, and DeLongis 1986; Lazarus and Folkman 1984; Roth and Cohen 1986; Zakowski, Hall, Klein, and Baum 2001) and have examined resilience as a means of "bouncing back" from adverse circumstances (Cameron and Brownie 2010; Fletcher and Sarkar 2013; Luthar and Cicchetti 2000). However, we believe that scrambling is different from both constructs in that it is the immediate marshalling of resources in response to an acute stressor. We draw on the crisis response literature, in addition to the literature on coping and stressor-management, in developing a model of scrambling as a process and ability.

Scrambling

Although overlooked in the literature, scrambling is not necessarily a novel concept. In American football, a "quarterback scramble" is a term used to describe an unplanned or impromptu manoeuvre that a quarterback must make when faced with unexpected pressure from the opposing team (National Football League 2014). To respond appropriately to the situation, the quarterback must be able to recognize the situation, remain calm, identify options or courses of action, and mobilize resources and support. Drawing on the crisis response literature, we suggest that these four steps outline a more general model of scrambling. To respond to a crisis, an individual must (1) recognize that there is a crisis situation or imminent threat, (2) remain calm under pressure (i.e., manage feelings of stress), (3) identify options or courses of action based on a variety of stimuli (i.e., make sense of available information), and (4) garner assistance and support from others.

Scrambling: An Ability and a Process

While one's ability to scramble is likely related to one's coping style and one's level of resilience and learned resourcefulness, an individual's personal characteristics and resources are also likely to impact scrambling. According to Bandura (1982) and Lazarus and Folkman (1984), individuals' resources, and their appraisal of these resources, impact the extent to which they perceive an event to be stressful. Their resources and resource-appraisals also impact how successfully they are likely to be in staving off the negative outcomes often associated with these events. Specifically, we propose that cognition and decision-making, emotion-management, affect, and personality are likely to influence how employees will appraise and respond to crisis situations.

Cognition and decision-making. A wealth of research on the relationships between stress, decision-making, and cognitive performance suggests that stress negatively and significantly influences the quality of individuals' information processing and decision-making abilities (Lepine, Podsakoff, and Lepine 2005). According to Chajut and Algom (2003) and much of the work on threat rigidity (Staw, Sandelands, and Dutton 1981), there are three models that reflect how individuals attend to and process information while experiencing acute stress. First, the "attentional model" posits that stress depletes an individual's attentional resources, resulting in increased attention to a few stimuli and less attention to others (Chajut and Algom 2003). Depending on the situation and the stimuli, this response can lead to either enhanced or reduced performance. Second, the "capacity-resources model" states that stress narrows attention and individuals attend to information that is most accessible or salient, regardless of its significance or relevance (Chajut and Algom 2003). Like the first response, the outcome of this approach depends on whether or not the information attended to is most critical to the situation. Third, the "thought suppression model" involves a more unconscious process or automatic search, in which the individual becomes sensitized to monitor for specific information or stimuli (Chajut and Algom 2003). This response draws on attentional resources and can lead to hyper-vigilance to irrelevant cues or "to-be suppressed" thoughts.

Neurophysiological studies have demonstrated that brain regions associated with decision-making are highly sensitive to stress and that stress exposure can impede memory processing and speed (Lupien, Maheu, Tu, Fiocco, and Schramek 2007). Specifically, both the adrenal-medullary systems and the adrenal-cortical systems impact the immediate physical consequences that individuals are likely to experience during stressful events or while scrambling (Gaillard and Wientjes 1994). "Fight or flight" responses, which are triggered by threatening or challenging events, result in increases in heart rate, blood pressure, muscle tension, concentration, and a narrowing in focus (Hartsough and Myers 1985).

While advantageous in moderation, if these "fight or flight" responses are prolonged, are too intense, or occur too frequently, they can become problematic and distracting for individuals trying to make decisions and take action (Gloria, Faulk, and Steinhardt 2013). For instance, nausea, muscle tremors, heart palpitations, ringing in the ears, and even fainting can occur when individuals experience acute stress during crisis situations (Hartsough and Myers 1985). For individuals who must scramble at work, it is essential that they be able to make decisions and take actions without being impeded by the negative consequences of heightened arousal.

Demands on cognition: Uncertainty and time. Defined as "the ability to choose between competing courses of action based on their relative value or consequences" (Balleine 2007, p. 8159), decision-making is essential to successful scrambling. Yet, much research suggests that humans do not always make strategic or advantageous decisions (Gigerenzer and Todd 1999). This is especially true during stressful, time-sensitive, and uncertain situations (Lepine et al. 2005; Salas, Driskell, and Hughes 1996). According to Weber and Johnson (2009), the difficulty of making well-calculated decisions is somewhat dependent on the degree of uncertainty in the current situation and the potential outcomes of the decision. Each decision lies on a continuum ranging from "complete ignorance," where no possible outcomes or consequences are known, through "ambiguous," where outcomes are known but their probabilities are not known, to "risk," where the probability of each outcome is known, and finally to "certainty," where only one outcome or consequence is possible (Lepine et al. 2005). The more information available about outcome possibilities and outcome probabilities, the higher the likelihood that decisions will be made strategically (Brand, Recknor, Grabenhorst, and Bechara 2007).

Unfortunately, crisis characteristics, such as time and pressure, have the potential to distract individuals from their ability to process information and consider different decision possibilities and their outcomes (Boggs and Simon 1968; Finkelman and Glass 1970). In fact, time pressure is thought to be one of the most central factors of all performance degradation issues, such as poor decision-making (Stokes, Kemper, and Marsh 1992) and reductions in visual and auditory search behavior (Janis and Mann 1977; Stokes et al. 1992; Wickens, Stokes, Barnett, and Hyman 1991; Wiggins and O'Hare 1995). Thus, individuals who are able to maintain composure and remain focused during crisis situations are likely to be able to make adaptive decisions under pressure – a hallmark of effective scrambling.

With heightened time pressure, individuals also tend to revert toward more familiar, but not necessarily more effective, information-processing and decision-making strategies (Lehner, Seyed-Solorforough, O'Connor, Sak, and Mullin 1997). During times of stress, individuals often make decisions based on the "intuitive-experiential system," which is often referred to as the heuristic system because it relies on fast, parallel, associative and emotional types of processing (Epstein, Pacini, Denes-Raj, and Heier 1996; Kahneman 2003). This type of processing is in stark contrast to the "rational-analytical system," which is associated with slow, serial, controlled, flexible, neutral, and rule-governed information processing (Epstein et al. 1996; Kahneman 2003). Thus, individuals who are making decisions based on heuristics, emotion, and previous experiences, without carefully considering the current situation, are likely to be employing intuitive-experiential decision-making and not rational-analytical decision-making.

In doing so, individuals making intuition-driven decisions or acting on "fight or flight" reactions may not be adequately managing emotions, shifting attention, or processing available information – all key components of effective scrambling. Consequently, the effectiveness of the response is likely to be limited by rapid, and pattern-based, decision-making that does not fully appreciate the details of the current crisis. Thus, rational-analytical decision-making is likely to be more strongly related to effective scrambling than intuitive-experiential decision-making.

Managing emotions and affect. During crisis situations or situations in which an individual must scramble, emotion-management is critical to response success (Gohm, Baumann, and Sniezek 2001). According to Baumann, Sniezek, and Buerkle (2001), affective reactions to acute stressors impede performance and decision-making by drawing attention away from normal cognitive processes. Individuals who are able to (1) identify the emotions that they are experiencing, and (2) divert attention away from these emotions are likely to experience relatively few cognitive difficulties in crisis situations (Gohm et al. 2001). Research by Salovey, Mayer, Goldman, Turvey and Palfai (1995) suggests that individuals who can easily identify the specific emotion that they are experiencing during stressful situations may allocate less attention to their emotional reactions and more to their cognitive responses.

Additionally, individuals who do not focus on their emotions may be less distracted by them than individuals who do attend to their emotions during crisis situations (Bachorowski and Braaten

1994; Salovey et al. 1995; Swinkels and Giuliano 1995). For instance, in an acute stress simulation study, firefighters who were able to identify and accept their emotional reactions to stressors spent less time attending to their emotions (Gohm et al. 2001). As a result, these firefighters had more cognitive availability to devote to the situation itself. Thus, the extent to which one is able to recognize and manage one's emotions and acute stress responses may be key to one's ability to perform under stress and scramble successfully (Worchel and Yohai 1979).

Acute stress responses and anxiety. According to MacLeod and Mathews (1988), individuals tend to respond emotionally to stressors as a result of their trait-level anxiety. For instance, individuals who are high in trait-level anxiety tend to have a persistent tendency to orient attention toward threat-related stimuli (Eysenck, Mogg, May, Richards, and Mathews 1991; MacLeod and Mathews 1988). As a result, these individuals are more likely to become hyper-vigilant under stressful circumstances (MacLeod and Mathews 1988; Mathews and MacLeod 1985). As contended by Eysenck et al. (1991), hyper-vigilance can be maladaptive in that it results in highly focused threat-detection behaviors that reduce attentional capacities and limit cognitive control over other activities.

Although maladaptive in excess, anxiety can also be an adaptive defense mechanism that helps individuals recognize and react to threats (Marks and Nesse 1994; Nesse 1990). For instance, while panic has been associated with an inability to respond appropriately and efficiently to threats, moderate levels of anxiety have been associated with the ability to cognitively formulate rational plans of action and mobilize defensive resources (Marks and Nesse 1994). Although panic is almost certainly maladaptive to scrambling, a certain level of anxiety may be tolerable, and even necessary, to successful scrambling. For instance, individuals who are low in trait-level anxiety tend not to recognize or adequately respond to threat-related stimuli (MacLeod and Mathews 1988; Mogg and Bradley 1998). In situations in which they must scramble, these individuals are also more likely to become avoidant of stress-provoking stimuli than individuals high in trait-level anxiety (MacLeod and Mathews 1988; Mogg and Bradley 1998). Consequently, an individual's ability to successfully scramble depends on a regulatory trade-off between the costs and benefits associated with anxiety – an inadequate level of anxiety is disadvantageous because it will prevent the individual from reacting to the threat, while excess anxiety will disable the ability to scramble and react successfully (Cook, Hodes, and Lang 1986; Marks and Nesse 1994; Ohman 1993; Seligman 1970).

Affect. While excessive anxiety and other emotional stress responses can harm performance and crisis response by diverting attention away from cognitive processes (Baumann et al. 2001; Gohm et al. 2001), positive emotions and positive affect have the potential to enable positive adaptation to stressors and encourage performance (Fredrickson 2001, 2004). According to Fredrickson's broaden-and-build theory of positive emotions, positive affect can expand one's attentional scope, increase flexible thinking, and improve creativity and innovation (Fredrickson 2004; Fredrickson and Joiner 2002; Isen and Daubman 1984, Isen, Daubman, and Nowicki 1987). Broadened attention and cognitive flexibility and creativity are especially important to responding to novel and stressful situations (Fredrickson 2004). Lower levels of positive affect have been associated with rigidity and narrow-mindedness during stressful situations, which limits one's capacity to expedite decision-making and make accurate appraisals of stressors (Staw et al. 1981).

Unlike those with lower levels of positive affect, those with higher levels of positive affect are more likely to experience a broadening of their "thought-action repertoire" during stressful situations (Fredrickson 2004). The broadening of this repertoire may help to facilitate adaptive decision-making and coping strategies, such as garnering social support and resources. As a result, individuals with higher levels of positive affect seem better able to think flexibly, expand their behavioral options, and increase their personal resources during times of adversity (Gloria et al. 2013). Ultimately, we believe that positive affect will play a significant role in determining whether or not an individual will be able to scramble successfully during stress-provoking situations

(Danner, Snowdon, and Friesen 2001; Duckworth, Quinn, and Seligman 2009; Lyubomirsky, King, and Diener 2005).

Identifying options and courses of action. Identifying options may be particularly difficult during times of crisis. Consistent with the Threat Rigidity Hypothesis (Staw et al. 1981) and much of the literature examining acute stress, most individuals do not perform particularly well when faced with acute stressors. When experiencing acute stress, anxiety, and psychological arousal, many individuals tend to experience a narrowing of their perceptual fields, a reduction in their critical information processing, and a reversion to previous experiences and well-learned processes (Staw et al. 1981). Commonly referred to as "tunnel vision," an individual's perceptual and cognitive difficulties stem from reductions in the extent to which he or she is able to attend to novel information, distinguish important stimuli from peripheral or unimportant stimuli, and manage affective responses, such as increased heart rate or fear (Baumann et al. 2001; Gohm et al. 2001; Salas et al. 1996; Staw et al. 1981).

Research also suggests that when individuals feel threatened or experience significant psychophysiological arousal, they tend to abandon their typical systematic scan patterns (Keinan 1987), and become hyper-vigilant – "a state of disorganized and somewhat haphazard attentional processing" (Staal 2004, p. 39). Janis and Mann (1977) posit that hyper-vigilance can result in frantic attentional shifting and an impeded ability to recognize viable options and potential courses of action. Similarly, Staw et al. (1981) draw from examples in cybernetics to demonstrate how individuals can become more rigid in their thoughts and behaviors when confronted by acute stressors.

Using their systems-based explanation, Staw et al. (1981) posit that crisis situations cause restrictions in the flow of information, making it difficult for systems to respond flexibly and adaptively (Staw et al. 1981). Part of this restriction is attributable to the system's attempt to reduce demands and economize information processing (Arrow 1974; Staw et al. 1981). Typically, systems do this by decreasing or limiting the amount of information that they intake (i.e., tunnel vision) and by re-allocating attention and resources (Arrow 1974; Staw et al. 1981). For instance, when a system is threatened, the necessity of system response output (i.e., behavior) takes precedence over all other functions (Staw et al. 1981). As a result, the information channels and codes that a system typically uses to intake information may become occupied by other tasks designed to identify, control, and coordinate possible outputs of the system (i.e., behavior; Staw et al. 1981). Ultimately, the behavioral repertoire of a system becomes limited by the quantity and quality of the information that it receives, as well as the amount of time that it has to process the information (Staw et al. 1981).

According to the concepts of threat rigidity and system processing, employee performance during a crisis situation is likely dependent upon the employee's ability to deal with the information overload, reduce the impact of inhibitory emotions, and make informed and well thought-out decisions based on the available information (Staw et al. 1981). Without these abilities, an individual's capacity to process and make sense of information becomes compromised.

Mobilizing resources. To a large extent, whether or not an individual is capable of performing well within a crisis situation can be explained using the Job Demands-Resources (JD-R) Model (Demerouti, Bakker, Nachreiner, and Schaufeli 2001). According to the JD-R Model, if an individual's resources outweigh the demands of a situation, the individual will likely be able to deal with the situation and limit feelings of acute stress or strain (Demerouti et al. 2001). While job demands are the physical, psychological, social, and organizational aspects of a job that are taxing and require effort (Demerouti et al. 2001), job resources are the aspects of a job that help achieve work goals, reduce job demands, and/or stimulate personal growth and development (Demerouti et al. 2001; Karasek 1979; Schaufeli and Bakker 2004). For instance, a teacher may have the demands of managing a classroom of 30 or more students, grading papers, and attending to the needs of parents. All of these demands can be taxing on the teacher's health, well-being, and ability to do his job (Bakker, Demerouti, Taris, Schaufeli, and Schreurs 2003; Bonanno 2005; Van Vegchel, De Jonge, and Landsbergis 2005; Xanthopoulou, Bakker, Demerouti, and Schaufeli 2007). However, the opportunities for professional development, support from school administration, and the comradery that he shares with colleagues are resources that help reduce him stress and improve her performance as a teacher. Unsurprisingly, job demands tend to be significant predictors of negative job strain (Bakker et al. 2003; Bakker, Demerouti and Verbeke 2004), while job resources tend to be significant and consistent predictors of work engagement (Hakanen, Bakker, and Schaufeli 2006). Thus, the extent to which the teacher's resources meet the demands of the situation determine the likelihood that he will experience stress and be able to do his job when faced with the stressors of a crisis situations (Demerouti et al. 2001).

In addition to more organic job resources, such as social support among colleagues, there are also more formal job resources that can improve an individual's ability to deal with stressors and overcome challenges. Training and experience have both been linked to improved performance and reduced levels of stress and strain (Bonanno 2005; Gohm et al. 2001; Wiggins and O'Hare 1995). For instance, in stress inoculation programs, individuals are taught how to self-monitor, problem-solve, and regulate their own emotions in order improve their ability to cope with and respond to stressors (Meichenbaum 1985). According to Meichenbaum (1985), these skills are critical to managing stressors and are linked to better performance during stressful situations. Similarly, Wiggins and O'Hare (1995) found that during high pressure situations, experienced pilots spent less time visually searching and re-searching their screens than novice pilots. These results suggest that experienced pilots are more efficient than novice pilots at distinguishing peripheral or unimportant information from critical information (Wiggins and O'Hare 1995). Given that speed is an important quality of scrambling, it is likely that individuals who are more experienced with certain situations will be quicker than less experienced individuals in their ability to distinguish important from unimportant information.

Still, some research findings also suggest that training or experience may actually be detrimental to performance (Gigerenzer and Todd 1999; Kahneman 2003). For instance, over-training may lead to a heavy reliance on heuristics, which can be maladaptive if the heuristics do not readily translate from a past crisis situation to a current crisis situation. Therefore, while training and experience can bolster job-related resources or act as resources in and of themselves, their utility during crisis situations may be dependent on a number of other factors or personal resources, such as an individual's personality composition (Xanthopoulou et al. 2007).

Individual Differences in Scrambling

Individuals are likely to vary considerably in their abilities to recognize a crisis, remain calm, identify courses of action, and mobilize resources. One source of such differences lies in the personality characteristics of individuals (Lazarus and Folkman 1984; Watson and Hubbard 1996). The remainder of this discussion is oriented around the "Big Five" model of personality (McCrae and Costa 1987).

Openness to Experience

Openness to Experience is a six-facet construct, consisting of (1) Fantasy, the capacity for vivid imagination, (2) Aesthetics, the appreciation for art of beauty, (3) Feelings, the value placed on emotions and emotionality, (4) Actions, the willingness to try new things, (5) Ideas, the pursuit of intellectual simulation, and (6) Values, the re-examination of social and/or political perspectives (McCrae and Costa 1987). Individuals high on Openness tend to score relatively highly on curiosity, imagination, and divergent thinking – all qualities that impact innovative behavior and that are likely to influence an individual's ability to flexibly adapt to challenging situations (Sinha and Srivastava 2013). Given that Open individuals seem to be more willing to consider new ideas and unconventional approaches (Ehrhart and Makransky 2007), and that individuals must be able to recognize these ideas, opportunities, and approaches when faced with novel crisis situations, it is expected that individuals high on Openness will be more likely to successfully respond to crises.

Extraversion

Characterized by six facets, Warmth (i.e., friendliness and positive feelings toward others), Gregariousness (i.e., getting enjoyment from being around others), Assertiveness (i.e., the desire to take charge and lead), Activity (i.e., the need to be busy and involved in activities), Excitement Seeking (i.e., the extent to which one enjoys excitement and stimulation), and Positive Emotions (i.e., the range of positive feelings that an individual experiences; McCrae and Costa 1987), Extraversion has been positively associated with support seeking during times of crisis or acute stress (Epstein 2011). Although Extraversion, at the factor-level, has significantly predicted problem-focused coping (Epstein 2011; Roth and Cohen 1986), very little crisis response literature has considered the role of Extraversion in an individual's ability to respond to stressors. Extraversion may enable successful crisis response by enabling individuals to communicate, disseminate information, and make decisions during times of crisis (Van de Walle and Turoff 2008). Similarly, Extraversion is likely to be highly and positively related to crisis response success, as positivity has been repeatedly linked to successful short-term and long-term resilience to stress (Luthans, Avolio, Avey, and Norman 2007). Thus, we expect Extraversion and scrambling effectiveness to be positively correlated, especially if the crisis situation requires a group or team-based approach.

Agreeableness

Categorized by a tendency to be cooperative, warm, and even altruistic (McCrae and Costa 1987), Agreeableness is often high among individuals who seek to serve and help others (Judge and Cable 1997). The six facets of Agreeableness are Trust (i.e., the extent to which one believes that others are honest), Straightforwardness (i.e., the extent to which one is honest), Altruism (i.e., one's unselfish concern for others), Compliance (i.e., one's approach to conflict), Modesty (i.e., one's level of humility), and Tender-Mindedness (i.e., the extent to which one empathizes with others; McCrae and Costa 1987). Although Agreeableness is theorized to measure the quality of the social interactions that an individual is likely to have, a host of empirical studies, as well as a number of case studies, have demonstrated a negative relationship between Agreeableness and creative thinking and innovation (King, Walker, and Broyles 1996). Given this negative relationship, it is unlikely that highly Agreeable individuals will be able to successfully respond to novel crisis situations. For instance, although individuals must be willing and able to work with others during a crisis event, they must also be unafraid to challenge the status quo and make difficult decisions without social support (Borins 2000; Teltumbde 2006). Given the dearth of research surrounding the relationships between Agreeableness and crisis response, it is difficult to hypothesize specifically about these relationships.

Conscientiousness

Characterized by dependability, organization, and responsibility (McCrae and Costa 1987), Conscientiousness is associated with efficiency, reliability, and a preference for conventionality (Judge and Cable 1997). According to McCrae and Costa (1987), Conscientiousness includes six facets, Self-Discipline (i.e., an individual's ability to persist and complete a task), Competence (i.e., the extent to which an individual is practical), Achievement Striving (i.e., an individual's level of aspirations), Deliberation (i.e., an individual's ability to thoroughly think about one's actions before acting), Order (i.e., an individual's level of organization or neatness), and Dutifulness (i.e., the extent to which an individual is governed by morals or ethics). Of the Big Five, Conscientiousness is consistently the most predictive factor of job performance and future work-related success (Judge and Bono 2001). Thus, we expect that Conscientiousness will also be predictive of individuals' success and job performance within crisis situations. Similarly, Conscientiousness has been associated with heightened awareness and better attention to detail – actions that could lead to improved decision-making and actions during crisis situations (Weick and Sutcliffe 2001). Thus, it is likely that Conscientiousness will be positively related to one's ability to scramble and perform adaptively during crisis situations.

Neuroticism

Individuals who are poised, self-reliant, and stable are typically considered to be high on emotional stability and low on Neuroticism (McCrae and Costa 1987). Conversely, insecurity and indecisiveness are characteristics of Neuroticism (McCrae and Costa 1987). Thus, the six facets of Neuroticism include Anxiety (i.e., nervousness), Angry Hostility (i.e., propensity towards anger or outbursts), Depression (i.e., feelings of sadness), Self-Consciousness (i.e., lack of self-confidence), Impulsiveness (i.e., inability to control one's whims), and Vulnerability to Stress (i.e., propensity towards panic). Given that all facets of neuroticism are associated with poor job performance (Barrick and Mount 1991) and poor stress responses (Gunthert, Cohen, and Armeli 1999), Neuroticism is likely to be significantly and negatively related to successful crisis response.

Although it is important to explore the relationships between each of the Big Five factors and scrambling, we encourage future research to examine these relationships at the facet-level. Closer examination will allow more detailed and insightful conclusions to be drawn about scrambling and how it is related to personality. Overall, the combination of personality factors, personal characteristics, and job-related resources are likely to influence the extent to which an individual is able to successfully scramble during crisis situations. No one factor or characteristic alone is likely to determine whether or not someone will be able to respond adaptively to crisis-related stressors. Thus, in the future, it will be important to explore a multitude of potential predictors and correlates in order to gain a more holistic perspective of scrambling and its outcomes.

Outcomes of Scrambling

Employees who demonstrate resilience, possess a high positive affect, utilize their resources, and manage their emotions are likely to be effective "scramblers." In sports, people who have these abilities are often referred to as "clutch players" – individuals who are capable of delivering results efficiently during high leverage situations. Described as being able to rise to the occasion, keep "cool under pressure," and "compartmentalize," these players often meet and surpass challenges just in the "nick of time" (Fromal 2014). Why is it that sports teams recruit and value these players?

Based on what we know about the hypothesized predictors and correlates of scrambling that have been outlined in this chapter, we believe that these clutch players, much like scrambling employees, are capable of delivering high levels of performance, both in the moment and in future crisis situations. We also believe that individuals capable of scrambling will experience higher levels of self-efficacy – an outcome that has been linked to improvements in overall work performance, productivity, and job satisfaction (Judge and Bono 2001; Judge, Jackson, Shaw, Scott, and Rich 2007; Stajkovic and Luthans 1998). Similarly, we expect that these increases in self-efficacy will lead to reductions in acute stress and anxiety during crisis situations, especially if individuals have the opportunity to exercise problem-focused coping and can engage in successful scrambling experiences at work (Jex, Bliese, Buzzell, and Primeau 2001).

Individuals who scramble effectively are likely to cultivate more personal and job-related resources (Fredrickson 2001, 2004). By successfully scrambling and rising to the challenge in crisis situations, an employee may develop other positive feelings associated with doing well and overcoming challenges (Bandura 1982; Bandura, Adams, and Beyer 1977; Fredrickson 2001, 2004). In turn, the employee is likely to carry these positive feelings into future endeavors, whether these endeavors are related to crisis situations or not (Bandura 1982; Fredrickson 2001, 2004). This assertion is supported by Fredrickson's broaden-and-build theory, which indicates that improvements in personal resources, such as self-efficacy, can lead to the cultivation of other resources, such as creativity and innovation (Fredrickson 2001, 2004). Thus, individuals who are capable of scrambling effectively during crisis situations are more likely to emerge with higher levels of self-efficacy, and in turn, are more likely to experience other positive outcomes.

Similarly, individuals who scramble effectively are also likely to be engaging in other positive activities, such as problem-focused coping, which is associated with improved well-being and reduced levels of chronic strain (Epstein 2011; Folkman et al. 1986; Roth and Cohen 1986; Sonnentag 2001). Employees who fail to scramble effectively may "fight," "flight," or "freeze" when faced with the stressors associated with a crisis situation. Often, individuals have these reactions to acute stressors because they become cognitively overloaded and emotionally strained (Chajut and Algom 2003; Hartsough and Myers 1985; Lepine et al. 2005). As a result, they are unable to efficiently process information and often become burdened by emotional or psychophysiological responses, such as feelings of fear or increased heart rate (Gloria et al. 2013; Hartsough and Myers 1985). Meanwhile, employees who scramble will be able to differentiate and process information and use their available resources to help them meet the cognitive and emotional demands of the situation. As a result, employees who are capable of getting in "the zone," so to speak, will be better able to make decisions that are adaptive for them, their work teams, and their organization.

Although individual scrambling will directly impact the employee who is engaging in the scrambling, scrambling is also likely to impact other employees in the workplace. For instance, if a newspaper editor scrambles effectively when she receives a last-minute news piece, her subordinates may be more likely to trust her and engage in adaptive followership or organizational citizenship behaviors (Dirks and Ferrin 2002). Employees who trust their leaders are more likely to have high levels of job satisfaction, affective commitment, and engagement (see Dirks and Ferrin 2002 for review) – all factors that are associated with healthy and productive workplaces (Karasek and Theorell 1990; Kelloway and Day 2005). If the newspaper editor fails to manage emotions, process information, delegate, and mobilize resources, not only might the newspaper suffer, but her employees may also suffer. By leading by example, and by rising to the occasion, the leader is demonstrating that crisis situations are manageable and that it is possible to scramble without panicking.

Implications and Future Research

Although firefighters, air traffic controllers, and emergency room personnel are among the professionals most likely to encounter acute stress situations during their typical workweek, acute stress situations have the potential to arise in any employment situation at any time. Not only this, but acute stress is the most common form of stress – even more common than chronic stress, which is far more researched and discussed in both the scientific and non-scientific communities (American Psychological Association 2014). Yet, we know very little about crisis response among general employee populations and we know even less about the impact that crisis response can have on these individuals' health, well-being, and performance. As such, we hope to introduce the concept of scrambling into the organizational psychology and crisis response literatures with the goal of improving upon the existing literature related to crisis response, resilience, learned resourcefulness, decision-making, and other relevant areas of research.

First, we hope that this chapter has provided a platform from which scrambling research can be launched. Although we recognize that the content of this chapter is not exhaustive and likely negates some important areas, such as cognitive ability and creativity, we believe that it serves as a starting point to better understanding how ordinary people, during ordinary work days, respond to short bursts of adversity and challenge. To begin this exploration, we need to better understand what scrambling is, both as an ability and as a process. Similarly, we also need to understand what scrambling is not – how it differs, both empirically and theoretically, from other abilities and processes. Although this chapter provides insight into how scrambling may be related to other constructs, such as positive affect, we hope that future conceptualization and research can add to our early theorizations.

Second, we hope that future research seeks to better understand the individual and situational differences associated with scrambling. Although we hypothesize that scrambling is present in almost all jobs and for almost all employees, it is necessary to confirm this. Future research must seek to determine whether or not there is variability in scrambling across occupations and circumstances. Specifically, it might be valuable to investigate what resources are required to meet the specific demands of a crisis situation at work, and which of these resources is most important to successful scrambling. Both job-related resources (e.g., support from co-workers) and personal resources (e.g., intelligence) may determine the extent to which an individual is able to scramble in any given situation. Thus, it will be important for future research to evaluate what personal and job-related resources improve one's likelihood of being able to scramble in order to meet the needs of a crisis situation.

Third, and perhaps most importantly, it is necessary to better understand the outcomes or consequences of acute stress and how effective scrambling can improve employees' health and performance both during and after crisis situations. Given that resilience and problem-focused coping have been linked to lower levels of chronic stress and strain, as well as improved well-being and performance (Epstein 2011; Folkman et al. 1986; Roth and Cohen 1986; Sonnentag 2001) we expect that scrambling will help to offset the stress that employees experience. At the very least, we expect that one's ability to scramble effectively will be related to how much stress one experiences during a crisis situation. If an individual is able to effectively process information, think clearly, manage emotions, and make adaptive decisions during crisis situations, it is unlikely that he or she will experience negative consequences, such as worry, stress, or guilt about decisions that were made or not made.

Similarly, if individuals are able to allocate attention toward important stressors or stimuli, process information, manage emotions, and mobilize relevant resources, they will be more likely to make well-informed, rational decisions. These decisions are likely to aid and benefit the employee and his or her colleagues. For instance, if an NFL quarterback is able to scramble effectively, he will be able to make a play that will further his team's position on the field. By doing so, he improves his team's likelihood of winning the game and the likelihood that his team will move up in the league rankings. Each of these outcomes has potential ripple effects on the team and the quarterback himself. If the team wins games, the team is likely to do well financially; if the quarterback does well, his teammates will be more likely to trust him, his confidence will improve, and his job security will rise.

Fourth, in order to be most practically relevant and applicable, the trainability or malleability of scrambling will have to be examined. Future research could seek to determine if, how, and to what extent scrambling can be trained. Of great importance will be determining the "how" – what exactly it is about scrambling that can or cannot be trained. For instance, training may be most effective if it focuses on learned resourcefulness or resilience, two aspects of adaptation that have been demonstrated to be malleable (Luthans, Vogelgesang, and Lester 2006; Meichenbaum 1985). On the other hand, attempts to train positive affect may not be as effective. Without understanding how these and other characteristics amalgamate to contribute to effective scrambling, one risks failing to understand how individuals can learn to scramble more effectively.

Conclusions

Just as crisis situations can arise during everyday life, they can affect everyday people. From the newspaper editor to the teacher to the NFL quarterback, it's likely that all employees will experience times of crisis at some point during their career. In fact, many employees will experience the acute stressors most commonly associated with crisis situations on a relatively frequent basis. Who hasn't experienced an unexpected situation that evokes a sense of threat, that must be dealt with quickly, and that involves some level of uncertainty? Many of us can say that we experience a situation like this on a yearly, if not monthly or even weekly basis. Yet, very little is known about how individuals respond to these acute stressors and how these acute stressors impact their health and performance. By introducing the concept of scrambling, we hope to encourage research and discussion that might provide insight into these responses and how they can be optimized.

References

American Psychological Association (2014). Stress: The different kinds of stress. Available at: http://www.apa.org/helpcenter/stress-kinds.aspx. Accessed 24th May 2015.

Arrow, K.J. (1974). The Limits of Organization. New York: Norton.

Bachorowski, J. and Braaten, E.B. (1994). Emotional intensity: Measurement and theoretical implications. Personality and Individual Differences, 17, 191–9.

Bakker, A.B., Demerouti, E., and Verbeke, W. (2004). Using the job demands–resources model to predict burnout and performance. Human Resource Management, 43, 83–104.

Bakker, A.B., Demerouti, E., Taris, T.W., Schaufeli, W.B. and Schreurs, P.J. (2003). A multigroup analysis of the Job Demands-Resources Model in four home care organizations. International Journal of Stress Management, 10, 16.

Balleine, B.W. (2007). The neural basis of choice and decision making. The Journal of Neuroscience, 27, 8159–60.

Bandura, A. (1982). Self-efficacy mechanism in human agency. American Psychologist, 37, 122–47.

Bandura, A., Adams, N. and Beyer, J. (1977). Cognitive processes mediating behavioral change. *Journal of Personality and Social Psychology*, 35, 124–39.

Barrick, M.R. and Mount, M.K. (1991). The big five personality dimensions and job performance: A meta-analysis. *Personnel Psychology*, 44, 1–26.

Baumann, M.R., Sniezek, J.A. and Buerkle, C.A. (2001). Self-evaluation, stress, and performance: A model of decision making under acute stress. In E. Salas and G. Klein (eds), *Linking Expertise and Naturalistic Decision Making* (pp. 139–58). Mahwah: Lawrence Erlbaum Associates.

Boggs, D.H. and Simon, J.R. (1968). Differential effect of noise on tasks of varying complexity. *Journal of Applied Psychology*, 52, 148.

Bonanno, G.A. (2005). Resilience in the face of potential trauma. *Current Directions in Psychological Science*, 14, 135–8.

Borins, S. (2000). Loose cannons and rule breakers, or enterprising leaders? Some evidence about innovative public managers. *Public Administration Review*, 60, 498–507.

Brand, M., Recknor, E.C., Grabenhorst, F. and Bechara, A. (2007). Decisions under ambiguity and decisions under risk: Correlations with executive functions and comparisons of two different gambling tasks with implicit and explicit rules. *Journal of Clinical and Experimental Neuropsychology*, 29, 86–99.

Cameron, F. and Brownie, S. (2010). Enhancing resilience in registered aged care nurses. *Australasian Journal on Ageing*, 29(2), 66–71.

Chajut, E. and Algom, D. (2003). Selective attention improves under stress: Implications for theories of social cognition. *Journal of Personality and Social Psychology*, 85, 231–48.

Cook, E.W., Hodes, R.L. and Lang, P.J. (1986). Preparedness and phobia: Effects of stimulus content on human visceral conditioning. *Journal of Abnormal Psychology*, 95, 195.

Danner, D.D., Snowdon, D.A. and Friesen, W.V. (2001). Positive emotions in early life and longevity: Findings from the nun study. *Journal of Personality and Social Psychology*, 80, 804–13.

Demerouti, E., Bakker, A.B., Nachreiner, F., and Schaufeli, W.B. (2001). The job demands–resources model of burnout. *Journal of Applied Psychology*, 86, 499–512.

Dirks, K.T. and Ferrin, D.L. (2002). Trust in leadership: Meta-analytic findings and implications for research and practice. *Journal of Applied Psychology*, 87, 611.

Duckworth, A.L., Quinn, P.D., and Seligman, M.E.P. (2009). Positive predictors of teacher effectiveness. *The Journal of Positive Psychology*, 4, 540–47.

Ehrhart, K.H. and Makransky, G. (2007). Testing vocational interests and personality as predictors of person-vocation and person-job fit. *Journal of Career Assessment*, 15, 206–26.

Epstein, R. (2011). How best to fight stress: Measuring and ranking relevant competencies. Paper presented to the *Western Psychological Association*, 91, 315–322.

Epstein, S., Pacini, R., Denes-Raj, V. and Heier, H. (1996). Individual differences in intuitive–experiential and analytical–rational thinking styles. *Journal of Personality and Social Psychology*, 71, 390.

Eysenck, M.W., Mogg, K., May, J., Richards, A., and Mathews, A. (1991). Bias in interpretation of ambiguous sentences related to threat in anxiety. *Journal of Abnormal Psychology*, 100, 144–50.

Finkelman, J.M. and Glass, D.C. (1970). Reappraisal of the relationship between noise and human performance by means of a subsidiary task measure. *Journal of Applied Psychology*, 54, 211–13.

Fletcher, D. and Sarkar, M. (2013). Psychological resilience: A review and critique of definitions, concepts, and theory. *European Psychologist*, 18, 12–23.

Folkman, S., Lazarus, R.S., Gruen, R.J. and DeLongis, A. (1986). Appraisal, coping, health status, and psychological symptoms. *Journal of Personality and Social Psychology*, 50, 571–9.

Fredrickson, B.L. (2001). The role of positive emotions in positive psychology: The broaden-and-build theory of positive emotions. *American Psychologist*, 56, 218–26.

Fredrickson, B.L. (2004). The broaden-and-build theory of positive emotions. *Philosophical Transactions of the Royal Society B: Biological Sciences*, 359, 1367–77.

Fredrickson, B.L. and Joiner, T. (2002). Positive emotions trigger upward spirals toward emotional well-being. *Psychological Science*, 13, 172–5.

Fromal, A. (March 6, 2014). The 10 most statistically clutch players of 2013–14 NBA season. Available at: http://bleacherreport.com/articles/1983612-the-10-most-statistically-clutch-players-of-the-2013–14-nba-season. Accessed 24th May 2015.

Gaillard, A.W.K. and Wientjes, C.J.E. (1994). Mental load and work stress as two types of energy mobilization. *Work & Stress*, 8, 141–52.

Gigerenzer, G. and Todd, P.M. (1999). *Simple Heuristics that Make Us Smart*. New York: Oxford University Press.

Gloria, C.T., Faulk, K.E. and Steinhardt, M.A. (2013). Positive affectivity predicts successful and unsuccessful adaptation to stress. *Motivation and Emotion*, 37, 185–93.

Gohm, C.L., Baumann, M.R. and Sniezek, J.A. (2001). Personality in extreme situations: Thinking (or not) under acute stress. *Journal of Research in Personality*, 35, 388–99.

Gunthert, K.C., Cohen, L.H. and Armeli, S. (1999). The role of neuroticism in daily stress and coping. *Journal of Personality and Social Psychology*, 77, 1087–100.

Hakanen, J.J., Bakker, A.B. and Schaufeli, W.B. (2006). Burnout and work engagement among teachers. *Journal of School Psychology*, 43, 495–513.

Hartsough, D.M. and Myers, D.G. (1985). *Disaster Work and Mental Health: Prevention and Control of Stress among Workers*. Rockville: National Institute of Mental Health.

Isen, A.M. and Daubman, K.A. (1984). The influence of affect on categorization. *Journal of Personality and Social Psychology*, 47, 1206–17.

Isen, A.M., Daubman, K.A., and Nowicki, G.P. (1987). Positive affect facilitates creative problem solving. *Journal of Personality and Social Psychology*, 52, 1122–31.

Janis, I. and Mann, L. (1977). *Decision Making*. New York: Free Press.

Jex, S.M., Bliese, P.D., Buzzell, S. and Primeau, J. (2001). The impact of self-efficacy on stressor–strain relations: Coping style as an explanatory mechanism. *Journal of Applied Psychology*, 86, 401–9.

Judge, T.A. and Bono, J.E. (2001). Relationship of core self-evaluations traits – self-esteem, generalized self-efficacy, locus of control, and emotional stability – with job satisfaction and job performance: A meta-analysis. *Journal of Applied Psychology*, 86, 80–92.

Judge, T.A. and Cable, D.M. (1997). Applicant personality, organizational culture, and organization attraction. *Personnel Psychology*, 50, 359–94.

Judge, T.A., Jackson, C.L., Shaw, J.C., Scott, B.A., and Rich, B.L. (2007). Self-efficacy and work-related performance: The integral role of individual differences. *Journal of Applied Psychology*, 92, 107–27.

Kahneman, D. (2003). A perspective on judgment and choice: mapping bounded rationality. *American Psychologist*, 58, 697–720.

Karasek, R.A. and Theorell, T. (1990). *Healthy Work: Stress Productivity, and the Reconstruction of Working Life*. New York: Basic Books.

Karasek Jr, RA. (1979). Job demands, job decision latitude, and mental strain: Implications for job redesign. *Administrative Science Quarterly*, 285–308.

Keinan, G. (1987). Decision making under stress: Scanning of alternatives under controllable and uncontrollable threats. *Journal of Personality and Social Psychology*, 52, 639–44.

Kelloway, E. and Day, A. (2005). Building healthy workplaces: Where we need to be. *Canadian Journal of Behavioural Science*, 37, 309–12.

King, L.A., Walker, L.M. and Broyles, S.J. (1996). Creativity and the five-factor model. *Journal of Research in Personality*, 30, 189–203.

Lazarus, R.S. and Folkman, S. (1984). *Stress, Appraisal, and Coping*. New York: Springer.

Lehner, P., Seyed-Solorforough, M.M., O'Connor, M.F., Sak, S. and Mullin, T. (1997). Cognitive biases and time stress in team decision making. *Systems, Man and Cybernetics, Part A: Systems and Humans, IEEE Transactions on*, 27, 698–703.

Lepine, J.A., Podsakoff, N.P. and Lepine, M.A. (2005). A meta-analytic test of the challenge stressor-hindrance stressor framework: An explanation for inconsistent relationships among stressors and performance. *Academy of Management Journal*, 48, 764–75.

Lupien, S.J., Maheu, F.F., Tu, M.M., Fiocco, A.A. and Schramek, T.E. (2007). The effects ofstress and stress hormones on human cognition: Implications for the field of brain and cognition. *Brain and Cognition*, 65, 209–37.

Luthans, F., Vogelgesang, G.R., and Lester, P.B. (2006). Developing the psychological capital of resiliency. *Human Resource Development Review*, 5, 25–44.

Luthans, F., Avolio, B.J., Avey, J.B., and Norman, S.M. (2007). Positive psychological capital: Measurement and relationship with performance and satisfaction. *Personnel Psychology*, 60, 541–72.

Luthar, S.S. and Cicchetti, D. (2000). The construct of resilience: Implications for interventions and social policies. *Development and Psychopathology*, 12, 857–85.

Lyubomirsky, S., King, L. and Diener, E. (2005). The benefits of frequent positive affect: Does happiness lead to success? *Psychological Bulletin*, 131, 803.

MacLeod, C. and Mathews, A. (1988). Anxiety and the allocation of attention to threat. *Quarterly Journal of Experimental Psychology*, 40, 653–70.

Marks, I.M. and Nesse, R. (1994). Fear and fitness: An evolutionary analysis of anxiety disorders. *Ethology and Sociobiology*, 15, 247–61.

Mathews, A. and MacLeod, C. (1985). Selective processing of threat cues in anxiety states. *Behaviour Research and Therapy*, 23, 563–9.

McCrae, R.R. and Costa, P.T., Jr. (1987). Validation of the five-factor model of personality across instruments and observers. *Journal of Personality and Social Psychology*, 52, 81–90.

Meichenbaum, D. (1985). *Stress Inoculation Training*. New York: Pergamon Press.

Mogg, K. and Bradley, B. (1998). A cognitive-motivational analysis of anxiety. *Behaviour Research and Therapy*, 36, 809–48.

National Football League. (2014). Quarterback scramble. Available at: http://www.sportingcharts.com/dictionary/nfl/quarterback-scramble.aspx. Accessed 24th May 2015.

Nesse, R.M. (1990). Evolutionary explanations of emotions. *Human Nature*, 1, 261–89.

Ohman, A. (1993). Fear and anxiety as emotional phenomena: Clinical phenomenology, evolutionary perspectives, and information processing mechanisms. In *Handbook of Emotions* (pp. 511–35). New York: Guilford Press.

Roth, S. and Cohen, L.J. (1986). Approach, avoidance, and coping with stress. *American Psychological Association*, 41, 813–19.

Salas, E., Driskell, J.E. and Hughes, S. (1996). The study of stress and human performance. In J.E. Driskell and E. Salas (eds), *Stress and Human Performance* (pp. 1–46). Mahwah: Erlbaum.

Salovey, P., Mayer, J.D., Goldman, S.L., Turvey, C. and Palfai, T.P. (1995). Emotional attention, clarity, and repair: Exploring emotional intelligence using the Trait Meta-Mood Scale. In J.E. Pennebaker (ed.), *Emotion, Disclosure, and Health* (pp. 125–54). Washington, DC: American Psychological Association.

Schaufeli, W.B. and Bakker, A.B. (2004). Job demands, job resources, and their relationship with burnout and engagement: A multi-sample study. *Journal of Organizational Behavior*, 25, 293–315.

Seligman, M. (1970). On the generality of the laws of learning. *Psychological Review*, 77, 406–18.

Sinha, N. and Srivastava, K.B.L. (2013). Association of personality, work values, and socio-cultural factors with intrapreneurial orientation. *Journal of Entrepreneurship*, 22, 97–113.

Sonnentag, S. (2001). Work, recovery activities, and individual well-being: A diary study. *Journal of Occupational Health Psychology*, 6, 196–210.

Staal, M.A. (2004). Stress, cognition, and human performance: A literature review and conceptual framework. *NASA Technical Memorandum*, 212824.

Stajkovic, A.D. and Luthans, F. (1998). Self-efficacy and work-related performance: A meta-analysis. *Psychological Bulletin*, 124, 240–61.

Staw, B.M., Sandelands, S.E. and Dutton, J.E. (1981). Threat rigidity effects in organizational behavior: A multilevel analysis. *Administrative Science Quarterly*, 26, 501–24.

Stokes, A.F., Kemper, K.L. and Marsh, R. (1992). Time-stressed flight decision making: A study of expert and novice aviators (Technical Report ARL-93–1/INEL-93–1). Urbana-Champaign: Aviation Research Laboratory, University of Illinois.

Swinkels, A. and Giuliano, T.A. (1995). The measurement and conceptualization of mood awareness: Monitoring and labeling one's mood states. *Personality and Social Psychology Bulletin*, 21, 934–49.

Teltumbde, A. (2006) Entrepreneurs and intrapreneurs in corporations. *Conceptualizations and Learning*, 21, 129–32.

Van de Walle, B. and Turoff, M. (2008). Decision support for emergency situations. *Information Systems Business Management*, 6, 295–316.

Van Vegchel, N., De Jonge, J. and Landsbergis, P.A. (2005). Occupational stress in (inter)action: The interplay between job demands and job resources. *Journal of Organizational Behavior*, 26, 535–60.

Watson, D. and Hubbard, B. (1996). Adaptational style and dispositional structure: Coping in the context of the five-factor model. *Journal of Personality*, 64, 737–69.

Weber, E.U. and Johnson, E.J. (2009). Mindful judgment and decision making. *Annual Review of Psychology*, 60, 53–85.

Weick, K.E. and Sutcliffe, K.M. (2001). *Managing the Unexpected: Assuring High Performance in an Age of Complexity*. California: Wiley.

Wickens, C.D., Stokes, A., Barnett, B. and Hyman, F. (1991). The effects of stress on pilot judgment in a MIDIS simulator. In O. Svenson and A.J. Maule (eds), *Time Pressure and Stress in Human Judgment and Decision Making* (pp. 271–92). New York: Plenum Press.

Wiggins, M. and O'Hare, D. (1995). Expertise in aeronautical weather-related decision making: A cross-sectional analysis of general aviation pilots. *Journal of Experimental Psychology: Applied*, 1, 305–20.

Worchel, S. and Yohai, S.M.L. (1979). The role of attribution in the experience of crowding. *Journal of Experimental Social Psychology*, 15, 91–104.

Xanthopoulou, D., Bakker, A.B., Demerouti, E. and Schaufeli, W.B. (2007). The role of personal resources in the job demands-resources model. *International Journal of Stress Management*, 14, 121–41.

Zakowski, S.G., Hall, M.H., Klein, L.C. and Baum, A. (2001). Appraised control, coping, and stress in a community sample: A test of the goodness-of-fit hypothesis. *Annals of Behavioral Medicine*, 23, 158–65.

Index

Note: italic page numbers indicate figures and tables.

Hargreaves, A. 232
Harkness, A.R. 10
Harris, K. 68, 69
Harrison, G.L. 293
Hartel, C.E.J. 247
Hattie, J. 224
Häusler, S. 248
Hawkins, A.J. 364
Hayes, A.F. 305
Hazan, C. 274–5
Hazlett-Stevens, H. 350–1
heart disease 18, 42, 316, *323*, 332
Hepburn, C.G. 241–2
Herriot, P. 47
Hill, G. 223
Hill, J.E. 364
hip hop musicians 313, 318, 319, 326
Hobfoll, S.E. 242, 243, 348, 363, 364
Hochwater, W.A. 109
Hofacker, C. 304
Hoffman, N.P. 109
Hofstede, G. 289, 292
Hofstede, G.J. 289
Holbrook, A. 32
Holmes, T.H. 239
Hong, J.Y. 184–5
Hong Kong *see* China
hope 17, 107, 108, 249
Horne, J.F.I. *138*, *148*, 151
Houle, L. 369
Houston (R&B singer) 335
Howard, S. 178, 182
HRS (US Health and Retirement Study) 58–9
Huang, G. 247
Hubbard, B. 11, 14
Hulin, C.L. 240
humour 111, 155, 185, 213, 230
Hutchence, Michael 322
hyper-responsivity mechanism 105

independence, psychological 90–3
individualism 90, 93, 141, 244
informational support 118–19
instrumental support 26, *29*, *30*, 118
interpersonal conflict 1, 67, 68, 69, *73*, *74*, *75*, 76, 77, 78, 96, 105
    measurement of 71–2
Interpersonal Conflict at Work Scale (ICAWS) 71–2
interrole conflict 109, 362, 364, 365, 366, 367, 369, 371
introversion 55, 56, 57, 106–7, 108, 109, 156, 231

Jackson, S. 84
Jahoda, M. 246–7
Jang, L.K. 232
Janis, I. 379
Japan 84
Jaramillo, D. 368, 369
Jaredic, B. 27
Jensen, S.M. 249
Jepson, E. 181, 232
Jex, S.M. 78
Job Demands–Resources (JD–R) model 242, 363, 366, 371, 379–80
job flexibility 364–5
job loss/insecurity 1, 2, 42, 56, 161, 239–52
    and adaptability 243, 249, 251
    and optimism 243, 248, 250
    outcomes of 240–2
        family/social 241
        health 239, 240–1
        job-related 242
    and personality 240, 242–51
        and Big Five traits 246–7
        broaden-and-build theory 242, 243
        COR theory 242–3, 249
        and cultural values 244
        and emotional intelligence 247
        and locus of control 247–8
        and positive/negative affectivity 245–6
        and psychological capital 248–50
        and spirituality 244–5
    and psychological distress 241, 245
    and resilience 243, 250
    and self-efficacy 249–50
job performance 68, 69, 77, 287, 291, 293–4, 301, 382
job satisfaction/dissatisfaction 1, 57, 67, 68, 69, 70, *73*, 77, 94, 118, 291
job search behaviours 172, 246, 249, 250
job skill transfer 299, *300*, 302–3, 304, 305, 306, *306*, 307, 309
    defined 302
    and P-E fit 303
job strain 46, 54–5
Johnson, B. 178, 182
Johnson, E.J. 377
Jongsma, A.E. 353–4
Jordan, P.J. 247
Judge, T. 240
Judge, T.A. 368

Kacmar, K.M. 68, 69, 71, 369–70
Kapsou, M. 27
Karasek, R.A. 242

For Product Safety Concerns and Information please contact our EU
representative GPSR@taylorandfrancis.com
Taylor & Francis Verlag GmbH, Kaufingerstraße 24, 80331 München, Germany

www.ingramcontent.com/pod-product-compliance
Ingram Content Group UK Ltd.
Pitfield, Milton Keynes, MK11 3LW, UK
UKHW051833180425
457613UK00022B/1227